DiCarlo

Volume I, To 1937

DiCarlo

Buffalo's First Family of Crime

Thomas Hunt and Michael A. Tona

DiCarlo: Buffalo's First Family of Crime
Volume I, To 1937

ISBN: 978-1-304-26581-4

Includes bibliographical references (p. 352) and index.

Copyright © 2013 by Thomas Hunt and Michael A. Tona
All rights reserved. No part of this book may be used or reproduced by any means, graphic, electronic, or mechanical, including photocopying, recording, taping or by any information storage retrieval system without the written permission of the authors except in the case of brief quotations embodied in critical articles and reviews.

Visit us on the web at: http://buffalomob.com

The views expressed in this work are solely those of the authors and do not necessarily reflect the views of the publisher, and the publisher hereby disclaims any responsibility for them.

Covers designed by Thomas Hunt and Michael A. Tona.

Dedicated

... To the memory of Arnold C. Brackman (1923-1983), whose strong shove so many years ago started me off on a journey I have always enjoyed.

T.H.

... To the memory of my father, Carmen J. Tona (1924-2001), whose lessons in tenacity, diligence and perseverance guided my motivation to complete this formidable project.

M.A.T.

Table of Contents

Acknowledgements .... *ix*
Author's Note .... *xi*
Introduction to Volume I 1
1. New World .... (1906-1909) 5
2. City of Light .... (1908-1919) 15
3. North of the Border .... (1918-1921) 35
4. Booze and Blood .... (1921-1922) 53
5. Succession .... (1921-1922) 66
6. Good Killer .... (1921-1922) 75
7. Unprotected .... (1922-1923) 93
8. Intimidation .... (1924) 112
9. To Prison .... (1924-1925) 134
10. Feds Targeted .... (1923-1925) 145
11. Feud in Buffalo .... (1923-1926) 157
12. Poison .... (1926-1927) 174
13. No One Safe .... (1927-1928) 182
14. Paroled .... (1926-1928) 219
15. Convention .... (1928) 222
16. War .... (1929-1931) 232
17. New Order .... (1931-1932) 264
18. Public Enemy No. 1 ...... (1931-1934) 285
19. Bookmaking .... (1935-1937) 328
    Endnotes 352
    Bibliography 443
    Index 452

Photographs are presented on Pages 207-218.

Acknowledgements

The authors wish to thank all who assisted in this project and to provide special acknowledgement for the contributions of the following individuals: Joe Giambra, former Buffalo Police Department detective, who served as a source of inspiration and support throughout the years of research; Ron Babcock, genealogist and Family History Center librarian, who aided in tracing the Sicilian roots of the DiCarlo family; Ronald Fino, who helped clarify the relationship between Laborers' Union Local 210 and the Buffalo Crime Family; organized crime researchers Richard N. Warner and Lennert van't Reit, who shared their discoveries; and crime historians Patrick Downey and Scott Deitche, who provided valuable feedback on the manuscript. The authors also wish to acknowledge the efforts of the FOIA officers of the Federal Bureau of Investigation and the U.S. Citizenship and Immigration Services, the archives technicians at the National Archives and Records Administration Northeast Region, and the librarians, archivists and staffs of the following libraries: *Buffalo Courier Express* Special Collections Library and Inter-Library Loan Department at the E.H. Butler Library of Buffalo State College, Grosvenor Special Collections Room of Buffalo and Erie County Public Library, Research Library of the Buffalo History Museum, Williamsville Family History Center of the Church of Jesus Christ of Latter Day Saints, Public Library of Youngstown and Mahoning County, Ohio, and the Local History and Archives Department of the Hamilton Public Library.

Author's Note

"Mike, meet Joe DiCarlo."

I was just a twenty-one-year-old college kid in 1973, possibly even less mature and worldly than most others of my age. And I had just been introduced to Joseph J. DiCarlo. A significant local celebrity, DiCarlo was a notorious gangster with a distinguished Mafia pedigree. Decades earlier, the police commissioner of Buffalo, New York, labeled him "Public Enemy No. 1." (That was an unkind label. It grossly exaggerated the danger DiCarlo represented to society in order to convey his degree of influence over the city's criminal rackets.) At the time of our meeting, he was reportedly retired, spending afternoons in "his office," a table beside the pay telephone in Santasiero's Restaurant on Niagara Street.

I put out my hand. As DiCarlo shook it, I managed to speak some small word, perhaps "Hello." I really don't remember.

The introduction accomplished, Joe Giambra led me to a seat at a nearby table. Giambra, friend of my family and part-time instructor of an organized crime course I was taking at the University of Buffalo, knew DiCarlo and other underworld characters through his full-time position – detective in the Buffalo Police Department. During our lunch, I could not take my eyes off DiCarlo. I'm sure other patrons had the same experience. His table was the focal point of the restaurant, and it seemed as though everyone who entered the establishment approached him with a warm greeting.

He was Buffalo royalty.

Growing up in and around the City of Buffalo in a Sicilian-Italian family, I was always intrigued by the region's underworld.

I recall stories told at family gatherings about relations who had been Prohibition Era bootleggers. And there were always whispered warnings about old neighbors who were believed to be "Mafia-connected."

However, that moment in DiCarlo's presence, changed things for me and made the subject far more real than it had ever been. Learning all I could about it and about the older gentleman holding court in Santasiero's became an obsession. That obsession has lasted through the past thirty-five years.

As I worked toward a degree in criminal justice, I accumulated newspaper clippings and copies of government documents about the Buffalo-area crime family known as "The Arm." And, of course, I remained in close touch with Joe Giambra. Giambra led the Buffalo Police Department's Criminal Intelligence Unit – a long title for a three-man office on a meager budget. The unit kept an eye on known outlaws and worked with the FBI on matters related to organized crime. Giambra allowed me to tag along on some routine surveillance tours through the city's old Italian neighborhoods, and he guided me in my research efforts.

I went regularly to Santasiero's to have lunch and to watch our local celebrity. Every now and then, I noticed that DiCarlo left his usual table to speak privately with some visitors in the restaurant's rear dining room. At those times, it was tough to keep my imagination in check.

One of those back room gatherings occurred just a few weeks after the May 1974 murder of John Cammilleri. Cammilleri had been a determined rival to Sam Pieri, a top man in Buffalo's underworld, as the regional crime family broke up into competing factions. I was able to identify Pieri and Carl Rizzo and a few others as they entered the restaurant. Then I noted Ron Fino's arrival. The son of Cammilleri confederate Joe Fino, Ron was also the business manager of Local 210 of the Laborers International Union of North America.

It was a peace conference of local underworld factions brought about by the Cammilleri murder, I concluded. I brought my theory to Joe Giambra at Buffalo Police Headquarters. He had me write everything down, and he put my report into the Cammilleri intelligence file. My conclusion was probably a bit off the mark. I later learned that the meeting was more likely to work out some details of union dental plan pilfering.

I managed to speak with DiCarlo on two other occasions.

My final DiCarlo encounter occurred in 1978, a couple of years before his death. My great uncle, Pete, who had moved away from western New York in the late 1930s, was in town for a visit. He was about ninety then, and DiCarlo was nearly eighty. I took Uncle Pete out to Santasiero's Restaurant. Over lunch, we got to talking about Buffalo during the Prohibition Era, and I mentioned that DiCarlo was seated at the front of the restaurant. Recalling DiCarlo's family from the old days, Uncle Pete insisted on seeing him.

I escorted Uncle Pete to DiCarlo's "office" and was astonished to find that the men seemed to recognize each other. They exchanged handshakes and cheek kisses and spoke together in Sicilian. After the conversation, I was told that DiCarlo pulled some strings at City Hall for Uncle Pete when he had trouble securing a liquor license in 1933. (The connection might have been deeper. Much later, a National Archives search uncovered Uncle Pete's 1931 bootlegging arrest record.)

In between my first and last DiCarlo meetings, I had a genuine sit-down with the retired gangster. I was terribly nervous. It didn't go at all as I hoped. Unfortunately, in such encounters, you don't get a second chance.

I had written a research paper on DiCarlo's impact on local mob history. Joe Giambra was evidently impressed with the paper, shared it with its subject and arranged in March 1974 for me to meet with DiCarlo to discuss it. Like others in local law enforcement, Giambra had a cordial relationship with DiCarlo.

There were about a million questions I wanted to ask DiCarlo. I actually rehearsed a few beforehand. But, just as in our first meeting, words didn't come easily.

At the table in Santasiero's, I introduced myself. We shook hands and sat down. "What's doin'?" DiCarlo's voice was deep and gravelly. I explained about Giambra and the research paper.

"That's nothin' kid." He called a waitress over. "Give the kid a drink."

I asked for Scotch and water. DiCarlo urged me to have something to eat. I thanked him but said the drink was fine. Then, before I could phrase my first question, someone I did not recognize sat down with us and began talking to DiCarlo. A few minutes later, that man surrendered his seat to another visitor. DiCarlo introduced me.

"Sam Pieri," he said.

I stood and shook hands with Pieri. When I returned to my seat, he dropped into the chair beside me, contributing significantly to a case of nerves that no amount of Scotch could relieve. I'm not sure how many more minutes I remained in Santasiero's that afternoon. It wasn't long before I excused myself and headed home without having asked a single question. That was two months before Cammilleri's underworld career came to an abrupt end.

Cammilleri's murder occurred around the time of my college graduation. With school behind me, work occupied much of my time and much of my concentration. I still worked in occasional lunches at Santasiero's, and I bumped into Joe Giambra now and then. Organized crime research was shoved onto a back burner until a startling event in 1980.

I returned home from work one afternoon and brought the newspaper with me to a chair on my front porch. Looking up from the pages, I noticed a man sitting in a parked car across the street. It was an odd sight. Our street was narrow and busy, and no one ever parked there. When my curiosity got the better of me, I strolled out to the mailbox. The car immediately moved forward and turned into my driveway.

A young man got out of the car, identified himself as an FBI agent and started asking me questions about the recent murder of Carl Rizzo. I only knew what I had read in the newspaper, and I told him that.

"What if I told you that I have something that belongs to you... which was found in his possession?" the agent asked.

"I'd be quite surprised," I answered. And I truly was when he reached into a briefcase and pulled out that old college research paper.

That sparked my interest in underworld research once again. I have been actively seeking information and trying to make sense of it ever since. One piece of the puzzle was especially difficult to acquire. That was Joseph J. DiCarlo's FBI file.

The DiCarlo file contained something like three thousand pages and required extensive FBI review. It took several years and quite a number of complaints by me in order to have it released under the Freedom of Information Act. When it finally arrived, I was impressed by how closely DiCarlo's life story matched the history of the Buffalo Mafia family. They appeared in western New York at about the same moment. The two matured together, growing in wealth and influence. As DiCarlo entered retirement, the Arm began to disintegrate. The organization did not survive long after his 1980 death.

The last section of the last part of the FBI file had a familiar look. It was that research paper again – this time with many of the names redacted. I honestly felt honored to have my work included in the official documentation of DiCarlo's underworld career. It reinforced a feeling I have had over and over since 1973: I was meant to write this story.

- Michael A. Tona

Introduction to Volume I

Joseph DiCarlo never rose to command the Mafia organization his father founded in western New York State. However, he was inextricably linked with that criminal society.

At a superficial level, DiCarlo and the Buffalo mob occupied the same place and the same time, and they were influenced by the same people and the same events. But they also shared a deeper connection. They were brought into existence by the same father. Through their parallel histories, they pressed toward similar goals, encountered similar obstacles and employed similar methods.

Though DiCarlo and the Mafia criminal society were bound together by their common heritage and their common experiences, there was little if any affection between them. Indeed, a sort of sibling rivalry seems to have developed over the years, intensifying as both reached old age and infirmity.

Just as the crime family had followed DiCarlo into life, it followed him into death. Shortly after he passed away in 1980, the criminal organization that had been both brother and nemesis to him also ceased to exist.

— — —

DiCarlo and the Mafia both arrived in Buffalo in 1908. In that year the DiCarlo family pulled up its shallow Manhattan roots and transplanted itself in the "City of Light" on the far end of the still busy Erie Canal.

Buffalo was ascendant, a rapidly modernizing center for industry, transportation and international commerce. The Pan-American Exposition of 1901, magnificently lighted through hydroelectric power generated more than twenty miles away in Niagara Falls, brought hemispheric recognition for the achievements of the eighth largest city in the United States.

The city's Canal District, long regarded as a center of debauchery, had begun to shed that old reputation. The process was aided by the settlement in the district of family-oriented Italian and Sicilian immigrants, who gradually squeezed the vice merchants from their midst.

For some time, the district remained a criminal breeding ground, but DiCarlo's father Giuseppe is believed to have brought organization to the local outlaws. In an era when a small number of America's leading capitalists monopolized major industry, Giuseppe's imposition of a formal Mafia structure on the business of crime must have seemed entirely appropriate.

Mafia structure and discipline, coupled with Buffalo's proximity to Canada, put the criminal organization in the perfect position to take advantage of bootlegging opportunities during the Prohibition Era. The western New York mob served as a pipeline for illegally imported alcohol, enriching itself and increasing its influence.

Both Joseph DiCarlo and the Buffalo-based crime family were shaken by Giuseppe's untimely death in the summer of 1922. The region's first Mafia boss was just forty-eight years old. Joseph was in his early twenties at that time, legally a man, but still adolescent in behavior and demeanor.

A DiCarlo relative, "Uncle" Angelo Palmeri, functioned briefly as guardian for Giuseppe's children and his growing criminal empire. Buffalo ceased to be the seat of regional underworld power a short time later, when Palmeri ceded his position as local Mafia chief to Niagara Falls-based Stefano Magaddino. Joseph DiCarlo, who must have been accustomed to deferential treatment, probably did not view the changes in a positive light.

At the conclusion of the Prohibition Era, as liquor lost much of its profit potential, DiCarlo and the Mafia organization began exploring alternative sources of income. Gambling, like alcohol consumption, was a pastime Americans enjoyed without much concern for its illegality. DiCarlo, then in his prime, sought to organize gambling ventures within the City of Buffalo, likely sharing his proceeds with the leadership of the regional

Magaddino Crime Family.

Frustrated by police crackdowns on his Buffalo gambling operations and seeing no role for himself in the Magaddino-run Mafia known as "the Arm," DiCarlo went to seek his fortune elsewhere. At the same time, the mob also went off in search of new rackets and new territories. As Magaddino established lucrative enterprises in concert with other crime families, DiCarlo formed his own relationships with underworld leaders around the country.

DiCarlo engaged in rackets in Cleveland and Youngstown, Ohio, and in southern Florida, before destiny and empty pockets brought him back to Buffalo in the mid-1960s. He and the criminal organization sired by his father were reaching old age.

DiCarlo's return coincided with a rebellion of a new generation of Buffalo Mafiosi against the authority of aging Magaddino. In his retirement, DiCarlo provided counsel to the rebel faction. He had lost the strength and the intestinal fire to do much more than that. The regional Mafia also had weakened. Magaddino, battling criminal charges as well as Buffalo rebels, advancing years and declining health, yielded to a heart attack in the summer of 1974 and left the crime family without a proven leader.

In frail health in the fall of 1980, DiCarlo entered a nursing home and passed away a short time later. Though the Mafia's younger generation had triumphed, their criminal organization was ailing. The Buffalo rebellion had fractured the crime family. Related bloodshed had depleted the ranks and had drawn the attention of federal law enforcement. Those who might have been capable of succeeding Magaddino were removed from contention through mob violence or successful prosecution. Within five years of DiCarlo's death, the crime family collapsed.

— — —

This is the story of Joseph DiCarlo's life and his death, his travels, his relationships, his successes and his failures. Because DiCarlo's story and that of the western New York Mafia are so closely interwoven, it also is the account of a Sicilian organized criminal society, which became rooted in the Buffalo area, thrived for decades along the waters of Lake Erie and then suddenly withered under the intense heat of government scrutiny.

In two volumes, *DiCarlo: Buffalo's First Family of Crime* chronicles a century of DiCarlo family history and related developments in the American Mafia organized crime network. This volume covers the period through 1937. Volume II focuses on the period 1938 to 1984 and includes an epilogue describing events as recent as 2012.

Chapter 1

New World

Joseph DiCarlo was six and a half years old as he boarded the steamship *Indiana* in the Italian port city of Naples on May 5, 1906.[1] He already was farther from his birthplace than he had ever been – farther than most of his relatives had ever been – and his journey was just beginning.

The boy must have felt both great excitement and great anxiety as he stepped from the gangway onto the deck of the *Indiana*. The excitement probably waned as he was led down steep metal stairs into the dimly lit steerage area in the bowels of the ship. He was comforted by the presence of his mother Vincenza, his brothers Francesco and Salvatore, his sister Rosaria and his uncle Luigi Grasso. Few among the other 1,519 third-class passengers could have looked at all familiar to him. Only three others were from the DiCarlo hometown of Vallelunga, Sicily.[2]

Together the steerage travelers would serve as human ballast through the next eighteen days, as they ate, slept and fought off seasickness in the cramped and foul-smelling quarters.

Their passage across the Atlantic was somewhat less unpleasant than that endured by many other emigrants from southern Italy. The *Indiana* was a very new vessel, with little accumulated filth and odor. It had been built in 1905 by the Riva Trigoso firm on order for Erasmo Piaggio's Genoa-based Lloyd Italiano Line. Three hundred eighty-one feet long and forty-seven feet wide with a modest service speed of 14 knots, she was one of four sister ships of Lloyd Italiano's "American States" Class.[3]

While Piaggio pioneered luxury trans-Atlantic cruises complete with gourmet dining, amenities were always reserved for first-class passengers, and *Indiana* was not among the Lloyd Italiano luxury ships. She could accommodate just twenty-five first-class ticketholders. Only nineteen sailed on the May 5 voyage.[4]

Passengers in steerage had nothing that could be considered luxury. They received scant attention from the crew, which neglected cleaning and maintenance duties until the ship approached its destination and an imminent inspection. Their meals were only the most economical imaginable, with the choicest bits being the leftovers from the first-class galley and whatever might be privately purchased from an enterprising steward. They had little in the way of sanitary facilities, ventilation or privacy.[5]

On the most pleasant sailing days, some of the passengers crowded into limited and out of the way areas of the deck to catch a few breaths of sea air mixed with engine exhaust and to be pelted with salty mist. On the less pleasant days, all remained below, distracting themselves as best they could from the acrid fumes of the unwashed and the ill. Many turned to song or to conversation to pass the time.

During the eighteen-day adventure, young Joseph DiCarlo and his family must have thought often of their Sicilian homeland, where many generations of DiCarlos had lived and worked and died.

― ― ―

Nestled in the fertile, oblong valley surrounded by the Madonie Mountains near the center of the Sicilian island, Vallelunga (literally translated as "long valley") served a farming population. It was far removed geographically, socially, economically and philosophically from bustling Italian port cities like Naples and Palermo. The Vallelunga community was homogenous, tightly knit and firmly rooted to the soil.

The municipality began as a feudal estate during the Middle Ages. The Notarbartolo family is credited with founding the town within its baronial right in the 16th Century. Feudal traditions lingered through the 19th Century, however, limiting access to farmland and holding much of the local population in a state of perpetual servitude.

Vallelunga experienced a building boom in the mid-1600s, when it was home to just seven hundred people. Its first Roman

Catholic house of worship was constructed in that period. The *Chiesa Maria Santissima di Loreto* (Church of Mary Most Holy of Loreto) was dedicated to the miracle of the Madonna of Loreto, a religious conviction that the house of Jesus' mother Mary was moved by angels from Nazareth in Palestine to the village of Loreto on the Sicilian coast.[6] The church's two bell towers dominated a piazza in the heart of Vallelunga. The piazza was eventually surrounded by tightly packed rows of sand-colored concrete homes and shops. The population grew along with the structures. By 1881, local residents numbered more than six thousand.[7]

The DiCarlo family had lived in the region for generations, though it had called Vallelunga its home only since the 1850s. At that time Joseph DiCarlo's grandfather, a stonemason named Francesco, moved to Vallelunga from his birthplace in neighboring Valledolmo. The documented presence of DiCarlos in Valledolmo can be traced back at least one hundred years earlier.[8]

Unlike low-lying Vallelunga, the community of Valledolmo was founded at the site of an old hill fortification known as Castelnormanno, constructed near the peak of the Cozzo Campanaro. Castelnormanno's 17th Century incorporation with neighboring Vallis Ulmi (Valley of the Elms) gave the town its name.[9]

With his move to the long valley, Francesco DiCarlo found masonry work and a bride. On January 4, 1857, he married Giuseppa Spera, descended from a long line of Vallelunga stonemasons.[10]

Francesco and Giuseppa Spera DiCarlo had two sons, separated by an interval of sixteen years. Marino, named according to Sicilian tradition for his paternal grandfather, was born in Vallelunga in October of 1857. Giuseppe followed on October 18, 1873. He was named for a great-grandfather, who lived in Valledolmo in the late 18th Century.[11]

Francesco retired from masonry to a farming life and died at the age of fifty-five,[12] when Giuseppe was only about seven years old. Marino learned his father's craft and became a mason. He likely served as head of the household until his mother's second marriage to Domenico Monteleone on New Year's Eve, 1883.[13]

Also married previously, Monteleone was a Palermo

native.[14] He earned a living as a merchant. It appears likely that he first encouraged young Giuseppe to break with DiCarlo family custom and to reach out for a life beyond the farms and pastures of central Sicily.

Giuseppe's marriage on December 11, 1897, also might have helped to guide him away from the DiCarlo tradition of manual labor in the region. He exchanged vows with Vincenza Grasso, daughter of a merchant from Santa Caterina Villarmosa, a fair-sized town east of Vallelunga and just north of the provincial capital of Caltanissetta.[15]

After his marriage, Giuseppe went in search of greater reward and an easier life than his ancestors had known. He became a merchant, possibly taking over the business of his stepfather, who had recently died. It took some time for Giuseppe to completely separate from the long valley, and he initially established a home there for his wife and their growing family. However, he spent considerable time in Palermo,[16] the island's center of commerce and the historic capital of the Mafia criminal society.

A secret brotherhood of outlaws, descended from ousted noble families of the island's medieval period, from urban guilds and from a long history of rural banditry, the Mafia was first recognized by outsiders after the Italian unification of the 1860s. By that time, it had penetrated virtually every corner of western Sicilian society.

The organization, most highly concentrated in the Palermo area, exacted tribute payments from peasants, professionals and tradesmen. It dominated local commerce, controlled elections, arbitrated disputes, dispensed justice and in every way behaved as Sicily's ruling class.[17]

Giuseppe certainly knew of the Mafia during his years in Vallelunga; he might have been part of it there. However, his known association with the underworld began during his stays in Palermo in the mid-1890s. There he established a friendship with Isidoro Crocevera, member of the Mafia brotherhood on both sides of the Atlantic Ocean.

Crocevera was just a few months younger than Giuseppe. He was medium height and medium build, with thick black hair and a black mustache molded into a handlebar, fashionable for the time. Though not physically intimidating, Crocevera's dark eyes gave him a sinister appearance. By the late 1890s, Crocevera moved to the United States,[18] but his relationship with Giuseppe continued for decades.

A first child was born to Giuseppe and Vincenza DiCarlo on September 20, 1898. The boy was given the name Francesco, in honor of Giuseppe's deceased father. Joseph DiCarlo was born November 1 of the following year. The family grew to include daughter Rosaria (Sarah) on February 6, 1902, and son Salvatore (Sam) on April 2, 1904.[19]

In the late summer of 1905, Giuseppe was ready to break with family tradition, sever his connection to Vallelunga and embark on a new life in a new land. Temporarily leaving his wife and children behind, he set out for America aboard the *S.S. Lombardia* of the Navigazione Generale Italiana steamship line. He landed in New York City on September 14 and made his way to the tenements of Oliver Street to meet with Pasquale Enea, whom Giuseppe described as his brother-in-law.[20]

Giuseppe found himself among an increasing number of Vallelunghesi in New York. Also in the city were his wife's cousins, Loretta and Rosaria (Sadie) Mistretta. The Mistretta sisters settled in lower Manhattan the previous summer, taking jobs in the clothing industry as dressmakers.[21] Several members of the Muscarella family, Mistretta in-laws, had also made the move across the Atlantic, as did the Bonasera clan, related by marriage to the Muscarellas.[22]

Probably aided by his numerous contacts in Manhattan, Giuseppe embarked on a business selling produce in partnership with grocer Salvatore Manzella from a storefront at 190 Elizabeth Street.[23] In spring of 1906, Giuseppe felt secure enough in his new surroundings to send for his wife and children.

— — —

Arrival in New York's hectic harbor was an emotional experience for new immigrants. As their ships steamed through the narrows between Brooklyn and Staten Island into Upper New York Bay, before them Liberty's stern but welcoming face came into view.

The Statue of Liberty at Bedloe's Island was just twenty years old, as Joseph DiCarlo and his family saw it for the first time on the morning of May 23, 1906. To them it must have represented the end of an arduous journey, the moment of family reunion, as well as the beginning of a new life full of hope and opportunity.

Behind Liberty, close to the New Jersey shore, the steerage passengers of the *Indiana* disembarked for processing at the Ellis Island facility. Having escorted his sister and her children safely into United States territory, Luigi Grasso separated from them at the island and returned to his wife and children in Sicily.[24]

The DiCarlos encountered one minor obstacle during processing. It was discovered that Giuseppe was late meeting the ship, and they were forced to wait for him. As a result, the first meal eaten by Joseph, his siblings and his mother on American soil was a box lunch provided by the immigration center. Though nothing to write home about, it was probably superior to the fare aboard the *Indiana*. At four-twenty in the afternoon, Giuseppe arrived, and the family was discharged into his care.[25]

Time in New York City went by in a blur for young Joseph DiCarlo. He later recalled that his family resided for a year in Brooklyn, but he was uncertain of the address and did not remember whether he attended school there.

Things became a little clearer following a move across the East River into Manhattan. That move occurred in time for the start of the 1907-08 academic year. Joseph recalled attending school on 105th Street between Second and Third Avenues in East Harlem, although he did not recall the name of the school.[26]

His first encounter with the American educational system probably was not a positive experience. In fact, it might have caused him some steerage flashbacks. Schools of the day typically were dilapidated, overcrowded and poorly ventilated.

The school Joseph attended appears to have been part of Grammar School No. 72. The grammar school proper was an exception to the rule of outdated educational facilities. It was a massive standalone building located on Lexington Avenue between 105th and 106th Streets, adjacent to St Cecilia's Roman Catholic Church. The school was constructed in the early 1880s with all the extravagant building comforts of that era, including indoor plumbing for sanitation and convenience, and tall, double-hung windows for light and fresh air.[27]

However, Joseph experienced none of those luxuries. The boys' primary school branch of G.S. No. 72 was not housed in the Lexington Avenue building. Instead, it occupied the former home of Primary School No. 19, a cramped and tightly enclosed rental space a block and a half away. In those dismal and stifling quarters Joseph began learning his three-Rs.[28]

Giuseppe DiCarlo continued to work on Elizabeth Street, in a neighborhood populated almost exclusively by Sicilian and Italian immigrants. At street level, the neighborhood was a confused collection of storefronts, sidewalk vendors, shoppers, pushcarts, wagons, barrels, crates, draft animals and abundant garbage. Awnings protruded from the front of many shops, shading the busy strip of walkway between the buildings and the curbside sellers. Above, the day's wash of hundreds of families typically could be seen draped across the balcony railings, fire escape ladders, and clotheslines of the upstairs tenements.

As in Giuseppe's Palermo days, his work brought him into regular contact with members and bosses of the Mafia criminal society. He remained in touch with his old friend Isidoro Crocevera, recently settled in Brooklyn after serving a three-year prison term for counterfeiting.

―――

Crocevera and his underworld colleagues Giuseppe Giallombardo and Giuseppe DePrima were arrested early in 1903 for passing phony five-dollar bills in Yonkers, New York. They were convicted of counterfeiting and locked away in Sing Sing Prison in Ossining, New York, on March 17, 1903. Of the three, Crocevera received the lightest penalty. Federal Judge E.H. Thomas sentenced Giallombardo to five years and DePrima to four years.[29]

Repercussions from that case were felt as far away as Buffalo, New York. The counterfeiting investigation led to the brutal murder of DePrima's brother-in-law and underworld associate, Buffalo resident Benedetto Madonia.

During interrogation of his suspects, William Flynn of the Manhattan office of the Secret Service came up with a plan he hoped would break down Crocevera and cause him to provide evidence against higher-ups in the counterfeiting organization: Flynn made it appear that DePrima was cooperating.

Between private questioning sessions, he treated Crocevera with contempt, while behaving in a friendly manner toward DePrima. Flynn's ruse achieved a result other than the one he desired. Crocevera did not break down, but instead managed to get word of DePrima's apparent cooperation to the leaders of the counterfeiting ring based in New York City.[30]

Giuseppe Morello, an immigrant from Corleone, Sicily, and supreme boss of the Mafia in the United States, was in command of that ring.[31] His brother-in-law Ignazio "the Wolf" Lupo served as his lieutenant and his enforcer.[32] In addition to counterfeiting, the two also supervised protection rackets, in which store owners paid a "tax" to be shielded from harm, corporate scams and a brand of extortion known as the Black Hand. In the Black Hand racket, well-to-do Sicilians and Italians were targeted with mailed demands for payment. Uncooperative victims faced penalties ranging from property destruction to death.[33]

After hearing of DePrima's apparent betrayal, Morello and Lupo decided that a demonstration of Mafia discipline was in order. Rather than wait years for DePrima's release, they met with the visiting Madonia in Manhattan in April of 1903. They had him murdered and left his nearly beheaded remains in a barrel on a Manhattan street corner.[34]

Giuseppe DiCarlo likely had regular contact with Morello gangsters and possibly with Giuseppe Morello himself.[35] A café operated by Morello family friend Pietro Inzerillo[36] sat just a block from DiCarlo's shop. Morello's Mafia organization regularly used the café at 226 Elizabeth Street as a meeting place, and authorities felt sure it was the site of the Madonia slaying. A wholesale grocery and importing business owned by Lupo was just around the corner at 8 Prince Street.

There are reasons to suspect Giuseppe DiCarlo of more than acquaintance with these Sicilian gangsters and of active participation in their underworld rackets.

The Pasquale Enea, whom Giuseppe first visited after arriving in the United States in 1905, is known to have served the fledgling American Mafia in a senior advisory role, while remaining a powerful leader in the underworld of Sicily.[37] Morello was deferential toward Enea and another important Sicilian Mafia boss named Vito Cascio Ferro.[38] Though Giuseppe indicated for the manifest of the *S.S. Lombardia* that Enea was a brother-in-law, Enea can be found nowhere in the DiCarlo family tree. He is similarly absent from federal and local census records of the era.

An additional link between Giuseppe and the Manhattan

underworld can be detected in the plight of his Elizabeth Street business partner Manzella.

Just months after the DiCarlo family's summer 1908 relocation to Buffalo, Manzella's creditors forced him into bankruptcy. The grocer told authorities he was financially ruined by regular payments he was compelled to make to Morello brother-in-law Ignazio Lupo. Believing his life was at stake, Manzella signed blank promissory notes for Lupo, which Lupo later sold at a discounted rate to others. Manzella said he provided thousands of dollars in notes and cash to Lupo through "two, three or four years, perhaps."[39]

Giuseppe appears to have been in business with Manzella for three years, possibly the entire duration of the grocer's reported troubles with Lupo. Giuseppe secretly could have served as an inside agent for the Morello gang, guiding his partner into making choices that would be profitable for the gang.

Morello's extortion technique was to get close to his victims and then win their friendship by guiding them through Black Hand ordeals. He would happen to be close to a well-to-do Sicilian immigrant's home or business just as an anonymous extortion letter was delivered. Knowing Morello to be an important figure in the underworld, the recipient typically would request his aid in negotiating with the Black Handers. Once Morello had assumed the ironic role of his victim's protector, many profitable manipulations were possible.

In one case, Morello secured the loyal service of a physician by posing as their representative in Black Hand negotiations. He told the physician's parents that he convinced an extortion gang to withdraw completely its cash demand. The family viewed him as a hero. In his gratitude, the physician served the Morello clan for years, even committing perjury in court to establish a Morello alibi.[40]

With DiCarlo as proxy, a similar technique might have been used against the Elizabeth Street grocer Manzella.

Lupo left New York City a very short time after the DiCarlo move to Buffalo. "The Wolf" abruptly closed his Prince Street grocery and importing businesses and vanished, leaving behind debts of nearly $100,000. When he returned to the city, he was arrested for extorting $4,000 from Manzella. He was arraigned in Jefferson Market Court on November 17, 1909. The magistrate released Lupo on bail, stating, "I have met Lupo before. I would be perfectly willing to parole him and don't think he would run away. If he did, it would be a good thing for the country." Manzella subsequently failed to make the scheduled court appearance, and the extortion charge against Lupo was dropped.[41]

Chapter 2

City of Light

Buffalo, New York, became the DiCarlo family's new home in summer of 1908. Considerable planning seems to have gone into the relocation. As in the case of the family's move across the Atlantic, Giuseppe went ahead first and scouted the area. His earliest presence there is documented by a trip across the Canadian border in March of 1907.[1]

At the time, Buffalo was already a major commercial and industrial center and the eighth most populous municipality in the United States.[2] Rail lines, the Erie Canal and port facilities on Lake Erie made the city a focus of international trade and travel. It served as the primary U.S. conduit for the export of grain produced in the nation's breadbasket. Massive grain elevators lined the city's lakefront. Abundant hydroelectric power produced at nearby Niagara Falls teamed with the city's accessibility to encourage the growth of industry. Located within easy reach of New York and Pennsylvania mining communities, Buffalo became a leading producer of iron and steel.

The growth of its factories and its docks meant an enormous increase in the demand for human labor. Immigrants flowed into the city to meet that demand, and Buffalo quickly became one of the nation's busiest immigrant ports. With newcomers arriving daily, the city's population more than doubled between 1880 and 1910. A large and growing immigrant Italian population, drawn by plentiful jobs in the manufacturing plants, on the rail lines and at the docks, had arrived from the southern Italy regions of Sicily, Calabria and Basilicata.[3]

Sicilians from the DiCarlo hometowns of Valledolmo and Vallelunga took a particular liking to the western New York region.[4] They and their fellow southern Italians joined earlier arrivals from Germany, Poland, Ireland, England, Canada and Russia to create a cosmopolitan community in Buffalo. People of many varied backgrounds mingled on the city streets.[5]

That mingling was not always harmonious. Buffalo experienced its share of ethnic violence.

A rivalry grew in the 1880s between a developing Italian community and a more established Irish community. The ethnic groups initially met in the slums of the West Side Canal District, also known as "the Hooks." Italian immigrants, seeking the least costly housing available, moved into the dockside region in large numbers, as slightly better off Irish families began moving from there toward the city's South Side. As the Italians displaced the Irish, cultural differences and extremely close quarters combined to produce some ethnic tension.[6] Heightening the tension was the overwhelming presence of the Irish in the local police[7] and fire departments, in the schools and in the workplace, even among the city's Roman Catholic clergy.

Genuine enmity between the groups resulted from economic considerations. As the city's unskilled laborers, including predominantly Irish dockworkers, attempted to improve their lot by organizing labor unions, Italian immigrants saw opportunity for themselves. Non-union Italian workers, willing to work long hours for little pay, undermined the labor movement and drew the lasting ire of the Irish.[8]

The groups came into direct conflict when two large shipping companies – the ironically named Union Steamboat Company and the Western Transit Company – were found to be using Italian and other non-union longshoremen exclusively. Out of work union members were incensed, and guards had to be assigned to protect the dockworkers. In 1884, a pro-labor mob violently attacked a group of Greek residents merely because they appeared to be Italians.[9]

Animosity between the Irish and Italian segments of the city became so intense that it reversed the political alignment seen in other major American urban centers of the period. Democratic Party organizations in New York City, New Orleans, Chicago, Kansas City and elsewhere typically absorbed first Irish and then Italian newcomers to the cities. With the benefit of a growing immigrant base, the supremacy of Democratic Party machines like New York's Tammany Hall was assured. Such an Irish-Italian combination proved impossible in Buffalo.[10] As a result, Italians there generally affiliated with the Republican Party.[11]

While those at the lower end of the Buffalo social scale viewed the newly arrived Italians as dangerous rivals, the city's elite viewed them as little more than animals. Conveniently forgetting that the City of Buffalo owed its existence to the foresight of Italian businessman Paolo Busti,[12] Italians were said to be dirty, lazy and prone to gambling and violence.

> ...there is hardly an Italian who does not carry a knife or a stiletto. This weapon they are only too ready to draw, and as they live so much together and are of such excitable temperaments they find innumerable provocations.[13]

Sicilian immigrants settled in large numbers in the Canal District, where the waters of an extensive canal system mixed with those of Lake Erie. Many were packed into filthy tenements similar to those on Manhattan's Elizabeth Street. But the Canal District also featured its own unique plagues.

Since the opening of the Erie Canal in 1825, that waterfront district had been home to numerous brothels and taverns, which catered to visiting sailors and local longshoremen. Canal District depravity became legendary. Robberies, drunken brawls and murders were commonplace.[14] Eventually, the area was deemed so perilous that even police officers dared not venture there alone.

The arrival of family-oriented Sicilians in need of affordable housing sparked a cleanup of the district. The process was a long and difficult one. Ultimately, neighborhood image-polishing resulted in the 1909-1910 renaming of Canal Street to Dante Place.[15]

Residents of the Canal District also dealt with a constant oppressive stench. The canal and its smaller, subsidiary waterways were used by the nearby tenements as a sewer system. The main canal generally had sufficient barge traffic to prevent stagnation and coax sewage toward the lake, but the smaller channels became stagnant pools full of human waste.[16] Livery stables added to the district's odor.[17]

The growth of the Sicilian colony helped push purveyors of vice from the district, but the immigrants brought another plague with them to their adopted homeland. That was the Mafia criminal society, also known at the time as the Black Hand.

As in New York City and other communities across the United States, wealthier Italian businessmen in Buffalo were harassed by anonymous Black Hand letter writers demanding cash. Before November 1906, there was little consequence to ignoring the demands. One local newspaper noted, "Since influential and prosperous Italian citizens have been receiving these threatening letters, none of which threats have been carried out, the police have been inclined to look upon 'Black Hand' methods as a joke..."[18]

The police took a different view after a bomb exploded outside the building at 140 Canal Street. That building belonged to fifty-two-year-old Dominico Bellissimo, who had been a Buffalo resident for more than a decade.[19] Within the structure were Bellissimo's butcher shop and a second floor apartment occupied by him and his family. The butcher had received and ignored two written demands to deliver $600 to the "Black Hand Society." Though no one was seriously hurt, the blast on the morning of November 20, 1906, shook an entire city block, tore the butcher shop's front door from its hinges, and shattered windows within a hundred-foot radius. It also convinced many in the community that Black Hand demands no longer should be taken lightly.[20]

In the wake of the incident, a number of Italians who had received threatening letters were granted pistol permits. Police Superintendent Michael Regan contemplated setting up a new detective bureau responsible solely for Black Hand matters and other criminal matters relating to the immigrant Italian population.[21]

Those who placed the bomb were never identified. Bellissimo's daughter spotted four men running from the building in an early morning fog just after the explosion tossed her from her bed, but she could not give a precise description of them. Police immediately arrested five men. There was little evidence upon which to base a formal charge. The men were arraigned on vagrancy charges but were then turned loose with an order to leave the city within twenty-four hours.

The authorities had better luck resolving a Black Hand extortion case a few months later. Nicola Vario, twenty-four, was charged with attempting to extort money from resident Bruno Cefoli by threatening to cut Cefoli's face with a knife. Cefoli brought the threat to the attention of police, and Vario was successfully prosecuted. On March 13, 1907, Vario was sentenced to a year in prison.[22]

Authorities believed for a moment that they had jailed the leader of the Black Hand Society and eliminated the extortion threat from the community. While Vario was a career criminal and gave every indication of serving as a gang boss,[23] his removal from Buffalo did not halt Black Hand operations.

In the summer of 1907, police were stunned to find that a Black Hand organization had brazenly attempted to extort $10,000 from the Buffalo Pitts Company, a highly regarded manufacturer of steam engines and vehicles located near the Lake Erie docks. Police arrested Frank Guarino and Liborio DiMarto for the attempted extortion. At arraignment, defense attorney Horace O. Lanza brought through police court such a parade of good character witnesses for his clients that they were discharged.[24]

--- --- ---

The DiCarlos arrived in Buffalo just as foreign-born residents became a majority of the city population. After two years of acclimation within the urban Italian colonies of Brooklyn and East Harlem, Joseph DiCarlo and his siblings probably took to Buffalo quite readily. Life in rural Vallelunga already had become a distant memory.

There are a number of possible reasons for the family's relocation. The DiCarlos might have wished to live near the Vallelunga and Valledolmo settlements of western New York. Many families from those sections of Sicily settled in the Buffalo area. Giuseppe DiCarlo's cousins from Valledolmo were among the recent arrivals.

It is possible that business opportunities attracted Giuseppe. Just before the move, the American economy bottomed out following the stock market crash and banking panic of 1907. The crisis hit New York City particularly hard. There were runs on banks and one prominent suicide, that of Charles Tracy Barney, former president of Knickerbocker Trust Company. Giuseppe's earlier trip to the Buffalo-Niagara Falls region and into Canada might have convinced him that prospects were better in that area.

However, a different sort of opportunity might have lured Giuseppe to the region: the opportunity to command the Buffalo Mafia.

The Morello gang of New York City had strong connections to the Buffalo area. Benedetto Madonia, the Buffalo resident who fell victim to the gang's wrath in 1903, had been a Morello associate. Morello lieutenant and brother-in-law Ignazio Lupo had friends and family in the area, including the Ingrassia and Oddo families.[25] Lupo is believed to have spent some time with Buffalo acquaintances during his absence from New York City between November 1908 and November 1909.[26]

A Morello desire to establish a Mafia subsidiary in Buffalo would not have been at all out of character. The underworld boss was known to have fostered the growth of allied crime families in places as far from his New York City base as Chicago and New Orleans.[27]

Giuseppe's ancestral ties would have made him an ideal enforcer of Morello's will in a region where so many Valledolmesi and Vallelunghesi lived and worked. The likelihood of shared experiences between Giuseppe and Morello in New York City and the continuing close relationship between Giuseppe and faithful Morello associate Isidoro Crocevera would have inspired Morello's trust.

Supporting the theory that Giuseppe moved west primarily for underworld opportunity is his apparently instantaneous rise to the position of local Mafia chief. Without the backing of an underworld authority like Morello, Giuseppe's rise would have been contested or at least delayed.

Giuseppe DiCarlo's presence in Buffalo appears to have aided the Morello counterfeiting racket. John A. Adams, Secret Service operative for the Buffalo District, worked with local police Detective Thomas O'Grady to uncover the region's bogus-bill distribution network. Their efforts resulted in the jailing of some street-level pushers of counterfeit notes but failed to identify top-level organizers.[28]

Months after the successful February 1910 counterfeiting prosecution of Morello, Lupo and much of their organization in

New York City, large numbers of phony two-dollar and five-dollar bills identified as "Lupo-Morello notes" continued to turn up in western New York. Some of the bills were believed to have been moved into the area as part of a shipment sold by Morello lieutenant Antonio Cecala to Buffalo saloonkeeper Calogero Pezzino.[29] Others apparently were brought in by Niagara Falls fish merchant Orazio Battaglia[30] and by Brooklyn racketeers Giuseppe Guarnieri and Salvatore Costanzo.[31] None of the counterfeit currency was connected directly to Giuseppe DiCarlo.

As Giuseppe established himself in business, he and his family lived for a short time in a tenement on West Eagle Street, near the Terrace and the Canal District.[32] The family moved after a few months to 120 Front Avenue, a short walk from the last leg of the Erie Canal on the city's Lower West Side.[33] Before spring of 1910, the family moved up the block into a rented home at 197 Front Avenue.[34]

In Buffalo, Giuseppe briefly sold produce on Front Avenue and then once again joined a Manzella grocery business – this time it was one owned by brothers Pietro and Carmelo Manzella, immigrants from Valledolmo and likely cousins to the Salvatore Manzella of New York City's Elizabeth Street.[35]

Pietro Manzella was born March 12, 1867.[36] He entered the United States through New York City within days of his twenty-fourth birthday and settled in the Buffalo area. There in 1893 he married Lucia LoGrasso, sister of Dr. Horace LoGrasso, a prominent physician specializing in the treatment of tuberculosis. Manzella gained American citizenship in 1897. He and his brother Carmelo established a wholesale grocery at Buffalo's Elk Street Market a year later.[37] Though he seemed to be the junior partner in the business, Carmelo was the older of the two immigrant brothers (a third brother Giovanni remained in Sicily). Carmelo was born December 8, 1864, and reached the United States a year before Pietro, in March 1890. Like Pietro, he became a citizen in 1897.[38] Both brothers were highly regarded businessmen in the Italian colony and were among the founding parishioners of St. Anthony of Padua Roman Catholic Church.[39]

In December of 1909 – one month after Lupo reappeared in New York City – Giuseppe DiCarlo, Pietro Manzella and a third partner, Carmelo Gugino, formed a stock corporation for the purpose of importing and wholesaling groceries, wines and liquors. They launched the Buffalo Italian Importing Company at 161 Court Street with an investment of $4,500. Each partner/director put up a third of that amount, individually purchasing fifteen shares of stock at one hundred dollars each. Fifty-five additional shares were created but unsold.[40] While not part of the ownership group, Carmelo Manzella served as president of the company. Luigi Cannatta, a Front Avenue resident who emigrated from Italy in 1902, was secretary and bookkeeper. In addition to his role as director, Giuseppe served as company treasurer.[41]

According to the articles of incorporation, the company's duration was to be "perpetual." It was hardly that. By the end of October 1910, the Buffalo Italian Importing Company was forced into Bankruptcy Court.[42]

A number of oddities were uncovered during the bankruptcy proceeding, which continued for more than a year and a half.[43] In January 1911, bankruptcy referee Chauncey J. Hamlin publicly accused the company officers with a fraudulent business failure. Hamlin had learned that in the firm's final two months of existence, almost $12,000 in cash and merchandise disappeared from its offices. The company directors could not explain those losses nor the disappearance of five barrels of wine on the final day the business was in operation. Financial records indicated the wine had been sold to a man named Francesco Chicanno. The court was unable to locate anyone by that name, and none of the three directors could provide any clue to his whereabouts.[44]

Arthur Lachman, a merchant from San Francisco, sought to recover those barrels of wine in addition to sixty-five others that had been delivered to the Buffalo Italian Importing Company just five days before it closed. The referee sided with Lachman, noting the purchase of the wine valued at over $1,400 was made on credit obtained by repeated misstatement of the business's inventory.

"I find that on August 15 the company made a fraudulent statement to Armour & Co." Hamlin said. "At that time it did not have on hand $7,000 of merchandise as stated or it has since fraudulently disposed of a large amount of goods. Three or four days after, it made a substantially similar statement to Bradstreet & Co."

Attorney Daniel N. McNaughton, representing the importing company's creditors, argued that further action should be taken to penalize company officers:

> It is seldom that so plain a case of fraudulent bankruptcy is uncovered. About $12,000 of the assets of the company disappeared during the last two months it was in business and not a word of explanation is offered. When asked for explanation of some of these transactions, each of the officers of the company points to the other two and in this way they are trying to escape individual responsibility. But assets amounting to $200 each day for the past two months of the company's existence have disappeared, and I don't believe they are going to be able to divide the responsibility.[45]

The circumstances were similar to the 1908 failure of Ignazio Lupo's importing business in New York City, though smaller in scale. Investigators determined that Lupo had used loans to make $50,000 worth of merchandise purchases in the week before his business closed and he vanished from the city. A court-ordered inventory of Lupo's Prince Street establishment discovered only about $1,500 in goods. A short time later, an estimated $50,000 of products associated with Lupo's name was found being loaded aboard a ship bound for Italy.[46]

The failure of the Buffalo Italian Importing Company appears not to have had a negative impact on the DiCarlo family finances. On January 17, 1911 – just three days after local newspapers hit the streets with stories of the importing company's "fraudulent failure" – the DiCarlo family purchased a large two-family home at 246 Seventh Street on the southwest corner of the intersection with Virginia Street. The neighborhood was middle-class residential, just a block from Front Avenue but a world away from the tenements of West Eagle Street. The house was purchased in Vincenza DiCarlo's name. That was likely a concession made to the possibility of legal action against Giuseppe, but it might also have been a simple effort to launder undisclosed proceeds of the business failure.

Giuseppe was not prosecuted in connection with the obvious frauds of his business venture. But it seems he did not get away scot-free. As the bankruptcy reached its resolution near the end of 1911, Carmelo Manzella won a civil judgment of $1,043.62 against Giuseppe.[47]

Italians had assimilated sufficiently into Buffalo society by 1910 to experience the other side of the organized labor issue. Italian union workers in the construction industry went on strike in June. Subsequent events showed that the Italian community had gained in confidence in the two and a half decades since first tangling with the Irish and was prepared to defend its interests.

The strike turned violent on the morning of June 8, when the contracting company of Joseph Metz & Sons brought in a crew of a dozen non-union Polish workers to complete construction of Faxon's bakery at Terrace and Court Street.

After completing a project at the YMCA building at Pearl and West Mohawk Streets in the early morning, the crew was loaded into a wagon. Police escorted the wagon part of the way to the bakery job site but then separated from the vehicle. At Terrace and Court Street, a group of striking Italian workers charged the unguarded wagon, while others hurled rocks and bricks at the Polish laborers within. The work crew scattered. Police rushed in, dispersed the crowd and arrested two men, Joseph Montana, thirty years old, of 53 Dante Place, and Serafino Carubba, fifty-two, of 198 Trenton Avenue.[48]

The following day, nearly two hundred Italians rioted at Upper Terrace and West Genesee Street. Union men and women from the railroad and garment industries joined the construction strikers in the violent protest. Twenty-five police officers succeeded in subduing the crowd. Seven people were arrested, including a man whose name was recorded in newspaper reports as Joseph DeCalo and Joseph DeCarlo.[49]

While this man could have been Giuseppe DiCarlo, it seems unlikely. There were at least four other men with similar sounding names in the city in 1910. One of those, a twenty-four-year-old hod carrier residing at 57 Front Avenue, seems a more likely participant in the construction workers strike.[50]

Following the morning riot, a gathering of several hundred Italian women, many with children in tow, gathered at City Hall to demand that Mayor Louis P. Fuhrmann take an active role in settling the local work stoppages. Fuhrmann refused to get directly involved, and referred the matter to Police Superintendent Michael Regan. The women marched the short distance to Police Headquarters. Regan met with representatives of the group but explained that he had no authority over labor matters. Displeased by the official reticence, the crowd created a noisy disturbance. A squad of police was assigned to clear the street, but quickly found it had its hands full.

> The women fought like wildcats, biting and scratching the officers, egged on by a few of the straggling strikers. Three of the women were arrested. Capt. [Edward] Forrestal led the squad of police. He and Detective [John] Murray and Patrolman [Joseph] Fitzgerald, who were in the very midst of the fray, were bruised and scratched.[51]
>
> Forrestal, with Detectives [Edward] Newton and Murray and Policeman Fitzgerald, gingerly assayed the task and one irate woman wrenched off a fence picket and cracked it on Murray's head. Another yanked off the captain's hat and tried to claw his face. It was a nasty job to tackle, but the police kept their tempers and finally induced the women to go home. Two ultraviolent ones were arrested.[52]

As the crowd disbanded, some of the women reportedly attacked Polish construction laborers and broke windows at a home at 179 Niagara Street.[53]

Those accused of rioting and of assaulting police officers during the two days of violence were arraigned on October 3, 1910. All pleaded not guilty. Convicted in early January 1911, each defendant received a reprimand and a twenty-five-dollar fine.[54]

― ―

Giuseppe DiCarlo and "Angelo" Palmeri possibly met as early as 1907-08 in New York City. They certainly became very well acquainted in Buffalo after 1912. Fast friends, the two men eventually shared their businesses, their households, even their families.

Benedetto Angelo Palmeri was born January 12, 1878, the second son to Francesco and Anna Caleca Palmeri of Castellammare del Golfo, Sicily. He was raised in an upper middle class household supported by Francesco's work as a merchant.[55]

Castellammare, which occupies a low-lying coastal area encircled by hills in the northwest portion of the island, appears to have been part of the ancient Sicilian settlement of Segesta. In the Middle Ages, the town was named for a prominent fortification built in its harbor and connected to the town by a drawbridge. A busy port city, Castellammare has traditionally handled the grain and produce exports for much of Sicily's Trapani province.[56]

At the time of Palmeri's birth, the town hosted two rival Mafia factions. One of the factions was a network of the Bonventre, Magaddino and Bonanno families and their allies. The Palmeri family apparently aligned itself with this faction. The other was comprised of the Buccellato clan and its allies. The two factions feuded in and around Castellammare for decades. When members of the rival groups settled in the United States, they brought their old alliances and the old feud with them.[57]

At the age of twenty-eight, Angelo Palmeri left Castellammare del Golfo and sailed aboard the *S.S. Lombardia* to New York City. He landed on September 7, 1906, and moved into a Stanton Street apartment with a cousin.[58]

Due to Stanton Street's proximity to the Elizabeth Street neighborhood where Giuseppe worked between 1907 and 1908 and where the Morello Mafia was based, it is possible that Palmeri met Giuseppe during that period.

Palmeri's eighteen-year-old brother Paolo joined him in New York on February 27, 1909, after a transatlantic voyage on the *S.S. Prinzess Irene*.[59] The eighteen-year-old was the third child of Francesco and Anna Palmeri to be named Paolo. Two earlier sons with that name died at young ages in 1890 and 1891. Their last son named Paolo was born October 1, 1892.[60]

Two years after Paolo's arrival, Angelo Palmeri moved to Buffalo, setting up a saloon at 103 Dante Place and living for a while in an upstairs apartment. He supplemented his income through gambling, a fact that came to the attention of law enforcement during an August 28, 1912, raid. Palmeri was one of eleven saloonkeepers arrested as police detectives swept through the Canal District looking for gambling houses. He and three others were convicted and fined fifty dollars each.[61]

There followed a period of unquestionable closeness between Palmeri and Giuseppe DiCarlo.

In the fall of 1913, Angelo Palmeri married Vincenza DiCarlo's cousin Rosaria Mistretta, at that time still a dressmaker in Manhattan. The Reverend Pasquale Beccaria presided over an October 5 wedding ceremony at Mary Help of Christians Church in New York City's East Village.[62]

By the end of the year, the newlyweds moved into the upper apartment of the DiCarlo family home at 246 Seventh Street in Buffalo. The two families became very close. Joseph DiCarlo and his siblings began calling Palmeri their "uncle," a title of respect and affection.[63]

The community knew Palmeri by another name, Buffalo Bill. That moniker resulted from his embrace of the American cowboy image. Palmeri was regularly seen around the city wearing a "ten gallon" hat and a holstered pistol.

Giuseppe, generally referred to at the time by the curious title "Don Pietro,"[64] entered into a partnership with Palmeri in a saloon business located at 103 Dante Place.[65] Giuseppe's level of involvement in the saloon is unknown. He also seems to have maintained a separate business of his own as a commission merchant on Michigan Avenue within the Elks Street Market.

Homes and businesses in the Italian neighborhood experienced a rash of unsolved Black Hand outrages in 1914. While Giuseppe was known at the time to be the leader of the regional Sicilian underworld, authorities could not link him to its criminal activities.

A saloon owned by Matteo Orlando at Trenton Avenue and Court Street was ripped apart by a July 14 explosion. The Orlando family, living in an apartment over the saloon, was not hurt.[66]

Three homes on Trenton were damaged in November bombings. Authorities revealed that the residents had ignored several Black Hand threats mailed from Postal Station C on East

Utica Street. The station was well outside of the immigrant Italian neighborhoods. That month saw complaints of Black Hand letters received in nearby Niagara Falls and Hamburg, New York. Recipients sought police assistance and demanded pistol permits.[67]

In December, two area businesses were targeted. Salvatore Vacante's saloon at 66 Carolina Street in Buffalo was wrecked in an explosion on December 9.[68] A December 20 attack destroyed the front of Joseph Basile's grocery in Niagara Falls. Basile reportedly had received cash demands mailed from Postal Station B on West Avenue on Buffalo's West Side.[69] The press reported that, "Suspicion has been directed to a group of men who have been living luxuriously without any apparent means of livelihood."[70]

That same month, Vincent Villardo of Niagara Falls came forward to reveal that he had received four Black Hand demands for money. The first letters instructed him to leave $500 with a man near the Log Cabin Hotel in Edgewater, New York. Villardo did not do as he was told. The fourth letter, which he rushed to authorities, contained a drawing of multiple daggers stabbing a human heart. All of his letters were said to have originated from Postal Station C in Buffalo.[71]

— — —

Joseph DiCarlo's early life in Buffalo, particularly the portion of it that followed the move to Seventh Street, was filled with advantages unknown by other young immigrants. These were not the result of merit or effort, but of his station in the community. His father was well respected, relatively wealthy and connected to powerful friends.

Joseph must have been aware of his good fortune as he mixed with fellow classmates in Buffalo schools. He first attended the No. 2 School on the Terrace in Buffalo for two years, beginning in the fall of 1908.[72]

No. 2 School had only opened its doors eight years earlier, primarily to serve Buffalo's burgeoning Italian community. In its first year, more than nine hundred of its one thousand pupils were children of Italian-born parents. Attendance was haphazard. Many schoolchildren also had jobs, selling newspapers, shining shoes or helping on farms.[73]

In fourth, fifth and part of sixth grade, Joseph attended No. 1

School on Front Avenue between Maryland and Hudson Streets. Attendees at that school, built in 1897, were also predominantly Italian.[74] The school was terribly overcrowded during Joseph's years there. The opening of an annex when Joseph was in fifth grade provided some relief.[75]

At No. 1 School, Joseph earned generally average grades, though he appears by that time to have fallen a year or more behind some of his peers. He was solid in reading, average in geography and language, and inconsistent in his spelling work. He showed considerable promise in arithmetic, turning in well above average marks in fourth and sixth grades. After the start of sixth grade in October 1912, he was transferred back to No. 2 School.[76]

There is reason to believe administrators of No. 1 were aware of Joseph's family connection to the local underworld. An unidentified employee of the school, who knew the DiCarlo family well, told federal investigators years later that Giuseppe was "generally regarded as the Buffalo representative of the 'Black Hand Society' or Mafia."[77]

Joseph eventually completed sixth, seventh and eighth grades there, graduating in spring 1917. Despite a decent academic record, he was uninterested in education. Perhaps he realized further learning could not be an asset to his preferred fields of endeavor. His father's status, probably achieved with little more than a grammar school education, already had opened many doors for him. He probably found those more attractive than the ones that might be opened by high school. Joseph put an end to his academic career in fall of 1917, after thirty-seven days at Hutchinson Central High School on Elmwood Avenue and Chippewa Street.[78]

His only further use for school came up a year later. The First World War was two bloody months away from its final armistice as Joseph registered for the draft on September 12, 1918. On his registration card, he indicated an October 1, 1900, date of birth – shaving almost a year from his actual age – and a continuing academic career as a Hutchinson High School student.

By that time, Joseph's United States citizenship was assured. That, too, was taken care of by his father, who submitted a Petition for Naturalization about eight months after Joseph left school. As a still-minor (under age twenty-one) child, Joseph earned his derivative citizenship when Giuseppe was naturalized July 7, 1920.[79]

———

Angelo Palmeri was arrested again in February of 1915. It was the start of a busy and sorrowful year for him and for his family.

Patrolman Edward McNamara was walking his beat along Dante Place (formerly Canal Street) at 7 p.m. on February 26. He heard a gunshot just as a drugstore window a few feet from him was shattered by a lead slug. The slug seemed to have been intended for McNamara.

Patrolman Soldano Frascella, a rookie working in plainclothes in the same Italian neighborhood, was alerted by the sound of the shot and grabbed a man running from the area of the drug store. As Frascella started for the patrol box at Dante Place and Evans Street, three men jumped him. The three men and Frascella's prisoner escaped into a nearby saloon.

Together, McNamara and Frascella entered the saloon. Frascella found the man he previously had in custody, and the officers took him again to the patrol box. Leaving McNamara with the prisoner, Frascella went in search of the others who attacked him.

It was then McNamara's turn to be assaulted. A group of men swarmed him. He tried to fight them off with his nightstick, but a growing mob wrested it from him as they gave him a severe beating. As the crowd called out, "Kill the cop," Frascella rushed back to his companion's aid.

With a revolver drawn, Frascella parted the crowd and made his way to McNamara, lying on the sidewalk beneath several of his attackers. A few pokes of Frascella's revolver muzzle ended the melee and earned the rookie three prisoners, Antonio Sacco, Charles Valarosa and Angelo Palmeri. The three men were charged with assaulting a police officer.[80]

Palmeri was convicted March 5 and fined the statutory maximum of $250. His codefendants, Antonio Sacco and Charles Valarosa, were discharged.[81]

The case was resolved just a few months before Rosaria Palmeri gave birth to the couple's first child, a daughter they named Anna.[82] Joseph DiCarlo and his sister Sarah served as godparents when infant Anna was baptized on November 11,

1915.[83]

Rosaria subsequently developed serious health problems. As the new year opened, she contracted influenza and pneumonia. Rosaria died at home on January 5, 1916. She and Angelo Palmeri had been married just two years and three months.[84]

Giuseppe DiCarlo was on hand to provide authorities with death certificate details. Curiously, he witnessed the document by making a mark instead of signing his name. Giuseppe's ability to read and write is documented elsewhere. The "X" he scratched onto the records might have been indicative of his emotional state at the time.

After a Mass of Christian Burial in St. Anthony Church, Rosaria was buried at Pine Hill Cemetery.[85]

Unable to care for an infant on his own, Palmeri separated from his three-and-a-half-month old daughter Anna. He brought her to New York City and left her in the care of the Mistrettas.[86]

With his family life suddenly in tatters, Palmeri also pulled away from Giuseppe to a degree. He moved to the Niagara Falls community. There he set himself up in a cigar store on Eleventh Street. He later opened a fruit store at 106 Niagara Street, just over a mile from his residence.[87]

The DiCarlo family was not immune to tragedy.

Just a few months after purchasing and moving into a cluster of homes at 270, 272 and 274 Prospect Avenue, the oldest of the DiCarlo children took ill. Francesco DiCarlo was eighteen years old when he was diagnosed with tuberculosis in January 1917.[88] Under the care of Dr. James Mangano, Francesco's condition nevertheless worsened over time.

During this period, Giuseppe continued in the nominal role of saloon operator at 88 Front Avenue and 211 Court Street, though it is likely that others handled the day-to-day functions of those businesses. After a year, he purchased a saloon property at 166 Front Avenue from the Ziegele Brewing Company. Like his other real estate dealings, that purchase also was made in his wife's name.

His commission merchant business soon became too much for him to manage, and he turned that over to Filippo Mazzara.[89] Mazzara, an immigrant from Castellammare del Golfo[90], occupied a leadership position within the DiCarlo Mafia organization and commanded a Castellammarese underworld crew in Buffalo.[91]

Giuseppe was ailing, and reported that fact on his World War I Draft Registration Card.[92] He indicated that he had been sick and unable to work. The specific nature of his illness was not stated. It is possible that he was simply consumed with worry over the health of his oldest son.

Francesco died on March 13, 1918, after a fourteen-month battle with tuberculosis. Giuseppe and Vincenza DiCarlo buried their first-born child at Pine Hill Cemetery on March 16.[93]

Less than a year later, Vincenza was diagnosed with cancer of the uterus. Giuseppe, likely still reeling from the loss of his son, summoned doctors from New York City, Boston and Rochester, New York, in a vain effort to find a cure for his wife.[94]

Vincenza was taken to Memorial Hospital in New York City for treatment in June 1919. In advance of the train trip, she prepared her will. Giuseppe, Angelo Palmeri and Palmeri's bodyguard Frank Rangatore were by her side as she revealed her intention to bequeath her property to her daughter Sarah, with her husband Giuseppe serving as executor.[95]

On July 3, surgeons at Memorial Hospital attempted to remove the cancer from Vincenza's body. She died following the procedure.[96]

Her death at the age of forty-six stunned the community and revealed the extent of her husband's influence:

> Buffalo's Italian colony was plunged in grief last week when death removed one of its most beloved and best known members in Mrs. Jennie DiCarlo… When news of her death was received in Buffalo, not only her relatives and friends mourned but the entire Italian colony of Buffalo was saddened by the news. Loved because of her wide charity among the Italians of the city and well known for her kindly disposition and sweet grace of personal charm, Mrs. DiCarlo was regarded by the sons and daughters of Italy as the most beloved Italian woman of the city.

The cortege from the DiCarlo home on Prospect Avenue to Holy Cross Church at Maryland and Seventh Streets was led by the Sons of Italy and accompanied by Serafino Scinta's elaborately uniformed band playing a funeral march. More than six hundred relatives and friends packed the requiem Mass celebrated by Pastor Joseph Gambino. Mourners needed over one hundred automobiles to travel from the church to Pine Hill Cemetery.

The church, the gravesite and the DiCarlo home overflowed with floral offerings, many of those testament to Giuseppe's underworld connections. Flowers were sent from locations across New York State, and from Massachusetts, Pennsylvania, Illinois and Michigan:

> Some of the prominent Italians who sent floral offerings were: Joseph Costello, Dr. Stephen Rosselli, Bartolo Aleide, Thomas Dyke, Anthony DeFusto, Mussio family of Brooklyn, Joseph Badinna of New York, Battaglia family of Pittsburgh, Sunceri family of Pittsburgh, Galboa family of Hornell, N.Y., Augustus Scalia of Erie, Pa., Charles Bonasera, Rangatore and Palmieri of Niagara Falls, Frank Fina, "Friends of Niagara Falls," Peter Silato, Philip Gandolfo of Boston, Mass., N. Caldais, G. Grammanco, Anastasi brothers, Frank Ulizzi, Orazio Tropeo, Pacini family, V. Malone, John Vitale of Detroit, Gasper Milazzo of Detroit, Andrea Macaldino of Detroit, Joseph Aiello of Utica, Carlo Gelsomino and friends, Miss Bessie Bellanca, Benjamin Carroll, N. Sciambra, Bellissimo brothers, Frank Battaglia, Dr. Giambrone, Frank Cappello, Frank DiCarlo, Sons of Italy, John Provino and Joseph Battaglia of Batavia, N.Y., Umbarto Randaccio, Vaccaro brothers and Sacco brothers.[97]

Among the senders were several future Mafia leaders. John

Vitale and Gaspare Milazzo rose to top positions in the Detroit "Partnership." Joe Aiello and Orazio Tropea moved to Chicago. Aiello, who was born in Bagheria, Sicily, and settled in Utica, New York, upon his arrival in the U.S., became boss of a Mafia family in the Windy City as well as an important figure in the Chicago-based Unione Siciliana organization. Tropea, a Catania native who settled in New York City and then married a Buffalo woman before heading further west, stepped into an enforcer's role for the Genna and Aiello Mafia clans. All of those important underworld figures died violently within the following decade.

The Vaccaro brothers were local Buffalo toughs. Charles Bonasera, Frank Fina, Frank Ulizzi and Umberto Randaccio were members of Giuseppe DiCarlo's Mafia organization. Bonasera, a relative of the Bonaseras who settled in New York City, was one of the many Vallelunga immigrants to western New York. Ulizzi might also have had underworld connections in Cleveland, Ohio, where he was found murdered six months after Vincenza DiCarlo's funeral.[98]

Vincenza was laid to rest in a large family plot Giuseppe purchased at Pine Hill Cemetery. Giuseppe had the remains of their son Francesco transferred next to Vincenza's, and he marked the family gravesite with a twelve-foot-high monument – a five-foot statue of the Madonna upon a seven-foot granite pedestal bearing the family name.[99]

Chapter 3

North of the Border

Shots were fired, and James Celona collapsed to the curb in front of his confection business. April 16, 1918, would be the last day of the twenty-nine-year-old's life. Three bullets had entered his body. One of those had passed through his midsection, damaging his liver, his pancreas and his left kidney and causing a massive loss of blood. He had just minutes longer to live.[1]

The shooting occurred in broad daylight on a busy spring afternoon in Hamilton, Ontario, and a crowd quickly gathered in front of Celona's York Street business.[2] When two young Italian men, Dominic Speranza and Dominic Paparone, attempted to flee the scene, a number of Hamilton residents and police officers pursued.

The desperate young men rounded the corner and ran up Park Street for several blocks. They turned left at Mulberry Street and kept running. Witnesses spotted Speranza tossing away a revolver behind a building at Mulberry and Bay Streets. After another block, the two men separated. Speranza ran down Railway Street and entered a private home near Cannon Street. Paparone continued on to Caroline Street, where he ran into the arms of Hamilton Constable Brady. Brady had borrowed an automobile from a York Street businessman and circled around to head off the fleeing suspects. Paparone was found to be carrying a handgun, which had not been fired.

Constable Joseph Duffy followed Speranza into the Railway Street residence. Searching the home, Duffy spotted a pair of legs emerging from beneath coats hung on the back of a door. The legs belonged to Speranza. As the constable grabbed him, Speranza – perhaps affected by the long run, by nervousness or by guilt – became violently ill.[3]

Speranza and Paparone were held on a preliminary charge of vagrancy while police conducted an investigation into Celona's murder.[4]

Celona had been a resident of Hamilton for less than a year,[5] but already was well known in the city's Italian colony. He had the appearance of a successful businessman, but no one attributed his obvious wealth to the legitimate earnings of his York Street candy and ice cream shop.[6] The shop was generally understood to be a front for criminal activity. Authorities received word of gambling on the premises,[7] and one neighbor complained that young girls were brought to the site for "improper" reasons.[8] In fact, Celona was a leading figure in an Ontario criminal network comprised of fellow immigrants from the Calabrian region of southern Italy[9] and headed by Domenic Sciaroni of Guelph.

Sciaroni, also known as Joe Verona, established himself in Guelph in 1912, after moving through Buffalo and Toronto.[10] Calabrians in those communities, including relatives in Buffalo, participated in his underworld rackets. However, Sciaroni scrupulously avoided doing business with Sicilians and avoided all contact with Toronto Mafia boss Toto Gagliardo.[11]

Celona's association with the Sciaroni network dated back at least four years to a time when he resided in St. Catharines, Ontario, near the U.S.-Canada border.[12] Among its other illicit enterprises, the Calabrian organization involved itself in the illegal transport and sale of liquor.

As Celona was taken to Hamilton's General Hospital, another underworld figure was by his side. Rocco Perri had arrived at Celona's shop minutes earlier and had witnessed the shooting.[13]

Like Celona, Perri moved to Hamilton from St. Catharines and was connected with the Calabrian criminal society in Ontario. In St. Catharines, Perri worked at a bakery operated by organized crime figure Filippo Mascato.[14] Perri settled in Hamilton in 1915, living first at 157 Caroline Street North[15] before moving several years later to 105 Hess Street North.[16] Outwardly an importer of pasta and olive oil, Perri, who had no qualms about dealing with the Sicilian Mafia, was quickly moving up through the ranks of the Calabrian criminal society.[17] The murder of Celona accelerated his climb.

Perhaps because he benefited from Celona's demise, Perri's account of the shooting placed the blame on Celona. He told investigators that Dominic Speranza acted only out of self-defense.[18] His story was not supported by other eyewitnesses.

According to J.S. Tallman, an official of Armstrong & Company at 68 York Street, Speranza's actions appeared deliberate and unprovoked. Tallman reported that he watched the shooting through his business's front window. He said he saw Celona walking toward the confection shop from the west at just after 2 p.m. Speranza walked into view from the east. The two men passed as if they were unacquainted, Tallman observed. However, Speranza then wheeled, drew a .38-caliber handgun and fired twice into Celona's back. Celona cried out and dropped to the sidewalk, as Dominic Paparone joined Speranza and the two began to walk away. Speranza spun about a second time and fired twice more at Celona. One of the shots missed its target and ricocheted off the sidewalk.[19]

Coroner G.E. Leach presided over an April 23 inquest into the killing. Perri was one of the witnesses. He testified that he had known Celona for four years, a period of time that stretched back to the time in which they both lived in St. Catharines. Perri said he had known Dominic Speranza for a year and Paparone for two months. Asked if Speranza was a friend of his, Perri responded, "All Italians are my friends."

The coroner's jury did not accept Perri's self-defense argument, and, after just fifteen minutes of deliberation, returned a charge of willful murder against Speranza and Paparone. The two young men responded without emotion when they were officially charged with murder the following day.[20]

Speranza was unable to keep his composure during the November jury selection in Chief Justice Falconbridge's court. A reporter noted that within a few minutes the defendant went from smiling to fighting back tears.

Speranza entered a self-defense plea to the murder charge. A number of Italian witnesses came forward to support his claim. Witness Angelo LaRose testified that he observed Celona grab Speranza, demand the payment of $50 and then strike Speranza on the face. Defendant Paparone told the same story. Speranza provided more details when he took the stand:

I heard footsteps behind me. When I turned,

> Celona was there and grabbed me by the coat... He held me by his left hand and struck me with his right hand... I did not strike him at all. He was too strong for me. I was dazed after he hit me the first time... He reached into his vest pocket and pulled a knife out... He said that would be my last day.[21]

Speranza said he shot Celona just to get away. When asked why he then returned to shoot the man two more times, the defendant claimed he did not remember doing so. "I was too excited to remember," he said. In a possible quest for leniency, Speranza insisted that he was only seventeen years old and had been just sixteen at the time of the shooting. A court observer suggested that he looked to be in his early- to mid-20s.

In his charge to the jury, Falconbridge noted that the testimony of Italian witnesses differed from that of non-Italian witnesses. "There is no witness who speaks of anything in the nature of an assault upon Speranza by Celona except the Italians," Falconbridge cautioned. The justice asked jurors to ignore testimony regarding the nature of Celona's business and to consider whether Speranza's actions were compatible with a plea of self-defense.

"If he was attacked by Celona, he has a perfect right to defend himself," Falconbridge said. "But he had no right to go away and then return to the attack later."

The jury deliberated for an hour before finding Speranza guilty of manslaughter. With no evidence that Paparone did anything more than run from the scene, the jury found him not guilty. Falconbridge immediately sentenced Speranza to spend the rest of his life in Kingston Penitentiary.[22]

While the not-guilty verdict kept Paparone out of prison, it could not protect him from vendetta. He was shot in the back on the morning of January 28, 1919, at the corner of Lincoln and South Main Streets in the city of Welland, Ontario, just about a dozen miles from the U.S. border. Authorities linked his murder to the Celona killing and speculated that a member of the Sciaroni criminal network from Hamilton was responsible.[23]

The Celona killing turned out to be merely the first of many high-profile murders involving bootlegging gangs in the region.

By the time of Celona's death, Ontario was already a year and a half into its Prohibition Era. The Ontario Temperance Act, banning the domestic sale but not the manufacture or export of beverages containing more than 2.5 percent alcohol, went into effect September 16, 1916. As in the U.S. years later, support for the measure was due in large part to wartime patriotism. Canada and other dominions of the British Empire entered the First World War in 1914.[24]

Prohibition laws brought new regulations for individuals and businesses and new opportunities for outlaws. They also brought dramatic changes to criminal organizations on both sides of the U.S.-Canada border. As underworld groups worked to link a reliable supply of alcohol with a thirsty market, they came together into sprawling networks. The potential for vast profits lured even groups as traditionally insular as the Sicilian Mafia into business relationships with outsiders.

Competition for bootlegging profits sparked feuds between and within the new criminal networks. Located along one of the busier liquor smuggling routes, western New York and nearby communities in Canada experienced a great deal of underworld bloodshed. The killings helped Rocco Perri rise to the exalted position of "King of Bootleggers."[25]

― ― ―

Angelo Palmeri rebounded from his losses in 1919, as he moved into an apartment at 558 Portage Road in Niagara Falls.

On December 21, Palmeri married Loretta Mistretta, the older sister of his late wife. The wedding, like his first, was held at Mary Help of Christians Church in Manhattan. The Reverend Ercole Anthony Maglio, assistant pastor, conducted the Mass. The witnesses to the ceremony were Filippo and Giuseppina Gandolfo.

The newlyweds returned to Palmeri's Niagara Falls apartment, along with Palmeri's daughter by his first marriage. Anna, then five years old, was emotionally bonded to Loretta by that time. The two probably had lived together for all but the first few months of Anna's life.

Palmeri's employment was unclear. A local directory listed him as a fruit dealer. His underworld aide Frank Rangatore was known to have been a commission merchant dealing in produce and might have welcomed an investment from or a partnership with Palmeri. However, census records point to a different position for Palmeri, calling him the keeper of a restaurant.

In truth, by the end of 1919 crime had probably become Palmeri's primary occupation. The positions listed in directories and government records were likely no more than sidelines or smokescreens. In this period Palmeri appears to have worked in Niagara Falls rackets with Calabrian boss Joseph Sirianni, fellow Castellammarese Mafioso "Don Simone" Borruso and an American-born Borruso underling named Joseph Henry Sottile. Through them, he came to be associated with Rocco Perri of Hamilton, Ontario.

Sirianni was one of several brothers raised in the town of San Pietro Apostolo in Calabria.[26] He reached the United States in 1897[27] and was followed by his siblings. Three of the Sirianni brothers – Joseph, Samuel and Saverio – operated a saloon on Eleventh Street in the Italian colony of Niagara Falls.[28]

Borruso was born in Castellammare del Golfo, Sicily, in May 1880.[29] He sailed to the U.S. from Palermo aboard the *S.S. Saxonia*, arriving in New York City on April 9, 1912.[30] He eventually settled on Whitney Avenue in Niagara Falls.[31]

Sottile was born in 1890 to Italian immigrant parents in Pennsylvania. Working as a barber, he moved into a rented home at 133 Eleventh Street before 1920.[32] With connections on both sides of the U.S.-Canada border, he became a key participant in Prohibition Era liquor smuggling networks.

— — —

America's "Noble Experiment" to ban the manufacture, transport and sale of intoxicating beverages was proposed as the 18th Amendment to the U.S. Constitution late in 1917. The amendment won the necessary state support for ratification in just over a year. But the idea of banning alcohol – forcing the country "dry" – was not something new.

An American Temperance Society, which urged abstinence from alcohol, was established in Boston in 1826. It sparked a temperance movement across the country. Various similar groups, including the Women's Christian Temperance Union, sprang up.[33] The groups initially strove for moderation in the drinking of alcohol. Over time, their objective became a complete ban on intoxicating beverages.

New York State's old patrician elite, feeling itself besieged by growing numbers of beer-drinking German and Irish immigrants in the middle of the 19th Century, managed to pass a ban on the sale of intoxicating liquor in the state in April 1855. The measure later was ruled unconstitutional.[34]

Distrust of immigrants and of liquor-fueled political organizations that catered to them prompted the creation of the politically savvy Anti-Saloon League in 1895. The league focused the attention of conservative Americans on the crimes committed by people under the influence of alcohol and on the resources diverted from productive economic uses to provide recreational alcohol. The league disseminated a Prohibition message through the nation's churches, making use of the oratorical skills of such prominent men as Howard Hyde Russell[35] and dry-sympathizer William Jennings Bryan.[36] It then used its wide base of support to persuade lawmakers to adopt dry measures.

With U.S. entry into World War I, Prohibition was changed from an issue of morality to an issue of survival. Bryan communicated a warning to America:

> We can't afford to take the children's bread and give it up to men to convert into alcohol. How can we justify the making of any part of our breadstuffs into intoxicating liquor...? We cannot have our men's strength impaired. We need men at maximum strength, with their brains clear and their nerves steady.[37]

The anti-immigrant feelings of prohibitionists were only intensified by America's participation in the global conflict. German immigrants were tainted by their ethnic connection to America's primary opponent in the war. Italian immigrants bore the stain of their country's pre-war alliance with Germany and Austria-Hungary. Irish immigrants were linked to the enemy through the Germany-supported activities of Ireland's separatist movement.[38]

After years of debate and failed efforts, Congress approved a proposed Prohibition amendment to the U.S. Constitution near the end of 1917. The measure outlawing the manufacture, sale or transportation of intoxicating liquors was sent to state legislatures for their approvals. Ratification required the approval of thirty-six out of the forty-eight existing states within a period of seven years.

Already twenty-eight states had individually banned or restricted the sale of intoxicating beverages.[39] Elsewhere laws were on the books closing saloons on Sundays. In addition, breweries had earlier agreed to modify their product so that it would contain no more than 2.75 percent alcohol for the duration of the war. The United States was gradually drying out. Ratification of a national prohibition amendment seemed inevitable.

Thirty-one states backed the amendment between January 8, 1918 and January 13, 1919. Five more states – Missouri, Nebraska, North Carolina, Utah and Wyoming – approved the proposal on January 16, 1919, giving the dry cause all the support it needed in a period of just 394 days. All states with the exception of Rhode Island eventually voted for the measure. New York State was slow to do so. It approved the 18th Amendment on January 29, 1919.

The amendment's effective date was one year from its ratification. However, the Anti-Saloon League and allied legislators pushed up the deadline through passage of the Wartime Prohibition Act on November 21, 1918. The reasoning behind the act was that communicated by Bryan – clear heads at home were necessary to properly equip and feed the army and no foodstuffs should be wasted in wartime to the production of alcoholic beverages. However, the act was not passed by Congress until ten days after an armistice had been signed, effectively ending the war. Act supporters nevertheless felt a measure should be in place to restrict alcohol consumption during the country's demobilization. The Wartime Prohibition Act took effect June 30, 1919, about seven months before enforcement of the 18th Amendment could begin.[40]

As the effective date of Prohibition measures approached, enforcement remained an unresolved question. The 18th Amendment allowed for concurrent jurisdiction by the federal government and the states, but there was no clear plan in place to apprehend, prosecute and penalize violators, and no precise definition for what constituted "intoxicating liquors."

The Volstead Act, passed over President Woodrow Wilson's

veto on October 28, 1919, sought to remedy those problems. It defined as intoxicating any beverage containing one-half of one percent or more of alcohol by volume.[41] That limit was far lower than limits set by various states and the meager 2.75 percent limit set by wartime breweries. The act also specifically empowered the Department of the Treasury to enforce the restrictions against the sale, manufacture and transportation of alcoholic beverages.

New York State issued licenses to allow certain saloon owners to continue operation during the postwar demobilization but also passed a state excise law commanding all saloons to close January 31, 1920, about two weeks after the effective date of the 18th Amendment. Officials noted that after February 1 the excise law would not be enforced against saloons opting to serve soft drinks or "near-beer" with less than 0.5 percent alcohol.[42]

By law, the City of Buffalo went dry with the rest of New York State on February 1. After that date, liquors could be purchased legally only as prescription medication and only in very small quantities. Anyone desiring a sip of something stronger than near-beer would need to turn to moonshiners, the operators of home distilleries, wineries and breweries, or to bootleggers, the black market smugglers of illegally imported booze.

Even at the opening stage of the Prohibition Era, Buffalo newspapers appeared skeptical that the 18th Amendment could change the habits of local drinkers while alcohol continued to flow more freely just a short distance away:

> ...the proximity of the dominion [Canada]. where "booze" is priced at $15 to $16 a case, will give rise to greater vigilance on the part of those charged with the enforcement of Prohibition.[43]

Due to its location on the Canadian border,[44] its busy international port and its access to domestic transportation networks, Buffalo was perfectly positioned to serve as a conduit for the smuggling of illegal liquor into the United States. While Giuseppe DiCarlo outwardly complied with alcohol restrictions by billing his Front Avenue drinking establishment as a soft-drink saloon,[45] behind the scenes he mobilized his underworld organization to take advantage of lucrative black market opportunities. The DiCarlo Mafia's increasing control of the liquor conduit greatly enhanced its wealth, its local influence and its prestige among the nation's organized criminal enterprises.[46]

However, Canadian bootlegging gangs held the upper hand in liquor smuggling deals at the dawn of U.S. Prohibition. With more than two years of experience in the racket and with easy access to legally produced alcohol, the Calabrian criminal association in Ontario was poised to take advantage as the U.S. gradually went officially dry. That network included Rocco Perri's Hamilton organization and the closely related Guelph gang of Domenic Sciaroni.

— — —

The U.S. Prohibition Era was only weeks old when the bodies of two murdered men were found in a ditch beside Bader Avenue S.W. in the Brooklyn District of Cleveland, Ohio.[47]

Mr. and Mrs. Sherman Ransopher, residents of Flowerdale Avenue were walking home from a Salvation Army meeting just after one o'clock on the morning of January 30, 1920, when Mrs. Ransopher spotted what appeared to be a man's foot sticking out of a Bader Avenue snowdrift near the intersection with Pearl Road. The couple rushed to the nearest home, that of Charles Leibold on Pearl Road. Mrs. Ransopher remained behind as Mr. Ransopher and Leibold returned to the snowdrift. Using matches for illumination, the men saw three bloody bodies in the ditch and immediately went to summon police. Upon their return, however, only two bodies remained in the ditch. A trail of blood led away from the site, indicating that the third victim spotted by Ransopher and Leibold was still alive.

Police followed the trail of blood about a mile. It ended at a well-traveled road. The person who left the trail was never found.

Detectives found a letter in the pocket of one of the victims. It was addressed to Salvatore P. Russo of Buffalo. Signed by his father, a New York accountant, the letter described Russo's recent financial difficulties. With the help of relatives, police positively identified the murder victims as Russo, age thirty, and fellow Buffalo resident Frank Ulizzi, forty. The authorities concluded that Russo and Ulizzi were both involved in smuggling liquor into Cleveland.[48]

Russo, an itinerant artist, was known to visit Cleveland in connection with bootlegging operations. His brother Michael, who went by the name Michael Valenzano, was arrested as a pickpocket and con-man in Buffalo in 1919 and was also believed to be involved in organized criminal activity. Men identifying themselves as police but behaving very much like gangsters had ordered the visiting Michael Russo out of Cleveland just a day before Salvatore Russo's murder.

Ulizzi was a fish dealer, a partner in a moving and trucking business and a member of Giuseppe DiCarlo's Mafia organization. Authorities believed he was involved in Black Hand extortion rackets and operated a safe house for Mafiosi on the run.[49]

The two victims had arrived in Cleveland just hours before their deaths, reaching Union Depot at nine-forty in the evening on the twenty-ninth. Police learned they were met at the train station by business associates.[50]

Detective Charles Cavolo investigated the murders for the Cleveland police and learned that more than bootlegging was involved. On February 22, he interviewed Buffalo resident Anthony Vaccaro, a friend of Ulizzi. Vaccaro said he last saw Ulizzi on January 28, when Ulizzi asked him for money and for the address of a place to stay in Cleveland. Vaccaro had no money to lend but gave Ulizzi the name and address of his brother-in-law, Antonio Zito, 2422 Woodland Avenue, Cleveland.

While Cavolo questioned Vaccaro, Buffalo police searched the Vaccaro home and discovered items that had been stolen from several stores around the city. Cavolo reported to his superiors, "Upon investigation I am satisfied that Frank Ulizzi; Tony Vaccaro; Mike Russo, alias Valinzano; and [associate] Mike Martino have been committing burglaries in and about Buffalo and Frank Ulizzi has been visiting other cities disposing of the goods."

Cavolo also learned from sources in Buffalo and Cleveland that an Ulizzi business address at 237 Seneca Street in Buffalo was a front. "It is known from coast to coast as a place for criminals to go there and be protected by Frank Ulizzi while they were there," Cavolo reported.

The detective was certain that Vaccaro knew more about the Ulizzi and Russo murders than he was revealing. Lacking evidence against Vaccaro, Cavolo was forced to release him.

Buffalo police held him on a charge of receiving stolen property.[51]

———

Shots were fired in the vicinity of Giuseppe DiCarlo's soft-drink saloon[52] at 166 Front Avenue shortly after midnight Sunday, August 8, 1920. Police investigators were unable to establish clearly who did the shooting or why, though they had theories and the basic building blocks of a criminal case.

They had two victims. Both were in Columbus Hospital on Niagara Street.[53] One could be of no help to the investigation, as he was held in the hospital morgue. The other was a local man, also of no help, as he was determined not to discuss how he came to have a bullet hole in his leg.

Police had two suspects in custody, neither of whom felt talkative. They also had a good number of likely witnesses, who claimed to have seen nothing at all and to have heard nothing helpful. They even had a confession of sorts from the surviving victim, though they did not consider it believable.

Mostly they had supposition unsupported by evidence. That was par for the course in the densely populated waterfront neighborhood where violent crimes occurred with regularity but only when no one was looking.

The fruitless investigation began when doctors were summoned at 1 a.m. to tend to an unidentified shooting victim, lying unconscious at Virginia and Seventh Streets. Doctors Anthony Barone and Salvatore Lojacono examined the man and quickly sent him on to the hospital. Little could be done for him. The man lingered for half an hour, never regaining consciousness, until he succumbed to his injuries.[54]

Medical examiners Earl G. Danser and Charles E. Long determined that a slug, fired into the victim's back, tore through his liver and intestines, causing massive internal bleeding. Death was the result of hemorrhage.

The deceased was said to be about forty-five years old, five-foot-eleven in height and two hundred pounds. He had graying black hair and wore a brown suit with a white striped shirt. He did not have a hat or shoes with him at the hospital and carried no identifying papers.[55]

Before three o'clock that morning, thirty-eight-year-old Buffalo resident Vincent Vaccaro was brought into the same hospital with a bullet wound in his left thigh. Vaccaro, who lived close to the DiCarlo saloon, would answer no questions about the cause of his wound. It was evident that he had changed his pants before going to the hospital. The pants his doctors saw had no bullet hole in them.[56]

Detectives focused their investigation on the area of the saloon. They spoke with residents of the neighborhood and took four men to police headquarters for questioning: Vincent Vaccaro's brother Anthony, the Vaccaros' uncle Rosalino Visconti, local grocer Peter Rizzo and bartender Joseph Fraterizo.[57]

They likely would have taken Giuseppe and his son Joseph, then twenty, into custody as well, but neither man could be located. The DiCarlo family told detectives that father and son had left home early Sunday morning and were not expected back until much later.[58]

Police discovered a revolver, loaded except for a single empty chamber, inside a garbage container behind the building at 174 Front Avenue. That location was just a couple of doors down the street from the DiCarlo business. Another handgun was found hidden in the icebox in Visconti's home, also on Front Avenue.[59]

During interrogation, Fraterizo reluctantly told police that he recalled hearing five gunshots after midnight – one shot, then a pause, then three more shots, another pause and the final shot. He said he was in the cellar beneath the saloon at the time and could not tell if the reports were from weapons fired within the business or outside of it. The bartender, apparently nervous about speaking with the police, refused to sign his name to a transcript of his brief statement.[60]

The other men initially refused to make statements at all. Eventually, Rizzo, who was secretly a member of the DiCarlo criminal society, made a statement. He told detectives he heard a distant gunfight shortly before seeing Visconti and Vincent Vaccaro's wife helping the injured man into Visconti's butcher shop, across Carolina Street from the DiCarlo saloon.[61]

The Vaccaro brothers had been in some trouble before. There were rumors that they were connected with local Black Hand extortion rackets, in which residents and businessmen were terrorized into sending cash payments. Anthony had been arrested and questioned in connection with the murders of Frank

Ulizzi and Salvatore Russo. At the time of his brother's shooting, Anthony was awaiting trial on a charge of receiving stolen property.[62]

No one could put a name to the remains in the morgue. However, after questioning dozens of residents, Chief of Detectives Charles F. Zimmerman learned that the deceased was a visitor to Buffalo from Brooklyn, where he had a wife and children. Zimmerman sent a description of the victim to police in Brooklyn.[63]

Before Brooklyn authorities could react on Monday, a man describing himself as a cousin of the deceased and a resident of Brooklyn showed up at the morgue to identify the remains of Isidoro Crocevera and arrange to transport the body back home. Police were puzzled by the man's arrival and his mention of an anonymous telephone call he received Sunday morning advising him that his cousin was dying in Buffalo.

The man stated that Crocevera was forty-six years old, worked as a foreman for the Pierce Brothers shipping company at the Brooklyn waterfront and had traveled from Brooklyn three days earlier to spend a vacation with some friends. He noted that Crocevera was survived by a wife, who did not yet know of her husband's death and assumed he was enjoying his trip, and seven children – five boys and two girls.[64]

For some reason, Buffalo detectives seemed not to recall Crocevera's name. And press reports of his identity neglected to point out his history of involvement with the Sicilian underworld in New York State.

If Buffalo police were genuinely unaware of Crocevera's involvement in these criminal matters, it was not through any fault of William Flynn of the U.S. Secret Service. By that time, Flynn had authored a series of articles and a book, entitled *The Barrel Mystery*,[65] about the Morello-Lupo gang and his lengthy and ultimately successful effort to put the Mafia leaders behind bars for counterfeiting. Crocevera was featured prominently in Flynn's work. The articles were published in newspapers around the country in 1914. His book was published in 1919 and was serialized the next year.

Back in Buffalo from whatever called him away early Sunday morning, Giuseppe DiCarlo walked into police headquarters Monday evening with an attorney at his side. He revealed his own lengthy personal connection with Crocevera. He recounted their friendship since first meeting about twenty-five years earlier in Palermo, Sicily, and their regular visits with each other.

Those visits, he said, had recently been interrupted by a period of two years, until the men met briefly at Giuseppe's saloon half an hour before the shooting. Giuseppe told police he saw his old friend step outside the saloon just three minutes before shots rang out. Immediately upon hearing five blasts, he rushed outside but did not see Crocevera.[66]

On the afternoon of Tuesday, August 10, police arrested Joseph DiCarlo for the shooting of Vincent Vaccaro, charging him with first-degree assault. Joseph refused to make any statement, and was released on bail.[67]

The following day, Detective Chief Zimmerman told the press that Vincent Vaccaro had confessed to causing Crocevera's death. Noting that the evidence did not support the confession, Zimmerman expressed his belief that Vaccaro was trying to protect his brother.[68] On the twelfth, Anthony Vaccaro was arraigned on a charge of murder. As news of the charge hit the newspapers, so did police officials' well grounded pessimism at ever bringing the DiCarlo and Vaccaro cases to trial:

> Although it was formally decided to charge Vaccaro with the crime, the police are dubious about getting a conviction or even having the case go to the grand jury because persons who are suspected of having witnessed the crime have steadfastly refused to admit it.[69]

Detectives finally attributed the gunfight to a disagreement over how best to split the proceeds of a liquor smuggling operation. They surmised that young Joseph grew angry with the Vaccaro brothers and intended to settle the argument with his revolver. He aimed low and inflicted the wound to Vincent Vaccaro's thigh. Anthony Vaccaro stepped to his brother's defense and quickly discharged a firearm in DiCarlo's direction, striking Crocevera in the back with an errant shot.[70]

Their hypotheses might have been right on the mark, but without the cooperation of witnesses, there was no chance of securing convictions in the case. All charges against Joseph DiCarlo and the Vaccaro brothers were dropped.

———

Giuseppe turned away from the saloon business in 1920[71] and became owner of the Venice Restaurant, 387 Washington Street in Buffalo. The business move might have represented a reach for respectability. But it could have been motivated by the rising expenses, diminishing returns and heightened suspicions related to Prohibition Era saloon keeping.

The Venice Restaurant was opened in September 1919 by Nino and Antonio Sacco.[72] It was at that time a family-run business providing quality Italian and American cuisine.

> It is the rendezvous of the gourmand, the elite who like to tuck their feet under a table laden with snowy napery, shining silver and palatable dishes.[73]

With a businessman's lunch offered at fifty-five cents a plate and dinners at seventy-five cents, the Venice was advertised as a means of combating the postwar "H.C. of L." (high cost of living).

Giuseppe reportedly operated the restaurant in partnership with his son Joseph. The degree to which Joseph and his younger siblings assisted Giuseppe at the restaurant is unknown. It is certain, however, that during this period Giuseppe's sons were a source of worry for their old man.

Sam, sixteen, got into trouble with the law in the early summer of 1920. He and friend Matthew Tagliarano, nineteen, of 133 Front Avenue, were arrested for assaulting two young women in their company.[74]

One of the women involved, Gladys Hemstock, eighteen, knew Sam from school.[75] The other was her sixteen-year-old friend Evelyn Hartman. The group reportedly met on the evening of June 26. They all agreed to take a ride in Tagliarano's car down to the Sunset Inn dancing resort on River Road in Tonawanda. The Sunset Inn was a popular summer spot overlooking the Niagara River. There they danced together until 2 a.m.

Rather than drive the young women home afterward,

Tagliarano drove them to an isolated spot on Two-Mile Creek Road. According to the complaint of the women, Sam then became physical with Hemstock while Tagliarano acted in a similar fashion toward Hartman.

"Sam told me that I would have to do what he said or I would have to walk home," Hemstock recalled.

Hemstock and Hartman resisted the advances. Tagliarano allegedly struck Hartman. The young women eventually succeeded in freeing themselves and in attracting the attention of police officers.[76]

Sam and Tagliarano were initially charged with rape before Tonawanda Justice of the Peace A.L. Cherry. The magistrate decided that the matter should be turned over to a grand jury. After three nights in Tonawanda's lockup, Sam and Tagliarano were released on bail in the amount of $2,000 each.[77]

Nothing but bad press came of the charges as they were dismissed.

During the same summer, Joseph was arrested twice. The first arrest resulted in a suspended sentence for a motor vehicle violation.[78] It was the first of many such offenses for Joseph. His arrest for shooting Vaccaro occurred little more than a month later.

In July of 1921, Joseph was again arrested on a motor vehicle charge. Convicted of reckless driving, he was forced to pay a thirty-five-dollar fine.[79] Three months later, Sam was fined fifteen dollars for a motor vehicle violation.[80] Joseph closed out the year with a driving offense that brought a ten-dollar fine.[81] Either the brothers had no regard for the laws of the road, or they had infinite confidence in their father's ability to fix things for them.

― ― ―

Prohibition enforcement agents managed to disrupt some Calabrian bootlegging operations early in 1921. They arrested Samuel Sirianni and Frank Carallo of Niagara Falls, charging the two men with smuggling whiskey in the largely rural Youngstown-Lewiston corridor north of Niagara Falls. The matter was of significant personal interest to Niagara Falls Calabrian gang boss Joseph Sirianni, as Samuel was his brother. The two men were convicted in Buffalo's federal court on February 9, 1921.[82]

Authorities arrested some suspected Sicilian rum-runners in the same area in April. Michael LoBosco,[83] James DiTulio and Charles Balli, all of Niagara Falls, were arrested as they sat in a parked touring car on the shoulder of River Road outside of Youngstown, New York. Sheriff's deputies found two bottles of whiskey and three revolvers in the vehicle.

On the same night, deputies took Thomas Morello, age thirty-seven, of Niagara Falls, into custody. Morello was caught driving a truck loaded with Green River whiskey valued at ten thousand dollars.[84]

Police began to suspect a feud between competing rum-running gangs later in the month. Early in the morning of April 22, three gunmen with pistols drawn approached a group of alcohol smugglers unloading a cargo of whiskey and liqueurs from a motorboat at the foot of Georgia Street in Buffalo. The gunmen, Peter Rizzo, Sam LoVullo and Pietro Barbera, stepped from the shadows and demanded the liquor, which was turned over to them.

The three men stashed their prize in the attic of a home occupied by Barbera's sister and her family at 71 Efner Street. The original smugglers, connected with important city and county officials, reported the theft to the authorities. Police raided the Efner Street home and recovered the liquor.[85]

Though Rizzo, LoVullo and Barbera appeared to have violated Prohibition laws and to have committed armed robbery, powerful people in Buffalo were happy simply to have their alcohol shipment returned. The three men were not prosecuted.

Less than a month later, the mutilated remains of a bootlegger provided additional evidence of a growing rivalry between gangs.

Chapter 4

Booze and Blood

Brothers William and Robert Winspear discovered the brutalized corpse near their farm just outside of Buffalo on the morning of Wednesday, May 18, 1921. They spotted the body in a ditch to the side of Harlem Road, midway between Genesee Street and Walden Avenue. A loaded .38-caliber revolver and a blood-covered hatchet sat on the road near the body.

Sheriff's department investigators found two .32-caliber bullet wounds on the victim. One was through the right eye. The other was under the right arm. They counted a dozen hatchet wounds to the head, face and chest. The victim's clothes were badly torn, indicating that he had struggled against his attackers. Despite the closeness of the discovered weapons, investigators determined that the man had been killed in a bootleggers quarrel elsewhere and then transported to the site.[1]

An autopsy revealed that death was not instantaneous. The medical examiner concluded that the victim, mortally wounded by the gunshots and hatchet gashes, was still alive when he was thrown into the ditch.[2]

The numerous wounds made his face unrecognizable. Efforts to identify the remains were aided by the discovery of letters in the dead man's pockets.[3]

The sheriff's office announced to the press that the murdered man was twenty-eight-year-old Frank Pizzuto, until recently a resident of New York City. Pizzuto had moved from the city with his wife Flo, a former chorus girl, about a month earlier. The couple rented an apartment at 155 Franklin Street in Buffalo. Pizzuto used the site of the old DiCarlo saloon, 166 Front Avenue, as his mailing address. However, no one at that location admitted knowing him.[4]

Questioned by deputies and by Assistant District Attorney Walter W. Hofheins, Flo Pizzuto pointed an accusing finger at Frank Vassallo, thirty-six, of 212 Front Avenue.[5] She said she last saw her husband as he entered Vassallo's "Grant Six" touring car near midnight on Tuesday, the seventeenth. She also noted that she had traveled in the same car several days earlier and saw a hatchet on the floor of the vehicle.[6]

According to Flo Pizzuto, she and her husband had fled New York City because he had committed some offense against Italian criminals there.[7] The couple spent a week in North Hempstead before deciding to relocate to Buffalo.[8] She acknowledged that her husband had been in the bootlegging business, but she claimed that he was trying to separate himself from the racket and planned to open a shoe store.[9]

Sheriff's deputies brought Vassallo in for questioning. Over the next few days, deputies also rounded up Constantino Leone, his wife Christina, Vincent Patricola, Peter Rizzo and a former prizefighter named Jack Martin.[10]

Investigators found some blood spots inside Vassallo's car. Vassallo said he did not know how they got there. He denied seeing Pizzuto after midnight on Tuesday.[11]

Constantino Leone, thirty-five-year-old olive oil merchant, was interesting to the authorities for several reasons. Leone used the same 166 Front Avenue mailing address as Frank Pizzuto. Leone also reportedly had an appointment to meet with Pizzuto on the night of his murder. In addition, investigators believed Leone was in Vassallo's car that night.

Leone was known to be a close friend of Vassallo and was suspected of involvement in bootlegging. Heightening the interest of sheriff's deputies was the fact that Leone's wife reported him missing on the eighteenth. Leone turned up two days later, saying he had just returned from a business trip begun on the seventeenth.[12]

Patricola was questioned because he was with Pizzuto the evening before his murder.[13] Rizzo was commonly seen at the soft drink saloon at 166 Front Avenue and was believed to have done business with Pizzuto.[14]

A Pizzuto tattoo that the sheriff's office initially thought was a clue turned out to be nothing of the sort. Noting the name,

"Rosalia Karvuglia," inscribed over the tattooed image of a heart, deputies suggested that the name referred to a secret society, to which Pizzuto belonged. However, they quickly determined that Rosalia was merely the name of a Pizzuto ex-girlfriend.[15]

Though the local media expected for days that a murder charge would be filed against one or more of the men questioned in the case, Assistant District Attorney Hofheins announced May 23 that the evidence was insufficient and all suspects were being released.[16]

— — —

The number of Palmeris in Niagara Falls increased near the end of 1920. A daughter was born to Angelo and Laura Palmeri on October 15 of that year. They named her Rosaria. That Rosaria's godparents were Cleveland Mafia boss Joseph Lonardo and his wife Concetta is testament to Angelo Palmeri's growing influence in the underworld.[17]

At roughly the same time, Angelo Palmeri's brother Paul decided to move to the community. Before the relocation, Paul and his wife Helen had been living in Manhattan, where he worked as a barber.

Angelo likely had need of his brother's assistance – bodyguard Frank Rangatore died months before at the age of forty-five.[18] The Palmeri brothers opened a business together at 1107 East Falls Street. They gave the appearance of working as importers and commission merchants selling produce. However, events in the summer of 1921 indicated that the Palmeris were engaged in a very different sort of business.

In the afternoon of August 29, Emilio C. Gnazzo, a twenty-five-year-old New York City resident who recently moved to Niagara Falls to find work, walked carelessly out the door of a store at 121 Eleventh Street. A gunman jumped from behind the cover of a parked car and fired a bullet into Gnazzo's head. As Gnazzo stumbled back into the store, the gunman followed, pumping several more lead slugs into his body before fleeing. Gnazzo collapsed onto a cuspidor, blood spurting from his wounds. The gunman hurried off. Another man near the store, believed to be an accomplice of the shooter, ran in the opposite direction.

Gnazzo's wife Lillian observed the attack from an upstairs apartment and watched her husband's killer flee through an alley beneath her window. She attempted to slow him by dumping a pot of water from the window. Drenched but unharmed, the man reached a rear yard and escaped over a fence. Lillian told authorities she could identify the killer.[19]

While the region was beginning to experience a rash of bootlegging-related violence, Niagara Falls police determined that Gnazzo was killed because he was slow to repay a loan obtained from Angelo Palmeri. Described as "an inveterate gambler and a regular loser," Gnazzo had borrowed less than five-hundred dollars, offering some jewelry as security.

However, Gnazzo failed to pay the five-dollars-per-month interest Palmeri charged on that underworld loan. The two men reportedly met and argued earlier on August 29 and then went their separate ways.

To their hypothetical murder motive, police added a contributing factor – Gnazzo's brash manner. A former U.S. seaman, Gnazzo had a physical nature and was quick to slap around those he felt he could handle.[20] He might have become pushy with the wrong man.

Detectives searching for Palmeri noted he was not at his usual haunts. They speculated he might be preparing to leave town. A local bank seemed to confirm that theory when it revealed the next morning that Palmeri had just cashed a check for $1,400.

Detective Sergeant George H. Callinan received a tip that Palmeri was hiding out with his friend Sam Rangatore, brother of the late Frank Rangatore, at 420 Eighth Street. Callinan paid a visit to a Rangatore neighbor on Eighth Street to check out the tip. He learned that the Rangatores had been acting suspiciously and ignoring all telephone calls.

Callinan called to the station for assistance. Three detectives and a patrolman met him at the Rangatore home. He positioned the patrolman and two detectives in front of the home with instructions to grab anyone leaving the premises. He and Detective Sergeant Terrence M. Reilly went to a side door. Mrs. Rangatore allowed them inside. The detectives found Palmeri in an upstairs bedroom, reclining fully clothed on a bed.

"Put up your hands and put them up high," Callinan ordered Palmeri.

Palmeri stood up with his hands in the air but said nothing.

The detectives searched for a handgun. None was found. Callinan handcuffed himself to Palmeri and led his prisoner from the house.[21]

On September 1 before Police Court Judge Charles Piper, Palmeri was formally charged with first-degree murder. Defense attorney Angelo F. Scalzo entered a plea of not guilty.

Palmeri seemed unconcerned by the charge. A press report described him as "cool and at ease."[22] In his jail cell, he reportedly passed the time singing songs from his favorite operas.[23] Friends brought pillows and blankets to make him comfortable.

As Palmeri sang away in his jail cell, his close associate Joseph Sottile was also charged with first-degree murder. That charge resulted from the September 5 shooting death of Samuel Mancusa.

Patrons of Tony Travis's soft drink saloon at 1126 East Falls Street, Niagara Falls, that evening were alarmed by the sound of gunshots coming from a rear room. Patrolmen Thomas Kelly and Ben Nichols were nearby. They rushed into the saloon and found a wounded Sottile backing out of the rear room while firing his handgun. They found Mancusa dead inside the room with two bullet wounds in his chest. Sottile was placed under arrest.[24]

Sottile insisted that he fired his .38-caliber handgun only in self-defense. He said he and Mancusa had been talking for about an hour, when they began to quarrel. Mancusa drew a revolver and shot him. Struck in the arm by the shot, Sottile said he returned fire as he withdrew from the room. Sottile did not reveal what the quarrel was about.[25]

Like his friend Palmeri, Sottile was represented by attorney Angelo F. Scalzo.[26] As Sottile was charged, Scalzo went to the press to support his client's story. The attorney insisted that the shot that killed Mancusa must have been fired after Sottile's arm was wounded. So that fatal shot, Scalzo argued, had to have been fired in self-defense.

Coroner W.L. Draper examined Mancusa's body and determined that he was killed by a slug fired into the right side of his chest. It severed the pulmonary artery between Mancusa's heart and his lungs and then exited the body under the left arm. The authorities revealed that Mancusa had been in and out of the United States over the previous dozen years. His wife and family lived in Italy, and he visited them regularly. He returned from his latest trip to Italy four months earlier.[27]

The Mancusa murder case became muddled on September 7 as Nicola Papaleo, age forty, surrendered to police in Utica, New York, and confessed to recently killing a man in Niagara Falls. Doubting Papaleo's sanity, police in Niagara Falls hesitated to link the confession to the Mancusa murder. However, Detective James Keenan was dispatched to Utica to speak with Papaleo and bring him back.

Papaleo told Keenan that Mancusa owed him twenty dollars. When Mancusa passed his home on the fifth, Papaleo asked for the money. Mancusa refused. Arguing over the loan, the two men went into Travis's saloon. Inside the rear room, Papaleo said, Mancusa drew a revolver and fired four times at him. Papaleo returned six shots. He then dropped his handgun and fled through a back door just as he saw Sottile entering the room. At eleven o'clock the next morning, he traveled to Buffalo and then on to Utica.[28]

Police attempted to question Papaleo on the details of his story, but came away only with additional evidence that the confessed murderer was insane. "...He was in such a nervous state that he could not answer them," the *Niagara Gazette* reported of the interrogation attempts. "He is wild-eyed and spends his time lying flat on his stomach in his bunk."[29]

Additional reasons to distrust the confession also came to light. According to one press report, Papaleo was an associate of Angelo Palmeri.[30] Another indicated that he recanted his confession when interviewed September 8 by Health Officer John L. Bishop.[31]

Angelo Palmeri had probably grown hoarse from his jailhouse singing by the time his police court hearing came up on September 14. At that time, Judge Piper noted the disappearance of the prosecution's main witness against Palmeri. With permission from Niagara Falls authorities, Lillian Gnazzo had accompanied her husband's body to New York City for burial. Then she vanished. Prosecutors had no other witnesses who would admit to seeing Palmeri anywhere near 121 Eleventh Street on the day Gnazzo was killed.

Attorney Scalzo asked Judge Piper to discharge Palmeri. The judge decided to allow the police some more time to track down

Mrs. Gnazzo, and ruled that Palmeri would remain in custody.[32] After two more days, police still could not locate the widow. Judge Piper found that there was insufficient evidence to hold Palmeri any longer and discharged him.[33]

Prosecutors had similar problems with their murder case against Joseph Sottile. At a September 23 hearing, witness Joseph Archie testified that he saw much of the gunfight between Sottile and Mancusa. Archie said he was playing cards in the saloon's front room when he heard a shot and rushed to the rear room. He saw Mancusa holding a smoking handgun and heard Sottile ask, "What are you shooting at me for?" Other shots were then exchanged.

Additional weight appeared to be given to Archie's statement because he was a relative of Mancusa. As a result of the hearing, Judge Piper reduced the charge against Sottile to second degree murder but refused to release him on bail.

Scalzo went over his head. One week later, Supreme Court Justice Charles A. Pooley, a Buffalo native, ordered that Sottile be released from the Niagara County Jail in Lockport, New York, on bail of $10,000.[34]

― ― ―

Authorities had no better luck with their early attempts to prosecute regional underworld figures for bootlegging.

On September 27, 1921, Vincenzo "James" DiNieri, a close associate of Palmeri and the Sirianni brothers, was arraigned in Niagara Falls Police Court on a charge of transporting liquor illegally. DiNieri was a native of Caltavuturo, Sicily, a town about eight miles northeast of Valledolmo. He had been in the United States since 1912 and was employed as a laborer for the Union Carbide Corporation.[35]

The sheriff's department claimed that it had seized hundreds of bottles of liquor from a cellar in a DiNieri-owned home on Fourteenth Street and that Undersheriff George W. Hoak had observed DiNieri moving the contraband into the building.

Hoak was not in court for the arraignment, but attorney Angelo Scalzo was. Scalzo, who had defended Palmeri and Sottile against murder charges, also represented accused liquor smuggler DiNieri.

Scalzo immediately launched a two-pronged attack on the smuggling charge. He asserted that any liquor seized by officials belonged not to his client but to one Joseph Toledo, an occupant of the building who had vanished since DiNieri's arrest. Scalzo also challenged the sheriff to produce the hundreds of bottles of liquor he claimed to have confiscated and introduce them as evidence.[36]

When DiNieri was questioned about the parcels Hoak reportedly saw him carry into the cellar, the defendant said they were merely sacks of potatoes.

The sheriff's department hesitated to bring forth the seized bottles of liquor, and Scalzo brought the matter before the U.S. commissioner. The 18th Amendment prohibited the manufacture, sale and transportation of liquor, not the possession of it. Without proof that the liquor confiscated from the Fourteenth Street cellar had been produced, sold or moved since the passage of the amendment, the sheriff's department had no right to confiscate it, Scalzo argued. The attorney boldly demanded that the seized liquor be returned to where it was found. The argument was as convincing as it was brazen. The U.S. commissioner agreed and ordered the sheriff's department to put the liquor back.[37]

The case against DiNieri had fallen apart. On September 30, Judge Piper dismissed the smuggling charge and released DiNieri. Attorney Scalzo went to the press to announce that he was filing a $10,000 lawsuit against Hoak for false arrest.[38]

Two months later, a liquor smuggling case against a Buffalo racketeer made it as far as the jury verdict.

Authorities had arrested Peter Bonventre[39] of 418 Front Avenue on June 3, 1921, catching the twenty-four-year-old with two other men inside a truck carrying a load of outlawed booze. Bonventre's two companions, Raymond Shelper and Albert Smith, quickly pleaded guilty to illegally transporting liquor. Bonventre, however, pleaded not guilty. He said he had gotten into the truck for a ride and knew nothing of its cargo.

The case went to trial in November, with Bonventre represented by attorney Michael Montesano. On the twenty-ninth of that month, the trial jury returned a not-guilty verdict, freeing Bonventre.[40]

Before the end of the year, DiNieri was in the news once again. A December 5 explosion and fire at his grocery, 1123 East Falls Street in Niagara Falls, caused damage estimated at four thousand dollars. The explosion ripped out the side of the one-story frame building, broke all the building windows and ignited a fire that consumed the shop and its contents.

DiNieri denied that the explosion had been caused by either a bomb or an alcohol still. Authorities found no evidence that a still had been located on the premises. DiNieri said no one would have planted a bomb in the store because he had no enemies..[41]

If DiNieri had no enemies at that time, his underworld associates certainly did. In February of 1922, the Sirianni brothers were attacked by rivals.

— — —

Joseph Sirianni drove his seriously wounded brother Samuel to Buffalo's General Hospital on the afternoon of February 17. Thirty-year-old Samuel had gunshot wounds to his groin and his right knee. Doctors decided the groin wound was mortal, as the slug that caused it had punctured his liver.

Police attempted to learn the details of the shooting from Joseph Sirianni. He told them that he and his brother had left their soft drink saloon in Niagara Falls and were on their way east to Alden, New York, when they stopped at a roadhouse outside the Buffalo city line on either Genesee Street or Broadway. Outside the roadhouse, two gunmen ordered them to raise their hands. The gunmen then opened fire, striking Samuel twice and then running off. Sirianni carried his wounded brother to their car and took him at once to the hospital, he told police.

The story did not ring true. Police took Sirianni for a drive along Broadway and Genesee, asking him to point out the roadhouse. He could not do so. The authorities went in search of more reliable information and announced they wanted Sirianni pal Vincenzo DiNieri for questioning.[42]

Within a day, Sheriff William Waldow began assembling a picture of what happened to Samuel Sirianni by merging Samuel's shooting with an incident reported later that evening. Twenty-two-year-old barber Stanley Nowakowski showed up at the same hospital with gunshot wounds early on the morning of the eighteenth. Nowakowski and witness Edward Closs told authorities that Nowakowski had just been shot by gunmen in a passing car. Nowakowski said he did not know why he was targeted. He suggested the gunmen mistook him for someone else.[43]

Waldow announced that both of the shooting victims were

lying. He said they both had been shot in the same bootleggers gunfight at three o'clock in the afternoon of the seventeenth. The shootout occurred on Broadway near Harlem Road in a neighborhood populated in large part by Polish and German families. The sheriff's view was supported by the discovery of Nowakowski's revolver at that location.

The late appearance of Nowakowski at the hospital was part of a smokescreen, according to Waldow. The sheriff said Nowakowski and his allies initially hoped to avoid the questioning that would result from hospital treatment of his wounds. By evening, it became apparent to them that Nowakowski would not survive without medical treatment, and the gang staged a phony drive-by shooting on Clinton Street to cover up the earlier gunfight and allow Nowakowski to get to the hospital with a plausible story.

Police arrested DiNieri as Waldow went public with details that could only have come from an informant. The sheriff said DiNieri and the Siriannis were in the process of delivering fourteen cases of Canadian whiskey valued at one thousand dollars to the owner of a roadhouse when rivals attempted to steal their liquor shipment. The Siriannis' car was directed toward an alley off Broadway where two gunmen opened fire. The ensuing gunfight caused the injuries to Samuel Sirianni and Stanley Nowakowski.[44]

Samuel succumbed to his injuries on February 21.[45] Two days later he was given a lavish funeral beginning at his Niagara Falls home at 248 Eleventh Street and continuing at St. Joseph's Church. More than one hundred and twenty automobiles participated in the funeral procession, which included delegations of Italian residents from many towns in western New York and Ontario, Canada. Floral offerings filled five automobiles.[46]

Upon Nowakowski's release from the hospital, he was arrested and charged with the murder of Samuel Sirianni. Police also arrested seventeen-year-old Stanley Gorski on the same charge.[47] Arrests related to the case continued for more than a month. Leo "the Jew" Kuhn, thirty-one, was taken into custody on March 2. He admitted arranging the liquor transaction that led to the attack on the Siriannis.[48] On March 3, twenty-three-year-old Leo Smolarek, operator of the roadhouse, became the third man charged with Samuel Sirianni's murder.[49] Joseph

Bartkowiak, twenty-seven, and Alexander Lakrewski, eighteen, both residents of Coit Street, were arrested in April.[50]

By the spring of 1922, three major Calabrian bootlegging gangs of roughly equal strength existed in western New York and adjoining regions of Canada. The Hamilton-based gang of Rocco Perri had grown in underworld power since the 1918 murder of James Celona and rivaled the Guelph-based network of Domenic Sciaroni and the Sirianni organization headquartered in Niagara Falls.[51]

Perri and Sirianni had established beneficial working relationships with Sicilian Mafia groups on both sides of the border. Only Sciaroni resisted such combinations. The fact that the fifty-five-year-old gang boss remained preeminent among the Calabrian racketeers was a problem for the other bosses of the region. But the problem had an obvious solution.

The body of Sciaroni's Niagara Falls ally Maurizzio Bocchimuzzo was found in early April 1922 about thirty feet off the side of Buffalo's River Road near the banks of the Niagara River. The body was found in a prone position with a portion of the face decomposed and clothing frozen to the ground. Police were drawn to the site by a hand-painted sign at the side of the road. The sign, a piece of white cardboard nailed to a broomstick, read, "Death! Here! Look!"[52]

A postmortem examination determined that Bocchimuzzo had been dead about a week. An indentation was found on the forehead and additional marks on the skull. These indicated that Bocchimuzzo had been struck on the head with a blunt instrument. Bullet wounds were found in the right temple and in the right side of the abdomen. An absence of blood at the spot where the body was found led investigators to conclude that Bocchimuzzo had been killed at another location. Due to his links to gangsters in Ontario, they speculated that the murder occurred across the border in Canada.[53]

At eleven-thirty in the evening on May 10, 1922, a bus driver noticed Domenic Sciaroni's dead body by the side of the road at Lewiston Hill. Police determined that the gang boss had been shot twice in the back of his head and once in his shoulder. All of the shots were fired at close range. It appeared that the body had been thrown from an automobile.[54]

Detectives pieced together Sciaroni's movements on the day of his murder. In the morning, he met with Rocco Perri in Hamilton before continuing on to Niagara Falls in the company of two other men. At eleven o'clock he purchased a gear for his McLaughlin automobile at Lammerts Auto Works on Sixth Street in Niagara Falls. He then drove on to Joe Sirianni's saloon on Eleventh Street and left his vehicle in Sirianni's garage.[55]

In the evening, he attended a bootleggers' banquet at DiVita's restaurant on Eleventh Street. Sciaroni reportedly left the banquet at ten-forty-five that evening in an automobile with four other men, all believed to have been Italian residents of Canada. Sciaroni's own car remained in Sirianni's garage.[56]

Domenic Sciaroni was buried in Guelph on May 13. Prominent in the funeral procession was Rocco Perri, the man who profited most from Sciaroni's murder.[57] Perri instantly became the senior member of the Calabrian criminal fraternity in the region. He very likely was also the wealthiest, as he absorbed many of Sciaroni's old rackets.[58]

Domenic Sciaroni's brother Joseph and cousin Salvatore attempted to hold the family criminal empire together. They were opposed by a force they could not identify. On June 15, Salvatore Sciaroni and his associate Jim Forti were attacked and wounded as they left a store in Brantford, Ontario, a small town about 25 miles west of Hamilton.[59] With Domenic killed immediately after visiting with Perri and Salvatore wounded in an area that could be considered Perri's back yard, the Sciaronis had reason to suspect that the Hamilton underworld boss was gunning for them.

Joseph and Salvatore Sciaroni confronted Perri with their suspicions on September 3. Perri insisted he had nothing to do with the recent attacks. He attributed the murder of Domenic Sciaroni to an incursion by "those dirty Sicilians." Perri noted that a Brooklyn Mafioso named Stefano Magaddino, leader of a band of killers originally from Castellammare del Golfo, Sicily, had been visiting the region. Magaddino, he said, was working with Toronto's Sicilian boss Toto Gagliardo to take control of Calabrian rackets in Ontario. The Sciaronis, already suspicious of the Sicilian criminal society in general and Gagliardo in particular, were easily convinced.

Within a few days of the meeting with Perri, Joseph Sciaroni was murdered.[60]

The remaining Sciaroni criminal operations were quickly consumed by Perri. With Ontario's Calabrian underworld solidly behind him, Perri established an alliance with the Siriannis of Niagara Falls. Though the purpose of the alliance was to prevent the expansion of the Sicilian Mafia in the region, each group formed working relationships with the Sicilian underworld.[61]

Chapter 5

Succession

Giuseppe DiCarlo's health was deteriorating as he sold the Venice Restaurant to local businessman and friend Thomas J.B. "Tommy" Dyke early in 1922.[1]

Dyke was an Italian-American native of New York City, born Gaetano Bellantoni on Mulberry Street in 1895.[2] His parents, Rocco and Angelina Bellantoni, were immigrants from the town of Scilla in Calabria, Italy.[3] During his adolescence, when he adopted the name of Tommy Dyke, his family lived on Elizabeth Street, about one city block south of the DiCarlo-Manzella grocery.[4] It appears likely that Giuseppe DiCarlo became aware of the Bellantoni family and young Tommy Dyke at this time.

Like many youths of that time and place, Dyke was drawn into the local street gangs. While working as a bartender for underworld chieftain Frank "Chick Tricker" Tricca,[5] Dyke and his friend Harry Lenny, a boxer and fight manager, formed the Harry Lenny and Tommy Dyke Association. It was a respectable name that provided some cover for a street gang that worked with politically linked Italian gangland organizers like Tricker, Paul "Kelly" Vaccarelli and Jack Sirocco.[6]

Sirocco's organization, a tool of the Tammany Hall Democratic machine,[7] emerged as the primary rival of a labor racketeering and extortion gang controlled by "Big Jack" Zelig and Benjamin "Dopey Benny" Fein.[8] The rivalry became a blood feud by the middle of 1912, as Zelig's forces quickly eliminated three Sirocco gangsters.[9] At the time, Chick Tricker characterized the conflict as "a religious war."

> It's a scrap between the Italians and the Jews... These fellows think they can come into our places and blackmail us. Well, they can't. We won't give up... This Jack Zelig gang is the descendants of Monk Eastman's bunch, only they haven't got the nerve of that tribe.

Tricker noted that he and his Italian allies had assumed control of old Irish saloons and other enterprises on the Lower East Side. Some of his associates, like Paul Kelly, had Celticized their names in the process.[10]

The October 5, 1912, murder of "Big Jack" Zelig quieted the feud temporarily but did not resolve it.[11] A November 1913 strike by workers at the Feldman hat frame factory brought about more bloodshed. The Zelig gang, then under the leadership of "Dopey Benny" Fein, supported the strikers. Management called in Sirocco's men as strikebreakers. The resulting clash resulted in the death of a close friend of Fein known as "Little Maxey" Greenwald.[12] When Sirocco gangsters gathered the next month to watch a bicycle race at Madison Square Garden, Fein's men also showed up. A running gun battle ensued around trolley cars and taxicabs on the city streets. Somehow, the dangerous spectacle resulted in no known casualties.[13]

A tragic event early in 1914 put Dyke's name on the front pages of New York newspapers and perhaps encouraged his move to Buffalo. The Harry Lenny and Tommy Dyke Association sponsored a January 9 ball at Arlington Hall, 19-23 St. Mark's Place in Manhattan. At eight o'clock that evening, as organizers arrived to set things up for the ball, Fein gunmen emerged from buildings across the street and opened fire with revolvers. The Lenny and Dyke men drew their own weapons and returned fire. Sixty-five-year-old Frederick Strauss, a clerk in City Court since 1888, was caught in the crossfire. He fell to the street, dead of gunshot wounds. The feuding gunmen scattered, leaving empty revolvers, a box of event badges and the lifeless body of Frederick Strauss behind for police.

Investigators found that a number of the badges intended for the ball had names already written on them and some of those names were familiar: Jack Sirocco, "Chick" Tricker, Harry Lenny, Tommy Dyke, and brothers Paul and Nick Vaccarelli.

Placards advertising the ball in area stores provided an additional link between the event and politicians and Italian underworld bosses by listing the officers of the Harry Lenny and Tommy Dyke Association. The list included First Vice President Paul Vaccarelli, Second Vice President Albert Marinelli, Treasurer Eddie Dyke, Recording Secretary Frank "Chick" Tricker and Marshal John Sirocco.[14]

An eyewitness to the Arlington Hall gunfight told police that, once the shooting had stopped, one of the gunmen ran to Arlington Hall bouncer Edward "Fat Bull" Morris, an off-duty special police officer, and begged, "Hide me, Fat Bull. Hide me."[15] Police arrested Morris, along with "Dopey Benny" Fein and three members of Fein's gang, "Little Abie" Beckerman, Rubin Kaplan and Irving "Waxey Gordon" Wexler. Morris broke down under police interrogation and named Wexler as the gunman who sought his protection.[16]

During hearings related to the gunfight, Lenny and Dyke did their best to provide some breathing room for gang bosses and politicians. They said the officer titles in their dance advertisements were purely honorary and had been assigned without the recipients' knowledge or permission. They insisted that the association itself was comprised only of the two of them. They claimed to know nothing about the shooting, but "they were certain it was not directed at them."[17]

Deputy Police Commissioner Harry Newburger scoffed at the explanation offered by the gangsters. "Just think of it, a bartender and a prizefighter calling themselves an association and running a ball for themselves!"

Police were unable to assemble a case against Fein and his men,[18] and the underworld conflict raged on.

About 1921, Dyke's brother Edward died and his widowed mother Angelina, a longtime resident of Broome Street, moved to Brooklyn.[19] In the same period, Dyke, by then the owner of the Italian Gardens restaurant on Broome Street, relocated to Buffalo and became prominent in business and political circles. In Buffalo, he gave his name to yet another association, but one with a charitable purpose. His Thomas J.B. Dyke Association raised money for local causes and sent performers to entertain at area hospitals each summer.

After purchasing the Venice Restaurant from Giuseppe

DiCarlo, he redesigned the establishment as more of a nightclub and provided it with air conditioning, entertainment and a new name: the Ritz.[20] The businessman's lunch and spaghetti dinners gave way to a jazz orchestra and bootleg whiskey. Within a year, Dyke was arrested for violation of the Prohibition laws.[21]

As Giuseppe retired from his legitimate enterprises, Joseph DiCarlo established himself as a businessman. On February 2, 1922, Joseph contracted with Frederick C. Beck for the purchase of the Auto Inn roadhouse on Main Street and Transit Road in Williamsville, a small village a few miles northeast of Buffalo. The purchase price was $3,000.[22] It appears likely that Joseph had his father's assistance in the deal.

Giuseppe probably was well acquainted with Auto Inn. To ensure the success of Mafia bootlegging ventures, he would have made it a point to get to know the managers of the roadhouses and speakeasies in the region. He reportedly got to know Auto Inn's manager – "Jew Minnie" Clark – better than most. Giuseppe and Minnie reportedly had a romantic relationship.[23] The situation benefited Minnie's business, as Giuseppe was able to provide it a measure of protection.

At the start of Prohibition, Auto Inn seemed to operate unnoticed by "dry" agents while its rival Transit Inn was repeatedly raided and fined. Transit Inn owner Peter Klippel was arrested three times during the warmer months of 1920. Early the next year, Klippel publicly blamed Minnie Clark for his troubles, saying she benefited from connections unavailable to him.[24] Klippel likely was referring to a rumored friendship between Minnie and the wife of the local Prohibition agent. It is also possible he was referring to the protection of her paramour Giuseppe DiCarlo.

After Klippel's protest, Minnie's luck changed. In July 1921, New York State Troopers raided her establishment along with Klippel's Transit Inn and two others in the area. They seized champagne, wine and home brew at all four locations and arrested the proprietors.[25] Another raid was conducted by the county sheriff and his deputies a month later at Auto Inn, Transit Inn and Dickey's Roadhouse. About a dozen bottles of whiskey were found in Minnie's possession. She was arrested for possessing prohibited liquor.[26]

In March 1922, the deal for the purchase of Auto Inn was

closed, and Joseph DiCarlo changed the name of the business to Auto Rest.[27] He added his sister, Sarah, to the deed in April.[28] Under Joseph's guidance, Auto Rest became a popular attraction for the nightclub crowd from Buffalo. The roadhouse featured a live orchestra and plenty of bootlegged beverages.

For relaxation, Giuseppe attended boxing matches. He became an avid fan of a local lightweight contender Rocky Kansas (born Rocco Tozzo). Giuseppe appears to have partly financed Kansas's career and likely did a fair amount of wagering on the short, powerfully built fighter.

Nicknamed "Little Hercules," the five-foot-two, 130-pound Kansas was described as "a man with a short pair of legs and muscles rippling up his back that one would expect of a weight lifter."[29]

On March 26, 1921, Giuseppe helped organize a testimonial dinner for Kansas in the Mahogany Room of the Lafayette Hotel. Nearly three hundred people attended the event. Other organizers of the dinner included Kansas manager Daniel J. Rogers (born Daniel Gaudiosa[30]), Lester Cameron, Thomas Petrella and Jack Lawrence. Entertainment was provided by various local musical groups, including the Bison Trio and the Rocky Kansas Jazz Band.[31]

The Buffalo locals had much to celebrate. Not only had Kansas recently defeated highly regarded Bronx native Willie Jackson in a twelve-round bout at New York's Madison Square Garden,[32] but he had also won for his followers quite a bit of cash. Sports writers estimated that three hundred Kansas backers from Buffalo won close to $75,000 by gambling on the match, as the odds were heavily in Jackson's favor. One unidentified Buffalo bettor managed to score $15,000.[33]

Arnold Rothstein was one of the 13,468 spectators at that sporting event.[34] The famous New York gambler and racketeer appeared regularly in the newspapers of the period. He was widely believed to have fixed the 1919 World Series for the underdog Cincinnati Reds. However, there was little reliable evidence of his involvement. Rothstein was called before a Chicago grand jury in the fall of 1920 to testify regarding the "Black Sox" scandal, but he was not among the individuals charged in the case. Prosecutors decided that a Rothstein associate and bodyguard,[35] a former boxer named Abe Attell, had used Rothstein's name without authorization to convince White Sox players they would be paid $100,000 for throwing the Series.[36]

Attell reportedly also influenced the betting odds for the Jackson-Kansas boxing match. He was observed making significant bets on Willie Jackson around New York City in advance of the fight. Attell's money and his known connection to Rothstein could have pushed up the "ridiculous odds" against Kansas.[37]

The possibility that Attell and Rothstein tinkered with the betting odds of the event ought not detract from Kansas's achievement in Madison Square Garden. The Buffalo boxer was universally respected as an honest competitor who always gave one hundred percent in the ring.[38]

Compared in the press to former greats George "Kid" Lavigne and "Jersey" Joe Wolcott as well as to reigning Heavyweight champion Jack Dempsey,[39] Kansas's victory over Jackson secured a summer championship match against reigning Lightweight Benny Leonard of New York City.[40] Kansas and his followers did not fare as well in that bout. Leonard proved to be Kansas's nemesis. During their careers, Kansas and Leonard faced each other four times, and Kansas never came out on top.

Rocky Kansas eventually won the Lightweight Championship of the World, battling Pennsylvania native Jimmy Goodrich through fifteen rounds in December of 1925. Giuseppe DiCarlo did not live long enough to see it.

— — —

Giuseppe was just forty-eight at the time of his death on July 9, 1922. He had been in a vague state of ill health at least for several years.[41]

Though abbreviated by fate and somewhat cheapened by his unwillingness to play by the rules, Giuseppe's life story was one of success. He had amassed a fortune through his business dealings and through the continuous stream of bootlegging, extortion, loan sharking, robbery and gambling income generated by the Buffalo Mafia organization under his command. In addition to wealth and underworld influence, Giuseppe had helpful allies in every stratum of Buffalo society – common laborers, government officials, captains of commerce, purveyors of recreation and respected professionals. With the strength of his allies behind him, he had overcome considerable obstacles.

Giuseppe's friends and his money proved of little use in the fight he faced in early summer of 1922. At that time, he left his home in lively Buffalo for the peace of a recently purchased country estate in the wooded eastern suburb of Bowmansville.[42] It was probably not a coincidence that the estate sat just two miles from Minnie Clark and Auto Inn.

In Bowmansville, Giuseppe fought the final rounds of a losing match against an assortment of health problems. His heart was enlarged and weakened, his kidneys were not functioning properly, and diabetes was wreaking havoc on his body. From June 1 to July 8, he was under the care of Dr. Salvatore Lojacono. At just after midnight on July 9, Dr. Lojacono pronounced Giuseppe dead, the result of acute pulmonary edema – fluid buildup in his lungs.[43]

The Buffalo underworld boss was given a lavish farewell, orchestrated by undertaker Louis Mascari of Dante Place and attended by noteworthy community leaders. The Saturday, July 11, funeral was one of the largest the Italian community had ever hosted.[44]

The funeral services began with a wake at the DiCarlo family home on tree-lined Prospect Avenue. DiCarlo's body was then driven a few city blocks to Holy Cross Church at Maryland and Seventh Streets.[45]

The church building then was still new. Bishop Charles H. Colton of the Diocese of Buffalo founded Holy Cross Parish in 1914 to serve the growing Italian population on the Lower West Side. He appointed the Reverend Joseph Gambino to be the first pastor. Construction began the same year. Father Gambino dedicated the brick church on September 5, 1915, four months after Bishop Colton's death.[46]

After a Mass of Christian Burial celebrated by the Reverend Donato Gregory Valente, a long cortege wound its way through Buffalo streets to Pine Hill Cemetery. The procession included the *Conte di Torino* Lodge of the Order Sons of Italy and the Italian musical band *Circolo Musicale Bellini*. Floral tributes packed 135 carriages. The flowers were sent by Giuseppe's friends and associates in Buffalo, Detroit, Cleveland, Milwaukee, Chicago, New Orleans, San Francisco, Boston and Youngstown,

Ohio.[47]

Eight honorary pallbearers stood with the casket and the numerous floral displays at the DiCarlo family plot within the United German and French Cemetery at Pine Hill.[48] The most easily recognized of the pallbearers was boxer and local hero Rocky Kansas. Kansas's manager Daniel Rogers and restaurateur Thomas J.B. Dyke also were pallbearers.

Vito V. Christiano's participation in the funeral brought in a political element. Christiano, active in local Democratic politics, served the Italian community as a court interpreter and a private investigator. He became an honorary member of the Thomas J.B. Dyke Association. (In 1923, he defeated Daniel Rogers in a Democratic primary for supervisor of Buffalo's 27th Ward.[49])

Medical professionals among the pallbearers were Dr. Salvatore Lojacono, Dr. Charles Panzarella and Dr. Anthony Barone. Panzarella and Barone were born to Italian immigrant parents and maintained practices on Front Avenue. The legal profession was represented by Alexander Taylor, a prominent local attorney and Buffalo native.[50]

Giuseppe's surviving children, Joseph, Samuel and Sarah, watched as their father's casket was lowered into the ground between the graves of their mother Vincenza and older brother Francesco.[51]

― ― ―

At the moment of his father's passing, twenty-two-year-old Joseph DiCarlo became the focus of the Buffalo Mafia family's attention. Key figures in the DiCarlo organization considered backing him as successor to his father's leadership position. However, the idea was quickly discarded, and Angelo Palmeri was selected instead.

Looking back at that moment, the Federal Bureau of Investigation later reported that Joseph was passed over because of his immaturity.

> ...The father of Joseph DiCarlo was in charge of the western New York area for the syndicate and after his death Joseph DiCarlo was suggested to succeed his father as czar, but was considered too young and irresponsible for the position.[52]

Palmeri immediately returned to Buffalo from Niagara Falls.[53] He moved himself and his family into the DiCarlo residence on Prospect Avenue. Joseph, Sam and Sarah DiCarlo likely viewed the move in a positive light. Their "uncle" had returned home.

Palmeri might have been selected to rule the regional Mafia in his own right, but his presence within the DiCarlo household, coupled with the organization's apparent desire to be led by a more mature version of Joseph, suggests that he functioned as a sort of regent. If Joseph's level of emotional development was the only obstacle standing between him and the boss's seat, Palmeri might have been chosen merely to keep that seat warm while Joseph acquired experience and wisdom.

Joseph did not have much of an opportunity to grow into the position. Subsequent events and the arrival of a powerful and ambitious underworld character in western New York conspired to keep him from the command of the regional crime family.

Chapter 6

'Good Killer'

On October 10, 1891, Stefano Magaddino was born into one of the warring Mafia factions of Castellammare del Golfo, Sicily. He was the third of Giovanni and Giuseppa Ciaravino Magaddino's eight children.[1]

The Magaddino family was allied with the locally prominent Bonventre clan. The two houses had been formally united through the July 14, 1876, marriage of Giovanni Magaddino's sister Carmela to Martino Bonventre.[2]

The Magaddino-Bonventre alliance grew significantly in size and status during Stefano Magaddino's childhood, as Martino and Carmela Bonventre's daughter Caterina married into the Bonanno family. Her husband Salvatore Bonanno traced his ancestors back through political leaders in Palermo, Sicily, to a medieval noble family of Pisa, on the Italian mainland.[3]

The Magaddinos, Bonventres and Bonannos of Castellammare comprised the local Mafia's old guard. As "men of respect," their guidance and their support was sought by much of the community. However, their dominance within the coastal town was repeatedly challenged by a Mafia faction led by the large Buccellato family.[4]

The factions engaged in a long and bloody feud, interrupted by brief and futile attempts at reconciliation.

One of the more promising peaceful overtures occurred shortly after Salvatore Bonanno's son Joseph was born in January, 1905. Salvatore extended an olive branch by inviting Felice Buccellato, leader of the rival clan, to serve as Joseph's godfather. As Buccellato accepted the honor, the villagers of Castellammare regarded newborn Joseph Bonanno as a "dove of peace." However, the old rivalries resurfaced just a few years later.[5]

The competing families of Magaddino and Buccellato made one known attempt at intermarriage. Stefano Magaddino's oldest brother Pietro took Anna Buccellato as his wife. Even that union could not prevent a flare-up of the old feud in 1916. Acts of violence and revenge took the lives of Pietro Magaddino and Giovanni Buccellato in that year.[6]

A desire to escape the feud must have been at least part of their motivation as Bonventres, Magaddinos and Bonannos began crossing the Atlantic and settling in the United States in the early 1900s. Many gathered in the Williamsburg section of Brooklyn, around the intersection of North Fifth and Roebling Streets. That area, which had been home to Irish-, German- and Russian-American families at the turn of the century, became host to the largest colony of Castellammaresi in the U.S.[7] Smaller concentrations of Castellammaresi were located in Manhattan, Buffalo and Endicott, New York; Detroit, Michigan;[8] and Philadelphia, Pennsylvania.[9]

The Magaddinos and their allies quickly learned that the old-country rivalry had followed them.

> The Magaddino family was not alone in having members in America; the Buccellato family did also. They were archenemies in Castellammare, and archenemies they remained in Brooklyn.[10]

The feud reached Brooklyn after a murdered member of the Bonventre family was found dismembered within a sack.[11] The ensuing conflict spread beyond Brooklyn to the growing Castellammarese community in Detroit.[12]

— — —

Stefano Magaddino was seventeen as he sailed from Palermo to New York City aboard the *S.S. San Giorgio*. He stepped onto Ellis Island on a cold winter day, February 7, 1909, and made his way to the Williamsburg home of his brother Gaspare. Gaspare Magaddino lived on North Fifth Street close to Roebling[13] and worked in a nearby bakery owned by relative Vito Bonventre.[14]

Stefano found work as a salesman for a Roebling Street

importing firm operated by Vito and Martino Mule, also natives of Castellammare del Golfo, Sicily.[15] Within months of his arrival in the United States, he was formally welcomed into the American branch of the Mafia society. The induction ceremony was held in Chicago.[16]

The details of the induction ceremony and Magaddino's reason for associating himself with the Chicago Mafia, so distant from his Brooklyn home, are lost to history. It seems likely that he hoped to provide some protection for himself and his fellow Castellammarese Mafiosi in Brooklyn, while also assuring the group's independence from expansive New York-area crime bosses.

It also is possible that Magaddino observed dramatic and worrisome changes within New York's underworld. The Manhattan-based Morello organization, already investigated for murders, counterfeiting, Black Hand extortion and bankruptcy frauds, was under constant Secret Service scrutiny by fall of 1909. Boss of bosses Giuseppe Morello and a dozen of his underlings were arrested in mid-November for counterfeiting.[17] At that time, a rival Mafia organization, led by Salvatore "Toto" D'Aquila, was gaining strength across the East River in Brooklyn. D'Aquila took over Morello's boss of bosses position after Morello was convicted and sentenced to a long prison term in 1910.[18] The obvious volatility of New York's Sicilian criminal society could have driven Magaddino to ally with a more stable regime.

Chicago's Sicilian underworld chieftain at that time was the "ferocious and greatly feared"[19] Anthony D'Andrea. President of the Unione Siciliana fraternal order, D'Andrea had enormous clout throughout the Sicilian colonies in the U.S. and also throughout the Mafia criminal organization.[20]

D'Andrea was born June 7, 1872, in Valledolmo, Sicily, to Giuseppe and Francesca Miceli D'Andrea.[21] Well educated in a Palermo seminary, he was an ordained priest when he crossed the Atlantic in the 1890s. He taught at Catholic schools in Maryland and Pennsylvania before an 1899 appointment as a parish priest at St. Anthony's Church in Chicago. After just two months in the city, D'Andrea left the priesthood in order to marry sixteen-year-old Lena Wagner, a German immigrant.[22]

D'Andrea was one of the early organizers of both the Unione

Siciliana[23] and the American Mafia network. Upon completion of a sentence in Joliet Prison for his role in a coin counterfeiting operation,[24] he became a political powerhouse in Chicago's West Side 19th Ward. With the help of Joseph D'Andrea, he engaged in early forms of labor racketeering.[25]

D'Andrea's lieutenant in the Chicago-area Unione was Michele "Mike" Merlo. Merlo earned a sterling reputation as an underworld diplomat and became a trusted adviser of Stefano Magaddino and other important Mafiosi. He eventually succeeded D'Andrea as Chicago's underworld chief.[26]

— — —

Gaspare and Stefano Magaddino married two sisters from the Castellammarese Caroddo family. Pietra and Carmela Caroddo, who had lived with their grandmother in Sicily, entered the U.S. on November 15, 1909, aboard the *S.S. Perugia*. They joined their brother Carlo in an apartment at 247 North Fifth Street in Williamsburg, Brooklyn.[27]

The Caroddo and Magaddino families had been very close while in Sicily. The older sister, Pietra, had taken care of Stefano when he was a boy in Castellammare. From that time on, he looked at her as a second mother.[28] The bond between the families continued within the confines of their Williamsburg neighborhood. Stefano and Carmela, the younger of the sisters, lived in the same apartment building, 126 North Sixth Street, before they were married.[29]

Gaspare took Pietra Caroddo as his wife in July of 1910.[30] Stefano and Carmela wed on October 19, 1913.[31] A third Caroddo sister, Rosaria, married Bartolo DiGregorio. Already a distant Magaddino relative, the marriage to Rosaria made DiGregorio also an in-law of the Magaddinos.[32]

Stefano and his wife broke with Italian tradition as they named their newborn son in February of 1917. Tradition called for a first-born son to be given the name of his paternal grandfather.[33] However, they named their first son Peter, rather than Giovanni.

Straying from naming convention ordinarily indicated a family rift. But there was no falling out between Stefano and his father. Stefano had other reasons for choosing the name Peter.

Stefano's oldest brother Pietro (Peter), husband of Anna Buccellato, had been murdered in Sicily just seven months before

Stefano's son was born. Stefano likely named his son in honor of the slain Pietro. Stefano also may have considered the continued use of the Pietro name within the Magaddino clan to be in jeopardy. Stefano's brother, named for their grandfather, apparently died without an heir who would have been obligated to name his first-born son Pietro. Stefano's break with tradition permitted the name of the family's patriarch to be passed on to future generations.

Soon after Peter's birth, Stefano Magaddino moved his wife and child to Philadelphia. The relocation was likely an effort to protect Carmela and Peter from the increasing violence of the feud with the Buccellatos.

Philadelphia was a safe haven, as Salvatore Sabella of Castellammare had recently been appointed Mafia boss there. Sabella had been groomed for the position by Giuseppe Traina, chief lieutenant of Brooklyn-based boss of bosses Salvatore D'Aquila.[34] Sabella must have known of the Magaddino clan from his days in Castellammare and might have been in contact with Stefano there or in Brooklyn. He became part of the Magaddino extended family in January 1919, when he married Stefano's cousin Maria Galante.

Magaddino continued to use a Williamsburg home address for himself through several more years, though he traveled extensively during that time. He visited Philadelphia, Buffalo and Chicago, and he likely traveled also to Detroit. Gaspare Milazzo, another important Castellammarese Mafioso, had set up shop in Detroit after leaving Brooklyn fearing prosecution for a Buccellato killing.[35]

The Magaddino family's documented Philadelphia addresses were 1444 South Eighth Street and 737 Reed Street, both located within the Italian immigrant community of South Philadelphia. While living at the South Eighth Street address in January 1919, Carmela gave birth to the couple's first daughter, Josephine. A second daughter, Angela, was born in June 1921, while the family lived on Reed Street.[36]

— — —

The "Good Killers" case of August 1921 brought public attention to the Bonventre-Buccellato feud and revealed Stefano Magaddino as a leader of a far-reaching Sicilian underworld organization.[37]

That case began August 8, as crabbers Isaac Sorrell, Charles Bennett and John Gant fished a dead man's body from the waters of Tucker's Cove, an inlet of Shark River near Neptune City, New Jersey. Authorities took the body to the Thomas Hardy funeral home in Belmar. There Monmouth County Physician Charles E. Jamison and Dr. Joseph Ackerman performed an autopsy.

The doctors determined that the man was probably Italian, about twenty-five years of age, and had been in the water of Tucker's Cove for about two weeks. They extracted a number of large shot from a gaping wound on the body's left side. Death was clearly the result of homicide.

In their report, the doctors noted that clothesline had been used to secure two red sandstone weights to the victim, causing the body to remain submerged in the cove. A twenty-seven-pound stone was tied to the neck and a twenty-five-pound stone was tied to the knees.

In a coat pocket was found an envelope mailed from Mahaffey, Pennsylvania, and addressed to "Caizzo, 44 Twelfth St., New York City." The name "Caizzo" turned out to be a close match to a missing person report on a Camillo Caiozzo filed August 1 in New York City.[38] Caiozzo relatives Julius Caietta of New York City and Paul Ladonna of Elizabeth, New Jersey, were called in to identify the body.[39]

Monmouth County detectives had no trouble tracing the clothesline and the peculiar red sandstone to the Riverview Inn close to Tucker's Cove in Neptune City. At the inn, run by Salvatore Cieravo (known locally as Salvatore Rose), investigators found a pile of the same sandstone used around the base of a prominent outdoor plant stand. They also found identical clothesline hanging from trees and poles in the Riverview Inn's yard.[40]

Cieravo was taken into custody on the morning of August 12 as a material witness to the murder of Caiozzo. He was confined in Red Bank borough jail for a few hours and then transferred to Monmouth County Jail in Freehold, where he was held without bail.[41]

While New Jersey police were sorting out Cieravo's role in the Caiozzo killing, a twenty-eight-year-old Castellammarese-immigrant barber named Bartolomeo Fontana approached acting

Captain Michael Fiaschetti of the New York Police Department's Italian Squad with a vague request for protection. Thanks to an informant, Fiaschetti already suspected Fontana of involvement in Caiozzo's murder, and he set himself to the task of extracting a detailed confession.

The burly, cigar-chewing Fiaschetti decided to allow Fontana to wrestle with his conscience for a time. He booked himself and Fontana into a room at the Broadway Central Hotel. Early in the morning, Fiaschetti was awakened by the sound of Fontana pacing across the room. The veteran detective remained still, feigning sleep, as Fontana stopped his pacing at the room's window and shouted in a Sicilian dialect at the late summer dawn.[42]

Fiaschetti, a native Italian, roughly translated Fontana's rant: "My God! He was my friend, my brother, and I killed him. But you know, my good God, I didn't want to do it. I had to do it. They made me kill him."

Fiaschetti rose, switched on the light and got to work on Fontana. "I don't want to see you go to the chair, when you are not to blame," he said. "They are to blame, and I want to get them. I want to get them for having made you kill your friend."[43]

That morning, Fontana told the complete story of the murder of Caiozzo and of a gang of assassins that became known as the "Good Killers."

The barber told of the gang's origin in Castellammare del Golfo, Sicily, its membership of immigrant Mafiosi from the Bonventre and Magaddino families and their allies, and its division into crews of about fifteen members each. He said the gang had been at war for a decade and a half since its leader, a Brooklyn baker from the Bonventre faction, was brutally murdered by the rival Buccellato clan.[44]

Fontana said he began associating with the Good Killers group around 1914 when he lived in a Castellammarese colony in Detroit, Michigan. When a group of Good Killers moved from Detroit to Brooklyn, Fontana went along.[45] Though never a full member of the group, Fontana became familiar with its contract-killing operations. He told Fiaschetti that the Good Killers leadership either terrorized young immigrants into working as its assassins or sponsored the immigration of men who would do the gang's bloody work. Assignments often ended badly for the gunmen.

"Whether he obeyed or not, his life was forfeit," Fontana said. "[The Good Killers] would kill the immigrant just to be sure he wouldn't tell."[46]

The barber gave Fiaschetti the details he could remember of fifteen murders committed by the gang and of the one he was ordered to commit under the threat of death. He provided the names of six gang leaders who had compelled him to slay his boyhood friend Caiozzo. Three of the leaders lived on Roebling Street in Williamsburg. They were Stefano Magaddino, Magaddino's brother-in-law Bartolo DiGregorio and Vito Bonventre. The other three were all from Manhattan: Giuseppe Lombardi of Elizabeth Street, Mariano Galante of Orchard Street and Francesco Puma of East Twelfth Street.[47]

According to Fontana, Caiozzo had been deemed responsible in some way for the death of Pietro Magaddino in 1916. The Magaddino clan initially attributed that death to direct action on the part of the Buccellatos. Caiozzo's involvement apparently came to light much later. As Caiozzo arrived at Ellis Island in June 1920,[48] word of his offense against the Magaddinos was sent from Sicily. The Good Killers began planning for revenge.

Caiozzo settled with his mother and siblings on East Twelfth Street in Manhattan but carefully avoided all contact with Puma. After a year, the Good Killers decided they could get to Caiozzo easiest by using his boyhood friend Fontana to catch him off guard. At a gang hangout, three of the Good Killers backed Fontana into a hallway, pressed the muzzles of their handguns into his stomach and assured him he would be shot to pieces if he did not immediately swear to kill Caiozzo. Fontana took a solemn oath to murder his friend.[49]

The two old chums became reacquainted in the summer of 1921 and might have shared an apartment briefly.[50] Late in July, Fontana proposed a combination business trip and vacation in New Jersey. Caiozzo had recently sold an embroidery business, earning between six hundred and seven hundred dollars, and Fontana urged him to invest the proceeds in a "disorderly house."[51] He offered to put Caiozzo in touch with a New Jersey acquaintance who managed such an establishment near Shark River in Monmouth County.[52] Fontana suggested they spend a few days there and enjoy some hunting in the countryside.

The pair arrived at the Riverview Inn on Thursday, July 26. On Saturday, Caiozzo took a train back into New York City. The purpose of that trip is unclear, but Caiozzo is known to have stopped in to see his family. During Caiozzo's absence from the inn, Fontana told his host Cieravo about the Good Killers' instructions to him. Cieravo knew of the gang and understood that Fontana had no option other than to murder his friend. The innkeeper offered Fontana the use of a shotgun and recommended that the deed be done in the woods away from the inn.[53]

Caiozzo returned to Cieravo's inn on Sunday. He and Fontana went duck hunting the following day. The two men ventured toward an overgrown and marshy area along Shark River. Fontana, holding the shotgun borrowed from Cieravo, lagged just a step behind Caiozzo as they hiked. When the men were just out of sight of the inn, Fontana put the muzzle of the shotgun against his old friend's back and jerked the trigger.

The weapon had been loaded for more than birds. Lead slugs ripped a large hole through Caiozzo's back and side.[54]

Panicked and stricken with guilt, Fontana rushed back to the inn, leaving Caiozzo where he had fallen. Close to two-thirty that afternoon, Cieravo saw Fontana and asked if everything was all right. Fontana said it was. Cieravo wanted to know where the killing had taken place, and Fontana indicated, "Right over there," pointing to a spot close by.

Cieravo was angered: "I told you to go far away. You'll spoil my house."

The innkeeper grabbed a shovel and had Fontana lead him to Caiozzo's body. When they reached the site, Cieravo tried to have Fontana bury his friend. Fontana refused. Disgusted, Cieravo dragged the body a dozen or so paces away and hid it in some brush.[55]

The two men then walked toward Cieravo's home on Embury Avenue, stopping along the way for Cieravo to have a brief discussion with his acquaintance Giuseppe Lombardi, a member of the Good Killers gang. Following the exchange, Lombardi departed for New York City.

Before dawn the next morning, Lombardi returned to Neptune City accompanied by Francesco Puma. With help from Fontana and Cieravo, they located Caiozzo's remains, tied stones to the body and sank it in the water of Shark River. The men adjourned to a 4 a.m. breakfast at Newton's Luncheon near the local train station and returned via train to New York.[56]

As he reached the city, Fontana became concerned for his future. Lombardi and Puma urged him to visit Brooklyn with them. Recalling the fate of other assassins used by the Good Killers, Fontana declined the invitation.[57] He approached Captain Fiaschetti at his earliest opportunity.

— — —

When Fontana finished explaining the Caiozzo murder to Fiaschetti, the police captain placed him under arrest. Fiaschetti and his Italian Squad quickly developed a plan to trap Stefano Magaddino under circumstances that would make him an accessory to the Caiozzo murder. Fontana telephoned Magaddino, told him he believed the police were on to him and asked the gang leader to bring money to Grand Central Terminal so he could get away.

Magaddino took the bait and brought $30 for Fontana to a Grand Central Terminal filled with undercover police detectives. Detective Silvio A. Reppetto, pretending to be a traveler, lurked nearby as Magaddino handed the money to Fontana and told the barber to take a train to Buffalo, where he would be well cared for by "the chief."[58]

Detectives immediately surrounded Magaddino. He resisted arrest but was overpowered. The Italian Squad then rounded up Bonventre, Lombardi, Galante, Puma and DiGregorio.[59] Two other key members of the group, Castellammarese Mafiosi named Gaspare Milazzo and Salvatore Sabella, avoided arrest and escaped the notice of the New York media.[60]

During processing at the police station, the arrested men were all in close quarters. Magaddino lunged at the much smaller Fontana, yelling, "I'll burn you up for this yet! You won't get away with it."

Fiaschetti attempted to block Magaddino's charge and was kicked in the stomach. Carleton Simon, deputy police commissioner in charge of narcotics cases, rushed to Fiaschetti's aid and wrestled for a moment with the prisoner. Fiaschetti recovered and resolved the matter with his nightstick. Magaddino was struck soundly on the head by the burly police captain and momentarily lost consciousness. He also lost a bit of blood and required stitches to close a wound to his forehead.[61]

As all seven arrested men were locked in the Tombs Prison, police informed the press that three of the prisoners made admissions concerning the Caiozzo murder. Details of the prisoner statements were not released.[62]

Back in Monmouth County, New Jersey, Detective Jacob B. Rue learned of Fontana's confession and of his accusations against the Good Killers gang. Rue made out a complaint against Fontana, Magaddino, Bonventre, Puma, Lombardi and Galante. He omitted DiGregorio from the complaint. It is not known if he did so by error or by design. Justice of the Peace Edward W. Wise reviewed Rue's paperwork and issued a warrant for the arrest of the named men.

A preliminary hearing on the matter was held before Magistrate Joseph E. Corrigan at the Tombs in New York City on August 17. Corrigan decided that the six men wanted by Monmouth officials would be held on fugitive from justice charges. He acknowledged a Sullivan Law weapons possession charge against DiGregorio, who was apparently not wanted in New Jersey.

During the proceedings, defense attorney Edward A. Wynne called the court's attention to injuries sustained by Magaddino and Puma since their arrest. Magaddino's head was stitched and bandaged, his hat and shirt were stained with blood. Puma's arms and eyes were blackened with bruises. Puma removed his shirt, revealing black and blue marks on his back.[63]

Wynne did not comment on the possible cause of the injuries. However, the attention he paid to the evidence of police brutality did cause an abrupt end to the rumors of prisoner confessions. Confessions believed to have been extracted through police administered beatings would be of no use in court.

All of the men were held without bail. Fontana was shuttled off to Raymond Street Jail in Brooklyn so he would not be intimidated into silence by the others. The remaining six men went back to the Tombs.[64]

While at Raymond Street Jail, Fontana spoke with visiting Detective Lieutenant Bert McPherson, head of Detroit's Italian Squad, and with Nicholas Selvaggi, first assistant district attorney for Kings County (Brooklyn). During the interrogations, Fontana admitted setting a number of arson fires in Detroit years earlier and provided what information he could recall of sixteen Good Killers attacks.[65]

In Manhattan, he said the gang had been responsible for the December 29, 1920, slaying of Salvatore Mauro in front of 232 Chrystie Street;[66] the May 1921 killing of Vincenzo Alfano on Delancey Street; the February 28, 1921, killing of Joseph "Longo" Granatelli in front of 189 Chrystie Street; and the murder of a man named Casileo, the details of which he could not recall.

In the Bronx, the gang had recently shot Angelo Lagattuta. Unknown to Fontana or to the Good Killers themselves was the fact that Lagattuta survived that attack and was recovering in a New York hospital.

Fontana indicated that the Good Killers were responsible for the deaths of Joseph Ponzo and Francesco Finazzo in Brooklyn, but he could not provide dates and locations for those murders.

His memory of Detroit slayings was helped by information Lieutenant McPherson was able to dig out of police files. Fontana said the Good Killers had murdered three Buccellato brothers, two Giannola brothers, father and son Pietro and Joseph LoBosco, Luca Sarcona and Andrea Lacatto.[67]

— — —

The American press, not yet fully recovered from its "yellow" period, delighted in sensationalizing reports about the Good Killers gang and in inflating the number of deaths attributed to it. As early as August 17, there were published claims that the Good Killers were responsible for as many as seventy murders. That figure came about by calculating the total number of suspicious Italian deaths in Detroit between 1917 and 1921.[68] The following day, one New York paper upped the total to eighty-seven,[69] while an Ohio paper hit the streets claiming one hundred were killed.[70] To reach the century mark, the newspaper had to expand the known territory of the Good Killers from New York, New Jersey and Michigan into Pennsylvania and Illinois.

Not to be outdone, a New York newspaper decided on August 19 that 125 people were massacred by the gang. Those included the estimated seventy from Detroit, twenty believed killed in Chicago, eighteen in Pittsburgh and seventeen in the New York area.[71]

Eventually, the press tired of merely inflating the body count and moved on to other unwarranted and irresponsible assertions.

After McPherson learned from Fontana that some Good Killers victims had been buried secretly in the area of Seven Mile Road and Gratiot Avenue on the outskirts of Detroit, newspapers proclaimed a nationwide search for gang burial grounds.[72]

Fiaschetti fanned the flames of sensationalism. He pronounced the Good Killers bust as "the most important capture ever made by him and his men."[73] On August 20, without any apparent justification, he announced to the New York media that the breakup of the band could finally resolve the 1909 assassination of Italian Squad founder Lieutenant Joseph Petrosino. Petrosino had been shot to death in Palermo during an official assignment for the New York Police Department.[74]

The press puzzled for just a few days over Magaddino's reported Grand Central Terminal mention of a "chief" located in Buffalo. While the title could have referred either to Giuseppe DiCarlo or Angelo Palmeri, Fontana revealed much later that he understood it to refer to Filippo Mazzara.[75] In the short time since Mazzara's 1920 move from Brooklyn, he had risen to command a Buffalo-based Castellammarese crew in the DiCarlo Mafia.[76]

Coverage of the "chief" portion of the story seemed to peak on August 18, with a stunning story in the *New York Telegram*:

> The chief, alleged leader of the Camorra murder gang charged with eighty-seven killings in New York and Detroit, is being sought with two companions in Buffalo today... "The Chief," who is a mysterious figure even to the members of his own gang, is the man who issues the murder orders, and he receives his directions from the headquarters in Sicily. He is declared to have at his disposal a fund exceeding half a million dollars and to be on intimate terms with seemingly respectable merchants...[77]

Buffalo Police Chief James W. Higgins and Detective Chief Zimmerman met with newspapermen that day to dispel the rumors. They characterized stories linking Buffalo criminals with crimes in other areas of the country as "bunk" and denied the existence of the gang "chief."

> Neither Chief Higgins nor Zimmerman had heard anything of a report that a man known as the chief was in this city and being sought by the New York police for his connections in several recent murders there.[78]

While that denial killed off speculation about the Buffalo "chief," press sensationalism continued. For weeks, newspapers across the country reacted hysterically to any report of homicide related to Italians. Each was said to be linked in some way to the Good Killers.[79]

By mid-September, long before the courts had resolved any of the issues relating to the gang's alleged crimes, the story had been played out. Major newspapers showed little interest in the actual legal proceedings in the case.

— — —

New York authorities initially held six men as fugitives from New Jersey justice and awaited the processing of extradition orders. When extradition papers were officially filed, however, only Fontana, Lombardi and Puma were named.

While Detective Rue was said to have been interested in all six men, Monmouth County prosecutors inexplicably left Magaddino, Bonventre and Galante out of the case filed with the county Court of Oyer and Terminer.[80] The omission of Magaddino was particularly glaring, as New York detectives could have testified that he acted in Grand Central Terminal as an accessory after the fact. It appears that the prosecutors decided to focus merely on those who had been physically present in New Jersey for the murder of Caiozzo and for the disposal of his remains.

In New York, Magaddino, Bonventre and Galante were released.

Puma's legal problems doubled as he awaited extradition. He was implicated in September along with Vito Caradonna in the April 14, 1914, stabbing death of Vito Buccellato in the basement of Buccellato's home, 203 Chrystie Street, Manhattan.[81]

Lombardi was the first of the three fugitives to be transported to New Jersey. His extradition papers were approved by New York Governor Al Smith early in September. Detective Rue and Detective Charles C. Davenport escorted Lombardi from the Tombs to the Monmouth County Jail in Freehold on September 7. Fontana and Puma followed soon after.[82]

Pleading not guilty to the charge of concealing a murder, Puma and Lombardi were freed on bail.[83] Though Fontana had confessed to the premeditated murder of Caiozzo, he pleaded not guilty to a first-degree murder charge, possibly hoping prosecutors would allow him to plead to a manslaughter charge in exchange for his testimony against the other accused.[84]

All hope for a plea bargain was dashed when Prosecutor Charles F. Sexton concluded that the appearance of a quid pro quo would make Fontana's testimony worthless.[85]

On March 22, 1922, Fontana appeared in court to change his plea to *non vult contendere*, announcing that he would not contest the first-degree murder charge. He was immediately convicted and sentenced by Judge Samuel Kalisch to life in prison at hard labor.[86]

Later that same day, Fontana was brought back into court to testify against Cieravo. The innkeeper's alleged participation in the Caiozzo murder triggered indictments for accessory before the fact, accessory after the fact and murder. The charges were divided into separate cases, with the accessory before the fact charge heading to trial first.

As Fontana reached the stand, he curiously refused to swear to the truthfulness of his testimony or to place his hand on the Bible. Sexton asked Judge Kalisch to compel the witness to take the oath. An amused Kalisch asked what he could possibly do to compel Fontana after having already sentenced him to life behind bars. A brief recess was called, after which the witness was more accommodating.[87]

Fontana testified to his conversations with Cieravo the day before the murder. He told of Cieravo's offer of the shotgun and his instruction to perform the murder away from the Riverview Inn. He also testified about the innkeeper's role in the temporary hiding and subsequent disposal of Caiozzo's remains, and about the stones and the rope that were taken from inn property in order to keep the body submerged in Tucker's Cove.

Judge Kalisch took issue with portions of Fontana's testimony, informing the jury that the current trial was on the charge of accessory before the fact. Any evidence relating to Cieravo's activities after Caiozzo's death were of no consequence.

Cieravo took the stand in his own defense. Questioned by his attorney J. Mercer Davis, he denied ever speaking to Fontana about the murder, even of knowing Fontana aside from the short vacation Fontana and Caiozzo spent at the inn. Cieravo also said he did not know Giuseppe Lombardi.

"I first learned of the murder from a taxicab driver on Springwood Avenue, who told me that a dead man had been found near my place," he said.

In a closing statement, Davis told the jury to disregard Fontana's testimony. As a convicted murderer, Fontana's words should carry little weight, he argued. Davis insisted that the entire Good Killers story was fabricated by Fontana to conceal the fact that he had murdered his longtime friend in order to rob him of several hundred dollars.

Cieravo's jury deliberated for four hours on March 24 before returning a verdict of not guilty.[88] Sexton, realizing that his chief witness had an enormous credibility problem, promptly dropped the other charges against Cieravo. The innkeeper was freed just as Fontana began his prison sentence.

The trials of Puma and Lombardi, initially scheduled for the end of January, 1922, were repeatedly delayed. Neither case would ever be heard in a courtroom.

On November 4, 1922, Puma took an evening walk from his home at 508 East Twelfth Street, Manhattan. With his hands in his pockets and a cigar in his mouth, he strolled around the corner onto Avenue A. Five gunshots sounded from close by. Several slugs passed into Puma's chest, abdomen and right wrist. One stray shot wounded a twelve-year-old girl playing nearby.

Puma drew his own handgun and spun to face his assailant. At that moment, the blade of a knife entered his stomach. He fell, bleeding badly, and lost consciousness, his cigar smoldering on the sidewalk beside him. He later died of his wounds at Bellevue Hospital.

With the report of his death, the *New York Times* revealed its suspicion that Puma had been cooperating with authorities on an investigation of the Mafia society. An attempt had been made on his life a month earlier. Puma kept that incident secret from all but his close family.[89]

One month after Puma's death, Sexton caused Lombardi's bail to be discharged and dropped the case against him.[90]

Of all the accused assassins in the Good Killers case, only Fontana – the informant – ended up serving a lengthy prison sentence. He was confined at New Jersey State Prison in Trenton, beginning on March 25, 1922. He was paroled temporarily on December 15, 1939. He was readmitted to the prison for observation August 1, 1940, and then permanently released January 21, 1941.[91]

--- --- ---

Stefano Magaddino's arrest was sufficiently unpleasant and the lingering Good Killers case sufficiently threatening to convince him to move from New York City in 1922.[92] Of all possible destinations, Buffalo was most inviting.

The region held enormous criminal potential during the Prohibition Era. The City of Buffalo also had become prestigious within the Mafia, as it hosted regular meetings of Sicilian underworld leaders.[93] A growing community of Castellammaresi in and around Niagara Falls was already familiar with Magaddino.

Magaddino had been on close terms over the years with both Buffalo boss Giuseppe DiCarlo and his lieutenant Angelo Palmeri. Magaddino's sponsor in the American Mafia, Anthony D'Andrea of Chicago, also had connections to Buffalo. Much of his family settled there, and D'Andrea himself resided in the city in 1895.[94]

As DiCarlo's health deteriorated around the start of Prohibition, he offered to bring Magaddino into his organization and groom him as the next boss. Magaddino declined that offer:

> When [DiCarlo] was alive, I was young and he wanted me to be *rappresentante*... I said, "But, what are you crazy?" He said, "I'm sick and I can't..." "So what? Pick one who is more qualified for it... For if you have a good *rappresentante*, everything would be maintained well..." I said, "I'm still too young yet. I got children to take care of."[95]

In October 1922, Magaddino purchased a building lot on Whitney Avenue in Niagara Falls. The deed was recorded in is wife Carmela's name.[96] Awaiting the construction of their new home, the Magaddinos moved in with the Palmeri and DiCarlo families on Prospect Avenue in Buffalo. Magaddino became active in the local Mafia society.

Magaddino's move to western New York occurred just three months after Giuseppe DiCarlo's death, as the Buffalo crime family found itself urgently in need of a powerful leader. The organization had begun splintering into two factions, the "Ins" and the "Outs." The Ins numbered thirteen men, while the Outs, with whom Stefano identified, numbered twenty-four.[97] To preserve order, each faction was given the power to approve or deny membership to the other faction's prospective inductees. When the Ins quickly inducted seven or eight men without approval from the Outs, the situation in Buffalo became critical.

Palmeri, possibly aware that he did not have the ability to be more than a lieutenant and possibly also aware that DiCarlo earlier had offered to turn the organization over to Magaddino, willingly stepped aside as the crime family drafted Magaddino as its new boss.

Magaddino still was reluctant. He stated a preference to serve under fellow Castellammarese Mafioso Filippo Mazzara. However, the family leaders demanded that he take the position.[98]

> They took me and put me there by force... I would have been satisfied to be an aide as long as Philip became rappresentante. But I didn't want to be *rappresentante*. They wanted me to become one. I didn't care. They grabbed me by force in order to save the situation. They believed that I was able to save the situation.[99]

The relationship between Stefano Magaddino and Joseph DiCarlo was civil but strained. Joseph quietly worked to undermine the man who had taken his father's position and who was effectively blocking his own ascension. Stefano considered Joseph to be a thorn in his side. However, out of respect for Joseph's deceased father, Stefano dealt with him with restraint.[100]

Chapter 7

Unprotected

Without the guidance and the protection of his influential father, Joseph DiCarlo drifted into increasingly risky criminal endeavors and found himself regularly targeted by law enforcement.

Just after midnight on September 11, 1922, shots were fired outside the Auto Rest roadhouse in Williamsville. Prohibition agents were responsible for the gunfire. The loud pops of their handguns caused many of the establishment's seventy-five patrons to jump from their seats and dash for the exits. No one was hurt. Agents claimed they directed their weapons at the tires of a high-powered automobile that sped from the scene as they arrived at Auto Rest for a liquor raid.[1]

A man in the crowd flashed a deputy sheriff's badge and attempted to block the "dry" agents. He forcefully ordered them out of the establishment. The four agents, confident of their jurisdiction, grabbed the man and threw him out of their way.[2] Fearful patrons, initially uncertain whether they were witnesses to a raid or victims of an armed robbery, were lined up along the walls as the building was searched.[3]

Only a pint bottle of whiskey and two highball cocktails were found on the premises and seized as evidence. Authorities concluded that Auto Rest's supply of alcohol had been stored in the automobile parked in the rear yard, where a chauffeur kept the engine running ready to drive away at the first sign of trouble.[4]

Joseph DiCarlo, the principal owner of the roadhouse, was arrested along with manager "Jew Minnie" Clark, head waiter Leo Laughlin and waitress Mae Crissey. A hearing on charges of selling liquor and maintaining a nuisance was scheduled for September 29. Bail was set at $1,000 each for Joseph and for Minnie Clark. Joseph posted bail for both. Bail was set at $500 each for Laughlin and Crissey.[5]

The close relationship between Joseph DiCarlo and Minnie Clark, more than ten years his senior, was represented by some newspapers as a marriage. The *Buffalo Enquirer* and the *Buffalo Morning Express* referred to the inn manager as "Minnie Clark DiCarlo" and reported she was Joseph's wife.[6] The couple apparently made no effort to correct the record and possibly encouraged the misrepresentation. Though not legally married, Joseph and Minnie shared a room at the Auto Rest and at that time probably considered their relationship a marriage.[7]

If Joseph DiCarlo had any lingering doubts that he and his business were being targeted by law enforcement, those were dispelled when agents paid a return visit to Williamsville less than a week later.

At 1 a.m., Sunday, September 17, a dozen federal Prohibition agents smashed their way into Auto Rest through three different entrances. They found about one hundred patrons inside the roadhouse. No alcohol was found, but it was not for lack of trying. The search was both thorough and destructive. Agents broke into cabinets in Auto Rest's kitchen, toppled cases of canned goods and tossed over tables. The lock on the establishment's rear door was broken.[8]

"One of the agents drew a revolver and told me that he would blow off some heads if anybody tried to make any false moves," recalled inn employee John Barbera. "Several other agents carried billies in their hands as they searched for liquor."[9]

Joseph DiCarlo was standing near an entrance as the raid began. He told reporters that agents grabbed him and threatened him with violence if he tried to escape or to destroy any beverages.

Joseph responded coolly, inviting the agents to inspect the roadhouse and instructing the Auto Rest's jazz orchestra to play an upbeat tune to keep the patrons entertained. When the agents were preparing to leave, Minnie, proving herself a gracious and understanding hostess, offered them a meal. The agents were probably very surprised by the invitation, but they did not refuse it.

In the wake of the second raid, questions were raised as to the legality of the enforcement action. The search warrant tossed in Joseph's direction when agents burst into the roadhouse appeared to have been signed by U.S Commissioner John H. Klein. But Klein later said he had signed no warrant for a search of Auto Rest. The other U.S. commissioners in the jurisdiction – Donald Bain, George P. Keating, Charles D. Stickney and Charles Doane – also had no recollection of signing such a warrant.[10]

The procedural question proved embarrassing for federal authorities, who quickly and quietly transferred away a number of the agents involved in the Auto Rest raids. Only one agent appeared before Commissioner Klein when the first set of liquor sale charges against Joseph, Minnie Clark, Laughlin and Crissey were reviewed at the end of September. The commissioner ruled that he could not accept as evidence the uncorroborated testimony of a single agent, and the charges were dropped.[11] Klein tossed out charges stemming from the second raid before the case had even officially come before him.[12]

— — —

Local and federal authorities began chipping away at a Buffalo narcotics trafficking ring in 1921. With each arrest, their attention moved closer and closer to Joseph DiCarlo.

Narcotics trafficking was a relatively new federal crime. Cocaine and heroin were imported, sold and purchased largely without significant federal restriction until 1914. The drugs were incorporated into patent medicines[13] and even soft drinks. Coca leaves, the source for cocaine, were included in Coca-Cola's recipe until about 1903.[14] The Harrison Narcotics Act of 1914 outlawed the recreational use of coca- and opium-derivative drugs and required sellers of medicinal cocaine and heroin to acquire federal licenses and pay special taxes on the transactions.

Harrison Act enforcement was inconsistent until 1919, when the U.S. Supreme Court ruled that intent to resell by an unlicensed party could be inferred from the purchase of a large quantity of drugs. Neither the court nor the Harrison Act attempted to define the specific quantity that indicated intent to sell.[15] The Supreme Court ruled in 1920 that satisfying a narcotics addict's craving was not a valid medicinal purpose for cocaine or heroin.[16]

On December 2, 1921, rooming house owner Belle Karnes and her lodger Joseph "Busy Joe" Patitucci, both 35, were arrested on drug charges after $5,000 worth of opium and heroin were discovered in Karnes' house at 265 Franklin Street. Though the drugs were found in a clothes closet off Karnes' own apartment, the case focused on Patitucci. U.S. Commissioner Doane released Karnes but held Patitucci with bail set at $2,000.[17]

Born July 4, 1893, in Licata, Sicily, Patitucci entered the U.S. through Ellis Island just before his seventeenth birthday.[18] Busy Joe's family grew influential in the American underworld. A cousin, Salvatore "Sam" Todaro became an important figure in the Mafia of Cleveland, initially partnering with the Lonardo brothers in Prohibition Era rackets[19] and later with the Porrellos.[20]

At trial, Patitucci admitted his drug use and testified that it dated from his service in the U.S. Army. Drafted in February 1917, Patitucci served in France during the Great War. He was introduced to cocaine and morphine at that time and brought a drug addiction home to Buffalo with him in 1919. Patitucci's jury found him guilty but urged leniency in light of his military service. He was sentenced to three months in the Erie County Penitentiary.[21]

William J. Donovan joined the law enforcement effort just as local and federal agencies began running up the score against drug criminals in the city. Widely known as Colonel Donovan for the rank he held at the conclusion of the Great War[22] (and in some circles as "Wild Bill"[23]), the Buffalo native was appointed to the post of U.S. Attorney for the Western District of New York in February 1922.[24]

Police believed they dealt local drug criminals a severe blow in April, 1922. Acting on a tip from federal investigators in New York City, they tailed a number of suspects for three weeks. When they felt certain how several of the individuals worked together, they made arrests.

Alleged drug ringleader John B. "Johnny" Dyke and his teenage truck driver John A. Fina[25] were taken into custody along with Kitty Fox, another rooming house owner. They were charged with peddling narcotics. Two other men and two other women were also arrested for addiction to drugs.

Quantities of cocaine and morphine and a number of hypodermic syringes were seized at Fox's residence, 709 Michigan Avenue. A subsequent raid of Dyke's cigar store at 156 Elmwood Avenue turned up a cache of drugs with an estimated value of $10,000. Hidden around the store, police found cocaine, morphine and gum opium. Authorities also seized a small truck, which they said Fina had used to make drug deliveries. The truck turned out to be partly owned by John Dyke's brother, Buffalo and New York City restaurateur Thomas J.B. "Tommy" Dyke.

Fox was held on $2,000 bail. Bail was fixed at $10,000 for Johnny Dyke and $5,000 for Fina. Both men made bail and were released.[26] Dyke and Fina later pleaded guilty to possession and selling narcotics. Dyke was sentenced to two and a half years in Atlanta Federal Penitentiary. Only nineteen, Fina was given a thirteen-month sentence at the Elmira Reformatory.[27]

One of the narcotics officers involved in the case told the press, "If things had broken better for us, we would have seized drugs valued at thousands and thousands of dollars in this city. The lead, which we got in New York, leaves little doubt that Buffalo is the clearing house for numerous larger cities, including New York."[28]

By December of 1922, U.S. Attorney Donovan announced that a police noose was closing on the leaders of the regional drug ring.[29]

Investigators had in fact been assembling a case for several months and were at that time gathering manpower and mapping out strategy.[30] Internal Revenue Service narcotics agents from Washington, Boston, Baltimore and Philadelphia were added to the staff of the New York office and placed temporarily under the command of New York division chief Ralph Hunter Oyler.[31]

On January 6, 1923, Joseph DiCarlo and two dozen others were arrested and charged with participating in a drug trafficking conspiracy.

Led by Oyler, agents first raided John J. Mangano's Niagara Street drug store.[32] The twenty-nine-year-old Mangano, a ward politician for the Democratic party, initially denied any involvement in the traffic of illegal narcotics and offered to assist in the law enforcement effort. However, a thorough search of his store revealed a secret stash of cocaine and morphine sulfate valued at more than $2,000. Mangano and two other men in the store – Thomas Agro and John Russo, also known as Joseph Puma – were placed under arrest.

Joseph DiCarlo happened to walk into the drug store while agents were there, and he was promptly arrested. His explanation that he had merely stopped in to buy a cigar was ignored. Agents already had his name on a list of suspected drug ring organizers.[33]

Oyler's agents then quietly swarmed into the Stella Restaurant on The Terrace, arresting "Busy Joe" Patitucci, who had only recently completed his three-month sentence in the Erie County Penitentiary. They also arrested Rosario Cavaretta and nineteen-year-old Samuel Gentile. The men were charged with possessing and selling narcotics. A search of the premises revealed significant quantities of cocaine and morphine and a smaller amount of heroin hidden in secret pockets behind the wainscoting of the restaurant's kitchen.[34]

With Patitucci, Cavaretta and Gentile removed from the establishment, Oyler and his men posed as Stella Restaurant employees. Oyler personally donned the white apron Patitucci typically wore, and agents Joseph Murphy and John Sheehan acted as waiters. As Patitucci's regular customers came calling and placed narcotics orders, the undercover men flashed their badges, arrested them and secured them in a rear room of the restaurant. A patrol wagon was called later to carry the prisoners to the federal building for processing.[35]

The federal agents continued their busy day with an 11 p.m. raid of the Ace in the Hole soft drink establishment at West Eagle Street and the Terrace, just a few doors away from the Stella Restaurant. They arrested proprietor Samuel Spica and his wife Mary. Undercover agents earlier had made cocaine purchases from both of the Spicas. During the raid, agents seized a loaded automatic pistol they found in Samuel Spica's possession and four ounces of cocaine they discovered in a cigar box hidden in the cradle of the Spicas' sleeping infant. Samuel Spica tried unsuccessfully to buy his way out of trouble with a $1,000 bribe. As the couple was charged at the federal building, Mary Spica carried their wailing, baby in her arms.[36]

Agents then proceeded to round up every suspected drug dealer in the city. U.S Commissioner John Klein kept his office open through the night in order to process a total of twenty-five arrests.[37]

Speaking to the press about the scope of the law enforcement action, Oyler expressed shock at the level of drug activity in the region. "In all my experience in narcotics work never have I seen anything like it. Peddlers plied their trade openly on the principal streets. Drug stores, soft drink places and restaurants dealt in drugs without fear."[38]

Joseph DiCarlo and John Mangano were quickly released on bail. Dan Rogers, manager of boxer Rocky Kansas, furnished the $5,000 bail for Joseph's release.[39] Many other suspects were released on lesser amounts. However, Joe Patitucci and another suspect, boxer Albert "Kid Ginger" Dominico, were not as fortunate. They were held in county jail until January 15, when they finally made bail. Bail for Patitucci, initially set at $10,000, had been reduced to $7,000. Dominico needed to raise $5,000 for his release.[40]

Mangano, disputing the validity of the federal agents' search warrant, attempted to have the charges against him dropped and brazenly insisted that the drugs found in his store be returned to him. That effort failed. Agents proved they had sufficient evidence against Mangano to justify their search warrant. They noted that undercover men had purchased illegal drugs within Mangano's store just two days before the raid.[41]

The case against Joseph DiCarlo went nowhere. Commissioner Klein soon discharged him.[42] Federal prosecutors focused their efforts on Mangano, Patitucci and the other men linked to drug sales at the Stella Restaurant.

As Buffalo residents came to grips with the scope of the drug network in their midst, another problem – the cooperation of local police officers with drug traffickers – became apparent. Federal agents learned from an informant that drug peddlers regularly paid police in exchange for immunity from arrest. There even was some evidence that police were willing to act as enforcers for the underworld. The local media reported that a Buffalo city detective personally threatened Oyler with harm if he went ahead with his planned raids.[43]

The community soon had reason to believe that corruption in the police department involved more than a few rogue cops. With drug traffickers reeling, Buffalo's police refused to press its advantage. In fact, police administrators began siphoning resources away from narcotics enforcement. Lieutenant Austin J. Roche, whose small narcotics squad had been involved in more than a hundred arrests and in the seizure of more than $100,000 worth of drugs in just a few months' time, found in late May 1923 that his squad was shrinking.

U.S. Attorney Donovan decried the police department's treatment of Roche. Once promised a squad of six men, Roche had been forced to get the job done with just two, and then found that enforcement of vice laws and other police duties had been added to his responsibilities. After Patrolman Simon Callinan was transferred out of the narcotics squad, leaving Roche with only one officer, Donovan threatened on May 31 to call a special grand jury session to investigate police corruption.[44]

Donovan's attention to the plight of the narcotics squad forced Police Chief John Burfeind to clarify Roche's responsibilities. The chief announced on June 2 that Roche was primarily responsible for suppressing narcotics traffic and vice, but he could be called upon to aid other branches of the department when necessary. Burfeind took the opportunity to chastise Roche for working more closely with the U.S. Attorney's Office than with his own commanders in the police department.[45]

Donovan countered by calling upon first-term Mayor Francis Xavier Schwab to investigate the transfer of Callinan. Schwab agreed to do so[46] but then turned the matter over to Burfeind, who objected to answering any questions about matters within his department. "I have nothing to investigate," the chief said. As his comment reached the press, Patrolman Donald Savini, the remaining member of Roche's narcotics squad, turned in his resignation from the police force.[47]

Savini subsequently brought allegations of police graft to the attention of the city administration and the press. He claimed that criminals were tipped off by corrupt police officers whenever a raid of the vice or narcotics squad was about to occur. He also charged that the only way for a legitimate officer to keep his job in the city's notorious "tenderloin" district was to do as corrupt officers told him. Chief Burfeind denied Savini's accusations,[48] even as a number of drug peddlers from the tenderloin came forward to say that they had sent weekly payments to one of his detectives, William "Stormy Bill" Jordan, in order to purchase protection from police raids.[49]

The new revelations sparked local and federal investigations into police misconduct in the City of Buffalo.[50]

— — —

In July, five of the alleged drug conspirators arrested in January's sensational raids went to trial. They were Busy Joe Patitucci, Albert Dominico, Rosario Cavaretta, Sam Gentile and Frank E. Barone.[51] Barone, who was Patitucci's partner in the Stella Restaurant,[52] also was indicted for using the mail to advertise and sell sulfate of morphine.[53]

During the trial, government witnesses, including federal agents and local narcotics addicts, testified that they had purchased morphine or cocaine from the defendants inside the Stella Restaurant. Drug sales were said to be such a common practice in the establishment that payments were casually rung up on the restaurant's cash register.[54]

Defense attorneys attacked the credibility of the drug-addicted witnesses and claimed that narcotics officers – including Ralph Oyler – had lied on the stand in order to notch a conviction.

"The only reason [witness] Belle Lawrence was in court is because they keep her out of jail for testifying against these men," attorney Michael H. Maher told the jury. "She gets arrested for various things and then squeals on someone to keep out of jail."

Prosecutor Harold V. Cook defended his witnesses, saying they were more credible than the accused.[55]

After five hours of deliberation on Thursday, July 19, the jury agreed with Cook, finding Patitucci, Cavaretta, Gentile, Dominico and Barone guilty as charged. The verdict prompted an emotional scene in the courtroom. Barone's father collapsed, Patitucci's mother cried loudly. "Kid Ginger" Dominico, the boxer, shouted threats to Stanley Kenney, a federal agent instrumental in the case: "I'll get you when I get out."

As the five convicted drug peddlers were led from the courtroom, a crowd of nearly one hundred young men gathered. Fearing a riot, deputy marshals forced the crowd out of the building.[56]

The following Monday, federal Judge John Clark Knox sentenced Patitucci, Barone, Cavaretta and Gentile to statutory maximum two-year sentences in Atlanta Federal Penitentiary. "It has been shown in the testimony that narcotics were sold freely as meatballs in the [Stella] restaurant," Knox said. "The crime of selling drugs calls for a severe penalty."[57]

The sentencing of Dominico was delayed a couple of days, as Judge Knox reviewed the trial testimony.[58] On Wednesday, July 25, the judge gave him the same two-year sentence as his conspirators. The start of that sentence had to be postponed, however, as Kid Ginger escaped on the way to his holding cell.[59]

Deputy U.S. Marshal Frank Rine was assigned to bring Dominico and another prisoner from their federal court sentencing hearings to cells in the county lockup. Neither of his prisoners was handcuffed. As the group reached the corner of Franklin and Church Streets, Dominico simply bolted, heading in the direction of Erie Street. Needing to look after his remaining prisoner, Rine was unable to give chase.[60]

A police dragnet was spread over Buffalo's Italian neighborhoods and a fifty-dollar reward was offered for information on Kid Ginger's whereabouts. But Dominico was not found in the city. He managed to elude law enforcement until October 1, when Ralph Oyler discovered him in Detroit, Michigan.[61]

The start of Busy Joe Patitucci's sentence also was postponed. Patitucci decided to cooperate with authorities, and he remained in Buffalo in order to give testimony relating to corruption in the municipal police department.[62]

Due to public pressure, investigation of police graft had become the focus of Mayor Schwab's administration. Testimony from tenderloin vice merchants implicated a large number of police officers and administrators.

In early August, Lieutenant Roche was called as a witness in the mayor's investigation. From the witness chair, he testified that Chief Burfeind, Deputy Chief John S. Marnon, Captain John J. Creahan and Patrolman Louis H. Rosenow each had extended their protection to one or more of the city's vice establishments.

Learning that Patitucci held information on police corruption, the mayor and Assistant Corporation Counsel Frank C. Westphal had several closed door discussions with the convicted drug peddler.[63] The secret meetings were necessary, Schwab told the press, because Patitucci could be killed for revealing what he knew. Among other things, Patitucci knew of at least one Buffalo policeman who was on the take. After a January narcotics arrest, Patitucci had slipped $100 to acting Detective William "Stormy" Jordan on the way to the police station. The bribe had caused Jordan to process Patitucci only on a minor charge of vagrancy.[64]

Two days after his secret meetings, Patitucci was a free man. Granted a writ of error, which made a new trial possible, he was released on $7,000 bail. A local newspaper remarked, "…it is possible that Pattituccio [sic], who has had several conferences with District Attorney Moore and United States Attorney Donovan, will never serve his sentence."[65]

— — —

In August of 1923, Joseph DiCarlo and Minnie Clark faced yet another round of bootlegging charges. On the sixteenth, Prohibition agent Henry N. Greenfield visited Auto Rest and purchased six glasses of whiskey for one dollar each and a bottle of whiskey for $15. Agent Charles Grill witnessed the transactions.[66]

Federal Prohibition agents led by James A. Hayes and Valentine Haas followed up with a search of the establishment on August 18. They found two fifth-gallon bottles of whiskey, and Joseph and Minnie were charged. To avoid a stay in prison, DiCarlo needed to provide $2,000 bail.

Just after noon on August 22, he drove himself to the office of U.S. Commissioner Donald Bain to deliver the bail money.[67] He had reason to feel optimistic about his case. Though federal authorities constantly hounded him, they had not been able to make any of their charges stick.

A short time later, Joseph drove narcotics peddler Peter Gallelli to his Delaware Avenue apartment. Gallelli stepped out of the car at one-thirty, crossed the street and greeted a man in front of the Ford Hotel. As Gallelli traded a small package of morphine for $35, another man approached.

Joseph, still in his car, apparently recognized the men with Gallelli. He shouted, "Look out for the two agents!" then he sped away up Delaware Avenue in his high-powered automobile.

Gallelli had no escape. Federal narcotics agents placed him under arrest and conducted a search of his apartment. They found four bottles containing cocaine valued in the thousands of dollars.

Gallelli's wife Helen, who was home during the search, was arrested for possession of narcotics. During questioning by agents, Gallelli made statements implicating Joseph DiCarlo in the drug deal.[68]

Joseph managed to avoid arrest for nearly twelve hours. Just after midnight on August 23, he was picked up and charged with conspiracy to violate the Harrison Narcotics Act. After a stop at the office of the U.S. Attorney, where he refused to answer any questions, he was locked up for the night at police headquarters.[69]

Press accounts of the Gallelli and DiCarlo arrests noted that police also took off the streets a drug dealer who worked as an informer and helped set up the Ford Hotel drug buy. Officials refused to reveal the name of the man they held as a material witness.[70]

William Donovan took personal charge of the DiCarlo case. In New York City at the time the arrests occurred, he hurried back to Buffalo to demand that Commissioner Klein set Joseph's bail at the enormous sum of $50,000.

"I want to make sure that DiCarlo does not get out easily," the U.S. attorney said. "We have him now and I don't want to take chances of his running away. Bail of $25,000 would be mighty cheap. He could produce it in no time."[71]

Donovan said he considered Joseph DiCarlo to be one of the most important drug dealers in the region. Evidence of his involvement with narcotics dated back four years, but prosecutors had been frustrated by his careful use of underlings to pass narcotics to purchasers.[72]

Federal agents went to the press with an accusation that Joseph was "the brains of the Buffalo dope ring." They suspected that it was he who supplied narcotics to convicted dealers Joe Patitucci, Frank Barone and Samuel Spica.[73]

Klein agreed with Donovan and set bail at the virtually unprecedented $50,000 amount. Joseph still managed to be back on the street by the end of the day. Joseph and his sister Sarah pledged their interests in the Auto Rest business, the summer home in Bowmansville and three homes on Prospect Avenue. Dan Rogers and Maryland Street resident Josephine Vacanti also contributed to the bail amount.[74]

Peter and Helen Gallelli remained behind bars. Their bail had been set at $25,000.

The government's material witness also was released. Still refusing to identify him, officials said he would be called to testify in the federal case against Joseph and the Gallellis.[75]

Joseph insisted that he was innocent of any drug dealing. He argued that his arrest was a case of mistaken identity. Through attorney John Knibloe, he claimed that he had not been on Delaware Avenue when Gallelli was arrested. He acknowledged seeing Gallelli that day, but that was at a lunch spot on Chippewa Street. He said he did not see Gallelli after leaving the restaurant. Joseph's alibi on the afternoon of August 22 included a stop at a Main Street store to purchase an athletic suit and a visit to the Central YMCA, where he paid for a membership and spent several hours playing handball.[76]

— — —

On the evening of Aug. 31, 1923, narcotics agents arrested another man they considered to be a leader in the Buffalo area drug trade. Sylvester Camerano, known around the city as Lester Cameron, was captured on Main Street. Agents had been watching for him for months. Investigators said Cameron partnered with John Mangano in the distribution of illegal narcotics.[77]

Cameron, about forty years old, was well known in the city. He frequented horse races and boxing events in the area, owned barbershops at two locations, dressed in the finest clothes and drove an ostentatious automobile. The buzz around Buffalo was that he had amassed a considerable fortune not through the barber trade but through bootlegging and gambling.[78]

"I am as innocent as a babe," Cameron protested as he was brought to the Federal Building for processing. "They are trying to connect me with a lot of greaseballs that I wouldn't even speak to."[79]

At the Federal Building, Cameron refused to be fingerprinted, complicating investigators' efforts to tie him to crimes in other jurisdictions. Donovan questioned Cameron for an hour before sending him to spend the night in the Franklin Street police station. The suspect was arraigned before Commissioner Klein the next morning.[80]

Investigators managed to piece together Cameron's background. They learned that he was born in Naples, Italy, around 1883 and had been in trouble on and off in the U.S. since

1900. In that year, he was arrested for assault but discharged. He served time in the Elmira Reformatory after a 1902 abduction conviction. He was sentenced to 150 days in the Erie County Penitentiary after a 1912 conviction on assault charges, and he earned a six-month sentence for assault in 1917. In 1922, he was tried for bootlegging and for bribing a federal agent in Newark, New Jersey, but he was acquitted by a jury.[81]

Donovan decided to try Mangano and Cameron together, along with Thomas Agro, John Russo and teenager August Mercurio, for possessing, selling and conspiring to sell narcotics. The case was added to the federal court docket for late in the year.[82]

Rumors circulated in October that Mangano was providing evidence to prosecutors in the hope of obtaining leniency.[83]

— — —

Rivals once again tried to eliminate Buffalo bootlegger Vincent Vaccaro in early autumn 1923. Vaccaro had been wounded in the 1920 gunfight that took the life of DiCarlo family friend Isidoro Crocevera. Vaccaro also had been arrested in July 1923 and charged with first degree assault, the result of an inconsequential duel with Charles Ragone on Porter Avenue.[84]

After attending a meeting of an Italian-American society, Vaccaro returned home to 181 West Tupper Street just after midnight on September 22, 1923. He was climbing the front stairs of his home, as a Ford touring car quickly drove up. Gunmen within the vehicle opened fire on Vaccaro. The automobile took off down West Tupper, turning onto Virginia Street. Vaccaro yelled out and fell onto the front porch with three bullet wounds in his side.[85]

Vaccaro's parents, who lived at the same address, heard the shots and rushed outside. They found their son lying in a pool of blood and caught a glimpse of the Ford touring car as it sped away. They carried Vaccaro into the house and called for an ambulance.[86]

At Columbus Hospital, doctors believed Vaccaro was near death. Two bullet strikes to his left shoulder were not considered life threatening, but a third bullet had pierced his left lung and passed through his abdomen. Doctors did not expect Vaccaro to recover from that final wound.[87]

Police combed the West Tupper Street neighborhood, trying

to identify Vaccaro's assailants. Two newsboys, who said they witnessed the shooting, told police they saw the shots come from a touring car with three men inside of it. They said darkness prevented them from getting the car's license plate number.[88]

During the day, Detective Sergeant Connolly of the homicide squad questioned Vaccaro several times. Vaccaro would not answer any questions relating to the attack.[89] Investigators brought Vaccaro's family and friends into police headquarters for questioning. Zimmerman, chief of detectives, told the press that no one could shed any light on the crime.[90]

As in the 1920 case, police decided that the Vaccaro shooting was the result of a feud between bootleggers.[91]

Despite the dire predictions of his doctors, Vaccaro did recover from his wounds. After his release from the hospital, he moved from Buffalo and divided his time between Cleveland, Ohio, and Detroit, Michigan.[92]

― ― ―

At the beginning of November, Assistant U.S. Attorney Ganson Goodyear Depew learned that attempts had been made by a suspected drug dealer to influence prospective jurors. Depew immediately informed Judge John R. Hazel. The judge responded by suspending a trial in progress and calling all active jurors before him for a warning:

> Reports that certain persons have been tampering with jurors in the corridors of this building with a view to influencing your verdict in cases soon to be tried have been called to my attention. You are hereby ordered not to hold any conversations relative to cases that have been tried, are now being tried or that may be tried in the future in this court, with any persons.
>
> For any juror to discuss a case with a person not in his own panel constitutes a serious offense. Both juror and the person approaching him are liable to a serious punishment. I am sure that none of you honorable gentlemen would be influenced by such persons, but, nevertheless, you must

be warned.[93]

The judge asked jurors if any of them had been approached in any manner. None came forward.[94]

Camerano, Mercurio and Russo went to trial before Judge Hazel on Tuesday, December 4. Two of their earlier codefendants were not with them. Agro had pleaded guilty to drug peddling before the trial began. Rumors of Mangano's cooperation with authorities immediately were proven true: The druggist was the first witness called to testify for the prosecution.

Due to telephoned death threats against the turncoat Mangano, dozens of Secret Service men and narcotics agents were assigned to mix with a courtroom crowd of several hundred people. Spectators the agents deemed suspicious were frisked for weapons.[95]

On the witness stand, Mangano described how he came to possess the drugs seized at his business in the January raid. He testified that Camerano, known to him for about five years, came to his drug store on December 20, 1922, and presented him with packages containing 30 ounces of morphine. The drugs had been received by Camerano as payment for a bootleg whiskey deal, Mangano said. Camerano wanted the druggist to hold them in his store. When Mangano refused, Camerano left the packages and walked out. He returned to Mangano's store the next day and offered to sell the morphine to Mangano at fifteen dollars an ounce. The druggist turned down the offer but agreed to keep the drugs at his store and to sell them as opportunities arose. Mangano testified that, within a few days, he sold two ounces of the morphine to Thomas Agro, who planned to resell them. The rest remained in a store filing cabinet.[96]

About two weeks later, Mangano thought he would finally be rid of Camerano's parcel. Agro and Russo came to the store, telling the druggist that a deal was being prepared by August Mercurio for the sale of all the remaining morphine. However, the man with whom Mercurio made the arrangements turned up short of cash and then disappeared. Soon after that, narcotics agents burst into Mangano's store, finding the morphine, Mangano, Agro and Russo. Mercurio was arrested later at his home.[97]

Mangano also testified about a falling out between Camerano and himself.

Released on bail after his January arrest, Mangano returned to his business. Camerano came to the store, expressing concern over the trouble he had caused the druggist but also demanding payment from Mangano for the drugs that were seized. Infuriated, Mangano shouted, "Get out of my store and never come in here again." According to Mangano's testimony, he and Camerano had not spoken since then.[98]

When asked on cross-examination if he knew Joseph DiCarlo, Mangano replied that he knew two people by that name. Asked about the younger Joseph, the druggist said they had been acquainted since childhood. He testified that they had a social relationship and did not engage in business together. Joseph stopped by the drug store a few times a week to buy cigars, Mangano said.[99]

Assistant U.S. Attorney Depew brought Chief Oyler to the stand, along with agents involved in the raids and some eyewitnesses to the argument between Mangano and Camerano.[100]

As the prosecution concluded its case. Defense attorneys asked for dismissal of the charges against Camerano, Russo and Mercurio on the grounds that Depew's case did not establish a conspiracy among all the defendants to sell illegal narcotics. Judge Hazel denied the motion, but noted a problem with the conspiracy charge:

> ...Russo and Mercurio were not original conspirators, in my analysis of the case, but I believe that Cameron and Mangano were. But if subsequent acts were sufficient to show them to be parties later to a conspiracy, that is something for the jury to decide.[101]

Each of the defendants adopted a different strategy as they attempted to poke holes in Depew's case.

Camerano's counsel Edward F. Shlenker brought a number of witnesses to the stand to testify that his client was not in Buffalo on the date he was charged with turning the morphine over to Mangano. Rooming house owner Harriet Fox stated that Camerano made frequent trips to New York, Detroit and Cleveland, and had left for New York the day before Mangano said he received the drugs.[102] Three New York City residents – Phoebe Feiner, Abe Kaufman and W. Engler – testified that they recalled seeing Camerano in New York on December 21, 22 and 23 of 1922. On cross-examination, however, they were unable to explain how those dates happened to stand out in their memories.[103]

Ernest W. McIntyre, attorney for Mercurio, drew attention to that fact that his client's involvement in the alleged conspiracy was limited to referring an undercover narcotics agent to Agro. Mercurio took the stand to testify that he only led Agent Stanley Kenney to Agro because Kenney represented himself as badly in need of drugs and Mercurio felt sorry for him. McIntyre classified the undercover agent's actions as entrapment.[104]

Russo's attorney, Samuel M. Fleischman, built a defense argument that one newspaper called "the most novel ever introduced in a federal court room." Fleischman claimed that Russo became caught up in the drug transactions after Agent Kenney told him that raids were being performed solely for the purpose of making a motion picture.[105]

Defense attorneys called to the stand May Patitucci, wife of Busy Joe, in an effort to prove that Mangano was the only true drug dealer of the bunch. The witness testified that she was a former drug addict and had made purchases of narcotics from Mangano without doctor's prescriptions. The defense attempted to establish that her husband was functioning as a government informant, but prosecutor Depew denied the claim.[106]

After Judge Hazel instructed the jurors and sent them to their deliberations on Wednesday, December 12, the general opinion in the courtroom was that Camerano would be acquitted. (In the courtroom gallery, gamblers reportedly had difficulty enticing wagers in favor of conviction even after offering two-to-one odds.) Camerano appeared confident of acquittal, as he loudly joked with companions in the courtroom hallway and announced plans for a post-trial visit to New York.

The jury deliberated for about three hours and returned with a stunning guilty verdict against Camerano. He was convicted of all six counts against him, including conspiracy and possessing and selling morphine. The jury found Mercurio and Russo not guilty of conspiracy but convicted them of the possession and sale of drugs.

Following the announcement of the verdict, Camerano called out, "Before God, I am innocent. Never in my life did I have anything to do with dope."[107]

At the December 17 sentencing hearing, Camerano once again protested his innocence. "I never sold Mangano anything," he said. "So help me God, Mangano lied on the stand." Camerano did come clean about other wrongdoing. He admitted to bootlegging and to gambling, noting that he had made $40,000 betting on boxer Rocky Kansas:

> I think a man who would lower himself to sell drugs is the scum of the earth. Send me to Atlanta [Federal Penitentiary] for bootlegging or for anything else, but not for a thing like that.

Judge Hazel imposed a prison sentence of four and a half years and a fine of $2,000 on Camerano. Attorney Shlenker stated his intention to appeal the verdict, and Camerano was freed on $25,000 bail. U.S. Attorney Donovan asked the judge to be lenient with the other defendants. They were sentenced to shorter terms in the Erie County Penitentiary. Mercurio was sentenced to three months in prison. Russo received two months.

Thomas Agro, who had admitted selling narcotics but would not testify against the other defendants, was sentenced to two years in Atlanta Federal Penitentiary.[108]

— — —

In an obvious appeal to public opinion as his trial date approached, Joseph DiCarlo announced December 23, 1923, that Auto Rest would provide a bountiful turkey dinner to the needy of the Buffalo community on Christmas Day. Joseph encouraged civic organizations to direct the "worthy poor" to the corner of Main and Genesee Streets between noon and four in the afternoon. He arranged for buses to pick up passengers there hourly and transport them to Auto Rest.

"Everyone who shows up will be fed," he said. "They will also be transported safely back to the city." In addition to dinner, Joseph promised entertainment – music, singing and dancing.[109]

Whatever goodwill was generated by the gesture quickly dissipated.

Chapter 8

Intimidation

Federal prosecutors issued a subpoena for Busy Joe Patitucci just after Christmas of 1923. He was summoned to testify as the principal witness in the government's drug case against Joseph DiCarlo and Peter Gallelli. Patitucci had already aided the prosecution of other drug traffickers in Buffalo and in New York City.[1]

On New Year's Day, 1924, after having gone to an evening movie, Patitucci and his wife May[2] had a late meal at Frank Lumia's Italian restaurant on Oak Street near Tupper Street.[3] Close to eleven o'clock, Lumia's telephone rang. The restaurant owner answered it and had a quiet conversation. Joe and May Patitucci left the restaurant shortly before eleven-thirty.

As the couple stepped out onto the sidewalk, an automobile parked at the northwest corner of Oak and Tupper Streets caught Busy Joe's eye. It was a new Overland touring sedan. He thought little of it and walked eastward along Tupper Street with his wife. When they crossed Elm Street, the automobile behind them started up with a roar. The vehicle sped up the street, stopped behind the couple at Elm Street to let out two men before continuing ahead to Michigan Avenue.

Patitucci recognized the two men. They were DiCarlo and Gallelli. Gallelli wore a dark, brown overcoat. DiCarlo was dressed all in black. Both of them were walking quickly in Patitucci's direction.

In an instant, a bullet struck Patitucci under his chin.

Seeing both DiCarlo and Gallelli holding handguns, Busy Joe spun about, yelled and ran. Multiple shots were fired, as he raced in the direction of Michigan Avenue. Reaching the corner, he passed the parked automobile, spotting Joseph Ruffino, Gaetano Capodicaso and a third man within. Patitucci turned right onto Michigan Avenue, as his assailants regrouped and sped off. He did not stop running until he reached Genesee Street, a block away.[4]

There he paused to check his injuries. In addition to bullet entrance and exit wounds under his jaw, he found three bullet holes in his overcoat. One was in the coat's right lapel. Another was in the left side. A third hole was in the center back of the coat. Patitucci also discovered a .32-caliber slug lodged in the fabric of his coat pocket. Patitucci hailed a police officer, who took him to Emergency Hospital.[5]

Police combed the area for witnesses and evidence. Oak Street resident Leonard Smith told detectives he saw the shooting and noted the license plate number of the gunmen's automobile as it fled from the scene. Records at the Auto Bureau revealed that the license plate was registered to Ruffino.[6]

As Patitucci's wounds were dressed in a hospital room guarded by police, Detective Sergeant William Connolly began searching for DiCarlo. He stationed police officers at Auto Rest to watch for DiCarlo there, while he explored DiCarlo's usual haunts in Buffalo. Connolly visited restaurants around Chippewa, Main and Huron Streets, as well as the Prospect Avenue home occupied by Angelo Palmeri. After a last stop at the Roma Café on Niagara Street,[7] an establishment owned by Filippo Mazzara and Philip "Phil Manor" Livaccori, Connolly returned to the detective bureau. There he found a message from the police at the Auto Rest. They had DiCarlo.

Connolly arranged to meet the officers and DiCarlo at Chippewa and Main Streets. The group then proceeded on to the No. 3 police station. Upon entering, they were confronted by "Busy Joe" Patitucci in the company of police Captain Edward Thierfeldt. Patitucci looked at DiCarlo and said, "There is one of them now."

Gallelli, Capodicaso and Ruffino were arrested at their homes. Each of them was also identified by Patitucci at the police station. Ruffino's automobile was seized from the garage and driven to the station. It was left at the curb in a line of three cars, and Patitucci was brought outside. Busy Joe walked to Ruffino's vehicle and stated, "This is the car."[8]

A fifth conspirator – the third man Patitucci saw in the automobile – was sought but could not be identified. Through agreement between County Attorney Guy B. Moore and U.S. Attorney Donovan, no state charges were filed against the suspects. Instead, the four men were turned over to federal authorities. Donovan personally handled their arraignment on charges of intimidating a government witness.[9]

Joseph DiCarlo and Peter Gallelli gave alibis. Joseph said he was in the New York Central railroad station on Exchange Street with a friend at the time of Patitucci's shooting. Gallelli claimed he was playing cards with five other men.

Joseph's alibi was shattered when Raymond Delahunt, a detective with the New York Central, told authorities he remembered seeing Joseph and four other men leave the station in an automobile just after eleven that evening. Another railroad employee supported Delahunt's statement.[10]

Gallelli's wife contradicted her husband's alibi. Helen Gallelli told authorities that her husband was home by nine o'clock on the night of the shooting and went to bed for the night an hour later.[11]

Indicating that DiCarlo and Gallelli already were free on bail of $50,000 each as they awaited their narcotics trafficking trial, Donovan pressed Commissioner Klein to impose heavy bail amounts on the prisoners. "I feel that $500,000 would not be excessive but demanded $100,000 each from these men," Donovan said. "It is an offense against public justice, and they are lucky they are not facing a murder charge."[12]

Donovan's request was unprecedented. The bail figure was the highest ever demanded in the history of the federal court. When Joseph DiCarlo said he could easily secure the required amount, Donovan considered the comment no more than a boast. A DiCarlo attorney, Harry Lipsitz, declared the bail amount excessive and asked for a lower figure. When Commissioner Klein sided with Donovan, Lipsitz brought the matter to Judge John R. Hazel.

However, Joseph's friends and family had little trouble raising bail for him, as well as for Ruffino and Capodicaso. Eighteen Buffalo residents came forward, pledging a total of $600,000 in property. The three men were released within hours. Gallelli, suspected of firing the shot that struck Patitucci, remained in custody. No apparent effort was made to secure his release.[13]

The ease with which such enormous bail amounts were raised prompted an investigation by Donovan's office.

— — —

Detective Sergeants William Connolly, Bartholomew O'Leary and George Bingeman brought in fifty people for questioning. They quickly released all but one: The detectives took a special interest in twenty-eight-year-old Philip Mangano.

A resident of Brooklyn and a suspect in a recent murder there, Philip Mangano had been in Buffalo only for a short time. He was said to be no relation to local druggist John Mangano. While in Buffalo, Philip Mangano had been staying at 272 Prospect Avenue, a DiCarlo family home sitting adjacent to another DiCarlo residence occupied by Angelo "Buffalo Bill" Palmeri. Authorities believed Philip Mangano was a key underworld ally of Joseph DiCarlo, but Donovan announced that Mangano was not the fifth shooting conspirator they were seeking.[14]

Donovan moved quickly to process criminal charges against the four suspects. He and his staff worked through much of the night, gathering and preparing evidence. On January 3, Donovan brought the assembled facts and his first few witnesses before a federal grand jury.[15] Police Captain Edward Thierfeldt of the Pearl Street Station was the first witness. He was followed to the stand by Delahunt and Patitucci.[16] Patitucci appeared before the grand jury for four hours wearing the same clothes he wore on the night of the shooting. The clothes had not been cleaned. Down the front of his gray shirt were large blood stains. Bullet holes were evident in his garments. On his right coat pocket, the cloth surrounding a small bullet hole was burned crisp, as if singed by a gunshot fired at extremely close range.[17]

During the day, Donovan made it clear he was not finished with Philip Mangano. Before Commissioner Klein, the U.S. attorney argued that Mangano was a material witness with information on the movements of the Patitucci shooting suspects. Klein agreed to hold Mangano under a $1,000 bond. Later in the day, the amount was increased to $15,000.

Mangano had no trouble raising the bail amount. Joseph Sanzone of Niagara Street and Rosario Barone of Erie Street came forward to pledge real estate valued at $30,000 for Mangano's release.[18]

On Friday, January 4, restaurateur Frank Lumia was called before the grand jury. Investigators believed that the telephone call Lumia received at his restaurant three days earlier had been placed by one of the shooting conspirators in order to keep tabs on Patitucci. Lumia denied the call had anything to do with Patitucci.

May Patitucci also was called to the stand on that final day of testimony. The *Buffalo Commercial Advertiser* took the occasion to advance a startling theory about her:

> The theory regarding the shooting of Pattitucci [sic] at first advanced was that May Gilmore, Pattitucci's wife, was an accomplice and that she had knowledge of the attempted assassination prior to the shooting.[19]

— — —

Detective Sergeant William Connolly of the Buffalo Police had a busy weekend.

On Saturday, Assistant U.S. Attorney Thomas Penney Jr. asked Commissioner Klein to issue an arrest order for Joseph DiCarlo's nineteen-year-old brother. Samuel DiCarlo was wanted as a material witness in the Patitucci intimidation case. Connolly found Samuel on Main Street on Saturday night and took him into custody. After processing, he was released on a $20,000 bond.[20]

Connolly placed John Geraci under arrest on Sunday afternoon. Geraci was employed as a watchman at the Auto Rest inn. Connolly convinced Geraci to lead him to three revolvers owned by Joseph DiCarlo. The weapons were found wrapped in newspaper and hidden in the pantry of the DiCarlo summer home in Bowmansville. A slender, spring-blade knife was also found. Two of the revolvers were .32 caliber. The third was .38 caliber.

Police believed that Joseph DiCarlo gave Geraci the revolvers shortly after the shooting of Patitucci and that Geraci had been attempting to dispose of the weapons since that time.[21] Geraci was held as a material witness.

On Monday, January 8, the federal grand jury returned indictments against the four suspects in the Patitucci shooting. An arraignment was scheduled for Friday.[22]

Buffalo police, working with railroad Detective Raymond Delahunt, arrested Angelo Palmeri on the eleventh as he stepped off a train arriving from New York City. Police believed Palmeri was the fifth man in the Overland touring sedan. Palmeri, who reportedly traveled to New York City after the Patitucci shooting, was taken to the Niagara Street police station. There he underwent questioning by Donovan, Assistant U.S. Attorney Ganson Depew and several other federal investigators.

Donovan also questioned a number of taxicab drivers, who claimed to have seen Palmeri, Philip Mangano and Joseph DiCarlo together at the train station a short time before Patitucci was attacked.[23]

Palmeri refused to answer any questions. Responding to a request by Assistant U.S. Attorney Samuel Dickey, Commissioner John Klein decided that Palmeri should be held as a material witness under bail of $10,000.[24]

Palmeri was still in custody as DiCarlo, Gallelli, Capodicaso and Ruffino entered not guilty pleas on Friday.

Donovan's office continued to investigate links between the suspects. A roadblock was encountered on January 15. John Geraci, the Auto Rest watchman arrested nine days earlier, refused to provide information to the federal grand jury. Petitioning that the witness be held in contempt of court, prosecutor Samuel Dickey classified Geraci's attitude on the stand as "very arrogant."

> He acted very arrogant in answering questions propounded by the petitioner... Geraci's general attitude and conduct before the said Grand Jury was such that he refused to answer numerous questions put to him by the members of the said Grand Jury and the petitioner, merely stating that he did not know and could not remember.[25]

District Court Judge George Morris hoped to loosen Geraci's

tongue with a stay behind bars. "You are committed to the Erie County Jail until you are ready to talk or until the court orders your release," Morris ruled.

Fearing Geraci might be intimidated by DiCarlo allies in the Erie County facility, the court later transferred him to a cell in Rochester's Monroe County Jail.[26]

On the morning of January 20, a Buffalo newspaper printed a staggering revelation. Citing unnamed sources within the U.S. Attorney's Office, the newspaper reported that a secret criminal society, with a Buffalo area membership totaling more than two thousand, was using death threats to silence government witnesses in the Patitucci shooting case. No justification was provided for the exaggerated membership figure.

Donovan's office saw evidence of the sprawling secret society within the quick generation of huge bail amounts for DiCarlo, Capodicaso and Ruffino.[27] Federal prosecutors turned their attentions to those who had pledged property to secure the release of the three suspects.

Donovan called nearly all of the bondsmen before the Grand Jury at the end of January. The witnesses included Joseph DiCarlo's sister Sarah; Dan Rogers; Joseph Mule; Carmelo, Angelo and Michael Montante; Biaggio and Elizabeth Testa; Philip Livaccori; Augustine Cridino; Thomas W. DePasquale; Vincenzo and Carolina Privitera; Joseph and Carolina Picogna; Salvatore and Jennie Zuzze; and Louis LoDestro.[28]

— — —

The government's case against DiCarlo, Gallelli, Capodicaso and Ruffino reached Judge Morris's federal courtroom at two o'clock in the afternoon of February 4, 1924. Donovan and his assistant Ganson Depew handled the prosecution. Attorneys Michael Montesano and Harry Lipsitz represented Joseph DiCarlo. Ruffino and Capodicaso were represented by attorney Ernest McIntyre. Samuel Fleischman represented Gallelli.

The four defendants were formally charged with conspiring to intimidate a government witness, and with attempting to restrain a government witness by force of arms.[29]

Jury selection took two and a half hours. Donovan asked prospective jurors if they knew any of the defendants or their counsels. Defense attorneys asked if they had formed any opinions about the case because of press reports or had any prejudice against Italian-Americans. The defense dismissed eight members of the jury pool. The prosecutors dismissed two.[30] Selected jurors included five farmers, two merchants, a butcher, a grocer, a shop foreman, a real estate broker and a retiree.

During the selection process, DiCarlo looked on, attentive but relaxed. Capodicaso and Ruffino were expressionless. The press noted that Gallelli appeared nervous. His eyes repeatedly darted around the courtroom.[31]

Witness testimony began the next morning. Busy Joe Patitucci was an early government witness. Patitucci described the drug addiction that had afflicted him since serving in the Army in 1918. He told of his convictions for using and selling narcotics. For the first time, he publicly revealed that Joseph DiCarlo supplied him with drugs.

> I bought dope from DiCarlo... I sold the narcotics; used them. Between October 1922 and January 1, 1923, DiCarlo called on me nine or eleven times. I bought from him sometimes 67 ounces, 65 ounces, 90 ounces. I paid him for it. I paid sometimes $16.50, $17, $14.50.[32]

Donovan attempted to discuss Patitucci's earlier purchases of narcotics from Joseph DiCarlo's father. Attorney Montesano objected, and Judge Morris ruled the subject of Giuseppe DiCarlo's alleged narcotics dealings out of bounds.[33]

Busy Joe related his role in the August 1923 arrests of Gallelli and DiCarlo. Waiting along Delaware Avenue close to Chippewa Street, he saw an automobile stop in front of a nearby rooming house. He spotted DiCarlo, inside the auto, handing a package of morphine to Gallelli. Gallelli turned the package over to a drug addict Patitucci knew by the name of Staley. When federal agents swarmed Gallelli and Staley, DiCarlo sped away in his automobile. Patitucci spotted DiCarlo later that night at a Chippewa Street restaurant and provided that information to police.

The witness then described the attempt on his life. Patitucci said he clearly recognized DiCarlo and Gallelli as the gunmen and Ruffino and Capodicaso as the men in the car. He suspected the shot that hit him under the chin was fired by Gallelli.[34]

On cross-examination, attorney McIntyre asked if the government had offered to reduce Patitucci's two-year drug conspiracy sentence in exchange for his cooperation. "I haven't the slightest expectation that the government will do anything for me," Patitucci responded. "I did it for the good of the community."

McIntyre asked about Patitucci's wife May. The witness said he and his wife were married at Buffalo City Hall the previous year. It was later revealed that the couple obtained a marriage license at City Hall but had never gone through a marriage ceremony.

The defense attorney also asked about the witness's vision. Patitucci admitted that his eyes were periodically blurry since returning from the war in France. "Since I got back," he said, "sometimes good, sometimes my eyes bother, sometimes it is blurred."[35]

Later in the day, prosecutors called a surprise witness, convicted drug dealer Lester Cameron. At the mention of Cameron's name, the crowded courtroom gallery filled with excited murmurs and defense counsel huddled for a whispered conference. Joseph DiCarlo sat bolt upright in his chair. Cameron made his way hesitantly to the stand.[36] He had attempted unsuccessfully to avoid the court appearance. He earlier showed court officials a telegram, which stated his mother was dying in New York City.[37]

Donovan questioned Cameron about his acquaintance with DiCarlo and with Patitucci. During the questioning, Cameron glanced nervously in DiCarlo's direction.

> "Where did you first meet Joe DiCarlo?" demanded Col. Donovan.
>
> Cameron's face blanched. Beads of perspiration broke out on his forehead. He could not keep his eyes from DiCarlo's face as the latter sat frowning at him.
>
> The federal prosecutor was forced to repeat the question twice before Cameron finally answered, "At a race track four years ago."
>
> ...Cameron then told, under questioning, of having met Pattituccio [sic]

frequently in the soft drink place operated by [Joseph DiCarlo's cousin] Lorenzo Lupo[38] at No. 22 Court Street, but denied ever discussing the DiCarlo case with him.

Contradicting himself five minutes later, Cameron said Pattituccio had told him he was a witness against DiCarlo. Cameron twice refused to answer questions put to him regarding John Mangano's connection with DiCarlo. All the time he kept his eyes shifting back and forth from DiCarlo to the federal prosecutor.[39]

During one meeting in Lupo's establishment, Cameron said, Patitucci "told me… he was going to be a witness against DiCarlo." The witness subsequently expanded on that statement: "He told me he was going to hang Joe DiCarlo if he never did another thing." Cameron said he responded to Patitucci's remark by calling Busy Joe "a chump."

Cameron admitted to being "not on unfriendly terms" with DiCarlo. But he denied telling DiCarlo that Patitucci was poised to testify against him.[40]

"Did DiCarlo ever say, 'Let us get up a collection and get rid of Pattituccio [sic] and Mangano'?" Donovan's question was drawn from a pretrial interview, in which Cameron told him of DiCarlo's remark. "Remember, you are under oath."[41]

Looking toward the scowling DiCarlo, a shaken Cameron decided to change his story. He shouted, "No!"

Donovan persisted, "Joe DiCarlo told you shortly before January 1, 1924, that he was going to get rid of Pattituccio for good, didn't he?"

"No, no, no!"[42]

— — —

On the second day of testimony, Donovan called May Patitucci to the stand, expecting her to corroborate Busy Joe's story. Instead, May did all she could to contradict her grand jury testimony and her statements to prosecutors.

May revealed that she was a recovering drug addict and a former prostitute. She explained that she and Joseph Patitucci had never been formally married, though they had obtained a license and had been living together as man and wife for about two years. Her name was May Gilmore, but she was generally known as May Patitucci. She testified that on the evening of January 1, she and Joseph Patitucci were both drunk:

> That night, I was intoxicated, and so was Joe... I had wine to drink that night. I don't know how much. I had more than one glass, about five or six, I guess... Joe is in the habit of getting intoxicated. He drinks now and then, generally wine. This was New Year's Day: We were drinking more or less throughout the day. I wouldn't say he was good and drunk, but he was intoxicated. He drank as much as I did and probably more.[43]

She said she was unable to identify the two men who fired handguns at her companion. She testified that, when she heard the shots, she was "dumbfounded and intoxicated." Though she turned toward the sound of the shots, she raised her hand in front of her face and could not see much beyond it. She recalled only that the car looked to be a sedan and the handguns used by the attackers were black rather than nickel-colored.

May also testified that Busy Joe confided in her that he could not positively identify his attackers:

> Joe Patitucci asked me if I really had seen the men that he said were the men, and I said, 'No" that I didn't. .. And Joe said that he was not positive that it was these men; he just had a suspicion of these men. That is what he told me last night.

Confronted with her own grand jury testimony, in which she named the attackers and made no mention of alcohol, May claimed that she had been instructed to lie to the grand jury. "Joe told me at that time that if I testified before the grand jury that I knew the men, it would help him, because he didn't want my story to go against his story." She explained that she and her husband believed the government might shorten his prison sentence if he helped to convict DiCarlo and Gallelli.

Donovan was flabbergasted. "Did you ever tell me before that you were intoxicated?" he asked May. She responded, "No, I did not." Judge Morris interrupted just to be certain: "This is the first time you have told that?" May answered, "Yes, sir."

Donovan asked the witness additional questions about death threats Busy Joe reportedly received. May denied that there had been any threats. Near the end of May's examination, Donovan admitted to Judge Morris that "the government has been taken entirely by surprise by the attitude of this witness." The judge responded, "The court can see that."[44]

When May Patitucci was excused from the witness stand, Judge Morris had some questions of his own for her.

"You were under oath before the grand jury?" he asked.

"Yes," she said.

"And you were under oath here?" he asked.

Her second answer was less certain: "I guess so."

"Well," the judge said, "I order you in the custody of the court and the United States marshal on a charge of perjury."[45]

To dispel any doubts introduced by May Patitucci's testimony, Donovan was compelled to bring to the stand a number of police officers who had spoken with Joseph and May Patitucci on January 1. They all testified that they saw no evidence of intoxication.[46] They also described what they knew of the events of that night.

One of the prosecution's final witnesses was John Geraci, who had been imprisoned three weeks for contempt of court after refusing to answer questions before the grand jury. Geraci was in a more talkative mood as he stepped to the witness stand on the morning of February 8.

Geraci told of his working relationship with Joseph DiCarlo. He said he served as a watchman at Auto Rest's parking yard but received no wages. His compensation was in the form of free lodging. He identified the three handguns, some ammunition and the knife taken by police from the DiCarlo home at Bowmansville. He also identified the pages of the January 4 *Buffalo Evening Times* that he had used to wrap the handguns.

Asked how he came to possess the handguns, Geraci responded that they were given to him by Minnie Clark: "When she gave me those guns, she said, 'Take these guns away from here... I'm sick.'"

Geraci said he had never seen two of the weapons before. He said the .38-caliber, blue steel, Smith & Wesson handgun belonged to him. "I found that gun three months ago at the Auto Rest, out in the yard," he said.[47]

Donovan followed up, "You said you owned all the pistols when I first asked you about them, didn't you?" Geraci admitted he lied to the prosecutor. He said no one instructed him to lie.

Looking for a place to dispose of the weapons, Geraci brought them first to the home of Minnie Clark's sister, Mina Scherer. He knew Scherer from Auto Rest, where she worked as a waitress. Geraci later placed the pistols in his car and returned to Auto Rest, leaving them in the vehicle. He finally headed out to Bowmansville.

"I went back in my car and drove out to the farm...," he testified. "I left the guns out there in the house. I did not tell anyone that I put them there. No one asked me where I put them, I am positive about that."[48]

Donovan completed his case with testimony from Detective Sergeant William Connolly. Connolly told of his investigation of the Patitucci shooting, his arrests of the suspects and his trip to Bowmansville with Geraci to retrieve the weapons hidden there.[49]

— — —

Defense witnesses included three of the four defendants. Only Joseph DiCarlo did not take the stand on his own behalf.

Joseph Ruffino testified that he barely knew his codefendant DiCarlo and did not know Capodicaso or Gallelli at all. He had been acquainted with Patitucci years earlier, and the two shared a mutual friend. Ruffino acknowledged that he owned an Overland sedan, which he kept in a garage across Niagara Street from his home. He said he took his wife and children for a drive on January 1 and returned home around eight o'clock in the evening. He went out in the car a short time later. He was not feeling well and needed some aspirin. He got back around ten and parked his automobile back in the garage. Ruffino said he did not go out again that night. As family members played cards in his house, he went to his bedroom to sleep.

"I was not on Tupper Street at any time, day or night, the first day of January... or on Michigan Street or in that vicinity at all," he testified.

On cross-examination, Donovan asked Ruffino about his job. Ruffino said he worked as a salesman for the Bond Chemical Company, manufacturer of perfumes and hair tonic.

"Is not the Bond Chemical Company engaged in bootlegging?" Donovan asked.

"Not that I know of," Ruffino replied. "I never seen any alcohol there. Perfume is all I saw."

Donovan then asked the witness about the people who helped to bail him out of prison, striving to link Ruffino more closely with DiCarlo than indicated in earlier testimony. Ruffino said Joseph and Carolina Picogna were his godparents. He was acquainted with Dan Rogers and knew Joe Spero for six or seven years.[50] He knew Sarah DiCarlo, but he said he had not been aware that she went on his bond. "I do not know if she went on my bond," he said. "I did not ask her."

He said Joe Mule and Vincent Privitera were his brothers-in-law; Louis LoDestro was his cousin; Thomas DePasquale, Salvatore LaMarca and Salvatore Zuzze were his friends; and John Barone was his automobile mechanic. He claimed to have no knowledge of Philip "Phil Manor" Livaccori or Augustine Cridino.

Donovan asked whether Ruffino and DiCarlo might have known each other as children. They lived in the same neighborhood for a time, and Giuseppe DiCarlo operated a saloon a few doors from the Ruffino's home. Ruffino said he never knew the DiCarlos lived in that neighborhood and he knew nothing of the DiCarlo saloon.

Donovan attempted to tie Ruffino to DiCarlo through their common birthplace of Vallelunga, Sicily.[51] However, Ruffino could not address the U.S. attorney's questions. He said he had no knowledge of his birthplace and had been in the Buffalo area since he was a small child.

When Ruffino's father took the stand, Donovan was able to confirm that, like DiCarlo, Ruffino had been born in Vallelunga. Ruffino's wife Anna and other relatives supported the defendant's alibi. Garage owners George Burg and LeRoy Fremming testified that Ruffino's automobile was parked in their facility at the time of the attack on Patitucci.[52]

Also testifying in his own defense, forty-six-year-old Gaetano Capodicaso said he knew DiCarlo but did not know

Gallelli or Ruffino. He said he knew Patitucci well enough to say hello when he saw him. Patitucci greeted him as "Zio Tani," which Capodicaso said translated to "Uncle Gaetano."

Capodicaso testified that he spent the evening of January 1 at a billiard hall at the corner of Spring and Seneca Streets, near the liquid soap factory he owned. He remained there until about midnight. He and the billiard hall's proprietor Tony Magistrale walked home together, as they both lived on Myrtle Avenue. Capodicaso reached his home at about a quarter past midnight.

"I was not on Tupper Street on New Year's night, nor on Michigan Street," he testified. "I was not in an automobile with Joseph DiCarlo and Mr. Gallelli or any person else. I do not know anything about any person shooting Joe Patitucci."[53]

Donovan's cross-examination initially focused on a fraudulent statement on a pistol permit belonging to Capodicaso. The witness claimed he signed but did not read the permit application. He said he did not know that the application contained a statement indicating that he was a citizen of the U.S. Capodicaso explained that he was not a citizen.[54]

Capodicaso said he once owned a Colt .38-caliber pistol. "I lost that more than five months ago. I haven't got a revolver now." He stated that he had never fired a handgun.[55]

When asked about the individuals who pledged their property to secure his release from prison, Capodicaso indicated that he was confused. Donovan went through the list of names on the bond. "I did ask some of those people to go on my bond," Capodicaso responded unhelpfully, "but I do not know who the persons were. I did not ask any of the persons whom you have named to go on my bond."[56]

Capodicaso's time on the stand spilled over from the session held on Friday, February 8, to an unusual Saturday session for the court. A number of witnesses also were brought in Saturday to confirm Capodicaso's alibi. Two of those witnesses, Edward Norvew and Charles Gerard, were little help. Through his cross-examination, Donovan was able to prove that the men were recalling events from New Year's Eve rather than the following night.[57]

Once in the witness stand, Peter Gallelli did what he could to set the record straight on a nickname that the newspapers had given him. "I have heard myself characterized as 'Pete the Slash.'

I do not know whether that is because of the slash on the side of my face. I suppose so." Gallelli explained that he had a scar from a childhood injury at his hometown in Calabria, Italy.

Gallelli testified that on January 1 he attended a prizefight between Rocky Kansas and Teddy Meyer[58] at Buffalo's Broadway Auditorium. The fight ended at about six, and Gallelli reached his home by a quarter to seven. He had dinner with his friend Raphael Cotroni, and then the two men went to pay their respects at the wake of Joseph Mascari. After the wake, Gallelli went to visit friend Gus Lama and his family. After a few hands of poker, Gallelli said he returned home around ten-fifteen and remained there the rest of the night.

While he knew Patitucci, he said he did not know Ruffino or Capodicaso. He testified that he became acquainted with Joseph DiCarlo at a Rocky Kansas-Ritchie Mitchell bout a year and a half earlier. "Joe DiCarlo was betting on Rocky Kansas, and I was betting on Ritchie Mitchell. I was betting $35 on Ritchie Mitchell. He got knocked out in the second round."[59]

Gallelli said he was unaware that Patitucci planned to testify against him in the narcotics case. He admitted to selling a small quantity of narcotics, but he denied that DiCarlo had anything to do with it. He explained that he was prepared to plead guilty to the drug charge, but his attorney talked him out of it.[60]

Sarah DiCarlo later took the witness stand to provide an alibi for her brother Joseph. She testified that she and Joseph had dinner January 1 with the Palmeris at 274 Prospect Avenue. The party broke up at about eleven-thirty, as Angelo Palmeri planned to take the 12:01 a.m. train into New York City.

Joseph drove Palmeri and several other men to the New York Central Station on Exchange Street, she said. Her brother returned about twelve-fifteen and took her to Joseph Mascari's wake. Mascari had been an undertaker and had arranged the funerals of her parents Giuseppe and Vincenza DiCarlo, she explained. Joseph, Sam DiCarlo and friend Joe Spero headed out to Auto Rest at about one, she said.[61]

The defense brought to the stand a number of witnesses, including New York Central Railroad chauffeur Joseph Crage and Buffalo Police Detective James Johnson, who supported DiCarlo's alibi. They testified that they saw DiCarlo at the train station between eleven-thirty and eleven-fifty-five on January 1.

On Monday, February 11, the defense called William Andrews, a Cleveland weapons expert, to the stand. Andrews said he examined the revolvers seized by police and the bullet retrieved from Patitucci's pocket. "That bullet was not fired out of any of these three pistols," he testified.[62]

Later that day, Donovan called Raymond Delahunt to the stand as a rebuttal witness. Delahunt damaged the defendants' alibis. He testified that he saw DiCarlo enter the train station on January 1 with Angelo Palmeri, a short man named Mangano and several other men. Delahunt identified Ruffino as one of the other men. "I saw him there," the railroad detective said. "He was sick. I was standing near the radiator, and he came over and spit right alongside of my leg." The group entered the station at eleven o'clock, he said, and left it no later than eleven-twenty-five.

Delahunt further testified that a few days later, a man saying he represented Joseph DiCarlo asked the railroad detective what he recalled of the evening of January 1. Delahunt mentioned the names of the men he recalled seeing. At that point, the man spoke of $1,500 that could belong to Delahunt if he would "go easy."[63]

New York Central Railroad yard foreman John Davis went to the witness stand to confirm the offer of a bribe to Delahunt. Davis testified that he overheard a man telling Delahunt, "I have $1,500 in my pocket if you can forget something."[64]

--- --- ---

In his summation, Donovan directly accused May Patitucci of complicity in the attack on her common law husband: "Why did they leave May Patitucci unharmed? Well, gentlemen, her appearance on the stand, her action in the witness box, has answered that question very clearly... Because she was there to take him along; because she had been talked to; because she was to betray this man by taking him, the man who thought he had married her, she was to deliver him over into the hands of those men who, in their code of morals, considered that he had betrayed them."

Donovan attacked the defendants' alibis. "Gentleman, when men set out to do a desperate deed, the first thing they do is to prepare their alibi. And could you or I go to the New York Central Station and be seen by so many people on a simple journey like that, unless we determined that we should be seen by them?"

The prosecutor noted that defense witnesses to DiCarlo's presence in the station seemed to have nothing else in the world to do other than note the times at which they saw DiCarlo. "Makes you wonder ... what others had been offered money in this case."[65]

Judge Morris took forty minutes to deliver his charge to the jury. Though he did not mention it in the charge, time had become an issue in the case. The judge was due to begin an assignment in the New England district the next morning.

The jury went out to begin deliberations at five-thirty. Expecting a verdict before morning, a large crowd of spectators remained in the federal courtroom. After an initial ballot, jurors took an hour-long break for supper. They resumed their deliberations at about seven. At nine-thirty, the panel returned to the courtroom for fifteen minutes of additional instruction from the judge. More instruction was required at 12:30 a.m. on February 12. Forty-five minutes later, the jurors reached a verdict and filed into the courtroom for the last time.

Even at that late hour, the gallery was filled beyond capacity. All seats were occupied, and additional spectators stood in the aisles and in an outer vestibule.

The jury found Joseph DiCarlo and Peter Gallelli guilty of conspiring to deter a government witness by force, intimidation or threat and also guilty of endeavoring to impede a witness. It found Joseph Ruffino guilty of conspiring with DiCarlo and Gallelli but not of making an actual effort to impede a witness. Gaetano Capodicaso was found not guilty of either offense.[66]

As the verdict was read, the defendants remained frozen in position, and the courtroom gallery was silent. DiCarlo's face grew flushed and covered with perspiration. Gallelli and Ruffino were pale and expressionless. Though he had been acquitted, Capodicaso showed no signs of happiness over the verdict.[67]

Judge Morris proceeded immediately with sentencing. He ordered the three convicted men brought forward to the bench. The scene was too much for Helen Gallelli, seated in the rear of the gallery. She screamed and fainted.[68]

The judge sentenced all three men to terms at Atlanta Federal Penitentiary:

> In the first place, I will say that as to two of these defendants, it seems fortunate that they

were not better marksmen... If they had been better marksmen, they might be headed for the death chair instead of the penitentiary. It is the order of the court that Joseph DiCarlo and Peter Gallelli be confined in the federal penitentiary at Atlanta, Georgia, for a term of six years, and pay a fine of $5,000 each. It is ordered that the defendant Ruffino be confined in the federal penitentiary at Atlanta, Georgia, for the term of two years, and pay a fine of $1,000. The other defendant, Capodicaso, is discharged.[69]

Ruffino bore a brooding look, as he stood before the judge's bench. Gallelli remained emotionless, with his arms folded across his chest. As DiCarlo heard his sentence, a smirk became visible on his still-flushed face. After the sentencing, a deputy marshal led the three men from the courtroom and took them temporarily to the Erie County Jail.[70]

— — —

Immediately after the trial, Donovan made several noteworthy announcements. He said first that he was putting the grand jury to work on the attempted bribery allegations made by Delahunt and Davis. A defense attorney in the Patitucci intimidation case reportedly offered to pay $1,500 if Delahunt would alter his recollection of January 1 events to benefit DiCarlo.

The identity of the attorney who made the bribe offer was not released. However, it became a simple matter to deduce. At the conclusion of the trial, defense attorneys Samuel Fleischmann and Ernest McIntyre denied having any part in the affair and Davis's testimony cleared them of any responsibility. After the trial, Donovan released a statement saying attorney Michael Montesano had no part in the offense. Only attorney Harry Lipsitz was not cleared.[71]

Fleischmann, Lipsitz, Delahunt and Davis were summoned before the grand jury.[72] Lipsitz was later indicted for attempting to bribe a government witness and attempting to obstruct justice.[73] He was acquitted of the charges after a 1925 trial.[74]

Donovan also announced the sudden reappearance of Joe Spero and Philip Mangano.

Donovan had considered Spero and Mangano material witnesses to DiCarlo's movements on January 1. Spero had been released on $10,000 bail. Mangano had been released on $15,000 bail. They were missing during the trial, though Delahunt said he once spotted Mangano in the courtroom during defense testimony. On the final day of the trial, Donovan contacted their bondsmen but learned that Spero and Mangano could not be located.

Spero and Mangano contacted prosecutors after the jury verdict was announced. Spero was called to Donovan's office on the morning of February 12. Mangano was called in that afternoon. The U.S. attorney wanted to be certain that the two men had not also been victims of witness intimidation.

Finally, Donovan publicly backed away from his earlier statements regarding a secret criminal society in the Buffalo area. He told the press that he was satisfied that no large secret underworld organization existed in the community. He said he had come to believe that a small group of outlaws was using fear to manipulate many in the community.[75]

Donovan's successful prosecution of DiCarlo, Gallelli and Ruffino became welcome news within the Federal Bureau of Investigation, which aided Donovan in the case. M.F. Blackmon, special agent in charge of the FBI's Buffalo field office, sent a two-page letter advising then-Assistant Director J. Edgar Hoover of the trial result.[76] Blackmon received an approving response from then-Director William J. Burns:

> My attention has just been called to the results obtained by you in an investigation of the case of Joseph DiCarlo et al – Conspiracy to Intimidate a Government Witness – and to the substantial sentence imposed by the court upon DiCarlo, Gallelli, and Ruffino, totaling fourteen years in the penitentiary and $12,000 fine.
>
> I want you to know that I consider the results obtained are splendid, and I take this opportunity to commend you.[77]

There was some initial uncertainty whether the intimidation verdicts against DiCarlo, Gallelli and Ruffino would be appealed. DiCarlo was asked about it on the afternoon of February 12. He said he had no idea what his attorneys planned to do.

"It's up to them," DiCarlo said, "and I am waiting to hear from them now."

DiCarlo managed to keep himself comfortable as he waited. On Friday, February 16, he and Ruffino were seen enjoying wine and food at Thomas J. B. Dyke's Ritz Restaurant, though they were supposed to be locked up in the county jail. Assistant U.S. Attorney Ganson Depew found reports of the unauthorized restaurant visit "perfectly astounding" and immediately investigated.[78]

Depew had met with DiCarlo, Ruffino and Gallelli at the federal building during the afternoon. The prisoners then were permitted a brief visit with their families and their attorneys. They were supposed to be back behind bars by five o'clock. Gallelli returned as ordered. However, DiCarlo, Ruffino and the deputy marshals assigned to them stopped off first at Dyke's Washington Street eatery. They were hours late reporting to the county jail.

"When this office heard of the liberties allowed the two prisoners, the two deputy marshals were asked for explanations," Depew told the press. "They informed me they took DiCarlo and Ruffino to supper at the Ritz and then back to jail. The irons, they claim, were on at all times."[79]

The press noted other reports that neither DiCarlo nor Ruffino were handcuffed while in the Ritz.

Depew said he sent a report of the incident to federal Marshal Joseph Fritsch at Rochester.[80]

On February 20, DiCarlo was released on $50,000 bail, as his appeal was processed by the U.S. Circuit Court. The release of Ruffino on bail was expected, as his attorney also was preparing an appeal. Gallelli did not pursue an appeal. He remained in the county jail waiting for transport to Atlanta.[81] Sarah DiCarlo, Niagara Street resident August Lascola and Niagara Street garage owner Herman Weinstein furnished the bonds for Joseph DiCarlo's release.[82]

Depew had promised that, if DiCarlo appealed the witness

intimidation verdict, federal prosecutors would immediately bring him to trial on the earlier narcotics charge. He followed through on that promise at the end of February by scheduling DiCarlo for trial in the federal court's April term.[83]

Chapter 9

To Prison

Busy Joe Patitucci was again in front of a judge on February 29, 1924. He appeared in Buffalo City Court to obtain a larceny warrant against the woman he had considered his wife. May Gilmore Patitucci, indicted for perjury in connection with her testimony in the witness intimidation trial and released only through Patitucci's insistence, was charged with stealing $175 from under Patitucci's pillow as he slept.

May said she would fight the charge on the grounds that she should be regarded as Patitucci's lawful wife.[1] May and Busy Joe had been estranged since the trial. May had been seen often in the company of Oak Street restaurateur Frank Lumia. She took a job in his establishment and moved into a second-floor apartment above the restaurant.

On March 10, Patitucci confronted May at the restaurant. He pleaded with her to return to him. When she refused, he created a disturbance, and Lumia forced him to leave. At twelve-forty-five the next afternoon, Patitucci telephoned Lumia. He asked Lumia to meet him at the corner of Chippewa and Main Streets in order to pick up May's belongings.

After Lumia left, Busy Joe showed up at the restaurant and again begged May to return to him. With her refusal, he drew a revolver, aimed it at her and pulled the trigger three times. He then ran from the restaurant, tossing his weapon into the street and putting five tablets into his mouth. May was struck in the throat by a single slug. Bleeding heavily from the wound, she collapsed to the floor.

Patitucci dropped onto the sidewalk at Oak and South Division Streets. A detective spotted him there. When the detective approached, Patitucci told him that he had just shot his wife and had taken bichloride of mercury tablets to kill himself.

May and Busy Joe were both taken to the Emergency Hospital. Doctors had Patitucci's stomach pumped as they tended to May's wounds.[2]

On March 13, hospital officials said May's condition was significantly improved.

Patitucci remained in critical condition.[3] His condition deteriorated through the next few days. He succumbed to the effects of the poison on the seventeenth. His death was ruled a suicide.[4] A stormy romance had succeeded where assassins' bullets had failed.

There was significant controversy over whether Patitucci made a statement before he died. Medical Examiner Charles E. Long said that Patitucci made no final statement, though Dr. Long and the police encouraged him to do so.[5] However, Patitucci's family told a different story.

Busy Joe's seventy-six-year-old mother and her son-in-law Rocco Bonadonna told Detective William Connolly that he wrote a confession. In his statement, they said, he admitted that he had falsely accused DiCarlo, Gallelli, Capodicaso and Ruffino of shooting him. He lied in court in the hope that securing their convictions would eliminate his own pending prison term and allow him to run off with May.[6]

Donovan closely examined the statement, scrawled in pencil in the Italian language onto a notebook page. He instinctively doubted its authenticity but promised to look into it. The U.S. attorney noted that the statement was not dated and was not witnessed. He felt certain the alleged confession would be insufficient reason to retry the witness intimidation case.

"There is nothing to show when Pattituccio [sic] made this statement," Donovan told the press. "He may have written it long before he committed suicide or it may have been forced from his lips by the Black Hand. We are investigating the whole matter."[7]

Patitucci's statement was translated into English for the newspapers:

> To Mr. W.J. Donovan,
> Joseph DiCarlo, Peter Gallelli, Joseph Ruffino and Gaetano Capodicaso were not the men who shot me New Year's night. I

> lied about them. May Gilmore caused all my trouble. I lied about them because of May Gilmore. I'm sorry, Mr. W.J. Donovan.
> Joe Patitucci.[8]

The suicide death of Patitucci eliminated the government's key witness in the narcotics trial against Joseph DiCarlo and Peter Gallelli. As the threat of additional jail time diminished, another threat appeared.

On Saturday night, March 15, Auto Rest's patrons were enjoying the fare and the jazz music of the Williamsville roadhouse. Just after midnight, a police traffic whistle was heard outside the roadhouse. Immediately, dozens of red flares were lit around the building and numerous figures dressed in white robes and hoods could be seen.

One female patron called out, "My God, the Klan!"[9]

Auto Rest became quiet as fifty of the robed men entered the building in a column of twos. Once inside, an older man who marched at the head of the group instructed all patrons to stand up, and he ordered the orchestra to play the Star Spangled Banner. After the anthem, the patrons returned to their seats, as fifty intruders marched around the dining room and formed a hollow square. [10]

One of them instructed, "Let us bow our heads in prayer." He then offered a prayer thanking God for the good, clean things in life and asking Him to aid the Ku Klux Klan in cleaning liquor out of Erie County.

Another Klansman stepped forward to make a lengthy announcement:

> It is the understanding of the Invisible Empire that this place is running in violation of the law and under the protection of the authorities. In the Invisible Empire, there is no such thing as partiality or protection. The Klan stands for law and order, and if this place is run on an orderly basis, no one will be molested. But if the owners persist in running it in violation of the law it will be

> closed... Last week we warned four other places. Our warnings were unheeded. Therefore they will be closed.

The Klan spokesman told the orchestra to play America, and the robed men exited in a column of twos while that music played.[11]

Erie County Sheriff Frank Tyler learned of the Klan activity and of the accusation of official protection of Prohibition violators. "No place or illicit traffic of any nature is being run under the protection of the sheriff's office," Tyler said on March 17. "If the Klan tries to close up the four places they referred to Saturday night, then they will run afoul of the law. But, thus far, they have violated no law."[12]

Minnie Clark did not object to the demonstration. She told authorities that the visitors "acted like gentlemen and molested no patron in the place."[13]

Noting that the Klan warnings occurred just outside his city, Buffalo Mayor Francis Schwab warned that police would act against demonstrations within Buffalo's city limits. Citing an opinion from District Attorney Guy Moore, Schwab said the Klan's interference in a business qualified as a breach of peace. Klansmen acting in a similar manner in the city "will get what is coming to them," he said.[14]

One local publisher was unimpressed with the Klan demonstrations. An editorial ridiculed the organization:

> As between Jew Minnie, who for the most part minds her own business, and the busybodies who want to regulate everybody's business, we should say off-hand that we consider the lady less a menace to the peace and dignity of the community than these midnight prowlers... We do not for one moment believe that the Klan is even slightly interested in the enforcement of law. Bent on having an excuse to wear their silly disguises in the same dramatic fashion that the amateur detective displays his tin star, they scrutinize hopefully rather than regretfully, every situation which may

> provide them with the opportunity to pose as guardians of the community and to parade in their clown clothes.[15]

The Klan activity ultimately resulted in little more than a continuing war of words with Mayor Schwab.[16]

— — —

Joseph DiCarlo's appeal of his witness intimidation conviction caused Cleveland mobster Sam Todaro to visit Buffalo. U.S. Attorney Donovan called Todaro to the Federal Building on March 31 to answer questions relating to his cousin Joe Patitucci's confession.

Todaro said he had been in possession of Patitucci's handwritten confession for about a week before turning it over to attorney Horace O. Lanza following Patitucci's death. Todaro had known Lanza for some time.

Todaro first learned of the confession when he visited his cousin at the hospital and Patitucci instructed him to find a black notebook at his mother's house.

> I said, "What you got in that book?"
> "I write down them fellows are innocent."
> And I says... "Why didn't you tell them before?"
> He said, "You keep that book. Don't give it to nobody. If I die, you give it to somebody; if not, you don't give. If I don't die, give me back."[17]

Todaro said he found the notebook on a bedroom dresser, pocketed it, and returned home to Cleveland. He placed the notebook in a safe at the grocery business he ran with his partner Joe Lonardo. Todaro admitted discussing the item with Lonardo and some others, including one other Lonardo brother, in Cleveland. Donovan asked Todaro if he tore the confession page from the notebook. Todaro answered that he did not.

A short time after learning of Patitucci's death, Todaro brought the notebook back to Buffalo and delivered it to Lanza.

> I says, "Mr. Lanza, I got this book from my cousin." I says, "I want to bring this book to the United States District Attorney." Mr. Lanza told me, "You leave it, and I will take care of it. That is all right."[18]

Donovan noted that DiCarlo knew of the Patitucci confession a few hours before Patitucci's death. The U.S. attorney said DiCarlo approached Lanza about the confession two days before Todaro brought it there.[19] Donovan attempted to determine how DiCarlo received his information.

Todaro said he was acquainted with Joseph DiCarlo. He said Patitucci introduced them four or five years earlier at the Venice Restaurant but he hadn't seen DiCarlo "for a while." He said he had met Capodicaso a couple of times but did not know Ruffino at all. Todaro said he did not tell DiCarlo or anyone else in Buffalo about the notebook he held for Patitucci.

"Does Joe Lonardo know Joe DiCarlo?" Donovan asked.

"I think so," Todaro replied.

Todaro recalled his cousin's difficult situation. At the time Patitucci began supplying evidence to federal prosecutors, Todaro offered to accommodate him and his mother in Cleveland.

> I have been telling him to come to Cleveland and live with me. When Joe told me nobody like him in Buffalo, just only one man like him in Buffalo, that is the district attorney... The rest is nobody like him, no believe him anybody. Nobody like him. I says, "Joe, come over to Cleveland, come and live with me at my house. Bring your mother to Cleveland."[20]

The cousins communicated with each other frequently. Donovan revealed two telegrams Patitucci sent to Todaro during the last month of his life. The first was dated February 13, 1924. It read, "Come to Buffalo as soon as possible." Todaro vaguely recalled that his cousin wanted to see him at that time.

The second telegram, dated March 1, read, "Come as soon as possible. You have twenty-four hours. After twenty-four hours you have no excuse. Very important." Todaro said he rushed to Buffalo and reluctantly spoke with Patitucci about pending court cases in Brooklyn.

> He says, "Listen, Sam. I made arrest of four fellows in Brooklyn, New York. I want you to go in Brooklyn, New York, and talk to this fellow."
> "Please, Joe, don't mix me up in that. What you call me that for? Won't you let me alone, Joe? What you want me for all right? For somebody else? Don't call me."
> "If you talk to them and tell one to plead guilty, the other three will be discharged."
> I says, "Don't tell me that, Joe. Don't bother me."[21]

With the help of a translator, Patitucci's mother composed an affidavit on the matter of her son's confession. Natalia Patitucci recalled that her son revealed the innocence of DiCarlo and his codefendants:

> About ten or twelve days before my son took poison, he confided to me that the defendants... were innocent. I asked him why he had them arrested and he said he had done that because he had suspected that they were the ones. [Several days after he was taken to the hospital] my son stated to me that he had left a paper or statement. He did not tell me what it was or where it was. Upon that occasion there was also present Salvatore or Sam Todaro, my cousin, and he called my cousin over to the bedside and said something to him which I did not hear.[22]

Detective Sergeant William Connolly's sworn statement noted the rumors of a Patitucci confession but introduced a contrary statement by the deceased man: "On March 12, 1924,

Joe said, in answer to my question if he had wrote any letters, 'What I got to write? No. I don't send any letters.'"[23]

Edward N. Wilkes, a handwriting expert in the employ of the Marine Bank of the City of Buffalo, examined Patitucci's signatures on the confession and on his marriage license and stated that "both of said signatures were written by one and the same person."[24] A similar result was obtained when Allen K. Brehm, vice president of the Buffalo Trust Company, compared the confession signature with Patitucci's banking account signature card.[25]

A sworn statement by U.S. Attorney Donovan helped to put some of the pieces together. Donovan said Patitucci had repeatedly expressed concern that he would be attacked. "He said that his life was in danger," Donovan recalled. "He told me that a relative of his from Cleveland had spoken to him about the current talk that he would get 'knocked off'..."

After the witness intimidation trial, Donovan spoke with Patitucci about reducing his own narcotics sentence in light of his cooperation with the government. Donovan noted that Patitucci remained infatuated with his common law wife. Even after she contradicted his testimony and moved out of his home, he continued to hope she would return to him.[26]

The U.S. attorney subsequently received some disturbing news about his key narcotics witness.

> It was alleged that Pattitucci [sic] had sent the message to the defendants that if they were convicted and could obtain a new trial that he would be out in California and would not appear against them. I charged Pattitucci with saying that but he denied it and said he had told only the truth.[27]

Donovan stated that he visited Patitucci in the hospital and heard nothing about a confession: "At no time did Pattitucci [sic] indicate in any manner that his testimony on the trial had been false."[28]

— — —

Though acquitted of the witness intimidation charge, Gaetano Capodicaso quickly became the focus of another legal action. He and Angelo Palmeri were accused of providing false information on pistol permit applications. Commissioner Klein presided over their April 13 perjury arraignment.

According to U.S. Attorney Donovan, Capodicaso's application was filed in February 1923 and Palmeri's was filed in July 1923. The prosecutor said both men swore under oath that they were citizens of the United States, while they were actually immigrants who never had been naturalized.[29] The two men were released after each posted $5,000 bail.

At the arraignment, Donovan revealed that the original pistol permit applications, including citizenship affidavits, had vanished from the county clerk's office sometime after the witness intimidation trial. County Clerk Arthur A. Atkinson could not explain the lost records. He promised to make a full investigation.[30]

Deprived of the official documents that proved the accusations, Donovan built his case on a less sturdy foundation. He filed an affidavit based on his own copies of the documents. In it, he noted that Capodicaso's application was witnessed by Main Street saloon owner Stephen Bellissimo and approved by notary public and former court interpreter Harry Evans. He said Palmeri's application was witnessed by Frank Sciarone of Dante Place and approved by Bartolo Oddo. A cousin of New York Mafioso Ignazio Lupo, Oddo was a former supervisor of Buffalo's 27th Ward.[31]

Assistant U.S. Attorney Thomas Penney presented the case against Capodicaso and Palmeri to the federal grand jury on April 15.[32] Lacking evidence to support the perjury charge, the grand jury refused to indict either man.

— — —

An effort by DiCarlo's attorneys to have his guilty verdict set aside due to Patitucci's apparent confession[33] was unsuccessful. Judge Morris, ruling on the Buffalo matter from his new jurisdiction in New England, decided in June 1924 that "the statement purported to have been given by Pattitucci [sic] is of such doubtful authenticity that the court is not satisfied that justice requires the setting aside of the verdict."

He explained that to justify a new trial, new evidence "must be of such a character and weight as to satisfy the court that if introduced upon a new trial it will probably, and not possibly, produce a different result." The judge felt that the document did not have the required weight.

Judge Morris also noted that the confession probably could not be admitted as evidence in a new trial. "The recanting statement is supposed to have been made by Pattitucci [sic] some days before his death. It cannot be admitted as a dying declaration and as Pattitucci is now dead it could not be admitted as impeaching testimony."[34]

One month later, DiCarlo attorney Louis Thrasher filed a legal appeal citing 108 "errors" made during the witness intimidation trial. In his twenty-six-page filing, Thrasher argued that Judge Morris had erred in allowing various elements of Patitucci's testimony, in permitting Donovan to treat Lester Cameron as a hostile witness, in permitting Donovan commentary during the questioning of May Patitucci and in having May Patitucci taken into custody on perjury charges while the jury was present. Thrasher also objected to instances of hearsay that incriminated the defendants and to references made to other offenses unproved against the defendants.[35]

Joseph DiCarlo's marriage to Salvatora "Elsie" Rose Pieri on November 29, 1924,[36] suggests that he was confident of winning his appeal. It also suggests a dramatic change in his relationship with "Jew Minnie" Clark, a change possibly linked to her earlier insistence that Joseph's firearms be removed from her home.

Elsie Pieri was born in Buffalo on September 5, 1901. She was the oldest of nine children born to Giovanni and Ignazia "Anna" Ciresi Pieri.[37] Her parents both were immigrants from Montemaggiore Belsito, Sicily, which is located a short distance northwest of Valledolmo. Giovanni Pieri arrived in the U.S. as a young adult in April 1893.[38] Anna Ciresi crossed the Atlantic at the age of fifteen, reaching New York in July 1898.[39] The two were married at St. Anthony's Church in Buffalo in November 1900.[40]

Giovanni Pieri was a wholesale grocer in business with his brothers, Stefano, Rosolino and Giuseppe, and became a leader in Buffalo's Montemaggiore colony. When he died of endocarditis at the age of forty on January 10, 1914, his funeral cortege was a spectacle. Despite snow and strong winds, the procession included a marching band, members and officials of two Montemaggiore societies, numerous carriages and many floral garlands.

As Joseph DiCarlo and Elsie Pieri applied for their marriage license, each reported that they lived in Cleveland, Ohio. Joseph reported his home address as 854 Orange Street in that city. Elsie said she lived at 125 East Avenue.[41] Joseph and Elsie were married in St. Anthony's Roman Catholic Church in Fredonia, New York. The Rev. Domenico Belliotti performed the ceremony. Filippo and Lena Mazzara served as witnesses.[42]

Joseph and Elsie spent less than half a year together before the judicial system forced them apart.

Despite the bulk of Thrasher's document, the U.S. Circuit Court of Appeals found it unconvincing. In April 1925, more than a year after the witness intimidation trial was concluded, the appeals court upheld the convictions against Joseph DiCarlo and Joseph Ruffino. The two men were sent to Atlanta Federal Prison on April 15, as their attorneys petitioned the U.S. Supreme Court to review the case.[43]

The appeals process came to an end on June 1, 1925, as the Supreme Court refused to hear from the DiCarlo and Ruffino attorneys.[44]

Chapter 10

Feds Targeted

Prohibition Era violence eventually spilled beyond the memberships of bootlegging gangs. Late in 1923, a federal Prohibition agent was gunned down within a nightclub in North Buffalo.

Before becoming a "dry agent," George H. Stewart designed bridges as a masonry engineer with the coal-hauling Buffalo, Rochester and Pittsburgh Railroad. He lived with his wife Nellie in Salamanca, New York, a small town near the border with western Pennsylvania. The couple had two grown children. In May 1922, Stewart went to work for the federal government. An assignment to interdict the flow of illegal alcohol into the Buffalo region caused him to leave his wife behind in Salamanca and take a room for himself at 21 Johnson Park in Buffalo.[1]

Working with his partner, "Lucky Lou" Kelley, the fifty-year-old Stewart quickly became familiar with the region's underworld figures and began hounding gangs of rum-runners.

Sixty miles away from his wife in Salamanca, Stewart became romantically involved with a young woman named Celia Nyler in midsummer 1923. Stewart provided the 19-year-old Nyler with gifts, took her to restaurants and made rent payments on her apartment at 609 West Utica Street. Troubled by the weighty responsibilities of his new job, Stewart was able to unburden himself in conversations with Nyler. He revealed to her the occasions when duty compelled him to draw his Terrier revolver and take others' lives. He was comforted by Nyler's willingness to listen to the stories and to pray for him.[2]

In fall 1923, federal officials received a number of reports regarding alcohol sales at the Genova Inn, a two-story brick building at Hertel and Elmwood Avenues in Buffalo.[3] Michael H. Stapleton, director of the local Prohibition enforcement office, assigned Stewart in early November to obtain evidence against the operators of the Genova Inn.[4]

On Saturday, November 10, Stewart spent much of his day working with two other agents at Niagara Falls to track the movements of an area bootlegging gang. The agents left the Falls after midnight, heading toward Buffalo.[5]

Stewart went to Celia Nyler's apartment, arriving there at two-thirty on Sunday morning. Felix Kamarek, brother of the landlady, answered Stewart's ring of the doorbell and told the agent that Nyler was not at home. Stewart explained that he had just shot a man and was feeling very nervous. He told Kamarek that he would drive around in his car and look for Nyler. As Stewart drove off, Kamarek noted that the agent was not alone. There were two other men and two women in his vehicle with him.[6]

Just before three o'clock, Stewart entered the Genova Inn alone. Even at that late hour, the club was busy. He checked his hat and coat at the cloakroom and seated himself at a table across the dance floor from a table used by the Genova Inn's twenty-seven-year-old owner Salvatore "Sam" Pinnavaia. Pinnavaia, well known in western New York and Ontario bootlegging circles, had recently promised that he would make sorry any dry agent setting foot inside the Genova Inn.[7]

Stewart ordered a whiskey and obtained it.

At that moment, a woman approached Stewart's table. Appearing to know him, she said, "Hello, George." The woman spoke quietly, asking Stewart if he wanted to go to a party with her and some friends. Stewart turned down her proposal and prepared to leave.

The woman strode over to Pinnavaia's table and whispered to the club owner, "That's a dry agent." She then continued on to intercept Stewart at the cloakroom.[8]

Stewart asked for his coat and hat but met with some resistance when he offered the counter attendant a dime for a tip. She said she should have a quarter. Stewart produced a quarter. The attendant then insisted that Stewart did not have the proper check for his coat.[9]

A small crowd of inn employees quickly formed at the

cloakroom. Salvatore Pinnavaia and his thirty-three-year-old brother Ralph, who worked as a musician and a waiter in the club, moved unnoticed by Stewart toward a trelliswork partition separating the cloakroom from the main room of the club. Samuel Provenzo, who shared ownership of the inn with Pinnavaia, observed the gathering and rushed to the cloakroom.

Stewart apparently felt threatened by all the attention. He drew his revolver. Provenzo stepped forward and urged Stewart to put away the weapon. "Please, mister, don't cause any trouble," Provenzo said. "This is a respectable place." Provenzo and Stewart exchanged shoves. Provenzo fell to the floor and crawled away toward the rest rooms, as the Pinnavaia brothers, pistols drawn, opened fire on Stewart through the trellis partition behind him.[10]

The dry agent attempted to return fire but managed just one shot, which struck the ceiling, before he collapsed. The Pinnavaias emptied their weapons into Stewart's body. Nine slugs hit the agent. Two pierced his heart.[11]

The gunfire startled the inn's patrons, and they stormed the exit. Some trampled Stewart's dead body as they rushed past the cloakroom. In the confusion, the Pinnavaia brothers and the woman who warned them of the dry agent's presence managed to slip away.[12]

News of the Stewart killing enraged Assistant U.S. Attorney Ganson Depew. He mobilized the forces available to him and sent a request for more:

> It was cold-blooded murder, and we will leave no stone unturned to secure the guilty persons. Not only have all the federal agents in this section of the state been ordered to work on the case, but I have already communicated with the attorney general's office in Washington and expect further aid.[13]

Sources in the police department speculated that bootlegging gangs, tired of being harassed by Prohibition agents, had planned to take violent action against a number of them. Police suggested the Stewart killing was merely the first of a planned series of slayings. The Pinnavaias had hoped their female friend would be able to lure Stewart away in a car so they could kill him at some other location, the authorities theorized. When Stewart refused the proposition, they decided to act against him within the Genova Inn.[14]

Taking seriously the possibility that the underworld was targeting his agents, Prohibition office administrator Frank E. Sayer immediately pulled "Lucky Lou" Kelley from his duties in the Buffalo region. After two weeks, Kelley was given a new assignment in Syracuse, New York.[15]

While the authorities searched for the Pinnavaias across the region, police in Buffalo put additional pressure on bootlegging gangs, drinking establishments and vagrants. Mayor Francis Schwab directed the police to raid soft drink saloons, close down those found in violation of Prohibition laws and arrest anyone found to be unemployed. Five drinking houses were raided on November 13. The owners, charged with liquor offenses, were ordered to show cause why their businesses should not be closed.[16]

The local pistol permit process was once again questioned. It was learned that Salvatore Pinnavaia was licensed to carry a revolver by Judge Thomas Hazard Noonan. Alerted to that fact, Judge Noonan took measures to ensure a review of pistol permits. He decided that no new permits would be issued until December 1 and that all existing permits would be revoked as of that date. Beginning in December, only permits deemed necessary would be renewed.[17]

Investigators trying to track the Pinnavaias discovered a number of possible trails.

Another Pinnavaia brother, Michele, was sought in Rochester, where the family was well known. Detectives could not locate him. They knew, however, that Michele had been charged in a murder and spent some time in Monroe County Jail before he and two alleged accomplices were released on bail. A fourth man charged in the same case, Louis Alessi, remained behind bars. Detectives went to speak with him. Alessi felt he had been framed for murder by his three codefendants. He helped point the police to Michele Pinnavaia's new residence in Jamestown, New York. The detectives found Michele and searched his home, but turned up no evidence of Salvatore and Ralph Pinnavaia.

Police also learned that a close friend of the family, Joe Baglio, operated the Iroquois Hotel in Batavia, about midway between Buffalo and Rochester. However, Baglio was little help to the investigation.[18]

Charles Zimmerman, chief of detectives in Buffalo, wrote to officials in Hamilton, Ontario, to ask if they had spotted the Pinnavaias. Hamilton Chief Constable S.J. Dickson responded that he had not seen the brothers but suspected they were linked with Rocco Perri: "There is no resort they would be more likely to connect with than one kept by Rocco [Perri]."[19]

Among the measures employed by the police in an effort to locate the Pinnavaias in fall 1923 was the examination of mail sent to known underworld figures. Joseph DiCarlo's mail was of particular interest. Detectives began recording the return addresses and postmarks of all letters delivered to him or to members of his family.[20]

— — —

While the Buffalo authorities searched for the Pinnavaias, Niagara Falls police had two more gangland murders to consider. In the early morning hours of November 15, Vincenzo "James" DiNieri and his close friend Charles Austaro were murdered in separate attacks.

Austaro, thirty-six-year-old driver for the Salvatore Guarino bakery at Nineteenth Street and Ferry Avenue, left his home in a thick morning fog at about forty minutes after four. As was typical, Austaro used the bakery's horse-drawn wagon – kept in a barn behind his Fifteenth Street boarding house – to get to work. He was dead by the time the wagon reached the bakery at four-forty-eight.

A half dozen slugs had been fired into his body. Four were steel jacketed, and two were lead, indicating that at least two weapons had been used. Police believed all the bullets were fired at close range.[21]

A native of Caltavuturo, Sicily, Austaro had sailed to the United States as an adult in July 1913.[22] Though he had a close relationship with his bootlegger friend DiNieri, Austaro had a good reputation in the community.[23]

Investigators believed Austaro was ambushed on Ferry Avenue between Fourteenth and Fifteenth Streets by gunmen concealed by roadside shrubs. Due to the downward angle of some wounds, the coroner's office suggested that a gunman might have jumped up onto the wagon before shooting Austaro.[24] Lacking any other motive, the police speculated that Austaro was killed to prevent him from taking action against those responsible for DiNieri's murder.[25]

Employees of Dold Farms in Wheatfield, New York, about eight miles east of Niagara Falls, found DiNieri's body within a seven-passenger Jordan touring car the same morning. The vehicle was parked on River Road near the entrance to the Dold Farms picnic area.[26]

Police took particular interest in the murder, as DiNieri was believed to be the second most powerful man in the Niagara Falls area bootlegging racket.[27] Escalation of an ongoing bootleggers feud was feared. Chief of Detectives George "Duke" Callinan told the press he was aware that two rival gangs of liquor smugglers had been warring for some time.[28] Investigators noted that DiNieri had aided in the prosecution of Stanley Gorski for the February 1922 murder of Samuel Sirianni. As a witness in Gorski's trial, DiNieri admitted working as a messenger to set up liquor deals for the Sirianni brothers. According to DiNieri, Samuel Sirianni was killed when Gorski and his men went back on a deal and attempted to rob a liquor shipment.[29]

DiNieri seemed to be the victim of a similar crime. The rear seats in the Jordan touring car were folded, as if to make room in the vehicle for a shipment of liquor. DiNieri had been struck and shot from behind. The back of his head showed a large bump, evidence that he had been struck by a heavy instrument, and two gunshot wounds. One of the slugs lodged in his brain. The other passed through and exited the skull through DiNieri's face. A third gunshot wound was found in his right shoulder.[30]

Callinan said the murder appeared to be the work of a professional killer.[31] The time of the murder was placed at between one and two o'clock that morning. Dold Farms employees reported they heard gunshots at that time.[32] Because the murders of Austaro and DiNieri were several hours apart, investigators considered the possibility that the same gunmen were involved in both. District Attorney Burt A. Duquette called in a ballistics expert to compare bullets taken from each body.[33]

Austaro and DiNieri were buried following elaborate funerals on November 17. Both funerals were attended by the

Italian Society of the Madonna.[34] DiNieri had been president of that society, and Austaro had been a member. Due to his lack of influence in the community and his lack of relatives in the United States, Austaro's ceremony was shorter and less conspicuous. DiNieri's, however, would have suited royalty.

Society of the Madonna members lined the street in front of the DiNieri home, each carrying flowers. The procession from the DiNieri home on Fourteenth Street to St. Joseph's Church on Pine Avenue was led by a marching band. DiNieri's casket, covered with a blanket of chrysanthemums, was transported on a horse-drawn carriage. A cortege of more than a hundred automobiles followed it to the church.

Joseph Sottile and Paul Palmeri were noted among the DiNieri mourners. After a requiem Mass sung by the Reverend Austin Billerio, the procession continued on to St. Joseph's Cemetery. There, Paul Palmeri delivered a eulogy for his murdered friend.[35]

Detectives tracked down a number of details related to the DiNieri killing. They learned that the Jordan touring car belonged to Peter Carillo of East Falls Street in Niagara Falls.[36] The car's license plate, however, was traced to a Chevrolet owned by a man named Brodie in Sanborn, New York.[37]

Friends of the deceased told police a rival gang showed up in Niagara Falls a few months earlier, intent on removing DiNieri and taking over his bootlegging enterprises. The friends said DiNieri succeeded in forcing the newcomers out. The names of DiNieri's rivals were not revealed.[38]

Two days after the funerals, local newspapers reported that a cousin of DiNieri had been missing since the day of the murders. Family friends believed the cousin might have been in the car with DiNieri at the time he was killed. Police surmised that the missing cousin either had been killed and disposed of at some other location or had been taken captive.[39]

— — —

The elimination of Vincenzo DiNieri did not interrupt the flow of alcohol across the United States-Canada border. By spring of 1924, alcohol was flowing in both directions, thanks to a bootlegging innovation by Joseph Sottile of Niagara Falls.

Sottile purchased large quantities of denatured alcohol. Because the denaturing process involved the addition of poisons to alcohol that made it undrinkable, denatured alcohol was unrestricted by the Prohibition laws. Within an abandoned Niagara Falls theater, Sottile created a redistilling plant. The poisonous chemicals added to denatured alcohol had a slightly different boiling point than the alcohol itself. With care and precise equipment, experienced chemists were able to boil off the toxic elements and produce raw alcohol – drinkable but unpalatable.

Sottile provided the raw alcohol to Rocco Perri and other bootleggers across the border in Ontario, who had a number of uses for it. They sometimes used the alcohol to dilute genuine imported liquors, producing greater quantities of the high-priced beverages and dramatically improving their profit margins. They also mixed the alcohol with coloring and flavoring agents to produce beverages that could pass for Scotch, gin, bourbon and other liquors. The new mixtures were then sent back across the border for sale to the underworld suppliers of drinking establishments.

For his efforts, Sottile received from Perri a steady supply of Canadian whiskey and beer, which he sold off to U.S. customers.[40]

To ensure that the flow of liquor was not interrupted, the region's bootlegging organizations made regular payoffs to border guards, customs officials and police.[41]

— — —

In March 1925, a second United States federal employee in the region lost his life in the war on bootlegging.

Orville A. Preuster of Niagara Falls became a U.S. customs inspector in August of 1921. A U.S. citizen born in Canada, Preuster had previously worked as a motion picture operator in a theater on Main Street in Niagara Falls. On May 22, 1924, the Customs Department assigned him to combat liquor smugglers along the border. In a short time, Preuster and his partner Ellsworth H. Shaw put together an impressive string of liquor seizures. They also confiscated more than a dozen automobiles and three motorboats that had been used in the illegal transport of alcohol.[42]

Sunday, March 1, 1925, was a day off for Preuster. At just after three-thirty that afternoon, he and his friend Elmer J. Whiteacre climbed into Preuster's Moon sedan. The car was parked in the driveway of Preuster's Tenth Street home.[43] Preuster and Whiteacre planned to drive over to a farm in Lewiston to buy a dog.

Preuster turned on the vehicle's spark and stepped on the starter. An explosion shook buildings throughout the residential neighborhood at the intersection of Ontario Avenue and Tenth Street. The sedan was completely demolished. Bits of the wreckage were embedded into the clapboards along the front of Preuster's home and the home of E.E. Hardy next door. The windows of both homes were shattered.

The explosion threw Whiteacre from the car. He had lacerations on his face, his left arm and his left leg. Though serious, his injuries were not life-threatening.

Preuster, then forty-two, was torn apart by the explosion. Part of his head and both of his legs were severed from his body. His torso was ripped open by flying debris and thrust by the force of the blast into the back seat of the vehicle.[44]

The explosion was attributed to a dynamite bomb rigged to the starter. Police called in mechanics familiar with Moon Motor Company vehicles to examine the wreckage and give their opinion of the bomb's construction. "There is not a criminal in this city clever enough to make such a machine and plant it as ingeniously as this one was placed," Chief of Detectives Callinan told the press.[45] After examining what remained of the sedan, expert G.F. Schmelzer revealed that the bomber clearly possessed automotive knowledge and a fair amount of nerve:

> The job was the work of a skilled mechanical electrician who took risks in the installation of the infernal machine, which was no more than a stick of dynamite, the concussion cap of which was connected with the starting switch on the motor of the car in such a manner that the cap would explode with the slightest movement of the starter.[46]

Detectives immediately suspected forty-year-old Pasquale "Patsy Cronin" Curione of the Village of La Salle of involvement in the bombing. La Salle was a small community sitting about six miles east of Niagara Falls, and Curione was known as "king" of the bootleg fraternity there[47] and as an underworld associate of

Joseph Sirianni and Joseph Henry Sottile.[48]

Curione and Preuster had crossed paths the previous December, when Preuster caught Curione bringing a car filled with twelve thousand dollars worth of Canadian ale into the Niagara Falls area. Curione offered the customs inspector a bribe of two thousand dollars to keep quiet about the ale. Preuster pretended to accept the offer, and told Curione to deliver the payment to him in the foyer of the Federal Building in Buffalo. Curione kept the appointment and was arrested as he presented the bribe to Preuster. The "king of La Salle bootleggers" was charged with bribery and scheduled for trial on March 10.[49]

Curione viewed the arrest as an act of betrayal, and Preuster was aware of his anger. Later that winter, however, things seemed to change between the two men. In an interview with police, Lucas Preuster recalled a recent difference in his murdered brother's demeanor.

> Only the other day, Orville came home feeling particularly happy. I asked him why he felt so good natured, and he said it was because he believed he had no enemies. "I thought I had one," said he, "Patsy Cronin, but he passed me in his car today and waved his hand to me."[50]

Following Preuster's murder, Curione was called in to police headquarters for questioning. He was interrogated for two hours by Police Chief Myron F. Blackmon, U.S. Attorney Richard H. Templeton, Prohibition Enforcement Chief Allan Bartlett and Secret Service Bureau Chief Edward J. McHugh. Though certain Curione was responsible for the bombing, the officials could not tie him to the crime.[51]

As Curione left the interrogation, he passed an office filled with police and newspaper reporters. He poked his head in and cheerfully said, "Good night, gentlemen." Hearing no response, he repeated his farewell. Police Sergeant Nelson spoke up for the group. "Never mind, Patsy," the sergeant told Curione. "We'll meet again, and when we do, it will be right."

"I'm sorry you have that feeling towards me," Curione responded. He left the building and drove off in a recently purchased Pierce Arrow.[52]

Officials interpreted the killing of Preuster as a warning to all who opposed the regional bootlegging gangs, particularly the gang led by Sirianni and Sottile. Thomas M. Hennessy, deputy collector of customs, told the press that Prohibition enforcement officers constantly received threats. "Unless the murderers of Preuster are caught and summary justice meted to them," Hennessy said, "there isn't a customs or Prohibition agent along the Niagara frontier whose life is worth a nickel."[53]

The Niagara Falls City Council approved a $5,000 reward for information leading to the arrest and conviction of those responsible for the bombing. The local Ku Klux Klan, of which Lucas Preuster was a member, offered a $1,000 reward.[54]

To protect him from gang wrath, the Customs Department ordered Preuster's partner Ellsworth Shaw and his wife to leave town.[55]

The underworld quickly discovered that Preuster's murder was a mistake. Law enforcement officers were not frightened into submission, they were enraged. Additional federal manpower was sent to western New York.[56] A grand jury directed to investigate the bombing expanded its focus and called in all known bootleggers and gangsters in the Niagara Falls area.[57]

Churches also mobilized against the underworld. At Preuster's March 3 funeral, the Reverend Herman Brezing of the Zion Lutheran Church said, "I can still hear the boom of that explosion. I trust to God that it will echo and re-echo until it has swept away every evildoer and those who love violence have been brought to justice."[58]

Days later, the Reverend A.B. Mercer, president of the Niagara Falls Council of Churches, stepped to the pulpit to put the blame for Preuster's death where it belonged:

> Do we know who killed him?... As we all know, it was the bootlegger crowd, and I might add at this point that it is not the first murder that they have been responsible for in Niagara Falls... We were aroused from our lethargy by the explosion of that bomb to the extent that we all said, "Something ought to be done." But what? One thing we ought to stop making bootleggers. Who makes them? Every man who drinks, the

respectable businessman, the man high up in the world, the respectable merchant, so-called, and in many instances the man whose name is on the church roll. Any person who takes a drink these days is making bootleggers. When we quit drinking and encouraging others to drink, we will rid ourselves of the bootlegger evil. Every man who drinks now, when liquor has been outlawed, is indirectly responsible for the death of Orville A. Preuster.[59]

Chapter 11

Feud in Buffalo

Brothers John and Carmelo Gambino spent the evening of July 13, 1925, walking along Buffalo's Dante Place and chatting. They were joined by Rosario and John Burgio of Peacock Street, a narrow road wedged between boat slips off the Erie Basin. The four men discussed their jobs and the high cost of living.

The group broke up at a quarter to eleven near the Erie Street canal bridge. John Gambino said goodnight to his companions and crossed the bridge. Carmelo and the Burgios walked back to Dante Place.

John Gambino stopped in for about fifteen minutes to visit a sick brother-in-law at 134 Erie Street. He then continued toward Seventh Street where he lived. He did not make it home.[1]

Gambino reached the corner of Church Street and Lower Terrace at eleven-fifteen. At that moment, a Ford automobile pulled up to him and stopped. Two men stepped out of the vehicle. Gunshots echoed through the neighborhood. The two men climbed back into the Ford, and it raced away on Church Street toward West Genesee.[2]

Gambino was dead on the sidewalk. He had been shot eight times.[3]

The Buffalo police knew Gambino well. They had linked him to a series of underworld killings between 1923 and 1925. The first was the murder of Calogero DiRosa, who was shot to death near the Erie Street bridge between Dante Place and Erie Street on April 30, 1923. Gambino was arrested by Detective Sergeant John Smaldino and was held in connection with the DiRosa slaying for three weeks. There was little evidence to tie Gambino to the crime, however, and he had to be released.[4]

Investigators apparently did not look into the possibility that Gambino murdered DiRosa to avenge an earlier killing. DiRosa in the spring of 1911 had been convicted of manslaughter and sentenced to serve a minimum of six years in Auburn State Prison after shooting and killing Peacock Street resident Sebastiano Gambino. A family vendetta could have grown out of Sebastiano's death.[5]

Gambino also was suspected of involvement in the November 26, 1923, murder of Frank Genovese. Genovese was the leader of a Buffalo criminal organization. His gang was blamed for the robbery and killing of Charles Spang in 1917.

Spang was a collector for the Broadway Brewing Company. While seated in a saloon at Georgia and Fourth Streets, counting his collection, five men entered and shot and robbed him of more than two thousand dollars.

One gang member, Joseph Roberto was arrested on the run in Holyoke, Massachusetts. He was tried, convicted and sentenced to death.[6] Genovese eluded authorities until his arrest in Rochester in February 1921.[7] He also was prosecuted for the Spang murder, but much of the evidence against him had been destroyed in a fire.[8] Genovese was acquitted and returned to lead his gang until he was shot to death at the intersection of Erie Street and Dante Place.[9]

Police could not assemble a case against Gambino, who they believed to be Genovese's underworld rival.[10] They focused their attention instead on Joseph Ferrigga, operator of a Court Street soft drink saloon. Weeks earlier, Ferrigga fired a handgun at Genovese when the gangster created a disturbance in the saloon. A grand jury did not find enough evidence to indict Ferrigga on a charge of murdering Genovese.[11]

Another murder occurred in the same vicinity on March 5, 1925. Police department employee Edward Grant found John Manestri's lifeless body behind the police station at West Seneca and Erie Streets shortly after midnight. Manestri had been shot twice. One bullet had entered his back. Another had been shot through the back of his head. The slug sliced through his brain and exited his forehead just above his left eye.[12]

During the course of their murder investigation, detectives learned that Manestri did not have a steady job. He gambled frequently and often spent his time at Anthony Bonadonna's pool room at 141 Dante Place. No one could tell police what Manestri was doing on the night he was killed or who might have wanted him dead.

On March 10, *Buffalo Courier* copy-reader Clarence E. Good acknowledged that he was in the neighborhood at the time of the killing. Good went to Police Headquarters and provided a largely unhelpful statement:

> I was waiting for a Hoyt streetcar at the corner of Franklin and Seneca Streets, standing in front of the See Mee restaurant. With me was another man, whose name I do not know. After I had waited a minute or two, I notice a big, black, enclosed car coming down Franklin Street toward Seneca from Erie... The car crossed the tracks and stopped in front of the building which I have later learned is the News Garage. In the car were three persons... One person was driving and two were sitting in the tonneau. Just as the car drew to a stop in front of the garage building, a passenger train came by. As the train was about halfway past the crossing, I heard three shots. At the time, I thought they were torpedoes on the track... As the train's last car passed the crossing, I noticed the automobile I have mentioned before leave the front of the News Garage and dash very rapidly around the next corner, turning to the left.[13]

As Good's streetcar arrived, he heard that someone had been shot. He went home, planning to tell the police the next day what he observed. His visit to Police Headquarters was delayed due to an illness, he said.[14]

As detectives linked Manestri with the Genovese gang, they brought Gambino in for questioning once again. He claimed to have no knowledge of the Manestri murder.[15]

Another mysterious murder occurred just weeks later. Forty-year-old Joseph LaPaglia was found dead at about ten o'clock on the night of March 26. His body was found at the intersection of

Georgia Street and Front Avenue. Medical Examiner Earl Danser determined that LaPaglia had been disabled by a shot from behind and killed by a gunshot to his left ear. Police had no suspects in the killing but believed LaPaglia was killed because he recently testified against Dante Place resident Joseph Zabito as the star witness in his murder trial.[16]

With Gambino long associated with gang violence, it was probably no surprise to Buffalo's law enforcement community when his bullet-riddled remains were found on the sidewalk. Police noted that he was the first of his underworld faction to be killed in retaliation for the murders of the Genovese gang members.[17]

Detectives discovered two handguns on the ground near Gambino's body. One was a blue steel Smith & Wesson .38 Special, and the other was a Spanish-made .32-caliber revolver with nickel plating and a pearl handle.

The detectives also discovered two witnesses, who watched the murder from a distance. Mildred Dovern of Church Street and Irene Griffin of Lower Terrace were returning home from Erie Beach when they saw two gunmen emerge from an automobile and shoot Gambino. One of the gunman was described as about five-feet-five inches tall and one hundred fifty pounds, wearing a light-colored "Palm Beach" suit and a Panama hat. The second looked to be about two inches taller and ten pounds heavier. He wore dark clothes. The women noticed a third man in the vehicle but could not provide a description of him. They were able to recall only the first two digits of the automobile's license number.[18]

Though there were more clues in the Gambino killing than in others related to the gangland feud, the media reported that police were "skeptical of chances of working out a solution."[19]

— — —

An appalling crime later that summer united Buffalo's Sicilian community and resulted in some positive press for the city's Mafia leaders.

At one-thirty in the afternoon on August 18, 1925, the dead body of twelve-year-old Joseph Gervase was discovered in some tall weeds near the canal towpath at the foot of Georgia Street. The boy had been sexually assaulted and strangled to death.

Police immediately went in search of Elmer Thompson. A

drifter, Thompson had earned some money in Buffalo through cutting hair and clog dancing at cheap theaters. He had also earned a reputation as a degenerate. A number of youngsters reported that Thompson had made "improper suggestions," attempting to lure them to a room on Swan Street to teach them new dance steps. Thompson and Gervase were seen together the day before. Thompson hired the boy to carry a suitcase for him. The two were observed walking in the direction of the canal.[20]

The authorities could find no clue to Thompson's whereabouts. A man said to be his brother was arrested and questioned in West Virginia. That man did not match Thompson's description.[21] Police also spoke with Samuel Garwood, a former prison guard at the Moundsville Prison outside of Wheeling, West Virginia, where Thompson had served time. "I talked with Thompson every day for four years and always thought he was half-witted," Garwood said. "He appeared lazy and often asked foolish questions."[22]

Mafia bosses Angelo Palmeri, Filippo Mazzara and Giuseppe DiBenedetto mobilized the Sicilian community to aid the Gervase family with funeral expenses. They and Joseph Colognia went to all the homes and businesses in Buffalo's Italian quarter asking for donations. Everyone contributed. Though the underworld clout of the three primary collectors was probably persuasive, the *Buffalo Times* saw the successful fund drive as evidence of Sicilian unity: "For the entire colony, always closely bound together, is touched as never before by the untimely death of little Joseph."[23]

The next day, Palmeri, Mazzara, DiBenedetto and Colognia paid an after-dinner visit to Joseph Gervase's father. Fortunato Gervase, with the help of his oldest son Vincent, had been trying to provide for his family of eleven on the small wages of a road worker. The group pulled Fortunato away from a gathering of sympathetic friends and spoke with him in a rear room.

"We can't tell you how sorry we are about your son," Palmeri said, "so we've brought along a little help for you." Mazzara presented him with a roll of small bills, totaling $565, and the group told Fortunato that his son's burial expenses had been paid. The grieving father broke down and wept.[24]

More than one thousand people gathered outside the Gervase home for the funeral procession to Mount Carmel Church on the morning of the twenty-first. Gervase's parents were overwhelmed with grief and anger. His mother shrieked in Sicilian, "Before the dead body of my little boy goes under the ground, I must kill the murderer with my own hands!" As the white casket draped with roses was carried from the family home at 109 Commercial Street, the woman loudly protested: "I must kiss my little Joe, my little Joe that I love!" As family members tried to calm his wife, Fortunato cried quietly.

People around the casket whispered to each other: "He was such a good boy. He gave his mother fifty or sixty cents every night. It was all his earnings. She waited every night for him to come home. He was such a good boy."[25]

The search for Elmer Thompson continued long after Joseph Gervase's burial and prompted a degree of cooperation between the underworld and the police. Mazzara and Mafia underlings Angelo Puma and Frank DeFusto – men referred to by the press as Italian community leaders – offered a $1,000 reward for Thompson's capture. To publicize the reward offer, five hundred circulars were printed. The Buffalo Police Department shipped those to law enforcement agencies in other cities.[26]

In February of 1926, authorities checked on rumors that Thompson had been seen in Buffalo.[27] They found no evidence of the accused killer.

In mid-July, 1927, a man precisely matching Thompson's description and his Bertillon data was arrested in Vermont and turned over to prosecutors in Massachusetts. The man, who insisted his name was George Taylor, was charged with killing a girl. He was caught after selling a watch that belonged to the victim. When questioned about the Gervase killing, Taylor denied any involvement. As Taylor went on trial for murder in Boston, Buffalo officials announced that it would be futile to try to have him extradited to New York.[28]

— — —

A 1926 gangland murder in Chicago exposed underworld connections among individuals and organizations across the United States. Victim Orazio Tropea, an enforcer for the Genna Mafia family in the Windy City and a part-time resident of Buffalo, was found to be in possession of a list of names, addresses and telephone numbers. The list revealed Tropea's personal, business and criminal contacts in Chicago, New York,

Buffalo, Detroit, Pittsburgh and Los Angeles.

Born April 29, 1880, in the city of Catania on Sicily's east coast, Tropea traveled to the U.S. as an adult.[29] He left his parents, his wife and two young children behind in Sicily.[30] Tropea first settled with relatives in the Bushwick section of Brooklyn and then moved westward to Buffalo.

In Buffalo around 1916, he became romantically involved with a woman named Helen Brown. Tropea and Brown lived together and had a son together in 1917. A short time later, Tropea and his new American family moved to Chicago. Within a few years of the move, Tropea learned that his wife back in Sicily had died.

At that time, he began a long-term affair with Beatrice Gold of Chicago, then just a teenager. Somehow, the question of marriage between the two arose. Apparently unaware of Tropea's common-law wife, Benjamin and Esther Gold forbade their daughter's marriage to Tropea on the grounds that he was not Jewish. Possibly in a vain effort to put an end to the relationship, the Golds moved from Chicago to South Haven, Michigan – about one hundred and twenty miles away on the opposite shore of Lake Michigan.[31]

In Chicago, Tropea associated himself with the South Side Mafia organization run by Sam Genna and his five brothers. The rest of the "Terrible Gennas" were Vincenzo "Jim," Pete, Antonio "Tony the Gentleman," "Bloody Angelo" and "Little Mike." The Genna mob engaged in extortion, gambling and bootlegging. It included such underworld characters as Samuzzo "Samoots" Amatuna, Vito Bascone, Ecola "the Eagle" Baldelli, John Scalisi and Albert Anselmi. Within this group of outlaws, Tropea emerged as a specialist in extortion. He quickly earned a nickname for himself among his helpless extortion victims in Little Italy, "the Scourge."[32]

The Chicago region hosted a number of criminal organizations in the early Prohibition Era. The ambitions of the various Italian and Sicilian gang leaders were held in check for a while through the savage discipline of regional Mafia chieftain Antonio D'Andrea. Michele "Mike" Merlo assumed the position of Mafia peacemaker and disciplinarian after D'Andrea's murder in May 1921. His reign was generally successful but very brief. Merlo died of natural causes on November 9, 1924.[33]

Merlo was not yet buried when the Gennas took up arms against a rival Irish and Polish gang.

Dean O'Banion, owner of a florist shop at 738 North State Street and boss of the North Side Gang, was busy on November 11 preparing floral displays for Merlo's extravagant funeral. Three men entered his shop at midday. O'Banion recognized at least one of the men, the tallest of the three, and greeted him with a handshake. As they clasped hands, the other two men drew weapons and opened fire. O'Banion dropped to the floor with six bullets in him. The three visitors retreated out of the store, jumped into a waiting automobile – described by a witness as a dark-colored, nickel-trimmed Jewett – and sped away.

Two slugs had pierced O'Banion's right chest. Two others had ripped through his throat. The final two had been fired into opposite sides of his head. During an autopsy, powder burns were found on O'Banion's left cheek, leading investigators to believe that the left side of the head was the location of the final shot, a coup de grâce.[34]

Suspicion focused on Genna gangsters. Some believed "Little Mike" Genna, Albert Anselmi and John Scalisi were responsible. But considerable police attention focused on two Mafiosi recently arrived in Chicago from Orazio Tropea's old haunts in Brooklyn. Acting on a tip from an informant, Chicago police arrested Brooklynites Frank Yale and Saverio Pollaccia on November 18 as they boarded the New York Central Railroad's express train for a return trip to New York.[35] Some suspected Tropea of involvement in the killing, though Tropea was not arrested.[36]

Yale was known as the Calabrian underworld boss of Brooklyn and as a boyhood friend of both Chicago gang leader Johnny Torrio and his lieutenant Alphonse "Al Brown" Capone. Authorities in the Windy City recalled that Yale had last been noted in town in 1920 when another underworld chieftain, Torrio's former boss "Big Jim" Colosimo, was shot to death.[37] Pollaccia had been a close personal friend of Brooklyn-based Mafia boss of bosses Salvatore D'Aquila. The friendship recently ended as Pollaccia sided with D'Aquila's Manhattan rival Giuseppe "Joe the Boss" Masseria in a New York underworld conflict.[38]

During questioning by Chicago police, Yale and Pollaccia

insisted that they had only arrived in Chicago on the day after O'Banion's murder. Investigators could produce no evidence that they had been in town earlier. The two men were freed.[39]

Following the murder of O'Banion, a number of Genna followers, led by "Samoots" Amatuna and a well-educated Sicilian known by the aliases of "schoolmaster" and "Cavallero," broke away to form their own gang.[40] Tropea, Anselmi, Scalisi and others sided with the rebel faction.[41]

Between May 26 and July 9 of 1925, three of the Genna brothers were killed.

Angelo Genna was the first to go. Gunmen ambushed him while he was driving his roadster at Hudson and Ogden Avenues.[42]

Mike Genna was slain in the company of Anselmi and Scalisi in a June 13 shootout with police. That gunfight also took the lives of police officers Charles B. Wilson and Harold F. Olson and resulted in capital murder charges against Anselmi and Scalisi.[43] Officer William Sweeney, who single-handedly pursued the cop-killers and fired the shot that resulted in the death of Mike Genna, was promoted and praised by the police department. The rewards were offset in large part by gangsters, who communicated their disapproval by bombing Sweeney's home.[44]

The nature of the Mafia rebellion became clear when Tony Genna, mortally wounded at a meeting with supposed friends early on July 8, was questioned by his brother Sam and Assistant State's Attorney John Sbarbaro in the hospital. Sam pleaded with Tony to reveal who had shot him. Tony responded, "Cavallero." Asked to repeat his answer for Sbarbaro, Tony first indicated that Cavallero was merely with him at Grand Avenue and Curtis Street when he was shot. Later, Tony clearly blamed Cavallero for the shooting. Police decided that Cavallero used the same technique as in the O'Banion murder, grasping Tony's pistol hand in a handshake while other gunmen shot him.[45]

The remaining members of the Genna family, certain that they were marked for death, decided to flee Chicago. They returned to Italy.[46]

The rebel faction in the local Sicilian Mafia lost a key man when Samoots Amatuna was murdered in November. Two men shot him inside a barbershop at 804 West Roosevelt Road near Halsted Street. Amatuna, clinging to life, was taken to Jefferson

Park Hospital. Arrangements were quickly made for him to marry his fiancée, Rose Pecoraro, sister-in-law of the late Mike Merlo. Before the ceremony could begin, Amatuna lost consciousness. He died of his wounds early the following morning.[47]

During this period, Tropea put his extortion skills to use, raising money for a Scalisi and Anselmi legal defense fund. Residents and businessmen in Sicilian and Italian neighborhoods were assessed fees. They received letters informing them of the amounts that were expected of them and promising severe retribution if the payments were not made. One letter included a reference to the bombing of Officer Sweeney's residence: "You will have to pay or you will die – you and your wife – and we'll blow up your store like we did the cop's home."

Though the assessments were large, Tropea had little trouble collecting. He raised tens of thousands of dollars in just a few weeks.[48]

Anselmi and Scalisi avoided the gallows for the killing of Officer Olson. After hearing defense counsel argue for the gunmen's right to "defend" themselves against the police, a jury decided on November 12 that fourteen years in prison was sufficient punishment. A second trial for the killing of Officer Walsh was scheduled for early in 1926. That called for another round of fundraising by "the Scourge."[49]

Tropea found collections far more difficult the second time around. One of those reluctant to pay into the defense fund was Henry Spingola, brother-in-law to the Gennas. After agreeably paying his assessed ten-thousand-dollar fee for the first trial, Spingola refused to contribute any more than two thousand dollars for the second. Rather than try to strong-arm the well-connected Spingola, Tropea invited him for dinner and a game of pinochle. On January 10, 1926, the men met at Amato's restaurant at Taylor and South Halsted Streets.

As they began their final hand of pinochle, Tropea stepped away to make a telephone call. After the game, the two men parted as friends. Tropea moved to Amato's front window and struck a match just as Spingola emerged from the restaurant. Spingola crossed to the opposite side of South Halsted Street, where his car was parked. As he approached the vehicle, shotguns erupted behind him. Spingola was killed.[50]

Tropea's role in Spingola's murder was apparent. The

Spingola family and its allies were determined to eliminate "the Scourge." Others were willing to help. Tropea had been caught skimming from the Anselmi-Scalisi defense fund, and the rebel Mafia faction was gunning for him too.[51]

On the evening of February 15, Tropea stepped off an eastbound streetcar at the corner of South Halsted and Taylor. As he crossed South Halsted, an automobile came up behind him, nearly bumping him. Tropea turned and angrily shouted, "Why the hell don't you blow your horn?" The automobile pulled alongside of Tropea. A man jumped out and unloaded both barrels of a shotgun into "the Scourge."

While Prohibition Era Chicago was well known for hosting extravagant gangland funerals, Tropea received no elaborate send-off. The burial was attended only by Beatrice Gold and her brother Donald.[52] Helen Brown's effort to have Tropea's remains brought to Buffalo for interment brought her significant public humiliation, as newspapers made an issue of Tropea's relationships.[53]

Detectives investigating the killing stumbled upon Tropea's list of contacts. The list included grocers, restaurateurs, produce merchants, confectioners and factory workers, in addition to Tropea's girlfriend, his common law wife and his son. Most interesting to the press and the police were the several entries for Antonio Lombardo. Home and business addresses and telephone numbers were shown, along with information for reaching Lombardo at the Unione Siciliana organization on South Dearborn Street.[54] A powerful underworld leader and a close adviser of underworld rising star Alphonse Capone, Lombardo denied any association with Tropea and objected to his name appearing in the newspapers:

> That's being done to ruin me. I have right now a loan from a bank and I owe for some of my goods. I have over $100,000 of stock in my place, but if I lose my credit it would hurt me. If the bankers think I am a bad fellow they would call my note. That's what my enemies are trying to do to me.[55]

Buffalo residents on Tropea's list included Mafioso Sam LoVullo of 85 Efner Street, who somehow had avoided prosecution after stealing a cargo of booze from politically connected rumrunners in 1921, and grocer Joseph A. Quattrone of 356 Terrace Street.

The list also included Chicago residents Amato Mongelluzzo and Caterina Amara. Mongelluzzo, the owner of Amato's restaurant where Henry Spingola was ambushed and murdered, was held for questioning by police after Tropea's murder.[56] Caterina Amara was the maiden name of the wife of Chicago underworld newcomer Joseph Aiello.

Aiello and the Amara family, both originally from Bagheria, Sicily, settled for a while in Utica, New York. While in Utica, Aiello and his business partner Salvatore LaFata were charged with the June 1917 shooting of Antonio Gagliano. In an affidavit, Gagliano identified saloonkeepers Aiello and LaFata as his attackers.[57] Several months later, Gagliano contradicted his sworn statement. He said he did not actually see who shot him and had been forced by Detective John B. Grande to sign a false statement. Gagliano subsequently was charged with perjury.[58] LaFata sold his interest in the saloon and moved to Buffalo with his wife and three young children. On October 7, he was found murdered on the roadway at Maiden Lane and Water Street. His face had been shot away, his lower jaw shattered and five teeth blown from his mouth.[59] Buffalo Police arrested Joseph Celona, who had exchanged angry words with LaFata earlier in the day, but they were unable to connect him with the killing.[60]

Aiello married Caterina Amara in Buffalo in 1917 and subsequently moved on to Chicago. Aiello and his kin would eventually fill the void left by the departure of the Genna clan.[61]

The only New York City contact named on Tropea's list was Brooklyn's Saverio Pollaccia, adviser to Manhattan crime boss Giuseppe Masseria and suspect in the O'Banion slaying.[62] The scribbled name and address of Pittsburgh Mafia boss Giuseppe Siragusa also appeared,[63] as did contacts in Detroit and Flint, Michigan, and Los Angeles, California.[64]

— — —

Buffalo's own underworld violence raged on during the warmer months of 1926.

In the early morning hours of June 13, Sam LoVullo, friend of the recently murdered Orazio Tropea and a powerful underworld figure on Buffalo's west side, was found unconscious and bleeding on the sidewalk a short distance from his Efner Street home. Joseph Giambrone of Virginia Street drove LoVullo to Columbus Hospital and then telephoned police.

Doctors treated a bullet wound in LoVullo's left shoulder. The wound was not life-threatening.

When LoVullo revived, he found inquisitive Buffalo police detectives at his bedside. The thirty-year-old Mafioso refused to provide any information. "It is no use asking me questions because I won't answer them," he said.

Detectives Michael Scanlon and Frank Leigh had slightly better luck when they questioned a number of residents of the Trenton Avenue neighborhood. They were unable to identify LoVullo's assailant, but they learned that LoVullo had been playing cards with three other men when an argument erupted. LoVullo and one other man went outside to settle the disagreement.[65]

Though they did not tell police, LoVullo's friends were aware that Santo Falsone fired the bullet that struck LoVullo. Falsone, LoVullo and others were playing cards within a poolroom beside a grocery store at the northwest corner of Trenton Avenue and Carolina Street. When the argument occurred, Falsone, a thirty-eight-year-old iron foundry worker who lived close by on Carolina Street, invited LoVullo to step outside to settle it.

LoVullo expected a fistfight. But, when the two men stepped onto the sidewalk, Falsone spun around and fired a handgun at LoVullo.[66]

— — —

A personal vendetta was believed responsible for the murder of thirty-two-year-old tailor Joseph Cicatello a few weeks later. Cicatello was shot to death just after midnight July 2 in front of 83 Dante Place, a building that held both his tailor shop and his residence.[67]

Earlier that evening, Cicatello and his brother Anthony attended a meeting of the Termini Italian Society at St. Anthony's Hall on Upper Terrace. After the meeting, the brothers went to sit and chat in front of Joseph's shop. They lingered there from nine-thirty until ten o'clock. Anthony Cicatello headed home after that. Joseph remained outside and was joined by his wife Anna and their eight-year-old son Salvatore.

After twelve, a dark touring car pulled up in front of the building. As Anna and Salvatore watched, two heavyset men in dark-colored suits stepped out of the car, strode over to Cicatello, pulled out handguns and shot the tailor repeatedly in the chest and abdomen. The men ran back to their vehicle and sped away north on Dante Place and then east on Erie Street.[68]

Joseph Cicatello slumped in his chair and tumbled to the walkway. An ambulance rushed to the scene, but Cicatello died on his way to Emergency Hospital.[69]

Detective William J. Madigan investigated the killing and decided that it was related to the previous murder of a "suitor of Anna."[70] A Buffalo newspaper reported more specifically that Cicatello was murdered because he was believed responsible for the killing of John DeCaro at Elmwood Avenue and Tupper Street on May 6.[71]

At first, police believed DeCaro's death to be a suicide. He was found lying on the ground with a bullet wound behind his right ear and a revolver resting on his chest. Medical Examiner Charles E. Long decided that DeCaro death was probably a homicide. He learned from witnesses that DeCaro had fired several shots at Cicatello earlier that evening. The two men previously had been friendly.[72]

— — —

Pietro Rizzo, forty-eight-year-old cousin of Filippo Mazzara's aide Peter Rizzo, went for a drive with his eighteen-year-old son Michael on the evening of July 15. Pietro was ailing, and nighttime drives with his son helped him to feel better.[73] That night, the two men drove around in Michael's Dodge roadster from six-thirty until about twenty-five minutes to ten. Michael let his father out of the vehicle at on Front Avenue, a few blocks from the Rizzo home at 70 Efner Street.

Michael drove off to pick up his cousin, Salvatore "Sam" Insalaco, as Pietro began strolling southeast on Front Avenue. Michael and Insalaco were together an hour and forty-five minutes. Michael dropped his cousin off at eleven-thirty and then continued to ride around town alone. A short time later, his drive was interrupted.

He later recalled, "When I was riding on Seventh Street alone, some kids hollered to me that my father was shot. When I heard that, I went right over to Sam's house."[74] Detectives met

Michael and Insalaco there and brought both in for questioning.

Pietro Rizzo had been shot to death on Front Avenue between Georgia and Court Streets. He fell after being hit on the right side by a shower of .32-caliber bullets. Authorities believed his assailants opened fire from the back of a passing touring car.

Police noted that Pietro's twenty-year-old son Joseph, Michael's older brother, was missing. Joseph had attended a boxing match that night in the company of Samuel LoVullo, Peter Montana and others. After his father's funeral, Joseph's sedan was found near a stream at Woodlawn, south of Buffalo.

Police knew that Pietro Rizzo's cousin was a key member of Mazzara's Mafia crew. They found records of two of Pietro's arrests. He was charged with Prohibition violations on January 9, 1924, when dry agents raided his Efner Street home and discovered a one-hundred-gallon moonshine still,[75] and with carrying a revolver without a permit on March 9, 1925. However, they were unable to explain Pietro's murder and his son's disappearance.

The Buffalo bootlegging fraternity had no such trouble.

According to some who knew the Rizzo family, Pietro had moved to Buffalo in the early 1920s from Pittston, Pennsylvania. He and his son Joseph became involved in bootlegging rackets in western New York, transporting alcohol to associates in the Rochester area.

Early in 1926, racketeers from New York City offered Pietro a large quantity of denatured alcohol at one-fifth the usual price of bootleg liquor. The alcohol required careful redistilling in order to separate drinkable alcohol from the denaturing contaminants, but the low price was enticing. With Filippo Mazzara brokering the deal, Pietro agreed to take the shipment on credit. He stored the shipment at 69 Efner Street and "recooked" it at his home across the street.

When Pietro was slow in paying the approximately fifteen-thousand-dollar bill for the alcohol, the New Yorkers went back to Mazzara, as he had vouched for Pietro. Mazzara, in turn, went to his lieutenant Peter Rizzo to explain the dire situation. Peter Rizzo, then operator of the Flower Basket business on Niagara and Virginia Streets, washed his hands of the matter. He told Mazzara he would not pay his cousin Pietro's debts and did not care what happened to him. Mazzara gave the New Yorkers permission to handle the matter as they saw fit.

Members of Mazzara's crew approached Joseph Rizzo, in an effort to convince him not to contest underworld discipline. But Joseph made it clear that he intended to avenge his father's murder. That sealed his fate. Within days of his father's funeral, Joseph disappeared.[76]

— — —

The unsolved Cicatello and Rizzo slayings of July 1926 prompted Buffalo Police to set up a special squad to deal exclusively with vendetta-related murders in the Italian districts.[77] Just two days after announcing the new squad, another apparent gangland killing occurred in the city.

The victim was John Anthony Vassallo, a twenty-eight-year-old barber. Just before one o'clock in the morning on July 20, Vassallo was shot as he cranked his automobile in front of 497 Seventh Street, near the Niagara Street police station.

Vassallo and his friend Fred Ippolito had been driving south on Seventh Street, when Vassallo's car stalled. Ippolito joined Vassallo in efforts to restart the car and then decided to walk to his home at 505 Front Avenue. After he left, Vassallo continued working on the car.[78]

A vehicle carrying three men approached him on Seventh Street. When it stopped and one of the occupants got out with a weapon in hand, Vassallo instantly recognized his peril and started begging for his life: "Don't kill me. Don't shoot me. Please don't."

Shots rang out. Vassallo was struck in the chest and the shoulder. Seriously wounded, he fled from his attackers, running down an alley to the police station. He entered the station and collapsed in the vestibule. Police rushed him to Columbus Hospital, where surgeons attempted to repair the damage.[79] Vassallo died at the hospital that afternoon.[80]

Detectives gathered information about Vassallo's troubled relationships with his in-laws. A recent family argument had resulted in an exchange of gunshots. No one was hurt, but charges were filed. At the time of his murder, Vassallo was awaiting trial for firing two shots in the direction of in-law Angelo Pulvino.[81]

Buffalo's Chief of Detectives Austin J. Roche refused to be distracted by the family quarrels. He was certain that Vassallo was killed by an organization of bootleggers. "There is no question in my mind this is a liquor vendetta," Roche told the press. "This is getting too much like the reign of terror created by the gangsters in Chicago. We are going to break it up before it goes any further."[82]

Roche believed the motive for killing Vassallo was linked to the price of alcohol in the Buffalo area. Vassallo was undercutting the prices of a bootlegging ring, and the ring hired killers to eliminate their competition.[83]

Detectives learned that the victim had a fistfight with two men earlier in the evening. The men attacked him on Niagara Street at about nine-thirty. The names of the assailants were not reported to police.[84]

Expecting some reprisal for the Vassallo slaying, Deputy Police Chief Frank J. Carr set up two squads to patrol the Italian neighborhoods on the west side of the city. The squads were equipped with police cars and sawed off shotguns. On July 22, Carr announced, "The vendetta squads will go on duty tonight with orders to use their weapons without hesitation."[85]

The same day, Detective William Madigan reported to Roche that Vassallo had spoken a name as he died. The name sounded like, "Toto."[86]

The police believed Vassallo was indicating he was killed by a twenty-five-year-old nephew of Filippo Mazzara who had been in the United States for just two or three years and worked for Mazzara at the Elk Street Market. Police had little luck in locating either the nephew or Mazzara. Word reached detectives that the Buffalo Mafioso was spending some time in Cleveland, Ohio.[87]

Chapter 12

Poison

A May 14, 1926, raid by Prohibition agents at the Third Ward Political Club in Niagara Falls uncovered Joseph Henry Sottile's massive alcohol redistilling operation. For about two years, Sottile had been acquiring legal denatured alcohol at a low cost and carefully recooking it to remove toxins, a process known to bootleggers as "cleaning." He sold the resulting raw alcohol to contacts in Ontario, Canada, who diluted it, flavored it and bottled it.[1]

Raiding agents led by Mark Crehan, head of the local alcohol division, seized Sottile's distilling equipment, twelve thousand gallons of alcohol and five thousand gallons of whiskey. Crehan's force arrested just one suspect at the site, a Sottile assistant named Joseph Spallino, who happened to show up as the law enforcement action was occurring.

Spallino was processed and released on bail. He returned to the Third Ward Political Club to find Crehan's agents still there. The agents had discovered a safe in a front room of the headquarters and asked Spallino to open it. He refused. Apparently satisfied for the moment that they had put Sottile out of business, the Prohibition agents departed.

Two days later, agents returned to the club headquarters, entering through a basement door. They went to the front room and drilled open the safe. The agents seized a variety of documents from the safe, reportedly including records and membership lists of a regional bootlegging ring, and left a receipt for "books and assorted papers."[2]

Sottile fled the U.S., finding refuge for a time with Rocco Perri in Canada. Political connections there allowed a special hearing on a Sottile application for Canadian citizenship. As a warrant for Sottile's arrest was issued in the U.S., his citizenship was approved by Judge Emerson Coatsworth in Toronto.[3]

Though the regional bootlegging syndicate easily adjusted to earlier enforcement activity by dry agents, the shutdown of Sottile's redistilling plant was a severe blow. Bootleggers scrambled to find a source of cheap alcohol for thirsty customers.[4]

The pressure to resume the flow of liquor in the region and the vast potential rewards for doing so prompted Pietro Rizzo and others to try their hands at redistilling. They apparently did not have Sottile's chemical expertise or access to his raw materials.[5]

Less than one week after Rizzo's gangland murder, people in the region began to die of wood alcohol poisoning.

Twenty-one-year-old Mary Gilman of 46 Race Street was the first Buffalo resident to die. Her painful death occurred July 21. Relatives insisted that Gilman fell victim to a sort of indigestion. Though no autopsy was conducted, Medical Examiner Charles E. Long declared he was certain that wood alcohol was the cause of her death.

By July 25, almost twenty deaths in the Buffalo area and adjoining Canada were blamed on the consumption of wood alcohol. In addition, two alcohol-related blindings were reported by Buffalo hospitals.[6] The victims suffered terribly as death approached – they typically became violently ill, experienced severe abdominal pain and seizures, and lost their eyesight.

One Canadian victim, Joseph Cusick, the married father of four children, was rushed to Hamilton General Hospital. He was blind and in physical agony when he arrived. Doctors spotted the signs of alcohol poisoning and informed his family that he would not live through the night.

Mrs. Forman, a Hamilton woman who had previously been in trouble with the law over the sale of liquor, died a short time after drinking some of the poison alcohol and seemed to have transmitted toxins through her breast milk to her four-month-old baby. The baby was brought to General Hospital in critical condition.[7]

By July 28, authorities had attributed as many as thirty-nine deaths to the consumption of poison alcohol.[8] The number quickly climbed over 40.[9]

Authorities managed to track the poison alcohol to a saloon in Buffalo's northern Black Rock section. Police arrested the saloon owner, Polish immigrant Joseph Sucharski of Hertel Avenue and his New York-born wife Carrie. Both were charged with homicide.[10]

Joseph Sucharski, who seemed to be ill from drinking his own liquor, told police he had purchased five gallons of alcohol three weeks earlier from a bootlegger he knew by the name of "Patsy." Carrie Sucharski also confessed to making a recent low-cost liquor purchase. She said she bought a shipment from a man named "Sam." She provided a physical description of the man. With the couple in custody, their three young children were removed from the family home by the Children's Aid Society.[11]

Police quickly arrested twenty-four-year-old Polish-American bootlegger Joseph "Patsy" Banas of Amherst Street. Banas was a small-time operator and authorities doubted he could have produced the deadly liquor.

Detective Chief Austin Roche directed his men to round up every bootlegger in the city in the hope that the original source of the contaminated booze could be located.[12] U.S. federal authorities became involved in the investigation. They gathered samples of alcohol seized from local saloons and the homes of the poisoning victims and tested them for the presence of toxic substances. By noting the components of the beverages, the authorities hoped to learn if one or more batches of liquor caused the recent deaths.[13]

At about the same time, five people were arrested in Canada. The suspects were William Maybee, his wife, their two sons and bootlegger Bert D'Angelo.[14] When arrested, William Maybee was showing signs of alcohol poisoning. He died immediately after the arrests.[15]

Thirty-one-year-old D'Angelo ostensibly worked as a Hamilton fruit peddler, but authorities knew him as a low-level alcohol retailer in the Rocco Perri organization. While police gathered evidence, D'Angelo was held on a vagrancy charge.[16] The charge was later changed to manslaughter. D'Angelo was imprisoned temporarily at Oakville, pending an August 2 preliminary hearing.[17]

Back in Buffalo, Joseph Banas attempted to aid the investigation and to clear himself of a homicide charge by issuing a detailed statement to the police:

> On Sunday, July 18, 1926, at three o'clock in the afternoon, James Voelker, 659 Amherst Street, called me up on the telephone and told me he had some "stuff" coming in from Germany. I knew by "stuff" he meant alcohol. I asked him if it was "A-1 stuff." He said he would not handle any junk, nothing but the best. I told him to ship me two drums Monday, July 19. These drums each contain 120 gallons, 240 gallons in all. The "stuff" arrived at my house at eight-thirty o'clock Monday morning. I was in bed. It was delivered to my garage in the rear of 386 Amherst Street. I left it go until Wednesday. I opened one of the drums Wednesday afternoon and put some of the alcohol in a water glass. I added some water and took a drink. I immediately found it unfit. I went up to Voelker and asked him what kind of stuff he had sent me. I mentioned the awful odor. He told me foreign alcohol had just such an odor. I came back to my place, took some more of the stuff and cut it with hot water. It was just as bad and I knew it was unfit for anybody to drink. I went back to Voelker and told him I wanted to return all the "stuff" and get my money back. Then he said to bring it back and he would give me my money back. I asked him if he wanted it back in the drums or cans. He said he wanted it in cans. I sent it back. Then one of his helpers came and took away the two drums. I never sold any of that batch to anybody.[18]

James C. Voelker was not entirely unknown to dry agents. He was indicted in 1922 by a federal grand jury in Canandaigua, New York, on a charge of conspiring to violate the National Prohibition Act. He was linked with a group that stole a quarter of a million dollars' worth of contraband liquor from railroad freight cars at the New York Central terminal. Twenty-five men were named as defendants in the case. Voelker never went to trial. U.S. Attorney General John G. Sargent decided not to prosecute him.[19]

As the authorities went in search of Voelker, acting Buffalo Police Chief John S. Marnon ordered closed every soft drink establishment in the Black Rock section of the city and directed that a patrolman be placed at the door of each one to see that his order was carried out.[20]

Voelker was tracked to New York City. Police there learned that he checked out of his rooms at the Pennsylvania Hotel on the morning of July 26. They expected they would soon catch up with him.

In Buffalo, Voelker's home was raided. Authorities found two cans containing white sticks of a chalklike substance in a garage at the rear of the property. Government chemists determined that the sticks were part of a chemical treatment for removing poisons from wood alcohol. They noted that expert chemists would be needed to oversee such a process.[21]

On the evening of the twenty-sixth, Buffalo police arrested James Mucha of Kensington Avenue. They found nearly one hundred gallons of alcohol in Mucha's garage and believed that all of it had been purchased from Voelker.

The same day, Prohibition agents raided a facility they called a "whiskey-cutting" plant above a saloon at 434 Connecticut Street. There they discovered stills and other equipment in addition to thirty-six bottles of synthetic gin, twenty-four two-ounce bottles of whiskey, ten quarts of moonshine liquor, five gallons of wine and a quart of brandy. They arrested two men, Donald B. McCall and Edward Henner, as the operators of the plant.[22]

— — —

James Voelker walked into Buffalo police headquarters July 27 in the company of his attorney and Detective Sergeant Charles Glor. Hearing he was wanted in connection with the poison alcohol case, Voelker had returned from New York City and surrendered himself to Glor.

The suspect was questioned by Roche for an hour. He was then photographed and fingerprinted and taken to a meeting with

District Attorney Guy Moore. Moore later sat down with local Prohibition Chief Leo Regan, U.S. Attorney Richard Templeton and Roche to review the evidence against Voelker. At the conclusion of the meeting, Moore announced, "I am satisfied this is a plain case of murder, first degree."

Acknowledging that Voelker probably did not intend to kill anyone, Moore explained that New York's definition of first-degree murder included acts imminently dangerous to others and neglectful of others' lives. Moore said Voelker knowingly distributed the poison liquor with no concern for the harm it would cause.

Moore noted that a number of suspected poisoning victims had not been through autopsies. He said he would order that those bodies be disinterred and thoroughly checked by medical examiners Earl G. Danser and Charles E. Long, in cooperation with poisoning expert Dr. Charles A. Bentz.[23]

Armed with a court order, authorities went to Voelker's Amherst Street home and broke into his safe. Inside they found papers relating to liquor deals. The papers indicated that several of those deals involved Voelker's sixty-year-old father Carl.

A resident of the Black Rock section since his arrival from Germany four decades earlier, Carl Voelker was the longtime manager of the Elmwood Hotel located at the intersection of Elmwood Avenue and Amherst Street. Eight hours after his son's arrest, Carl also was taken into custody.[24]

Four additional men were arrested during raids of two adjacent homes on Thompson Street. Distilleries were found and seized in both buildings. At 62 Thompson Street, dry agents found four large stills in operation. They arrested the four men and seized eight hundred gallons of whiskey mash and one hundred fifty-five gallons of liquor. Next door, they found a still on the second floor. That raid netted more than a thousand gallons of mash and one hundred sixteen gallons of the finished product.

When the arrested men were asked their occupation, two responded frankly, "moonshine makers." One of the men said he had come to the city from Canada specifically for the purpose of "showing these Buffalo boys how to make moonshine."[25]

— — —

On July 29, 1926, U.S. Attorney Templeton announced

ninety federal indictments stemming from the raid on the Niagara Falls Third Ward Political Club and the investigation of the liquor poisonings. The defendants included American and Canadian bootleggers and directors of the Buffalo-based Jopp Drug Company and the Falls Tonic Company of Niagara Falls. The two manufacturing companies, holders of permits to purchase denatured alcohol from U.S. government warehouses, were accused of funneling the alcohol to redistilling operations. According to the authorities, Falls Tonic Company had just two directors, Sottile and Spallino.[26]

Among the more prominent of the accused were two "bootlegging kings": Rocco Perri of Hamilton, Ontario, and Pasquale "Patsy Cronin" Curione of the Niagara Falls suburb of La Salle. Also facing charges were Perri associates John Benjamin "Ben" Kerr, Joe Romeo, Harry Goldstein and Max Wortzman. Goldstein and Wortzman reportedly ran a Jewish alcohol smuggling gang based in Toronto. Romeo was a veteran racketeer in the Perri organization. Ben Kerr was regarded as an expert at transporting contraband across the U.S.-Canada border and became known as "king of the smugglers." Sottile and Spallino also were named in the indictments, as were regional Mafiosi Simone Borruso and Paul Palmeri.[27]

Some of the same individuals faced charges north of the border. Perri was charged there with manslaughter. A number of his underworld associates, including Goldstein, Kerr, Romeo and Wortzman, also were charged.[28] Perri surrendered to Canadian authorities on July 31. Within a week, he also was charged with customs violations.[29]

Little would result from all the arrests and indictments. Most of the defendants never went to trial. Only James Voelker of Buffalo and Bert D'Angelo of Hamilton, Ontario, were convicted of crimes. Both were convicted of manslaughter in their respective countries and sentenced to serve prison terms.[30] Voelker was sentenced to fifteen years. While an inmate at Auburn, he worked as a clerk in the facility's drug room.[31] D'Angelo was sentenced to four years. He appealed the guilty verdict and won a retrial. At his second trial, D'Angelo successfully argued that he had sold alcohol he believed was safe for consumption. He was acquitted of the manslaughter charge and freed.[32]

At the end of January, the customs charges against Rocco Perri were dropped. Perri and his colleagues went right back to work, as if nothing had happened. Events apparently took a toll on Sottile, however. Using an assumed name, he fled to Europe. Though the authorities were alerted to his movements, by that time he reportedly was so thin that he did not at all resemble the description provided to police.[33]

In mid-June of 1927, U.S. Judge John R. Hazel guaranteed that no further prosecutions would occur when he decided that Prohibition agents had improperly obtained the records and membership lists of the regional bootlegging operation by breaking into the safe at the Third Ward Political Club without a warrant. Judge Hazel ordered that the papers be returned to their owners and that their information not be used in any legal proceeding.[34]

Chapter 13

No One Safe

By the middle of the 1920s, ripples of an ongoing struggle within the Mafia of New York City began to be felt across the country and reached the Buffalo region by 1927. The New York conflict began in 1920, as former boss of bosses Giuseppe Morello and his lieutenant Ignazio Lupo returned to the city from Atlanta Federal Prison. After serving more than ten years of his original twenty-five-year counterfeiting sentence, Morello was released on March 18. Parole was granted to Lupo on June 30.[1]

Reigning Mafia boss of bosses Salvatore "Toto" D'Aquila became terribly insecure following the release of his predecessor Morello. A former Morello underling, D'Aquila owed his underworld status to the 1910 counterfeiting convictions that removed Morello's administration from New York.[2]

To combat the new threat to his standing, D'Aquila attempted to incite Morello, Lupo and their supporters into an open rebellion during a Mafia gathering late in 1920. The Morello faction attempted to avoid conflict by leaving the meeting. However, D'Aquila interpreted the move as an unpardonable offense and used it as justification for passing death sentences against twelve Mafiosi. He also decreed that the same severe sentence awaited anyone found to be giving them quarter.[3]

At least one of those condemned men seems not to have been a Morello supporter. Umberto Valente was a skilled gunman, who had previously helped D'Aquila eliminate rivals and project his power from Brooklyn into the hotly contested underworld of Manhattan. Valente was so effective in approaching his targets without their knowledge and in disappearing after a completed "job," that he became known as "*lo Spirito*" - "the Spirit" or "the Ghost."[4]

Born in the Barcellona Pozzo di Gotto section of Messina, Sicily, on August 14, 1891, Valente entered New York City at the age of 19 on July 6, 1910.[5] He quickly went to work for the Mafia's new supreme boss, D'Aquila. Valente was responsible for the D'Aquila-ordered May 23, 1914, murder of East Harlem Mafia chieftain Fortunato "Charles" LoMonte.[6] Based in Manhattan's East Village, Valente grew so powerful within Manhattan that his sponsor D'Aquila eventually considered him dangerous and decided to dispose of him along with the Morello faction.[7]

Following the D'Aquila death sentences, the dozen condemned men went into hiding. D'Aquila's underworld network was extensive and powerful. Over the previous decade, the supreme boss had insisted on the absolute obedience of other crime bosses around the country, had aided his allies into leadership positions and had installed spies into organizations that worried him.[8]

One of D'Aquila's strongest supporters was Cleveland boss Joe Lonardo. Originally from Licata, Sicily, Lonardo traveled to the U.S. as a teenager in February 1901.[9] He settled among his fellow immigrant Licatesi in Cleveland and established a reputation among the young toughs in the area: a few years after his arrival, a knife fight earned him a term in the reformatory.[10] Lonardo's brother Frank quickly joined him in the U.S. Two other brothers Dominick and John crossed the Atlantic by 1912.[11] Backed by D'Aquila and with the support of his brothers, his childhood friend Salvatore "Black Sam" Todaro and the Porrello family, Lonardo became leader of Cleveland's Sicilian underworld. By his thirty-fifth birthday, police had suspected him of involvement in one robbery and two murders, but he had not been prosecuted for those offenses.[12]

The Lonardos established a wholesale grocery business. At the beginning of the Prohibition Era, they managed to monopolize the supply of corn sugar in the region. Because the sugar was a necessary ingredient for moonshining, control of that commodity also meant a measure of control over distilling operations and the alcohol supply.[13]

> Police declare that [Joseph] Lonardo's

> power was such that the operators of bootleg stills were forced to buy their sugar from him. Those that balked, police say, did not stay in the bootleg business. Often lieutenants of Lonardo working under cover caused the rebels to be raided. Others were driven out thru force.[14]

Joseph Lonardo's devotion to D'Aquila went beyond ordinary loyalty almost to the point of worship. Nicola Gentile, a longtime associate of Lonardo, observed, "Lonardo was completely submissive to the personality of the ferocious "Toto" D'Aquila: he admired the ruler to the point of venerating him like a God..."[15]

Philadelphia Mafia boss Salvatore Sabella also was a D'Aquila disciple. Originally from Castellammare del Golfo, Sicily, Sabella was welcomed into D'Aquila's Brooklyn Mafia organization. There he served an apprenticeship under D'Aquila lieutenant Giuseppe Traina before moving to the City of Brotherly Love at the start of the Prohibition Era.[16]

Buffalo boss Stefano Magaddino and senior Buffalo-area Mafioso Angelo Palmeri had strong attachments to D'Aquila. Magaddino was linked to the boss of bosses through their shared underworld interests in Brooklyn and through Magaddino's kinship ties to D'Aquila pupil Sabella.[17]

Palmeri was linked through a close relationship with Lonardo[18] and connections to D'Aquila henchmen Silvio Tagliagambe and Mike LoBosco. Tagliagambe served as best man at the wedding of Palmeri's brother Paolo.[19] LoBosco was godfather to Paolo Palmeri's youngest son Frank.[20] An additional tie between Palmeri and D'Aquila is revealed in pistol permit applications of Erie County, New York. In 1926, D'Aquila used Angelo Palmeri's home address when applying for a pistol permit in Buffalo.[21]

With much of the American Mafia gunning for them, a number of the condemned Mafiosi – including Morello, Lupo and Valente – traveled to Sicily during the summer and fall of 1921. They sought refuge there and attempted to bring Old World Mafia pressure to bear on D'Aquila. One of those making the transatlantic trip in that period was Saverio Pollaccia, another former close associate of D'Aquila who experienced a sudden falling out with the boss of bosses.[22]

While Morello and the others were overseas, Nicola Gentile worked in the U.S. to have another Mafia assembly summoned so the charges against the Morello faction could be reviewed.[23] He was unsuccessful in that effort, but he appears to have found success in patching up the relationship between Valente and D'Aquila. The boss of bosses' differences with Pollaccia also appear to have been resolved at the same time. Valente and Pollaccia returned to New York together on January 18, 1922.[24]

Valente went back to work for the Mafia boss of bosses. D'Aquila agreed to rescind the death sentence against him if he would eliminate the rapidly growing threat posed by new Manhattan Mafia boss Giuseppe Masseria.[25]

— — —

Giuseppe Masseria was born January 17, 1886,[26] to parents Giuseppe and Vita Marceca Masseria in the small town of Menfi, Sicily. He, his parents and his siblings sailed across the Atlantic between 1899 and 1904. He reached New York as a teenager in 1902. The family's first residence seems to have been in the Little Sicily neighborhood of Manhattan's Elizabeth Street.[27]

While Masseria held a legitimate job as a tailor,[28] he moonlighted as a criminal. He was convicted of burglary on February 25, 1907. Just twenty years old with no other criminal record, he received a suspended sentence. He was arrested again in mid-April on a charge of attempted extortion. Evidence was insufficient, and Masseria was discharged.[29]

The following year, Masseria married. He and his wife Marie moved into an apartment with Masseria's family at 213 Forsyth Street. Though just a few city blocks from Elizabeth Street, the new neighborhood was culturally very different. Most residents were Eastern European Jewish immigrants.[30]

Married life agreed with Masseria, and he began packing extra pounds onto his five-foot-three-inch frame.[31] In November of 1908, the young couple had a son and named him Joseph. A second son was born in the summer of 1910, and a daughter followed two years later.[32]

Masseria's 1907 brushes with the law did not deter him from criminal activity. In June 1913, just as his daughter was born, he was convicted of the April attempted burglary of John E. Simpson's pawnshop at 164 Bowery.[33]

Pawnshops owned by the Simpson family had become institutions within New York City, and robbing them had become a tradition within the New York underworld. The very first pawnshop in the city was opened in 1822 by English immigrant Walter Stevenson, an uncle of later pawnbrokers J.B. and William Simpson. By the 1830s, the Simpsons were opening shops of their own. Future generations followed suit. The Bowery on Manhattan's Lower East Side became the favorite location for Simpson family pawnbrokers.[34]

The John E. Simpson establishment was by no means the most conspicuous of the family pawnshops, but for Masseria and his small gang of burglars, it was a convenient target. Sandwiched between the rear of the three-story Bowery shop and a structure at 148 Elizabeth Street was a narrow space, about five feet deep by twenty feet wide. That small area was shielded from the view of pedestrians by deeper buildings on either side of the pawnshop.

In the early morning of April 13, 1913, an unknown person alerted a local patrolman that an attempt was being made to break into Simpson's. By the time the patrolman reached the building, the would-be burglars had fled. Additional police from the Mulberry Street station were called out. They found a swinging scaffold hanging from the roof of the building and a man-sized hole cut into the rear wall. A number of burglars' tools – including saws, crowbars and hammers – were found on the scaffold and inside the pawnshop.[35]

It appeared that those who cut the hole in the wall were familiar with the structure. On the inside of the rear wall were two large steam radiators. Though the location of the radiators could not be seen from the outside, the hole seemed to have been carefully placed between those obstacles.

A search of the neighborhood was conducted. Four Italian men were quickly arrested in a tenement at 150 Elizabeth Street. Giuseppe Masseria, Salvatore Ruffino and his brother Giuseppe Ruffino were picked up as they stepped out of the building.[36] They could not explain their presence in the house. Masseria lived on Forsyth Street at the time, and the Ruffinos were residents of Brooklyn. Pietro Lagattuta was arrested in a three-room apartment at the rear of the Elizabeth Street building. He also was obviously out of place. His known address was 96 East

Houston Street.[37]

Under a mattress within the Elizabeth Street apartment, police found a loaded .38-caliber handgun.[38] Returning the next day, they ventured into the building's basement. Inside a coal bin, they discovered a hidden cache of tools valued at four hundred dollars. There were pipe cutters, chisels, rope, hacksaws, a motorized drill and two loaded pistols. Detectives traced many of the tools to purchases recently made from the Hammacher, Schlemmer & Company hardware store at Thirteenth Street and Fourth Avenue.[39] The investigators said it was the finest and most complete set of burglars' tools they had ever seen.

Police officials attempted to link the four arrested men to a series of twelve burglaries that dated back to the theft of fifty dollars from the Walkover Shoe Company on Bowery Street in January 1912. The most recent of those crimes – just one month before the attempted robbery of Simpson's pawnshop – resulted in estimated losses of between five thousand and seven thousand dollars from the Herman Shapiro pawnshop.[40] The authorities also suggested that Masseria had been involved in Black Hand extortion activities and possibly the 1910 kidnapping of young Michael Scimeca from his home on Prince Street.

In the end, Masseria was convicted only of the attempted burglary of Simpson's pawnshop. He was sentenced to four and a half years in state prison.[41]

Masseria earned an early release. By June of 1917, he and his wife and their three children lived at 136 East Houston Street. Masseria was employed by the Independent Ice Company of 239 Elizabeth Street.[42] Much of the ice business within New York City was a monopolistic racket run by local Mafiosi in concert with the Tammany Hall political machine. If Masseria's earlier criminal activities had not brought him in contact with underworld organizers, his work for the ice company surely did.[43] The 239 Elizabeth Street address of the company was also the business address of Salvatore Mauro, a Sicilian merchant and underworld figure.[44]

Masseria moved his family to 323 East Sixteenth Street before January of 1920. There he ran a poolroom and became involved in gambling rackets. As the Prohibition Era began and alcoholic beverages became a black market commodity, great wealth came his way. Masseria was in a superior position to capitalize on the thirst of Italian-Americans in the borough and to build a vast criminal enterprise on the foundation of bootlegging profits.

Within Masseria's Lower East Side territory and under the protection of his organization and the police who were on his payroll, younger Mafiosi set up a cooperative exchange for New York-area bootlegging gangs. At the curbside Liquor Exchange, gangs could negotiate mutually beneficial swaps of surplus liquor shipments. Those swaps were always brokered by young, well-dressed Italian men, who were paid commissions for their services.[45]

The curbside Liquor Exchange became known to federal Prohibition agents by September 1920 but the floating nature of the market and the complicity of local law enforcement made shutting it down impossible. According to officials, the market was conducted nightly at a randomly selected intersection within a district defined by Canal Street, Mulberry Street, Prince Street and Bowery. Exchange business was often noted at Mulberry and Broome Streets, just a city block from New York Police Headquarters.[46]

In mid-October, federal agents trying to track down the administrators of the Liquor Exchange announced that they had learned that a man known as "Tom" was the leader of the operation. Boyd's men tried without success to locate and arrest "Tom."[47] It seems certain that authorities were searching for "Tommy the Bull" Pennachio, a Masseria lieutenant widely regarded as the organizer of the Liquor Exchange.[48] However, at the time of their search, Pennachio was off in Atlanta Federal Prison, serving a one-year sentence for selling opium.[49]

Late in 1920, Masseria had a serious falling out with his former neighbor, Salvatore Mauro.

Mauro was born August 13, 1864, in Baucina, Sicily.[50] He emigrated to the U.S. early in 1890, settling first in Brooklyn. He was naturalized a citizen in 1898.[51] Within a decade of acquiring his citizenship, Mauro had achieved a measure of success, and was living and working in Manhattan's Little Sicily.[52] Mauro moved to 121 East Houston Street by spring of 1910.[53] Located near the intersection with Chrystie Street, his home was roughly across East Houston from the residence occupied by the Masserias seven years later.[54]

Just before nine o'clock on the morning of December 29, 1920, Mauro was noticeably disturbed as he left his home. Rumors around the neighborhood indicated that he had an angry exchange with a fellow gambler. The other man reportedly threatened to kill Mauro. As Mauro walked southward on Chrystie Street, he looked nervously side to side. He seemed to be carrying a bulky object in the right side pocket of his overcoat. He was just a few feet beyond the entranceway to the tenement at 232 Chrystie Street when a stocky gunman ran out of the building. Within two feet of Mauro, the gunman drew a pistol and shot Mauro through the back.

Several men standing nearby moved to disarm or capture the gunman, but a threatening wave of the pistol allowed him time to escape through the entrance of 230 Chrystie Street. Observers believed he passed through that building and its backyard to Allen Street.[55]

Police surmised that Masseria was the stocky gunman who took Mauro's life. Masseria was arrested and charged with murder. He was not brought to trial. Witnesses to the shooting became suddenly forgetful, and Masseria was later discharged.[56]

At that moment, Masseria became known locally as "the boss." With Mauro out of the way, Masseria became the single most influential and most feared Mafioso on Manhattan's Lower East Side.[57]

— — —

On the morning of May 8, 1922, restaurateur and bootlegger Vincent Terranova was shot down at 116th Street and Second Avenue in Manhattan's East Harlem neighborhood. Terranova, the half-brother of former boss of bosses Giuseppe Morello, was walking near his home when he was approached by an automobile. Several gunmen within the vehicle opened fire. Wounded, Terranova dropped to one knee on the sidewalk and drew a revolver. He shot several times in the direction of the automobile as it sped away.

When police arrived, Terranova was dead of gunshot wounds. He had thrown his revolver far into the street, in an apparent effort to avoid a repeat of an earlier gun possession arrest. The authorities were unable to identify Terranova's killers, but they believed the murder was the result of a feud that predated Prohibition.[58]

Late in the afternoon of the same day, a gunfight erupted on Grand and Mulberry Streets, one block east of Police Headquarters. Two rival bootlegging bands exchanged sixty shots on the crowded street. Of the six people struck by the flying lead, only one, D'Aquila subordinate Silvio Tagliagambe, seemed to have been deliberately targeted. The other five victims, including two young women, appeared to have been innocent bystanders.

Nearby police officers pursued two of the gunmen. One disappeared into the hallway of a tenement house at 173 Mulberry Street. The other tossed away a .38-caliber pistol and ran north along Mulberry. He also might have escaped in the rush-hour crowd, but a police car pulled directly into his path at Kenmare Street. The exhausted and staggering gunman was arrested by Detective Sergeants Edward Tracey and Joseph Coonan. He later was identified as Giuseppe Masseria.

Though Masseria was an ex-convict, he was found to be in possession of an unlimited pistol permit issued by Justice Selah B. Strong of the Supreme Court of Suffolk County, New York. Authorities could not explain the permit. Justice Strong had no recollection of issuing it. Masseria added to the mystery by denying he had ever been in Suffolk County.

Witnesses told police that three well-dressed Italian-looking men were seen loitering in front of a cheese shop at 194 Grand Street just before the shooting began. At five-forty-five in the afternoon, two other men – believed to be Tagliagambe and Umberto Valente[59] – walked out onto Grand Street from Mulberry. When the pair was still two doors from the cheese shop, the three loitering men drew pistols and fired. With hundreds of frightened pedestrians on the block, the situation became chaotic.[60]

Tagliagambe, a 28-year-old clothing presser who lived with his wife and young son at 60 Fourth Street,[61] initially was not counted among the casualties of the gunfight. He arrived at Bellevue Hospital by ambulance at eight that evening. Seriously wounded by two bullets, Tagliagambe told police he was shot in the street battle two hours earlier. Doctors rushed him into surgery but could not save his life.[62]

Masseria refused to make any statement concerning the gunfight on Grand Street. He was charged with the murder of Tagliagambe and was released on bail of $15,000. Three months after the Terranova and Tagliagambe murders, Joe the Boss was attacked as he strolled from his new home at 80 Second Avenue, between Fourth and Fifth Streets.

Witnesses noted a blue Hudson touring car driving up Second Avenue at just before one in the afternoon on August 8. The car stopped at Fifth Street in front of the Finkelstein Brothers butcher shop. Umberto Valente and a companion stepped out and walked to a restaurant on Second Avenue, across the street from the three-story brownstone where Masseria lived. The men positioned themselves at the front of the restaurant, looking out onto Second Avenue.

They were still inside the restaurant an hour later, when Masseria emerged from his house alone, climbed down the front steps and turned north onto Second Avenue.

The two men immediately rushed from the restaurant, Valente drawing an automatic pistol. Masseria spotted them and turned to flee. He considered escaping into the Mathilda Millinery Company, then moved back toward his house, decided it was too far off, and ducked into the Heiney Brothers women's wear shop at 82 Second Avenue. Valente followed him into the shop, cornered him and fired at him several times. Displaying great agility, Joe the Boss managed to dodge each of the shots. One of the store owners later described the scene for reporters:

> The man with the revolver came close to the other fellow and aimed. Just as he fired the man jumped to one side. The bullet smashed into the window of my store. Then the man fired again and this time the man being shot at ducked his head forward. Again the man fired and again his target ducked his head down. The third shot made a second hole in my window.[63]

Valente gave up and ran out of the store, rejoining his companion on the street and getting back into the Hudson car. As the men attempted to make their escape, a large number of striking cloak makers emerged from a union meeting at Beethoven Hall nearby. Their presence on the street held up traffic. To clear the route, one of the Hudson's passengers stepped out onto the car's running board and shot at the ground in the direction of the strikers. The sound of the gunfire scattered the crowd. Several in the group were hit by shrapnel, one of those later died of his injuries. Two were injured as they were trampled by their fellows.

Police arrived to see the car driving northeast on Second Avenue. They pursued, as the car turned west onto Fourteenth Street and then north onto Fourth Avenue. They lost sight of the Hudson about a mile away near the intersection of Madison Avenue and Thirty-First Street.

Masseria quickly returned home. Police later found him there, sitting on the edge of his bed, wearing a straw hat punctured by a bullet hole.[64]

Just two days later, an apparently delighted Umberto Valente was seen walking with five or six companions at Twelfth Street and Second Avenue. The men chatted in a friendly manner at the southwest corner of the intersection. Valente suddenly took fright and ran from the other men, who drew handguns and fired in his direction.

Valente drew a revolver as he darted into the street toward the northeast. One of his attackers followed him into the street, took careful aim and emptied his revolver at Valente. "The Spirit" managed to leap onto the running board of a taxi driven by Samuel Zuckenberg before the effect of a gunshot wound beneath his heart brought him to the ground. Valente's assassins ran off in different directions.

Detective William D. Kirk heard the gunshots from two blocks away and sprinted to the scene. He found Valente unconscious and two bystanders, including an eleven-year-old girl, wounded. Valente was taken to St. Mark's Hospital, where police hoped he would regain consciousness and make a statement. Valente died within an hour.[65]

Police assumed Masseria was responsible for the shooting. When they went to his home, Joe the Boss said he had not left the house since his close call two days earlier. He was at a loss to explain how he had acquired a brand new straw hat.[66] Masseria was arrested and charged with the Valente murder.[67] Also charged in the case was Joseph Biondo, an aide to Masseria lieutenant Salvatore "Charlie Luciano" Lucania. The charges were eventually dismissed.[68]

— — —

Without Valente to champion D'Aquila's interests in Manhattan, the boss of bosses was no longer able to challenge Masseria. The D'Aquila-Masseria conflict within New York was suspended.

Joe the Boss increased his power and extended his reach through unconventional alliances. Neapolitan gangsters from Little Italy and the West Side, who had been excluded from traditional Mafia crime families, were welcomed into the Masseria organization. In this way, West Side Neapolitan gang boss Vito Genovese became a powerful Masseria lieutenant.[69]

Masseria forged an alliance across the East River with Brooklyn Calabrian gang boss Frankie Yale. Strengthening the bond between the organizations of Masseria and Yale was a close personal friendship between Masseria and Yale's right-hand man, racketeer and prizefighter Anthony Carfano, also known as Little Augie Pisano.[70]

In this period, Masseria also formed a relationship with another longtime Yale friend, Alphonse Capone of Chicago. In the mid-1920s, Capone was formally welcomed as a vassal to Joe the Boss. Masseria appointed Capone a *capodecina* – leader of ten – and allowed him to select ten Mafia soldiers from the Masseria organization to bolster his Chicago operations.[71] The Masseria-Capone relationship upset the balance of power in the Chicago underworld, as existing Sicilian Mafia bosses found themselves in direct competition with a powerful New York organization.

Masseria's presence also was felt in Cleveland, where much of his family resided and where his brother participated in Mafia rackets.[72] Joe the Boss worked to undermine D'Aquila disciple Joe Lonardo by supporting the ambitions of "Black Sam" Todaro and the Porrello family.[73]

A major underworld power in the Bath Beach-Bensonhurst area of Brooklyn for many years, D'Aquila abandoned the region by 1925-26.[74] He moved his wife and children into a newly constructed two-family home at 2295 Southern Boulevard near Grote Street in the Bronx, New York. The building sat behind some roadside trees in a residential section roughly across the street from the Southern Boulevard entrance gate to the Bronx Zoo.[75] While remote from the old D'Aquila territory in Brooklyn,[76] the location was quite close to a vibrant Italian community in the west Bronx.

D'Aquila's power in the New York underworld was probably nearing its end at the time of his move. However, the boss of bosses continued to have great influence through his national network of supporters and spies. Friction continued between the D'Aquila and Masseria camps. Across the country, numerous Mafiosi – even top-level bosses – lost their lives to the violent rivalry.

— — —

A factional struggle occurred in Chicago, as Masseria support for gang boss Capone caused a deep and violent division in the Italian underworld. Largely a bystander to the war between Mafia forces under the Genna family and the Irish and Polish gangsters of the North Side, Capone was the primary beneficiary of the murders of local D'Aquila-aligned Mafia leaders Angelo, Mike and Tony Genna in the spring and early summer of 1925.[77]

Orazio Tropea's February 1926 murder also appeared to be a loss for D'Aquila and a gain for Masseria-sponsored Capone. The remaining members of the Genna clan fled from Chicago as the Aiello family of Utica, New York, moved in and became Capone's new nemesis.[78]

The community believed Joseph Aiello was responsible when Antonio Lombardo, leader in the Chicago-based Unione Siciliana[79] and adviser to Capone, was murdered on September 8, 1928. Aiello and Lombardo had been partners in a wholesale grocery business but a quarrel had turned them to enemies.[80]

Walking along a crowded Madison Street in the middle of the afternoon, Lombardo was shot twice in the head, just behind his left ear. He died instantly. His bodyguard Tony "the Pelican" Ferrara, was shot twice in the back and died later at Bridewell Hospital.

A second Lombardo companion, Joseph Lolordo, apparently was not targeted in the attack.[81] The police and the press were certain that Lolordo, like Ferrara, worked as a Lombardo bodyguard.[82] The fact that Lolordo was spared led the authorities to speculate that he was a conspirator in the murders.[83]

— — —

In Cleveland, boss Joe Lonardo made an aggressive move against a potential rival in the middle of 1926. He issued a death sentence against his business partner and fellow Licata countryman. Lonardo ordered his lieutenant Lorenzo Lupo to execute Salvatore Todaro. The order was an apparent overreaction to reports that Todaro mistreated a Jewish Lonardo employee while Lonardo was vacationing in Sicily. Nicola Gentile, a friend of both Lonardo and Todaro, mediated the dispute and convinced Lonardo to revoke the death sentence.[84]

The temporary truce between Lonardo and Todaro did not prevent bloodshed on Cleveland streets.

In the early morning hours of February 20, 1927, Biagio DePalma was shot gunned to death outside his Scoville Avenue home. After he fell to the ground, his attackers stood over him and emptied their weapons into his body. Police believed DePalma was murdered because he had provided information to authorities about local liquor dealers. Two months later, Sam Nobile, was shot to death at a garage on Ensign Avenue. It appeared he was killed as he attempted to steal a quantity of corn liquor from the premises.[85]

Lorenzo Lupo, Lonardo's lieutenant and a cousin of Joseph DiCarlo[86], made headlines in Cleveland in August 1927. Lupo turned himself in to police on August 15 and admitted fatally shooting former Deputy Sheriff Ralph H. Meyer at the city's White Rock Inn three days earlier. Authorities believed the two men were competitors in the slot machine racket, but Lupo denied any involvement with the gambling devices. He claimed that his only business was managing and promoting prizefighters.[87]

Lupo insisted that he did not know Meyer and that Meyer attacked him without provocation, striking him from behind and knocking him to the ground. He said he drew his own revolver merely to frighten his assailant. "I had no intention of shooting [Meyer]," Lupo said, "but it appeared he walked right into the path of the bullet. I had no intention of even wounding him."[88] Lupo was charged with second-degree murder and released on bail of $20,000.[89]

While awaiting a hearing on the charge, Lupo found himself the victim of a shooting. On September 9, he and his bodyguard, Mayfield Road gangster Albert "Chuck" Polizzi,[90] were getting into an automobile in front of Lupo's Cedar Road home, when they were fired upon by gunmen in another car. Lupo was seriously wounded. He lost his right eye and needed one thousand dollars' worth of plastic surgery to repair his nose. Polizzi suffered a neck wound.[91]

The second-degree murder charge against Lupo was considered by Justice of the Peace Stephen Vamos on October 4. The defendant was still badly scarred by his recent gunshot wounds.[92] Vamos decided that the shooting of Ralph Meyer was done entirely in self-defense and freed Lupo. County Prosecutor Edward Stanton announced that the case was not over. He pledged to seek an indictment against Lupo from a county grand jury.[93] The grand jury completed its investigation on October 11 and voted unanimously against indicting Lupo for murder.[94]

Two gangsters from the East attempted to move in on Cleveland vice, gambling and bootlegging rackets that fall. Jack Brownstein had been a minor hoodlum in Philadelphia. Ernest J. Yorkell formerly performed as circus strongman "Young Hercules." The two men, who had moved through Chicago, Detroit and Buffalo, began pushing around minor Cleveland racketeers. Their reign of terror ended quickly. Just after midnight on October 8, 1927, their remains were discovered by a milkman on his way to work. With hands and feet bound with clothesline, the two men had been shot numerous times, and their bodies were dumped near East Boulevard.[95]

Lonardo's top gunmen Charles Colletti and Lorenzo Lupo were jailed as suspects in the Brownstein and Yorkell killings.[96]

While Colletti and Lupo were behind bars, the Lonardo-Todaro feud erupted once again. With support from Masseria in New York, "Black Sam" ordered the murders of Joe and John Lonardo at a Porrello-owned Woodland Avenue barbershop.[97]

Joseph Lonardo received a telephone call at his Shaker Heights home on October 13. He and his brother John were asked to come to Angelo Porrello's barbershop to join the Porrellos in a game of cards. The Lonardos arrived at about eight-fifteen in the evening. As they walked into the shop, Joseph Lonardo was struck by seven bullets and collapsed to the floor. The forty-two-year-old Mafia chieftain died with gunshot wounds to his head, his right side and his left shoulder. Two slugs wounded John Lonardo.[98] He dropped to one knee but was able to rise and pursue his attackers out onto Woodland Avenue. He fell to the sidewalk and died in front of Angelo Caruso's butcher shop.[99]

Angelo Porrello, who stood at the shop entrance greeting the Lonardo brothers at the time of the attack, told police two unknown gunmen were responsible for the murders. He claimed he saw the gunmen shoot from a rear room at the shop while he was welcoming the Lonardos at the front door.[100] Detectives determined that Angelo Porrello's account was not credible. They found powder burns on Joseph Lonardo's head wounds, indicating the bullets were fired by an assailant standing just a few feet away.[101]

As the Lonardos were buried within silver caskets on October 17, the Porrello brothers were arrested. Angelo Porrello was charged with the Lonardos' murder. Bail was set at $20,000. His five brothers – Rosario, James, Joseph, Ottavio and John (another brother, Raimondo, was an inmate at the Dayton Workhouse at the time) – were booked on suspicious person charges. Bail for each was set at $5,000.[102] Police reports indicated that all the Porrello brothers except Angelo, who was in the barbershop, and James, whose whereabouts were unknown, had alibis for the time of the Lonardo murders.[103]

Following the deaths of the Lonardos, Lorenzo Lupo attempted to assume control of the Lonardo corn sugar monopoly and other rackets. Though Lupo reportedly was assisted for a time by Colletti and Polizzi, he had little success. Todaro and the Porrellos won the business of the Lonardos' former clientele.[104]

Lupo's efforts to keep alive the Lonardo Mafia faction ended on May 31, 1928. Late in the afternoon, his dead body was thrown from a yellow roadster as it passed the corner of Orange Avenue and East Twenty-Fifth Street. Five bullets had been fired into his head, one ripping apart his surgically repaired nose.[105] Lupo had just concluded a meeting with Colletti. When interviewed by police, Colletti said he did not know where Lupo was headed after their meeting.[106]

A witness told police he saw Colletti and another man get into a yellow car with Lupo at the corner of Broadway and East Ninth Street on the afternoon of the thirty-first. Police arrested Colletti and John Angersola.[107] Only Colletti, who was known to own a yellow car but would not tell police where it was, was charged with the Lupo murder. When the matter came before a grand jury, the story of the prosecution's only witness changed. He no longer recalled the men getting into a yellow car. The charge against Colletti was reduced to second-degree murder on June 8 and then dropped completely on the twenty-second.[108]

― ― ―

Ripples from the D'Aquila-Masseria conflict reached Buffalo, as a gang led by Vincenzo "Big Jim" Callea and his brother Salvatore "Sam"[109] began competing with the Magaddino organization for a share of bootlegging profits.

Magaddino's Mafia family was aligned with boss of bosses D'Aquila and had been friendly with Joe Lonardo of Cleveland. The Callea brothers – natives of Licata, Sicily, the same hometown as Todaro, the Lonardos and the Porrellos – were backed by the Porrello family of Cleveland, which in turn drew its support from Masseria in New York.[110] The Calleas set up speakeasies and distilleries in Buffalo and Niagara Falls in defiance of the powerful Magaddino.[111]

Magaddino was well settled in the area at that time. He had moved into his new residence on Whitney Avenue in Niagara Falls by 1923. That home was on the same quiet block – between Fifteenth and Seventeenth Streets – as the homes of fellow Castellammarese Mafiosi Paul Palmeri and "Don Simone" Borruso.[112] About 1926, Magaddino established the Falls Bottling Works on Walnut Avenue. While the company's legitimate business was the bottling and distribution of soft drinks, including Prohibition Era Budweiser ginger ale,[113] it likely also figured into Magaddino bootlegging endeavors. Magaddino was joined in the bottling company in 1927 by soft drink and cigar maker Peter Certo.[114]

As the Callea brothers began establishing themselves in the underworld of western New York rackets, Magaddino was out of the country. He traveled to Sicily in February 1927 in the company of Giuseppe DiBenedetto and Giuseppe's nephew Calogero "Charley Buffalo" DiBenedetto.[115] The men were away for a period of about three months. They returned to New York City aboard the *S.S. Presidente Wilson* on May 4.[116]

The leading Castellammarese Mafioso in Buffalo was murdered just before the end of the year. Filippo Mazzara, once considered as a successor to regional Mafia boss Giuseppe DiCarlo, was shot to death December 22.[117]

Mazzara's documented residence in Buffalo dated from 1920, when he moved from Brooklyn. However, he already was familiar with the area by that time. He and Giuseppe DiBenedetto married sisters – Antonina and Rosaria Pampalona – at St. Anthony's Church in Buffalo in August of 1910.[118] Both men were Brooklyn residents at the time but reported West Eagle Street, Buffalo, addresses in their marriage license applications.

Their decision to be married so far from home is unexplained. It might have been influenced by the presence of a growing Castellammarese colony in western New York, by the proximity of honeymoon spot Niagara Falls or by a possible seasonal migration between New York City and Buffalo.

Mazzara moved permanently to Buffalo one year before the anti-Castellammare publicity of the Good Killers case. He roomed at that time with Angelo Puma,[119] before bringing his family to Buffalo from Brooklyn. A Castellammarese immigrant and Canal District saloonkeeper, Puma settled in the region in 1903.

DiBenedetto followed his brother-in-law to western New York in 1921, about the same time as Magaddino's arrival. For a time, the two men shared a two-family home at 418 Front Avenue.[120] By 1925, both Mazzara and DiBenedetto were wealthy men, living in spacious homes in the same Italian neighborhood in Buffalo. Mazzara and his family resided at 203 Porter Avenue. DiBenedetto and his family lived in a newly built home at 710 Seventh Street. Mazzara commanded a Buffalo-based arm of the Magaddino Crime Family, and DiBenedetto was his trusted aide.

On the evening of December 22, 1927, Mazzara was at Joseph Ruffino's LaRu restaurant at 340 Niagara Street, near Virginia Street,[121] when he received a telephone call. After taking the call, Mazzara told his friend Ruffino he had to leave and asked to borrow his Nash automobile. Mazzara's Cadillac was being repaired. Ruffino, released from prison a year earlier after serving time for the intimidation of "Busy Joe" Patitucci, agreed without asking Mazzara his planned destination.

About one hour later, Mazzara was driving northeast along Maryland Street when two other autos – a large touring car and a medium-sized sedan – forced him to the curb about a hundred feet past Cottage Street. A half-dozen gunmen jumped out of the two autos and opened fire. The attack was performed so swiftly that Mazzara had no opportunity to defend himself. The pistol he kept strapped to his waist was not drawn.

A double-barreled shotgun was fired within two feet of the driver's side of the vehicle driven by Mazzara. The blast shattered all of the car's windows, crushed the left side of Mazzara's head and tore off part of the thirty-eight-year-old gang leader's scalp. Mazzara was killed instantly.

The gunmen returned to their cars and sped away. Witnesses did not note the license numbers of the vehicles.[122]

At the time of his murder, authorities were attempting to have Mazzara tried in a Detroit federal court for concealing assets during bankruptcy proceedings of the Detroit-based International Groceries Corporation. He was free on $10,000 bail posted by Angelo Puma.[123]

Buffalo Police immediately connected the Mazzara killing to the recent murders of Joseph and John Lonardo in Cleveland. They concluded that the same gang was responsible.[124] Detective Sergeant Ralph Guastaferro told newspaper reporters he believed that out-of-town gangsters were brought into Buffalo to eliminate Mazzara and that the killers never would be apprehended.[125]

On December 27, hundreds of mourners swarmed the Mazzara home at 203 Porter Avenue to pay their respects. Numerous floral tributes filled three rooms of the home. The most conspicuous display was an eight-foot-tall heart of roses surrounding a life-size photograph of Mazzara. Two large doves adorned the top of the heart. Over the gang leader's casket was draped a floral blanket created from hundreds of white Killarney roses.

Mazzara's Mafia career disqualified him from the usual Mass of Christian Burial celebrated for deceased Roman Catholics.[126] The Reverend Joseph Gambino, pastor of Holy Cross Church in Buffalo since its 1914 founding, refused the church funeral.[127]

William Cullen of the local Elks Lodge conducted a ceremony at the home in advance of a funeral procession to St. Mary's on the Hill Episcopal Church on Vermont and Niagara Streets. The cortege was led by a thirty-piece band and included more than one hundred and fifty cars of mourners. Marchers included members of the *Societa Castellammare del Golfo*, of which Mazzara had been president, and the Elks Lodge. Mazzara's honorary pallbearers were Angelo Puma, Angelo

Perna, Andrew Sciandra, Paul Viola, Sam Viola, Philip Tuanos and Frank Bonventre.[128]

Mazzara's estate was valued at $11,238.58. Of that amount, $2,700 was designated for support of his five minor children. Another $532.51 was paid out for mourning clothes and accessories for Mazzara's grieving widow Antonina. The remainder of the funds went to business creditors, funeral director Joseph Mascari and attorney Philip Catalano.[129]

The brutal murder of Filippo Mazzara prompted the creation of a new "Italian Squad" in the Buffalo Police Department. The squad, composed of Detective Sergeants John Smaldino, Peter Perry, Anthony Marinaccio and Ralph Guastaferro, was assigned with investigating gangland murders in the city's Italian neighborhoods.[130]

A month later, Mazzara henchman and business partner Philip "Phil Manor" Livaccori was shot to death in Erie, Pennsylvania, by unknown gunmen.[131] Livaccori's bullet-riddled remains were found in blood-spattered snow at four-thirty in the morning of January 27, 1928.

Police determined that he had spent some of that early morning with a friend in the Wayne Lunch diner on Twelfth Street between Peach and Sassafras Streets. When he left the eatery, he was shot from close range. Three slugs entered his right chest. Three other slugs struck him in the head. Another hit his left arm. One slug was stopped by Livaccori's pocket watch.[132]

Three gunmen escaped in an automobile bearing a Buffalo license number. The license was traced to a Studebaker owned by Pasquale "Patsy" Corda, a former convicted bank robber[133] and Neapolitan underworld figure with addresses in both Buffalo and Erie. When police questioned Corda, he said he knew nothing of the murder. Corda said he drove his automobile to Erie, Pennsylvania, with Livaccori the day before the murder. When a snowstorm hit the area, he decided to leave the vehicle in Erie and return to Buffalo by train. He arrived in Buffalo about five hours after Livaccori was murdered.[134]

Believing Corda to have been one of the three Livaccori murderers, Pennsylvania officials sought his extradition from Buffalo. Police in Buffalo disputed their theory, noting that Corda had been a loyal part of the same underworld faction as

Livaccori and Mazzara.[135] At a coroner's inquest in Erie, witnesses to the killing became suddenly forgetful. Evidence against Corda was determined to be insufficient to warrant extradition, and the case was dropped.[136]

Police surmised that Livaccori was murdered because he attempted to seize the underworld leadership position vacated by Mazzara's murder. Livaccori had operated a restaurant in Niagara Falls, New York, until about 1918, when he moved to Buffalo. He later became Mazzara's partner in the Roma Café.[137] Early in 1921, Livaccori was convicted of running a Niagara Falls "disorderly house." He was sentenced to serve one year in the Niagara County Jail.[138] During his court appearances, Livaccori was expensively dressed:

> Mannor, slim of build, was dressed in a tight fitting brown overcoat, a dark suit of faultless cut, a silk shirt of attractive design and a neatly tied black four in hand tie. His face was cleanly shaven. His hair was combed back and shone from the application of oil or brilliantine. Mannor's dark eyes and his heavy brows almost met over a sharp aquiline nose. He appeared very composed as he listened to the detective's story.[139]

Known as the "Beau Brummel" of the district, Livaccori drove a sedan of expensive make and late model and was a conspicuous figure in the downtown streets of Niagara Falls. He relocated from the Buffalo area to Erie in the fall of 1927, following an arrest for Prohibition violations. In Erie, he opened the LaSina Restaurant at 15 West Eighth Street.[140]

The Buffalo Elks Lodge made arrangements for Livaccori's funeral and for his burial in an unmarked grave in Erie's Calvary Cemetery.[141]

Hamilton, Ontario, fruit merchant Salvatore Guagliano was killed in March 1928 during a visit to Buffalo.

Guagliano drove a truck to the city's Elk Street Market three times a week to pick up loads of produce for his employer, Joseph Pelletier.[142] At seven o'clock in the evening of March 7, Guagliano parked the truck in a Front Avenue garage and walked along the west side of Front Avenue between Georgia and

Carolina Streets. The neighborhood sidewalks were filled with playing children, as a touring car pulled up to the curb near Guagliano and two men jumped out. Guagliano started to run when he spotted the men. They reentered their car and pursued the fruit merchant, firing handguns as they passed him. Frightened by the gunshots, neighborhood children hurried to their homes.

Police found Guagliano's body beneath a street lamp in front of Albert Bonfiglio's grocery and poultry shop. No witnesses to the killing could be found. Police determined that Guagliano had been shot by .38-caliber and .32-caliber firearms. He had gunshot wounds to his head, neck, chest and abdomen. The authorities concluded that the head and neck wounds caused his instant death.

Investigators discovered a Canadian liquor withdrawal application in one of the victim's pockets. It had been used to withdraw two dozen bottles of ale from a warehouse on February 29.[143] They also learned that Guagliano drove to Buffalo in the company of another Pelletier employee, Richard Licato, and the two men separated after their arrival. Police suspected Guagliano smuggled booze from Canada to Buffalo and returned to Hamilton with produce.[144]

On May 6 and May 7 of 1928, two men related by marriage were murdered in Buffalo's Italian colony. Stanley Lazzi, who worked as a plumber's helper but had three known aliases, was killed May 6 in front of his home at 68 Efner Street. With his wife hospitalized following the birth of the couple's fifth child, Lazzi was caring for their four other children. He stepped outside to call in his son, who was playing on the sidewalk. The boy looked over as two men jumped from a large touring car and fired two shots at his father. The gunmen returned to their automobile and sped away.[145]

The next night, a similar escape vehicle was used after laborer Santo Falsone was shot to death as he, his wife and their daughter walked home from Lazzi's wake. The wives of Lazzi and Falsone were cousins.[146]

Mrs. Falsone noticed a blue touring car trailing them for two blocks as they walked east along Georgia Street. As they passed Mogavero's grocery store, 168 Georgia Street, the car drew up to the curb. Two men, with revolvers in hand, jumped out. They pushed Falsone away from his wife and ten-year-old daughter and fired pistols at him at point-blank range. Mrs. Falsone rushed at the men and managed to knock a revolver from the hand of one of the killers. He retaliated by striking her in the face and knocking her down. The gunmen returned to the car and drove away eastward on Georgia Street.

Police said the killings were related to an underworld feud that dated back to the 1926 shooting of Sam LoVullo.[147]

Falsone's wife Carmela gave police a description of the two men who killed her husband. They were both about thirty-five years old. She estimated that one stood five-feet-eight-inches tall and the other was shorter and thinner. Both wore caps and light gray clothes with no overcoats. "I never heard of my husband saying he had trouble with anyone," she said. "He always stayed home nights. He very seldom went anywhere unless I went with him."[148] Within nine days of providing those details, Carmela Falsone became less cooperative. Investigators concluded that someone advised her to stop talking to police.[149]

On May 12, the funeral of respected Buffalo grocer Frank A. DeFusto drew the attention of the city's Italian residents. DeFusto, a native Calabrian and a Buffalo resident since 1896, had died of natural causes several days earlier at Sisters Hospital. While his six grandsons served as his pallbearers, honorary pallbearers included Thomas J.B. Dyke, Samuel Borruso of Niagara Falls, as well as men from New York, Akron, Cleveland and St. Catharines, Ontario.[150]

— — —

A series of underworld conflicts in Philadelphia also may have been related to the ongoing hostilities between the D'Aquila and Masseria camps. More than twenty murders involving relatively small Italian bootlegging gangs were counted in Philadelphia between 1925 and 1928.[151] The most noteworthy of these occurred as the D'Aquila-supported Sabella Mafia fought off challenges by the Neapolitan Lanzetti gang and the Sicilian Zanghi gang.[152]

While the July 1, 1928, assassination of Masseria partner Frankie Yale on a Brooklyn street[153] looked at first to be a victory for D'Aquila and a setback for Masseria, later evidence suggested that Masseria sanctioned the killing.

Detectives linked Yale's murder to Masseria's Chicago ally

Capone. They learned that three Capone gunmen traveled to New York from Capone's retreat in Miami, Florida, just before the killing. Police also discovered that the formerly friendly relationship between Yale and Capone had deteriorated in recent months.[154]

The elimination of Yale proved to be not at all costly to Masseria's organization, as Joe the Boss already had a stronger relationship with Yale's chief lieutenant Anthony Carfano.[155]

— — —

One final killing directly related to the D'Aquila-Masseria conflict occurred on a Manhattan street corner.

In the summer of 1928, D'Aquila and his wife Marianna developed health problems. They both began treatment for heart conditions by Dr. Daniel Cascio of 211 Avenue A in Manhattan. The nature of the conditions and the treatments are unknown, but their doctor visits became a daily ritual. The family drove into Manhattan every evening at about dusk. D'Aquila's own illness reportedly was cured by fall, but he continued driving his wife to Dr. Cascio.

On October 10, 1928, D'Aquila drove his wife to Dr. Cascio's office as usual. Four of the couple's six children went along for the ride. D'Aquila walked his family upstairs into the doctor's office and then returned to the street to examine the engine of his expensive new automobile.

Louis Realbuto, a druggist at the corner of Avenue A and East Thirteenth Street, reportedly witnessed what happened as the Mafia boss of bosses checked under the hood of his car. Realbuto initially reported that he saw three men walk up to D'Aquila. He watched as the group engaged in conversation for several minutes. The conversation evolved into an argument, Realbuto reported, and then shots were fired.[156] The three men rushed from the area, got into a waiting car and drove off.[157]

When police arrived, D'Aquila was lying dead in a pool of blood beside his automobile.[158] As police investigated the murder, D'Aquila's body was brought inside Realbuto's drugstore. D'Aquila had been shot nine times in his back, his chest, his left eye, his left leg and his groin. Slugs passing through his lung, heart, stomach and other organs caused massive hemorrhage.[159]

When detectives went to question Realbuto, the druggist

denied his earlier remarks. He insisted that he hadn't been in his store at the time of the shooting. He added that his pharmacy clerk also saw nothing of the incident until D'Aquila's lifeless body was brought into the store.[160]

Marianna and the four children were questioned at the Fifth Street Police Station. Marianna insisted that her late husband had been an importer of cheese and olive oil and had never been in trouble with the law. Detectives used his fingerprints to determine that D'Aquila had been arrested in 1906 as a con-man and in 1909 as a suspicious character. Each time he was discharged.[161]

After an autopsy, D'Aquila's body was brought back across the East River. Funeral services were held in downtown Brooklyn on October 15. D'Aquila was buried in St. John's Roman Catholic Cemetery in Queens.[162]

Though Giuseppe Masseria probably had been the most powerful Mafia boss in the United States for several years and had projected his power into underworld organizations across the country, official recognition had eluded him. The death of D'Aquila allowed Masseria to step into the coveted position of boss of bosses.

Giuseppe DiCarlo, Sr.

Jennie DiCarlo

Francesco DiCarlo

Chiesa Maria Santissima di Loreto, Piazza Umberto I, Vallelunga, Sicily.

Elizabeth Street, Manhattan, c. 1900

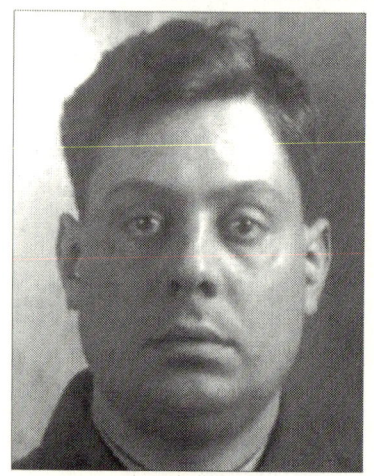

Ignazio Lupo

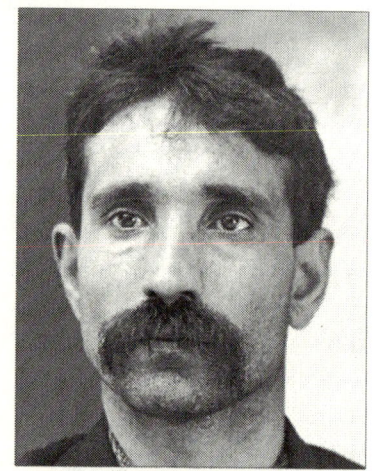

Giuseppe Morello

Isadoro Crocevera

Vito Cascioferro

Joseph DiCarlo, seventh grader at Buffalo Public School No. 2, is photographed (standing at top right) with the school basketball team. "P.S. 2" appears on the cager jerseys. The basketball held by Sam Bongiovanni at the center of the photo indicates the team won a 1915-16 championship. DiCarlo graduated from the school in the spring of 1917. He concluded his academic career the following autumn, after thirty-seven days at Hutchinson Central High School.

Joseph DiCarlo in 1918    Joseph DiCarlo in 1922

Dante Place in Buffalo

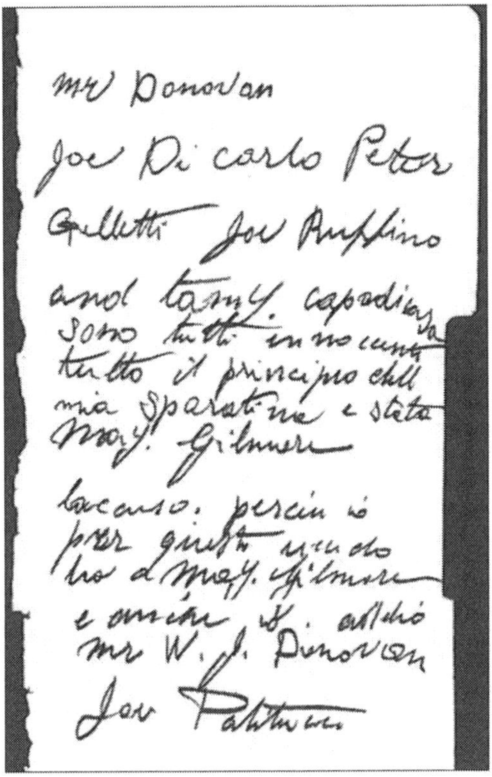

"Busy Joe" Patitucci

"Busy Joe" Patitucci's alleged suicide note (above) attempted to exonerate Joseph DiCarlo (right), Gaetano Capodicaso, Peter Gallelli and Joseph Ruffino (below, left to right) of witness intimidation charges.

1. Bartolo Fontano
2. Stefano Magaddino
3. Francesco Puma
4. Giuseppe Lombardi
5. Vito Bonventre

Photos by INTERNATIONAL.

Arrested in the Good Killers case

Filippo Mazzara

Angelo Palmeri

John Montana

Paul Palmeri

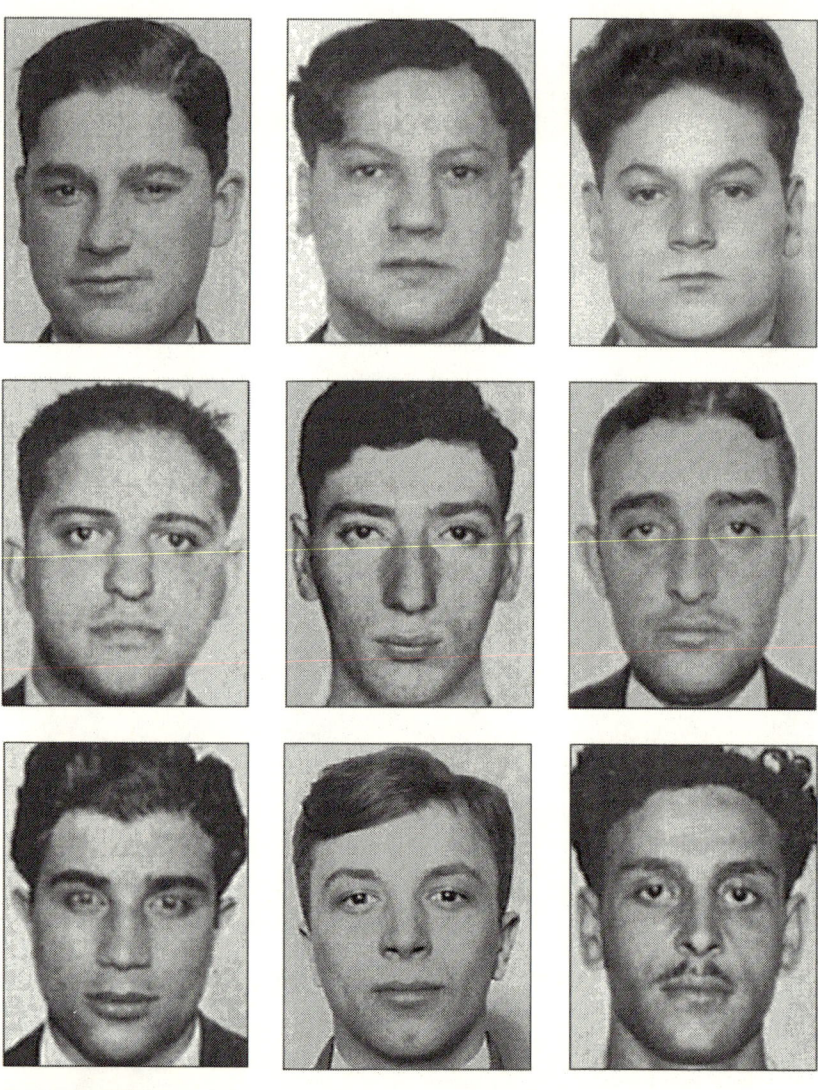

DiCarlo Gang members (by rows, left to right): Joe Pieri, John "Johnny Rai" Pieri, Salvatore "Sam" Pieri, Salvatore "Sam" DiCarlo, John "Peanuts" Tronolone, John Fina, Frederico Randaccio, Pasquale Natarelli, John Cammilleri, Salvatore Coppola.

DiCarlo Gang members (by rows, left to right): John Barbera, Frank DeGoris, Charles Bonasera, Angelo Acquisto, Joseph "Goose" Gatti, Tony "Baby Face" Palmisano, Sam "Shoes" Dolce, William "Billy" LaChiusa, Anthony "Lucky" Perna, Salvatore Bonito.

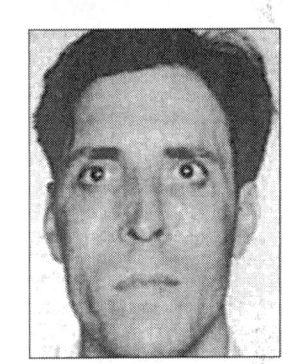

Mafia bosses Giuseppe DiBenedetto (seated) and Stefano Magaddino

Thomas J.B. Dyke (seated far left) celebrates his birthday with friends at his Ritz Café in 1922. Joseph DiCarlo is seen among the guests (seated far right). John Barbera sits beside him.

Joseph Sirianni

Rocco Perri

Rocky Kansas

Minnie Clark

Arnold Rothstein

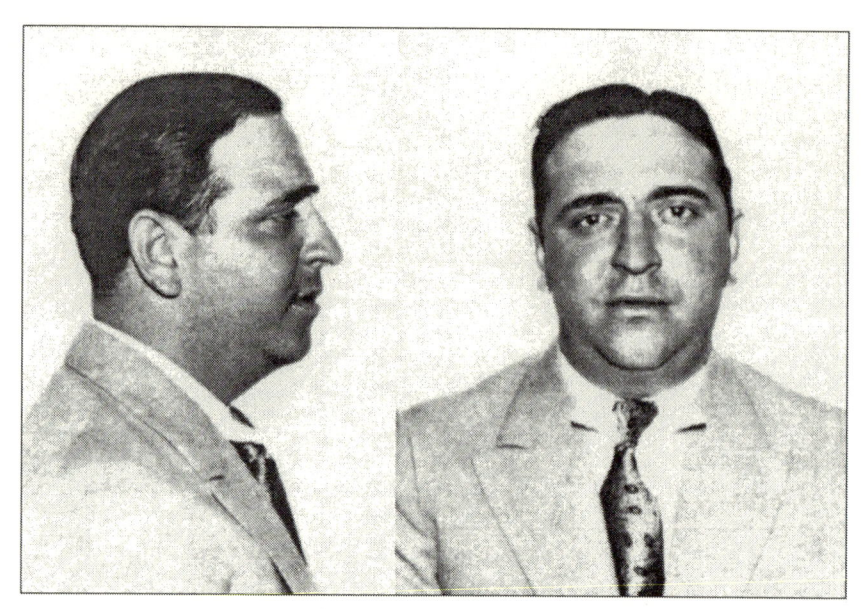

Joseph DiCarlo police mug shots from 1934 (above) and 1936 (below left). In 1937, DiCarlo is photographed with his trademark cigar (below right).

Thank you to Angelo F. Coniglio for the 1916 basketball team photo, to Rose Lombardo for DiCarlo portraits from 1918 and 1922 and the Angelo Palmeri photo, to Sharon Manning for photos of Filippo Mazzara, Stefano Magaddino and Giuseppe DiBenedetto, to Fran Lucca for the photo of John Montana, to Clark Bono for the photo of Minnie Clark. Mugshots of DiCarlo Gang members originated with the *1934 Higgins Pocket Gallery*. Dante Place image appeared in *America's Crossroads* by Michael N. Vogel, Ed Patton and Paul Redding. Other images are from newspaper archives and archives of national, state, county and city government agencies.

Chapter 14

Paroled

While underworld feuds were heating up, Joseph DiCarlo was cooling his heels in federal custody. His stay in Atlanta Federal Prison ended with a transfer on July 23, 1926. DiCarlo was moved from Atlanta to the under-construction United States Industrial Reformatory in Chillicothe, Ohio.[1] The move brought him about six hundred miles closer to his Buffalo home.

The Industrial Reformatory was conceived in 1925 as part of new approach concentrating on vocational training and rehabilitation of first-time federal prisoners between the ages of seventeen and thirty.[2] Assistant Attorney General Mabel Walker Willebrandt explained the philosophy in a 1928 letter:

> The establishment of the reformatory at Chillicothe has made it possible for us to separate the young men first offenders from the old and hardened criminals in the large penitentiaries, which is an important step toward helping them prepare for their successful return to society.[3]

Its first inmates arrived in January of 1926. They were housed in old military barracks at the World War I-era Camp Sherman base and were put to work on the construction of a permanent correctional facility on the site.[4] Construction could not have progressed very far by the time of DiCarlo's arrival.

DiCarlo was received on July 24 as prisoner number 126-C. His presence at the reformatory seems to have been a contradiction of the new criminal justice philosophy. At twenty-six years old, DiCarlo met the age requirement. However, he had already proven himself a habitual criminal, with eight arrests on his record. The transfer to Chillicothe may have been the result of string pulling by influential friends rather than of any official hope of reforming DiCarlo.

Underworld legend suggests that DiCarlo had the run of the institution. According to one story, he was often permitted to venture off prison grounds and once used the warden's automobile to attend a party. Drunk after that affair, he slammed the vehicle into a telephone pole on his way back to the reformatory. Ohio state troopers took charge of DiCarlo and returned him to federal custody.[5]

In February of 1927, DiCarlo's sister Sarah sold the Auto Rest roadhouse.[6] Her purpose for doing so is unclear. Sarah was made a co-owner of the property shortly after it was purchased in spring 1922. When Joseph DiCarlo was jailed on drug charges the following year, she pledged her interest in the roadhouse to help provide his bail. It is possible that she was in need of money by 1927.

It also is possible that the sale was made out of concern that the business might be seized by the government. U.S. District Court Judge John R. Hazel had recently ordered federal marshals to locate assets that could be used to pay the fine that was part of Joseph DiCarlo's witness intimidation sentence. DiCarlo owed $5,000 plus interest. Marshals reported that they could find no assets to pay that amount or any portion of it.[7]

In October of 1928, DiCarlo won parole from the United States Industrial Reformatory[8] and returned to his wife Elsie in Buffalo. Though Joseph and Elsie were a month from celebrating their fourth wedding anniversary, they still were very much like newlyweds. They had spent just four and a half months together between their November 1924 wedding and Joseph's April 1925 imprisonment.

Apparently unreformed, DiCarlo immediately went back into the rackets. He gathered his brother Sam, brothers-in-law John, Joseph and Sam Pieri, and other former associates into a new criminal organization:

> ...He formed what was known as the DiCarlo Gang. This gang engaged in any sort of illegal activity in Buffalo, New York,

that was profitable to them, from bootlegging through the scale of shaking down houses of prostitution, gambling joints and even going so far as to demand cuts from bookmaking establishments and cheap night clubs.[9]

The matter of DiCarlo's fine remained unresolved as he was paroled. At the end of August 1929, with Elsie about five months pregnant with the couple's first child, DiCarlo was sent back to prison. He returned to the Chillicothe facility to serve a term of thirty days for nonpayment of the fine. He was released September 29, 1929, after swearing to a pauper's oath:

I, Joseph J. DiCarlo, do solemnly swear that I have not any property, real or personal, to the amount of twenty dollars, except such as is by law exempt from being taken on civil precept for debt... and that I have no property in any way conveyed or concealed, or in any way disposed of, for my future use of benefit. So help me God.[10]

U.S Commissioner Harry E. Harding accepted the pauper's oath and decided that DiCarlo should be discharged. However, federal prosecutors would not forget DiCarlo's sworn statement and the $5,000 fine. They would pursue payment of the fine for many years.

Elsie gave birth to a daughter at St. Mary's Maternity Hospital on December 19, 1929. Their child was named Vincinetta Sarah DiCarlo in honor of Joseph's late mother.[11]

Chapter 15

Convention

Cleveland Patrolman Joseph Frank Osowski was walking his downtown beat at four-thirty Wednesday morning, December 5, 1928, when he spotted several newcomers to the city chatting with a known member of the local underworld. Osowski watched as the strangers ended their discussion, unloaded heavy leather luggage from a dust-covered automobile and checked in at the Hotel Statler on Euclid Avenue and East Twelfth Street.

After the men went to their rooms, the patrolman quietly looked over the hotel register. He noted that a significant number of out-of-town visitors with Italian-sounding names had checked in over the past two days and were lodging in expensive suites on the hotel's second through sixth floors.

Osowski reported his findings to Cleveland Police Lieutenant Kurt Gloeckner. At ten o'clock, Gloeckner and a few of his men arrived at the Statler to assess the situation. Gloeckner decided to move quickly and to take all the visitors in for questioning. He called Central Police Station for assistance. Seventy-five officers responded. Patrolmen were stationed at the hotel entrances, while Gloeckner and detectives went upstairs.

Using a list they created from the names in the hotel register, the detectives went from room to room, gathering their suspects. The visitors, just returning from a large breakfast, offered no resistance. Twenty-three men were arrested. Eighteen of those were found to be carrying firearms. The suspects were taken downstairs using the Statler's rear elevators. They were then loaded into patrol wagons waiting by the back doors.[1]

At police headquarters, the suspects were booked as suspicious persons, photographed singly and in groups and fingerprinted. A few immediately were linked to the underworld of Chicago. Others were from New York City, Buffalo, Tampa, St. Louis and other cities. It became apparent that the Cleveland Police had stumbled onto a Mafia convention.

While local authorities had little evidence regarding the purpose of the gathering, they jumped to the conclusion that it had something to do with recent gang violence in Cleveland. Factions in the city's underworld had been feuding over control of a corn sugar monopoly.[2] The police were not yet aware that the corn sugar war had concluded more than a year earlier with the murders of sugar baron brothers "Big Joe" and John Lonardo[3] by a Mafia faction commanded by Salvatore "Black Sam" Todaro and Joseph Porrello.[4]

The possibility that the gathering intended to be a coronation of a new Mafia boss of bosses occurred to no one. Cleveland authorities, who knew little or nothing of Giuseppe Masseria, his bloody rise to power or his local connections, never suspected such a thing was possible.

— — —

While the twenty-three suspects were being processed, Detective Captain Emmett Potts learned that additional out-of-town hoodlums were lodging in other sections of the city. Potts and a squad of detectives found and arrested four other suspicious strangers near East 110th Street and Woodland Avenue. On the register of an exclusive local hotel, they found the names of three other men believed to be part of the underworld convention. Those men could not be located.[5]

Captain Potts admitted to the press that there was little chance of holding the suspects on anything more than suspicion, despite the fact that many of them had been carrying concealed weapons. Potts noted that Ohio courts did not permit police officers without warrants to enter residences – even hotel rooms – in order to search for weapons.[6]

The twenty-three men arrested at the Hotel Statler included a number of high-ranking Mafiosi from the East and Midwest. Several were well known to law enforcement at the time of the arrests. Others would become infamous in the years ahead.

The largest group of convention attendees came from Chicago. Two of the better known Chicagoans were Pasqualino "Patsy" Lolordo and Giuseppe "Hop Toad" Giunta.

Lolordo was a top-level underworld diplomat in the Chicago region, a successor to Anthony D'Andrea, Michele Merlo and the recently slain Antonio Lombardo. Lolordo's brother Joseph, who served ineffectively as Lombardo's bodyguard, was widely believed to have been an accomplice in the killing that advanced Lolordo's underworld career.[7] At the time of the Cleveland convention, Lolordo had just one month more to live. He would be shot to death by underworld guests in his North Avenue home on January 8, 1929.[8]

Giunta was also a powerful figure in the Sicilian underworld. He would assume leadership of the criminal society in Chicago after Lolordo's death.[9]

Other Windy City representatives at the Cleveland convention included Frank Alo, Emanuele Cammarata, Sam Oliveri, James Intravia, Tony Bella and Giuseppe Sacco. Local Prohibition enforcement chief G.J. Simon recognized Alo as an employee of a Chicago firm that illegally produced beer. Learning of the arrests, authorities in Chicago checked their records and communicated to Cleveland Police that Lolordo and Cammarata each had been arrested twice and Giunta and Intravia each had a single arrest on their records.[10]

When he was booked, Alo provided the same 1715 Adams Street home address as "Hop Toad" Giunta. That address also was given to police by Paul Palazzola, the lone convention representative from Gary, Indiana, and a leading figure in the underworld of Chicago Heights.[11]

A large contingent from Brooklyn was led by Giuseppe Traina, Vincenzo Mangano, Giuseppe Profaci and Giuseppe Magliocco.

Traina, known to his underworld colleagues as "*lu viddanu*" or "the peasant," had been a top lieutenant under recently murdered American Mafia boss of bosses D'Aquila.[12]

Mangano was a leading Brooklyn waterfront racketeer of the period and the brother of Philip Mangano. He would quickly rise to command one of the largest crime families in the United States.[13]

Profaci, who had recently settled in Brooklyn after spending a few years in the Chicago area,[14] was already in command of a small Mafia organization in southern Brooklyn. Magliocco was Profaci's brother-in-law, trusted underboss and handpicked successor.[15]

Also among those arrested were Brooklyn Mafiosi Salvatore Lombardino and Giuseppe Palermo. New York police turned up arrest records for five of the six Brooklynites. Lombardino was wanted at the time by police back East. He was a suspect in the April 1927 killing of a truck driver in Belleville, New Jersey.[16]

New Jersey was represented at the convention by Michael Russo of Iselin and Andrea Lombardino of Newark. Russo, also known as Michael Valenzano, was frequently in trouble with the law since his 1919 arrests in Buffalo. A native of Cerda, Sicily, Russo was linked with criminal organizations in Buffalo, Cleveland and Pittsburgh before his move to New Jersey. Two of Russo's partners in a regional burglary ring – his brother Salvatore and Frank Ulizzi – were murdered in Cleveland in 1920.[17]

Tampa, Florida, sent two representatives. They were Ignazio Italiano and Giuseppe Vaglica.

Vaglica was born in Monreale, Sicily, arrived in the U.S. through New York's Ellis Island in 1912[18] and spent some time in Chicago. Within a decade of the Cleveland meeting, he met with a violent end. He was killed by shotgun blasts outside his Tampa eatery in July 1937.[19]

Italiano was considered one of the founding bosses of the Mafia in Tampa. A grocer by trade,[20] Italiano was one of the three "old-time heads" (along with Ignazio Antinori and Santo Trafficante Sr.) of a Tampa regional criminal network.[21] Italiano had strong connections to the New York area and to Giuseppe Profaci. Italiano and Profaci's father were acquainted in their native Sicily. In the U.S., Profaci reportedly provided Italiano's grocery with imported olive oil through the Mama Mia Importing Company.[22] Already in his late 60s at the time of his arrest in Cleveland, Italiano had less than two years left to live.[23]

Two attendees, Giovanni Mirabella and Calogero SanFilippo, were from the St. Louis area. Cleveland Police noted vaguely that one of those men had been arrested forty-seven times in his home city in connection with murders, burglaries and extortion plots there.[24]

Salvatore "Sam" DiCarlo was the only known representative of Buffalo's powerful Mafia organization. Brother of Joseph DiCarlo and youngest son of the late crime boss Giuseppe

DiCarlo,[25] Sam became a relatively minor figure in the organization after it was taken over by Stefano Magaddino. Sam's presence at the Cleveland convention could be evidence that Magaddino understood recent changes in the American Mafia and wished to send a representative agreeable to the new national leadership.

The final arrested convention attendee was local hoodlum Sam Tilocco. Tilocco, a Licata native, had been a member of the Lonardo Mafia in Cleveland before breaking away to join the Todaro-Porrello faction. At the time of the convention, he was serving as a bodyguard and top aide to Joseph Porrello.

Immediately following the arrests, Porrello instructed his personal attorney Martin McCormack to represent the suspects. McCormack began his work by badgering Safety Director Edwin D. Barry. The defense attorney correctly noted that the discovered weapons were of no legal consequence. He demanded the release of the suspects. Barry listened for a while before losing his patience and ordering McCormack out of his office.[26]

— — —

Though Patrolman Osowski and the Cleveland Police were initially lauded for breaking up the underworld convention, by Friday, December 7, some criticism was offered.

"I think more could have been gained had the police kept the gunmen under observation," Cleveland City Manager William R. Hopkins told the press. "Then, perhaps, it would have been possible to learn their plans and prevent their fulfillment if illegal."[27]

There was also concern that the quick-moving police failed to arrest all of the convention attendees. According to one report, as many as a dozen other gangsters fled the city after learning of the roundup at the Hotel Statler. Five checked out of a single city hotel moments after the arrests were made.

Evidence suggested that the police action occurred before all expected attendees had even arrived in Cleveland. Police found reservations for suspected gangsters at a residential hotel on the city's East Side. Officers were stationed at the hotel, but the anticipated guests never arrived.[28]

The idea that police acted too hastily was further supported by rumors that Alphonse Capone was spotted in Cleveland two days after the arrests. Attorney Salvatore LoPresti, defense counsel for Salvatore Lombardino, brought the rumors to the press: "Someone who knows told me that Capone came here in an automobile, but left immediately because friends advised him that it would be dangerous to stay."[29]

Despite his revelation of what seemed to be sensitive information, LoPresti eventually replaced McCormack as attorney for most of the suspects.

— — —

Almost immediately and without much explanation, Cleveland Police released Brooklynites Vincenzo Mangano and Giuseppe Traina. Safety Director Barry announced that he was satisfied Mangano and Traina had nothing to do with the other arrested men.[30]

The remaining twenty-one suspects from the Hotel Statler were questioned by police and immigration officials.[31] During police interrogation, the men refused to provide any meaningful information, told conflicting stories to explain their presence in Cleveland and denied even knowing each other. (One of the suspects admitted to being employed as a bootlegger and said he was in the area to rest after a liquor-buying visit to Canada.[32]) When questioned by Immigration Inspector William H. Flynn, the suspects were more cooperative. Flynn said he found no evidence that the arrested men had entered the country illegally.[33]

On Friday, December 7, the suspects were officially arraigned on suspicious person charges. They all pleaded not guilty. Bail for all but one of the prisoners was set at $10,000 – Salvatore Lombardino was held for the New Jersey truck driver murder investigation. Local officials were shocked to learn that, even before the hearing was held, bail in the form of $400,000 worth of residential and business property (twice the cash bail amount of $200,000) had been offered to secure the freedom of the twenty men. Authorities quietly concluded that the local corn sugar barons had arranged for their friends and neighbors to furnish the bonds. All twenty men were released, though they were obligated to remain in the city and to appear for court hearings on the suspicion charges.

City Manager Hopkins was incensed. "It is peculiar that these men, apparently strangers in the city, can come into Cleveland and have bond of such high value produced in so short a time," he said.[34]

Hopkins criticized the municipal court clerk's office for failing to investigate the value of properties put up as bond, and he asked Acting Law Director Alfred Clum to check into the land and business records for the pledged parcels. Clum immediately found a number of problems relating to the worth of the properties and existing liens against them.[35]

Pasqualino Lolordo's bondsman, Luigi Gattozzi of St. Clair Avenue, had pledged several properties, but the net value of the parcels was nowhere near the $20,000 required to serve as his bond. The first property, which had been used to cover other still-active bail bonds, was assessed at more than $15,000. However, it had two mortgages on it that totaled $11,000. A second property, assessed at $12,150, was mortgaged for more than half that amount. A third parcel assessed at $4,100 was mortgaged for $2,000.

A single property pledged by "Hop Toad" Giunta's bondsman, teamster Biagio Consolo of Murray Hill Road, was found to have been mortgaged for a greater amount than the $9,720 assessed value of the property.

Joseph and Mary Porrello, bondsmen for Giuseppe Profaci and Ignazio Italiano, pledged several properties in the area of Woodland Avenue and East 110th Street. One was found to have been used to cover other still-active bonds. All were heavily mortgaged.

Properties pledged by Raimondo Porrello and John and Antoinette Greco for the bond of Sam DiCarlo and Giuseppe Magliocco also had large mortgages. One property assessed at just over $19,000 had been mortgaged twice for a total of $18,000. A second property, which could not be found in the assessment records, had two mortgages totaling $8,000.

Sam Oliveri's bondsmen, Angela and Ernest Bertoni of Mayfield Road, pledged a parcel that could not be located in tax assessor's records. Clum noted that the property was vacant and padlocked due to a liquor traffic assessment. He said it was also mortgaged for $2,000.[36]

Similar problems were noted with the other properties, prompting Hopkins to declare all the bonds "worthless" and to call for the rearrest of the twenty suspects.[37]

Hearings on the bonds were held the following week. Despite the many problems, the bonds for just three of the suspects, Sam DiCarlo, Magliocco and Tony Bello, were ruled inadequate. City Law Director Carl F. Shuler decided there was insufficient unencumbered value in the Porrello and Greco properties to secure the DiCarlo and Magliocco releases. Chief Justice John P. Dempsey of Cleveland Municipal Court cancelled Bello's bond, finding that bondsman Giuseppe Vinciguerra improperly committed property owned solely by his wife.[38]

Deputies from Essex County, New Jersey, arrived in Cleveland on December 14 to take custody of Salvatore Lombardino. Ohio Governor A. Victor Donahey issued the appropriate extradition paperwork, and Lombardino was taken out of the state.[39]

The next day, under the guidance of attorney LoPresti, fifteen of the remaining twenty suspects agreed to plead guilty to the suspicion charge. The other five – Giuseppe Profaci, Ignazio Italiano, Giuseppe Vaglica, Sam Tilocco and Giuseppe Palermo – retained McCormack as counsel and continued to plead not guilty. Municipal Court Judge Charles Selzer accepted the guilty plea of the fifteen LoPresti clients and sentenced them to thirty days in the workhouse and a $50 fine. However, he suspended the sentences on the condition that the fifteen men immediately leave Cleveland and stay out of the city for at least a year.

An unidentified member of the group later indicated he would be glad to observe the judge's condition: "...There's no danger of our coming back before the year is out. We'll never come back if we can help it. We're sick of Cleveland."[40]

Following the December 15 hearing, authorities decided to rearrest Giuseppe Palermo. They had received word that he was wanted in Trapani, Sicily, in connection with the murders of eight people on February 20, 1920.[41]

Giuseppe Profaci's trial on the suspicious person charge began immediately. Profaci walked into the courtroom with the help of a cane. He explained that he had been injured in a steamship accident during a trip to Florida the previous May. He claimed that he had been on his way to Mount Clemens, Michigan, when he was arrested at the Hotel Statler.

Patrolman Frank Osowski was the first prosecution witness. He testified that he initially noticed several of the out-of-town visitors as they stepped from their automobile on the morning of

December 5. "The men looked both ways and pulled their hats down as they entered the hotel," he said. On cross examination, Osowski admitted that Profaci was not among the men he saw acting in that sinister manner.

The charge was difficult to prove. First Profaci and then the other four defendants were found not guilty. Profaci, Italiano, Vaglica and Tilocco were freed.[42] Not satisfied with his courtroom victory, Profaci pressed for more. He successfully petitioned the court to have his mugshot removed from the Cleveland Police files.[43]

Authorities never were able to define the purpose of the 1928 underworld convention. In the end, their list of possible purposes included preparation for a corn sugar gang war,[44] an effort to set up Chicago gang leader Joe Aiello for assassination,[45] a reorganization of rackets in the wake of the murders of Arnold Rothstein in New York[46] and Frankie Yale in Brooklyn,[47] and an assembly to elect a successor to murdered Chicago underworld leader Antonio Lombardo.[48]

However, the timing and the location of the gathering indicate that it was intended to be an official underworld recognition of Giuseppe Masseria's new status as supreme leader of the Sicilian-Italian criminal society in the New World.

Masseria had been the most feared Mafia leader in the New York region for several years, since defeating Umberto Valente, the champion of previous boss of bosses Salvatore D'Aquila, and sending D'Aquila scurrying from his Brooklyn base. However, there had been no recognition of Masseria's status at the national level through October of 1928, when D'Aquila's reign was ended with his murder on a Manhattan street. December was an appropriate time to recognize D'Aquila's successor.

With a Masseria coronation on the agenda, attendance at the Cleveland convention should have been far greater than the twenty-three men rounded up by local police at the Hotel Statler and should have included representatives of other major Mafia organizations across the U.S. At Mafia conventions of national importance in the period, attendees numbered in the hundreds and came from every region.[49] A large majority of convention attendees must have avoided arrest either by finding less noticeable accommodations than the Statler or by scheduling their arrivals after December 5.

Conspicuously absent from the list of those arrested were members of Masseria's own criminal organization. However, Joe the Boss had a number of friends and close relatives living in Cleveland and would not have required hotel accommodations.[50]

The City of Cleveland was the likeliest of all possible locations for a Masseria coronation. Its Midwest location allowed easy access for Mafiosi across the country. Much of his Masseria's family had settled in the city, and allies of the new boss of bosses – "Black Sam" Todaro and the seven Porrello brothers – had recently come to power in the local Mafia. Cleveland essentially had hometown appeal for the new boss while it also served as a symbol of his recent gangland victories.

Chapter 16

War

New Mafia boss of bosses Giuseppe Masseria learned no lessons from the self-serving and meddlesome behaviors that gradually eroded D'Aquila's underworld popularity and ultimately cost the previous boss of bosses both his position and his life. Masseria employed many of his predecessor's oppressive techniques in an effort to secure the loyalty of underworld factions.

At the start of his tenure as supreme Mafia ruler, Masseria installed his close allies Manfredi "Alfred" Mineo and Steve Ferrigno (also known by the names Fanuzzo and Ferraro) as leaders of the old D'Aquila organization.[1] While this secured for him the loyalty of the crime family's leadership, it did little to win the affection of family lieutenants or the rank and file. Many members, including important group leaders Giuseppe Traina, Vincenzo Mangano and Toto Chirico, quietly resented Masseria's imposition.[2]

Bosses of New York's three other Mafia families viewed Masseria with fear and suspicion. "Joe the Boss" solidified his hold on the regional underworld by appointing the revered Giuseppe Morello as his chief counselor.[3] However, many Mafiosi found Masseria's intrusions into the affairs of other crime families disturbing and his liberal policies toward Neapolitans and Calabrians distasteful.

Gaetano Reina, ruler of a Mafia organization in the Bronx, and Giuseppe Profaci, whose crime family operated in Brooklyn and Staten Island, personally disliked "Joe the Boss" but were careful to stay on good terms with him.[4] Brooklyn-based boss Nicola Schiro made every effort to avoid underworld politics.

More of an administrator than a leader, Schiro exhibited a conciliatory nature as he strove to hold together the factions of his criminal organization. The organization included Castellammarese Mafiosi in Brooklyn and Manhattan, who still considered Stefano Magaddino their leader.[5]

In 1929, the new boss of bosses was called upon to mediate the increasingly violent rivalry between the Chicago gangs of Alphonse Capone and Joseph Aiello. "Joe the Boss" made the trip to Chicago and met in the basement of Aiello's home with Aiello, Capone and Gaspare Milazzo (also known by his wife's maiden name Scibilia) of Detroit. A Castellammarese Mafioso, Milazzo had been part of Stefano Magaddino's Brooklyn organization before setting out for Detroit and establishing himself as an effective underworld peacemaker. Milazzo had a close relationship with Aiello and had served as godfather to the Mafia leader's son.

The meeting resolved nothing. Conservative Sicilian Mafia boss Aiello accused upstart Capone of aggressive expansion throughout the region. Masseria promised he would put Capone on a short leash but only if Aiello ceded the racket rights to the east side of Chicago. If Aiello accepted the terms, the boss of bosses offered to recognize him as the Mafia authority over all territory west of Chicago.

That failed to sweeten the deal. The western U.S. of 1929 offered a Mafia boss nothing comparable in value to half of the Windy City.

> Aiello blew up at Joe the Boss and told him to go back to New York before it got unsafe for him in Chicago. The parlay was over. In a dither, the fat man returned to New York and immediately spread the word that Joe Aiello was crazy and that he, Masseria, had narrowly escaped with his life.[6]

Masseria encouraged his vassal Capone into further aggression against Chicago's Sicilian crime family. Aiello, already supported by the Castellammarese Mafia clans of Detroit and Buffalo, entered into an alliance with Chicago's non-Italian North Side gangsters, then led by George "Bugs" Moran.[7]

"Joe the Boss" tried diplomatically to separate Aiello from

his Castellammarese backers. He reached out to Milazzo with an offer similar to the one presented to Aiello. If Milazzo would abandon Aiello, Masseria would allow Milazzo to oversee all Mafia enterprises in the western U.S. Milazzo, who valued principle more highly than power, refused.

The diplomatic failure and the continued Castellammarese support for Aiello enraged Masseria. The boss of bosses summoned Milazzo and Stefano Magaddino, the senior Castellammarese Mafiosi in the country, to appear before him in New York City. Fearing what might result from a face-to-face confrontation with "Joe the Boss" on his home turf, the Castellammarese leaders did not reply.

Masseria ultimately ruled that Milazzo and Magaddino, heads of the Castellammarese underworld network, were guilty of insubordination. Just as D'Aquila had rashly condemned to death the Morello faction, Masseria issued a death sentence against Milazzo, Magaddino and all their Castellammarese followers in the U.S.[8] As in the earlier case of D'Aquila's abuse of power, Masseria's action triggered the rise of a new and powerful rival.

— — —

Born July 31, 1886 into an affluent Castellammare del Golfo family, Salvatore Maranzano[9] was raised under the influence of the Bonventre-Magaddino-Bonanno Mafia. As a young man, he became a fearsome warrior for that organization. His heroic exploits in the long war against the Buccellato clan made him an underworld legend.

Maranzano later moved to Palermo. He was educated at a seminary and became a successful businessman in western Sicily's most important city. He enhanced his stature in the Sicilian Mafia through marriage to Elisabetta Minore, daughter of Trapani underworld chieftain "Don Toto" Minore.[10]

In the mid-1920s, Maranzano crossed the Atlantic. His presence in the Buffalo area is documented. On August 10, 1925, he was granted a pistol permit from Erie County, New York. In the permit application, Maranzano claimed residence at Angelo Palmeri's 295 Jersey Street, Buffalo, address.[11]

Maranzano then was noted in New York City near the end of 1925. The local Castellammarese colony held a large banquet to welcome the man they knew as *"Don Turridru"* to America,[12] and the Schiro Mafia organization formally inducted him as a member. [13] His presence was uplifting to many of the Castellammarese Mafiosi, including Stefano Magaddino's young cousin Joseph Bonanno:

> I felt honored and privileged just to be near him. I suppose it was like falling in love, only it was between men. When I was around Maranzano, I felt more alive, more alert, more called upon to fulfill my potential... He had a sweet voice, not at all gruff or *basso profundo*. His voice had an entrancing quality. When Maranzano used his voice assertively, to give a command, he was the bell knocker and you were the bell.[14]

Maranzano rented an apartment near Fourteenth Street and Second Avenue in Manhattan,[15] but he also established a residence north of the U.S.-Canada border in the area of Hamilton, Ontario. He seems to have participated in bootlegging rackets during this period and perhaps learned some of the tricks of the trade through exposure to Rocco Perri's operation in Canada.

When Maranzano crossed into Canada from Niagara Falls, New York, on February 5, 1926, he informed Canadian immigration authorities that he had never been in Canada before. Yet he indicated that he was the owner of a fifty-acre farm in Saltfleet Township, just east of Hamilton along the Lake Ontario coast.[16]

In spring 1927, Maranzano was joined by his forty-one-year-old wife Elisabetta and four of their children, aged four to thirteen. Elisabetta and the children sailed first class from Palermo to New York City aboard the *S.S. Martha Washington*, arriving in the city on May 19.[17] They then continued by railroad on to Canada, crossing the border at Niagara Falls on May 22. Their destination was Maranzano's home at 21 Mill Street in Hamilton.[18]

At roughly the same time as Elisabetta's arrival, a home at 2706 Avenue J in Brooklyn was purchased in Maranzano's name. The home seems to have been rented for a while by Maranzano's older brother, Giuseppe.[19]

Maranzano very quickly established a legitimate import-export business as well as his own bootlegging operation. He set up whiskey distilleries in Pennsylvania and upstate New York and coordinated his illicit enterprises through headquarters at a farm just outside Wappingers Falls, New York.[20]

Maranzano instantly disliked "Joe the Boss" and his liberal ideas. He privately referred to the supreme Mafia leader as "the Chinese." According to Bonanno, the nickname was due to the rotund Masseria's bloated cheeks, which made his eyes look like narrow slits.[21]

Maranzano's feelings toward Masseria could have been prompted by the boss of bosses' tyrannical nature. However, they also could have been the result of Maranzano's great ambition. The former Castellammarese Mafia warrior aspired to Masseria's position and had little regard for the Americanized Mafia set up by "Joe the Boss."[22]

— — —

The unconventional policies and dictatorial stance of the new boss of bosses prevented a successful reunification of the two major factions in the American Mafia. The old Masseria and D'Aquila networks across the country remained at odds.

The more liberal Masseria faction drew strong support from an alliance of Mafiosi originally from the Sciacca region of Sicily as well as from major Neapolitan and Calabrian criminal organizations. A conservative faction was dominated by a Trapani-based criminal league, by immigrant Castellammarese Mafiosi and by D'Aquila loyalists.[23] While other forces were also at work, friction between the two American Mafia divisions sparked violent outbursts.

In Chicago, the conservative Aiello Mafia targeted the city's top underworld diplomat, Pasqualino Lolordo.

On January 8, 1929, Lolordo spent the early afternoon in downtown Chicago with his wife Lena. The couple returned to their apartment building at 1921 West North Avenue at about two-thirty. They were met at the door by two men. All went up to the Lolordo's third-floor apartment. Lena served lunch for her husband and his guests. The meal concluded at about three o'clock and the two visitors left the apartment. Lena went to the kitchen to do ironing.

After about five minutes, there was a knock on the door. Lena watched from the kitchen as her husband let three men into the living room and then closed the door between that room and the kitchen, his common practice when transacting business at home. For most of an hour, Lena heard the four men talking, drinking and laughing. At four o'clock, she was shaken by the sound of gunshots.[24]

She rushed into the living room, and the three visitors pushed by her and out the door. She found Pasqualino Lolordo lying on the floor, bleeding from gunshot wounds to his head and body.[25] Lena knelt beside the body and placed a velvet pillow beneath her husband's head.

Moments after the shooting, Lena's sister-in-law Anna entered the apartment. Anna pulled Lena from her husband's body and telephoned for the police.

Investigators found a .38-caliber handgun on the second landing of the apartment building's staircase. They found another on the Lolordo's living room floor. A table held three half-filled drinking glasses. A fourth glass was found broken in Lolordo's lifeless hand.[26]

Aware that Lolordo and Capone worked closely together, police suspected the Aiello Mafia Family of involvement in Lolordo's assassination. Rumors had circulated to the effect that Joseph Aiello alerted Cleveland officials to the Hotel Statler meeting two months earlier in an effort to rid Chicago of Lolordo and other Capone allies. Police surmised that Aiello gained access to Lolordo by offering a truce in their underworld war.

When detectives showed Lena Lolordo a photograph of Joseph Aiello, she screamed. The detectives tried to have her positively identify Aiello as one of the men who killed her husband, but Lena refused to answer any questions.[27]

Capone's organization responded to the Lolordo slaying by arranging its own peace conference with top members of the Moran gang on the morning of February 14. At the scheduled time of the meeting, gunmen posing as police officers entered Moran's headquarters in the S.M.C. Carting garage at 2122 North Clark Street. They disarmed the seven men they found in the garage, lined the seven against the wall and opened fire with Thompson submachine guns. Among those murdered were two men who had little or nothing to do with Moran's operations.[28]

That gang leader George "Bugs" Moran had been the primary target of the St. Valentine's Day Massacre appears certain.[29] However, Moran was late getting to the garage that morning, and Capone lookouts across the street probably believed similar looking gangster Albert Weinshank was Moran. Learning of the loss of his underworld colleagues, "Bugs" fled the city. Suspicion focused on Capone and allied gunmen formerly associated with the St. Louis Egan's Rats gang.[30] Capone, however, was out of town. He was vacationing at his home at Palm Island, Florida.[31]

Lolordo's former position in the Chicago underworld was assumed by Giuseppe "Hop Toad" Giunta. Giunta was known to be friendly with Capone. In spring 1929, however, Capone received word that Giunta and Capone's Sicilian underlings John Scalisi and Albert Anselmi were plotting against him.

Giunta, Scalisi and Anselmi reportedly met their ends at an elaborate dinner at the Hawthorne Inn in Cicero, Illinois, on May 7. The bodies of the three men were found inside an automobile the next day. They had been beaten nearly to a pulp and shot.[32]

At that moment, the liberal forces of Chicago's underworld appeared to have the upper hand.

― ― ―

The Castellammarese underworld society in Buffalo suffered a serious loss early in 1929. On February 27, Giuseppe DiBenedetto was assassinated in Vincent Paladino's grocery at 116 Dante Place. DiBenedetto, who had succeeded Filippo Mazzara as the leader of a powerful underworld faction in Buffalo's Italian colony, was conversing with Paladino's brother James at five-thirty in the afternoon, when he was shot six times in the back and once in the stomach.[33]

Mortally wounded, DiBenedetto was transported to Emergency Hospital. On the way, Buffalo Detective Sergeant Ed Kenny asked DiBenedetto if he knew who shot him. The Mafia leader answered, "I know who shot me all right."

"Why don't you tell me?" Kenny asked.

"Oh, that fellow will be taken care of," DiBenedetto responded.[34]

Though James Paladino stood in front of DiBenedetto as the shooting took place, he told police he saw nothing.[35] Mrs. Ida Paladino, who had been cooking in a kitchen behind the grocery, said she recalled seeing two men in blue suits and caps running into the store. The first of the two was screaming, she said. She heard gunshots and saw DiBenedetto fall. Her memory failed after that, she said, because she fainted. Detectives were certain that James Paladino knew the identity of DiBenedetto's murderer. When they pressed him for the information, he responded, "What am I going to do, tell you his name and be killed myself a few days later?"

The authorities succeeded in learning that DiBenedetto had been lured to the Italian colony at Dante Place for a meeting with liquor racketeers. It was the first time in more than a year that he traveled to Dante Place without his bodyguard.

Following the shooting an estimated crowd of one thousand people gathered at the Paladino grocery.[36] A similar crowd might have turned out for DiBenedetto's funeral, but his family transported his remains back to Brooklyn for burial in Calvary Cemetery.[37]

Two months after the slaying of DiBenedetto, a series of explosions and fires destroyed a three-story building at 981 Niagara Street and damaged others in the neighborhood. The blasts, which occurred at about one-forty-five on the morning of April 28, were heard by motorists on the Canadian shore.

The destroyed structure had been home to the old Frontier Hotel owned by Angelo Puma. The building had been padlocked for a year after it was found to be part of a regional bootlegging operation, but it was recently reopened. No one was on the premises at the time of the explosions, though it was generally a busy location. The first floor accommodated a soft drink saloon run by Joseph Geraci. Puma ordinarily occupied living quarters on the second floor, while renters occupied other rooms. That night, Puma, who reportedly had not been feeling well, decided to stay at the Statler baths.[38]

The building withstood the initial shock of the explosions, but it "was a roaring furnace a few minutes after the concussion." Its front collapsed after about ten minutes. Fifteen minutes later, the side walls fell inward. Rubble struck Carmen's service garage nearby. The Buffalo General Electric building across the street lost all its windows to the blast. In all, the damage was estimated at fifty thousand dollars.

During their investigation of the explosions, police heard

rumors that the contents of the building had recently been insured for a large amount of money. They also found witnesses who said the occupants of the building had been warned of a bombing and all left just a half-hour before the first explosion.

Police considered various explanations for the incident, including arson and whiskey still explosions, but they were certain that an underworld vendetta was at work.[39] Puma left Buffalo shortly after the hotel explosion. It was rumored that he sailed back to Sicily. The power of the Mazzara group in Buffalo appeared to have been broken. The Callea brothers emerged as the dominant bootlegging faction in the city.

— — —

Cleveland's underworld boss was killed in June of 1929. Salvatore "Black Sam" Todaro, who guided the Cleveland Mafia into the Masseria camp following the elimination of former boss Joseph Lonardo, was targeted for entirely personal rather than factional reasons.

Lonardo's widow, Concetta Paragone Lonardo, had serious financial problems. Since her husband's murder, she had been entangled in litigation against another Lonardo widow.[40] Concetta was the long-time common law wife of Joseph Lonardo and mother to their five children. The couple separated about 1925, however.[41] At that time, Lonardo moved in with another woman named Fannie Lansone. Lansone claimed that she and Lonardo had been formally married in Sandusky, Ohio.[42] With the family fortune tied up by the litigation, creditors had seized a Lonardo family car, and Concetta faced the possible loss of her home at 13700 Larchmere Boulevard.[43]

Early in 1929, Concetta began making regular visits for advice and financial aid to Todaro at the Porrello corn sugar warehouse at Woodland Avenue and 110th Street. Her son Angelo, then eighteen, typically chauffeured her from home to the warehouse[44] in a new, maroon and black Chrysler Model 75 coupe.[45] During the visits, Concetta never left the automobile but waited for Todaro to come out to speak with her. Observing gangland protocol, Todaro dutifully did so.[46]

On the afternoon of June 11, Concetta's twenty-two-year-old nephew Dominic Sospirato accompanied her and her son on the drive to the Woodland Avenue warehouse. As usual, Todaro went out to the car. When he reached the sidewalk, gunshots were heard and the Cleveland boss fell to the ground, dying. He had been shot five times.[47]

The Chrysler sped away. Police found Concetta an hour later and took her into custody as a material witness to the Todaro slaying. She insisted that the gunshots had not come from the inside of her vehicle but said she did not know who was responsible for the murder. Angelo Lonardo and Dominic Sospirato could not be found. Cleveland Police sent bulletins to the police departments in surrounding communities, asking them to watch for the two young men.[48]

A grand jury quickly returned indictments for first-degree murder against the three known occupants of the Lonardo vehicle.[49] Concetta was held without bail. Prosecutors offered to set bail at $50,000, if her son and her nephew would surrender themselves to police.[50] That proved to be an insufficient lure, and the search for Angelo Lonardo and Dominic Sospirato continued.

"Black Sam" Todaro's funeral was well suited to his station in the Cleveland underworld. Services at Our Lady of Peace Church on Shaker Boulevard and East 126th Street drew attention to Todaro's expensive coffin and floral decorations costing thousands of dollars. Todaro's partner Joseph Porrello sent a unique "gates ajar" floral display. Numerous mourners paraded just over half a mile along Woodland Avenue from East 126th Street to East 110th Street. The cortege then headed south to Calvary Cemetery. Safety Director Edwin D. Barry forced some alteration in the funeral plans. He ruled that there would be no marching band, and he restricted the route of the cortege. Barry also refused to provide any police escort for the marchers.[51]

The murder of Joseph Syracuse in Buffalo occurred two weeks after the shooting death of Salvatore Todaro.

Thirty-three-year-old Syracuse worked during the day as a shoemaker and at night as a banjo player in local orchestras.[52] Police believed that he was also a bootlegger. Cases of liquor had once been found in his car, and the authorities connected him with liquor-running operations between Buffalo and Batavia, New York, his former home.[53] There were rumors that he relocated from Batavia after receiving death threats from former business partners who felt that Syracuse had betrayed them.[54]

Just after seven in the morning on June 25, Syracuse left his home at 96 Tenth Street and started on his daily walk to Caruso

Brothers Shoe Repair on Delaware Avenue. His walk was immediately interrupted, as an elderly man stepped out of a doorway and shouted at him. The man called Syracuse, a "double-crosser," and an argument ensued.

As the men argued, a large, black Packard touring car with side curtains drawn pulled up and stopped. Gunmen sprang from the car and opened fire on Syracuse at close range. Wounded in the first volley, Syracuse reached out to one of his assailants, pulling a button off the gunmen's coat. Syracuse pleaded for mercy: "Don't do that. Please don't."

Five more shots were fired, and Syracuse fell to the street with bullets in his head, chest and abdomen. A black button was clenched in his hand. The gunmen dropped their weapons and sped away in the Packard.[55]

While the police had no luck identifying Syracuse's killers, they seemed to have better luck with regard to the Packard. The vehicle was found later in the day at Auburn and West Avenues. Police traced the registration to the fictitious name of Anthony Palvoni. They then approached the Main Street automobile dealer who sold the car, and he identified a photograph of Umberto Randaccio as the man who purchased it.

Police went in search of Randaccio. When they arrived at his cigar store at 480 Michigan Avenue, they found a well-stocked speakeasy. They seized forty quarts of rye, Scotch and gin, all bearing Canadian labels, and called in federal Prohibition agents.[56]

Randaccio, resident of 161 Auburn Avenue, and his son[57] Fred "Lupo" Randaccio were placed under arrest and held on an open charge. The Randaccios protested that they knew nothing of the automobile or of Syracuse's murder.[58] Investigators found it impossible to assemble a case.

"Witnesses will not talk," Detective Chief John G. Reville told the press. "They are afraid to talk, and every effort seems to be put forth to shield the killers."[59]

The Randaccios' defense attorney tried to free his clients by filing a writ of habeas corpus. At a June 28 hearing, police witnesses admitted they did not have sufficient evidence to warrant criminal charges against the two men. Supreme Court Justice Alonzo G. Hinkley ordered the Randaccios released.[60]

In Cleveland, the ire of Todaro supporters became focused

upon Frank Lonardo, a surviving brother of the murdered Joseph and John Lonardo. Frank was shot to death from behind during a card game on October 19. The killer could not be identified, but authorities were convinced that the murder was an act of vengeance.[61]

Concetta Lonardo was tried for the Todaro murder on November 12, 1929. Prosecutors argued that she aided and abetted Angelo Lonardo and Dominic Sospirato in the murder. "She knew when she summoned Todaro to her auto that he was going to be shot down," attorney John Fitzmartin said. A jury of six men and six women found her not guilty.[62]

Their confidence buoyed by Concetta's courtroom victory, Angelo Lonardo and Dominic Sospirato came out of hiding and turned themselves in to police in February 1930. They were initially held at Cleveland's Central Station Jail, but Lonardo accusations of police brutality caused them to be transferred to the Cuyahoga County Jail.[63]

On June 11, a jury convicted them of second-degree murder. When Judge James Ruhl sentenced both to life terms in the Ohio State Penitentiary, Lonardo and Sospirato relatives in the courtroom gallery erupted in anger and disbelief. Law enforcement officers escorted the judge and jurors home to ensure their safety.[64]

Lonardo and Sospirato successfully appealed the verdict. They were subsequently acquitted of murder charges at a retrial.[65]

While the Salvatore Todaro and Frank Lonardo murders apparently resulted from personal vendettas and did not change the factional alignment of Cleveland's underworld leadership, they intensified feelings of insecurity within the American Mafia.

In the summer of 1929, the American Mafia was further shaken by an event in Pittsburgh, Pennsylvania. Thirty-nine-year-old Pittsburgh boss Stefano Monastero was assassinated August 6 outside St. John's Hospital.[66] Based on Pittsburgh's North Side, where he supplied equipment and supplies to local moonshiners, Monastero became the region's most powerful Mafiosi around 1925. He had successfully fought off rivals through four violent years.[67]

After Monastero's death, Giuseppe Siragusa emerged as leader of the region's Sicilian underworld. A native of Palermo and a resident of Pittsburgh's East End, Siragusa was personally devoted to the conservative Mafia faction. However, there were dissident elements within his organization.[68] While Siragusa forged valuable alliances with the Castellammarese Mafiosi in New York,[69] the Monastero loyalists of the North End resisted his leadership.[70]

The underworld status quo also was upset in the Bronx, New York. Ciro Terranova, liberal-aligned Mafia chieftain of East Harlem and half-brother of Giuseppe Morello, had interests in the Bronx.[71] The borough also was the home territory of the underworld organization of conservative sympathizer Gaetano Reina and his lieutenants Tommaso Gagliano, Thomas Lucchese and Dominick "the Gap" Petrelli.

Like Morello and Terranova, Reina originally was from Corleone, Sicily. He was born there on September 27, 1889.[72] He entered the U.S. about 1904[73] and settled with his brother Antonino in an East Harlem neighborhood within the underworld territory of Morello and Terranova. In 1917, Reina and his brother appear to have operated separate businesses from the same East 103rd Street address.[74] As the Prohibition Era approached, Reina began assembling a monopoly on ice distribution within New York City. During the 1920s, his rackets became concentrated in the Bronx. Near the end of the decade, he began construction of a grand, four-thousand-square-foot home on Rochambeau Avenue in the Norwood section of the Bronx, just west of the Bronx River.[75]

Gagliano, another Corleone native, was born May 17, 1884. He entered the U.S. a year after Reina. He resided for a time near Reina on East Harlem's First Avenue.[76] In the 1920s, Gagliano moved his family to East 227th Street on the east side of the Bronx River. While Gagliano seems to have had little affection for Terranova, he had a strong business link with Morello. Both were directors of the United Lathing Company, incorporated in 1926.[77]

Late in 1929, Gagliano approached a Bronx hoodlum named Joseph Valachi with a vague offer. Valachi had not yet been inducted into the Mafia, but he had been a street gangster and a burglar. Through his work with Irish gangsters, Valachi had become an annoyance to Terranova. At one point, Terranova had sought to have Valachi killed.[78]

"There's some trouble in the air," Gagliano told Valachi, "and I'm sure it's with people you don't like."

"Who's the trouble with?" Valachi asked.

When Gagliano mentioned Terranova, Valachi responded, "Count me in."

Gagliano told Valachi he might be called upon to shoot someone. The young hoodlum became uncomfortable with that thought because he recalled that his good friend Frank Livorsi was part of Terranova's organization. However, Valachi said he could be counted on to murder for the Reina Mafia Family.

Two days later, Gagliano underling Girolamo "Bobby Doyle" Santuccio ordered Valachi to kill Livorsi. Valachi steadfastly refused, though it hurt his new relationship with the Reina group and placed him in some jeopardy. Acting as a mentor for the young gangster, Petrelli defended Valachi's decision, and the murder "contract" was withdrawn.[79]

Prevented from bloodying Terranova, the Reina organization may have opted merely for humiliating him.

After working to secure an impressive victory for Tammany Hall Democrats in the November 5 elections,[80] Albert H. Vitale, New York City magistrate and honorary president of the Bronx-based Tepecano Democratic Club, took a month off to relax in western Virginia.[81] The magistrate's fatigue might have been brought on by campaign revelations that he had obtained a sizeable loan through the recently murdered criminal mastermind Arnold Rothstein.[82]

Vitale returned to his Bronx home[83] on Saturday, December 7, and learned that his political friends planned a dinner that night to celebrate his return. At eight-thirty, he visited the Tepecano clubhouse, 747 East 187th Street. He entered the Roman Gardens restaurant, East 187th Street and Southern Boulevard at about nine o'clock.[84]

Terranova and his top men were among the guests gathered in the private dining area of the Roman Gardens. Also attending were leaders and members of the Tepecano club, Bronx businessmen and political figures, and at least one New York Police detective.[85]

At close to one-thirty, Vitale rose to speak. He had just begun to thank attendees for their warm welcome home, when seven gunmen entered the dining room and robbed its occupants of cash and jewelry. The intruders also took the service revolver from veteran Detective Arthur C. Johnson. One of the bandits, apparently concerned that he would be recognized, wore a handkerchief over the lower half of his face. The others made no effort to disguise themselves.[86]

Terranova seemed to recognize at least the ethnicity of the robbers. As they gathered their loot, he scolded, "We are all *paesani*. You should be ashamed of yourselves."[87]

A few hours after the robbers left, Vitale called Detective Johnson to an executive office of the Tepecano club. The magistrate handed Johnson the revolver that had been stolen from him. When asked how he had acquired the weapon, Vitale refused to answer.[88] Later rumors suggested that some of the stolen jewelry items also had been sent back to their rightful owners.[89]

The story of the robbery made front-page headlines in the New York newspapers. The press noted that at least seven known gangsters attended the Vitale dinner and were robbed along with the other guests. Terranova, who had a long police record including charges of murder, robbery and disorderly conduct, was the most noteworthy. Known as "the Artichoke King" for the fortune he amassed by monopolizing the artichoke supply in New York City, Terranova was regularly seen in Vitale's company at Tepecano events and elsewhere.[90]

Joseph "Joe the Baker" Catania and his brother James, nephews of Terranova,[91] also were well known to police. Joseph had been repeatedly arrested on various charges but never convicted. James served time in Sing Sing Prison for robbery. A second robbery accusation against him had been discharged by Magistrate Vitale.

Daniel J. Iamascia, who served in Terranova's Mafia Family and also was a top aide to Bronx gang boss Arthur "Dutch Schultz" Flegenheimer,[92] had the longest "rap sheet." He had been accused of numerous robberies, burglaries, assaults and other felonies between 1918 and 1924. He was never convicted. In some of the cases, the charges were dismissed. In at least one, the primary witness against him failed to appear in court. Several other cases against him were closed with no disposition on record. It appears likely that he benefited from his brother Anthony's important political position as a director of the

Tepecano club.[93]

The remaining known hoodlums at the event were James and John Savino and Paul Marchione.

Police Commissioner Grover A. Whalen told the press that others with police records also were at the dinner. He did not reveal the names of those he suspected, but he said, "This [Tepecano] Democratic Club has been under police scrutiny for some time. It will get plenty of attention from now on."[94] The Commissioner said he heard that other police officers also attended the event but had left before the robbery occurred.[95]

Chief Magistrate William McAdoo demanded an explanation from Vitale. After some hesitation, Vitale responded with denials. According to Vitale, the group at his dinner included only thirty-two men. They included twenty directors of the Tepecano club and a dozen other guests.[96] His total was about half of the figure of sixty presented in early press accounts of the gathering.[97] Vitale explained the discrepancy and the apparent inclusion of known criminals in the event by noting that the Roman Gardens was open to the public at the time and that no barrier separated the private party area from the rest of the dining room.[98]

Investigations into the incident uncovered the close relationship between organized crime and organized politics in the Bronx. Public indignation over that relationship revealed a new Depression Era morality, in which gangsters and politicians could no longer rely on each other for protection.

For the Masseria organization, the Vitale dinner robbery may have signaled serious problems in the Bronx.[99] "Joe the Boss" took immediate action to resolve those problems.

At just after eight o'clock on the evening of February 26, 1930, Gaetano Reina was killed by the blast of a double-barreled shotgun as he left an apartment house at 1521 Sheridan Avenue in the Bronx. Police learned that Reina had been visiting his mistress at that location.[100]

Bypassing Reina's top lieutenants, Masseria inserted his own ally Bonaventura "Joseph" Pinzolo as boss of the former Reina Mafia organization. Pinzolo, a former Black Hand extortionist in Manhattan, had served several years in prison after being caught preparing to bomb an apartment building.[101] Gagliano, Lucchese and Petrelli momentarily accepted the intrusion into their crime family's business, while they secretly mobilized opposition to Pinzolo and Masseria.[102]

Following the Reina murder, Masseria took a brief vacation in Miami, Florida. Accompanying "Joe the Boss" were his lieutenant Charlie Luciano and Masseria's brother John. While in Miami, the Mafia boss attended a boxing event headlined by a bout between British heavyweight champion Phil Scott and American contender Jack "Boston Gob"[103] Sharkey. The Sharkey-Scott fight was one-sided. Scott repeatedly claimed that he had been fouled. In the third round, Scott refused to continue and forfeited the match.[104]

Luciano, one of the young Mafiosi who became wealthy through liquor dealings on the Lower East Side of Manhattan, apparently had enough financial resources to show his boss a good time after the boxing match. Luciano bankrolled a high-stakes card-gambling event that monopolized the entire top floor of a Miami Beach hotel. Luciano was unable to keep the event secret from the authorities. In the early morning hours of March 1, ten sheriff's deputies raided the games and placed nineteen men under arrest. Only Luciano was found in possession of a firearm.

Fortunes apparently had changed hands at the card tables. Deputies noted that one player held more than sixty thousand dollars, while another had just twelve cents.[105]

— — —

The boss of bosses also encouraged a change of leadership within the Mafia of the Detroit region. Masseria ally Cesare "Chester" LaMare[106] controlled bootlegging operations in Wyandotte, a city southwest of Detroit, and was influential in rackets in the Detroit-surrounded municipality of Hamtramck. With Masseria's support, the ambitious and ruthless LaMare began encroaching on territory controlled by an eastern Detroit Mafia organization led by Angelo Meli.[107]

Gaspare Milazzo, the Castellammarese Mafioso who earlier had drawn the ire of "Joe the Boss" by backing Aiello in Chicago, was a senior adviser in the Meli Mafia.[108]

Increasingly violent encounters between the two rival Detroit organizations prompted a call for a peace conference. LaMare saw that as an opportunity. The meeting was scheduled for May 31, 1930, at a fish market at 2739 Vernor Highway in Detroit.

Rather than attend himself, LaMare sent gunmen to set up an ambush for Meli and his top men.

Meli apparently suspected a trap and avoided the fish market. In his place, he sent the underworld peacemaker, Milazzo, and Sam Parrino.[109] Meli's men arrived at the market at about twelve-thirty and sat in a rear room to await LaMare.

They had not waited long when LaMare's gunmen silently entered the room, drew pistols and opened fire. Milazzo quickly bled to death. Parrino, with mortal wounds to his chest and abdomen, lingered for three hours. Before he died, he told Detroit detectives that he and Milazzo had been shot by two men they did not recognize. He said he knew of no reason why anyone would want to kill them.[110]

Following the double-murder at the Vernor Highway market, Meli's Mafia outwardly submitted to LaMare's control of the Detroit underworld. However, the new boss would have a brief and uneasy reign.

In Cleveland, in the Bronx and in Detroit, "Joe the Boss" had succeeded in eliminating the most visible leader of the conservative movement and in installing one of his own supporters as boss. He attempted to deal with the upstart Castellammarese in Brooklyn in a similar manner.

— — —

Masseria's first move against the Brooklyn conservatives was to demand a $10,000 tribute payment from boss Nicola Schiro. The passive, non-Castellammarese Schiro made the payment and subsequently went into hiding.[111]

With Schiro gone, "Joe the Boss" endorsed Giuseppe Parrino as the new leader of the Brooklyn organization. Parrino initially seemed a strange choice for Masseria, as he was the brother of Sam Parrino of Detroit, recently slain on orders from Masseria ally Chester LaMare. However, Parrino outwardly accepted that his brother's death was an accident and appeared willing to take orders from Masseria.

The Castellammarese underworld in Brooklyn saw Parrino as a "despicable sort." He had traded the life of his kin for a role in underworld leadership. "For a chance at becoming a Father [boss], Parrino was willing to serve a tyrant. He was also willing to overlook the slaying of his brother..."[112]

Like the slighted Reina lieutenants in the Bronx, the

Castellammarese in Brooklyn began plotting against the leader imposed on them by Masseria.

In an attempt to gauge the opposition, Masseria called relative newcomer Salvatore Maranzano to a meeting. Fearing for his safety but aware that a refusal could alert "Joe the Boss" to his insecure position in Brooklyn, Maranzano agreed to sit down with Masseria.

The meeting was held at a private home in uptown Manhattan. Maranzano was welcomed by Masseria and his top aide Giuseppe Morello. After an exchange of greetings, Masseria sat back and allowed Morello to speak for him. The former Mafia boss of bosses began by saying he knew of Maranzano's warrior reputation in Sicily and of his great business successes in America.

Morello readily admitted the Masseria faction's responsibility for the Milazzo murder. He explained that Masseria believed the leaders of the Detroit and Chicago Mafias had been plotting against him. The killing of Milazzo was an act of self-defense, Morello argued.

The conversation then turned to Stefano Magaddino. Morello noted that the western New York Mafia boss had not responded to repeated Masseria meeting requests. That had given "Joe the Boss" reason to suspect that Magaddino might be conspiring against him. Morello asked Maranzano to try to persuade Magaddino to come to New York City and meet with Masseria to put the suspicions to rest. Maranzano said he would try.

> Do try, *Don Turridru*... Something must be done... If something isn't done... there might be bloodshed. And if there is fighting, I think the wisest course for an intelligent man such as yourself would be neutrality. On that we can all agree.[113]

Masseria allowed Maranzano one month in which to convince the Buffalo-based Mafia boss to appear before him. If Magaddino refused, the boss of bosses promised to condemn him to death.

When Maranzano personally delivered that message, Magaddino was enraged: "Condemn me, will he? I'd like to see him do that. Why doesn't Masseria come to see me in Buffalo?

I'll take good care of him if he does. I'll blow his brains out."

Despite his angry threat, Magaddino apparently did not intend to confront the boss of bosses personally. Instead, he decided to back Maranzano in efforts to rally the Castellammarese Mafiosi in New York City against Masseria. Even that decision was not reached easily. Magaddino already had developed a jealous dislike for the ambitious Maranzano and hesitated to grant the newcomer any additional authority.[114]

At that moment, the most important man among the Castellammarese Mafiosi of Brooklyn was the wealthy Vito Bonventre, known as "the King" of bootleggers.[115] A fifty-five-year-old former baker,[116] Bonventre was a second-cousin of Joseph Bonanno. Maranzano foresaw a Masseria move against Bonventre and warned the Mafioso to take precautions.

> Bonventre wouldn't change his daily routine. His relatives also urged him to take a few simple precautions, just in case, but Bonventre would not listen. He said he was old and respected, that he had made many friends and that no one would dare touch him. He couldn't believe that Masseria would try to kill him.[117]

At seven o'clock in the morning of July 15, Bonventre was in a garage behind his newly constructed two-story home at 69 Orient Avenue in Brooklyn, when a shotgun discharge ended his life. Slugs tore through his chest and perforated his heart and lungs.[118] Bonventre's wife and children were living at the family's summer home in Seaford, Long Island, and did not learn of his murder until several hours later.[119]

At eleven that morning, Patrolman John H. Snyder found a Plymouth sedan parked near the intersection of Fairview Avenue and Linden Street in Ridgewood, Queens. He noted a double-barreled shotgun and about twenty shells inside the vehicle. Police determined that the car had been stolen from the Bensonhurst area of Brooklyn. They concluded that the Bonventre assassins used the Plymouth to make their escape.[120]

The authorities recalled that Bonventre, a thirty-year-resident of Brooklyn, had a criminal record dating back to a 1919 liquor-related charge, for which he received a suspended sentence. In

1921, he was among those arrested and later freed in the Good Killers case. In 1928, police raided a Bonventre business and seized four five-gallon tins of alcohol. The alcohol was assigned to the care of Sergeant Joseph Benk. Some of the alcohol subsequently disappeared. While police conducted an investigation, Sergeant Benk apparently killed himself.[121]

Following a July 18, 1930, funeral Mass at Mount Carmel Roman Catholic Church on North Eighth Street and Union Avenue, Bonventre was buried at Calvary Cemetery. To prevent an escalation of gang violence, more than one hundred police officers were assigned to keep order at the ceremonies, and the detective forces at the Bedford Avenue and Herbert Street police stations in Brooklyn were bolstered.[122]

With Schiro and Bonventre out of the picture and with Magaddino reluctant to face Masseria in New York City, Salvatore Maranzano had a clear path to the leadership of the predominantly Castellammarese Mafia organization in Brooklyn. He called a meeting of the crime family membership and laid out a case for a gangland war against "Joe the Boss":

> He has condemned all of us, Maranzano said. He wants to eat all of us like a sandwich. If you choose to stay out of the fight, it will gain you no safety. Masseria will only devour you in time. Masseria intends to subjugate us all. You can't make a separate peace with him. He is insatiable.[123]

Maranzano made an emotional appeal to those outraged by Masseria's violence. He reached out to Castellammaresi through references to the Milazzo murder and to Palermitani through mention of the earlier D'Aquila assassination.[124] When convinced that he had successfully made his case, he suggested that the gathered Mafiosi hold a vote to elect a war leader for the fight against Masseria. Maranzano was chosen overwhelmingly.[125]

— — —

Violence continued in Cleveland through this period.

Joseph Porrello had succeeded to the top spot in Cleveland's Sicilian underworld after the murder of "Black Sam" Todaro. Porrello held the job for just nine months.

On July 5, 1930, Cleveland Detective Sergeant Charles Cavolo saw Porrello and his bodyguard Sam Tilocco drinking coffee at a restaurant at Woodland and 110th Street. Cavolo spoke with them casually and learned that they were about to leave to see Frank Milano at his Venetian Café saloon at 12601 Mayfield Road.

Milano was the leader of an underworld faction known as the Mayfield Road Gang. His organization included a number of Lonardo loyalists. Milano, Albert "Chuck" Polizzi, John "King" Angersola and Charles Colletti were present at the Venetian Café when Porrello and Tilocco arrived and sat down.

Shots were fired, and two men were seen running out the front of the café to an automobile across the street. Tilocco, bleeding from gunshot wounds to his head, staggered out the front door and moved in the direction of his vehicle. He fell to the sidewalk and died there.

Porrello never got up from the table. He was instantly killed as three slugs smashed through his skull.

As police investigated the killings, they searched Milano's house, next door to his business. There they found quantities of whiskey and beer, slot machines and several firearms, as well as account books related to bootlegging operations. They noted a number of canceled checks that had been made out to bootleggers, lawyers and local politicians.[126]

Three weeks later, Vincenzo "James" Porrello, an older brother of the late boss, was riddled with five shotgun slugs and revolver bullets as he stood in a Woodland Avenue grocery waiting for a clerk to wrap up lamb chops for the Porrello evening meal. The fusillade was fired from an auto as it passed the store. James Porrello died later at St. Luke's Hospital.[127] The murder of Vincenzo "James" Porrello left his wife to care for their six children.[128]

The murders of Joseph and James Porrello and Sam Tilocco were the violent climax of several bloody months in Cleveland.

Back on March 26, two cousins, both named Anthony Borsellino, were found strangled to death in an automobile left halfway between Akron and Cleveland. Police concluded that they had been working as middlemen in the bootlegging industry.[129]

The following month, an in-law of the late "Black Sam"

Todaro turned up dead. Carmelo Licata's lifeless body was found in a gutter on Gay Avenue S.E. in Cleveland. He had been shot through the head.

The authorities recalled that Licata years earlier was convicted of killing Patrolman Elmer Glaefke. He was sentenced to spend the rest of his life in the Ohio State Penitentiary. However, Governor A.V. Donahey commuted that sentence so Licata could be deported in 1925. Licata somehow reentered the country without being noticed.[130]

— — —

The underworld violence of the period spread north across the border and reached the home of Rocco Perri, boss of the Calabrian bootlegging network in Ontario.

On August 13, 1930, Rocco Perri and his wife Bessie went to visit a relative. They returned to their home in Hamilton at eleven-thirty-five that evening. Bessie was driving their car. She parked the car in their garage, and the Perris stepped out.

Bessie took just a few steps when shotgun blasts erupted from inside the garage. Rocco Perri jumped into a back alley and spotted a neighbor who was out walking his dog. The two men cautiously returned to the garage. There they found Bessie dead in a pool of blood.

Rocco collapsed, crying in grief over the loss of his wife and rackets partner.[131]

The authorities were aware that Bessie had been an active participant in her husband's bootlegging enterprises. Some considered her the financial brains of the illicit business. The investigation of Bessie's killing was built upon the assumption that gunmen deliberately targeted her.

The police were able to assemble a long list of Bessie's enemies. She was not well liked and had a reputation for greed. One of the suspects was Tony Papalia, a friend and fellow countryman of Perri who had become a supporter of western New York boss Stefano Magaddino.[132] However, the police could not build a convincing murder case against Papalia or anyone else on their list of suspects.[133]

In the Ontario underworld, Bessie's murder was viewed as a message: Stefano Magaddino's western New York Mafia, which had been the junior partner of the Calabrians for years, was ready to take control of the region.[134]

That summer, the two secret Mafia splinter groups in New York City separately planned counterattacks against the tyrannical boss of bosses.

The members of Maranzano's Brooklyn force broke with their usual routines so they would not fall victim to Masseria ambushes. Their new war leader separated them into small guerrilla-like squads and appointed commanders over each. Maranzano arranged a network of secret "safe houses" for himself and his lieutenants and a system for supplying the locations with food, arms and ammunition.

The Castellammarese chief was constantly on the move, traveling between secret hideouts in a Cadillac specially fitted with metal armor and bulletproof glass.

Maranzano called in assistance and money from Castellammarese enclaves in other cities. With the members of his force living like bandits on the run, their underworld enterprises suffered from neglect and their income fell off dramatically.[135]

Philadelphia boss Salvatore Sabella and nine of his men relocated to Brooklyn to support their countrymen.[136] From the Chicago area, came Bastiano "Buster" Domingo, considered an expert marksman, a "virtuoso" with a machine gun.[137] Chicago Mafia leader Joe Aiello sent $5,000 each week to aid the war effort.[138] Pro-Castellammarese groups within the Detroit Mafia also provided financial backing for Maranzano.[139]

Like Chicago, the Buffalo region sent $5,000 weekly payments.[140] In addition, Magaddino sent Calogero "Charley Buffalo" DiBenedetto, who became Maranzano's personal driver.[141]

The first Maranzano counterattack against the Masseria regime occurred on August 15, 1930.

Giuseppe Morello spent much of that day in his office on the second floor of 352 East 116th Street in East Harlem. The building, one of a block-long series of four-story tenements between First and Second Avenues, was owned by Morello. His sister, Mary Lima, and her family lived in an apartment on the third floor.[142]

At ten minutes to four in the afternoon, a Morello conversation with two visitors was interrupted as Morello answered a knock on his office door. Bastiano Domingo and another gunman shoved their way into the office, immediately opening fire. Morello and his companions, construction contractors Joseph Piraino and Gaspare Pollaro, all were wounded. Morello, struck by slugs in the face and neck, did his best to complicate the intruders' job.[143]

Valachi recalled, "Buster told me... that this Morello was tough. He said he kept running around the office, and Buster had to give him a couple of more shots before he went down."[144]

Piraino apparently hoped to save himself by jumping out the second-floor window. He had already suffered a gunshot wound to his left chest and died on the sidewalk below.[145] Pollaro was seriously wounded but survived.

Alerted by the sound of the gunshots, Mary Lima ran downstairs. She reached the street in time to see two men getting into an automobile and driving off toward First Avenue.[146]

Giuseppe Morello, the sixty-three-year-old former boss of bosses, died on his office floor. He had been shot five times. Slugs had torn holes in both of his lungs, his aorta and his small intestine, causing massive amounts of blood to fill his chest and abdominal cavities.[147]

When rebel leaders within the former Reina Mafia Family learned of Morello's assassination, they instantly became aware they were not the only ones plotting against Masseria's underworld administration.

> "...When Morello got his, the Gagliano people knew they didn't do it. So naturally they figure somebody else is in trouble with Joe the Boss. Then they found out that it was Salvatore Maranzano's doing."[148]

Perhaps emboldened by Maranzano's move against Morello, the Gagliano group in the Bronx took action early the following month.

At ten o'clock on the evening of September 5, a scrubwoman working on the tenth floor of the Brokaw Brothers Building at Times Square discovered the body of a dead man inside the offices of the California Dry Fruit Importers. Police later identified the man as Bonaventura Pinzolo.

The Masseria-imposed leader of the old Reina crime family

had been shot five times, twice in the back, twice in the chest and once in the side. The slugs had pierced Pinzolo's heart, lungs, stomach and spleen. After an autopsy, Chief Medical Examiner Charles G. Norris estimated that Pinzolo's death occurred at four o'clock in the afternoon, when the Brokaw Brothers Building had been bustling with activity.[149]

Detectives learned that the California Dry Fruit Importers office had been leased four months earlier by Thomas Lucchese. The business imported and sold legal pressed-raisin "bricks," which could be reconstituted and fermented into wine. Lucchese was questioned in connection with the Pinzolo murder, but no case could be made against him.[150]

Following the slaying of Pinzolo, Gagliano and his allies reached out to Maranzano. The two forces decided to combine.[151]

― ― ―

While events were turning against Masseria's faction in New York City, his protégé Alphonse Capone was concluding a successful gangland war in the Windy City.

Maranzano had conveyed a warning to Capone not to directly meddle in the affairs of New York. For a time, Capone heeded the warning. His own war against Joseph Aiello and George "Bugs" Moran kept him occupied.

In the wake of the St. Valentine's Day Massacre, which decimated Moran's North Side Gang, Aiello had been forced to continue the war against Capone with just his own Sicilian organization. That group also had been depleted by killings and defections during the war.[152]

Aiello left the city for a while in the summer of 1930, seeking refuge with his allies in the Buffalo area.[153]

At about that time, one of Buffalo's former racketeers, Calogero "Charley Buffalo" DiBenedetto, ran into some trouble in New York City. On September 16, 1930, he and Joseph Bonanno were stopped by city police as Bonanno entered DiBenedetto's car at Park Row in Manhattan. Police found that DiBenedetto was carrying a revolver and arrested both men.[154] The police and their prisoners used DiBenedetto's car to travel to police headquarters, DiBenedetto was observed reaching under the seat. Police discovered another pistol, several machine gun clips and a quantity of bullets under the seat.[155]

Police connected Bonanno with the Bonventre clan of

Brooklyn[156] and decided that he had armed himself to pursue a vendetta against the murderers of Vito Bonventre. Detectives attempted to beat information out of Bonanno. They failed to learn anything of value but succeeded in breaking the young Bonanno's nose.

DiBenedetto feigned cooperation. He said he had been in town only a short time and had borrowed the automobile from a friend in Brooklyn. He agreed to take the police to see that friend, and then pretended to become lost on the Brooklyn streets. DiBenedetto's act was well received, and he avoided the brutal beating that Bonanno endured.[157] Back in Buffalo, however, authorities learned of DiBenedetto's arrest and decided to search his home on Prospect Avenue.[158] Within a trunk, they found a bloodstained, large-caliber revolver wrapped in a Cleveland newspaper dated August 21, 1929.[159]

New York Police released DiBenedetto and Bonanno the following day.[160]

In the autumn of 1930, the situation in Chicago changed dramatically. Stefano Magaddino and Salvatore Maranzano both urged Aiello to remain safely in Buffalo. Against their advice, Aiello returned to Chicago and to his deteriorating war effort against Capone.[161]

In mid-October, Aiello visited the home of Pasquale "Patsy Presto" Prestogiacomo, 205 North Kolmar Avenue in the West Garfield Park section of Chicago. Aiello and Prestogiacomo were partners in the Italo-American Importing Company on Randolph Street. Aiello asked if he could stay with Prestogiacomo and his family for a week or so. Prestogiacomo agreed. Over the course of the next ten days, Aiello did not leave the premises.[162] Then, on October 23, he telephoned for a taxi and said goodbye to his host.

As Aiello left the house to get into the taxi, an apartment window across the street at 202 Kolmar Avenue opened. Machine gun fire poured from the open window. Aiello was struck multiple times. The Mafia boss shouted, turned and stumbled around the corner to the cover of a building courtyard.

As he entered the courtyard, a second machine gun opened fire from a third-story window above him. Steel-jacketed rounds rained down on Aiello. He dropped to the ground, his life ended by dozens of bullet wounds.[163]

Prestogiacomo's front window and living room were ripped apart by the machine gun fire. He and his family barely escaped injury. "I fell to the floor of the vestibule" at the sound of the first shots, Prestogiacomo later told investigators. "I scrambled back into the house, gathered my family about me, and we all lay down to escape the fire of bullets."[164]

After Aiello's death, underworld resistance to Capone crumbled. Masseria's protégé became lord of the Chicago underworld. Freed from the burdens of his own war, Capone was able to send additional financial and manpower aid to "Joe the Boss" in New York.[165]

― ― ―

The Maranzano and Gagliano forces decided to seal their pact by jointly acting against another important Masseria supporter, Steve Ferrigno. Valachi was assigned to rent a room at the Alhambra Apartments, a large U-shaped complex on Pelham Parkway South in the Bronx. Valachi took second-floor quarters in the western side of the complex, directly across a courtyard from the entrance to Ferrigno's residence in the eastern building. Valachi was to keep an eye on Ferrigno's apartment and signal gunmen when he was vulnerable.

On Tuesday, November 4, Valachi spotted Ferrigno entering his apartment in the company of "Joe the Boss." He excitedly reported the news and continued to keep watch. Bastiano Domingo, Girolamo Santuccio and Nick "the Thief" Capuzzi quickly arranged the rental of a first-floor apartment with windows looking out on the same courtyard. News of Masseria's presence caused a change in plans: They hoped to eliminate the boss of bosses as he left Ferrigno's home. During the night, Valachi saw additional Masseria men enter the building. He counted as many as twenty. No one left.

The next afternoon, men began filing out of Ferrigno's apartment. The Maranzano and Gagliano gunmen watched for Masseria. When Ferrigno and Alfred Mineo stepped out into the courtyard, the gunmen concluded that Masseria had somehow eluded them. As their original target, Ferrigno, passed in front of their window, the gunmen opened fire with twelve-gauge shotguns.[166]

The blasts killed Mineo and Ferrigno before they had a chance to draw their pistols. Mineo, boss of the former D'Aquila

Mafia in Brooklyn, had his head split open by a shotgun discharge.[167]

Immediately following the shootings, witnesses saw three men running from the Alhambra Apartments. Two exited the west side of the western building onto Holland Avenue. The other passed through the main gate of the complex.

Police found Mineo in possession of no identification other than business cards, which indicated he was the vice president of the A.D.L. Holding Corporation of 55 West Forty-Second Street. Using his fingerprints, they were able to locate a short arrest record, a residential address on Fourth Avenue in Brooklyn and a former address near Thirty-Eighth Street in Brooklyn.

In Ferrigno's pockets, police found a driver's license issued to Sam Ferrarra of 384 Broome Street, Manhattan; an automobile registration certificate for Giuseppe Gangarraso of 97 Bay Thirty-Eighth Street in Brooklyn; and a pistol permit approved by a judge in Yonkers, New York. Police records showed he had been arrested twice for grand larceny.[168]

The Maranzano forces later learned that Masseria was still inside Ferrigno's building at the time of the shooting.[169] It seemed "Joe the Boss" still was dodging the bullets intended for him. His New York organization, however, was in shambles. Within a three-month period, four top Masseria men had been murdered.

Masseria had to press on without those aides and with a loosening grip on crime families in Brooklyn and the Bronx. Much of the old Reina group in the Bronx had joined the revolt against his underworld administration. The elimination of Mineo splintered his large Brooklyn-based criminal organization. Frank Scalise, Giuseppe Traina and Carlo Gambino defected from the Masseria camp and sided with Maranzano.[170]

Masseria was further hampered by two other developments.

The first occurred as an official of the New York Police Department met with the Mafia leader and demanded that he bring a stop to the bloodshed. If the underworld violence continued, the official warned, a special order would be issued to arrest Masseria and all his men.[171]

The second bordered on underworld impeachment. Mafia bosses across the country called for a convention to hear charges against the Masseria administration. A meeting was planned for

Boston in the first week of December. Masseria's authority as boss of bosses was temporarily suspended, so the charges could be considered fairly. The boss of bosses mantle was awarded to respected Boston Mafia leader Gaspare Messina for the duration of the hearing.[172]

Perhaps welcoming the opportunity to regroup after the series of devastating losses, Masseria responded by disarming. He ordered his underlings back to a peacetime posture, and prepared himself for the judgment of the Mafia assembly. Masseria's men were unhappy with his decision, believing it played into the enemy's hands. They were correct. Maranzano stepped up his guerrilla activities in Masseria territory, increasing his strength and his prestige.[173]

The Boston assembly attempted to bring the war to a close by sending a delegation to meet with Maranzano at his Wappingers Falls farm. Maranzano resisted.[174] He turned down a proposal that would have permanently unseated Masseria and triggered the election of a new boss of bosses.[175] He informed the delegation that he would make peace only if Masseria was assassinated. He privately indicated that Vincenzo Mangano, the last of the old D'Aquila group leaders to remain loyal to "Joe the Boss," should be the assassin.[176]

A second assembly of the American Mafia was called. Hundreds of underworld representatives gathered at a mountain resort hotel in New York State. Maranzano presided over the meeting and used it to air his grievances against Masseria. Yet another meeting quickly followed.[177]

Diplomacy seemed unable to produce meaningful results, but Maranzano's faction had more effective tools available to it.

— — —

Just before six o'clock on the evening of January 19, 1931, an argument erupted at a table in the Del Pezzo Restaurant, 100 West Fortieth Street in Brooklyn. Giuseppe Parrino, Masseria-installed boss of the former Schiro organization, had been dining there with three other men when the conversation became angry. Shots were fired behind Parrino, and he fell forward with bullet wounds to the back of his head and neck.[178]

Masseria's faction suffered far more serious losses two weeks later.

Masseria lieutenant Joseph "Joe the Baker" Catania was

walking to a Bronx business appointment just after noon on Tuesday, February 3. As he passed a candy store at 2375 Belmont Avenue,[179] a shotgun fired from a building diagonally across the street. Slugs struck Catania in his neck and chest, and he dropped to the sidewalk.

Daniel DeStefano, a friend of Catania, was nearby at the time of the shooting. DeStefano called for help and put Catania into an ambulance. "Joe the Baker" was rushed to Fordham Hospital.[180] He died at seven-forty-eight the next morning of internal hemorrhaging from wounds to his lungs, trachea and pharynx.[181]

Bastiano Domingo and Joseph Valachi brought Maranzano news of their successful ambush of Catania. The news was cause for celebration in the Castellammarese camp.[182] The opposite was true for Masseria's organization. Terranova was emotionally devastated, and he publicly swore he would avenge his nephew's death.[183]

Ten thousand people lined the route of the Catania funeral cortege on Saturday, February 7. The procession, the largest gangland funeral the Bronx had ever seen, included sixty-five mourners' vehicles and forty automobiles filled with flowers. Catania's bronze coffin was said to have cost ten thousand dollars. Three priests celebrated a requiem high Mass for Catania at the Church of Our Lady of Mount Carmel at 187th Street and Belmont Avenue. His remains then were temporarily interred at Woodlawn Cemetery, while a permanent mausoleum was built at St. Raymond's Cemetery.[184]

The day of Catania's funeral brought Masseria more bad news. Very early that morning, two bullets fired at close range took the life of his Detroit ally Cesare "Chester" LaMare.

LaMare had been a hunted man almost from the moment of Gaspare Milazzo's murder. Pursued by underworld rivals and by Detroit area law enforcement, he fled to New York for a while in the summer of 1930, before returning to Detroit and setting up a heavily armed hideout for himself and his wife on Grandville Avenue. On January 27, 1931, LaMare traveled to Louisville, Kentucky.

He returned to the Grandville Avenue house on the evening of Friday, February 6. An unidentified man accompanied him. After midnight, LaMare asked his wife Anna to drive their guest to the intersection of Harper and Connors Avenues and to pick up a medicinal ointment for him at a drugstore.[185] When Anna returned home, she found LaMare dead in the kitchen, with two gunshot wounds in the back of his head. There were powder burns around one of the wounds.[186]

Anna LaMare told the authorities her husband's killer must have been someone he knew well:

> Whoever killed Chester entered the house as a friend, for only our friends were ever admitted. We had a certain signal – three rings of the bell – which always identified our friends before we opened the door. Someone must have come to the house after I left. I'd know the man I drove to Connors and Harper, of course, but I really do not think he had a hand in this affair.[187]

Noting the continued aggression of the Maranzano faction, Masseria's lieutenants demanded that they be permitted to rearm. When "Joe the Boss" refused, his own top men began conspiring against him.[188]

Chapter 17

New Order

Masseria's group leaders and their allies in New York secretly consulted with Chicago's Capone and with other important Mafia leaders.[1] The conspiracy grew to include Charlie "Lucky" Luciano, the strongest of Masseria's remaining lieutenants. In the spring of 1931, Luciano represented the mutinous Mafiosi in negotiations with the Maranzano faction.

Near the beginning of April, Luciano and his aide Vito Genovese met with Salvatore Maranzano and some of his underlings at a private home in Brooklyn. Luciano offered to eliminate Masseria in order to bring the Mafia war to an end.[2]

"How much time do you need to do what you have to do?" Maranzano asked.

"A week or two," Luciano replied.

"Good." Maranzano said. "I'm looking forward to a peaceful Easter."[3]

At one o'clock in the afternoon of April 15, Masseria's steel-armored sedan drove up to Gerardo Scarpato's Nuova Villa Tammaro restaurant at 2715 West Fifteenth Street on Coney Island.[4] The business was closed to the public at that time, but a special welcome was extended to the Mafia boss of bosses. Surrounded by three trusted bodyguards,[5] Joe the Boss entered the restaurant to have lunch and play cards with men he considered his closest friends.[6] The guest list for the event is uncertain but probably included Luciano, Genovese, Vincenzo Mangano, Joseph Biondo, Nicola Gentile, Salvatore LoVerde, Saverio Pollaccia, Anthony Carfano, Frank Livorsi and Joseph Stracci.[7]

At two o'clock, gunshots were heard, and witnesses saw

several men quickly exit the restaurant, climb into an automobile and drive away.[8] A large crowd assembled in front of Scarpato's restaurant.[9]

When police arrived, they found Anna Tammaro, mother-in-law of the restaurant owner, crouched over the bloody remains of "Joe the Boss" Masseria.[10] He had been shot three times in the back, once in the neck and once just above his eye.[11] Several nearby chairs had been overturned. Playing cards were scattered on the floor. Police counted about thirty-five dollars in coins and bills, apparently the pot in a card game. They also found a number of coats and hats, worn either by Masseria's lunch guests or by his murderers.[12]

Anna Tammaro said she knew nothing of the murder. She had been in the kitchen when she heard the gunshots. Gerardo Scarpato also claimed he had no information on the crime. He said he had been out taking a walk.

Police found two handguns discarded in an alley beside the restaurant. Later in the day, they recovered what they believed was the assassins' getaway car. It was abandoned at West First Street near Kings Highway, about two miles from the restaurant. Three handguns were found in the back seat. The automobile was traced to its owner, Ercole Marchino of Manhattan, who had reported it stolen five months earlier.[13] Fingerprint experts studied the vehicle and the weapons, but could not identify the killers.[14]

After speeding away from the Nuova Villa Tammaro restaurant, Gentile and LoVerde went to Luciano's home. They were met there by Vincenzo Troia, a leading figure in the Maranzano Mafia organization. Luciano instructed Troia to relay a message to his boss: "Tell your compare Maranzano that we have killed Masseria for our own personal reasons, not to serve him." Luciano warned that if Maranzano took any further hostile action, "we will make war to the bitter end."[15]

The next day, Maranzano held a meeting at the Brooklyn home of a friend, Stefano LoPiccolo. Luciano and other former members of the Masseria organization attended and brought the years-long struggle known as the Castellammarese War officially to a close. Maranzano came to terms with Chicago boss Alphonse Capone through intermediaries and telephone conversations.[16]

Masseria received an appropriately gaudy gangland funeral

on the morning of April 20. He was laid to rest in a silver coffin said to cost fifteen thousand dollars. A funeral cortege of sixty-nine cars – including sixteen automobiles filled with floral tributes – began at the new, fifteen-story apartment hotel at 15 West Eighty-First Street, where "Joe the Boss" had lived with his family in Penthouse E. The procession continued to the Church of Mary, Help of Christians, on East Twelfth Street and then on to Calvary Cemetery.

At the funeral, there were indications that Masseria's old friends were distancing themselves from his memory. Five cars set aside for honorary pallbearers remained empty. Most of the flowers had been sent anonymously, except for a single heart of roses carrying a card from "A.C." – Capone's initials.[17]

— — —

While the war was over, underworld bloodshed continued.

On the evening of Saturday, May 9, Mike LoBosco and his old friend Joe Cosenza were chatting outside LoBosco's Cleveland butcher shop, 14707 Kinsman Road. At close to eleven o'clock, a Ford roadster drove slowly westward on Kinsman Road and came to a stop in front of the men. Shotguns were fired from the vehicle, and both LoBosco and Cosenza were struck by slugs. LoBosco was hit in the head and chest. Cosenza suffered a wound to his left thigh.

The roadster drove off, turning north on East 147th Street. A column of smoke produced by the vehicle prevented witnesses from clearly seeing its license plate number.

LoBosco and Cosenza were both known for their involvement in bootlegging rackets. LoBosco was a long-time adherent of the conservative Mafia faction. A former member of the D'Aquila organization, he had strong connections to the Niagara Falls region and to the Palmeri family. Locally, LoBosco was known as the "alky can king" for a monopoly he held on five-gallon tins.[18]

While receiving treatment for their wounds at St. Luke's Hospital, the forty-six-year-old LoBosco admitted to police investigators that he had spent a lot of time with the Porrello Brothers until he opened his butcher shop about four months earlier. Neither of the victims could provide police with any motive for the shooting.[19] The police concluded that the incident represented a new flare-up in the old Lonardo-Porrello feud.[20]

The Ford roadster was recovered after an Ashwood Road resident reported that it had been abandoned in front of his home. A loaded .32-caliber revolver was found within the vehicle. The license number on the roadster, 702-187, was traced to Sam Masseria, 2383 East Forty-Sixth Street. When police arrived at that address, they found that no one by the name of Masseria had lived there for at least six years.[21]

The following day, New York detectives found the body of Brooklyn waterfront racketeer Johnny "Silk Stockings" Giustra at the bottom of a tenement stairway at 75 Monroe Street in Manhattan. Giustra, twenty-eight, had come out on the losing end of a gunfight within the tenement. Bullet wounds were found in his chest, abdomen and head. The detectives believed he had been put "on the spot" by underworld associates.[22]

Authorities linked the Giustra murder to the assassination of Masseria. One of the coats left at the Nuova Villa Tammaro restaurant had been identified as belonging to Giustra. A confidential informant told investigators that Giustra was the triggerman for the assassination. At least one staffer from the office of the Kings County District Attorney believed Giustra's death closed the Masseria case.[23]

However, New York Police soon received additional details of the Giustra story. They learned that Giustra and his close friend and business partner,[24] undertaker Carmelo Liconti, had fallen into disfavor with some Mafia superiors following the assassination of Joe the Boss.[25] Both Giustra and Liconti had been summoned to the Monroe Street tenement on May 10. They were driving there together when a tire on their vehicle went flat near the corner of Canal and Lafayette Streets. Liconti tended to the tire, while Giustra went ahead into ambush.

When he learned of his friend's murder, Liconti suffered an emotional collapse and was admitted for observation to Kings County Hospital in Brooklyn. Upon his release, Liconti went into hiding.[26]

Giustra's funeral was arranged by the Guariano, Liconti and Giustra undertaking firm on Henry Street, a business in which he had been a partner. Johnny "Silk Stockings" was buried at Holy Cross Cemetery on May 15.[27]

In Cleveland, residents Emil and Sylvia Benovitz found a shotgun near the southeast corner of Milverton Avenue and East

146th Street, about one half mile from the LoBosco butcher shop. They turned the weapon over to police. Detectives determined that it had been used in the attack upon LoBosco and Cosenza. They traced it to a Youngstown, Ohio, store operated by Albert Antonelli.

The same store had sold a weapon used in the recent gangland murder of Frank Alessi. At the time of Alessi's death, Antonelli told authorities he had sold more than a hundred firearms through a period of two years. He estimated that two dozen of those had been sold to Joseph Porrello.[28]

LoBosco succumbed to his injuries on May 18. He was buried four days later in Calvary Cemetery.[29]

— — —

Following his underworld triumph, Maranzano scheduled a series of regional and national Mafia conventions. Attendance figures at each reached into the hundreds.

The first assembly, limited to New York regional Mafiosi, was held at a banquet hall on Washington Avenue in the Bronx. Its purpose was the reorganization of the crime families and the recognition of their new bosses. The most complicated business on the agenda was the untangling of the Maranzano and Gagliano organizations, which had been merged during the Castellammarese War.[30]

In May, important Mafiosi from across the country gathered at a resort in Wappingers Falls, New York, near the Maranzano farm. The clear victor in the recent underworld conflict, Maranzano explained that the old alliances were ended. "What's past is past," he insisted. "What's important now is peace." The Castellammarese leader conveyed to all the gathered underworld leaders that he personally had the strength to enforce the peace. Maranzano's armed guards were evident at the resort, they searched attendees for weapons, and they escorted any who had to step out of the meeting hall. While the meeting was taking place, all could hear the engine of a Maranzano-hired airplane as it continually circled the resort providing security.[31]

Later that month, Capone hosted a Mafia national convention at the Hotel Congress in Chicago.

Maranzano traveled by train from New York City to Chicago. Traveling with him were Joseph Bonanno and Charlie Luciano. Their train stopped in Buffalo, where leaders of the western New York Mafia boarded. Those included regional boss Stefano Magaddino, cousin Pete Magaddino and top lieutenant John Montana.

Montana was immediately called upon to use his considerable local influence. At the Buffalo station, Maranzano stepped off the train to make a telephone call. He had not returned as the train was preparing to leave. Montana arranged for the train to wait until Maranzano returned. The incident caused Stefano Magaddino to beam: "See what kind of men I have under me? John can stop trains."[32]

By 1931, Montana's influence was felt across the City of Buffalo. A resident of the community for more than 30 years[33] and a product of the public school system, he started a trucking and taxi business. In 1930, his Yellow Cab Company merged with the Van Dyke Taxi Company to form the largest taxi business in western New York. Montana served as vice president of that company, as well as director in other transportation-related firms. He also involved himself in local politics. Montana was elected to the Common Council in 1928 and won reelection two years later. He served on the council's finance committee.[34]

The convention was an impressive debut for the undisputed boss of Chicago's "Outfit":

> Capone was an extravagant host... He picked up the tab for everyone's accommodations and provided the food, the drink and the women. He sent Maranzano a gold watch studded with diamonds. Capone also gave us his unimpeachable assurance that the police would not meddle in our business while we were at the hotel.[35]

Many smaller meetings and parties occurred during the days spent at the Hotel Congress, but the main event was the assembly meeting in the hotel's basement. At that meeting, the membership of the American Mafia considered the mistakes of the past and how best to proceed for the future.[36]

A group of Mafiosi opposed a continuation of the traditional boss of bosses position. They argued that future disagreements between factions should be mediated by a panel of six respected underworld leaders, and they turned to Vincenzo Troia to select those leaders. Maranzano quietly undermined Troia, and the concept of rule by a representative panel was abandoned. Instead, the assembly endorsed Maranzano as its new boss of bosses.[37]

— — —

Pittsburgh's delegation to the convention was led by regional Mafia boss Giuseppe Siragusa, whose personal prestige had been enhanced by his wartime support of Maranzano. Other attendees from the Steel City included its rising star John Bazzano and veteran Mafioso Nicola Gentile. Unlike the others, Gentile's attendance was involuntary, the result of an ill-conceived effort by Siragusa to score additional points with Maranzano.

A Palermo native, Siragusa entered the U.S. in 1910 and lingered for two years in New York before moving west.[38] He opened a bakery in Pittsburgh in 1912 and later became proprietor of a confectionary and general manager of the Empire Yeast Company on Cedarville Street. Those positions provided him useful access to the moonshine necessities of sugar and yeast as the Prohibition Era began. Connections with conservative Mafia bootleggers in New York also proved valuable. Siragusa eventually moved into a large home on manicured grounds on Beechwood Boulevard in Pittsburgh's eastern Squirrel Hill district. The basement of that home became his headquarters. Following the August 1929, assassination of Stefano Monastero, Siragusa was recognized as the leader of the Mafia in the Pittsburgh region.[39]

Bazzano, born in 1888 on mainland Italy's southern coast, entered the U.S. at age twenty. He lived for a time in West Virginia and then moved to Johnstown, Pennsylvania. He became a naturalized citizen of the U.S. in 1916 and entered military service during the Great War. After the war, he moved to New Kensington, Pennsylvania. A Mafia protégé of Nicola Gentile, Bazzano became wealthy through business investments, including involvement in the Virogo Yeast Company.[40] Though Bazzano had little affection for either Maranzano or Siragusa, he managed to keep his feelings to himself during the convention.

With no interest in joining the conventioneers, Gentile was relaxing at home when he was summoned to Chicago to answer charges initiated by Siragusa. The precise nature of the charges is unknown, but continuing Gentile opposition to Maranzano was implied.

As Maranzano, some of his allies and the rest of the Pittsburgh delegation waited in another room, convention host Alphonse Capone personally interrogated Gentile in the bar of the Hotel Congress. The unwilling guest took a firm stand. "I came with a clear conscience," he told Capone. "I believe that some trap has been set for me. But, I warn you, if the accusations are nothing but false, malicious statements, I will claim the heads of those who made them."

Gentile's resolve impressed Capone, who fondly recalled an earlier meeting between them during the Mafia reign of the late Mike Merlo.

Siragusa's stature within the underworld plunged when Capone went to confront him with Gentile's threat. The Pittsburgh boss immediately recanted, trusting in Gentile's good nature to let the matter go. Bazzano brought word out to the waiting Gentile that the charges against him had been dropped. Noting that the convention represented an opportunity to resolve all differences peacefully, he urged Gentile not to act against Siragusa. Gentile saw the worth of letting bygones be bygones and withdrew his threat.[41]

― ― ―

The convention was a momentary success for both Maranzano and Capone. After years of struggling against elements of the Mafia, Capone finally had secured its unanimous endorsement as underworld leader of Chicago. Maranzano had moved from guerrilla leader and gangland outsider to a position of unparalleled power within the Sicilian-Italian criminal network. Their time in the sun would be brief.

Just a couple of weeks after the Chicago convention, Capone was indicted for tax evasion. Though the Windy City underworld boss reportedly offered as much as four million dollars to settle his affairs with the U.S. Bureau of Internal Revenue, federal officials decided to reject the offer and move ahead with his prosecution.[42]

Capone was arraigned June 16 for evading taxes for the years 1924 through 1929 and for conspiracy to violate the liquor law. The authorities had spent several years carefully assembling a case against Capone's operations. They moved first against a number of his underlings, winning tax convictions against his brother Ralph Capone, as well as Frank "the Enforcer" Nitti, Jake

"Greasy Thumb" Guzik and Sam Guzik.[43] Internal Revenue agents were able to document more than one million dollars of Alphonse Capone's income for the 1924-1929 period. The total tax and penalties owed on that income were calculated to be $383,705.21.[44]

The Chicago boss orchestrated a deal in which prosecutors recommended a sentence of no more than two and a half years in federal prison. Capone then pleaded guilty to the charges. However, when Judge James H. Wilkerson refused to be bound by the terms of that deal, Capone withdrew his guilty plea and prepared for trial.[45] His reign in Chicago would last just eleven more months.

That would be far longer than the reign enjoyed by the new boss of bosses.

Chambermaid Pauline von Hagen was cleaning rooms at Manhattan's Hotel Paramount[46] on the morning of July 9, 1931, when she discovered a dead man in one of the bathrooms. The fully clothed body was wedged against a washstand. Its head was pointed toward the bathtub. A rope was knotted about its neck, and stab wounds were evident on the chest and the throat.

Police identified the victim as Carmelo Liconti of Brooklyn, one of the suspects in the assassination of Giuseppe Masseria. An autopsy revealed that Liconti had been killed about twelve hours before he was found. It appeared that he had been struck twice on the head and that his lips had been injured in a deliberate effort to mutilate them.

Investigators learned that two men had rented the hotel room the day before under the probably fictitious names of W. Harris and G. Grossman. Arriving at two-thirty in the afternoon, they paid thirty-five dollars for the room, saying they expected to be there for a week. While they were registering, Grossman received a telephone call in the lobby. Grossman was heard to say on the phone, "Come on up."

No one at the hotel recalled seeing Liconti enter the building. Harris and Grossman left secretly during the night.[47]

Maranzano invited Mafiosi from across the country to purchase tickets to a three-day banquet beginning August 1.

Mafia bosses interpreted the invitation as a command, purchasing tickets, attending the banquet and bringing large cash gifts for the new boss of bosses.[48]

Coming as it did on the heels of a number of other expensive functions held for Maranzano's financial benefit, Buffalo's Stefano Magaddino objected to the expense. In doing so, the Buffalo boss drew attention to a growing division within the formerly monolithic Castellammarese underworld faction.

"Who is throwing this banquet, you or I?" Magaddino protested.[49] Decades later, the Buffalo leader was still grousing over the event:

> ...He throws a banquet that lasted three days, always taking advantage of the situation. It did not cost him a penny. It cost me and the others a lot of money. It cost much more than $200,000... I have never had an opening or a closing or a banquet..., I never had anything.[50]

The banquet was held at Gerardo Scarpato's Nuova Villa Tammaro restaurant, the scene of the Masseria assassination four months earlier. Police took note of the gathering and its attendees and raided the event several times, searching the guests for illegal weapons. The only weapons found, however, were accompanied by legal permits.

Official attendance estimates for the event ran between five thousand and twenty thousand people. Meals were served in sittings of five hundred at a time, beginning at noon and lasting until long after midnight each day. As an orchestra played Italian songs, diners feasted on salads, artichokes, spaghetti and roast chicken.[51]

Conspicuous in the restaurant was a table holding a large tray. As Mafiosi entered the dining room, they placed large cash contributions onto the tray.[52] "I never saw such a pile of money in my life," Joseph Valachi later recalled.[53]

When newspaper reporters inquired about the purpose of the banquet, a man calling himself Marty Salvatore – not an unlikely alias for Salvatore Maranzano – said it was a fundraiser for a mid-August holiday festival on Elizabeth Street organized by the Maritime Society of Sciacca. Salvatore said he was president of that society.[54]

While the main purpose of the dinner is for the religious celebration, Mr. Salvatore said that an energetic effort would be made to create peace and harmony among the factions of Italians and Sicilians of New York.[55]

Though the three-day banquet greatly enriched Maranzano – he took home as much as one hundred and twenty thousand dollars – it did little to create harmony. At one point in the event, a seemingly intoxicated Maranzano called out to Troia, asking him, "What would you do if you had one hundred thousand dollars?" Troia answered coyly, "When I have it, I will decide what to do with it."

Maranzano followed with a statement that conveyed mistrust of his colleagues and lack of commitment to his position: "I would like to go to Germany to be more secure."[56]

While Maranzano's detractors were riled by the statement, his friends were upset by the boss of bosses' actions following the banquet. Many believed they would receive a share of Maranzano's windfall as compensation for their wartime service.[57] However, the new underworld leader gave his followers nothing more than vague promises of future financial reward. To some, he communicated the possibility of yet another war within the American Mafia.[58]

Making matters worse were Maranzano's mood swings and a growing rift between the boss of bosses and the Castellammarese underworld leaders in western New York. Events in August revealed the extent of those problems.

Sometime after the Coney Island banquet, a group including Angelo Palmeri of Buffalo and Joseph Bonanno of Brooklyn waited at a restaurant for Maranzano's arrival. Conversation turned to a box that Palmeri had brought with him. Palmeri said it contained a felt hat costing one hundred dollars. It was to be a gift to the boss of bosses, an atonement for something Palmeri said during a previous visit that offended Maranzano.

"He got so upset that for a moment I thought Maranzano was going to kill me," Palmeri explained. "Tell me, is he still angry at me? Is this hat going to do any good?"

While kidding Palmeri for his fears, the group understood that explosions of Maranzano's temper had been occurring more frequently.[59]

A short time later, Maranzano made some disparaging remarks about Stefano Magaddino. Mafioso John DiCaro overheard and told Bronx boss Tommaso Gagliano about the remarks. Gagliano shared them with his underboss Thomas Lucchese. Through Lucchese, word of the leak got back to Maranzano, who became greatly concerned that his comments might have reached Buffalo.

"Such information, if it had reached Magaddino, might have been taken very badly and might have sparked an open row between Magaddino and Maranzano...," Bonanno later recalled. "The two men seemed to be headed for collision, but until then I didn't realize how close to it they already were."

The Buffalo boss subsequently met with Bonanno and Gaspare DiGregorio at DiGregorio's Brooklyn home. Magaddino expressed vague dissatisfaction with the new boss of bosses and complained that he had been kept waiting for more than an hour during a recent visit to Maranzano's office. "Many people are upset with him," Magaddino said.[60]

At three-forty-five in the afternoon of September 10, four armed men entered the offices of the Eagle Building Corporation on the ninth floor of the New York Central Building, 230 Park Avenue in Manhattan.[61] They found seven men waiting in an anteroom along with secretary Frances Samuels. The armed men identified themselves as government agents. One of the gunmen told Samuels and the seven men to line up against the wall, while the other three gunmen proceeded into the private office of Salvatore Maranzano.[62]

Within that room, the three men attacked Maranzano, stabbing and shooting him to death. Maranzano, who had been alerted to the possibility of a police raid of his office, made sure no weapons would be found by the authorities and was therefore defenseless against his attackers.[63]

The gunmen rushed out of the offices, and the seven men who had been waiting for Maranzano's attention were right behind them. Frances Samuels entered the inner office to find her employer dead.[64] For the second time in five months and the third time in three years, the reigning American Mafia's boss of bosses had been assassinated.[65]

Homicide investigators followed a number of leads in vain.

Two hats were found lying on the office floor. They were

traced to Chicago retailers. That raised the prospect of Capone involvement in the murder, but detectives quickly ruled that out.[66]

They examined a memorandum book that had notes of Maranzano's activities on the day of his murder. The notes related to telephone contacts with Stefano Magaddino, Paul Palmeri, Thomas Lucchese and others. One entry called to mind the business card found on Alfred Mineo's body ten months earlier. It was for A.D.L. Corporation, though the address was different from that on the Mineo card.[67] An entry for the Anawanda Club provided a link with Tammany Hall Democrats, who ran the club.[68]

Detectives traveled upstate to investigate Maranzano's affairs in Dutchess County. Records of an April 9, 1931, Maranzano pistol permit, endorsed by Poughkeepsie Town Supervisor Lee Jackson[69] and two other well known residents, raised questions of the Mafia leader's connections to local officials. Detectives considered briefly that a disagreement in the Wappingers Falls area could have led to the murder. Local resident Rocco Germano claimed that Maranzano cheated him out of his farm in 1928, then promised to make restitution in the amount of twelve thousand dollars but paid only five hundred dollars.[70] Germano was able to prove that he was in Poughkeepsie on the day Maranzano was killed.[71]

The investigators were left with a number of possibilities. They felt Maranzano was killed due to his apparent involvement in the smuggling of aliens into the country, to a factional struggle in the Italian underworld or to a bootlegging rivalry. The investigation of his alleged alien smuggling ring took detectives to Buffalo and to Chicago.[72]

As in the Masseria assassination, Charlie Luciano stepped forward and admitted to his underworld colleagues that he orchestrated Maranzano's killing. He claimed he did so in self-defense after learning that Maranzano had hired Vincent "Mad Dog" Coll to kill him and his organization's underboss Vito Genovese. Maranzano confidant Thomas Lucchese supported Luciano's story.[73]

Luciano quickly communicated with Stefano Magaddino.[74] The Buffalo boss was not at all upset by the news. Magaddino called Joseph Bonanno, who succeeded Maranzano as the most influential Castellammarese Mafioso within New York City, and told him that Luciano was prepared to offer a full explanation for his actions at yet another underworld convention in Chicago.[75]

--- --- ---

When word of the Maranzano assassination reached Pittsburgh, John Bazzano saw opportunity and immediately moved against local boss Giuseppe Siragusa.[76]

Siragusa had been in a precarious position for some time, though he seemed not to know it. His efforts to curry favor with Maranzano, even at the cost of a trusted and resourceful associate like Nicola Gentile, had eroded support within his organization. His insistence on holding down the prices of supplies he sold to moonshine operations undercut and angered competitors on Pittsburgh's North Side.

A meeting of local gang chiefs in late August failed to resolve the pricing dispute, as short-sighted Siragusa – protected through his personal friendship with the boss of bosses – saw no reason for compromise.

Just three days after Maranzano's assassination, Siragusa's wife returned home from church to find her husband's bullet-riddled body at the bottom of the basement stairs. Gunmen had apparently interrupted the boss's morning shave in his basement bathroom. His face was covered with lather.

Investigators noted that a pet parrot in the home, apparently the only witness to Siragusa's murder, incessantly repeated the words, "Poor Joe, Poor Joe..."[77]

--- --- ---

Gathering once again in Capone's city, the Mafia general assembly heard testimony from men who had been close to the late boss of bosses. Witnesses included Girolamo Santuccio, a Maranzano soldier,[78] and Frank "Ciccio" Scalise, a senior member of the old Mineo organization. "On that occasion, thanks to the testimony of Ciccio Scalise, there were revealed many deeds and misdeeds committed by Maranzano in the period of his dictatorship."[79] The Mafia assembly exonerated Luciano.

Noting the vast potential for abuse and factional violence within the traditional boss of bosses system, the assembly decided to move in a new direction. Above the hierarchies of individual Mafia families, it placed a panel of powerful leaders:

> The most consequential aspect of this post-Maranzano era was our adoption of a new form of leadership consensus. We revised the old custom of looking toward one man, one supreme leader for advice and for the settling of disputes. We replaced leadership by one man with leadership by committee. We opted for a parliamentary arrangement whereby a group of the most important men in our world would assume the function formerly performed by one man. This group became known as the Commission.[80]

The first Commission had seven members. It included the five Mafia bosses of New York – Charlie Luciano, Joseph Bonanno, Tommaso Gagliano, Giuseppe Profaci and Vincenzo Mangano – as well as Cleveland boss Frank Milano and Chicago boss Alphonse Capone, whose career-ending conviction on tax charges was just days away.[81] National meetings of the Commission were scheduled for every five years.[82]

The ability of the new system to maintain order in the Italian underworld was tested almost immediately, as violence flared up in Pittsburgh.

— — —

Luciano's underboss Vito Genovese settled a personal vendetta and removed a potential problem for the new order in the autumn of 1931: He took Saverio Pollaccia for a ride.

Pollaccia had a long and violent history in the American Mafia. Originally a supporter and personal friend of boss of bosses Salvatore D'Aquila, he turned his back on D'Aquila, and probably also Umberto Valente, to become a top adviser to "Joe the Boss" Masseria in the early 1920s. He traveled with Brooklyn's Frankie Yale to Chicago at the time of the Dean O'Banion murder. Just two years later, Pollaccia's contact information was found in the personal papers of the murdered Chicago gangster Orazio Tropea. Pollaccia was questioned by police in connection with the Mineo and Ferrigno murders of November 1930 and with Masseria's assassination.

As Luciano became the most powerful man in the former Masseria organization, he must have been concerned about

Pollaccia's treacherous past. It seems certain that Luciano quietly approved Genovese's plan to take Pollaccia along on a one-way automobile trip to Chicago, where Paolo Ricca had taken over as boss after Capone's October 1931 conviction on tax evasion charges.[83]

Pollaccia accepted Genovese's invitation, and the two drove west. They stopped briefly in Pittsburgh, where Genovese confided in new boss John Bazzano that he was traveling to Chicago to have Pollaccia eliminated. Once in Chicago, Genovese and Ricca murdered Pollaccia and buried him.[84] Pollaccia's wife and children never learned what happened to him.[85]

The elimination of the distinguished Sicilian Mafioso by the Neapolitan Genovese was enormously upsetting to Nicola Gentile and his protégé Bazzano. "This deed saddened me greatly," Gentile later wrote. "I don't have any trouble recalling that I said the following to Bazzano: 'This deed should never have happened or permitted, because one does not take the life of a father of five children for trivial reasons or spite.' To which Bazzano replied: 'Dear Uncle Cola, Genovese told me this in confidence. What could I have done?'"[86]

Bazzano lashed out at Pittsburgh's Neapolitan racketeers in midsummer of 1932, ordering the murders of three brothers – John, James and Arthur Volpe. The murders were committed July 29 within the Rome Coffee Shop on Wylie Avenue, a business operated by Bazzano and his brother Santo.[87]

After some investigation, the police were satisfied that Bazzano had not been involved in the Volpes' deaths. However, the underworld knew better.

A vacationing Gentile learned about the killings through a newspaper report in Syracuse, New York. He immediately concluded that Bazzano was responsible. Gentile understood that Bazzano, as a newcomer to the rank of Mafia boss, would not have acted against the well-connected Volpe brothers without the approval of some higher-up. Gentile assumed that Cleveland boss Frank Milano, a friend of Bazzano and a newly appointed member of the Mafia Commission, endorsed the hit.

Gentile was concerned that he would receive some of the blame for the murders. The close mentor-protégé relationship he had with Bazzano was widely known. His worry increased when he learned that Bazzano had assigned members of Gentile's Pittsburgh crew to perform the hit.[88] Further, the timing of Gentile's vacation from Pittsburgh could have been viewed by some as evidence that he had foreknowledge of plot against the Volpes and was trying to establish an alibi.

Vito Genovese was enraged by the news from Pittsburgh. He initially believed that Bazzano's prominent friends, Gentile from Pittsburgh and Albert Anastasia and Joseph Biondo from New York, all had conspired against the Neapolitan Volpes. Anastasia arranged a meeting with Genovese and assured him that he, Gentile and Biondo had no part in the attack. Anastasia persuaded Genovese to give him some time to look into the matter.

Using the democratic approach of the Mafia's new order, Anastasia quickly assembled a panel of Mafiosi from various organizations and summoned Bazzano to New York to explain himself.[89] Pittsburgh racketeers Joe Tito and Giuseppe "Big Mike" Spinelli also were summoned.[90]

Bazzano, Tito and Spinelli arrived in New York by August 4, taking rooms in the Pennsylvania Hotel. Bazzano took private quarters, while Tito and Spinelli roomed together.[91] Spinelli and Tito checked out of the hotel on August 6 and vanished.[92] Bazzano also left the establishment that day, but he did not check out.

That evening, the Pittsburgh boss was brought before Anastasia's assembly of senior Mafiosi in an empty building on Hicks Street in the Red Hook section of Brooklyn. Bazzano sat at a table as he was interrogated over the unauthorized murders of the Volpe brothers. One inquisitor charged that Bazzano had not only provoked retribution against himself but had also exposed his closest friends to Neapolitan wrath.

Bazzano grew indignant at the proceedings. He acknowledged his involvement in the Volpe slayings and insisted that he had done the right thing. Rather than mitigate his offense by citing Volpe antagonism or other justification, he incited his judges by calling for an expanded war against Neapolitan gangsters: "We finally can eliminate these Neapolitans!" he shouted, slamming his fists onto the table.[93]

The gathered mobsters had heard enough. John Bazzano was a loose cannon, a danger to shaky year-old underworld alliances.

As a group, they jumped at Bazzano and held him down. One fastened a rope around the struggling Pittsburgh boss's neck, while others punched small but deadly holes into his chest with ice picks. After the life had drained from Bazzano, the assassins folded his body up, tied it with clothesline and crammed it into burlap sacks. They dropped the parcel near a Center Street refuse pile known as Tin Can Mountain.[94]

Anastasia, Biondo and Vincenzo Mangano then met with Genovese and described to him how the matter had been resolved. Genovese decided that justice had been done and that Anastasia and Biondo had vindicated themselves.[95]

Bazzano's body was found on August 8. Detectives counted more than twenty puncture marks in its chest. There were no identifying papers.[96] Investigators tracked labels in the victim's clothing, circulated photographs of the dead man and compared dental casts to the records of missing persons. Clues eventually pointed to John Bazzano of Pittsburgh. Bazzano's brother-in-law Andrew Zappala traveled to New York to identify the remains and bring Bazzano's body back to Pittsburgh for a military burial.[97]

With the victim's identity established, New York Police began watching the movements of local Italian underworld figures. They learned, most likely through informants, that a group of Mafiosi planned a social gathering at a midtown Manhattan hotel on the evening of August 16. In advance of the party, police flying squads were sent to hotels in Manhattan and Brooklyn where Mafiosi were believed to be staying. Fourteen men were arrested.[98]

Five of the arrested men were from Brooklyn. They were Albert Anastasia, John "Johnny Bath Beach" Oddo, Cassandro "Tony the Chief" Bonasera, Ciro Gallo and Giuseppe Traina. Oddo and Bonasera, members of the Profaci Crime Family in Brooklyn, were close friends for many years.[99] Bonasera, a native of Vallelunga,[100] came to the U.S. as a child and reportedly attended school with Charlie Luciano. Bonasera had strong connections to the DiCarlo family and to other Vallelunghesi living in the Buffalo area.[101]

Arrested visitors to the city included Joseph DiCarlo's brother Sam DiCarlo and Paul Palmeri from the Buffalo area; Santo Volpe[102] and Angelo Polizzi from northeast Pennsylvania;

Peter Lombardo of Trenton, New Jersey; and Pittsburgh-area residents Calogero Spallino, Michael Bua, Frank Adrano and Michael "Valenzano" Russo. The arrests brought DiCarlo, Traina and Russo once again to the public's attention. Those three men also had been arrested as Cleveland underworld convention delegates in 1928.

The exposure was particularly dangerous for Sam DiCarlo. At the time, he was out on bail pending an appeal of a federal auto theft conviction. He had been found guilty on May 4 of violating the Dyer Act by stealing a vehicle in Chicago and transporting it across state lines to Buffalo. On the ninth, he was sentenced to serve two years in prison.[103]

The fourteen arrested men were ably defended by attorney Samuel Simon Leibowitz, who already had won seventy-seven out of seventy-eight murder cases in his career. Leibowitz went immediately to the press, arguing that his clients had merely assembled for a reunion of old friends in the grocery and restaurant businesses:

> There is not a scrap of evidence on which to hold these men. This is the most wholesale homicide arraignment in the history of criminal procedure in this country. And it will also be the most wholesale discharge of defendants in the history of criminal procedure. There is nothing against these men, absolutely nothing.[104]

On August 18, prosecutors admitted to Magistrate George H. Folwell of the Brooklyn Homicide Court that they had no credible evidence to connect the fourteen defendants to the murder of Bazzano. As Folwell ordered the defendants released, a police source explained to the press, "You can't bring your stool pigeons into court. Nobody ever testifies in a gang case. They know what happens to them if they do."[105]

John Bazzano's slayers escaped punishment, and his ice pick murder remains unsolved.

Perhaps hoping to avoid a similar end, Cleveland boss Frank Milano, an apparent supporter of Bazzano's private war against Neapolitan racketeers, went into exile. He moved his racketeering operations to southern California and Mexico. Dr. Giuseppe

Romano, highly regarded surgeon and longtime Mafioso, took over as boss of Cleveland's Italian underworld. Milano was removed from the American Mafia's ruling Commission. His Commission seat was awarded to Buffalo boss Stefano Magaddino.

— — —

An invisible force within the Mafia's new order continued to move against those connected with the final moments of the Masseria regime. It already had eliminated Johnny "Silk Stockings" Giustra in early May of 1931 and had caught up with Giustra's close friend Carmelo Liconti two months later. One loose end remained.

Gerardo Scarpato had been in a state of panic since the Masseria assassination in his Coney Island restaurant. Involved in Brooklyn racketeering for some time, the restaurateur knew how his associates operated.[106] When questioned following the assassination, he demanded that police fingerprint him, just in case his corpse should someday need to be identified: "Take my fingerprints. Take them for your books. I think you will need them. I may be next." Scarpato took the added precaution of having his own name tattooed on one of his arms.[107]

The restaurateur and his wife Elvira left Coney Island immediately after the Maranzano banquet at Nuova Villa Tammaro. The couple sailed for Italy, where Scarpato was able to rest his nerves. They returned to the United States nearly a year later, June 1, 1932, aboard the *S.S. Saturnia*.[108]

Scarpato apparently was rejuvenated by the trip. When he returned to Coney Island, he aggressively involved himself in local politics, becoming an executive member of the Surf Democratic Club. He invested in bicycle racing and boxing exhibitions at the Coney Island Velodrome arena.[109] He also opened a new café, the Seaside Inn, on busy Surf Avenue next door to the Nathan's Famous delicatessen.[110]

At the end of the summer, Elvira Scarpato took a short vacation away from her husband. She went to the Catskill Mountains and stayed at the Acra Resort. She returned to Coney Island on the evening of Friday, September 9, to find her husband not at home. Police later learned that Scarpato spent that evening at the Seaside Inn and was last seen as he left the establishment about one o'clock on Saturday morning.[111]

At six o'clock that morning, James Ormand, of 214 Windsor Place in the Prospect Park South district of Brooklyn, noticed a strange black sedan parked by the curb. He assumed that his neighbor Charles Baer had visitors and thought no more about the car that day. At eleven o'clock Sunday morning, Ormand and Baer met each other outside. Ormand asked about the car. Baer said he had no visitors. Examining the vehicle, the men saw a large burlap sack in its rear seat and decided to get the police involved. Each went to summon detectives who lived in the neighborhood.

Detectives James Dwyer and George Gallagher went out to take a look. Dwyer broke a rear window on the vehicle, unlocked and opened the door. The burlap sack was sewn closed. Dwyer used a knife to cut a slit in the sack and saw a dead body inside. Neither of the detectives recognized the victim.

The remains of Gerardo Scarpato were quickly identified after the sack and its contents were transported to the Fifth Avenue police station. The restaurateur had been strangled to death. A single length of sash cord had been used to bind him and to cause his death. The cord held his wrists behind him, bound his legs together and raised them to his chin, and surrounded his neck with a noose. Investigators determined that Scarpato gradually had tightened the noose as he struggled to free himself from his bonds.[112]

Police brought Anthony Carfano in for questioning. The Brooklyn underworld leader and former Masseria partner admitted that he had known Scarpato for many years, had grown up with him. Carfano said he could not imagine why anyone would want to harm his old friend.[113] The Scarpato murder was never solved.[114]

Chapter 18

Public Enemy No. 1

While much of the American Mafia was directly or indirectly engaged in the Castellammarese War, one arm of Stefano Magaddino's western New York organization focused its attention on building rackets within the City of Buffalo. During the early 1930s, law enforcement gradually became aware of the "DiCarlo Gang" commanded by Joseph DiCarlo.

In September 1930, Sam DiCarlo and six other men were arrested in connection with the kidnapping, torture and attempted murder of Fort Erie, Ontario, bootlegger William Shisler.

Missing for several days, Shisler was rescued from the Buffalo River at the foot of Michigan Avenue. The crew of the *S.S. Fitch*, moored at the Washburn-Crosby Mill on the Blackwell Canal, heard Shisler's screams at about two o'clock in the morning and went to investigate. The bootlegger had been struggling for half an hour to free himself from ropes tying his arms and legs together. When rescuers pulled him onto the deck of the *Fitch*, Shisler was unable to speak coherently, but moaned about men who were trying to kill him.

Shisler later told police of his abduction. He said he received a telephone call asking him to meet two men at Delaware Avenue and Bryant Street in Buffalo. He went to the meeting and was confronted by four men. They took Shisler away in a large sedan. The men demanded a $6,000 ransom for his release and instructed him to contact family members to arrange the payment.[1] Shisler wrote a letter, stating, "I am held in $6,000 ransom by a bunch of fellows who will stop at nothing. Please send it."

Shisler's father received the letter and took it at once to the

Fort Erie Police. They notified Buffalo Police. While awaiting a reply to the ransom demand, Shisler's captors subjected him to beatings. When it became apparent that no payment would be made, the men tied Shisler, struck him over the head and dropped him into the river.[2]

Buffalo Police quickly focused their attention on Sam DiCarlo. They went to his Prospect Avenue home and found Joe Aleo and Sam DiCarlo. Both men were arrested. Police quickly made five other arrests in connection with the case. Four of those arrested were arraigned on vagrancy charges in city court and quickly released.[3]

At Sam DiCarlo's home, investigators searched through notebooks and other documents. They confiscated a notebook, which held entries apparently related to bootlegging accounts, as well as a collection of "Old Log Cabin" whiskey bottle labels and revenue stamps. The evidence was turned over to Prohibition officials.

Police said they hoped to locate and question Joseph DiCarlo about his brother's activities.[4]

The authorities concluded that Shisler had been kidnapped after he received a quantity of liquor from a Windsor, Ontario, supplier and failed to provide payment.[5] By September 14, Buffalo's new Police Commissioner Austin J. Roche[6] announced that the Shisler investigation was closed.

Roche further declared that the city of Buffalo was entirely free of racketeers. Any plans by underworld organizations in the region to move into the city had been thwarted by constant police surveillance, he said.

"We are ready to throw any or all of these gamblers or racketeers in jail if they set foot inside the city limits," the police commissioner added. [7]

Just nine months after pronouncing the city free of racketeers, Roche found himself supervising a large racketeering investigation of Joseph DiCarlo's operations. In June 1931, Roche's police force began a crackdown on a bootleggers "union" they found operating in the region. He explained to the press that a band of extortionists had been compelling rumrunners to pay fees to the union or face dire consequences.

The union investigation dovetailed with the earlier investigation of William Shisler's kidnapping. As in the Shisler case, police learned that a local rumrunner had been terrorized by a gang.

After smuggling one thousand seven hundred cases of Canadian whiskey into the U.S., the rumrunner was confronted by the DiCarlo gang. Gang members told him that he would have to pay a fifty-dollar initiation fee and a protection "tax" of two dollars per case. When he refused, the racketeers delivered their ultimatum: "Make no mistake about this. We have the means of breaking you and your business at a moment's notice. If you want to continue to do business, membership in our union is the only means by which you will be allowed to do so."

The investigation revealed that about one hundred and twenty-five bootleggers and speakeasy proprietors had been enrolled in the union.[8]

On June 23, police gathered thirty-three people from a bootleggers union office at 88 West Chippewa Street. All were brought to police headquarters for questioning. Twelve were kept in custody. Ten others were ordered to appear before a grand jury. Commissioner Roche promised that he would obtain indictments for extortion against the ringleaders. In the raid, police also seized boxes of records, including membership and price lists.[9]

The next day, as more than fifty witnesses testified before the grand jury, Roche informed the press that Joseph DiCarlo was being held incommunicado in an outlying police station. DiCarlo had been arrested at his Prospect Avenue home. The police believed he was the leader of the bootlegger extortion ring. John J. Barbera, rumored to be DiCarlo's top lieutenant in the extortion operation, was held in another police station. Samuel Coppola, John Fina, Michael Menneci, Joseph Santasiero and Joseph Aleo, also described as DiCarlo lieutenants, had been arrested and held by police.

Roche said he uncovered a connection between the extortion ring and a New York syndicate that supplied liquor bottle labels and official-looking Canadian strip stamps. The labels and stamps were an added incentive for bootleggers to join the union. Other benefits for union members, Roche said, included access to armed guards for liquor shipments and to bail bondsmen in case of arrest.[10]

On the twenty-fifth, the local press ran a story that depicted

DiCarlo as the victim of an extortion ring, rather than as the leader of one. The story said that an unidentified man riding around Buffalo in a large, black touring car in the company of three other men had been making threats against DiCarlo.

That man and DiCarlo reportedly ran into each other at a Chippewa Street restaurant in mid-June. DiCarlo challenged the man to "Come and take me." The man ignored the taunt but assured others in the restaurant, "Joe can be taken, and I am the guy that can do it. If he can't listen to reason, maybe he'll listen to muscle."

According to the news story, the unidentified man and his companions had been extorting payments from Buffalo gamblers, speakeasy operators and other characters in the city's night life. Because it targeted only illicit businesses, the group did not need to fear that any of its victims would report the extortion to the police.[11]

Four indictments were returned by the grand jury on June 26. They named DiCarlo gang members John Barbera, Samuel Coppola, John Fina and Joseph Aleo as participants in the bootleggers union. Bail for each was set in the amount of $20,000. No indictments were returned against Joseph DiCarlo or Joseph Santasiero. They both were freed.[12]

Police subsequently expressed their disappointment that the top-level leaders of the coercive union escaped justice. The case against Barbera, Coppola, Fina and Aleo began to fall apart at the end of June. By the first week of July, there was wide expectation that the charges would be dismissed.[13]

— — —

As Buffalo authorities were rounding up the bootlegger extortion ring, a period of intense underworld bloodshed was concluding about seventy miles to the south, along the New York-Pennsylvania border. The violence, which included more than fifty murders during the thirteen years of Prohibition,[14] ended with the slaying of flashy bootlegger Alberto "Buffalo Al" Ritchie.[15]

Born in 1886 to a Neapolitan family,[16] Ritchie entered the United States at the age of eighteen and resided just long enough in Buffalo to acquire his nickname. He then lived for a time in Scranton, Pennsylvania, where he became a prizefighter and later a boxing promoter. At the start of the Prohibition Era, he turned from boxing to underworld rackets and began running alcohol into southwestern New York.[17] His illegal activity focused on the clustered communities of Olean and Salamanca, in Cattaraugus County, New York, and Bradford, in McKean County, Pennsylvania. In that busy, oil-rich region, well-established Neapolitan and Calabrian criminal organizations were already engaged in a feud.

After refusing to make tribute payments to the local Camorra leader, Ritchie agreed to provide the Camorra with a supply of low-cost alcohol. After a few years, Ritchie purchased an old inn on the Hinsdale Highway just north of Olean. He converted the building into a roadhouse and brothel named the Sunset Inn and shielded his illicit enterprises from the police by cooperating as an informant.[18]

A rivalry developed between Ritchie and underworld leaders Joe and John Barber.[19] On the morning of May 15, 1925, forty-year-old John Barber was murdered as he left his Wayne Street home in Olean.[20] Ritchie later told the authorities that the Barbers were targeted for punishment after defying the will of a regional criminal tribunal.[21] Joe Barber believed Ritchie was responsible for the death of his brother.

Ritchie's expansion of his rackets into Bradford in 1929 coincided with an attempt on his life. Late in the evening on September 26, Ritchie entered his small roadster, parked in front of the Christopher Columbus Lodge on Olean's North Union Street, started the vehicle and began to pull away from the curb. Another automobile immediately pulled up behind him and a gunman inside it opened fire on Ritchie with a shotgun.

A load of buckshot tore through the fabric top of the roadster and struck Ritchie's face, neck and shoulder. Severely wounded, he managed to draw a pistol and fire several shots at the gunman's vehicle as it drove away. Ritchie survived the attack, but his face was deeply scarred. He interpreted the shooting as an act of retaliation by the Barber faction.[22]

After recovering from his wounds, Ritchie abandoned Olean in favor of Bradford. In that community, he allied himself with McKean County Detective Jack Allison and obtained a county law enforcement badge, along with the officially meaningless title of assistant county detective. While Ritchie claimed to be working to rid Bradford of its Italian criminal element, many believed he was using his position to extort tribute from minor racketeers in the Italian colony while also diminishing the strength of his underworld rivals.[23]

In Bradford, Ritchie married a recent high school graduate named Anna Ciscone. The couple settled into a home at 46 Boylston Street, as Ritchie began a new career as a journalist.[24]

Focusing on the subject he knew best, the underworld of the Olean-Salamanca-Bradford region, Ritchie composed a series of articles for *True Detective Mysteries* magazine. The first of the series was published in September 1930 under the title, "Black Hand Exposed – At Last!" In that article, "Detective" Ritchie claimed that, during a 1928 murder investigation in Olean, he came into possession of a "little black book" of rules and rituals of a secret Italian criminal society. The book, he said, was written in Italian and published in Seville, Spain.[25]

Detective Jack Allison was awakened by the telephone at four-thirty in the morning, May 4, 1931. The anonymous caller told him to travel from Eldred to Bradford, watching the left side of the road for "a friend." Allison did as he was instructed. Along the route, he found local resident Charles Clark and Bradford's Acting Police Chief Garner R. Fairbanks at Red Rock Hill, already examining the dead body of thirty-year-old underworld boss Joe Barber. The body, wearing a blood-covered cap, was found propped up against a tree stump on the roadside. Barber had been shot once in the head, the slug removing a portion of his skull.[26]

In a celebratory mood, Ritchie appeared at John A. Still's funeral home and made arrangements for the funeral of his old rival.[27] Ritchie's own days were numbered, however, and the racketeer seemed to know it. He soon made another visit to the funeral home to select a casket for himself. "I may be the next to go," Ritchie told Still. "I'm getting ready."[28]

At three o'clock in the afternoon of June 5, Ritchie and a passenger, forty-five-year-old Tony "Mike" Maccio, were driving along Bradford's River Street in Ritchie's Chrysler Eight Coupe, when Ritchie spotted Loreto "Jumbo" Sarandrea to his left and pulled his car to the curb on the wrong side of the street to talk with him.

Sarandrea leaned into Ritchie's open driver's side window, as the men chatted. Another man darted to the automobile and thrust a .38-caliber pistol under Sarandrea's right arm. Shots were fired, as Sarandrea ran for cover and Maccio attempted to exit the car. Three steel-jacketed slugs struck Ritchie in the head, and another grazed his left arm. Two slugs struck Maccio in the back.

The gunman ran off. Ritchie and Maccio stumbled from the car. When an ambulance arrived, the mortally wounded Ritchie had sufficient strength to walk to it without assistance. He died at Bradford Hospital at five o'clock. Witnesses identified his murderer as Tony Lorenzo, who relocated to Bradford from Brooklyn, New York, about a half year earlier. Police concluded that Lorenzo had been hired to eliminate Ritchie.[29]

Ritchie's funeral on June 8 was not exactly as he had planned it. A warning reportedly was issued by the local underworld that anyone participating in the event would meet the same end as Ritchie. Local and county law enforcement officers turned out to St. Bernard Church to provide protection for Ritchie's six pall bearers and to maintain order.[30]

— — —

The Buffalo investigation of the DiCarlo Gang had an unfortunate side effect for Angelo Palmeri. While cooperating with local police, federal authorities in June stumbled across an old perjury indictment against Palmeri. The charge stemmed from a 1922 pistol permit application, on which he falsely claimed American citizenship. Palmeri had been released on $5,000 bond, but the matter never went to trial.[31]

Additional law enforcement attention was focused on Palmeri in September 1931 after four of his associates were arrested on charges of extorting money from a Niagara Falls restaurateur. Anthony Falcony complained to police that men sent by "Buffalo Bill" – Palmeri's nickname – had repeatedly demanded that he provide financial support for a friend in distress. According to Falcony, his brother Frank had been murdered after similar requests were made of him the previous fall. Police arrested Joseph and Michael LaBarbara, Louis Burgio and Nicholas Cerrito.[32]

Palmeri was not without enemies, and later in September it appeared that his enemies had gained the upper hand. "Buffalo Bill" suffered a severe beating followed by a death threat. He withdrew into his home on Buffalo's Jersey Street, where police kept watch over him. On September 28, detective sergeants stationed around the Palmeri residence spotted three men leaving his home.

A heavy rainstorm prevented identification of the men on the spot, and Joseph DiCarlo, Peter Rizzo and Rochester resident Patsy Amico all were placed under arrest. Authorities took note of a twelve-and-a-half-carat diamond ring worn by Amico. When the suspects were able to identify themselves as Palmeri's friends, they were released.[33]

Police turned their attention to Palmeri's brother Paul in November. Paul Palmeri, a Niagara Falls undertaker, was one of five men arrested in Chicago as suspected accomplices in the St. Louis, Missouri, kidnapping of wealthy fur dealer Alexander Berg.

On Friday evening, November 6, two gunmen forced Berg into a waiting automobile. They covered his eyes with bandages and took him to an apartment over a store.[34] Berg's family received a ransom demand for one hundred thousand dollars. Police learned that New Yorker Louis Spinelli, reportedly a friend of Berg, was positioning himself as an intermediary between the family in St. Louis and Berg's captors, apparently based in Chicago.[35]

Police followed Spinelli on Monday, November 9, as he went to a scheduled meeting with representatives of the kidnappers at the intersection of Harrison Street and Wabash Avenue in Chicago. Spotting an automobile with no license plates parked at the southeast corner of the intersection, the police converged. As other officers stood by with weapons drawn, Lieutenant Robert Carr went up to the vehicle, threw open its door and arrested its occupants.

The kidnapping suspects were Paul Palmeri, "Dago Lawrence" Mangano, Frank Chiaravalloti, Sylvester Agoglia and Angelo Caruso.[36] The thirty-nine-year-old Mangano was a prominent member of Alphonse Capone's Chicago Outfit. Newspapers regarded him as underworld leader of the city's West Side.[37] Chiaravalloti and Agoglia also were residents of Chicago. (Agoglia shared a common Brooklyn gangland background with Capone.[38]) Caruso was a resident of New York City and second in command of the Castellammarese Mafia faction led by Salvatore Maranzano.[39]

In Niagara Falls, Palmeri's wife learned of his arrest and told the local newspaper that it was an error. "Of course, it's all a mistake," she said. She acknowledged that Palmeri had gone to Chicago. When asked the purpose of his trip, she responded, "I don't know."[40]

As police were questioning their kidnapping suspects, Alexander Berg showed up at his St. Louis home in a taxicab. He was apparently unharmed but nervous and initially refused to speak with newspaper reporters.[41] He and his attorney Adrian Levinson later met with newsmen.

"At no time did I feel in danger of brutal treatment," Berg told the press. "But I will never forget what I went through. It was a terrible and most trying ordeal." Levinson added that Berg was "treated fine, given juicy steaks and plenty of fresh fruit to eat. He also was given magazines."[42]

Chicago Police released Palmeri and the other kidnapping suspects on November 10, 1931. Chief of Detectives William Shoemaker explained that no evidence had been found connecting the men to Berg's abduction.[43]

— — —

On November 21, 1931, Buffalo resident Faulkner E. Vanderburg walked into a building at 421 Niagara Street, climbed the stairs to the second floor and entered an apartment occupied by a bookmaking establishment. Neighbors overheard a loud argument, physical scuffling and then gunshots. Alarmed, building occupants rushed for the exit. At the stairway landing between the first and second floors, they found Vanderburg's dead body.[44]

Public records indicated that Vanderburg worked as an electrical engineer specializing in telephone equipment.[45] His actual occupation since late in 1929 was collector for a horseracing wire service known as the General News Bureau.[46]

Founded in 1907 by Chicago gambling czar Mont Tennes, General News Bureau used telegraph lines to provide horse race results to subscribing bookmakers. The service quickly became invaluable to sports gambling operations. Tennes survived rivals' repeated attempts on his life and squeezed out a number of competing firms, including the older Payne News Agency, to assemble a nationwide wire service by the start of World War I. Tennes retired from the business by 1927, turning it over to a group of investors including Philadelphia publisher Moses

Annenberg and John L. Lynch. Annenberg and Lynch aggressively expanded the enterprise into a coast-to-coast monopoly.[47]

Buffalo police attributed the murder of Vanderburg to a robbery attempt. Surprisingly, they appeared not to consider that Vanderburg's shooting was the result either of race wire service competition or of a disagreement over service fees. They noted that a gang had been holding up local bookmaking establishments for about a year and assumed that gunmen trailed Vanderburg as he made his collections.[48]

Detectives concluded that two men shot and killed Vanderburg and then retreated back up the stairs and out the second-floor window of the "bookie joint." They climbed to the building roof and leaped to an adjoining roof to make their getaway.[49]

Police brought in a number of local men for questioning. They seized apparently blood-stained shoes from one of their suspects, Anthony Iraci. Tests by the city chemist later revealed that the stains were not caused by blood. Authorities also questioned John Monaco, owner of the bookmaking establishment, and eight other men, including Anthony Perna and Russell Bufalino, but learned nothing helpful.[50]

With the investigation seemingly at a dead end, police brought Joseph DiCarlo to headquarters for questioning on December 1. DiCarlo, interrogated repeatedly since his release from prison, strenuously objected. "Why don't you let me alone?" he shouted as he was taken into Police Headquarters. "I'll go back to Italy if necessary to get away from this kind of stuff."[51]

Commissioner Roche apparently had a similar idea. On December 2, Roche had DiCarlo arrested for illegally registering to vote and simultaneously asked federal officials to begin deportation proceedings against the Buffalo racketeer.[52]

DiCarlo registered to vote October 16 in the Niagara Street District. While registering, he swore an oath that he was legally qualified as a voter. Authorities asserted that DiCarlo's 1924 federal conviction had cost him his right to vote. Under the law, convicted felons were ineligible to vote unless they secured an executive pardon. Detectives followed DiCarlo on Election Day and noted that he did not cast a ballot.[53]

Roche announced that he was also investigating how DiCarlo and others with criminal records had managed to obtain New York licenses to drive. The police commissioner mentioned to the press that DiCarlo was licensed to drive his "big, new limousine."[54] When questioned about the license, DiCarlo responded vaguely, "Someone fixed it for me in Albany."[55]

On December 3, Assistant District Attorney Walter W. Hofheins recommended that bail for DiCarlo be set at $1,500. An initial hearing on the illegal voter registration charge was postponed at the request of the prosecutor. DiCarlo attorney Frank Gugino objected to the delay. DiCarlo insisted that he was being persecuted by police and that Commissioner Roche was holding the voter registration charge over his head in an effort to compel him to aid the investigation into Faulkner Vanderburg's murder.[56]

That evening, Judge George H. Rowe appeared unexpectedly at Buffalo Police Headquarters to fix the bail amount and approve a bail bond presented by DiCarlo's attorney Frank Gugino. Roche immediately questioned the propriety of Judge Rowe's after-hours personal appearance. According to the police commissioner, a prisoner's bondsman traditionally approached a judge at court or at home after the amount of the bond has been fixed. Rowe answered that he did not care to have bondsmen at his home and preferred to handle the matter at Police Headquarters. The judge explained that he was going to be in the city for a dinner engagement and felt it was convenient to handle the DiCarlo bond in that manner.[57]

While a grand jury looked into the Vanderburg case, authorities pursued the illegal voter registration charge against DiCarlo. At a December 10 hearing in Buffalo City Court, police Captain Edward Thierfeldt testified about DiCarlo's 1924 witness intimidation conviction, and Board of Elections Secretary Glen Schultes described the oath taken by DiCarlo when he registered.[58]

In January of 1932, Commissioner Roche compiled a list of Buffalo "public enemies." He presented the list to Special Assistant Secretary of Labor Murray Garson, asking that the named individuals be considered for deportation from the United States. First on the list, Joseph DiCarlo was labeled "Public Enemy Number One."[59] The list also included Sam DiCarlo,

Angelo Palmeri and many of their underworld colleagues.[60]

Garson and Immigration Inspector John Kaba questioned Joseph DiCarlo on January 11. DiCarlo, claiming that he was employed as a Niagara Street florist, provided information on his family's Sicilian background and immigration to the U.S. He indicated that he became an American citizen as a minor when his father was naturalized.

"Do you know what year your father attained his final naturalization?" Garson asked.

"I don't know whether it is 1914 or 1915, but if I could get his papers I could tell you more about it." DiCarlo responded, perhaps unconsciously moving his father's naturalization far backward in time. "I have his papers somewhere."[61]

Immigration officials were unable to locate documentation to support DiCarlo's story.[62] Early in March, he provided authorities with his father's citizenship papers. Those proved that DiCarlo was twenty years old, a minor under the law at the time his father was naturalized.[63]

On March 7, County Judge F. Bret Thorn dismissed the illegal voter registration charge against DiCarlo. Defense counsel Frank Gugino convincingly argued that the federal intimidation offense on which DiCarlo was convicted in 1924 was not a felony under New York State law and could not have terminated DiCarlo's citizenship rights in the state. After a long legal squabble between the competing attorneys in the case, Judge Thorn ruled in favor of a Gugino motion to dismiss.[64]

DiCarlo's disputed driver's license was returned to him. Commissioner Roche first extracted a sworn promise that DiCarlo would not use his automobile in the commission of any illegal acts. Roche then sent a favorable recommendation to the Motor Vehicles office in Albany.[65]

— — —

The Porrello family's influence within the Cleveland underworld ended in February 1932 with the murders of Rosario and Raimondo Porrello.

The remaining Porrello brothers had been in hiding until reaching a truce with the Mayfield Road Gang earlier in the year. After the truce, Rosario and Raimondo were seen regularly, but always in the company of bodyguard Dominic "Mangino" Gueli.

At about three-thirty on the afternoon of February 25, the

two brothers and Gueli entered a Woodland Avenue tobacco shop owned by Joe Todaro.[66] The men sat at a table in the front room and began playing cards, as they did nearly every afternoon. Todaro stood behind the shop's counter and served a bottle of soda to patron Joe Damanti.

At three-fifty, three gunmen stepped into the shop's doorway, drew weapons and fired at the seated men. Todaro dropped down behind the counter to shield himself.

Raimondo Porrello fell to the floor with a bullet wound to the back of his head. Rosario rose to his feet before being felled by three shots to his head. Gueli managed to stumble to the center of the room despite suffering two gunshot wounds to his right temple. One of the slugs sliced completely through his brain. After three or four steps, Gueli collapsed.

The gunmen paused to view their work and then vanished into the street.

When police arrived, they found Joe Damanti unconscious on the sidewalk thirty yards from the shop with a bullet in his abdomen. Damanti was taken to St. Luke's Hospital, where his condition was graded critical. Police determined that he was an innocent bystander and was not at all acquainted with the Porrellos.

Three handguns were found on the shop floor near the doorway. Two of the weapons were empty and still warm. The third – a .45-caliber automatic pistol – had not been fired. The Porrellos were already dead, but Gueli still clung to life. He succumbed to his wounds two hours later.

At close to eight o'clock that evening, Cleveland racketeer Frank Brancato arrived at St. John's Hospital saying he had a pain in his stomach. It quickly became evident that the pain was the result of a gunshot wound. Though Brancato refused to say how or where he was wounded, police concluded that he was one of the gunmen who attacked the Porrellos.

Brancato was well known to police as a member of the Lonardo underworld faction. He had been questioned in connection with several recent murders and had been tried and acquitted for the 1930 killing of Frank Alessi.

Of the seven Porrello brothers who once dominated Sicilian organized crime in the Cleveland region, only three remained alive.[67]

While local and federal authorities were tangling with Joseph DiCarlo over voter registration and citizenship issues, they were also assembling a case against his brother Sam. On April 6, 1932, a federal grand jury indicted Sam DiCarlo for violating the Dyer Act, which prohibited the transport of stolen automobiles over state lines. The indictment included separate counts for interstate transportation of a stolen vehicle and for possession of the vehicle.[68]

Police had noted Sam driving around in a new 1931 Ford Victoria Coupe between August and December of the previous year. The vehicle was regularly parked in front of his house. They found that the car's engine number had been altered and that it was registered to a fictitious name and address.[69] Authorities eventually were able to trace the automobile to its legal owner, Jack Stone of Chicago. Stone had reported it stolen on August 6, 1931.[70]

Following the indictment, a warrant was issued for Sam DiCarlo's arrest. He was taken into custody on April 15, 1932.[71]

Federal prosecutors brought a number of witnesses from Chicago to Buffalo for Sam's trial. One of those was Edward Riccio, a notary public. A few days before the trial began, Riccio was returning to his room at a Buffalo hotel when a stranger accosted him. The stranger asked if Riccio was from Chicago and if he planned to testify in Sam DiCarlo's trial. As Riccio started to answer, a large automobile drove past. A man inside of it yelled out and threw a wad of paper at Riccio's feet.

Riccio opened the paper to find a scribbled warning on the back of a patent medicine advertisement. It read, "Leave town by Thursday nite or you will go in a coffin. This is yore chance to go hom alive." The Chicago notary turned the note over to federal prosecutors.

On May 3, U.S. Attorney Frederick T. Devlin opened the trial by calling six witnesses. Riccio was not on the witness list. A jury returned a guilty verdict the following day. Judge John Knight sentenced Sam DiCarlo to serve one year and one day in prison on each count, with the sentences running concurrently.[72]

Defense attorney Frank Gugino immediately filed an appeal. Sam DiCarlo was released on bail of $10,000 provided by three women with strong links to the local underworld: Laura Palmeri, wife of Angelo Palmeri; Lucia Rizzo, widow of the late Pietro Rizzo; and Antonia Bonventre, sister of Calogero "Charley Buffalo" DiBenedetto.[73]

While free on bail, Sam traveled to New York City with Paul Palmeri to attend a mid-August regional conference of Mafiosi. Both men were arrested there August 16 in connection with the recent murder of Pittsburgh underworld boss John Bazzano in Brooklyn. They and a dozen other suspects were released two days later.

— — —

A July 4, 1932, explosion at Albert Beyer's business in the eastern Buffalo suburb of Cheektowaga demolished the building's front entrance and shattered all of its windows. Initial reports indicated that Beyer's Doat Street establishment was a cigar and confection store. Authorities later revealed that liquor was sold on the premises.

Witnesses spotted an automobile pulling away from the building just before the explosion. Police traced the vehicle to Charles Bonasera, a close friend of the DiCarlos. However, Bonasera had reported it stolen on July 3.

Law enforcement's attention turned once again to Joseph DiCarlo. Erie County Sheriff Charles F. Freiberg brought DiCarlo in for questioning on July 11.

DiCarlo admitted that he knew Albert Beyer and that he had spoken with him at the end of June about a business deal. He denied a rumor that he had sought a loan of two thousand dollars but would not disclose the nature of the business deal. DiCarlo said he knew nothing about the explosion. He was out of town attending the funeral of restaurateur Thomas J.B. Dyke's brother on the fourth. He had returned from his trip only hours before the sheriff took him into custody. After four hours of questioning, Freiberg released DiCarlo.[74]

Buffalo Police Commissioner Austin Roche had more questions for DiCarlo in September as local law enforcement launched a drive against slot machines and other coin operated wagering devices.[75] It became clear that DiCarlo was shifting his attention from bootleg liquor to gambling.

According to an earlier decision by the Court of Appeals at Albany,[76] gaming machines in use around Buffalo were entirely legal for entertainment or vending purposes because prizes were limited to articles of small value – metal slugs or pieces of candy. By September 8, Roche had evidence of a secret agreement between machine distributors and the shopkeepers hosting the games. Under the agreement, the small prizes were redeemable for cash and merchandise.[77]

Roche immediately ordered the seizure of all gaming devices, including one hundred mint-vending machines from the Niagara Storage Warehouse, 220-226 Niagara Street. During the raid, information was recovered that led police to the main office of the Niagara Mint Company, 305 Root Building, 70 West Chippewa Street. That location was also DiCarlo's business address.

Investigators discovered that the placement and operation of the machines was overseen by the DiCarlo Gang. Stickers were placed on approved devices. Out-of-town distributors were required to pay the Niagara Mint Company two dollars a week for each machine they placed in Buffalo. After each weekly payment, new stickers would be affixed to identify approved machines.

Without the correct sticker, machines could be seized and destroyed. Roche told the press about two recent cases in which slot machines were forcibly removed from local restaurants.[78]

— — —

Prohibition agents were called out to an Erie, Pennsylvania, home in early August. Firefighters battling a blaze at the location discovered a liquor still inside.

Two agents arrived to place former Buffalo resident Pasquale "Patsy" Corda and John Solomon under arrest for bootlegging. Corda, the Neapolitan racketeer earlier suspected of involvement in the Erie murder of Philip Livaccori, managed to free himself from the agents and ran off. The agents caught up with him a block away. When Corda further resisted, the agents delivered a severe beating with blackjacks.

The agents returned to the burning home and attempted to dismantle the thousand-gallon still they found there. As they worked, the still exploded. The blast hurled the agents against a wall and caused burns to their hands and faces. In addition to the still, large quantities of mash, alcohol and gin were found on the premises.

Authorities determined that the illegal distillery had provided liquor to a large clientele in northwestern Pennsylvania.[79]

Despite continued enforcement, Prohibition's days were numbered. The midsummer Democratic National Convention in Chicago made repeal of the Eighteenth Amendment a plank of the party's campaign platform. Democratic Presidential Nominee Franklin Roosevelt pledged to work for repeal if elected. On November 8, 1932, Roosevelt won a landslide victory over incumbent Republican Herbert Hoover, who favored continuation of the Noble Experiment. Roosevelt had not yet taken office when, on December 6, 1932, Senator John Blaine of Wisconsin proposed a Twenty-first Constitutional Amendment to annul Prohibition.

Near the end of the year, Roche's lengthy "public enemies" list was reduced by one. Angelo Palmeri, longtime DiCarlo mentor, died on December 21, 1932.

The fifty-four-year old Mafioso attempted to leave his home at 295 Jersey Street at about one o'clock in the afternoon. He reportedly had an appointment to meet a friend uptown. Palmeri lost consciousness as he climbed into his automobile, which was parked in his driveway. A passer-by saw him slump behind the steering wheel and summoned the help of firemen from the station across the street from his house.

The firemen pulled Palmeri from his car and attempted to resuscitate him. He did not respond.

No autopsy was done. Physician August Lascola, who had treated Palmeri through the last eight months of his life, concluded that Palmeri died of cerebral hemorrhage. Dr. Lascola named parenchymatous nephritis (chronic inflammation of the kidneys) and hypertension as contributing factors. Palmeri had experienced symptoms of those disorders for at least eight months.[80]

As they heard news of his death, local police said Palmeri was "one of the last of the old guard of Buffalo's underworld." They grudgingly acknowledged that they had never notched a criminal conviction against him. One police official callously noted, "That's one more man we won't have to watch." A local newspaper, playing on Palmeri's affinity for five-gallon hats and holstered sidearms, quipped, "'Buffalo Bill' died with his boots on."[81]

The news was met with a different response within Buffalo's West Side Italian colony, where "Don Nitto" Palmeri was recalled with genuine affection and respect:

> His death Wednesday brought sincere expressions of sorrow from hundreds of American citizens of Italian ancestry whom he had befriended in times of need... To the police he was known as a man who had close contact with many illicit enterprises, who had such power that he was able to bring peace between warring liquor runners – but to the citizens of the lower West Side he was their individual welfare department, a man who could and would aid them when pride kept them from appealing to the organized charities... Especially sad were the members of upwards of a score of families whose only source of food each Christmas for years had been Angelo B. Palmeri.[82]

Palmeri's December 24 funeral procession was estimated to be the "largest ever turnout for an Italian-American citizen of Buffalo." Ceremonies began at the Palmeri home and continued with a Mass at Holy Angels Church on Porter Avenue. Palmeri was interred in a large family plot at Pine Hill Cemetery on Christmas Eve.[83] The funeral arrangements were handled by the Panepinto and Palmeri Funeral Home of Niagara Falls with the assistance of the Mascari Funeral Parlor of Buffalo.[84]

— — —

Early in 1933, twenty-five-year-old Angelo Porrello became the fifth member of his family to meet with a violent end within a two-year period. His father Rosario and three of his uncles had been murdered in Cleveland bootlegging feuds. Though he left Cleveland behind and settled in Buffalo in July 1932, Angelo Porrello could not avoid a similar fate. He was slain in a gunfight on Buffalo's Dante Place on January 13.

Widely considered a casualty of the continuing Magaddino-Callea conflict, Angelo actually lost his life due to a combination of a quick temper and poor luck at the billiard table.

Porrello spent the evening of January 12 playing pocket billiards in the poolroom of the Bagheria Club, 98 Dante Place. His opponent was Samuel Varisco, Republican committeeman from the city's Twenty-seventh Ward and son of the club's manager. Porrello repeatedly lost one-dollar game wagers and became quarrelsome. Varisco wanted to end the contests, but Porrello insisted that they continue playing and that they double the stakes. An argument ensued, the two men grappled and Varisco slapped Porrello's face.

"You'll pay dearly for that," Porrello said, as he left the poolroom.

The next afternoon at the Bagheria Club, Varisco learned that Porrello and his uncle John had been scouring the neighborhood looking for him. Varisco borrowed a handgun for protection. When he stepped out of the club just after six o'clock, he found Angelo Porrello waiting outside. Porrello called him over and walked him to the southwest corner of Dante Place and Evans Street. John Porrello emerged from a Callea brothers-operated soft-drink saloon at 124 Dante Place to join them.

Varisco attempted to explain the events of the previous night to John Porrello and apologized for slapping his nephew. Angelo Porrello cried out, "Why did you want to slap me?" as he threw a punch toward Varisco. The men scuffled, drew handguns and opened fire.[85]

Varisco's first two shots struck Angelo Porrello's head. One creased his forehead. The other smashed through his skull, killing him.[86]

As Varisco retreated behind a parked automobile, John Porrello pursued him, shooting repeatedly. The automobile absorbed much of the punishment meted out by Porrello's revolver. After the gunfight concluded, police counted a half dozen bullet holes in its side. Varisco escaped. He ran west down Dante Place, turned into an alley, climbed up onto a building roof and then dropped down onto a second-floor rear porch. Detective Sergeant William Fitzgibbons of the Buffalo Police apprehended him there minutes later.[87]

Varisco was charged with first-degree murder. He was arraigned February 14 before city Judge Clifford McLaughlin.[88] John Porrello was arrested and charged with first-degree assault.

Varisco's sixty-seven-year-old father Antonio also was arrested. He was charged with illegal possession of a handgun.[89]

Angelo Porrello's mother Josephine and his uncle Ottavio traveled from Cleveland to Buffalo on January 15. While they were making arrangements to transport Angelo's remains back to his home city for burial, Angelo's sister Frances, who remained behind in Cleveland, apparently attempted suicide. Despondent over the killing of her brother, Frances drank a small amount of poison. She was treated and released from St. Luke's Hospital.[90]

Despite a recommendation for dismissal by the district attorney's office, city Judge Patrick J. Keeler decided that Varisco should remain in custody while a grand jury considered the case. Keeler dismissed the assault charge against John Porrello.[91]

The grand jury refused to indict Varisco for first-degree murder. In May of 1933, Varisco stood trial for illegal possession of a revolver. While his trial was under way, Varisco pleaded guilty to a misdemeanor weapons charge. He was sentenced to one year in prison, but Judge F. Bret Thorn suspended the sentence.[92]

― ― ―

At one-thirty in the morning on January 25, 1933, two steel-jacketed .38-caliber bullets were fired through the door of Buffalo's Reuben Social Club, 288 Franklin Street. A police investigation determined that the bullets had been intended for Joseph DiCarlo.

According to the police report, DiCarlo had been targeted by rivals since a bomb exploded December 22, 1932, in front of a bookmaking establishment in Lackawanna. Following that explosion, police said, two men showed up in Buffalo inquiring about DiCarlo's activities. One night, the men waited for DiCarlo at the intersection of Pearl and Chippewa Streets to intercept him on his way to the club on Franklin Street.

Perceiving a threat, DiCarlo avoided his usual haunts and was not seen for three weeks. In mid-January, police noted his return to Buffalo nightspots.

Informants told the authorities that DiCarlo was being pursued by a hostile "mob" when he darted into the Reuben Social Club on January 25. Another man, who was not a member of the club, tried to enter behind DiCarlo. He was stopped at the entrance and then fired two shots into the door. One of the slugs cracked through the glass in the upper part of the door. The other punched a hole in the door's wooden panel. No one inside the club was injured.

Police took several men, including Vincent "Jimmy the Tough" Anconitano[93] and William "Billy" LaChiusa, into custody for questioning. Anconitano and LaChiusa allegedly had been with DiCarlo at the time of the incident.

Newspaper reporters found DiCarlo at his home. Wearing a mauve robe and bedroom slippers, he disputed the police version of the shooting.[94]

"That's not true," he said. "I have no quarrel with anyone, and I have no enemies that I know of. The reason I haven't been around much lately is because I've been home sick for the last ten days. I couldn't very well have been at the Reuben Club when I was home sick, could I?"[95]

DiCarlo continued, "What's this about a Lackawanna mob trying to put me on the spot? Why would they be trying to get me? ...There's nothing to it."

Told that police were holding Anconitano, DiCarlo responded, "Jimmy the Tough? What they got him for? He knows I've been sick."[96]

Less than a month later, the U.S. Congress took action that ultimately would end bootlegging and send organized criminals across the country scrambling for new rackets. On February 20, after favorable votes in the House of Representatives and the Senate, the Congress officially proposed the Constitution's Twenty-first Amendment to the individual states. To become the law of the land, the amendment repealing Prohibition required the approval of conventions in thirty-six of the forty-eight states.

― ― ―

The United States Secret Service revealed a two-year investigation into an international counterfeiting ring as it arrested alleged ringleaders in Buffalo. Joseph Ruffino and Anthony Perna were taken into custody on February 22, 1933.

Ruffino, who temporarily occupied the second slot on Commissioner Roche's list of public enemies, was accused of paying for drinks at a Lackawanna speakeasy with a counterfeit ten-dollar bill. The authorities believed Ruffino was the Buffalo agent of the counterfeiting ring. Perna was Ruffino's companion and alleged accomplice at the time the phony bill was passed. Perna's name also appeared on Roche's list as Public Enemy Number Five.[97]

Secret Service officials noted that the bills produced by the international ring had a bleached appearance and used poor quality paper. They suspected that the bogus notes were produced in New York City.[98]

The first hint that local Mafiosi were engaged in the counterfeiting operation came seven months earlier, when Umberto Randaccio was arrested for handing a Cities Service Station attendant a phony ten-dollar bill as payment for gasoline and oil. Randaccio, also listed by Roche as a public enemy, denied the charge.[99]

After a trial of five days, Umberto Randaccio was convicted April 5, 1933, on four counts of conspiracy to defraud the U.S. government. Judge John Knight sentenced him April 10 to serve seven years in federal prison.[100]

Just nine days later, Ruffino was convicted in the same courtroom.[101] With his sentencing still a week away, Ruffino attempted to win release on bail. However, as his bondsmen were appearing before the federal court clerk, Ruffino happened to see Manuel Cacera, speakeasy proprietor and the government's chief witness against him. Momentarily blinded by rage, Ruffino lunged at Cacera, shouting, "I'll get you for this when I get out!" The men were separated, and the incident was reported to Judge Knight, who promptly canceled Ruffino's bail. On April 26, the judge sentenced Ruffino to three years in federal prison.[102]

Secret Service agents continued to work on the case, and in August they arrested Anthony "Baby Face" Palmisano, another of Roche's public enemies. Two young women, Ann Maier and Charlotte Gryniewicz, identified Palmisano as the person who gave them eleven counterfeit five-dollar bills. Agents arrested Palmisano for possessing and distributing fraudulent notes. They also arrested Maier and Gryniewicz for the same offenses.

When Maier and Gryniewicz were taken to the Buffalo Police Detective Bureau, Palmisano saw them through the glass of a cell block door. He attracted their attention and then drew his finger across his throat.

The two young women agreed to testify against Palmisano before a federal grand jury. They identified Palmisano as the man who provided them with five-dollar bills, and they admitted passing the bills but denied knowing that they were counterfeit. They said Palmisano drove them to Buffalo area shops and gave them five-dollar bills with which to purchase cigarettes, fruit or candy. Each time, he presented them with a new bill, collected the change and allowed the women to keep the purchased items.

Echoing claims made in the Ruffino prosecution, authorities called Palmisano the Buffalo distributor of counterfeit dollars manufactured in New York City.[103] Palmisano pleaded not guilty to the charges. Bail was set at $50,000, and he was held for trial.[104]

However, detectives heard that a Palmisano lookalike, a Syracuse racketeer named Caesar Sposato, actually was responsible for the counterfeiting operation. Sposato volunteered to come to Buffalo to clear his name. When he arrived, Ann Maier and Charlotte Gryniewicz changed their story. They said Sposato, not Palmisano, was the man who handed them the counterfeit bills.[105]

― ― ―

The summer of 1933 was a hectic period for the DiCarlo family.

Beer had made a successful comeback in spring, with passage of the Cullen-Harrison amendment to the Volstead Act.[106] Breweries across the U.S. responded by stepping up production. Joseph DiCarlo responded by jumping at a fresh business opportunity.

In June, DiCarlo contracted with a Chicago brewery to be its sole sales representative in Buffalo. DiCarlo plans to undercut the prices of local breweries came to Commissioner Roche's attention. Buffalo beer was sold for $12 to $15 a barrel. Rumors indicated that DiCarlo had arranged for Chicago beer to be sold for $10 a barrel. On June 20, Roche again called DiCarlo in for questioning. Detectives were assigned to look into DiCarlo's new business.

Speaking with the press, DiCarlo confirmed his role as brewery sales representative. "The beer business is legitimate, isn't it?" he asked. "Why should there be any investigation of me going into the business?"[107]

On June 27, 1933, New York became the ninth state to vote for complete repeal of Prohibition by ratifying the Twenty-first

Amendment to the U.S. Constitution. The amendment required support from twenty-three more states.

The next morning, DiCarlo's sister Sarah was wed in grand style to Cassandro Bonasera of Brooklyn. The DiCarlo and Bonasera families shared a common birthplace in Vallelunga, Sicily, and both had family links to the Mistretta family. Bonasera had a number of relatives in the Buffalo area. Known in Brooklyn as Profaci Mafia Family soldier "Tony the Chief," Bonasera had been arrested one year earlier in connection with the murder of John Bazzano. By 1933, Bonasera's criminal record included more than twenty arrests.[108]

DiCarlo gave away the bride and saw to it that the ceremony performed by Monsignor Joseph Gambino was the most elaborate ever held in Buffalo's Holy Cross Church. John "Johnny Bath Beach" Oddo, Bonasera's close friend and associate from Brooklyn, and Margaret Cortelli, friend of the bride, stood as witnesses to the marriage.

The event drew an enormous crowd. The church was filled to capacity with family and friends, and a multitude gathered outside. More and more people gathered as the ceremony went on. By the time the new bride and groom stepped out of the church, the crowd was so large that it blocked the street.

After the ceremony, the bridal party breakfasted at the DiCarlo home. A wedding dinner was later served at the Hollywood Inn, 634 Main Street in Tonawanda. The festive day concluded with a lavish evening reception for the newlyweds and more than one thousand guests at Buffalo's Hotel Statler.[109]

Two weeks later, Joseph DiCarlo attempted to assist the politically powerful O'Connell family in recovering kidnapped twenty-four-year-old John J. O'Connell, Jr. As he left July 12 to meet with the O'Connells in Albany, DiCarlo revealed to friends that he had already been in touch with contacts in upstate New York, Cleveland, Detroit, Pittsburgh and eastern Pennsylvania.[110]

DiCarlo explained to newspaper reporters, "The O'Connells and their friends are my friends, and they can rest assured that I'll do all I can to get in touch with the men who kidnapped John O'Connell, Jr. [Thomas] Dyke called me personally and asked me to help him. That I am now doing."[111]

The extent of DiCarlo's assistance in the case is not known.

O'Connell's kidnappers initially demanded a ransom of a quarter-million dollars for the young man's return. As state and federal agents and segments of the American underworld mobilized to locate O'Connell, his captors reduced their demand to $75,000. The family made a counteroffer of $40,000, which the kidnappers accepted. Bound and blindfolded, John J. O'Connell, Jr., was turned loose on a New York City street corner on July 30.[112]

The *Buffalo Evening Times* reported on August 22 that DiCarlo was looking to expand his slot machine enterprise. The newspaper learned through "unofficial reports" of a secret meeting between DiCarlo's Buffalo organization and another slot machine group that operated just outside of the city. DiCarlo earlier demanded that restaurants and saloons in the area remove all machines controlled by the rival group. The meeting was held to resolve the dispute, but the *Evening Times* did not reveal if it was successful in doing so.[113]

Through the summer, Sam DiCarlo exhausted the legal appeals to his May 1932 Dyer Act conviction. The U.S. Court of Appeals for the Second Circuit affirmed his conviction at the end of August. On September 12, 1933, Sam DiCarlo began to serve his federal prison sentence of one year and one day.

― ― ―

The Magaddino Mafia organization's six-year rivalry with the Callea brothers ended abruptly on Friday, August 25, 1933.

Vincenzo "Big Jim" Callea and Salvatore "Sam" Callea stepped out in front of their Connecticut Street saloon[114] just after eleven o'clock that evening. They noticed two armed men walking toward them from an eight-cylinder Ford sedan parked nearby at the corner of Connecticut and Fourteenth Streets. The Calleas scrambled.

Salvatore jumped into a Ford coupe parked at the curb. Vincenzo started to run across Connecticut Street but was struck by shotgun blasts fired by one of the gunmen. Vincenzo reached the opposite sidewalk, but another discharge of the shotgun felled him in front of the Emky Shoe Company, 374 Connecticut Street. While he lay helpless and bleeding on the sidewalk, his assailant fired again into his body. The other gunman, carrying a revolver, trapped Salvatore in the parked car and fired two slugs into his head.

Connecticut Street, the major artery of a business district on

Buffalo's West Side, was busy that evening. Two bystanders, one of them a fourteen-year-old girl, were injured by stray bullets during the attack. The girl, June Bauder, suffered wounds to her forehead and left elbow, apparently from ricocheting slugs. A piece of flying lead struck Joseph Pariso in the left leg.

The assassins ran back to their car to make their escape. The vehicle traveled only a few feet before stalling in the intersection. The gunmen abandoned the murder weapons – a Remington 12-gauge automatic shotgun and a Smith & Wesson .32-caliber revolver – in the car and, with the driver, walked away along Fourteenth Street in a leisurely manner.

Vincenzo Callea was dead by the time police arrived on the scene. Salvatore, still clinging to life, was rushed to Columbus Hospital. He succumbed to his wounds shortly after his arrival. In Vincenzo's wallet, police found a receipt for three hundred pounds of yeast bearing the name and Jamestown, New York, address of John Porrello; a postal telegraph from Roy Carlisi; and an electric bill for a building in Amherst, New York, where Prohibition agents had uncovered a large distillery two months before. Salvatore's wallet contained a pistol permit issued on December 15, 1930.[115]

Local and federal authorities cooperated in the double-homicide investigation. Detective Sergeant Richard C. Mack suggested almost immediately that the Calleas were murdered due to their recent efforts to monopolize bootlegging in the region. Mack said he heard that the brothers had compelled area alcohol dealers to purchase liquor only through them. Deputy Commissioner William R. Connolly went to the press with the opinion that the gunmen had been brought to Buffalo from Cleveland specifically to put the Callea brothers on the spot.[116]

The investigation revealed that both Callea brothers had received telephone calls shortly after sunset on the twenty-fifth, summoning them to a meeting at their saloon later that night. The brothers drove separately to the saloon, arriving around eleven. They entered the establishment and spoke with bartender Charles Mancuso, before walking back outside.[117]

The sedan abandoned by the gunmen had been purchased with cash on the day of the murders. William M. Hudson, salesman at the Ford dealership at Main Street and Lafayette Avenue told police that he initially sold a four-cylinder two-door

1931 Ford Model-A sedan to an Italian man for $200 about a week earlier. Then, on the morning of August 25, the same man and a companion returned the vehicle and asked for a more powerful one, paying the $230 difference for a 1932 Ford V-8. The automobile was found to be registered to a fictitious name and address.[118]

Police initially suspected that Roy Carlisi purchased the murder car. The other man, described as an Italian about fifty years old, five feet four inches tall with a slim build, appeared to be a match for Carlisi's father Joseph. The Carlisis were known to be involved in bootlegging activities in Chicago and had recently relocated to the Buffalo area. At police headquarters, Hudson failed to identify Carlisi as the purchaser.[119]

By August 27, the authorities were convinced that the Callea murders were the result of a breakdown in distillery partnerships. They learned that the Calleas had invested in the operation of a large still controlled by an East Cleveland bootlegging gang led by the Porrellos and their cousin Angelo Tardino. That still was shut down after a federal raid months earlier, and the Cleveland gang looked to the Calleas for funds to build another. The brothers refused to finance the operation, instead investing in their own distillery plants around Buffalo. According to investigators, the Callea brothers and their allies controlled distilleries in Amherst, Forks and Cheektowaga, New York, as well as other locations.[120]

Funeral services for Vincenzo and Salvatore Callea were held in the Church of the Annunciation on August 29. Vincenzo's wife Giovannina and Salvatore's wife Carmela were left to raise their eleven children. Arrangements were handled by the *Societa Sant'Angelo di Licata*, to which both brothers belonged. As they were buried in Mount Calvary Cemetery, a detail from Fort Niagara's Company F, Twenty-eighth Infantry, fired a salute in honor of Salvatore Callea's service in the Great War.[121]

On the same day the brothers were laid to rest, the authorities traveled to Jamestown and took John Porrello and Philip Lombardo into custody. At Lombardo's address, 5 Howard Avenue, a large still was found to be operating. The men were transported back to Buffalo for questioning.[122]

In a special police lineup, Joseph Pariso, the wounded witness to the Callea murders, was unable to say whether Porrello or Lombardo had been at the scene of the shooting. "I don't know if they were there," he said. "Anyway, it was very dark and hard to see, and the men were running."[123] Porrello revealed during questioning by police that he had been friendly with the Calleas for thirteen years and had no reason to wish them dead.[124] The authorities found insufficient evidence to hold Porrello and Lombardo, and the men were released.

Buffalo police detectives checked long distance telephone records from the Calleas' homes and from their Connecticut Street saloon. They found recent calls to Stefano Magaddino and Patsy Curione, as well as to Peter Certo's Mello Bottling Works in Niagara Falls and a Porrello residence in Cleveland.[125]

At the beginning of September, investigators interviewed the wives of the murder victims. They learned much about the family and friendship connections of the brothers. Former Cleveland Mafia boss Joe Lonardo was godfather to Salvatore Callea's daughter Carmela. Calogero Romano,[126] father-in-law of Roy Carlisi, was godfather to Salvatore's son Joseph. Salvatore had long friendly relationships with the Porrello family in Cleveland and with Buffalo's Joseph DiCarlo, Joseph Ruffino and Patsy Corda. Calogero Romano was also a friend of Vincenzo Callea. Niagara Falls businessman Peter Certo was godfather to Vincenzo's daughter Carmela.[127]

Buffalo authorities had another murder on their hands just a few days later. They tried without success to link the murder of Buffalo resident James DiStefano to the Callea case. DiStefano reportedly went for an automobile ride with a group of men late on the night of September 4. DiStefano's body was found in a shack in Cheektowaga. His throat had been cut after he had been slugged on the head with an iron bar. A .38-caliber bullet had been fired into his skull to finish him off. Detectives found an unfired .32-caliber revolver in the dead man's hand.[128] The notion that DiStefano was linked to the Calleas was discarded within a couple of days.[129]

Police announced on September 12 that they were holding three men in connection with the murder of the Callea brothers. The suspects were Anthony "Lucky" Perna, Cerio DiSalvo and Joseph Mangus. The men were not officially charged, but Police Commissioner Roche made his suspicions clear: "It is our understanding that there were three men in the car used by the gunmen the night the Calleas were killed. We have three men under arrest. I am not looking for anyone else." Roche noted that Perna "has been in about every racket I can think of, and alcohol was one of them. He knew the Calleas and was working either with them or against them in the business."[130]

Within twenty-four hours, whatever case Roche had against the three suspects collapsed, and they were released.[131]

Joseph Callea, cousin to the murdered brothers, came to the attention of law enforcement one month later. In the ruins of a burned out house in Jamestown, police discovered a thousand-gallon distillery, thousands of gallons of mash, about a ton of corn sugar and a driver's license belonging to Joseph Callea of 533 Fargo Avenue. The address used on the license was a former address of John Porrello.

Free on bail pending the trial for an earlier bootlegging offense, Joseph Callea was arrested and questioned. Buffalo Police interrogated him on the circumstances of his cousins' murders. He admitted working for them as an alcohol "cooker" but claimed he knew nothing related to their deaths. "They were not the kind of fellows who would let working men like me, or anyone else, know their business," he told detectives. Satisfied that he could be no help in the murder investigation, Buffalo authorities left Joseph Callea to the federal Prohibition agents.[132]

The investigation reached a standstill. Even an October 28 report that Ford dealership employees had identified Calogero "Charley Buffalo" DiBenedetto as one of the men who purchased the car used in the Callea murder could not move it forward.[133]

--- --- ---

With his murder investigations thwarted, Police Commissioner Austin Roche initiated a city-wide offensive against racketeering. He issued a special order to all precinct captains and detectives on September 7, commanding them to round up all persons known to be involved in moonshine operations.[134] He made his intentions clear in an interview with the press:

> We plan to kick the known racketeer around as much as we can. Complaints are coming into this office from various sources regarding the operation of alcohol stills, and

> several have been raided. These stills, I believe, are being operated on a chain-store basis by the alcohol ring, who want to make all the money possible before the Eighteenth Amendment is repealed and to have a stock on hand to compete with legalized alcohol.[135]

Deputy Commissioner William R. Connolly explained that federal agents were being pulled away from Prohibition enforcement duties and city police were moving to fill the void. Connolly added, "The racketeers figure that with the 'dry force' cut to a minimum, and with the repeal of Prohibition imminent, they can get away with their game... They are mistaken. When repeal takes effect, enforcement of the liquor laws again will fall on our shoulders, so we're going to get busy now."[136]

Reportedly led by the smell of cooking mash on September 8, Buffalo detectives raided an enormous alcohol distilling plant at the rear of 373 Vermont Street. The plant included a thousand-gallon still and five vats. The total capacity of the operation was estimated at thirty thousand gallons, the largest alcohol plant ever seized by the city police. The distillery was dismantled and carted away by police.[137]

The next day, Roche mobilized his anti-gambling squad for additional liquor raids. The squad swept through known speakeasies, rounding up the operators. Its most sensational raid was at 145 Franklin Street. Police found a legitimate beer saloon on the first floor of that building and a speakeasy serving harder drinks upstairs.

"We have had that spot under watch for some time and know for a fact that [Joseph] DiCarlo has a large interest in it," Roche told the press. "DiCarlo was not in the place when it was raided."[138]

Acting on orders to arrest all out of town racketeers and any local men "who do not look good," detectives on October 4 arrested Buffalo residents John Tronolone[139], Joseph Gatti, Anthony Battaglia and Joseph Pieri. The men were charged with vagrancy.

Roche linked the latest crackdown to information he obtained while attending a U.S. Senate rackets committee hearing in Detroit. He said he learned that recently enacted anti-hoodlum laws in Detroit and Chicago were driving racketeers toward Buffalo.[140]

That evening, plainclothes officers of the Buffalo Police Department were uninvited guests at the Fifth Annual Shadow and Confetti Ball of the Niagara District Association in the roof garden of Moose Hall. Police determined that the dance was being used to raise funds for the defense of accused counterfeiters Anthony "Baby Face" Palmisano and Joseph Ruffino. As many as forty detectives infiltrated the event, mixing with one hundred twenty-five invited couples.

No arrests were made, but police learned from a souvenir program that the event was chaired by Joseph Gatti and John Fina. Fina had recently become Joseph DiCarlo's brother-in-law through his marriage to Adeline Pieri.[141] Salvatore "Sam" Pieri was listed on the program as a co-chairman. The program showed Joe Augello and Anthony Battaglia were responsible for the "arrangements," Horace Pieri was one of those involved in "wardrobe," Nick Gatti provided the refreshments and Angelo Polizzi handled event tickets.

An honorary membership roll included names familiar to local law enforcement: Joseph Gatti, John Tronolone, Joseph DiCarlo, Salvatore Pieri, Steve Pieri. Other names on the roll were Steve, Sam, Iggy and Frankie Coppola; James "Julie" Caputo; Joseph and Horace Pieri; Johnnie Fina; Sam Brancato; John Cammilleri and Sam "Doc" Alessi.[142]

— — —

In local elections on November 8, 1933, Buffalo ended a string of Republican city administrations that stretched back to 1918.[143]

Prevented by charter from succeeding himself,[144] incumbent Mayor Charles E. Roesch was preparing to return to his wholesale meat business. Republican standard-bearer Philip C. Schaefer fell short in his contest against Democratic candidate George J. Zimmerman in a general election that nearly swept Republicans from local government.[145]

Divisions within his own party handicapped Schaefer. Former Republican Mayor Frank Schwab ran against Schaefer in a party primary. After losing the Republican nomination to Schaefer, Schwab announced that he would run for mayor as an independent. Schwab abandoned that plan in October, but then strongly endorsed the Democrat Zimmerman.[146]

Less than a month after the elections, state conventions in Ohio, Pennsylvania and Utah approved the Twenty-first Amendment to the Constitution. Their December 5 votes completed the ratification of the amendment. While the liquor restrictions of individual states were left in place, national Prohibition was repealed.

In Buffalo, Roesch's departure from public office on January 1, 1934, left Austin Roche out of a job. The unpopular police commissioner had no place in the Zimmerman Administration. Zimmerman turned instead to former Commissioner James W. Higgins, who began a third term atop the police force. From 1919 to 1921, Higgins had served as commissioner in the administration of Frank Schwab. He was removed by Schwab at the end of 1921 but reinstated four years later. Higgins was again forced into retirement in 1930, when Roesch took office and appointed Austin Roche to lead the police.[147]

As Higgins returned to work, he disposed of Roche's public enemies list and demoted Joseph DiCarlo from Public Enemy No. 1 to private citizen.

"We shall have no more public enemies publicized at the expense of the police department," Higgins told the press. "Joe [DiCarlo] rode the wave of publicity and built himself up until he believed he was a big shot. I believe he was overrated as a so-called public enemy by my predecessor in office, for they never fastened anything on Joe."[148]

— — —

Four gunmen entered the Smoker club at 62 Youngs Street in Tonawanda on January 7, 1934. They held up a dice game inside the club and escaped with more than two thousand dollars in cash.

On the eighteenth, Buffalo Police arrested Pasquale Natarelli, twenty-three; Salvatore "Sam" Pieri, twenty-two; Anthony DeSalvo, twenty-four; and Joseph Pieri, twenty-four. Witnesses to the robbery were brought to police to view a lineup. They positively identified DiCarlo Gang member Natarelli as the gunmen who handed his revolver to one of his fellows in order to gather up money.

After identifying Natarelli, a number of the witnesses changed their stories. They told police they were drunk at the time of the robbery and could not be sure that Natarelli was there.[149]

———

Police learned in January 1934 that government witness Ann Maier had been threatened, apparently by friends of accused counterfeiter Anthony "Baby Face" Palmisano. Maier reported that at one-thirty in the morning on January 18 she was walking along South Division Street near Michigan Avenue, when a large sedan containing three men pulled up to the curb. One of the men got out of the vehicle, grabbed her and pushed against the wall of a building.

"You're the one who jammed up a pal of mine," the man said. "You'd better watch your step."

Police officers were assigned to guard Maier, while detectives went in search of the three men.[150]

A month later, Palmisano was no longer a concern, but his murder was. Early in the morning of February 20, 1934, the racketeer's body was found inside his luxurious 1933 Buick coupe, parked on River Road north of the Buffalo city line. Twelve bullets had been fired into his skull. An expensive cigar remained clasped between fingers of his right hand.[151]

Patrolman Elmer Bromley of the Tonawanda Police discovered the body at ten minutes after six. He estimated that Palmisano had been dead only ten or fifteen minutes. "I saw an automobile parked in the lane of traffic in the River Road," Bromley later recalled. "I stopped, got out and saw a man slumped on the right side of the front seat. The man was dead, and blood was still streaming down his face, over his blue overcoat and white scarf."[152]

Palmisano was born October 15, 1898, in Montemaggiore, Sicily.[153] He came to the United States with his mother Maria, uncle Salvatore, sister Benedetta and brother Vincenzo aboard the *S.S. Re D'Italia* on May 15, 1913.[154] The group traveled to Buffalo to rejoin Palmisano's father Domenico, whose first trip across the Atlantic occurred years earlier,[155] and other extended family. Domenico Palmisano's sister had married into the Pieri family, and Anthony Palmisano was a first cousin to Salvatore Pieri. Through the Pieris, Palmisano became an in-law of Joseph DiCarlo.

As a young man, Anthony Palmisano worked in local rackets

supervised by Angelo Palmeri. Upon Palmeri's death, Joseph DiCarlo assumed control of many of those rackets and likely worked closely with Palmisano.

The Mascari and Palamara undertaking establishment handled the elaborate funeral arrangements for Palmisano. Numerous friends and relatives crowded into a wake at the funeral home on February 20, 1934.[156]

Detectives investigating the murder learned that Palmisano had many powerful friends and just as many powerful enemies. Local racketeers went into hiding following the murder and could not be located by the police. A telephone call to Joseph DiCarlo's home revealed that his line had been temporarily disconnected. Detectives went in search of two known Palmisano aides, Frank DeGoris and Anthony Perna, hoping they could shed some light on the killing.[157] Joseph Mule, Palmisano's regular chauffeur, was brought in for questioning but provided no helpful information.[158]

A number of possible motives were proposed for the murder. One suggested that Palmisano had offended rivals in Niagara Falls. Another linked his murder to a vendetta resulting from the slaying of the Callea brothers.[159] Police learned of a rumor that Palmisano had double-crossed a New York City gang in a bootlegging deal, refusing to pay two thousand dollars owed for a shipment of alcohol.[160]

James L. Carroll, assistant chief of the Buffalo Police, suggested that Palmisano had been murdered either for "framing" Syracuse racketeer Caesar Sposato or for failing to provide him with adequate compensation. Sposato took the blame for Palmisano's counterfeiting operations. He was convicted and sentenced to five years in prison. The Syracuse gangster reportedly had threatened Palmisano: "That rat Palmisano will not live a year!"[161]

Commissioner Higgins seemed unconcerned by the killing. "It happened outside our jurisdiction," he told the press. "The activities of the gang which filled Palmisano with bullets are outside my territory, and I am not going to worry about this case for the victim was no great loss to society."

Tonawanda Police Chief Elmer Mang expressed the futility of his situation: "I have no theories and have no means of learning who committed the murder."[162]

Buffalo's gambling slot machine-related conflicts resumed April 6, when three men destroyed nickel-operated "digger" machines in two Allen Street cafés. Armed with sledgehammers, the men demolished machines in the Roosevelt Café and the Jamestown Café.

The machines featured electric crane-like devices and payoffs in novelty prizes. They became popular after law enforcement forced the removal of other coin-operated gaming devices. Buffalo City Judge Peter Maul had ruled that gambling restrictions did not apply to the digger machines because they were games of skill rather than chance.[163]

On April 8, additional machines in Niagara Street businesses and some in Lackawanna were wrecked. The authorities believed all the machines were destroyed by the same gang.

According to the police, local racketeers demanded a percentage of the earnings of digger machine owners. Any owner who refused to pay risked losing a machine valued between $225 and $250 to organized vandalism.[164]

On April 12, Buffalo Police Officer Robert McTigue was eating in an Elmwood Avenue restaurant when three men entered. One of the men stood near the restaurant door with his hand in his pocket. Another advanced to the restaurant bar, while the third used an eighteen-inch crowbar to smash a digger machine in the establishment.

McTigue drew his revolver and ordered the men to stay where they were. The man by the door slipped away, but McTigue handcuffed and arrested the other two. The man with the crowbar was identified as William LaChiusa. The man who stood by the bar was identified as Philip Gerace. The authorities determined that the group was employed by a criminal organization that was trying to control digger machine concessions in Buffalo.

John H. Winfield, owner of the machine McTigue saw vandalized and of other coin operated machines placed throughout the city, told police that he received several calls during the past week demanding protection money. He was instructed to pay two dollars per machine each week or his machines would be "wiped out."[165]

LaChiusa and Gerace were sentenced to serve a year in Erie

County Penitentiary for their wrongdoing. However, they were released after serving just three months of that sentence.[166]

— — —

Police may never have learned for certain who was responsible for the September 1931 beating of Angelo Palmeri, but Palmeri's Mafia associates seemed to have solved the crime. Two and a half years later, they exacted vengeance on behalf of their deceased comrade.[167]

At about one o'clock in the morning, April 29, 1934, Buffalo undertaker Marcantonio "Mike" Palamara was conversing and playing cards with friends Antonino "Nino" Sacco, Stephen Sacco, Michael Pellettiri and Vito DeNitto at a table in the rear sitting room of the Caruso Restaurant, second floor of 93 West Chippewa Street. Antonino Sacco was co-owner of the restaurant and brother of Stephen Sacco. DeNitto was the chef.

Palamara was seated with his back toward the door. His brother Anthony had left the restaurant a few minutes earlier.[168]

Two young men walked into the restaurant and strode over to Palamara's table. One reached out to Palamara, shook his hand and said, "Hello, Mike," before stepping to the side. The second man reached out with a revolver.[169]

A shot was fired into the back of Palamara's head. As he slumped in his chair, the man who shook his hand also drew a revolver. The two young men fired repeatedly into Palamara's body, as the other men at the table ran for cover. The gunmen then waved their weapons toward the restaurant's other patrons and backed down a stairway to make their escape. They dropped their handguns behind a shoeshine stand located at the restaurant's entrance.

Palamara fell dead clutching the Three of Clubs in his hand. Just a few feet away, his coat hung from a wall hook, a fully loaded .32-caliber Smith & Wesson revolver in its outside pocket.[170]

Marcantonio Palamara was born thirty-nine years earlier in Calabria, Italy. He settled in Buffalo in 1905 and became an apprentice in the undertaking establishment of Joseph Mascari around 1920. He later married Mascari's daughter Rose. Upon the death of Joseph Mascari in 1924, Palamara became a partner in the undertaking firm with Mascari's brother Samuel.[171]

Palamara was well acquainted with Buffalo's underworld

figures. He was friendly with Anthony "Baby Face" Palmisano and served for a time as Palmisano's chauffeur. Police said the two men had been inseparable. Both had been on unfriendly terms with the Callea brothers.[172] When Angelo Palmeri died in December 1932, Palamara was the undertaker of record on Palmeri's death certificate.[173]

Following Palamara's murder, police questioned the Sacco brothers, Pellettiri and DeNitto and briefly held the four men as material witnesses. The witnesses swore they did not know Palamara's killers and had never seen the men before.[174]

Detectives initially linked the Palamara slaying to the beating of Palmeri. Within a few days, they had abandoned that theory and focused instead on the animosity between Palamara and the Callea underworld faction.

Hundreds turned out to view Palamara's remains at the Mascari funeral parlor, 860 Niagara Street. Funeral services were conducted May 2 at Holy Cross Church. Six of Palamara's cousins, serving as pall bearers, carried the bronze casket draped by a blanket of roses. In the funeral cortege, flowers filled the hearse and two other automobiles. A total of forty-nine vehicles took part in the procession to Mount Calvary Cemetery, where Palamara was buried.[175]

After the funeral, police arrested Joseph Mule, Salvatore Fraterrigo and Angelo Sciascia on an open charge. Assistant Police Chief James Carroll spent five hours interrogating Mule about Palamara's murder. Mule, known to be a friend of Palamara, provided no information.

Fraterrigo, who had been a bodyguard to Palmisano and a close friend of Palamara and Sciascia, also denied any knowledge of the murder. After questioning, the three men were charged with vagrancy and released.[176] The Palamara murder remained unsolved.

— — — —

Paul Palmeri, brother of the late Angelo Palmeri, and his companion Samuel Constantino scuffled with a Niagara Falls police officer in May and earned prison sentences.

Patrolman Thomas Nickerson responded to an automobile accident on May 19. He exchanged hostile words with Palmeri and Constantino and members of a gathering crowd. The disagreement turned physical.

The police officer was left beaten and bleeding. He later charged that Palmeri wrenched his nightstick from his hand and struck him over the head with it. When Nickerson tried to subdue Palmeri, Constantino produced a knife and slashed the officer's face. Palmeri also was hurt. Following the incident, he was confined to his home with a broken jaw. Palmeri said that injury resulted from a nightstick blow administered by Nickerson.[177]

Palmeri and Constantino were arrested and arraigned before Acting Police Justice Angelo F. Scalzo. They pleaded not guilty to charges of second degree assault. The men were released after each posted a $1,000 bond.[178]

Later that month, a grand jury indicted Palmeri and Constantino. They went on trial in Judge Bertram E. Harcourt's Niagara County Court in July. Prosecutors identified the defendants as the men who injured Nickerson as he was attempting to keep back a crowd gathered at the scene of a traffic accident. The defendants denied injuring the officer. They said others in the crowd assaulted him when he called them disparaging names and charged them with his nightstick.[179]

After deliberating for seven hours on July 11, a jury found Constantino guilty of second degree assault and Palmeri guilty of third degree assault.[180] They were sentenced the following day. Constantino was sent to Attica Prison to serve one and a half to three years. Palmeri was confined in Niagara County Jail for a term of thirty days.[181]

The smashing of coin operated machines, halted for several months, threatened to resume in midsummer. On July 31, the *Buffalo Evening News* reported that racketeers had delivered an ultimatum to owners of the devices: Either pay a portion of machine proceeds to organized crime or "lose your bankroll in wrecked machines and hospital bills." The source of the ultimatum was described as a leading racketeer prominent in the local nightlife.

The warning was provoked by the recent placement of more than fifty new digger machines in Buffalo cigar stores, saloons and other establishments.[182]

Ten days later, Buffalo Police arrested Anthony "Lucky" Perna and Salvatore "Scarface" Coppola for stealing a digger machine from the Old Timer's Tavern on Main Street and installing it at the Jamestown Tavern on Allen Street. Perna and Coppola were charged with petit larceny. John Peschio, proprietor of the Jamestown Tavern, was charged with criminally receiving stolen property. With the arrests, police announced they had thwarted an effort to organize a slot machine hijacking ring.[183]

An explosion rocked an Elmwood Avenue neighborhood at just after three o'clock in the morning of August 16. A bomb destroyed John Winfield's automobile, parked in front of 250 Elmwood. Police announced that the bomb was the second placed on Winfield's car in as many days. The first, two sticks of dynamite left on the vehicle's running board, failed to detonate after its fuse was dampened by water sprayed from a city street cleaning wagon. The second bomb – a pipe filled with gun powder – was placed under the hood of the car.

Police officials explained that Winfield had been targeted by racketeers because he failed to pay demanded protection fees. "I operate a legitimate business and don't need any protection," Winfield stated.[184]

Joseph DiCarlo was taken into custody on the seventeenth. He was held under an open charge. In reporting DiCarlo's arrest, the press noted that Commissioner Higgins' view of the racketeer was similar to his predecessor Austin Roche. Though Higgins discarded the "public enemy" moniker, DiCarlo's photo was shown first among racketeers in a pocket rogue's gallery Higgins issued to his detectives.

Police brought Anthony Elardo and Joseph Mule in for questioning.[185] They decided to hold Elardo and Mule in addition to DiCarlo and five other men: Frank Barone, Sam "Shoes" Dolce, Frank "Cakes" Custodi, Joseph Iacuzzo and Joseph Gatti.[186] The next day, the police hauled in Anthony "Lucky" Perna, Samuel Pieri, Frank Minnolera, Michael Albano and Albert LaChiusa.[187] LaChiusa was brother to the William LaChiusa imprisoned for vandalizing coin operated machines in the spring.

All except DiCarlo were charged with vagrancy and released on August 20. Police admitted that they learned nothing from questioning the men.[188] John Tronolone and Joseph Pieri were arrested the following day. On the twenty-second, they and DiCarlo were let go.[189]

Joseph Mule, who had received some police notice in connection with the Palmisano and Palamara murders and through the slot machine conflict, became the focus of a law enforcement investigation when his dead and mutilated body was found October 21, 1934, in a muddy ditch in the town of Tonawanda. The ditch sat in the shadows of St. Peters Evangelical Church on Knoche Road.

Mule had earned a local reputation for ruthlessness since he moved to Buffalo from Brooklyn, New York, where his police record included arrests for murder, assault and robbery. Though he never served time in prison, the authorities were certain that he earned his living through bootlegging and other rackets.[190] Mule, whose real name was Giuseppe Mongiovi, was born in Racalmuto, Sicily, on December 15, 1904.[191] He first arrived in the United States on February 23, 1912, with his mother, two older sisters and a younger brother. They joined his father Calogero in New York City.[192] After a visit to Italy, he returned to New York at age sixteen on January 21, 1921.[193]

Acquitted of a murder charge in 1926, he changed his name to Joseph Mule – adopting his mother's maiden name – and moved west to Buffalo. For a time, he worked as an enforcer for local Mafia chieftain Filippo Mazzara, though he remained available to others as a killer for hire.[194] Through friendships with Anthony Palmisano and Marcantonio Palamara, Mule, a flashy dresser and restaurateur, became an important figure in local rackets. He briefly owned the Tivoli Restaurant, purchasing it from Antonino Sacco shortly before Palamara's murder and then selling it back to Sacco.

Though Mule's body was discovered outside Buffalo city limits, Buffalo Police launched an investigation into the murder.

Detectives theorized that the racketeer had been picked up in an automobile by men he considered his friends. The car usually driven by Mule, an expensive five-passenger coupe owned by his brother, was found in front of the Sicilia Bella tavern, 66 Carolina Street, where it had been parked since six o'clock, the evening of October 20. They considered the possibility that Mule may have driven off with a woman.

Evidence indicated that Mule attempted to fight off a number of attackers. An autopsy performed by Medical Examiner Charles

E. Long revealed that Mule had been, beaten, stabbed and garroted. There was a lump on the back of his head and bruises on his legs and body. One eye was blackened, and the other had a large bruise and abrasion over it. Numerous small stab wounds, which appeared to have been made with an ice pick, were found on the lower part of his chest and abdomen. The medical examiner also found injuries he believed were caused by the repeated tightening of a garrote made of insulated wire. A loop of wire, Doctor Long concluded, had been passed over Mule's eyelids and then tightened. It was then passed over his lower lip, where it left another indentation. It finally was tightened around Mule's throat. The medical examiner speculated that Mule was killed at another location and then driven to Tonawanda.[195]

Though the detail was left out of news reports, rumors around the city indicated that Mule's murderers had mutilated his genitals.[196]

This last fact may have led detectives to conclude that Mule's killing had something to do with a romantic dalliance. Leading them further in that direction was an anonymous letter sent to the police on August 6. The letter asked the authorities to "get" Mule for a number of criminal offenses: "He has past crimes in other cities. Why should these men take the law to themselves? If you get him, you would save many other families heartaches." The letter was written in what was described as a feminine handwriting, and it was signed, "One who has a broken heart." A sample of handwriting from Mule's wife allowed detectives to rule her out as the author of the letter.[197]

Though the murder was unsolved, it was widely believed to have been an act of gangland discipline. Mule had became an underworld menace, a disturbance to peace in the rackets, and it was necessary to eliminate him.[198]

Even while police detectives and county deputies continued their investigation, official sources felt there was little chance of discovering Mule's killers and little reason to try. Mule's passing, they said coldly, would be mourned only by the members of his immediate family.[199]

In the summer of 1935, the underworld faction to which Anthony Palmisano, Marcantonio Palamara and Joseph Mule had belonged suffered yet another loss. Anthony Palamara, brother of the late Marcantonio, was shot five times as he sat in his automobile in the early morning hours of Sunday, August 18.

The pop of handguns at a quarter to three in the morning awakened residents near the intersection of Fargo and Porter Avenues. Those drawn from their homes by the noise found Palamara's 1933 Plymouth parked in front of 167 Fargo Avenue. The vehicle's lights were on, and its passenger side door was open. Palamara's dead body was slumped behind the steering wheel, bleeding from three wounds in his head, one in his neck and one in his abdomen.[200]

When police arrived, they noted that each of the bullet wounds was surrounded by a circular powder burn. Palamara had been shot at extremely close range. Investigators found a .32-caliber revolver on the floor of the car and a .38-caliber revolver on the front seat.

Detectives found no one in the neighborhood would admit to witnessing the murder. They had Palamara's automobile, with his remains still within it, towed to the morgue for examination.[201]

Palamara's wife Rose told police that five men came calling for her husband at two o'clock in the morning on August 17. She told the men that he was asleep, and they left in an automobile bearing Ohio license plates.[202] She said she last saw her husband at seven that evening, when he left the house without mentioning where he was going.[203]

Rose Palamara explained that her husband for months had been in constant fear. He never went outside after dark, she said.[204]

Detectives seized business records from Palamara's office in Dante Place. The documents suggested that he had been active in bootlegging. Over the course of the previous year, Palamara had bought and resold at a profit several hundred thousand gallons of corn sugar syrup, a necessary ingredient for moonshine operations. Much of the sweetener had been purchased through the Joseph Quattrone, Fred Slade and the Pennsylvania Sugar Company during the summer of 1935. Authorities noted that Palamara had been arrested in 1928 for bootlegging and had been suspected of involvement in the racket for years.[205]

Police in Cheektowaga, to the east of Buffalo, were alerted to an abandoned automobile with Ohio registration. Witnesses said several unidentified men left the car and drove off in another.[206]

Like the other gangland killings of the period, the murder of Anthony Palamara remained unsolved. The slayings of the two Palamara brothers left two widows tending to a total of eight fatherless children.[207]

Chapter 19

Bookmaking

On May 15, 1935, New York Governor Herbert H. Lehman signed into law the Brownell bill, amending state penal code related to the consorting of known criminals. Previously, the code had allowed disorderly conduct prosecution against anyone with an "evil reputation" who consorted with others of similar reputation for unlawful purposes. However, the burden had remained with law enforcement to prove the unlawful intent of the contacts. The new Brownell Law eliminated law enforcement's burden of proof, viewing contact between known criminals as *prima facie* evidence of some criminal purpose. It placed upon defendants the legal burden of proving their innocence.[1]

Though many questioned the constitutionality of the Brownell law,[2] law enforcement wasted no time putting its new tool to use. New York City Police Commissioner Lewis J. Valentine was eager to have the Brownell law tested in court and predicted, "A lot of public enemies are going to leave town." Valentine's detectives arrested ten men in the Brownsville section of Brooklyn on May 20. The men, all in their twenties and all with police records, were found gathered outside a nightclub at Sutter Avenue and Amboy Street.[3]

A few days later, Buffalo Police also arrested ten men under the Brownell law. John "Peanuts" Tronolone, Anthony "Lucky" Perna, Samuel Pieri, Joseph Pieri, Carmen Scola, Sam Romano, Alphonse Travale, Angelo Talluto, Louis Burgio and Edward Scillia were charged with unlawful consorting. Arraigned before city court Judge George P. Burd, the men pleaded not guilty. At the hearing, defense attorney Samuel Fleischman criticized the new law as unconstitutional and unreasonable. Fleischman pledged to move for dismissal of the charges at trial. Assistant District Attorney George E. Wisch defended the law as an effective tool for preventing former convicts from meeting to plan new crimes. Judge Burd released the defendants on $500 bail each.[4]

At their first opportunity, Buffalo authorities used the Brownell law to take Joseph DiCarlo into custody. He and Anthony Battaglia were arrested June 2 as they chatted in front of the Gayety Theater at Pearl and West Huron Streets. Like DiCarlo, Battaglia had a criminal record.

"You ain't got nothing on me," DiCarlo said as he was arrested. "I ain't bothering nobody."

DiCarlo and Battaglia were processed and released on $1,000 bail each.[5] One local newspaper took the opportunity to publish DiCarlo's extensive arrest record. "Last night's arrest marks the first time he has run afoul of the law since Commissioner Higgins resumed leadership of the department one and a half years ago," the article noted. "During the regime of Austin J. Roche, however, Joe's name was in the news quite often."

At arraignment the following day, DiCarlo pleaded not guilty. A trial date was set, and he was released on $500 bail,[6] but the charge against DiCarlo was quietly dropped.

Adherence to the anti-consorting law would have been especially burdensome for DiCarlo. Many of his family members had criminal records. His brother Sam had been jailed on federal auto theft charges. Sam also had also been suspected of involvement in local kidnapping and bootlegging operations and had been arrested at Mafia conventions in Cleveland and New York City. DiCarlo in-laws included Brooklyn Mafioso Cassandro "Tony the Chief" Bonasera, the Pieri brothers and John Fina, all of whom had police records.

On June 11, Buffalo's first group of Brownell defendants appeared in Judge Robert J. Summers' city courtroom. The hearing focused on the constitutionality of the new anti-consorting law. The defendants all agreed to let attorney Fleischman argue on their behalf. He was opposed by Assistant District Attorney Wisch.[7] Though Fleischman noted the negative effect of the law on personal rights guaranteed by the United

States Constitution and the impracticality of all ex-convicts spending their lives in virtual seclusion, Judge Summers sided with Wisch on the constitutionality issue. The judge, however, discharged most of the defendants.

Four men, Anthony Perna, John Tronolone and Sam and Joseph Pieri, were convicted, despite their insistence that the "consorting" on May 24 amounted to nothing more than a discussion of which movie theater to visit that night. At the conclusion of the trial, a newspaper reporter noted Joseph DiCarlo in the courtroom gallery. DiCarlo refused comment when the reporter asked his opinion of the verdict.

Judge Summers delayed sentencing to allow all parties to review the case record.[8] On June 18, he imposed the maximum prison term of six months on each of the defendants, but suspended the sentences, citing the newness of the law under which they were convicted. Though the defendants escaped without punishment, Fleischman announced his intention to appeal the conviction all the way to the Supreme Court.[9]

In the same month, "Peanuts" Tronolone was convicted of running a bookmaking establishment at 67 Main Street. Tronolone was sentenced to thirty days in prison.[10]

A July appeal to County Judge F. Bret Thorn did not go Fleischman's way. Judge Thorn upheld the city convictions.[11] In August, Fleischman filed an appeal with the state's highest court.[12]

The earlier Brownell test cases in New York City had similar results. Seven of the ten defendants were convicted of illegal consorting and sentenced on June 1 to ninety-day terms in the workhouse. Defense attorney Emanuel Rosenberg ridiculed the law and jokingly suggested that individuals with "evil reputations" should be compelled to wear a sign reading, "I've been arrested and convicted. Stay away from me or the cops will arrest you for consorting."[13]

The Buffalo and New York City cases reached the New York Court of Appeals on November 25.[14] In a six-to-one decision returned January 7, 1936, the court essentially nullified the Brownell law. While stopping short of declaring the law unconstitutional, the court stated that prosecutors must prove that the accused have evil reputations, that the accused were consorting with unlawful intent and that the persons with whom they consorted were current unreformed criminals:

> Persons who have been convicted of a crime and served the sentence imposed are not thereafter barred from society or intercourse with other human beings; they are not outcasts, nor to be treated as such. The Legislature did not intend to close the door to reformation, repentance or a new try at life... Mere association with people of ill repute with no intent to breach the peace or to plan or commit crime is too vague a provision to constitute an offense. Neither can reputation alone – bad reputation – be made a crime. Suspicion does not establish guilt.[15]

--- --- ---

As the Brownell appeals were working their way through the New York courts, the police department of the City of Detroit expressed an interest in Joseph DiCarlo. Detroit Chief of Detectives Fred W. Frahm, investigating a number of gangland killings in his city, wrote to Buffalo Police on September 23, 1935.

> Will you kindly furnish us with photographs and fingerprints of one Joe DeCarlo [sic], a known character in your city, of Joe Gatti, alias The Goose, alias The Guinea, and also of a man known as Dad, alias The Butcher, described as an Italian; 55-60 yrs.; 5 ft. 6 in.; about 140 lbs.; medium dark complexion.
> Information has come to use that Gatti and DeCarlo, along with the man known as Dad, made frequent trips to Detroit in the years 1930-1931 by the way of Toledo, Ohio. If possible, we would like to have information as to the character and type of these men and what their purpose was in travelling from Buffalo to Detroit, as about that time there

was a number of murders here and in Toledo in which Italian gangsters were involved. We would appreciate any information in reference to this group as to whether they are known killers of their purpose in making several trips here.
Information in our possession is that your Deputy Chief of Detectives Frank McCarthy knows DeCarlo.[16]

The response of the Buffalo Police Department to Frahm's request has been lost. No information on the mysterious "Dad" appears to survive in Buffalo police records.

Frahm's letter further links the underworld organizations of Buffalo and Detroit, particularly during the period in which the Castellammarese War was raging and Gaspare Milazzo, Sam Parrino and Chester LaMare were murdered.

— — —

Sam Pieri, then in his mid-twenties, had grown into a significant figure in the DiCarlo Gang of the western New York Mafia.

Born in Buffalo on January 11, 1911, Salvatore Joseph "Sam" Pieri was the seventh child born to Giovanni and Ignazia "Anna" Ciresi Pieri.[17] Pieri and his siblings had difficult childhoods. Following the 1914 death of Giovanni Pieri, the family had little money and many mouths to feed. Ignazia, who was pregnant with her ninth child at the time of her husband's death, temporarily placed all of the children in local orphanages. As she found employment, she gradually brought the children back home.

Sam Pieri returned home at age six, but money remained a problem. He began working for the *Buffalo Evening News* before his thirteenth birthday and quit school after completing the seventh grade. He continued to work for the *Evening News* on and off until about 1934. However, he found ways of supplementing his newspaper income.

Pieri first ran into trouble with the law when he was just ten years old. He was arrested for malicious mischief on August 7, 1921, but was later discharged. In 1926, he also wriggled free of grand larceny and juvenile delinquency charges.

He was tried in June of 1928 on burglary and grand larceny charges. He was convicted of second-degree grand larceny and sentenced to an indefinite period of probation. His first conviction did not convince Pieri to mend his ways. He was caught shoplifting in October of 1930 and discharged, and was arrested on a Rochester, New York, warrant for first-degree robbery early the next year. The district attorney of Rochester eventually dropped the robbery charge against him.

Pieri served time in Erie County Penitentiary in 1931. He and two other men were arrested September 2 as they unloaded three hundred quarts of Canadian ale from a rowboat onto a dock at the foot of Hudson Street. As the arrest was made, a fourth member of the gang escaped by swimming away.[18] Pieri was turned over to federal agents. He was convicted of a bootlegging-related violation of tariff regulations and sentenced to sixty days in the county prison.

A week after the New York Court of Appeals robbed the Brownell Law of its teeth, Pieri and his underworld associates were again receiving attention from the authorities. On January 14, 1936, Pieri and his brother Joseph, along with John "Peanuts" Tronolone, Anthony "Lucky" Perna and Joseph DiCarlo, were arrested as they emerged from a downtown hotel in Cleveland. They were charged as suspicious persons. DiCarlo, Perna and Salvatore Pieri were freed. Tronolone and Joseph Pieri were convicted later in January and sentenced to serve thirty days in the workhouse and to pay a fifty-dollar fine.[19]

During trial, it was revealed that authorities had trailed the five men for several days after their arrival in Cleveland. Police officers testified that the men had no visible means of support and that Tronolone and Joseph Pieri were observed visiting Cleveland men with lengthy criminal records.

As he sentenced the two Buffalo men, Judge Louis Petrash said, "We have enough potential criminals to contend with without having them move from other cities. We plan to jail on suspicion charges every hoodlum brought into court who has no visible means of support."[20]

— — —

Just a few days after Judge Petrash took his stand against visiting criminals, another of Buffalo's Pieri brothers – John Pieri, also known as John Rai – went on trial for murder in

Toledo, Ohio. John Pieri and his codefendant Ralph Carsello were charged specifically with aiding and abetting in the murders of Abe "Punk" Lubitsky, Norman "Big Agate" Blatt, Louise Bell and Jack Kennedy.[21]

Both defendants were recognized members of Thomas "Yonnie" Licavoli's Detroit Mafia organization,[22] which swept into the Toledo region in the early 1930s to establish a monopoly over bootlegging, vice and gambling rackets.[23] Other key figures in the Licavoli Gang were "Yonnie's" brother Jimmy, his brother-in-law Leo Moceri, John Mirabella, Russell Syracuse and Ernest LaSalle.[24]

Abe Lubitsky and Norman Blatt were killed late in the evening of October 6, 1931. They were in Lubitsky's automobile at the intersection of Franklin Avenue and Bancroft Street, when they were raked by machine gun fire. A companion, Hyman Abrams, was wounded in the attack. Abrams claimed to be able to identify the gunmen. The murders of Lubitsky and Blatt were interpreted as a disciplinary measure for their refusal to provide a share of their gambling racket income to the Licavoli Gang.[25]

Despite the killings, local beer baron Jack Kennedy stubbornly resisted the Licavoli takeover. Through connections on the local police force, Kennedy encouraged law enforcement raids of Licavoli enterprises, including nightclubs and distilleries. "Yonnie" quickly understood the situation and complained to police, "Kennedy is behind these raids. You don't raid his businesses."[26]

On the evening of November 30, 1932, Kennedy was ambushed during a drive home from the Paramount Theater. Kennedy managed to avoid a hail of bullets, but his companion Louise Bell, twenty-two, was struck several times and died of her injuries two hours later.[27] While Kennedy refused to assist the police in their investigation, another witness to the shooting identified Licavoli underlings Pieri, LaSalle and Pete Corrado as the gunmen.[28]

Another Licavoli ambush the following summer achieved the desired result. At nine o'clock in the evening of July 7, 1933, Kennedy was walking with Audrey Rawls at his Point Place cottage near Lake Erie,[29] when two gunmen crept up behind them, shoved Rawls aside and opened fire on Kennedy. After the Toledo beer baron fell to the ground mortally wounded, the gunmen continued to pump bullets into his head and body. Investigators later found powder burns on Kennedy's right ear. Toledo residents were outraged by the brutal killing. Caught up in the emotion of the moment, county prosecutor Frazier Reams angrily announced to the press, "Yonnie and his gang will be stopped!"[30]

A series of law enforcement errors and Licavoli legal maneuvers prevented prosecution of any of the gang members before November of 1933. Licavoli gangster Joseph "Wop" English was the first to be tried. He was convicted of participating in the murder of Kennedy and sentenced to die in the electric chair.[31] That sentence was later commuted to life in prison.[32]

"Yonnie" Licavoli was brought into court eleven months later. After a month-long trial, he was convicted of conspiring in the murders of Kennedy, Bell, Lubitsky and Blatt. The jury, however, recommended mercy, sparing Licavoli the death sentence that had been imposed on English. "Yonnie" was sentenced to life in prison.[33]

As the trial of Pieri and Carsello began at the end of January 1936, prosecutor Reams informed the press that he intended to demand the death penalty for both. During trial, state witnesses identified the defendants as members of the Licavoli Gang. Taxi driver Clarence Ash, a witness to the murder of Louise Bell, testified that Pieri was one of her killers and Carsello and Leo Moceri[34] had been in the car with Pieri.

As Ash pointed to Pieri in the courtroom, the defendant's face noticeably reddened and then paled. Pieri subsequently kept his hand in front of his face.[35]

Elsie DiCarlo, wife of Joseph DiCarlo and sister of John Pieri, played a prominent role in the defense case. She testified that Pieri and other family members were gathered at her Buffalo home on November 29 and 30, as the DiCarlos celebrated their eighth wedding anniversary. On the twenty-ninth, she explained, "they all had a little too much to drink and they stayed all night." She said the group began playing pinochle at four o'clock the next afternoon. "I went to bed at twelve, after telling them they would have to get their own coffee." On cross-examination, prosecutors challenged Elsie DiCarlo on the date of her wedding.

Other defense witnesses supported a Carsello alibi for the

time of Kennedy's murder. They testified that Carsello was in Detroit that day, attending the wake of Licavoli's father-in-law Joe Moceri.[36]

In his closing argument, Assistant County Prosecutor Harry Friberg asked jurors to show the defendants that "the heat is still on in Toledo by sending them to the electric chair where they belong."[37] Defense attorney Cornell Schreiber closed by waving the November 29, 1924, DiCarlo marriage certificate in front of the jury. As he began reading the certificate, the prosecutor jumped to his feet and objected to the use of a document never entered into evidence during the trial.[38]

The jury convicted both Pieri and Carsello of first-degree murder but recommended mercy. Pieri was found guilty of participating in the Bell and Kennedy murders. Carsello was found guilty of involvement in all four murders. Instead of the death penalty sought by prosecutors, both defendants were sentenced to life in prison.

A newspaper reporter asked Pieri what he thought of the verdict. "Tough break, tough break," Pieri replied. "And I'm still insisting I'm innocent."

"It could have been worse," the reporter said.

"It could have been a hell of a lot better," Pieri answered.[39]

———

In western New York, the Stefano Magaddino Mafia organization and the affiliated DiCarlo Gang in Buffalo began forcing bookmakers and other operators of gambling rackets in the region to pay a "tax" on their illicit earnings. Those who refused to make the regular demanded payments were subjected to beatings and robberies. In the spring of 1936, opponents of the Magaddino tax clearly communicated their displeasure.

Just after five o'clock in the morning of May 19, 1936, an explosion rocked Magaddino's Niagara Falls neighborhood. Homes were shaken along Whitney Avenue between Fifteenth and Eighteenth Streets. Firefighters and police officers rushed to the area and found that the home at 1651 Whitney Avenue had been the target of an attack involving two dynamite bombs – one had been left outside the front door, and the other had been thrown through a window of the door. The home belonged to Magaddino's brother-in-law and sister, Nicholas and Arcangela Longo. The combined explosion of the bombs lifted the two-and-a-half-story brick home from its foundation and dislodged its roof.

Nicholas Longo was in New York City on business at the time, but Arcangela and their three daughters were asleep on the second floor of the home when the bombers struck. Awakened by the sound of breaking glass, Arcangela rushed downstairs in her nightdress. She had just reached the ground floor when the bombs exploded. Investigators said she was thrown back and immediately enveloped in flame. Missiles of torn plaster, wood and bomb fragments bruised and tore her flesh. The fire quickly burned through her clothing and seared her entire body.

Rose Longo, fourteen, and her sisters Josephine, thirteen, and Antonina, eleven, were grouped at the top of the stairway at that moment and escaped serious injury.

Arcangela was rushed to Mount St. Mary's Hospital. She died there at twelve-twenty in the afternoon. She was forty-two years of age.[40] The cause of death was determined to be burns and shock.[41] Her daughters Josephine and Lena were treated at the hospital for minor injuries and shock.

Investigators found that the bombs shattered glass and damaged walls at the neighboring Magaddino home, 1653 Whitney Avenue, and the Peter Battaglia home, 1649 Whitney Avenue. In addition, some of the contents of the Longo home had been tossed around the neighborhood. A large chair from the Longo dining room was found on Magaddino's front lawn.[42]

Niagara Falls Chief of Detectives George Callinan sought in vain for some motive in that attack on the Longo family. When Nicholas Longo returned home from New York City that evening, he was called to police headquarters. The dazed and grieving Longo requested that any questioning be done at Magaddino's home. Under the circumstances, officials agreed to the request. Callinan, District Attorney Raymond A. Knowles and Assistant District Attorney Clarence W. Greenwald interviewed Longo but found no reason that he would be a bombing target.[43]

Like the Magaddinos, Longo was a native of Castellammare del Golfo, Sicily. He was the son of Matteo and Rosa Ruggieri Longo, born on December 13, 1887.[44] He first entered the United States through New York City in the spring of 1910 and went to Metropolitan Avenue in Brooklyn to stay with his brother

Francesco.[45] He subsequently returned to Castellammare and married Arcangela Magaddino on November 6, 1920. He and his new bride sailed to New York early in 1921.[46] Their first child, Rose, was born in New York City on November 8, 1921. The following year, the young family settled in Niagara Falls, where their two other daughters were born. Nicholas Longo was naturalized a U.S. citizen in 1924.[47] Later that year, Longo traveled to Sicily in the company of Giuseppe DiBenedetto.[48] Arcangela Longo was naturalized in 1935.[49]

The investigators found sufficient reason to believe that the Longo home was targeted by mistake. Longo had left for New York City several days before the attack. If an enemy wished to kill him in the bombing, police reasoned, that enemy would have made an effort to ensure he was home.

"Longo was not connected with any rackets, as far as we know," Callinan told the press. The detective chief noted that Longo had been arrested only once, when he was charged with the illegal transportation of alcohol.

Police considered several theories. One was that Longo was targeted by some personal enemy unknown to authorities. A beer distributors' war was also deemed plausible. Magaddino, who lived next door, was known to be involved in breweries and owned the Power City Distributing Company. Authorities also mulled whether an underworld feud related to bookmaking rackets might be erupting in the Buffalo-Niagara Falls area.[50]

By May 20, investigators concluded that the bombers were not from Niagara Falls. "We are convinced from our investigation so far that no local element is responsible for the outrage," Callinan told the press. Callinan said he discarded the bookmaking war theory because "there is no such war, as far as we know."

That day, many mourners gathered at the Magaddino home, where the body of Arcangela Longo lay in a large bronze casket enclosed within a glass case. The visitors recalled Arcangela as a woman highly respected in the community.[51]

Almost two thousand people gathered at the home the following morning as funeral services began. Arcangela's casket was blanketed with roses. The flag of the United States and the flag of the Castellammare del Golfo Society were assembled into an arch over the bier. Pallbearers included John C. Montana,

Salvatore Lagattuta and Angelo Acquisto of Buffalo; Salvatore Falcone of Utica; Augustus Scalia of Erie, Pennsylvania; and Salvatore Rangatore Jr. of Niagara Falls.

After a ceremony within the home, more than four hundred cars carried mourners to St. Joseph's Church. A Requiem Mass was celebrated by Pastor George O'Neill with assistance from Reverend Alfonso Bernardo, assistant pastor, and Reverend James Collins of Our Lady of the Rosary Church.

The crowd of friends and associates of the Longo and Magaddino families overwhelmed St. Joseph's Church and spilled outdoors. Among the attendees were out-of-town friends from all areas of New York State and as far away as Detroit and Chicago. Conspicuous at the front of the church were Arcangela's male relatives. Following Sicilian custom, they had not shaved since learning of her death. Nicholas Longo was accompanied by daughters Rose and Josephine. Antonina remained confined in the hospital.

Following the Mass, the cortege moved on to St. Joseph's Cemetery, about one mile from the church. The procession included four large trucks and two automobiles filled with floral offerings. The line of vehicles was so long that the first cars arrived at the cemetery before the last ones left the church.

Beside the gravesite, two large floral displays – one a cross made of roses and the other a pillar of lilies topped with a white dove – stood erect. The remaining flowers were placed around the site and covered a large area of the cemetery.

Reverend O'Neill delivered a final blessing. Paul Palmeri, a lifelong friend of the Magaddinos, then stepped forward to speak to the mourners in Italian:

> Few persons acquire nobility by birth, most of those having this virtue acquiring it during their life and some after death. Mrs. Longo was one of those and we hope that the sincere sympathy of the hundreds who are here will tend to alleviate, in some small measure, the sorrow of those she leaves behind.[52]

Stefano Magaddino's underworld reputation had changed considerably since his days leading the Good Killers gang. By

1936, he was widely seen as deliberate and slow to anger.[53] The bomb-murder of his sister, however, was met with immediate Magaddino retaliation. The focus of the Mafia boss's wrath was a rebellious bookmaking organization headquartered in Batavia, New York.

— — —

Frank LoTempio, a thirty-eight-year-old bookmaker, arrived in Buffalo early on Saturday morning, June 27, 1936. He drove from his Batavia home with his wife Josephine Mancuso LoTempio and his sister Anna Panepinto[54] to attend the wedding of a cousin[55] at Holy Cross Church. The group met LoTempio's other sister, Rose Panepinto of Niagara Falls,[56] at the church. Sam Pieri, related to the LoTempios through his wife,[57] also was in attendance.[58]

The various branches of the family had fallen out of touch until just a few weeks earlier, when Pieri made a determined effort to convince LoTempio to attend the Buffalo wedding. The situation was especially puzzling for Josephine LoTempio, who later told police, "Five years we had been married and [Pieri] had never been down here, and all at once he got a notion he wanted to look up his cousins?"[59]

Born in Batavia in 1898, LoTempio was the oldest son of Antonino and Pietra Castellana LoTempio of Valledolmo, Sicily.[60] He worked for a local steel company as a young man and served in the U.S. Army during the Great War. By 1920, he and his brother Russell opened a poolroom and became involved with gambling. Horse race bookmaking became their primary activity, but they also ran casino rooms with roulette wheels and card games. LoTempio was arrested several times by Batavia Police for gambling but never served any time in jail. After his most recent arrest, he pleaded guilty to operating a gambling establishment and received a suspended three-month jail sentence and a fifty-dollar fine.[61] The authorities in his hometown were aware of recent tensions between LoTempio and organized criminals in Buffalo. They had received repeated warnings that Buffalo gangsters planned to rob LoTempio gambling establishments and had foiled those robberies through the placement of police guards. They also had heard that LoTempio made a visit to underworld leaders in Buffalo, warning them to stay away from his businesses.[62]

The wedding ceremony was held at Holy Cross Church at nine-fifteen in the morning. Afterward, the wedding party and some relatives and friends attended a breakfast reception at the bride's home, 546 Seventh Street. At eleven-thirty, the bride and groom went to a photographer's studio to have pictures taken, and the party began to break up.

LoTempio informed his wife and sisters that he needed to return to Batavia. Sam Pieri insisted that the women stay for the day in Buffalo and promised to drive them home to Batavia that night. The Pieri invitation appealed to the women, and they were escorted toward Rose Panepinto's automobile. Pieri and LoTempio stood alone in the street talking for a few minutes. When the conversation concluded, Pieri shook LoTempio's hand and turned away.

LoTempio moved toward a new, blue Oldsmobile parked at the curb. As he reached for the handle of the car door, two men emerged from the car in front of his and opened fire on him with handguns. Nine slugs struck LoTempio near the center of his chest. A tenth was fired as a coup de grâce into the right side of his face as he lay sprawled in the street, leaving a black powder burn.

The gunmen jumped back into their automobile, a black, 1936 Ford sedan, and sped away north toward Porter Avenue. Screaming and wailing, LoTempio's wife and sisters rushed to his side.

Detective Sergeant Frank N. Felicetta was one of the first police investigators to arrive at the scene.[63] He recognized LoTempio and knew of his criminal activities. He told newspaper reporters, "I noticed him in town just a week ago and asked him what he was doing here. The minute I saw the new car, I knew he was up to something."[64]

Investigators traveled to Batavia and quickly learned of LoTempio's resistance to a Buffalo-imposed tax on his gambling rackets. An anonymous informant indicated that LoTempio had been having trouble with the DiCarlo Gang. Police Commissioner Higgins issued orders to bring in Joseph DiCarlo and Sam Pieri for questioning. It was suspected that LoTempio's killers were imported from another region and that Pieri identified their target by shaking hands with LoTempio in the street.

Higgins publicly lashed out at the residents of Buffalo's Italian colony for failing to assist in the investigation. Many witnesses to the murder were found, but only a single witness, a nine-year-old girl, supplied any information of value to detectives.[65] "We've experienced these circumstances in all other gangland murders," Higgins told the newspaper reporters. "...If the people of Buffalo want crimes like these cleaned up and the perpetrators brought to justice, we must have their cooperation."[66]

On June 29, the getaway car used by LoTempio's killers was found abandoned on Normal Avenue near Hampshire Street. Detectives determined that the Ford had been purchased just a week before the murder for $664 in cash. In dealing with the Cooley Motor Company of West Huron Street, the purchaser used the fictitious name and address of John Gallo, 148 Roma Street. The auto salesman recalled him as an Italian male of average height and average build.

Following the discovery of the car, one detective boasted to a reporter that the Buffalo Police Department was the owner of a brand new Ford. "Are you going to keep it?" asked the reporter. "Well," the detective responded, "we'll only be too glad to return it to its rightful owner if he wants to come down to headquarters and claim it."[67]

DiCarlo was taken into custody June 30 by Immigration Service inspectors at the Peace Bridge, as he returned to Buffalo from a trip to Canada. He was turned over to Buffalo Police. Detectives picked up Pieri later that day. DiCarlo's attorney, John S. Knibloe, cut short the police interviews by obtaining a court order that DiCarlo be charged or released and by threatening to obtain a similar order on Pieri's behalf. Investigators later announced that their questioning of DiCarlo and Pieri shed no new light on the LoTempio murder.[68]

Frank LoTempio's funeral was among the largest ever held in Batavia's Italian colony. More than two hundred friends and relatives gathered at his home on Trumbull Parkway. The total number of mourners grew during the Requiem Mass at St. Anthony's Church. Five hundred people filled the church, and an estimated three hundred stood outside. The funeral procession to St. Joseph's Cemetery included one hundred and fifty cars and a police escort. In honor of LoTempio's military service, an honor guard fired a salute at the gravesite.[69]

———

A month later, bookmaker Roman C. "Whitey" Kroll, of 37 Linden Park, complained to the police that Joseph DiCarlo and John Tronolone beat and kicked him at the Maryvale dog track in Cheektowaga. Kroll said the beating followed a DiCarlo July 27 demand for a share of Kroll's bookmaking profits.

Badly bruised and limping – the limp was the result of the much earlier loss of his lower left leg during employment as a railroad detective – "Whitey" Kroll formally reported the incident on July 31. "I'm going through with this," he told police. "I won't kick in to the racket men, and I won't let DiCarlo or any of his mob get away with this."

According to Kroll, DiCarlo made his first protection payment demand the previous February. At that time, Kroll learned that his bookmaking partner Frank "Cakes" Custodi had been making regular payoffs to the DiCarlo Gang. Kroll severed his relationship with Custodi and went back into the gambling business independently a couple of weeks later. In March, DiCarlo and another man entered Kroll's establishment and hit him repeatedly until he fell to the floor.

"You're brave guys," Kroll told them, "hitting a one-legged man." DiCarlo answered the sarcasm with a kick that landed on Kroll's neck.

Another encounter between "Whitey" Kroll and the DiCarlo Gang occurred on July 5. "Peanuts" Tronolone spotted Kroll stepping from his automobile. He teased Kroll about his earlier beating, grabbed paperweights from a nearby newsstand and hurled them in the bookmaker's direction. Kroll drew a revolver and fired twice at the ground. Both men were arrested following that incident. Kroll was charged with first-degree assault. Tronolone was charged with second-degree assault.[70]

Police linked the ongoing difficulties between Kroll and the DiCarlo Gang to the July robbery of a poolroom and bookmaking establishment. Kroll was present at the time and lost $270 to the robber. Authorities noted that robberies of gambling establishments were occurring at a rate of three or four per week, though most went unreported.[71]

Tronolone eluded police for some time. DiCarlo was arrested as he exited a theater about midnight on July 31. He denied any wrongdoing and stated that he was nothing more than a local florist. He was booked preliminarily in Buffalo's detective headquarters and then transported to Cheektowaga. He was arraigned before Justice of the Peace Benjamin P. Milne. Asked if he was ready to be tried on an assault charge, DiCarlo responded that he needed until September to prepare his defense. A trial date was penciled in for September 9.

Bail was set at $5,000, and DiCarlo was held briefly at the Erie County Jail. He was released after Samuel Lombardo of Trenton Avenue and Florence Vacanti of Lakeview Avenue posted properties valued at $13,000. Bail was approved by Judge George A. Larkin. As DiCarlo walked out of Larkin's courtroom, he told reporters, "I don't know what all this is about."[72]

County prosecutors in August launched an investigation into reports of a widespread protection racket imposed on local bookmakers. Assistant District Attorney George E. Wisch offered immunity from prosecution to any bookmakers willing to testify against the protection racketeers. "If we can get any bookie to talk, we'll blow this thing wide open and stop this gangster terrorization," Wisch told the press.[73]

On August 3, Buffalo Detective Sergeants Frank Felicetta and John F. Mahoney found and arrested John "Peanuts" Tronolone. At arraignment, the case against Tronolone was adjourned until the same September 9 date set for DiCarlo's trial. "Peanuts" was remanded to the county jail.[74]

— — —

Buffalo detectives were called in the early morning hours of August 26, 1936, to investigate a shooting. They pulled up to the corner of Seventh and Virginia Streets at forty minutes after three to find an unconscious man lying in the gutter, bleeding from head wounds. The victim was identified as thirty-eight-year-old Sam "Salvie" Izzo, also known as Samuel Yates. Izzo was transported to Columbus Hospital, and a detective was posted at his bedside in case he regained consciousness and could name his assailants. Izzo died less than an hour after arriving at the hospital.

Police learned that Izzo, like Frank LoTempio, was a Batavia resident paying a visit to Buffalo. Izzo had come to the city on the evening of August 25 with seven other Batavia residents to attend the wake of a close friend's mother.[75] The men traveled in two vehicles. Izzo and his companions Domenic Valle and Anthony Panepinto rode in an automobile driven by Ben Bonarrigo.

The group remained at the wake from about ten-thirty that night until three o'clock in the morning. As they walked to their cars, Izzo was the first of the men to reach the street. He was shot at close range by gunmen who ran out from the dark shadows on the side of a house.

None of Izzo's companions could identify his killers.[76]

The Erie County medical examiner determined that Izzo was shot four times. Two bullets entered his skull. One penetrated his back under the left shoulder blade and pierced both of his lungs. The last caused a flesh wound on his right cheek.[77]

The murder weapon was discovered on August 27 by some children playing in an alley behind Trenton Avenue. Police described it as a .32-caliber Spanish-type revolver.[78]

Police efforts to link the Izzo and LoTempio killings initially were fruitless. Izzo had no police record. His friends from Batavia knew of no reason anyone would want to kill him,[79] though rumors spread that Izzo had made threatening remarks against those responsible for Frank LoTempio's murder.[80]

— — —

The September 9 date for the DiCarlo and Tronolone assault trial passed uneventfully, as a grand jury investigated Roman Kroll's accusations and the broader issue of the alleged protection racket.

On the nineteenth, witness Edward J. Scott, proprietor of Scott's Roller Rink and friend of "Whitey" Kroll, was charged with perjury in connection with his testimony before the panel. Though he earlier told police he was with Kroll at the dog track and saw the beating, he swore before the grand jury that he did not witness the incident. Scott pleaded not guilty to perjury. He was released on $5,000 bail provided by Mariner Street resident Ralph S. Davis.[81]

Two days later, the grand jury returned indictments against DiCarlo and Tronolone. Arrest warrants were issued for both men. DiCarlo was picked up the next day by police Lieutenant Vincent J. Connors and Detectives John Mahoney and Thaddeus Wisniewski.

DiCarlo entered police headquarters with a cigar protruding

defiantly from the corner of his mouth. Accompanied by his attorney John Knibloe, DiCarlo was processed on a charge of second-degree assault by Assistant District Attorney John Hillery. He pleaded not guilty.[82] He once again won his release after Sam Lombardo and Florence Vacanti provided his bond.

Knibloe confidently predicted, "This case will never come to trial. My first move will be to ask for an inspection of the minutes of the grand jury as a basis for a motion to dismiss the indictment. There is no evidence against DiCarlo. He was indicted on his reputation only and he has been much maligned."[83] When Tronolone was processed a short time later, Knibloe also served as his attorney.

Following a formal arraignment of DiCarlo and Tronolone on September 23, Knibloe went through a number of legal maneuvers in an effort to make his prediction come true.

--- --- ---

While DiCarlo and Tronolone awaited trial, attacks on Batavia bookmakers continued.

William Yates and Russell LoTempio of Batavia were driving along South Main Street just outside the Village of Medina, New York, at ten-thirty in the evening of October 29, 1936, when their Oldsmobile sedan suddenly exploded. The incident immediately provided a link between the recent killings of Sam Izzo and Frank LoTempio in Buffalo. Yates was a cousin of Izzo. Russell LoTempio was Frank LoTempio's brother and partner in his bookmaking business.

The explosion was heard for several blocks and shattered windows in some South Main Street homes. Yates jumped from the vehicle and suffered only minor injuries. Russell LoTempio, however, was trapped inside as the car exploded, crashed through a telephone pole and came to rest in a ditch. He was rushed to Medina Memorial Hospital. Doctors were forced to amputate his left foot, which had been mangled in the explosion.[84]

After learning that the two men had spent about an hour and a half that night at Van's Grill on East Center Street in Medina, authorities theorized that a bomb was attached to the underside of the automobile's floorboards while they were in the restaurant. The visit to Van's Grill, police determined, was related to gambling. Yates and LoTempio were called there to collect receipts of a football pool they operated in Medina. Yates and

LoTempio also were known to be involved in horse race bookmaking and other gambling rackets.[85]

After leaving the restaurant, Yates and LoTempio went to the Socony service station for gasoline and oil. They then drove up Orient Street to South Main. The bomb was set to explode, detectives said, when heat from the vehicle's engine rose to the point where it caused a fuse to ignite. That occurred just beyond the Medina village limits.[86]

––––

In November of 1936, DiCarlo and Tronolone defense attorney John Knibloe requested a list of the witnesses who appeared before the grand jury. It took until the final day of December for Judge Samuel J. Harris to rule against the request and until early February for a formal order denying the request to be composed and signed. During his attorney's maneuvers, DiCarlo was away, vacationing in Miami Beach, Florida.[87]

After the formal order was issued, the DiCarlo-Tronolone trial date was scheduled for February 24. DiCarlo flew in from Florida a few days early. The day before trial, he changed his attorney. Knibloe continued to represent Tronolone, but Thomas L. Newton was hired to represent DiCarlo. On the twenty-fourth, Newton asked the court for another postponement. The attorney said he recently suffered an attack of the grippe (flu) and had not yet recovered.

Noting that the case had already been delayed five months, Judge Harris reluctantly agreed to postpone the trial until March 1. He admonished the defense attorneys to be ready at that time, "and no excuses."[88]

As the trial began, "Whitey's" memory failed him. Kroll recalled that DiCarlo and Tronolone saw him at the dog track and made some comments. He also recalled that he ran off, fell and was kicked repeatedly. However, he did not remember seeing who kicked him.

Kroll testified that DiCarlo was the first to notice him at the track and told Tronolone, "There goes your friend, Peanuts," After that, DiCarlo was heard saying, "I wonder if he has a gun with him tonight," a reference to the earlier altercation between the two men. Kroll testified that he began walking toward an exit with Edward Scott. Scott then dropped back. The bookmaker heard a shouted warning and started to run for his automobile.

According to his testimony, he lost his footing and fell face-first on gravel behind the grandstand. As unknown men began kicking him, Kroll threw his arms up over his head.

Assistant District Attorney John T. Walsh confronted Kroll with a signed statement he earlier provided police. That statement named DiCarlo and Tronolone as Kroll's attackers. Kroll acknowledged he made the statement but attributed the details to his own hasty conclusions.

"Did DiCarlo kick you?" Walsh asked.

"I don't know who kicked me," Kroll replied.

Edward Scott was little help to the prosecution. He testified that he saw DiCarlo and Tronolone pursue Kroll at the track, but he then ran for a policeman and did not see what happened next. Walsh called police officers to the stand who testified about DiCarlo's callous response when he learned Kroll's condition. After reporting that Kroll was in "pretty bad" shape, Lieutenant Connors recalled, "[DiCarlo] said, 'He should have died.'"[89]

Walsh rested the prosecution's case at the end of the day, and the defense attorneys immediately asked Judge Harris to dismiss the charges on the grounds that insufficient evidence had been introduced regarding Kroll's physical injuries and that the prosecution had not connected the defendants with the crime. The judge denied the defense motions.[90]

The next day, as rumors circulated that DiCarlo would take the stand in his own defense, Judge Harris stunned the packed courtroom with an announcement: "...Certain information has been given to me which requires me to declare a mistrial. I discharge the jury." The office of the district attorney later revealed that two of the jurors in the case, George A. Trench and Norman J. Neeb, had received telephoned death-threats.

Defense attorneys, citing the prejudicial nature of recent newspaper coverage, asked that a new trial be postponed. Judge Harris refused and started selection of a new jury at once.[91] That jury was confined overnight to the Buffalo Athletic Club under supervision of sheriff's deputies. Jurors were prevented from any contact from the outside, including newspapers, magazines, letters and radio programs.[92]

Before court reconvened on March 3, Joseph DiCarlo spoke with newsmen about the juror threats. "It was done by an enemy of mine who was trying to make trouble for me," DiCarlo charged. "It would be silly for me to countenance any such thing. What good would it do me if a juror was threatened and didn't show up for duty?"

That day, the prosecution repeated its case against DiCarlo and Tronolone. The defense repeated its motions for dismissal, also adding an argument that the jury did not have sufficient grounds for returning a verdict beyond a reasonable doubt. Judge Harris once again denied the dismissal motions.[93]

The jury began its deliberations at seven-fifteen that evening and returned its verdict two hours later. DiCarlo and Tronolone were acquitted.

With friends gathered around him in the courtroom, DiCarlo told reporters, "I am innocent of this charge, and whoever tried to intimidate the first jury must have been an enemy of mine." Tronolone said he was "satisfied that the jury agreed I was innocent."[94]

Following DiCarlo's acquittal, law enforcement officials from his new Florida vacation spot asked Buffalo police about him. In a March 5 letter, H.V. Yocum, chief of the Miami Beach Police Department, and E.H. Adkins, commanding officer in the department's Identification Bureau, wrote, "Would appreciate greatly if you would send us photograph of one Joseph DiCarlo whom you had arrested in May, 1930, and June and December, 1931."[95]

― ― ―

Twenty-five-year-old John Tronolone had less than two days to enjoy his courtroom victory. At five o'clock in the afternoon of March 5, Buffalo police raided a Pearl Street bookmaking establishment, arresting Tronolone and fifty-year-old William Miller for taking bets on horse races. Three other men, Anthony Peters, William Bryant and Anthony Barone, were taken into custody as material witnesses and then released on $100 bail each.

Tronolone and Miller pleaded not guilty during arraignment before city Judge Robert J. Summers the next morning. They were freed on $500 bail each.[96] Bail for both defendants and the three witnesses was provided by Samuel Polino of Massachusetts Avenue.

On March 9, defense attorney Samuel Fleischman demanded a jury trial for Tronolone and Miller. Noting that no long delays would be permitted, Judge Summers set a trial date for the fifteenth.[97]

Two days before trial, Tronolone's earlier bookmaking conviction was appealed in Erie County Court. Defense attorney Knibloe argued that police failed to produce evidence connecting Tronolone to the gambling business. Knibloe asked for the conviction to be reversed and the prison sentence to be revoked. To counter the defense arguments, Assistant District Attorney David F. Doyle had police officers testify to conversations they had with Tronolone. In those conversations, the witnesses said, Tronolone admitted running the bookmaking operation and said he did so at the behest of Joseph DiCarlo. County Judge F. Bret Thorn decided to postpone a decision on the appeal until the more recent bookmaking charges could be tried.[98]

The police testimony about Tronolone and DiCarlo earned headlines in local newspapers and possibly forced a change in legal strategy. On the fifteenth, Tronolone pleaded guilty to bookmaking. He was sentenced to a month in prison. His codefendant Miller was discharged.[99]

— — —

Alfred Panepinto, a thirty-five-year-old former business partner of Paul Palmeri in Niagara Falls and brother-in-law of Frank LoTempio,[100] became the final casualty in Stefano Magaddino's war against Batavia bookmakers.

Panepinto was an undertaker by trade. In 1928, he moved from Batavia to Niagara Falls and, in partnership with Palmeri, established the Panepinto and Palmeri Funeral Home at 496 Nineteenth Street[101]. Early in 1937, after having some trouble with gangsters in Buffalo and Niagara Falls, a fearful Panepinto dissolved the partnership and moved back to Batavia.[102]

On the evening of August 13, 1937, Panepinto was playing poker at a table near the rear doorway of LoTempio's Pool Room on Ellicott Street. Just after midnight on the fourteenth, two men appeared in the doorway. One held a pump shotgun. The other had a .38-caliber revolver. Both fired at Panepinto. The force of the shotgun discharge threw Panepinto backward off his chair and into Michael Cesare, seated behind him.

Cesare later recalled, "Panepinto made a kind of gurgling noise in his throat, twitched a few times, and then lay dead with his eyes wide open."

The eleven other men inside the poolroom were unable to identify the gunmen. Some witnesses outside the establishment reported seeing two men run from an alley and leap into a green sedan.[103] The vehicle drove away in the direction of Buffalo with its lights off, and the witnesses could not read the license plate.[104]

Batavia Police sent bulletins to the New York State Police and Buffalo Police calling on them to watch for three or four Italian fugitives in a green sedan. At two o'clock in the morning, a Buffalo patrolman spotted a green sedan parked in front of Bowles Lunch, 211 Main Street. Looking into the rear of the vehicle, he saw a revolver on the floor. He also noted that the vehicle's engine was very hot, indicating it had just traveled a considerable distance at high speed. The patrolman arrested four men standing near the sedan as suspects in the Panepinto murder.

The four men were Salvatore Lagattuta, Samuel Fraterrigo, Joseph Lumetto and Sam LoVullo. Lagattuta was the owner of the green automobile.[105]

Buffalo Police ballistics experts studied the revolver taken from Lagattuta's vehicle and determined that it was not the same weapon that fired at Panepinto in Batavia. Lacking any other substantial evidence tying Lagattuta and his companions to the murder, the police set the four men free.[106]

Alfred Panepinto's funeral drew a large and emotional crowd. Services began at the South Jackson Street home of his brother Anthony. A Mass of Christian Burial was celebrated by Reverend Thomas Ciolini at St. Anthony's Church. Nearly five hundred people – many from the communities of Buffalo, Rochester, Niagara Falls, Medina and Albion – attended.[107] At the gravesite in St. Joseph's Cemetery, Panepinto's grief-stricken wife had to be restrained by family members as she attempted to throw herself on the bronze casket.[108]

Notes

Abbreviations of frequently cited newspapers:

BCA – *Buffalo Commercial Advertiser*, BCE – *Buffalo Courier Express*, BDC – *Buffalo Daily Courier*, BEN-*Buffalo Evening News*, BME – *Buffalo Morning Express*, BN - *Buffalo News*, BT – *Buffalo Times*, CP – *Cleveland Press*, CPD – *Cleveland Plain Dealer*, CT – *Chicago Tribune*, NG – *Niagara Gazette*, NYT – *New York Times*, PP – *Pittsburgh Press*, RDC – *Rochester Democrat and Chronicle*, RTU – *Rochester Times-Union*, YV – *Youngstown Vindicator*.

Chapter 1

[1] Manifest of the *S.S. Indiana*, sailed from Naples, Italy, on May 5, 1906, arrived at New York City on May 23, 1906.

[2] Eighty-eight names were deleted from the 1,613 originally recorded on the *Indiana* manifest. None of the other passengers from Vallelunga intended to establish residence in New York City as the DiCarlos did. One was headed to Buffalo, one to North East, PA (near Erie), and the last to Rochester, NY.

[3] "*I pioneri dell'armamento marittimo*," AIDMEN *Associazione Italiana di Documentazione Marittima e Navale* (www.aidmen.org). Details of the *Indiana* were obtained through the American Family Immigration Center (www.ellisisland.org) and Lloyd Italian – Navigation Company (1904-1918), Genoa (http://www.ips.it/scuola/concorso_99/rex/Il Lloyd Italiano6.htm). Erasmo Piaggio, a respected Genoese businessman, left the shipping giant Navigazione Generale Italiana (NGI) in 1904 to form his independent Lloyd Italiano Line, offering passenger service between Italy and ports in North and South America. The *Indiana's* sister ships in the American States Class were the *Florida*, the *Louisiana* and the *Virginia*. Financial problems later brought the Lloyd Italiano Line under the control of NGI.

[4] *Indiana* manifest.

[5] "Reports of the Immigration Commission," Senate Document No. 753, 61st Congress, 3d Session, Washington, D.C.: Government Printing Office, 1911. (Open Collections Program: ocp.hul.harvard.edu/immigration/outsidelink.html/http://nrs.harvard.edu/urn-3:FHCL:925102) Two years after the DiCarlo's crossing, the U.S. Immigration Commission conducted a study of steerage travel on the larger steamship lines. Commission agents in the guise of immigrants traveled steerage on a dozen ships finding deplorable conditions. Improvements were noted to vessels serving northern European ports, in accordance with U.S. regulations passed in 1882. However, southern European lines treated third-class passengers "as so much

freight, with mere transportation as their only due." The commission's report was presented to Congress on Dec. 13, 1909.

[6] Maria, Sister Katherine, M.I.C.M., "The Holy House of Loreto," *Slaves of the Immaculate Heart of Mary*, Etomite Project, 2004, www.catholicism.org/loretohouse.html; Thurston, Herbert, "Santa Casa di Loreto," *Catholic Encyclopedia*, www.newadvent.org/cathen/13454b.htm. The small stone home, 13 feet in width by 31 feet in length, currently stands within the *Basilica della Santa Casa* (Hall of the Holy House) in Loreto. The house is said to have been the spot of Mary's birth, as well as of Jesus' birth. Its miraculous journey to Sicily was a complicated one. The house is believed to have landed first in Tersato, on the Dalmatian coast, and to have remained there between 1291 and about 1294. It then moved again, making additional stops before finally coming to rest in Loreto.

[7] King, Russell, *Sicily*, Harrisburg: Stackpole Books, 1973, p. 32; "The Town of Vallelunga Sicily," *The Vallelunga Site*, www.vallelunga.com/town.aspx.

[8] Birth records of Valledolmo, Sicily. Giuseppe DiCarlo, great-great-grandfather of Joseph DiCarlo, was born in Valledolmo about 1773. He and his wife Luigia Scibetta had five children, including Joseph's great-grandfather Marino, who was born about 1794.

[9] Montanti, Giovanni, *Valledolmo: Storie, Paesaggio, Tradizioni*, sicilia.indettaglio.it /eng/comuni/pa/valledolmo/editoria/editoria.html; "Valledolmo," *Palermo Sicilia*, www.palermo-sicilia.it/english/valledolmo.htm.

[10] Cipolla, Giuseppe, *Le Famiglie Di Vallelunga*, Commune di Vallelunga Pratameno, 1995. Giuseppa Spera's father, grandfather and uncles were masons in Vallelunga. She was the daughter of Giachino Spera, born Feb. 20, 1819. Giachino's father Vincenzo Spera was born in Vallelunga on April 26, 1788. Giuseppa's sister Francesca married Francesco DiCarlo's cousin Antonino, a blacksmith of Valledolmo, on Oct. 13, 1869.

[11] Birth records of Vallelunga, Sicily. Marino DiCarlo was born Oct. 25, 1857.

[12] Death record of Francesco DiCarlo, Jan. 10, 1881, Vallelunga, Sicily.

[13] Cipolla, Giuseppe, *Le Famiglie Di Vallelunga*, Commune di Vallelunga Pratameno, 1995. Dominic Monteleone's daughter by a previous marriage also joined the Spera-DiCarlo clan by marrying Giachino DiCarlo on March 10, 1898.

[14] Cipolla, Giuseppe, *Le Famiglie Di Vallelunga*, Commune di Vallelunga Pratameno, 1995.

[15] Marriage records of Vallelunga, Sicily. Giuseppe DiCarlo and Vincenza Grasso were married in *Santa Maria di Loreto* Church on Dec. 11, 1897. Vincenza Grasso's father Giuseppe was born in Santa Caterina on Oct. 5, 1841, the son of Luigi and Angela Celistino Grasso of that town. It appears that Giuseppe Grasso moved to Vallelunga shortly after his July 1, 1869, marriage in *Santa Maria di Loreto* Church to Rosaria Sanfratello of Vallelunga. Rosaria was born April 15, 1846, in Vallelunga to Calogero and Vincenza Pelliteri Sanfratello. Giuseppe's parents, Francesco and Giuseppa Spera DiCarlo were also married in *Santa Maria di Loreto* Church.

[16] Manifest of the *S.S. Lombardia*, arrived in New York City Sept. 14, 1905. Giuseppe DiCarlo reported that Palermo was his last home city.

[17] Fentress, James, *Rebels and Mafiosi: Death in a Sicilian Landscape*, Ithaca NY:

Cornell University Press, 2000, p. 250; Hess, Henner, translated by Ewald Osers, *Mafia and Mafiosi: Origin, Power and Myth*, New York: University Press, 1998, p. 17-19, 42-43; Lewis, Norman, *The Honored Society*, New York: G.P. Putnam's Sons, 1964, p. 63, 316-317; Schiavo, Giovanni, *The Truth About the Mafia*, New York: Vigo Press, 1962, p. 38-44; Servadio, Gaia, *Mafioso*, London: Secker & Warburg, 1976, p. 10; Smith, Dennis Mack, *A History of Sicily: Medieval Sicily, 800-1713*, New York: Viking Press, 1968, p. 72-76.

[18] U.S. Census of 1920. In the census, Crocevera was listed as Isadore Crotaro, 45, of 63 Duffield Street, Brooklyn, a stevedore living with his wife and seven children. The document indicated that he entered the U.S. in 1897.

[19] Birth records of Vallelunga, Sicily, Nov. 1, 1899, the date of Joseph DiCarlo's birth

[20] Manifest of the *S.S. Lombardia*, arrived in New York City Sept. 14, 1905. Giuseppe DiCarlo declared his intention to meet his brother-in-law Pasquale Enea, 66 Oliver Street. According to Critchley, David, *The Origin of Organized Crime in America*, New York: Routledge, 2009, p. 66, Enea owned a grocery at 66 Oliver Street, which served as "a meeting place for Italian blackmailers and thieves."

[21] US Census 1910.

[22] Manifest of the *S.S. Algeria*, arrived in New York City Jul. 15, 1904.

[23] 1906 Trow Business Directory of Greater New York; SS *Indiana* manifest May 23, 1906, Record of Detained Aliens.

[24] Cipolla, Giuseppe, *Le Famiglie Di Vallelunga*, Commune di Vallelunga Pratameno, 1995. Luigi Grasso, born Feb. 11, 1879, was married on Sept. 20, 1899, to Giuseppa Piraino, born Nov. 5, 1877. The couple had six children born in Santa Caterina Villarmosa between 1902 and 1919. Giuseppa Piraino Grasso died May 22, 1937. Six months later, Luigi Grasso married Calcedonia LoCastro, 13-plus years his junior. He died Feb. 11, 1947.

[25] *Indiana* manifest, May 23, 1906, Record of Detained Aliens.

[26] Record of Examination, Jan. 11, 1932, Immigration and Naturalization Service file on Joseph DiCarlo, p. 133.

[27] "Overcrowded city schools," *NYT*, July 31, 1879, p. 8; "School accommodations," *NYT*, Oct. 1, 1879, p. 8; "Grammar school reception," *NYT*, June 17, 1881.

[28] Dierickx, Mary B. and Jeffrey Baumoel, "Public School 72," report to the Landmarks Preservation Commission, New York City Board of Education, June 25, 1996.

[29] Sing Sing Prison Inmate Registers, Series B0143-80, Box 13, Vol. 35, New York State Archives.

[30] Flynn, William J., *The Barrel Mystery*, New York: The James A. McCann Company, 1919, p. 21.

[31] Flynn, *Barrel Mystery*, p. 91-94, 262-263; Gentile, Nick, *Vita di Capomafia*, Rome: Editori Riuniti, 1963, p. 60 (translations by the authors). Gentile remembered being visited in Sicily by his friend and fellow Mafioso Umberto Valenti, who brought along Giuseppe Morello: "Fra questi vi era Piddu Morello, che era il capo dei capi dell'onorata societá all'inizio della mia inscrizione." (With him there was Piddu Morello, who was the boss of bosses of the Honored Society at the start of my membership.) Though Gentile also had Mafia credentials from Sicily, his induction into the American branch of the Mafia can be placed in Philadelphia in 1906.

[32] Flynn, *Barrel Mystery*, p. 119. Through the recollection of Antonio Comito, Flynn provided a scene of interaction between Morello and Lupo. As the counterfeiting gang split up $800 in genuine cash, Lupo claimed $200 as his share before Morello stepped in: "'Don't do things all your own way, Ignazio,' Morello warned in his husky voice. 'Let us deliberate and argue this thing out. There are eight hundred dollars. You have spent two hundred dollars. You get seventy-five dollars now...'"

[33] White, Frank Marshall, "The Black Hand in control in Italian New York," *The Outlook*, Volume 104, Number 16, Aug. 16, 1913, p. 857-865.

[34] "Eight Sicilians held for Barrel Murder," *NYT*, April 16, 1903, p. 1; Flynn, *Barrel Mystery*, p. 3-6.

[35] Morello also commuted to Elizabeth Street from a home address in East Harlem.

[36] Manifest of the *S.S. Martha Washington*, arrived in New York City on July 27, 1908. Inzerillo accompanied Giuseppe Morello's wife Lina Salemi and daughter Angelina as they traveled "second cabin" from Palermo to New York.

[37] Reid, Ed, *Mafia*, New York: Random House, 1952, p. 44; Critchley, David, *The Origin of Organized Crime in America: The New York City Mafia, 1891-1931*, London: Routledge, p. 66. Reid referred to Enea as Don Pasquale Anea. According to Critchley, Italian police suspected Enea of coordinating with New York Mafiosi on the 1909 assassination of NYPD Lieutenant Joseph Petrosino in Palermo, Sicily.

[38] Flynn, *Barrel Mystery*, p. 210-211. Flynn quoted a Morello letter to Rosario Dispenza of Chicago, in which Morello criticized a Mafia induction policy instituted by Cascio Ferro and Enea: "You see in this that I was right in resenting de Vito Casiaferro and Enea, and saying that it is not done that way, in making a person, by not asking information of the townsmen before making [him]..."

[39] "Ruined by Lupo, the Mafia leader," *NYT*, March 17, 1909; "Lupo a Black Hand artist?" *New York Sun*, March 17, 1909, p. 6; "Hold Lupo as counterfeiter," *NYT*, Nov. 23, 1909.

[40] Flynn, *Barrel Mystery*, p. 174-198.

[41] "Ruined by Lupo, the Mafia leader;" "Lupo a Black Hand artist?" "Hold Lupo as counterfeiter;" "Lupo once more arrested," *New York Sun*, Nov. 18, 1909, p. 12.

Chapter 2

[1] List or Manifest of Alien Passengers Applying for Admission to the United States from Foreign Contiguous Territory, Port of Niagara Falls, NY, month of Feb. 25 to March 24, 1907.

[2] "Parishes face a drastic pruning / 1906: A year of growth," *BN*, May 26, 2006.

[3] Vogel, Michael N., Ed Patton and Paul Redding, *America's Crossroads: Buffalo's Canal Street / Dante Place: The Making of a City*, New York: Western New York Heritage Institute, 1993.

[4] Augello, Michael P., "A History of Italian Immigrants in Buffalo, New York, 1880-1925," master's thesis, History Department of Canisius College, May 1960, p. 15. Augello asserts that as many as 8,000 of Valledolmo's 12,000 residents settled in the Buffalo area.

[5] Shelton, Brenda K., *Reformers In Search of Yesterday / Buffalo in the 1890s*, Albany: State University of New York Press, 1976, p. 6-11.

[6] Shelton, p. 10-11.

[7] "Buffalonians from sunny Italy," *BME*, April 5, 1908. As late as 1908, when the Italian colony had achieved a population of 30,000, there was only a single Italian officer on the police force. "Italians to be appointed to the police force," *BDC*, April 19, 1914, p. 81. A police department effort to hire several Italian-speaking police officers drew 50 applicants in 1914.

[8] Shelton, p. 10-14.

[9] Vogel, p. 191-193.

[10] The City of Boston appears to have had a similar political experience to that of Buffalo. Philadelphia's Democratic Party, though unable to secure the allegiance of the Italian American bloc, at least did not drive the group to the opposition.

[11] Shelton, p. 10-11.

[12] While Paolo Busti is generally credited with guiding the settlement of Buffalo, "Buffalonians from sunny Italy," *BME*, April 5, 1908, described him merely as being "of some prominence in the community." The reporter apparently noted the Busti name attached to early street names – Busti Avenue and Busti Terrace – in making his assessment of Busti's importance.

[13] "Buffalo's Little Italy," *BDC Illustrated Express*, May 24, 1891.

[14] The annual dredging of the district waterways regularly produced the whole and partial remains of a number of murder victims.

[15] Vogel, p. 200-203; Buffalo City Directory of 1910. The street was named for Italy's "supreme poet" Dante Alighieri, author of *The Divine Comedy*.

[16] Vogel, p. 225.

[17] Lothrop, Thos., M.D., and Wm. Warren Potter, M.D., *Buffalo Medical and Surgical Journal*, Volume XXXII, Buffalo, 1893, p. 174; "Buffalo's Canal District According to Historian Marvin Rapp," Buffalonian.com (www.buffalonian.com/history/articles/1851-1900/RappPortofBuffalo.html). Writing in the 1880s, Rapp considered the livery stables worthy of note: "Farmers near Buffalo would draw in hay and draw out manure. But business during the season would become so brisk, they could not draw the supply away so fast as it accumulated. [Rapp's source E.E.] Cronk saw manure piled over two stories high in back of the barns. As one approached, the pile would give the appearance of shaking, quivering. Closer examine this, if your nose could stand it and you could cut through the clouds of flies, would reveal millions of crawling impure maggots feeding on the excrement." A decade later, Lothrop indicated the livery stables remained a health concern.

[18] "Black Hand sets off bomb at door of a Canal Street butcher," *BDC*, Nov. 21, 1906.

[19] U.S Census of 1900. According to the census, Bellissimo was born in December of 1853 and entered the U.S. in 1892.

[20] "Black Hand sets off bomb at door of a Canal Street butcher."

[21] "Black Hand baffles police," *BDC*, Nov. 22, 1906.

[22] "Black Hand case on trial," *BDC*, March 8, 1907; "'Black Hand' man gets one year," *BDC*, March 14, 1907.

[23] According to "Black Hand case on trial," Vario invited his extortion victim Cefoli to join the Black Hand gang. Though sentenced in 1907 only to a year for his extortion offense – the maximum penalty then allowed – Vario turned up as an

inmate of Auburn State Prison in the U.S. Census of 1910.

[24] "May take that Black Hand case to grand jury," *BDC*, July 20, 1907. Horace (Orazio) Lanza was born in Valledolmo, Sicily, on June 5, 1880. He became the first Italian graduate of the University at Buffalo Law School in 1901.

[25] Testimony of Ignazio Lupo, defendant, U.S. v. Giuseppe Calicchio et al., #2-347, U.S. Circuit Court, Southern District of New York, p. 471-472; "Killing that made Wolf an exile," *NYT*, Feb. 17, 1910, p. 4; Atlanta Federal Prison inmate file #2883, Ignazio Lupo, National Archives. In his court testimony, Lupo stated that he was the cousin of Giuseppe and Bartolo Oddo of Buffalo. The Times article of Feb. 17, 1910, noted that Lupo first entered the U.S. across the Canadian border at Buffalo, after fleeing a murder charge in Italy. Prison records from 1917showed that Lupo corresponded with a nephew Michelangelo Ingrassia of Buffalo.

[26] Testimony of John Lupo, U.S. v. Giuseppe Calicchio et al., #2-347, U.S. Circuit Court, Southern District of New York, p. 452; "Black Hand suspect was bled himself," *NYT*, Nov. 13, 1909, p. 1. In U.S. Circuit Court in 1910, John Lupo testified that his brother Ignazio traveled "to Buffalo to try and get money to pay his creditors." The *Times* described Lupo returning to New York City and appearing before bankruptcy referee Peter B. Olney. In that appearance, Lupo claimed that he initially went to Baltimore in an effort to raise money, then went on to Buffalo for the same reason.

[27] Flynn, *The Barrel Mystery*, p. 32, 208-211. Flynn discussed Morello correspondence with a Rosario Dispenza relating to admission of a new Chicago Mafia member. In that letter, Morello also instructed Dispenza on the proper conduct of Mafia membership meetings. Flynn noted Secret Service surveillance of Morello during his trip from New York to New Orleans: "On his arrival there certain Italian confederates were waiting for him and escorted their chief to a little Italian café where a conference was held..."

[28] Adams, John A., Daily reports of agent, United States Secret Service, National Archives and Records Administration. Adams referred to O'Grady in a number of reports from 1911. In his report of activities of March 2, 1911, he noted, "O'Grady speaks Italian and is more familiar with the Italian population than any other Buffalo police officer." A native of Buffalo, O'Grady was raised in an Irish-Italian neighborhood on the city's lower west side. He reportedly learned to speak Italian before age 14. O'Grady became highly regarded in the region. After leaving the police force, he established the O'Grady Detective Agency, praised as the "Scotland Yard of America." He died after appendix surgery on Jan. 30, 1920. ("Noted detective near death after operation for appendicitis," *BDC*, Jan. 30, 1920, p. 16; "Detective is to be buried on Monday," *BCA*, Jan. 30, 1920; "Detective O'Grady dies in hospital," *BDC*, Jan. 31, 1920.)

[29] Adams, Daily report for March 2, 1911, dated March 4, 1911.

[30] Adams, Daily report for March 12, 1911, dated March 13, 1911; Daily report for April 8, 1911, dated April 9, 1911; Daily report for April 12, 1911, dated April 13, 1911. According to the report for April 8, Niagara Falls Chief of Police Thomas H. Lyons placed Battaglia's arrival in the community about three years earlier, roughly the same moment as Giuseppe DiCarlo's arrival in Buffalo. Battaglia appears to have been a Buffalo resident before moving to Niagara Falls. Adams' report for April 12 indicates that Battaglia, his brother and Vincenzo Muscarello were

arrested in Buffalo in 1898 in connection with the murder of a man named Barone.

[31] Adams, Daily report for April 13, 1911, dated April 14, 1911; Daily report for May 10, 1911, dated May 11, 1911; Daily report for May 12, 1911, dated May 13, 1911. Guarnieri and Costanzo reportedly entered the U.S. about 1910. The Secret Service determined that they began circulating phony currency in Brooklyn in February 1911, a year after Giuseppe Morello and a number of his men were convicted of counterfeiting and sentenced to long terms in Atlanta Federal Prison. They arrived in Buffalo in March 1911. On May 10, they were convicted of possessing and passing counterfeit bills. They both were sentenced to serve two-and-a-half-year terms in Atlanta Federal Prison.

[32] Record of Examination, Jan. 11, 1932, Immigration and Naturalization Service file on Joseph DiCarlo, p. 133.

[33] Buffalo City Directory of 1909. In order to be listed at the Front Avenue address in the 1909 directory, the DiCarlo family must have lived there by the end of 1908. Front Avenue was renamed Busti Avenue in 1928.

[34] U.S. Census of 1910.

[35] Birth records of Valledolmo, Sicily. A cousin of Pietro and Carmelo Manzella named Salvatore Manzella was born in Valledolmo, Sicily, on Feb. 27, 1859.

[36] Birth records of Valledolmo, Sicily.

[37] U.S. Passport Application, April 15, 1909 (Pg. 2577).

[38] U.S. Passport Application, April 15, 1909 (Pg. 2576); Birth records of Valledolmo Sicily.

[39] St. Anthony of Padua Roman Catholic Church was founded in 1891.

[40] Certificate of Incorporation of the Buffalo Italian Importing Company, Dec. 10, 1909.

[41] "Is guilty of failure by fraud," *BDC*, Jan. 14, 1911, p. 7; U.S. Census of 1910; Manifest of the *S.S. Lombardia*, arrived New York City on April 17, 1902. Cannatta came to the U.S. to work on Buffalo railroad projects for Luigi Giambrone. A Sicilian immigrant from Valledolmo, Giambrone had been in Buffalo since 1889.

[42] Bankruptcy docket, Buffalo, NY. According to the docket, a petition was filed in the afternoon of Oct. 25, 1910.

[43] Bankruptcy docket, Buffalo, NY. The docket indicates that the final actions in the case occurred on July 25, 1912.

[44] "Is guilty of failure by fraud;" "Failure declared to be fraudulent," *BEN*, Jan. 14, 1911, p. 4.

[45] "Is guilty of failure by fraud."

[46] "Rich Italian gone; once Mafia leader," *NYT*, Dec. 5, 1908, p. 1. The *Times* indicated that the merchandise was found at a transatlantic pier in Jersey City.

[47] "Judgments," *BDC*, Nov. 18, 1911, p. 10.

[48] "Poles attacked by Italian strikers," *Buffalo Enquirer*, June 8, 1910, p. 6; "Hurl stones at laborers," *BME*, June 9, 1910, p. 6; "Laborers in a riot," *BME*, June 10, 1910, p. 6; "Striking laborers riot in the Terrace," *BDC*, June 10, 1910. Joseph Montana was an older brother of John C. Montana.

[49] "Riot on Terrace quelled," *Buffalo Enquirer*, June 9, 1910, p. 1.

[50] Buffalo City Directory of 1910; U.S. Census of 1910.
[51] "Assault follows call on his honor at the City Hall," *BT*, June 9, 1910, p. 1.
[52] "Laborers in a riot."
[53] "Assault follows call on his honor at the City Hall."
[54] "Fined for rioting," *BME*, Jan. 4, 1911.
[55] Birth record of Benedetto Palmeri, Castellammare del Golfo, Sicily, Jan. 12, 1878, certificate # 37.
[56] Galante, Camillo, http://www.castellammareonline.com, 2002.
[57] Bonanno, Joseph, with Sergio Lalli, *A Man of Honor*, New York: Simon & Schuster, 1983, p. 25-28, 31, 41, 63.
[58] Manifest of the *S.S.Lombardia*, sailed from Palermo, Sicily, on Aug. 22, 1906, arrived at New York City on Sep.7, 1906.
[59] Manifest of the *S.S.Prinzess Irene*, sailed from Naples, Italy, on Feb. 12, 1909, arrived at New York City on Feb. 27, 1906.
[60] Birth record of Paolo Palmeri, Castellammare del Golfo, Sicily, Oct. 1, 1892, certificate # 635.
[61] "Fined For Gambling" *BME*, Sep. 25, 1912. p.9
[62] Certificate of Marriage, Benedetto Palmeri and Rosaria Mistretta, Oct. 5, 1913. Giuseppina Crivello was Rosaria's maid of honor.
[63] Palmeri's marriage to Rosaria Mistretta technically made him a cousin the DiCarlo children.
[64] "Dead man's hand seen upper one in police hunt for Joe DiCarlo," *BCE*, Nov. 5, 1939; "Salvatore DiCarlo" FBI file, Report MM 92-103, p. 13. The *Courier Express* repeatedly refers to Giuseppe as "Don Pietro." The FBI report uses the name "Don Pedro." "Don" is a southern European title of respect with its roots in Spanish culture. The title traditionally precedes a person's given (first) name. In Sicilian usage, the title accompanies a familiar form of the given name often created by combining a later syllable in the name with a diminutive suffix. A common nickname for Giuseppe is Peppino. In similar fashion, Salvatore becomes Turridu, Francesco becomes Ciccio, Antonio becomes Nino. However, Pietro is not known as a nickname for someone named Giuseppe. Interestingly, DiCarlo's underworld superior in New York City, Giuseppe Morello, also became known in some circles as Peter or Pietro. The nickname seemed in his case to be the result of confusion over his actual nickname, which was Piddu. It is possible that DiCarlo's nickname came about in the same way, though there is no evidence he was ever called "Piddu."
[65] Buffalo City Directory of 1914.
[66] "Black Hand terror grows after bomb shatters saloon," *BDC*, July 15, 1914.
[67] "Black Hand notes spread fear in suburban districts," *BDC*, Nov. 26, 1914.
[68] "Police find leads in bomb explosion at Italian saloon," *BDC*, Dec. 10, 1914.
[69] "Black Hand at work in Falls," *BDC*, Dec. 21, 1914, p. 9.
[70] "Police find leads in bomb explosion at Italian saloon."
[71] "Black Hand sends fourth letter to resident of Falls," *BDC*, Dec. 4, 1914, p. 13.
[72] Record of Examination, Jan. 11, 1932, Immigration and Naturalization Service file

on Joseph DiCarlo, p. 133; Buffalo Public School records of Joseph DiCarlo.

[73] "Italian children make good Americans," *BT*, Nov. 24, 1901.

[74] "Buffalonians from sunny Italy." The article noted that School No. 2 and School No. 3 hosted the largest numbers of Italian children in the city.

[75] "School No. 1 holds rich page in educational progress of city," *Buffalo Express*, Jan. 10, 1926.

[76] Buffalo Public School records of Joseph DiCarlo.

[77] Report of the Buffalo Office of the FBI, "BU 92-68," p. 4.

[78] Joseph DiCarlo registered for the World War I draft during his brief time as a student at Hutchinson High School.

[79] Certificate of Naturalization for Giuseppe DiCarlo dated July 7, 1920. Giuseppe declared his intention to become a citizen Sept. 19, 1912. His petition for naturalization was submitted June 13, 1917, at Erie County NY Supreme Court. Buffalo Police Detective Thomas O'Grady, who aided Secret Service operative John A. Adams in his 1911 counterfeiting investigation, served as a character witness on Giuseppe DiCarlo's naturalization petition.

[80] "Crowd makes attack on copper," *BDC*, Feb. 27, 1915; "Police battle with Italians," *BCA*, Feb. 27, 1915; "Attack officer," *BT*, Feb. 27, 1915, p. 3; "Officer attacked by a mob," *Buffalo Enquirer*, Feb. 27, 1915, p. 2.

[81] "Is fined $250," *Buffalo Enquirer*, March 5, 1915, p. 11; "Given maximum sentence for attacking policeman," *BEN*, March 6, 1915, p. 9.

[82] Birth certificate of Anna Palmeri dated Sept. 29, 1915.

[83] Baptism record, Holy Cross Church, Buffalo NY, Nov. 11, 1915.

[84] Death certificate of Rosaria Palmeri, Jan. 5, 1916.

[85] Death certificate of Rosaria Palmeri.

[86] Interview with Rose Lombardo, Aug. 5, 2005.

[87] World War I Draft Registration Card dated Sept. 12, 1918.

[88] "Frank DiCarlo," *BDC*, March 17, 1918, p. 62.

[89] Buffalo City Directory of 1924; Filippo Mazzara, Commission Merchant "Mazzara & Perna".

[90] Birth records of Castellammare del Golfo, Sicily, to Camillo and Caterina Palmeri Mazzara; Manifest of the *S.S. Brasile* arrived New York City on Feb. 22, 1907. Mazzara was born in Castellammare del Golfo, Sicily, on Oct. 17, 1889, and immigrated to the U.S. on Feb. 22, 1907. He initially settled with a brother-in-law at 19-22 Stanton Street in Manhattan.

[91] Report of the Buffalo office of the FBI, "BU-280-C," June 3, 1963, p. 13-14. The report was a translation and transcription of a surveillance recording of a Stefano Magaddino conversation. The FBI translator appears to have misidentified Filippo Mazzara as "Philip Maranzano" and as "Marzare" on these pages. It is likely that other mentions of "Maranzano" within this report actually referred to Mazzara. Magaddino was speaking of a time before Maranzano was in the United States.

[92] World War I Draft Registration Card dated Sept. 12, 1918.

[93] Cemetery Records; Pine Hill Cemetery.

[94] "Italians of Buffalo Pay Tribute to Memory of Mrs. DiCarlo, Friend of Colony, at

Remarkable Funeral" *BT*, Jul. 13, 1919.

[95] Last Will and Testament of Vincenza DiCarlo, Surrogate's Court, Erie County, New York.

[96] Certificate of Death for Jennie DiCarlo, Department of Health of the City of New York, July 3, 1919. The certificate was completed by Dr. M.S. Vogt, surgeon at Memorial Hospital. Vogt noted that the causes of death were carcinoma of the uterus and pyelonephritis, an infection of the kidneys.

[97] "Italians of Buffalo pay tribute to memory of Mrs. DiCarlo…" A number of the names contain obvious misspellings: "Galboa" for Balboa, "Silato" for Sileo, "Gelsomino" for Bellissimo and "Sciambra" for Giambra.

[98] Cavolo, Detective Charles, Cleveland Police Department, Memo to Deputy Inspector Chas. N. Sterling, Feb. 28, 1920. Cavolo learned that Ulizzi operated a Buffalo safe house for on-the-run gangsters and regularly traveled around the region selling stolen merchandise. Cavolo felt that Ulizzi, Tony Vaccaro and Michael Russo (alias Valenzano) ran a burglary ring. Russo was connected to Mafia organizations in Buffalo, Cleveland and New York City. On Jan. 28, 1920, Ulizzi reportedly told Tony and Vincent Vaccaro that he had been called to Cleveland "on business" and needed the address of someone there he could stay with. Vincent Vaccaro provided him with the Cleveland address of a Vaccaro brother-in-law, Antonio Zito. Ulizzi and Salvatore Russo, brother of Michael Russo, were found dead on Pearl Road in Cleveland on Jan. 29, 1920.

[99] Cemetery records. Record of Lot Owners; Lot 76, Section 10. United German and French Roman Catholic Cemetery.

Chapter 3

[1] Ontario Canada death record, County of Wentworth, Division of Hamilton, p. 184, No. 044205, recorded April 17, 1918; "Murder verdict against both men," *Hamilton (Ontario) Herald*, April 24, 1918; Dubro, James and Robin F. Rowland, *King of the Mob: Rocco Perri and the Women Who Ran His Rackets*, Markham, Ontario: Viking, Penguin Books Canada, 1987, p. 82. The death record notes that Celona was born in Italy to Dominico and Theresa Celona. He was buried in Hamilton Cemetery.

[2] York Street was renamed York Boulevard in 1976.

[3] "Two arrests made in murder case," *Hamilton (Ontario) Herald, April 17, 1918;* Nicaso, p. 60-61.

[4] "Two Italians were charged with murder," *Hamilton (Ontario) Herald*, April 25, 1918.

[5] "Murder verdict against both men."

[6] "Two arrests made in murder case." Celona had sought permission to expand his business to include a tobacco shop and a restaurant. His application was refused on April 4, 1918.

[7] "Speranza goes down for life," *Hamilton (Ontario) Herald*, Nov. 15, 1918.

[8] "Two Italians on trial on murder charge," *Hamilton (Ontario) Herald*, Nov. 14, 1918. Businessman Anthony Spicuzza testified about the goings-on during the trial of Celona's alleged assassins. He stated, "It was supposed to be a candy store, but I

had suspicion that young girls were being brought there. I advised the police to this effect and asked that the place be watched." Asked why he did so, Spicuzza replied, "Because I live directly opposite and did not wish to have an improper place near my home."

[9] Dubro and Rowland, p. 82; Nicaso, Antonio, *Rocco Perri: The Story of Canada's Most Notorious Bootlegger*, Mississauga, Ontario: John Wiley & Sons Canada, 2004, p. 60. Celona had been arrested and held for questioning after the 1917 murder of Salvatore LaFata in Buffalo.

[10] Dubro and Rowland, p. 80.

[11] Nicaso, p. 59.

[12] "Murder verdict against both men;" "Two arrests made in murder case." At the time of Celona's death, Rocco Perri, a leading figure in the same criminal network, acknowledged knowing him for four years. The sources disagree on Celona's home before his December 1917 move to Hamilton. They point to St. Catherines, Ontario, and Buffalo, New York. It is likely that Celona was well acquainted with both locations.

[13] "Murder verdict against both men."

[14] Nicaso, p. 36.

[15] Nicaso, p. 36; Ontario Canada death record, No. 044205, April 17, 1918.

[16] Nicaso, p. 36; "Two arrests made in murder case."

[17] Nicaso, p. 36.

[18] Nicaso, p. 60-61.

[19] "Two arrests made in murder case."

[20] "Murder verdict against both men;" "Two Italians were charged with murder."

[21] "Speranza goes down for life," *Hamilton (Ontario) Herald*, Nov. 15, 1918.

[22] "Speranza goes down for life;" Nicaso, p. 61. Speranza served eight years before he was paroled on condition that he leave Canada immediately.

[23] Ontario Canada death record, County of Welland, Division of Welland, p. 267, No. 034057, recorded Jan. 29, 1919; Nicaso, p. 61; "Dominic Paproni killed at Welland," *Hamilton (Ontario) Herald*, Jan. 29, 1919, p. 1; "Paproni victim of vendetta, police think," *Hamilton (Ontario) Herald*, Jan. 30, 1919.

[24] Nicaso, p. 37.

[25] "'King of Bootleggers' won't stand for guns," *Toronto Daily Star*, Nov. 19, 1924, p. 1. During an interview with the *Star* reporter, Perri stated, "Yes, they call me the king of the bootleggers."

[26] U.S.-Canada border crossing record of Joseph Sirianni, Niagara Falls, New York, Aug. 15, 1929.

[27] U.S. Census of 1930.

[28] World War I draft registration of Samuel Sirianni, June 5, 1917. Petition for naturalization of Saverio Sirianni, Supreme Court of Niagara County, Dec. 30, 1915.

[29] Birth records of Castellammare del Golfo, Sicily.

[30] Manifest of the *S.S. Saxonia*, arrived at New York City on April 9, 1912.

[31] U.S. Census records of 1920 and 1930, 1649 Whitney Avenue.

[32] U.S. Census of 1920.

[33] "The Volstead Act and related Prohibition Documents," The National Archives (http://www.archives.gov/education/lessons/Volstead-act/).

[34] Allen, Oliver E., *The Tiger: The Rise and Fall of Tammany Hall*, Reading, MA: Addison-Wesley Publishing Company, 1993, p. 66-67.

[35] "History: The saloon must go," Anti-Saloon League Website (http://www.wpl.lib.oh.us/), Westerville OH Public Library.

[36] "Many city pulpits join saloon attack," *NYT*, Jan. 28, 1918, p. 13.

[37] "Many city pulpits join saloon attack."

[38] Germany attempted to arm the Irish Republican Brotherhood for its 1916 Easter Rising in Dublin. The weapons shipment was intercepted by the British. Leaders of the uprising were later executed by British authorities for treason.

[39] "Prohibition wins in national House by 282 to 128," *NYT*, Dec. 18, 1917, p. 1.

[40] Fenwick, Charles G., *Political Systems in Transition: War-Time and After*, New York: The Century Co., 1920, p. 154.

[41] Fenwick, p. 156.

[42] "Saloons may keep open and sell mild brew, commissioner states," *BDC*, Feb. 1, 1920, p. 69.

[43] "Saloons may keep open and sell mild brew, commissioner states."

[44] Dubro, James, *Mob Rule: Inside the Canadian Mafia*, Toronto: Macmillan of Canada, 1985, p. 267. Canadian provinces had also passed measures prohibiting the local sale of alcoholic drinks. They did not ban the manufacture of alcohol for export, effectively allowing a flood of it to cross the border into the U.S.. According to Dubro: "The Canadian government allowed any exporter with the flimsiest of credentials to purchase from a Canadian distillery, as long as the shipment was destined for an offshore location that did not have Prohibition legislation in place. Cuba and the West Indies were the preferred locations. The situation was so clearly ludicrous that one boat was advertised as leaving for Cuba four times daily."

[45] Buffalo City Directory for 1920.

[46] Dubro, James and Robin F. Rowland, *King of the Mob: Rocco Perri and the Women Who Ran His Rackets*," Markham: Penguin Books Canada, 1987, p. 80-85. DiCarlo's Sicilian Mafia was not the only Italian criminal organization in the region smuggling Canadian liquor into the U.S. Dubro noted that a Calabrian group straddling the border was also actively involved. Principals in that operation included Rocco Perri of Hamilton, Ontario; the Scaroni family of Guelph, Ontario (with relatives in Buffalo, NY); and the Serianni family of Niagara Falls and Buffalo, NY.

[47] Though the U.S. Prohibition Era had just started, Ohio's own alcohol restrictions had been in place since May 27, 1919.

[48] Kelly, Ralph, "Murder in Cleveland: The Prohibition Toll, Chapter 1," *CPD*, January 1933.

[49] Cavolo, Detective Charles, Memo to Deputy Inspector Chas. N. Sterling, Cleveland Police Department, Feb. 28, 1920.

[50] Kelly, Chapter 1.

[51] Cavolo.

[52] The establishment was later known as the "Black and Green," 166 Busti Avenue. It was a notorious night spot through the 1940s and 1950s. The name of Front Avenue was changed to Busti Avenue in 1928.

[53] Columbus Hospital, 298 Niagara St., was built in 1908 to serve the growing immigrant Sicilian-Italian population of Buffalo's Canal District. Charles R. Borzilleri, M.D., born 1873 in Valledolmo, Sicily, and naturalized an American citizen, served as director of medicine at the facility during this period. Walsh, James J., M.D., *History of Medicine in New York, Vol. III*, New York: National Americana Society, Inc., 1919.

[54] "Pistol battle ends in death of unidentified man' another wounded," *BDC*, Aug. 9, 1920, p. 12; "Police baffled at slaying of man in Italian section," *BME*, Aug. 9, 1920, p. 4.

[55] "Pistol battle ends in death of unidentified man' another wounded;" "Police baffled at slaying of man in Italian section;" "Bullet in back kills stranger found in road," *BN*, Aug. 9, 1920, p. 22.

[56] "Police baffled at slaying of man in Italian section."

[57] "Pistol battle ends in death of unidentified man' another wounded;" "Police baffled at slaying of man in Italian section." Rosalino Visconti suffered five gunshot wounds in 1919 in Cleveland, Ohio. The attempt on his life was made after he received a Black Hand letter demanding a large sum of money. Visconti was murdered in a Cleveland bootleggers' war on June 1, 1931.

[58] "Pistol battle ends in death of unidentified man' another wounded."

[59] "Police baffled at slaying of man in Italian section."

[60] "Pistol battle ends in death of unidentified man' another wounded;" "Police baffled at slaying of man in Italian section;" "Police unable to solve mystery in murder of Italian," *BME*, Aug. 10, 1920, p. 7.

[61] "Police unable to solve mystery in murder of Italian."

[62] "Police baffled at slaying of man in Italian section;" "Not identified," *Buffalo Enquirer*, Aug. 9, 1920, p. 10.

[63] "Police baffled at slaying of man in Italian section;" "Police unable to solve mystery in murder of Italian."

[64] "Police unable to solve mystery in murder of Italian;" "Little progress in clearing up murder of Brooklyn Man," *BT*, Aug. 10, 1920, p. 4; "Seek Crocivera's slayer," *Brooklyn Daily Eagle*, Aug. 10, 1920, p. 2; "Wife in ignorance of husband's death," *Brooklyn Standard Union*, Aug. 10, 1920, p. 1.

[65] Flynn, *The Barrel Mystery*. Former Secret Service agent Flynn also recounted his campaign against the Morello-Lupo counterfeiting gang in a series of articles titled, "Black Hand: Inner secrets laid bare," in the *Washington Post* and other newspapers in spring-summer 1914. His book was serialized across the country in 1920 through the Wheeler Syndicate.

[66] "Police unable to solve mystery in murder of Italian;" "Find no clues," *Buffalo Enquirer*, Aug. 10, 1920, p. 10.

[67] "Assault charge for shooting," *Buffalo Commercial Advertiser & Journal*, Aug. 10, 1920; "Find no clues;" "Italian murder witnesses won't give information," *BME*,

Aug. 11, 1920, p. 5; "Assumes blame for man's death," *BDC*, Aug. 11, 1920, p. 4.

[68] "Assumes blame for man's death."

[69] "Charged with murder," *BME*, Aug. 13, 1920, p. 5.

[70] "Little progress in clearing up murder of Brooklyn man;" "Assumes blame for man's death;" "Italian murder witnesses won't give information;" "Charged with murder."

[71] The saloon at 166 Front Avenue served as a transition. Though described as a saloon, it was equipped with a kitchen and served meals.

[72] Business certificate #9266 filed Sept. 11, 1919, with the Erie County NY Clerk's Office.

[73] "Venice restaurant excels in service and fine cooking," *BT*, Feb. 21, 1920, p. 11.

[74] "Two girls allege men with an auto lured them away," *BME*, June 27, 1920, p. 1.

[75] "Girls are freed from jail; men under $2,000 bail," *BME*, July 1, 1920, p. 4.

[76] "Girls in prison but the ravishers go free," *BME*, June 30, 1920, p. 11.

[77] "Young men held, girls complaint," *BDC*, July 1, 1920, p. 5.

[78] Buffalo Police arrest record; FBI arrest record, Joseph DiCarlo INS file, p. 44.

[79] Buffalo Police arrest record; FBI arrest record, Joseph DiCarlo INS file, p. 44, 86.

[80] FBI file on Samuel DiCarlo, file #313235.

[81] Buffalo Police arrest record; FBI arrest record, Joseph DiCarlo INS file, p. 44.

[82] "Convict alleged runners," *BDC*, Feb. 10, 1921, p. 12; "Falls men convicted," *NG*, Feb. 10, 1921.

[83] Marco "Mike" LoBosco, a prominent figure in the bootlegging rackets in Cleveland, Ohio, was a close friend and lieutenant of Cleveland boss Joe Lonardo. LoBosco had a monopoly on five-gallon tin cans used for liquor and was known as the "alky can king." When arrested in April 1921, LoBosco gave authorities Paul Palmeri's address (1113 East Falls Street). LoBosco and his wife stood as godparents for Paul Palmeri's son, Frank, in Niagara Falls, NY, Dec. 27, 1924. Shotguns took LoBosco's life in Cleveland, Ohio, on May 9, 1931.

[84] "Seize four men, $10,000 in liquor and two autos," *BME*, April 4, 1921, p. 10; "Falls alleged bootleggers fall into trap set by Sheriff Bigelow," *NG*, April 4, 1921, p. 1.

[85] "Whisky runners held up by a rival band; liquor taken, but police get it," *BME*, April 23, 1921, p. 1.

Chapter 4

[1] "Six persons, blood stained car in custody," *BCA*, May 18, 1921; "Police questioning friend of victim," *BEN*, May 18, 1921, p. 1; "Slew man to get his liquor stock, theory," *BME*, May 19, 1921, p. 1.

[2] "Slew man to get his liquor stock, theory."

[3] "Six persons, blood stained car…;" "Police questioning friend of victim."

[4] "Gotham man is hacked to death," *BT*, May 18, 1921, p. 1; "Killed as an informer," *NYT*, May 19, 1921, p. 3; "Slew man to get his liquor stock, theory."

[5] The same address of Frank Vassallo – a two-family home at 212 Front Avenue – was also listed as the address of Mafioso Filippo Mazzara in the 1920 and 1921 Buffalo municipal directories.

[6] "Slew man to get his liquor stock, theory;" "Expect arrest in murder of Pizzuto near," *BT*, May 19, 1921, p. 2.

[7] "Gotham man is hacked to death."

[8] "Killed as an informer."

[9] "Friends of Pizzuto grilled for clue," *BEN*, May 19, 1921, p. 1.

[10] "Detain Jack Martin in Pizzuto murder," *BEN*, May 23, 1921; "Grills chorus girl, 4 men in Pizzuto murder," *BEN*, May 20, 1921, p. 1.

[11] "Friends of Pizzuto grilled for clue."

[12] "Murder victim's wife helps to solve mystery," *BEN*, May 21, 1921, p. 1; "Officials make second arrest in murder case," *BCA*, May 20, 1921; "Grill woman in murder mystery," *BDC*, May 20, 1921, p. 14; "Holding five in Pizzuto murder," *BDC*, May 21, 1921, p. 3.

[13] "Holding five in Pizzuto murder."

[14] "Pretty wife of murdered man is questioned again," *BME*, May 20, 1921, p. 5; "Friends of Pizzuto grilled for clue."

[15] "Hold one and seek one in murder," *BDC*, May 19, 1921, p. 1; "Ready to put charge against one suspect," *BCA*, May 19, 1921.

[16] "No murder charge," *BEN*, May 23, 1921, p. 39.

[17] Baptismal record; St. Joseph's Roman Catholic Church, Niagara Falls, NY. Further evidence of Palmeri's underworld connections can be seen in the baptism of his youngest daughter, Rose, born in 1924. Rose's godparents were Vincent and Caroline Mangano of Brooklyn.

[18] Frank Rangatore, prominent Niagara Falls fruit commission merchant, died June 15, 1920, at St. Mary's Hospital following two surgical procedures on a badly infected left leg. Rangatore was said to be connected to the aristocracy of Trabia, Sicily, his native town. His father was mayor of Trabia, and his uncle represented the district in the Italian parliament (*NG*, June 16, 1920, p. 9).

[19] "Gunman gets his victim at Falls," *BCA*, Aug. 29, 1921; "Killer shoots from ambush and follows victim into store," *NG*, Aug. 29, 1921; "Assassins murder man in front of Falls store," *BME*, Aug. 30, 1921, p. 1.

[20] "Gnazzio was shot over money dispute, police say; may arrest slayer soon," *NG*, Aug. 30, 1921, p. 1.

[21] "Suspect arrested in connection with killing of Emilio Gnazzio said to have drawn money and planned getaway," *NG*, Aug. 31, 1921, p. 1.

[22] "Alleged slayer of Emilo C. Gnazzio arraigned today," *NG*, Sept. 1, 1921, p. 1.

[23] "Suspect arrested in connection with killing of Emilio Gnazzio said to have drawn money and planned getaway," *NG*, Aug. 31, 1921, p. 1.

[24] "Kills man in Falls saloon; vendetta duel," *BME*, Sept. 6, 1921, p. 1; "Pistol duel in East Falls Street has fatal ending," *NG*, Sept. 6, 1921, p. 1.

[25] "Shot to death in Falls café; blame vendetta," *BN*, Sept. 6, 1921, p. 28.

[26] Anthony F. Scalzo, son of Italian immigrant parents, was born in Ossining, New York, in 1888. His father Salvatore, a grocer, moved his family and business to Niagara Falls in 1889. Angelo Scalzo earned a law degree from the University of Buffalo Law School in 1910. While attending law school, he worked as a clerk in the office of Horace O. Lanza, prominent Buffalo attorney.

[27] "Pistol duel in East Falls Street has fatal ending."
[28] "Confession of slayer puzzle to the police," *NG*, Sept. 7, 1921, p. 1; "Insists he murdered man," *BCA*, Sept. 8, 1921, p. 9; "Self accused slayer believed to be demented," *NG*, Sept 8, 1921, p. 1.
[29] "Self accused slayer believed to be demented."
[30] "Confession of slayer puzzle to the police."
[31] "Papaleo repudiates murder confession made in Utica," *NG*, Sept. 9, 1921, p. 1.
[32] "Judge Piper refuses to free man accused of killing Gnazzo," *NG*, Sept. 14, 1921, p. 1.
[33] "Discharge Palmiero, accused of murder; witness is away," *NG*, Sept. 16, 1921; "Free Palmiero of murder charge," *BDC*, Sept. 17, 1921, p. 10.
[34] "Recall old tragedy when former actors appear in court," *NG*, Sept. 23, 1921, p. 1; "Man charged with murder released on $10,000 bail," *BME*, Oct. 1, 1921, p. 6.
[35] U.S. Census of 1920; World War I draft registration, June 5, 1917.
[36] "Sheriff must put liquor in evidence to convict Denario," *NG*, Sept. 27, 1921, p. 1.
[37] "Falls officer refuses to give up seized liquor," *BME*, Sept. 30, 1921, p. 11.
[38] "Dinerio is freed, to sue undersheriff for $10,000 balm," *NG*, Sept. 30, 1921, p. 1.
[39] Pietro Bonventre was the brother-in-law of racketeer "Charley Buffalo" DiBenedetto. Bonventre married Antonia DiBenedetto June 4, 1921, in Brooklyn, New York, according to Declaration of Intention, Antonia Bonventre, May 2, 1938.
[40] "State Troopers Are Scored In Case; Bonventre Acquitted," *BME*, Nov. 29, 1921. p.10
[41] "Fire follows explosion in East Side store," *NG*, Dec. 5, 1921, p. 1; "Explosion wrecks store at Falls; loss is $4,000," *BME*, Dec. 6, 1921, p. 11.
[42] "Falls man in hospital," *BME*, Feb. 18, 1922; "Auto gunmen run wild on East Side; two shoot from passing machine," *Buffalo Enquirer*, Feb. 18, 1922; "Holdup men fire in effort to rob roadhouse guest; mystery shooting," *BDC*, Feb. 18, 1922, p. 1.
[43] "Pedestrian is shot down by bandits," *BME*, Feb. 18, 1922.
[44] "Police brand tale of victims false," *BN*, Feb. 18, 1922, p. 1; "2 victims of rum runners' fight dying," *BME*, Feb. 19, 1922, p. 1; "Say wounded men cover up battle over booze load," *BDC*, Feb. 19, 1922, p. 91; "Rum runners in gun battle," *BT*, Feb. 19, 1922; Sirianni shot in bootleggers war, Buffalo police say," *NG*, Feb. 20, 1922.
[45] "Alleged victim of gunmen died today," *NG*, Feb. 21, 1922, p. 6.
[46] "The funeral of Sam Sirianni…," *BME*, Feb. 24, 1922, p. 7.
[47] "Victim of liquor runners' battle dies of wounds," *BME*, Feb. 22, 1922, p. 7.
[48] "Another man is held in fatal shooting case," *BME*, March 2, 1922.
[49] "Arrest one more in Sirriani case," *BN*, March 4, 1922.
[50] "Sought on Falls murder charge, trapped in backyard," *BDC*, April 11, 1922, p. 4; "Arrest fifth man for the killing of Samuel Serriani," *NG*, April 11, 1922, p. 10; "Held for murder," *BME*, April 11, 1922, p. 4; "Arrest suspect in murder of Sirianni slain February 17," *BME*, April 24, 1922. Leo Smolarek became a prosecution witness. Stanley Gorski was convicted of first degree murder and sentenced to die in the electric chair. New York Governor Alfred E. Smith

commuted the sentence to life in prison. Nowakowski and Bartkowski pleaded guilty to a reduced charge of first degree manslaughter. They were both sentenced to 10 years in Auburn State Prison.

[51] Dubro and Rowland, p. 85.

[52] "Mystery slaying discovered when victim's body is seen by hunters," *BDC*, April 3, 1922, p. 1; "Find body of Italian near River Road," *BME*, April 3, 1922.

[53] "Find body of Italian near River Road;" "Think death of Bocchimuzzo result of feud," *BDC*, April 4, 1922, p. 16; "Predicts arrest soon in murder," *BDC*, April 5, 1922, p. 16; "Bocchimuzzo slain by secret society gang, police claim," *BME*, April 6, 1922. Police learned that Bocchimuzzo left Italy at age 16 and lived in Niagara Falls, Ontario, for five years. In late 1921, he moved to 1011 East Falls Street in Niagara Falls, New York, where he operated a soft drink café with Angelo Muncho. Bocchimuzzo had not been seen since Feb. 1. Police believed he was kidnapped and held for some time before he was murdered.

[54] Dubro and Rowland, p. 91-92; Nicaso, p. 61; "Think man murdered in car and thrown in road by killers," *NG*, May 11, 1922, p. 1.

[55] "Body of murdered Dominick Sciaroni shipped to Canada," *NG*, May 12, 1922.

[56] Dubro and Rowland, p. 91-92; Nicaso, p. 61; "Body of murdered Dominick Sciaroni shipped to Canada;" "Murdered man with bootleggers, police learn," *BDC*, May 12, 1922, p. 5.

[57] Dubro and Rowland, p. 92-93.

[58] Dubro and Rowland, p. 101.

[59] Nicaso, p. 62.

[60] Nicaso, p. 62-63.

[61] Nicaso, p. 64.

Chapter 5

[1] "Thomas J.B Dyke," *BDC*, July 21, 1922, p. 9; "Birthday party given at Ritz cafe," *BDC*, Sept. 22, 1922, p. 9; *BME*, Nov. 26, 1922, section 6, p. 4.

[2] "Thomas Bellantoni, East Side figure, 49," *NYT*, June 22, 1945, p. 12; U.S. Census of 1910.

[3] "'Angel' laid in tomb as East Side prays," *NYT*, Feb. 24, 1924; "Death takes 'Angel of Broome Street,'" *NYT*, Feb. 23, 1924; Passenger manifest of *S.S. Alsatia*, arrived New York City on June 16, 1893.

[4] U.S. Census of 1910. The Bellantoni family – Rocco and Angelina Bellantoni and their seven sons – resided at 168 Elizabeth Street.

[5] "Police raid saloon of Chick Trigger in search for weapons," *New York Evening World*, Jan. 16, 1914, p. 19; Asbury, Herbert, *The Gangs of New York: An Informal History of the Underworld*, Garden City, NY: Garden City Publishing Co., 1928, p. 325-326, 366-367, Keefe, Rose, *The Starker: Big Jack Zelig, the Becker-Rosenthal Case, and the Advent of the Jewish Gangster*, Nashville: Cumberland House, 2008, Chapter 3; "'Chick' Tricker says gunmen are waging a battle of races," *New York Evening* World, June 6, 1912, p. 4. Frank "Chick Tricker" Tricca was sometimes referred to in the press as "Chick Trigger." Asbury stated that Tommy Dyke served

as manager of a Tricker-owned "dive" known as the Fleabag at 241 Bowery. The *Evening World* placed the saloon at 271 Bowery. According to the *Evening World*, Tricca was a native New Yorker, born on Crosby Street. Keefe noted that Paul Kelly, Jack Sirocco and Chick Trigger feuded among themselves.

[6] "Gangs in battle kill court clerk," *NYT*, Jan. 10, 1914; McPhaul, Jack, *Johnny Torrio: First of the Gang Lords*, New Rochelle, NY: Arlington House, 1970, p. 45; Asbury, p. 325. According to Asbury, Jack Sirocco learned his trade under the infamous New York gang boss Monk Eastman. One of Jack Sirocco's henchmen was Johnny Torrio, leader of the James Street Gang, who later achieved notoriety as an underworld boss in Chicago and as the mentor of Al Capone.

[7] "Repeaters in gun fight on Broadway," *New York Sun*, Sept. 17, 1913, p. 1; "Senator's friend swears Carroll hired repeaters," *New York Evening World*, Nov. 18, 1913, p. 1.

[8] Oddly, the Zelig organization also was supported by the Tammany Hall Democratic machine.

[9] "Police declare war on gunmen; six held for street battles," *New York Evening World*, June 5, 1912, p. 1. The *Evening World* named the three Zelig gang victims as Rizzi, Ranezi and Morello.

[10] "'Chick' Tricker says gunmen are waging a battle of races."

[11] "Big Jack Zelig shot and killed in crowded car on eve of Becker's trial for murder of Rosenthal," *New York Sun*, Oct. 6, 1912, p. 1; "'Big Jack' Zelig killed by man with police gun," *New York Tribune*, Oct. 6, 1912, p. 1.

[12] "Chief and gangmen held for murder," *NYT*, Jan. 11, 1914; "Gangsters up to-day," *NYT*, Jan. 15, 1914.

[13] "Indict 9 gangsters for an old murder," *NYT*, June 1, 1916.

[14] "Chief and gangmen held for murder." Despite his continuing connections to the underworld, Albert Marinelli served as Tammany's Second Assembly District leader and was New York County Clerk. Eddie Dyke, Tommy Dyke's older brother, was an aide to Tammany boss Big Tim Sullivan.

[15] "Gangs in battle kill court clerk."

[16] "Chief and gangmen held for murder;" "Gangsters up to-day;" "Ban on Harburger badges," *New York Sun*, Jan. 14, 1914, p. 5.

[17] "Captain faces gangsters when placed on trial," *New York Evening World*, Jan. 17, 1914, p. 4.

[18] Building on information provided by jailed gangster Joseph "Jo the Greaser" Eisenzweig, prosecutors were able in 1916 to secure indictments against nine members of the Fein gang and a woman companion of one of the gangsters for participating in the gunfight that killed Frederick Strauss.

[19] "Death takes 'Angel of Broome Street,'" *NYT*, Feb. 23, 1924; "'Angel' laid in tomb as East Side prays," *NYT*, Feb. 24, 1924. Thomas Dyke's mother, Angelina Bellantoni, was known as the Angel of Broome Street because of her generous giving to neighbors in need. Her funeral was said to be "the greatest Italian funeral the city has known, greater even than the procession for Lieutenant [Joseph Petrosino]." Her honorary pallbearers included Congressman Christopher D. Sullivan, State Senator Philip Klienfeld, Alderman James F. Kiernan and New York Port Warden Albert Marinelli. Included in the funeral cortege were State

Senator James J. Walker, New York Supreme Court Justice Salvatore A. Cottillo, Magistrate Max S. Levine, Assistant District Attorney P. Francis Marro, Assemblyman Frank P. Galgano and featherweight and junior lightweight boxing champion Johnnie Dundee.

[20] "Thomas J.B Dyke;" "Birthday party given at Ritz café."

[21] "Ritz to open the dansant on two afternoons of week," *BDC*, May 25, 1922, p. 4; "Teck and Ritz owners held for a hearing," *BME*, Dec. 11, 1922, p. 1.

[22] Contract for sale dated Feb. 2, 1922, Erie County NY land records.

[23] A 1952 FBI report noted that both Giuseppe DiCarlo and his son Joseph had been romantically involved with Minnie Clark: "At one time [Joseph DiCarlo] was engaged in business with, and apparently had as his paramour one Jew Minnie Clark, and with this woman for several years prior to 1924 operated a road house and speak-easy known as the Auto Rest in Williamsville, New York. It has been reported that this woman was formerly the paramour of DiCarlo's father."

[24] "Dry sleuths pounce on Transit Inn for second time; nab 3," *BDC*, Sept. 20, 1920, p. 12; "Agents raid Transit Inn for third time; arrest owner and 2," *BDC*, Oct. 18, 1920; "Blames Minnie Clark for Transit Inn raids," *BEN*, Feb. 23, 1921, p. 13.

[25] "Road houses raided by troopers," *BDC*, July 13, 1921, p. 14; "Four road houses near Buffalo are raided by state," *BME*, July 13, 1921, p. 8; "Roadhouse proprietors arraigned on dry charges," *BME, July 14, 1921, p. 7.*

[26] "Sheriff raids roadhouses; has battle at one," *BME*, Aug. 22, 1921, p. 4.

[27] Business certificate No. 11466 dated March 8, 1922, Erie County Clerk's Office. Auto Rest is now the Buffalo Brew Pub, 6861 Main Street, Williamsville, New York.

[28] Erie County NY land records.

[29] Reed, Herbert, "Rocky Kansas proves too rugged a battler for the Bronx favorite," *New York Post*, March 22, 1921.

[30] Daniel Gaudiosa later adopted an Americanized version of his mother's maiden name Rogirio

[31] "Hail Rocky Kansas as next Lightweight champ at testimonial banquet," *BT*, March 27, 1921, p. 49; "Rocky Kansas is hailed at banquet as boxer and man," *BDC*, March 27, 1921, p. 64; "Rocky Kansas guest of honor," *BME*, March 27, 1921.

[32] Kelly, Billy, "Buffalo boy batters Jackson all over ring before 14,000," *BDC*, March 22, 1921; Reed, Herbert, "Rocky Kansas proves too rugged a battler for Bronx favorite," *New York Post*, March 22, 1921; Matrison, Charles F., "Kansas is victor over Bronx bomber," *New York Herald*, March 22, 1921.

[33] "Rocky Kansas to remain idle until championship go; is honored at big banquet," *BDC*, March 23, 1921, p. 12; "Rocky Kansas slips crowd and goes directly to home," *BDC*, March 24, 1921, p. 10; "Kansas signs for Dundee and Ward, passes up Schoell," *BDC*, March 25, 1921, p. 12. The March 25th story indicated that one of Kansas's backers had won $30,000 betting on his fights over the course of a single month. That unnamed backer contributed $500 to the testimonial dinner.

[34] Matrison; "Rocky Kansas to remain idle until championship go." The crowd would have been significantly larger, but the New York Fire Department reportedly turned away 3,000 at the gates after the Garden reached its reasonable limit.

[35] Pietruszka, David, *Rothstein: The Life, Times, and Murder of the Criminal Genius Who Fixed the 1919 World Series*, New York: Carroll & Graf, 2004, p. 136.

[36] "Ask why Rothstein was not indicted," *NYT*, Aug. 2, 1921, p. 28; "Rothstein cleared in baseball fixing," *NYT*, Oct. 27, 1920, p. 13; "New witness tells of baseball plot," *NYT*, Sept. 28, 1920, p. 1. In the Oct. 27 story, one of the organizers of the fix Billy Maharg told authorities that Attell lied about Rothstein's participation. Attell reportedly showed Maharg a telegram as evidence of Rothstein's backing. "The wire was signed with the initials 'A.R.,'" Maharg stated. "We learned later that this was a fake telegram and that somebody had wired to New York to have it sent... As a matter of fact, Rothstein was never involved. Attell was lying."

[37] "Rocky Kansas slips crowd and goes directly to home;" Pietruszka, p. 176-186. The *Courier* called the odds against Kansas "ridiculous" and noted Attell's betting. Pietruszka described what must have been a falling out between Rothstein and Attell in the fall of 1920, as the World Series fix was discovered. Attell left the country for a time, staying in Montreal, Canada. From there, he accused Rothstein of fixing the Series. Rothstein held a press conference and directed the blame toward Attell. The relationship might have been patched up after Attell returned to New York in November but could not be positively identified as the man involved in 1919 World Series gambling.

[38] "Hail as next lightweight champ at testimonial banquet," *BT*, March 27, 1921, p. 49.

[39] "Rocky Kansas to remain idle until championship go." The *Courier* noted that Kansas's "rugged" style was similar to Lavigne and Wolcott and that his combination of a heavy punch and little ring finesse was reminiscent of Dempsey.

[40] "Rocky Kansas to remain idle until championship go."

[41] World War I Draft Registration Card filed Sept. 12, 1918. Giuseppe DiCarlo noted that he was sick and unable to work. However, the registrar's report detected no physical problem that would disqualify Giuseppe from military service.

[42] "Joseph DiCarlo," *Amherst Bee*, July 13, 1922. DiCarlo had purchased the A.J. Cooke home on the Sanford Road (later Maple Street). The newspaper noted, "Mr. DiCarlo's death is especially sad, coming so soon after his purchase of a beautiful country home, where he expected to enjoy life."

[43] Joseph Peter DiCarlo Certificate of Death, New York State Department of Health, issued July 10, 1922, with registered number 3970. The causes of death were listed as "acute oedema of lungs" and "acute cardiac dilatation." Contributing factors were "nephritis (chronic)" and "diabetes mellitus."

[44] "Death of Joe De Carlo, Sr., grieves great many friends," *BDC*, July 11, 1922. Undertaker Louis Mascari is named on Joseph Peter DiCarlo Death Certificate, above.

[45] "Joseph DiCarlo, retired commission merchant, to be buried Tuesday," *Buffalo Enquirer*, July 10, 1922, p. 11; "La morte di Giuseppe Di Carlo," *Il Corriere Italiano*, July 13, 1922.

[46] Hill, Henry Wayland, editor in chief, *Municipality of Buffalo, New York: A History, 1720-1923*, New York: Lewis Historical Publishing Company, 1923, Volume II, p. 647; "Parish history," Holy Cross, Buffalo, NY (holycrossbuffalo.org/aboutus/history.htm); "Holy Cross Church, Buffalo, New York," Rootsweb (www.rootsweb.com/~nyerie/buffalo/church10.htm). According to Hill's book,

Bishop Colton died May 9, 1915.

[47] "La morte di Giuseppe Di Carlo," *Il Corriere Italiano*, July 13, 1922; "Joseph DiCarlo, retired commission merchant, to be buried Tuesday," *Buffalo Enquirer*, July 10, 1922; "Death of Joe De Carlo, Sr., grieves great many friends."

[48] "Death of Joe De Carlo, Sr., grieves great many friends."

[49] "Fraud Charges in 27th Ward Start Factional Battle" *BDC*, Sep. 24, 1923. p.14

[50] Panzarella, Barone and Taylor records were found in the 1920 U.S. Census. Panzarella and Taylor also were found in the 1930 U.S. Census. Details related to Lojacono and Taylor were found in their World War I draft registrations.

[51] Burial records of Pine Hill Cemetery.

[52] "Salvatore DiCarlo" FBI file, Report MM 92-103, p. 13. The report quotes an unnamed informant providing information to the Bureau in September of 1946.

[53] Niagara Falls Directory for 1922. The directory indicates that Palmeri "removed to Buffalo."

Chapter 6

[1] Birth and marriage records of Castellammare del Golfo, Sicily. Stefano Magaddino's older brothers were Pietro, born Sept. 26, 1883; and Gaspare, born June 6, 1886. His younger siblings were sister Arcangela, born May 5, 1894; brother Antonino, born June 18, 1897; sister Rosaria, born about 1901; sister Giuseppa, born about 1902; and Maria, born about 1905.

[2] Marriage records of Castellammare del Golfo, Sicily, July 14, 1876.

[3] Bonanno, Joseph, with Sergio Lalli, *A Man of Honor: The Autobiography of Joseph Bonanno*, New York: Simon and Schuster, 1983, p. 49-50; Feuerstein, Gary, "Bonanno Pisano," Leaning Tower of Pisa (http://www.pisabelltower.com/ltpinfo/pisano.htm), 1998. A 12th Century artist named Bonanno is traditionally believed to have served as architect of the Leaning Tower of Pisa, though there is some controversy on the point.

[4] Bonanno, Joseph, p. 25-28, 41, 63.

[5] Bonanno, Joseph, p. 28; Bonanno, Bill, *Bound by Honor*, New York: St. Martin's Press, 1999, p. 40-41; Birth Certificate of Giuseppe Bonanno, Castellammare del Golfo, Sicily. Sources disagree on the date of Joseph Bonanno's birth. His autobiography places it on Jan. 18, 1905. However, his birth certificate indicates Jan. 21, 1905, as his date of birth.

[6] Death records of *chiesa cattolica Maria Santissima del Soccorso* in Castellammare del Golfo. Giovanni Buccellato, 28, died July 13, 1916. Pietro Magaddino's killing followed one week later on July 20, 1916. Antonino Magaddino, brother of Pietro and Stefano, was arrested and charged with two murders on Aug. 14, 1916.

[7] Bonanno, Joseph, p. 63.

[8] Bonanno, Joseph, p. 62.

[9] Morello, Celeste A., Before Bruno: The History of the Philadelphia Mafia, Book 1, 1880-1931, published by the author, 1999, p. 44-45.

[10] Bonanno, Joseph, p. 63.

[11] "Italian band held for killing of 16," *NYT*, Aug. 17, 1921, p. 1; "Gang sought booze

control, gunman says," *Detroit Free Press*, Aug. 17, 1921, p. 1. While these and other news stories from 1921 refer to the killing of a baker named Bonventre 15 years earlier, there are no earlier reports relating to such an event.

[12] "Gang sought booze control, gunman says;" "Police reopen old mysteries on revelations of death ring," *New York American*, Aug. 20, 1921, p. 1.

[13] Manifest of the *S.S. San Giorgio* arrived at New York on Feb. 7, 1909.

[14] Bonanno, Joseph, p. 67; World War I Draft Registration of Gaspare "Michael" Magaddino, dated June 5, 1919. Bonanno noted that his Uncle Vito was an established baker in Brooklyn in the 1920s. The draft registration card indicated that Gaspare Magaddino was employed by Vito Bonventre's bakery, 115 Roebling Street, Brooklyn. In addition to Gaspare Magaddino, Joseph Bonanno is known to have been an employee of Bonventre's bakery.

[15] World War I draft registration of Stefano Magaddino dated June 5, 1919, and of Vito Mule dated Sept. 12, 1918; "New York charters," *NYT*, March 29, 1924, p. 24. The Vito Mule Importing Company dissolved in March of 1924. These Mule brothers appear not to have been related to a Manhattan baker/Black Hander Pellegrino Mule, who was arrested Feb. 7, 1909.

[16] Report of the Buffalo Office of the FBI, "BU 92-61," Stefano Magaddino FBI file #92-2924. A note regarding electronic surveillance of Magaddino described his Jan. 21, 1965, conversation with two men: "At this time, Magaddino launches into a long, detailed discussion of the growth of the Cosa Nostra in the United States, starting when he was 17 years old. He indicates that he first became a member of the Cosa Nostra in Chicago, Illinois."

[17] Flynn, William J., Daily reports of the New York office of the U.S. Secret Service, National Archives and Records Administration, microfilm T915 - 116, Nov. 15, 1909, p. 4-6.

[18] Gentile, Chapter IV. Gentile explained that D'Aquila became boss of bosses after Morello was convicted of counterfeiting and sent to prison early in 1910. D'Aquila had a difficult time consolidating his power in Morello's old strongholds, lower Manhattan and East Harlem, and his position was threatened by Morello's release from prison 10 years later.

[19] Gentile, p. 48, 51. Gentile's descriptions were: "*il capo di Chicago, il D'Andrea, uomo feroce e temutissimo in tutti gli Stati Uniti*" (the boss of Chicago, the D'Andrea, a ferocious man and very fearsome in all of the United States), and "*l'uomo che faceva tremare gran parte degli Stati Uniti*" (the man who makes a large part of the United States tremble).

[20] Gentile, p. 48, 51. Gentile explained that D'Andrea was feared across the United States. He indicated that Mafia bosses in Cleveland and Pittsburgh felt compelled to assassinate a man named Paolinello because they received a letter from D'Andrea condemning Paolinello to death.

[21] Birth records of Valledolmo, Sicily.

[22] "Former priest recovers his bride," *CT*, Aug. 19, 1899, p. 8; "Catholics bar D'Andrea's body from the church," *CT*, May 17, 1921, p. 3. D'Andrea is known to have had at least five brothers and four sisters. His brother Horace (Orazio) became a priest and served in St. Anthony's Parish in Chicago.

[23] "Catholics bar D'Andrea's body from the church," *CT*, May 17, 1921, p. 3. The

newspaper reported that D'Andrea personally founded the Unione Siciliana and served as its first president. However, there is no evidence that D'Andrea was in the United States at the time of the Unione's 1895 founding in Chicago. D'Andrea's arrival in Chicago is dated from 1899.

[24] Nelli, Humbert S., *The Business of Crime: Italians and Syndicate Crime in the United States*, Chicago: University of Chicago Press, (Phoenix edition) 1981, p. 125; "Raid flat; get bad coin," *CT*, Sept. 19, 1902, p. 11; "Federal grand jury holds alleged 'get rich' men," *CT*, March 8, 1903, p. 36; "D'Andrea free for a week," *CT*, April 18, 1903, p. 3; "Bad money gang raided," *CT*, May 21, 1903, p. 5; "D'Andrea's story," *CT*, Feb. 8, 1916, p. 15. Nelli indicated that D'Andrea's jail sentence was commuted by President Theodore Roosevelt in 1908. However, press reports in 1903 stated that D'Andrea was sentenced to just 13 months. Roosevelt's action appears to have been clearing D'Andrea's criminal record so he could run for public office.

[25] The press of the period inaccurately referred to Joseph and Anthony D'Andrea as brothers. They were not related.

[26] Gentile, p. 72-73.

[27] Manifest of the *S.S. Perugia* arrived at New York on Nov. 15, 1909.

[28] Report #KC 92-1259, FBI file of Stefano Magaddino, p. 10; FBI report BU 92-61 (NARA 124-10204-10421), p. 48. Electronic surveillance caught Magaddino expressing his grief over the death of his sister-in-law: "She was like a second mother to me and not like a sister-in-law. But my conscience is clear, because she did not want for anything." When Magaddino was young, she reportedly washed Magaddino's clothes, cooked his food and took care of him when he was sick.

[29] Certificate of Marriage #10807 dated Oct. 19, 1913, Brooklyn, NY.

[30] Petition for Naturalization of Gaspare Magaddino #7938 filed with Supreme Court of Niagara Falls NY.

[31] Certificate of Marriage #10807 dated Oct. 19, 1913, Brooklyn, NY.

[32] Report #BU 92-594, FBI file of Salvatore Sabella, p. 2.

[33] Nelson, Lynn, *A Genealogist's Guide to Discovering Your Italian Ancestors*, Cincinnati: Betterway Books, 1997. According to Nelson, the second male child traditionally was named for the maternal grandfather, the first female child for the paternal grandmother and the second female child for the maternal grandmother.

[34] Morello, p. 46-47; Report #DN 92-222, FBI file of La Cosa Nostra, Cover page C.

[35] Bonanno, Joseph, p. 63.

[36] Commonwealth of Pennsylvania Certificates of Birth: Josephine Magaddino, Jan. 11, 1919, file #0136740-1919; Angela Magaddino, June 2, 1921, file #1156350-1921; Petition for Naturalization of Carmela Magaddino.

[37] "Italian band held for killing of 16," *NYT*, Aug. 17, 1921, p. 1. This and other press accounts of Aug. 17 appear to be the earliest published references to the gang name. It seems unlikely that gang members ever used this name before it was published. "Good Killers" might have been a Michael Fiaschetti-inspired translation of Bartolomeo Fontana's Italian language description of the gang. It is possible that Fontana sought to differentiate the group from its rivals as good guys vs. bad guys. It is also possible that he referred to the group with a term such as *Bonventre assassini* (Bonventre assassins). The "bon" portion of the Bonventre

name might have been translated as "good."

[38] "Body of murdered man is found in Shark River cove by crabbing party," *Long Branch (NJ) Daily*, Aug. 9, 1921, p. 1; "Body of missing man found sunk in cove," *NYT*, Aug. 10, 1921, p. 9.

[39] "Body of missing man found sunk in cove."

[40] "More details of crime told of," *Long Branch (NJ) Daily*, March 24, 1922.

[41] "Arrest in Caiozzo mystery," *NYT*, Aug. 13, 1921, p. 4; "Held in Belmar murder," *NYT*, Aug. 13, 1921, p. 9; "Suspect held in Belmar shooting," *Long Branch (NJ) Daily*, Aug. 13, 1921, p. 13; "Road house proprietor is held under $10,000 bail on murder charge," *Long Branch (NJ) Daily*, Aug. 16, 1921, p. 1.

[42] Fiaschetti, Michael, as told to Prosper Buranelli, *The Man They Couldn't Escape: The Adventures of Detective Fiaschetti of the Italian Squad*, London: Selwyn, 1928, p. 81; "Leader of murder gang is trailed," *New York Telegram*, Aug. 18, 1921, p. 3. According to the *Telegram*, Fontana roomed not with Fiaschetti but with Detective Pelligrino, and Fontana talked about Caiozzo's murder in his sleep.

[43] Fiaschetti, p. 81-83.

[44] Critchley, David, "Vito Bonventre (born 1891) and the Good Killers," *The American Mafia Yahoo! Group*, Aug. 8, 2008 (http://groups.yahoo.com/group/americanmafia/message/477). According to Critchley, Fontana misunderstood the legend of a Bonventre death. Critchley argued that the legend could have grown out of the 1908 murder of Giovanni Carollo, in which a baker named Vito Bonventre was a suspect. Carollo's remains were found tied up inside of a sack in Brooklyn. While Critchley's suggestion is an interesting one, it is difficult to accept that so profound an event in the lives of Castellammaresi could have become so confused in such a short time.

[45] "Link confession to 70 murders", *Lima (OH) News*, Aug. 17, 1921, p. 1; "Italian band held for killing of 16."

[46] "Sixteen murdered by Good Killers," *Trenton (NJ) Evening Times*, Aug. 17, 1921, p. 4.

[47] "Three more admit death band killing," *NYT*, Aug. 18, 1921, p. 1.

[48] Passenger manifest of the *S.S. LaSavoie*, June 28, 1920.

[49] "Italian band held for killing of 16."

[50] "Italian band held for killing of 16."

[51] "Disorderly house" was an idiom referring to a house of prostitution.

[52] "Suspect held in Belmar shooting." Cieravo was already under indictment for running a brothel located at Springwood Avenue, Asbury Park, NJ.

[53] "Fontano balks at taking oath," *Long Branch (NJ) Daily*, March 23, 1922.

[54] "Italian band held for killing of 16;" "Confessed slayer is chief state witness," *Asbury Park (NJ) Evening Press*, March 23, 1922.

[55] "Fontano balks at taking oath."

[56] "Fontano balks at taking oath;" "More details of crime are told of."

[57] "Organized to commit murder," *Mansfield (OH) News*, Aug. 17, 1921, p. 1; "Exposes murder gang," *BT*, Aug. 17, 1921, p. 1.

[58] The two men likely conversed in Sicilian. So, the term "chief" could have been a

376 · DiCarlo

police translation of "*capo*" or "*capodecina*."

[59] "Italian band held for killing of 16;" "Assassin roundup bares plans for six new murders," *New York World*, Aug. 18, 1921.

[60] Moen, R.A., Report of Investigation No. B 8969 into the Power City Distributing Company, Division of Alcohol Beverage Control, State of New York Executive Department, Jan. 3, 1958.

[61] Downey, Patrick, *Gangster City: The History of the New York Underworld, 1900-1935*, Fort Lee, NJ: Barricade Books, 2004, p. 97; "Murder gang informer attacked by prisoner," *Brooklyn Standard Union*, Aug. 17, 1921; "Three more admit death band killing."

[62] "Three more admit death band killing;" "Death ring may have killed 87," *New York Evening Journal*, Aug. 18, 1921.

[63] "Three more admit death band killing."

[64] "125 murders laid to band as police get new details," *New York World*, Aug. 19, 1921.

[65] "Confesses he set two Detroit fires and knew slayers," *New York World*, Aug. 20, 1921, p. 5.

[66] Downey, p. 97. Police considered Mafia big shot Giuseppe Masseria the prime suspect in the Mauro slaying but could not find sufficient evidence linking him with the crime.

[67] "Italian band held for killing of 16;" "Gang sought booze control, gunman says," *Detroit Free Press*, Aug. 17, 1921, p. 1; "Guilt in feud murders may mean chair," *Detroit Free Press*, Aug. 18, 1921, p. 1; "Police reopen old mysteries on revelations of death ring," *New York American*, Aug. 20, 1921, p. 1.

[68] "Link confession to 70 murders", *Lima (OH) News*, Aug. 17, 1921, p. 1.

[69] "Death ring may have killed 87."

[70] "100 murdered by Good Killers," *Lima (OH) News*, Aug. 18, 1921, p. 2.

[71] "125 murders laid to band as police get new details."

[72] "Seek graveyards of 'Good Killers'," *Trenton (NJ) Evening Times*, Aug. 20, 1921, p. 2.

[73] "Italian band held for killing of 16."

[74] "Confessions here give clue to Petrosino slayer," *New York World*, Aug. 21, 1921, p. 1; "Killer gives clue to Petrosino death," *NYT*, Aug. 21, 1921, p. 17.

[75] Moen, R.A., "Power City Distributing Co., Inc.," Report of Investigation B 8969, State of New York Executive Department, Division of Alcoholic Beverage Control, Jan. 3, 1958, p. 4. Organized crime historian Lennert van't Riet located this summary of New York's investigation of the Good Killers case.

[76] Moen.

[77] "Leader of murder gang is trailed."

[78] "No secret orders connected with Buffalo murders," *BME*, Aug. 19, 1921, p. 4.

[79] "New York police suspect Good Killers active," *Clearfield (PA) Progress*, Sept. 6, 1921, p. 4; "'Good Killers' shoot New Jersey merchant," *Appleton (WI) Post-Crescent*, Sept. 29, 1921, p. 1; "Fear 'Good Killers' did stabbing and shooting," *Appleton (WI) Post-Crescent*, Oct. 31, 1921, p. 1; "'Good Killers' band feared in

action again following two more murders," *Clearfield (PA) Progress,* Nov. 1, 1921, p. 1.

[80] "State of New Jersey v. Bartolomeo Fontana, Francesco Puma, Giuseppe Lombardi," Requisitions February 1921-1922, Box 77, Extradition records 1844-1968, New Jersey State Archives.

[81] "Indict 2 as slayers; Mafia crime charged," *NYT,* Sept. 15, 1921, p. 3.

[82] "Camorra slayer now in Freehold," *Monmouth (NJ) Democrat,* Sept. 18, 1921.

[83] "State v. Joseph Lombardi," Monmouth County Quarter Sessions Minutes, 1920-1922, January term 1922, p. 507; "State v. Joseph Lombardi," Monmouth County Quarter Session Minutes, 1920-1922, October term 1922, p. 29; "Held in $10,000 bail in Neptune murder," *Trenton (NJ) Evening Times,* Dec. 17, 1921, p. 5; "Foes shoot gunman full of bullets," *NYT,* Nov. 5, 1922, p. 32.

[84] "Seek extradition of slayer Fontano," *New York American,* Aug. 22, 1921, p. 9.

[85] "Salvatore Rose acquitted," *Monmouth (NJ) Democrat,* March 30, 1922.

[86] "Confessing murder gets life sentence," *Monmouth (NJ) Democrat,* March 23, 1922; "Acquit Cieravo on serious charge," *Long Branch (NJ) Daily,* March 25, 1922.

[87] "Confessed slayer is chief state witness;" "Acquit Cieravo on serious charge;" "Fontano balks at taking oath."

[88] "Salvatore Rose acquitted;" "Acquit Cieravo on serious charge;" "Verdict of not guilty given after four hours' deliberation," *Asbury Park (NJ) Evening Press,* March 25, 1922.

[89] "Foes shoot gunman full of bullets;" "'Murder farm' Italian is slain during stroll," *New York Tribune,* Nov. 5, 1922, p. 9.

[90] "State v. Joseph Lombardi," Monmouth County Quarter Session Minutes, 1920-1922, October term 1922, p. 29.

[91] Inmate Registers 1894-1975, Register I (1920-1926) #6166-9547, Vol. 13; Inmate Registers 1894-1975, Register M (1940-1945) #21414-#24764 and #53A-152A, Vol. 17; and Inmate Registers 1894-1975, Descriptive List No. 6 (1921-1923) #6484-7663, Volume 29, New Jersey State Prison at Trenton, New Jersey State Archives.

[92] Gaspare Milazzo, who escaped arrest in the Good Killers case, also moved from New York in this period, settling in Detroit.

[93] Report #BU 280-C, FBI file of Steve Magaddino, p. 8.

[94] Buffalo City Directory of 1895. Anthony D'Andrea is shown living at the 651 Elk Street address of his older brother, also named Anthony. In addition to their presence in the Buffalo area, the D'Andrea and DiCarlo families were linked in Sicily. Anthony D'Andrea's niece, Giuseppa Giuffre, married into the DiCarlo family of Valledolmo.

[95] Report #BU 280-C, p. 6-7. The term *rappresentante* was often used interchangeably with *capo* or boss. The leader of a crime family served as *rappresentante* – representative – of the family when the various bosses gathered for group decision-making.

[96] Land records of Niagara County, NY.

[97] It is tempting to view the "Outs" as roughly equivalent to the Castellammarese Mafiosi, many of whom settled outside of the City of Buffalo. The "Ins" therefore

378 · *DiCarlo*

could have referred to Mafiosi, primarily non-Castellammarese, who were based within the city proper.

[98] Mazzara could have been proposed as a compromise candidate. As a Castellammarese immigrant established within the City of Buffalo, he was in a position to reconcile the differences between the Ins and the Outs.

[99] Report #BU 280-C, p. 8.

[100] Report #BU 280-C, p. 6.

Chapter 7

[1] "Shooting marks dry raid at Auto Rest," *BN*, Sept. 12, 1922, p. 1; "Dry sleuths pull wild, wooly, west raid at Auto Inn," *BDC*, Sept. 12, 1922, p. 14.

[2] "Many shots fired at speeding auto taking booze away," *Buffalo Enquirer*, Sept. 11, 1922, p. 1. It seems this was the same man, inn employee John Barbera, who complained that he was severely beaten at the hands of the agents: "Shooting marks dry raid at Auto Rest."

[3] "Dry sleuths pull wild, wooly, west raid at Auto Inn."

[4] "Three arrested when agents raid Auto Rest," *BME*, Sept. 12, 1922, p. 5; "Dry sleuths pull wild, wooly, west raid at Auto Inn;" "Shooting marks dry raid at Auto Rest."

[5] "Many shots fired at speeding auto taking booze away."

[6] "Many shots fired at speeding auto taking booze away;" "Three arrested when agents raid Auto Rest." The *Enquirer* story spelled her name "Minnie Clarke DeCarlo."

[7] "Tommy Dyke's racket draws a huge crowd," *BME*, Nov. 26, 1922, Section 6, p. 4. The *Express* described the third annual ball of the Thomas J.B. Dyke Association, a social event run by and attended by men who knew Joseph DiCarlo well. The story noted, "The silver cloth gown of Mrs. Joseph DiCarlo, formerly Minnie Clark, proprietor in the past of several places where one could get a bit to eat and a drop to drink and, with her husband, now host at a roadhouse near Williamsville, was the envy of most of the fair sex..."

[8] "Dry sleuths again smash way into inn," *Buffalo Enquirer*, Sept. 18, 1922, p. 5; "Dry agents smash their way into Auto Rest; comb resort for liquor but find nothing," *BDC*, Sept. 18, 1922, p. 5; "Twelve dry agents raid Jew Minnie's," *BME*, Sept. 18, 1922, p. 6.

[9] "Dry agents smash their way into Auto Rest." Barbera seems to be the same man roughed up by dry agents the previous week.

[10] "Dry agents smash their way into Auto Rest."

[11] "Dry raid sleuths slip up in court," *BDC*, Sept. 30, 1922, p. 16; "Discharges four persons taken in raid on Auto Rest," *BME*, Sept. 30, 1922, p. 4.

[12] "Dismiss charges against DiCarlo," *BDC*, Oct. 4, 1922, p. 16.

[13] "House votes to expose secrets of drug trade," *NYT*, June 23, 1906, p. 3. Congress engaged in a heated debate in 1906 over whether to require the makers of patent medicines to disclose on labels the amounts of alcohol, opium, cocaine and "other poisonous substance" contained in their products.

[14] Hays, Constance L., *The Real Thing: Truth and Power at the Coca-Cola Company*, New York: Random House, 2005, p. 101-102; "Coca-Cola case goes to trial,"

Atlanta Constitution, Feb. 4, 1903, p. 8; "Coca-Cola and Peruna must pay a heavy tax," *Atlanta Constitution*, July 21, 1904, p. 1. The removal of trace amounts of cocaine from the Coca-Cola syrup seems to have been prompted at least as much by financial concerns as by mounting public pressure. The U.S. government had attempted to tax Coca-Cola as a medicinal concoction because of its small cocaine content. In 1907, Coca-Cola newspaper advertisements drew attention to recent tests that showed no "cocaine or other deleterious substances" in the drink.

[15] Rowe, Thomas C., *Federal Narcotics Laws and the War on Drugs: Money Down a Rat Hole*, Binghamton NY: Haworth Press, 2006, p. 14-17.

[16] Jin Fuey Moy v. United States, Supreme Court of the United States, Dec. 6, 1920; Rowe, p. 18.

[17] "Belle Karnes arraigned on narcotics law charge," *BME*, Dec. 3, 1921, p. 4; "Petittucti is held for jury on narcotic charge," *BME*, Dec. 7, 1921, p. 4.

[18] Birth records of Licata, Sicily; Manifest of the *S.S. Venezia*, arrived in New York June 23, 1910.

[19] Statement of Sam Todaro, taken by U.S. Attorney William J. Donovan, March 31, 1924, at Buffalo, NY.

[20] Porrello, Rick, *The Rise and Fall of the Cleveland Mafia: Corn Sugar and Blood*, Fort Lee, NJ: Barricade Books, 1995, p. 66. Like Todaro, the Lonardos and the Porrellos were also from Licata, Sicily. Seven Porrello brothers, immigrants from Licata, were known in Cleveland: Rosario, Vincenzo, Angelo, Giuseppe, Ottavio, Giovanni and Raimondo. Birth and death records of Licata, Sicily, reveal an eighth brother. Born to Angelo and Francesca Tardino Porrello on March 21, 1879, this first-born son was named Ottavio after his paternal grandfather. He died on April 2, 1890, at the age of 11. His parents named their next son Ottavio. He was born on Aug. 16, 1891.

[21] "Indict Smith and others in big booze raid," *BME*, July 20, 1922, p. 14; "Four Rochester men plead guilty to selling liquor," *BDC*, July 21, 1922, p. 3.

[22] "Colonel Donovan gets Congressional Medal of Honor," *BME*, Dec. 3, 1922; "Eight new heroes who won Congressional Medals of Honor," *NYT*, Jan. 7, 1923, p. XX4. The Medal of Honor was presented to Donovan for his heroic leadership of New York's "Fighting 69th" (U.S. Army 165th Infantry, 42nd Division) near Landres et St. Georges, France, in October 1918. Donovan personally led an assault on a strongly defended German position. After taking a machine gun bullet to the leg, he refused to be evacuated and remained with his unit until it withdrew. Donovan became the most decorated American officer of World War I. By the time of his death on Feb. 8, 1959, he was the only American to have received the country's four highest service awards, the Medal of Honor, the Distinguished Service Cross, the Distinguished Service Medal and the National Security Medal.

[23] "Gen. William J. Donovan dies; lawyer headed O.S.S. in war," *NYT*, Feb. 9, 1959, p. 1. The *Times* indicated that his "Wild Bill" nickname was awarded by his troops during World War I.

[24] Fenimore, William E., "William Joseph Donovan," FBI special inquiry dated June 26, 1953. Donovan held the post for two and a half years. He was promoted to assistant to the attorney general on Aug. 14, 1924. Later in his career, he served as director of the World War II-era spy agency, the Office of Strategic Services

380 · DiCarlo

(OSS). OSS was the forerunner of the Central Intelligence Agency.

[25] John A. Fina's father Frank was a member of Giuseppe DiCarlo's Mafia organization and one of the flower donors at Vincenza DiCarlo's funeral.

[26] "Dope ring gets jolt by arrests, agents believe," *BME*, April 22, 1922, p. 2; "Big chiefs in dope ring are caught, claim," *BME*, April 26, 1922; "Start crusade on narcotic traffic; Assert Buffalo is distribution base," *BDC*, April 26, 1922, p. 1; "Big drug haul is made here," *BT*, April 26, 1922.

[27] "Woman who sells narcotic drugs sent to penitentiary," *BDC*, Jan. 5, 1923.

[28] "Start crusade on narcotic traffic..."

[29] "Promises action against 'dope ring' in Buffalo," *BDC*, Dec. 12, 1922, p. 16.

[30] "Federal agents look for others; narcotics worth thousands taken," *BDC*, Jan. 7, 1923, Section 9, p. 1; "40 caught in federal net," *BT*, Jan 8, 1923.

[31] "Narcotic men get to heart of local gang," *BME*, Jan. 8, 1923, p. 1; "Seize drugs in Mangano's," *BME*, Jan. 8, 1923, p. 1.

[32] Mangano's drug store was located at 209 Niagara Street.

[33] "Seize drugs in Mangano's."

[34] "Seize drugs in Mangano's;" "Federal men nab thirteen, hunt others," *BME*, Jan. 7, 1923; "More arrests expected in drug scandal," *BME*, Jan. 9, 1923.

[35] "Seize drugs in Mangano's;" "Stella's profits $1,000 per day," *Buffalo Commercial Advertiser and Journal*, Jan. 8, 1923; "Oyler disclaims any interest in narcotic bribes," *BDC*, Jan. 10, 1923, p. 5.

[36] "Federal agents arrest forty in city wide raid; lasts all night," *BDC*, Jan. 8, 1923, p. 1.

[37] "Federal agents arrest forty in city wide raid; lasts all night."

[38] "Narcotic men get to heart of local gang."

[39] "Seize drugs in Mangano's."

[40] "Police check up dope work of last year," *BME*, Jan. 16, 1923, p. 6.

[41] "Court refuses application for return of seized drugs," *BDC*, Aug. 10, 1923, p. 7.

[42] "Is caught after chase," *Buffalo Evening Times*, Aug. 22, 1923.

[43] "Narcotic chief tells of threat detective made; Marnon defends," *BDC*, Jan. 9, 1923, p. 1; "Oyler disclaims any interest in narcotic bribes." Initially, Oyler did not confirm that a Buffalo detective threatened him. Later he claimed to have no knowledge of or interest in the threat.

[44] "Say police laxity in aiding fight against dope evil may bring federal jury probe." *BDC*, June 1, 1923, p. 16.

[45] "Order is issued by Chief Burfeind after conference with lieutenant," *BDC*, June 3, 1923, p. 83.

[46] "Executive adopts suggestion made by Col. Donovan in latest letter," *BDC*, June 5, 1923, p. 16.

[47] "Burfeind spurns Donovan's 'dope' probe suggestion," *BDC*, June 5, 1923, p. 5.

[48] "Former narcotic squad member to face mayor today," *BDC*, June 28, 1923, p. 6.

[49] "Examining charge that 'Stormy Bill' took 'hush money,'" *BDC*, June 7, 1923, p. 16; "End investigation in Jordan graft case tomorrow," *BDC*, June 8, 1923, p. 18; "Jordan got hush money dope peddlers testify," *BME*, July 3, 1923, p. 5; "Negro 'hop' peddlers swear they get police protection in return for 'hush' money," *BDC*,

July 3, 1923, p. 1.

[50] "U.S. grand jury to probe dope and vice conditions," *BDC*, July 10, 1923, p. 4; "Federal grand jury opens inquiry into dope trade," *BME*, July 12, 1923, p. 4; "Tenderloin resort keeper tells mayor of paying police for protection," *BME*, July 13, 1923, p. 5; "Paid hush money to some coppers, woman says, but captain had go-between," *BDC*, July 13, 1923, p. 1; "Oak Street woman 'squeals' on cops; Savini tells of hidden influence," *BDC*, July 13, 1923, p. 1; "Witnesses state detectives levy heavy payments from Tenderloin," *BDC*, July 21, 1923, p. 1.

[51] "Five go on trial for alleged plot to beat drug act," *BDC*, July 17, 1923, p. 3.

[52] "Five go on trial for alleged plot to beat drug act."

[53] "Sold narcotics through the mails, federal men say," *BME*, Sept. 28, 1922; "Charged with using mails to promote sale of narcotics," *BDC*, Sept. 28, 1922, p. 16.

[54] "Five go on trial for alleged plot to beat drug act."

[55] "Dope trial draws fugitive from justice to U.S. court," *BME*, July 19, 1923, p. 5.

[56] "Convicts five on charge of selling 'dope' in Buffalo," *BDC*, July 20, 1923, p. 14; "Five men are found guilty in dope case," *BME*, July 20, 1923, p. 5.

[57] "Two years for 'dope' peddlers," *BDC*, July 24, 1923, p. 5; "Dope peddlers sentenced to Atlanta pen," *BME*, July 24, 1923, p. 5.

[58] "Two years for 'dope' peddlers"; "Dope peddlers sentenced to Atlanta pen."

[59] "Dope peddler escapes from U.S. marshal," *BME*, July 26, 1923, p. 14.

[60] "Dope peddler escapes from U.S. marshal"; "Escaped peddler of dope is caught by narcotic chief," *BME*, Oct. 2, 1923, p. 16. The *Express* account stated that Dominico broke away from Rine at Church and Pearl Streets.

[61] "Escaped peddler of dope is caught by narcotic chief."

[62] "Pattitucci, on way to prison, gives new lead," *BME*, July 27, 1923, p. 1.

[63] "Pattitucci, on way to prison, gives new lead."

[64] "Pattitucci, on way to prison, gives new lead"; "Dope peddler, afraid that he will be shot, refuses to testify in open against police officers," *BDC*, July 27, 1923; "Detective, on stand, makes denial, swears charges all 'frame-up,'" *BDC*, Aug. 4, 1923, p. 8; "Grafters in police department will get no sympathy, Schwab declares," *BDC*, Aug. 5, 1923, p. 77.. Patitucci was among the witnesses who testified in Officer Jordan's corruption trial: "While we go to the stationhouse, Jordan sit in front with me and Murphy, the other cop, sat with the other man in the back. I slipped $100 in Jordan's hand while he drive the car. When he got to headquarters Jordan placed a charge of vagrancy against me. The judge discharged me the next day. The other fellow was told to leave town." Patitucci was credited with aiding in the conviction of Jordan.

[65] "Convicted narcotic peddler, who 'saw' mayor, appeals case," *BDC*, July 29, 1923.

[66] Deposition of federal Prohibition Agent Henry N. Greenfield before U.S. Commissioner Donald Bain, dated Aug. 17, 1923.

[67] "Is caught after chase."

[68] "Is caught after chase;" "Arrest two men, woman accused of narcotic sales," *BDC*, Aug. 22, 1923, p. 1.

[69] "Arrest two men, woman accused of narcotic sales."

70 "Is caught after chase;" "Arrest two men, woman accused of narcotic sales;" "Bail of $50,000 furnished by DiCarlo in dope case," *BME*, Aug. 23, 1923.

71 "Bail of $50,000 furnished by DiCarlo in dope case."

72 "Bail of $50,000 furnished by DiCarlo in dope case."

73 "Bail of $50,000 furnished by DiCarlo in dope case;" "DiCarlo gets his freedom, raising bail of $50,000," *BDC*, Aug. 23, 1923, p. 16.

74 "Bail of $50,000 furnished by DiCarlo in dope case."

75 "DiCarlo gets his freedom, raising bail of $50,000;" "DiCarlo makes claim of 'mistaken identity.'" *Buffalo Evening Times*, Aug. 23, 1923.

76 "DiCarlo gets his freedom, raising bail of $50,000;" "DiCarlo makes claim of 'mistaken identity.'"

77 "Suspected leader of dope ring captured by federal agents," *BME*, Sept. 1, 1923, p. 1.

78 "Cameron faces 27 years in prison, $32,000 fine," *BME*, Dec. 13, 1923, p. 1.

79 "Held in $25,000 bail," *BT*, Sept. 1, 1923, p. 9. Camerano's "greaseballs" slur was directed either at more recent Italian immigrants or at Sicilian codefendants – Camerano was born in Naples, Italy, and appears to have done much of his growing up in New York City. Barber Sylvester Camerano, 17, appears in the 1900 U.S. Census, living in Manhattan with parents Felix and Beatrice and sisters Mary and Stella. The family immigrated in 1891. On a 1918 World War I draft registration card, then-Buffalo resident Sylvester Camerano, 34 years old, indicated that his closest living relative was his mother Beatrice of Brooklyn, New York.

80 "Probe possibilities of previous convictions in case of Buffalo man held," *Buffalo Enquirer*, Sept. 1, 1923, p. 12.

81 "Camerone has checkered career," *BCA*, Dec. 12, 1923.

82 "Federal jury gets evidence in dope case," *BME*, Oct. 23, 1923, p. 4.

83 "Federal jury gets evidence in dope case."

84 "Poor duelists are these two," *BDC*, July 9, 1923, p. 5; "Noisy duel this morning at foot of Porter Ave.," *BME*, July 9, 1923, p. 1. Police were told that the duel resulted from an automobile accident in which Vaccaro lost an eye.

85 "Shot down on steps of home in Tupper St.," *BME*, Sept. 22, 1923, p. 1; "Shot down on steps of home," *Buffalo Enquirer*, Sept. 22, 1923, p. 12; "Vaccaro shooting puzzles police; dying man silent," *BDC*, Sept. 23, 1923, p. 107.

86 "Man shot 3 times by gang in auto in front of home," *BDC*, Sept. 23, 1923, p. 1.

87 "Vaccaro shooting puzzles police…," "Man shot 3 times…"

88 "Shot down on steps of home…"

89 "Vaccaro shooting puzzles police…"

90 "Vaccaro shooting puzzles police…"

91 "Vaccaro shooting puzzles police…," "Shot down on steps of home…"

92 "2 Buffalo men quizzed in Ohio gang murders," *BEN*, Oct. 11, 1927.

93 "Punish severely fixer or bribed juror detected, court's warning," *BDC*, Nov. 24, 1923, p. 1.

94 "Punish severely fixer or bribed juror detected, court's warning;" "Judge interrupts court to warn panel of jurors," *BME*, Nov. 24, 1923, p. 14.

95 "Mangano witness for government; life threatened," *BDC*, Dec. 5, 1923, p. 4;

"Braves death to bare dope secrets," *BME*, Dec. 5, 1923, p. 1. The *Express* story erroneously reported that the death threats were received a few hours before Mangano's appearance on the stand. According to the *Courier*, the most recent death threat had been telephoned to Mangano's business two weeks earlier.

[96] "Braves death to bare dope secrets."

[97] "Mangano witness for government; life threatened." The man who offered to buy the drugs but then vanished turned out to be Stanley Kenney, a federal narcotics agent.

[98] "Braves death to bare dope secrets;" "Mangano witness for government; life threatened."

[99] "Mangano denies talk of immunity," *BCA*, Dec. 5, 1923.

[100] "Testimony of Mangano is corroborated," *BCA*, Dec. 7, 1923; "Testifies Mangano threatened life of Cameron," *BDC*, Dec. 7, 1923; "Women gives testimony on dope traffic," *BME*, Dec. 7, 1923, p. 4.

[101] "Government in Cameron trial rests its case," *BME*, Dec. 8, 1923, p. 9.

[102] "Government in Cameron trial rests its case."

[103] "Cameron is attempting to make alibi," *BCA*, Dec. 10, 1923; "Cameron attempts to prove alibi," *BT*, Dec. 10, 1923, p. 1.

[104] "Cameron is attempting to make alibi;" "Expect dope trial to wind up soon," *BCA*, Dec. 11, 1923; "Accuses Mangano of death threat against lawyer," *BDC*, Dec. 12, 1923, p. 5.

[105] "Cameron faces 27 years in prison, $32,000 fine;" "Government in Cameron trial rests its case."

[106] "Expect dope trial to wind up soon."

[107] "Cameron faces 27 years in prison, $32,000 fine;" "U.S. jury declares Camerano guilty on all six counts," *BDC*, Dec. 13, 1923, p. 18; "Cameron is guilty on all 6 counts," *BCA*, Dec. 12, 1923.

[108] "Sentences Lester Cameron to four and half years," *BDC*, Dec. 18, 1923, p. 3; "Cameron wins right to appeal dope conviction," *BME*, Dec. 18, 1923, p. 7; "Cameron gets four and half year sentence," *Buffalo Commercial Advertiser and Journal*, Dec. 17, 1923.

[109] "Joe DiCarlo to serve free Christmas dinner to needy at Auto Rest," *BDC*, Dec. 24, 1923; "Free holiday dinner for all at Auto Rest," *BT*, Dec. 24, 1923, p. 3.

Chapter 8

[1] "Drug ring exposed bringing in gunmen," *BEN*, Jan. 3, 1924.

[2] Though Joseph Patitucci stated that he married May Gilmore in City Hall, their relationship appears to have been a common law marriage.

[3] The address of Lumia's restaurant was 411 Oak St.

[4] Testimony of Joseph Patitucci, United States v. DiCarlo, Capodicaso, Ruffino and Gialelli, Buffalo, NY, Feb. 5, 1924; Affidavit of Joseph Patitucci, Arrest Warrants for Joseph DiCarlo, Peter Gallelli, Gaetano Capodicaso and Joseph Ruffino, Jan. 2, 1924.

[5] Testimony of Joseph Patitucci, Feb. 5, 1924; "Pattucci shot down in street," *BT*, Jan. 2, 1924. What May Patitucci did as Joseph Patitucci ran for his life is not known

for certain. The *Buffalo Times* account indicated that after the first shots were fired Joseph Patitucci merely "staggered from his wife's side," but she was right beside him again an instant later. She later testified that she hid in an alley and did not see the gunmen.

[6] "Federal authorities are aroused by shooting of Pattitucci by gunmen," *BME*, Jan. 3, 1924; "Fear new attacks in dope peddler's war," *BT*, Jan. 3, 1924.

[7] The Roma Café was located at 225 Niagara Street, Buffalo, NY.

[8] Testimony of Detective Sergeant William Connolly, United States v. DiCarlo, Capodicaso, Ruffino and Gialelli, Buffalo, NY, Feb. 8, 1924.

[9] "Drug ring exposed bringing in gunmen."

[10] Federal authorities are aroused by shooting...;" "Fear new attacks in dope peddler's war;" "30 witnesses in attempted assassination," *BCA*, Jan. 3, 1924.

[11] Federal authorities are aroused by shooting...;" "30 witnesses in attempted assassination."

[12] "Federal authorities are aroused by shooting..."

[13] "Federal authorities are aroused by shooting...;" "Drug ring exposed bringing in gunmen;" "Swift justice for men who shot Pattitucci," *BME*, Jan. 4, 1924.

[14] "Fear new attacks in dope peddlers' war;" "30 witnesses in attempted assassination." Philip Mangano had recently been questioned in connection with a New York City gunfight in March 1923 that resulted in the death of John Peccori. Mangano later served in the leadership of a New York-area crime family commanded by his brother Vincent. Philip Mangano was found murdered near Sheepshead Bay, Brooklyn, on April 19, 1951. His brother, Vincent, disappeared and was never found.

[15] "Fear new attacks in dope peddlers' war."

[16] "Swift justice for men who shot Pattitucci."

[17] "U.S. grand jury gets evidence in witness shooting," *BDC*, Jan. 4, 1924.

[18] "U.S. grand jury gets evidence in witness shooting;" "Jury renews dope witness shooting probe," *BEN*, Jan. 4, 1924.

[19] "Dope traffic chief known to federals," *BCA*, Jan. 4, 1924.

[20] Subpoena for Samuel DiCarlo, United States v. DiCarlo, Capodicaso, Ruffino and Gialelli, Jan. 5, 1924; "Young DiCarlo held," *BME*, Jan. 6, 1924, p. 1; "Watchman at Auto Rest Inn being held," *BCA*, Jan. 7, 1924.

[21] "Watchman at Auto Rest Inn being held;" "Find weapons at DiCarlo's Inn," *BT*, Jan. 7, 1924; "Find supposed weapons of gunmen in DiCarlo's home," *BME*, Jan. 8, 1924.

[22] "Indict four for shooting Pattitucci, U.S. witness," *BME*, Jan. 9, 1924, p. 14.

[23] "Arrest fifth man in shooting case," *BDC*, Jan. 11, 1924; "DiCarlo and his companions deny shooting," *BME*, Jan. 12, 1924, p. 14.

[24] Subpoena for Angelo B. Palmeri, United States v. DiCarlo, Capodicaso, Ruffino and Gialelli, Jan. 11, 1924.

[25] Contempt of court order against John Geraci, U.S. District Court Judge George F. Morris, Jan. 15, 1924; "Silence to grand jury brings jail," *BME*, Jan. 16, 1924, p. 18.

[26] "Death threats silence witness, official fears," *BDC*, Jan. 26, 1924, p. 14.

[27] "DiCarlo case may disclose dark mystery," *BME*, Jan. 20, 1924.

[28] Praecipe of witnesses before grand jury, U.S. v. Joseph DiCarlo, et al, Jan. 22, 1924.

[29] Indictments No. 4227 and 4228, U.S. v. DiCarlo, Gallelli, Ruffino and Capodicaso, U.S. District Court for the Western District of New York, Jan. 7, 1924; "Jury complete for trial of DiCarlo and his pals," *BME*, Feb. 6, 1924.

[30] "Jury complete for trial of DiCarlo and his pals;" "DiCarlo, three others on trial in shooting case," *BDC*, Feb. 6, 1924, p. 4.

[31] "DiCarlo, three others on trial in shooting case."

[32] Testimony of Joseph Patitucci, Feb. 5, 1924.

[33] Testimony of Joseph Patitucci, Feb. 5, 1924.

[34] Testimony of Joseph Patitucci; "Chief witness tells story in DiCarlo trial," *BCA*, Feb. 6, 1924; "Braves death to testify baring Buffalo dope ring," *BME*, Feb. 7, 1924.

[35] Testimony of Joseph Patitucci; "Chief witness tells story in DiCarlo trial."

[36] "Cameron denies hearing DiCarlo make threat to 'get rid of' Pattituccio," *BDC*, Feb. 7, 1924.

[37] "May Gilmore switches testimony in DiCarlo case; perjury charged," *Buffalo Express*, Feb. 8, 1924, p. 14; "Sick mother is better; trip off," *Buffalo Commercial Advertiser and Journal*, Feb. 8, 1924. According to the *Commercial Advertiser and Journal*, U.S. Attorney Donovan called the New York City home of Cameron's mother and learned that she was feeling better. Cameron subsequently dropped a request to leave Buffalo to be by her side.

[38] Lupo had recently been questioned in connection with a New York City gunfight that resulted in the death of Michael Carraro.

[39] "Cameron denies hearing DiCarlo…"

[40] Testimony of Lester Cameron, United States v. DiCarlo, Capodicaso, Ruffino and Gialelli, Buffalo, NY, Feb. 5, 1924; "Cameron denies hearing DiCarlo…"

[41] "Cameron denies hearing DiCarlo…;" Affidavit of William J. Donovan, United States v. DiCarlo, Gallelli, Ruffino and Capodicaso, April 23, 1924.

[42] "Cameron denies hearing DiCarlo…"

[43] Testimony of May Patitucci, United States v. DiCarlo, Capodicaso, Ruffino and Gialelli, Buffalo, NY, Feb. 6, 1924.

[44] Testimony of May Patitucci, Feb. 6, 1924.

[45] "Refuses to identify 4 alleged gunmen," *BN*, Feb. 7, 1924; "Testimony as to identity of four gunmen conflicts," *BT*, Feb. 7, 1924.

[46] "Testimony as to identity of four gunmen conflicts;" "Pattituccio's wife deserts govt case," *Buffalo Commercial Advertiser and Journal*, Feb. 7, 1924, p. 1.

[47] Testimony of John Geraci, United States v. DiCarlo, Capodicaso, Ruffino and Gialelli, Buffalo, NY, Feb. 8, 1924.

[48] Testimony of John Geraci; "DiCarlo's wife had guns, says witness," *BEN*, Feb. 8, 1924; "Geraci breaks silence by testifying in trial of DiCarlo shooting case," *BME*, Feb. 9, 1924.

[49] Testimony of Detective Sergeant William Connolly, Feb. 8, 1924.

[50] Joe and Maria Spero were witnesses to the marriage of Joseph Ruffino and Anna

Privitera at St. Anthony of Padua Roman Catholic Church, Buffalo, New York, on June 4, 1913 (Certificate and Record of Marriage).

[51] Joseph Ruffino was born March 4, 1890, in Vallelunga, Sicily. He was the son of Michele Ruffino and Calogera LaMartina (Birth Certificate #57). He entered the U.S. through the port of New York aboard the S.S. Britannia on Feb. 2, 1894. He was three years old and accompanied by his parents and his brothers Vincenzo, five years old, and Rosario, seven months old.

[52] Testimony of Joseph Ruffino, United States v. DiCarlo, Capodicaso, Ruffino and Gialelli, Buffalo, NY, Feb. 8, 1924; "DiCarlo's fate may be in hands of jury tonight," *BDC*, Feb. 9, 1924, p. 12.

[53] Testimony of Gaetano Capodicaso, United States v. DiCarlo, Capodicaso, Ruffino and Gialelli, Buffalo, NY, Feb. 8-9, 1924.

[54] Testimony of Gaetano Capodicaso; "DiCarlo's fate may be in hands of jury tonight."

[55] "Ignorance of this witness is profound," *BCA*, Feb. 9, 1924.

[56] Testimony of Gaetano Capodicaso, Feb. 8-9, 1924.

[57] Testimonies of Edward Norvew and Charles J. Gerard, United States v. DiCarlo, Capodicaso, Ruffino and Gialelli, Buffalo, NY, Feb. 9, 1924; "Ignorance of this witness is profound."

[58] Testimony of Peter Giallelli, United States v. DiCarlo, Capodicaso, Ruffino and Gialelli, Buffalo, NY, Feb. 9, 1924. The trial transcript reported that the prize fight in Buffalo on January 1 was between Rocky Kansas and Patty Meyers. Kansas' opponent appears to have been named Teddy Meyers. According to "Rocky Kansas victor," *NYT*, Jan. 2, 1924, p. 22, Kansas won a decision against Meyers despite being knocked down twice in the early rounds.

[59] Testimony of Peter Giallelli. It seems Gallelli was referring to a bout between Rocky Kansas and Milwaukee fighter Richie Mitchell in Buffalo on February 18, 1921. However, according to "Richie Mitchell loses," *NYT*, Feb. 19, 1921, p. 15, Kansas scored a knockout against Mitchell in the first round of that fight. The first-round KO is confirmed by Sugar, Bert Randolph, *The Ring Record Book and Boxing Encyclopedia*.

[60] Testimony of Peter Giallelli; "Giallelli owns he sold dope to Pattitucci," *BN*, Feb. 9, 1924.

[61] Testimony of Sarah DiCarlo, United States v. DiCarlo, Capodicaso, Ruffino and Gialelli, Buffalo, NY, Feb. 9, 1924; "Nine witnesses construct alibis about DiCarlo," *BDC*, Feb. 10, 1924.

[62] Testimony, United States v. DiCarlo, Capodicaso, Ruffino and Gialelli, Buffalo, NY, Feb. 9, 1924; "Nine witnesses constrict alibis about DiCarlo."

[63] Testimony of Raymond A. Delahunt, United States v. DiCarlo, Capodicaso, Ruffino and Gialelli, Buffalo, NY, Feb. 11, 1924; "Extra: DiCarlo is guilty gets six years; 2 others sentenced," *BME*, Feb. 12, 1924, p. 1.

[64] Testimony of John H. Davis, United States v. DiCarlo, Capodicaso, Ruffino and Gialelli, Buffalo, NY, Feb. 11, 1924.

[65] Summation by U.S. Attorney Donovan, United States v. DiCarlo, Capodicaso, Ruffino and Gialelli, Buffalo, NY, Feb. 11, 1924.

[66] Transcript, United States v. DiCarlo, Capodicaso, Ruffino and Gialelli, Buffalo, NY,

Feb. 11-12, 1924; "Extra: DiCarlo is guilty gets six years; 2 others sentenced;" "Sentenced to six years, $5,000 fine; Capodicaso only one who escapes," *BDC*, Feb. 12, 1924.

[67] "Meddling with U.S. witnesses charged," *BEN*, Feb. 12, 1924.

[68] "Meddling with U.S. witnesses charged."

[69] Sentencing by Judge Morris, United States v. DiCarlo, Capodicaso, Ruffino and Gialelli, Buffalo, NY, Feb. 12, 1924; "Meddling with U.S. witnesses charged." The judge's quote was approximated from pieces in both sources. In the transcript, he reportedly said, "If they had been better marksmen, they might be headed for Sing Sing instead of for Atlanta." Sing Sing Prison in Ossining, New York, was the location of the electric chair.

[70] "Meddling with U.S. witnesses charged."

[71] Testimony of John H. Davis; "Grand jury to hear story of alleged bribe," *BME*, Feb. 13, 1924, p. 12.

[72] "Grand jury to hear story of alleged bribe;" "Evidence in alleged bribe case to jury," *BCA*, Feb. 13, 1924; "Donovan in personal charge," *Buffalo Enquirer*, Feb. 13, 1924, p. 14.

[73] "Lawyer Lipsitz indicted; faces trial for bribery," *BME*, March 15, 1924, p. 16.

[74] "Federal jury returns not guilty verdict in Lipsitz bribery case," *BME*, Dec. 4, 1925, p. 5; "Lipsitz made bribe offer, sleuth says," *BDC*, Dec. 2, 1925, p. 9; "Lipsitz bribery charges to go before jury today," *BME*, Dec. 3, 1925, p. 9. The Lipsitz defense countered the bribery accusations from Delahunt and Davis by putting Lipsitz himself on the stand and following with a large number of distinguished character witnesses. After the acquittal, among those happily congratulating Lipsitz was U.S. Attorney Richard T. Templeton, who prosecuted the case.

[75] "Grand jury to hear everyone concerned," *BN*, Feb. 13, 1924; "2 turn up as trial ends," *Buffalo Enquirer*, Feb. 13, 1924, p. 14.

[76] Blackmon, M.F., Letter from SAC Buffalo to the attention of Mr. Hoover, Feb. 19, 1924.

[77] Burns, William J., Letter from FBI director to SAC Blackmon, Buffalo, Feb. 27, 1924.

[78] "Wants DiCarlo to eat jail food," *BDC*, Feb. 17, 1924, p. 83.

[79] "Gunmen dine in downtown night café," *BME*, Feb. 17, 1924.

[80] "Wants DiCarlo to eat jail food;" "Gunmen dine in downtown night café."

[81] "DiCarlo obtains $50,000 bail," *BDC*, Feb. 20, 1924; "Gallelli not to file appeal," *BDC*, Feb. 19, 1924.

[82] "DiCarlo's bail," *BME*, Feb. 21, 1924, p. 16.

[83] "DiCarlo to face narcotics charge," *BDC*, Feb. 28, 1924.

Chapter 9

[1] "'Busy Joe' charges common law wife stole his money," *BDC*, March 1, 1924, p. 12.

[2] "Pattitucci shoots wife, takes bichloride poison," *BME*, March 12, 1924, p. 14; "U.S. witness attempts to kill woman," *BCA*, March 11, 1924; "Pattituccio tries to kill Gilmore woman and self," *BDC*, March 12, 1924.

[3] "Pattitucci and woman may live," *BT*, March 13, 1924.
[4] "Pattituccio, informer, dies of poison taken after attempt to kill wife," *BDC*, March 18, 1924, p. 16.
[5] "Pattituccio, informer, dies of poison taken after attempt to kill wife."
[6] "Claim Pattitucio, dying, retracted DiCarlo charges," *BDC*, March 22, 1924, p. 14.
[7] "Probe confession clearing DiCarlo," *BDC*, March 27, 1924, p. 16.
[8] "Probe confession clearing DiCarlo."
[9] "Klan says it will close roadhouse this week," *BCA*, March 17, 1924, p. 1.
[10] "Klan says it will close roadhouse this week;" Lay, Shawn, *Hooded Knights on the Niagara: The Ku Klux Klan in Buffalo , New York*, New York: New York University Press, 1995, p. 71.
[11] "Klan says it will close roadhouse this week."
[12] "Denies charge inn protected," *BCA*, March 17, 1924, p. 16.
[13] Lay, Shawn, p. 71.
[14] "Mayor warns Klan to stay out of city," *BCA*, March 17, 1924, p. 16.
[15] "The Ku Klux Klowns," *Heacocks*, April 1924, p. 15.
[16] Meyer, Joseph J., *The Wet City: Buffalo, New York, During the Prohibition Era, 1920-1933*, Allegheny College, 1996, p. 17-18.
[17] Statement of Sam Todaro, March 31, 1924.
[18] Statement of Sam Todaro, March 31, 1924.
[19] Morris, Judge George F., Rescript on motion to set aside the verdict because of newly discovered evidence and for errors committed during the progress of the trial, United States v. DiCarlo, Gallelli, Ruffino and Capodicaso, June 28, 1924.
[20] Statement of Sam Todaro, March 31, 1924.
[21] Statement of Sam Todaro, March 31, 1924.
[22] Affidavit of Natalia Patitucci, United States v. DiCarlo, Gallelli, Ruffino and Capodicaso, March 25, 1924.
[23] Affidavit of Detective Sergeant William R. Connolly, United States v. DiCarlo, Gallelli, Ruffino and Capodicaso, March 27, 1924.
[24] Affidavit of Edward N. Wilkes, United States v. DiCarlo, Gallelli, Ruffino and Capodicaso, March 27, 1924.
[25] Affidavit of William H. Wilson, United States v. DiCarlo, Gallelli, Ruffino and Capodicaso, March 28, 1924.
[26] Affidavit of William J. Donovan, April 23, 1924.
[27] Affidavit of William J. Donovan, April 23, 1924.
[28] Affidavit of William J. Donovan, United States v. DiCarlo, Gallelli, Ruffino and Capodicaso, April 25, 1924
[29] "Black Hand involved in federal case," *BME*, April 14, 1924, p. 4.
[30] "Black Hand involved in federal case;" "Pistol permit vanishes from clerk's office as alien holder is seized," *BDC*, April 14, 1924, p. 16; "Supervisor to be grilled by Donovan," *Buffalo Commercial Advertiser and Journal*, April 14, 1924, p. 10.
[31] "Fake pistol permit case before jury," *BME*, April 15, 1924, p. 18; "Federal grand jury gets perjury evidence," *BDC*, April 15, 1924, p. 5.

32 "Jury hears evidence against two men in pistol permit case," CE, April 16, 1924, p. 5; Testimony of Ignazio Lupo, defendant, U.S. v. Giuseppe Calicchio et al.

33 "DiCarlo applies for new trial on shooting charges," BDC, April 14, 1924, p. 16.

34 Morris, Rescript on motion to set aside the verdict; "Argue DiCarlo's new trial plea at Concord, N.H.," BDC, April 19, 1924, p. 16.

35 Thrasher, Louis L., Assignments of error, United States v. DiCarlo, Gallelli, Ruffino and Capodicaso, July 25, 1924.

36 Marriage license of Joseph DiCarlo and Elsie Rose Pieri, registered no. 1100, Town of Pomfret, County of Chautauqua, New York, Nov. 29, 1924; Marriage certificate of Joseph DiCarlo and Elsie Rose Pieri, Village of Fredonia, County of Chautauqua, New York, Nov. 29, 1924.

37 Birth certificate of Salvatora Pieri, No. 380, City of Buffalo, New York, Sept. 5, 1901.

38 Manifest of the *S.S. San Giorgio*, arrived New York City April 20, 1893.

39 Manifest of the *S.S. Bolivia*, arrived New York City July 1, 1898.

40 Certificate and Record of Marriage #104, City of Buffalo, New York, Giovanni Pieri and Ignazia Ciresi, Nov. 16, 1900.

41 Marriage license of Joseph DiCarlo and Elsie Rose Pieri; Marriage records of St. Anthony's Roman Catholic Church, Fredonia, New York, Nov. 29, 1924.

42 Marriage certificate of Joseph DiCarlo and Elsie Rose Pieri, Nov. 29, 1924.

43 "Ruffino and DiCarlo on way to jail," BME, April 16, 1925.

44 "DiCarlo and Ruffino to serve terms for shooting Pattitucci," BME, June 2, 1925, p. 5.

Chapter 10

1 U.S. Census of 1920; "Nine bullets are fired into victim's body," BME, Nov. 12, 1923, p. 1.

2 Statement of Celia Nyler to Buffalo Police, Nov. 13, 1923.

3 The address of the Genova Inn was 822 Hertel Avenue.

4 "Nine bullets are fired into victim's body."

5 "Dry agent is killed in Buffalo cabaret," NYT, Nov. 12, 1923, p. 19.

6 Statement of Celia Nyler.

7 "Girl tells of threat by Pinnavaia against federal dry agents," BME, Nov. 15, 1923, p. 1. Sam Pinnavaia and his brother Ralph were born in Serra di Falco, Sicily. Sam LoVullo, with whom the Pinnavaias were friendly, was also a native of Serra di Falco, Sicily.

8 "Woman's 'tip-off' followed by shower of shots in place at Hertel and Elmwood Avenues," BDC, Nov. 12, 1923, p. 1.

9 "Girl tells of threat by Pinnavaia against federal dry agents."

10 Statement of Sam Provenzo to Police, Nov. 11, 1923; "Girl tells of threat by Pinnavaia against federal dry agents."

11 "Woman's 'tip-off' followed by shower of shots in place at Hertel and Elmwood Avenues;" "Nine bullets are fired into victim's body."

[12] "Woman's 'tip-off' followed by shower of shots in place at Hertel and Elmwood Avenues."

[13] "Nine bullets are fired into victim's body."

[14] "Scent plot to slay Buffalo dry agents," *NYT*, Nov. 13, 1923, p. 23; "Agent Stewart victim of plot, woman states," *BME*, Nov. 14, 1923, p. 1.

[15] "Upstate 'Izzy' in Syracuse to foil death ring," *Syracuse Herald*, Nov. 27, 1923, p. 4.

[16] "Police begin cleanup of city," *BME*, Nov. 14, 1923, p. 9.

[17] "All revolver permits revoked," *BME*, Nov. 14, 1923, p. 9.

[18] Supplementary Investigation Report, Buffalo Police, Nov. 13, 1923.

[19] Dickson, Chief Constable S.J., Letter to Buffalo Chief of Detectives Charles Zimmerman, Nov. 16, 1923.

[20] Buffalo Police homicide file on Stewart murder.

[21] "Killers' war may result from two Falls murders," *BME*, Nov. 16, 1923, p. 10; "Crime wave scene moves to Niagara," *BCA*, Nov. 15, 1923, p. 1. The *Commercial Advertiser* initially reported that Austaro "bullet-riddled body" was struck by eight slugs. The *Express* story, noting six slugs, was written following the autopsy.

[22] Manifest of the *S.S. Napoli*, arrived New York City on July 19, 1913.

[23] "James DiNiere is shot to death in his auto in Wheatfield and Charles Austaro is slain in city," *NG*, Nov. 15, 1923, p. 1.

[24] "Kill men, friends, at same hour but different places; leave few clues," *BDC*, Nov. 16, 1923, p. 1.

[25] "Killers' war may result from two Falls murders."

[26] "Crime wave scene moves to Niagara."

[27] "James DiNiere is shot to death in his auto…;" "Fear outbreak of gang war in Niagara County," *BT*, Nov. 16, 1923.

[28] "Fear outbreak of gang war in Niagara County."

[29] "Dead man was witness in rum murder,' *BCA*, Nov. 16, 1923, p. 1; "Falls police baffled by murder mysteries," *BT*, Nov. 17, 1923, p. 4.

[30] James DiNiere is shot to death in his auto…."

[31] "No arrests are made in murder mysteries – will call in expert to see if same gang killed two," *NG*, Nov. 16, 1923, p. 1.

[32] "Crime wave scene moves to Niagara."

[33] "Murder of pair still baffles Falls police," *BME*, Nov. 17, 1923.

[34] *Madonna del Perpetuo Soccorso*, also known as Our Lady of Perpetual Help, is the patron saint of the DiNieri and Austaro home town of Caltavuturo, Sicily.

[35] "East side stilled as funeral corteges of slain men wend way from church to final resting place on Pine Avenue," *NG*, Nov. 17, 1923, p. 1; "Murdered Italians given last homage by friends," *BME*, Nov. 18, 1923, Section 5, p. 10.

[36] "Murder auto still being held by police," *BME*, Nov. 22, 1923, p. 10.

[37] "Crime wave scene moves to Niagara."

[38] "Is vendetta involving DiNiere family broadening to include members of murdered man's family in this city?" *NG*, Nov. 19, 1923; "Cousin with murdered man now missing," *BME*, Nov. 19, 1923, p. 5.

[39] "Cousin of DiNiere sought," *Buffalo Enquirer*, Nov. 19, 1923; "Is vendetta involving DiNiere family broadening…;" "Cousin with murdered man now missing."

[40] Dubro and Rowland, p. 15-17, 155.

[41] Nicaso, p. 100.

[42] U.S. Census of 1920; World War I Draft Registration, Sept. 12, 1918; "Orville A. Preuster, enemy of Niagara rum runners, is killed by bomb in his car," *Niagara Falls Gazette*, March 2, 1925. Preuster was a widower. His wife Ida died sometime between the 1920 census and Preuster's 1925 murder.

[43] Orville A. Preuster's home address was 2115 Tenth Street, Niagara Falls, NY.

[44] Dubro and Rowland, p. 153; "Orville A. Preuster, enemy of Niagara rum runners…;" "Blackhand bomb hidden in his car rips customs man to death at Falls," *BDC*, March 2, 1925. The *Daily Courier* reported that Whiteacre was on the vehicle's running board at the time of the explosion. However, the *Gazette* reported that Whiteacre entered the vehicle from the driver's side – initially planned to drive the car himself – but then slid over to the passenger's side when Preuster decided to drive.

[45] "Orville A. Preuster, enemy of Niagara rum runners…;" "City council at Falls acts in aid of hunt started by federal men," *BDC*, March 3, 1925.

[46] "Auto expert certain dynamite blast used to murder Preuster," *NG*, March 5, 1925; "Tells officials dynamite job was work of expert," *BDC*, March 6, 1925.

[47] "Blackhand bomb hidden in his car…"

[48] Nicaso, p. 100.

[49] "Blackhand bomb hidden in his car…;" "Federal sleuths spread net for bomb slayers of Falls customs inspector," *BME*, March 3, 1925.

[50] "U.S. starts search for bomb slayers," *BEN*, March 2, 1925.

[51] "Orville A. Preuster, enemy of Niagara rum runners…;" "U.S. starts search for bomb slayers,"

[52] "Orville A. Preuster, enemy of Niagara rum runners…"

[53] "Hunt threat notes as clue in murder," *BEN*, March 3, 1925.

[54] "Offer reward in bomb explosion," *NG*, March 3, 1925; "Trail found in bomb murder, says official," *BEN*, March 4, 1925; "Orville A. Preuster, enemy of Niagara rum runners…"

[55] "Companion of slain sleuth under cover," *BME*, March 7, 1925; "Hide customs agent to protect him from wrath of dynamiters," *BDC*, March 7, 1925.

[56] "Federal sleuths spread net for bomb slayers of Falls customs inspector," *BME*, March 3, 1925.

[57] "Grand jury takes up Preuster case," *BDC*, March 11, 1925.

[58] "Trail found in bomb murder, says official."

[59] "Head of Falls church council directly charges bootleggers with Orville Preuster murder," *NG*, March 8, 1925.

Chapter 11

[1] Madigan, William J. and squad, Supplemental Investigation Report to Acting Chief of Detectives John Reville, July 20, 1925.

[2] Madigan, July 20, 1925; Statement of Mildred Dovern to Buffalo Police, July 13, 1925.

[3] "Shooting victim fourth to die in gangsters' feud," *BDC*, July 15, 1925, p. 5.

[4] "Shooting victim fourth to die..." Buffalo Police Headquarters was located at Franklin and Seneca Streets.

[5] "Amino dies of wound and Ross faces murder charge," *BDC*, May 31, 1911, p. 6; "Murder in first degree charged against DiRosa," *BDC*, June 7, 1911, p. 6; "Murder scene re-enacted in courtroom to show man shot to defend himself," *BDC*, p. 6; "Seven hours out, jury in murder case fails to agree and is discharged," *BDC*, p. 7; "DiRosa to Auburn for not less than six years," *BDC*, p. 7; U.S. Census of 1910. While *Courier* accounts referred to DiRosa's victim as Sebastiano Amino and Sebastiano Gambrino, census records show the name as Sebastiano Gambino. It is supposed that Sebastiano Gambino and John Gambino were related, but the precise relationship between them is unknown.

[6] "Shooting victim fourth to die...;" "Believe they will find slayers," *BDC*, July 6, 1917; "Whole detective force is seeking Spang's slayer," *BDC*, July 8, 1917, p. 5; "Man under arrest in connection with Spang murder case," *BDC*, July 9, 1917; "Men sought for quiz in Spang murder," *BDC*, July 17, 1917, p. 4; "Man accused of part in Spang's murder is caught," *BME*, Feb. 15, 1921, p. 7.

[7] "Man accused of part in Spang's murder...;" "Advised to flee after murder, is Genovese's story," *BDC*, Feb. 16, 1921.

[8] Buffalo Police Headquarters, located at Franklin and Seneca Streets, was destroyed by fire on Dec. 11, 1919.

[9] "Frank Genovese shot; old feud, police claim," *BME*, Nov. 27, 1923, p. 1; "Victim once held in Spang murder case' police see plot for revenge," *BDC*, Nov. 29, 1923; "Genovese is shot in old feud," *BT*, Nov. 27, 1923, p. 1; "Gangster is dying from five wounds," *BCA*, Nov. 27, 1923; "Man believed shot in spite feud dies; hold drinker owner," *BDC*, Nov. 28, 1923, p. 3; "Genovese, gunman's victim, dies of wound," *BME*, Nov. 28, 1923, p. 16.

[10] "Shooting victim fourth to die..."

[11] "Dismiss charge in Genovese murder," *BDC*, Dec. 28, 1923, p. 4; "Genovese, gunman's victim..."

[12] "Shot dead on street nearby police office," *BME*, March 5, 1925, p. 4; "Police unable to find trace of murderers," *BME*, March 6, 1925, p. 4.

[13] Statement of Clarence E. Good to Buffalo Police, March 10, 1925. "Tonneau" refers to the rear passenger compartment on early automobiles. Railroad track torpedoes were explosive charges placed on the tracks behind disabled trains. The devices detonated loudly under the weight of an approaching train, providing warning of the obstruction ahead.

[14] Statement of Clarence E. Good.

[15] "Shooting victim fourth to die..."

[16] "Homicides," *Annual Report*, Buffalo Department of Police, 1925, p. 42; "Unknown gunmen escape in auto after shooting Italian on Front Ave.," *BME*, March 26, 1925.

[17] "Shooting victim fourth to die..."

[18] Madigan, Supplemental Investigation Report, July 20, 1925.

[19] "Shooting victim fourth to die..."

[20] "Homicides," p. 42; "Think Boston prisoner man wanted here," *Buffalo Courier*, July 17, 1927; "Suspect is indentified in Boston," *BT*, July 17, 1927, p. 57; "Man may be suspect in Buffalo murder," *BEN*, July 18, 1927, p. 3.

[21] "West Virginia police fail to identify man held there as slayer of Buffalo boy," *BDC*, Aug. 23, 1925, p. 1.

[22] "Former guard in prison knows man sought as slayer," *BDC*, Aug. 23, 1925, p. 1.

[23] "Near panic as Joseph is laid to rest," *BT*, Aug. 21, 1925, p. 14.

[24] "Near panic as Joseph...;" "Italian colony raises fund of $565 to pay for Gervase funeral," *BDC*, Aug. 21, 1925, p. 14. While the *Courier* indicated that the $565 was given to Fortunato Gervase to pay funeral expenses, the *Times* indicated that the cash was in addition to the payment for funeral expenses.

[25] "Near panic as Joseph..."

[26] "West Virginia police fail..."

[27] "Seek slayer here," *BME*, Feb. 16, 1926, p. 16.

[28] "Think Boston prisoner man wanted here," *Buffalo Courier*, July 17, 1927; "Suspect is indentified in Boston," *BT*, July 17, 1927, p. 57; "Man may be suspect in Buffalo murder," *BEN*, July 18, 1927, p. 3; "Suspect identified as Elmer Thompson," *BEN*, July 20, 1927, p. 34.

[29] Manifest of the *S.S. La Gascogne* arrived New York City on Feb. 1, 1909. The ship sailed out of Havre, France. Tropea reported that he was to meet his cousin Francesco Cundari of 217 Van Buren Street in Brooklyn. In the summer of 1924, as Tropea filled out a travel certificate for American aliens making temporary visits abroad, he reported that he entered the U.S. on April 1920 aboard the *S.S. Conte Rosso*. Tropea is known to have been in the U.S. long before April 1920. While he could have left the country and returned in that month, he could not have returned aboard the *S.S. Conte Rosso*. That ship was not in service until 1922.

[30] "Rival loves weep for Orazio but his real widow is sought," *Chicago Daily Tribune*, Feb. 18, 1926, p. 3.

[31] "Rival loves weep for Orazio...;" U.S. Census of 1920; U.S. Census of 1930. The newspaper recorded the name of Tropea's teenage lover as "Beatrice Gould." However, census records for 1920 and 1930 show the family name as "Gold." The Golds' move from Chicago to South Haven, Michigan, occurred between January 1920 and Tropea's death in February 1926. Their South Haven address was recorded in Tropea's address book.

[32] Kobler, John, *Capone: The Life and World of Al Capone*, New York: G.P. Putnam's Sons, 1971, p. 88-89; Keefe, Rose, *Guns and Roses: The Untold Story of Dean O'Banion*, Nashville: Cumberland House, 2003, p. 112-113.

[33] Gentile, Nick, *Vita di Capomafia*, Rome: Editori Riuniti, 1963, p. 47-50; "Crowds honor the memory of Michael Merlo," *CT*, Nov. 13, 1924, p. 5; "Ten thousand at funeral of Michael Merlo," *CT*, Nov. 14, 1924, p. 2.

[34] "Girl an O'Banion death clue," *CT*, Nov. 11, 1924, p. 1.

[35] "N.Y. gangster held by Crowe in gun inquiry," *CT*, Nov. 19, 1924, p. 1. Yale and Pollaccia were a good fit for a witness's description of the O'Banion gunmen. The

witness, quoted in "Girl an O'Banion death clue," reported that two shorter Italian-looking men, quite similar in appearance ("might have been twins"), entered O'Banion's flower shop on either side of a taller man "who might have been a Jew or a Greek." Yale and Pollaccia differed in appearance mainly in weight and hairline, two features that would have been concealed by typical November attire. There was no such resemblance between Scalisi and Anselmi, often suspected of being O'Banion's killers.

[36] "Deportation or death seen as gangster fate," *CT*, Feb. 17, 1926, p. 2. This article, published shortly after Tropea's death, stated, "Police say they can trace Orazio's death back to the murder of Dean O'Banion a year and a half ago. They believe he was one of the murderers..."

[37] "N.Y. gangster held by Crowe..."

[38] Rosa Pollaccia certificate of Baptism, Shrine Church of Our Lady of Solace, Coney Island, New York, Oct. 17, 1920; communications with Pollaccia descendant, Louis Cafiero, 2008; Gentile, Nicolo, *Translated Transcription of the Life of Nicolo Gentile*, p. 115-116. The baptism certificate indicated that Salvatore D'Aquila served as godfather for Rosa Pollaccia. The Gentile transcription, apparently a government translation of notes for Gentile's later *Vita di Capomafia*, reported that Pollaccia served as a "personal consigliere of Masseria."

[39] "Suburb gun center shut," *CT*, Nov. 21, 1924, p. 1.

[40] "Death marked for 3 more of Genna family," *CT*, July 10, 1925, p. 1.

[41] "Trace Sicilian killer in fight for deportation," *CT*, Feb. 18, 1926, p. 3; "Police raid Mafia; get 121," *CT*, Feb. 23, 1926, p. 1.

[42] "New rich rum chief slain by gunmen in car," *CT*, May 27, 1925, p. 2; Kobler, p. 160. Kobler blamed the North Side Gang for Angelo Genna's murder. According to Kobler, six blocks from the Hotel Belmont, where Genna and his wife lived, a touring car containing four North Side gangsters darted out of a side street and headed after Genna's roadster. However, Kobler did not explain how the North Siders could have known that Genna would be passing that spot at that time. The trip was not usual business for Genna, as he reportedly was on the way to close on the purchase of a house.

[43] "Kill two cops; city aroused," *CT*, June 14, 1925, p. 1; Kobler, p. 161-163. According to Kobler, the arrival of police interrupted a plan by Anselmi and Scalisi to assassinate Mike Genna.

[44] "Kill two cops...;" "Bare plot to help gunmen by blackmail," *CT*, Oct. 22, 1925, p. 1.

[45] "Gennas in terror; Tony dies," *CT*, July 9, 1925, p. 1.

[46] "Back to Italy, plan of Gennas; Spingolas stay," *CT*, Jan. 14, 1926, p. 3.

[47] "Samoots dies in silence; fails to wed," *CT*, Nov. 13, 1925, p. 1.

[48] "Bare plot to help gunmen by blackmail," *CT*, Oct. 22, 1925, p. 1; Kobler, p. 164.

[49] "Report second Genna trial to be delayed," *CT*, Nov. 16, 1925, p. 28; "Genna killers get 14 years." Scalisi and Anselmi were acquitted of the murder of Officer Walsh and appealed the 14-year sentence imposed for the killing of Officer Olson. After serving just seven months of their sentence, the Illinois Supreme Court granted the gunmen a new trial on the Olson killing. A jury found the pair not guilty.

[50] "Genna slaying revenge for O'Banion, claim," *CT*, Jan. 12, 1926, p. 1; "Feudists slay

Sicilian ally of Genna gang," *CT*, Feb. 16, 1926, p. 1; Kobler, p. 169.
[51] Kobler, p. 170; "Orazio the 'Scourge' buried without friends or clergy," *CT*, Feb. 21, 1926, p. 4.
[52] "Orazio the 'Scourge'…"
[53] "Rival loves weep…;" "Son-in-law is killed by gang in Chicago row," *BME*, Feb. 17, 1926; "Say man killed in Chicago son-in-law of Buffalo woman," *BDC*, Feb. 17, 1926, p. 16. The *Tribune* published photographs of the two women claiming to be Tropea's common law wives.
[54] "Deportation or death…"
[55] "Trace Sicilian killers in fight for deportation," *CT*, Feb. 18, 1926, p. 3.
[56] "Genna slaying revenge…"
[57] "Clear up shooting case," *Utica Daily Press*, June 23, 1917, p. 15; "Two men wounded by revolver shots," *Utica Daily Observer*, June 22, 1917, p. 6. Bystander Samuel Clegg was also wounded in the attack. The shooting occurred at about 11 p.m. June 21, 1917, near the intersection of Bleecker and Niagara Streets. Aiello and LaFata, walking west on Bleecker, opened fire on Gagliano when they were within ten feet of him. Clegg's injury was the apparent result of Gagliano's attempt to return fire.
[58] "Forgot all about who shot him twice," *Utica Daily Observer*, Sept. 18, 1917, p. 10; "Victim of shooting accused of perjury," *Utica Daily Observer*, Sept. 19, 1917, p. 12. Witnesses asserted that Grande was not present when Gagliano made his initial deposition.
[59] "Grocer is shot, slayers escape," *BME*, Oct. 8, 1917; "Sunday murder in lower part of city gives police mystery as to slayers," *BDC*, Oct. 8, 1917.
[60] "Shooting back in slain man's life," *BME*, Oct. 9, 1917; "Auto pops into murder mystery without solving," *BDC*, Oct. 11, 1917. The *Daily Courier* reported that Celona's first name was Vincenzo or "Jimmy." Also arrested was a man named Michael Rossi. James Celona was murdered in Hamilton, Ontario, six months later, on April 16, 1918.
[61] Certificate of marriage, Holy Cross Church, Buffalo, New York, Joseph Aiello and Catarina Amara, Oct. 17, 1917; Passenger manifest of *S.S. Principe di Piemonte* arrived New York on Nov. 6, 1911. The manifest indicated that the Amaras were born in Bagheria but had lived in the U.S. since 1896.
[62] "Deportation or death…;" "Genna slaying revenge…"
[63] "Deportation or death…;" Giuseppe Siragusa Petition for Naturalization, certificate number 1956822, U.S. District Court for Western Pennsylvania, May 23, 1923. The *Tribune*, apparently having trouble deciphering Tropea's handwriting, recorded the surname as "Louogniao" and the address as 4310 Liberty Avenue in Pittsburgh. Careless penmanship could transform the name "Siragusa" into something closely resembling what was recorded in the *Tribune*. Siragusa's naturalization petition shows his address as 4510 Liberty Avenue – also a difference that can be attributed to handwriting.
[64] "Deportation or death…;"
[65] "Victim refuses to give name of assailant," *BCE*, June 14, 1926; "Bullet victim will not talk," *Buffalo Evening Times*, June 14, 1926.

[66] Tona, Carmen, March 1981 interview with Pete Barbera, close acquaintance of Sam LoVullo.

[67] "Shot twice, man dies, en route to the hospital," *BCE*, July 2, 1926; "Shot to death at doorway of Dante Pl. home," *Buffalo Evening Times*, July 2, 1926.

[68] Statement of Anna Cicatello to Buffalo Police, July 2, 1926. One news story – "Gunman kills tailor; makes escape in car," *BEN*, July 2, 1926 – indicated that Cicatello's murderer did not get out of the car. The story stated: "The slayer thrust an arm between the curtains of the machine and fired a volley of bullets at the tailor."

[69] "Shot twice, man dies..."

[70] Madigan, W.J., Report to Chief of Detectives Austin J. Roche, Buffalo Police, July 22, 1926.

[71] "Shot twice, man dies..."

[72] "Street shooting mystifies police," *BDC*, May 2, 1924, p. 9; "Police continue grilling of pair held in DeCaro shooting," *BDC*, May 3, 1924, p. 12; "Probably murder, official verdict in DeCaro case," *Buffalo Enquirer*, May 2, 1924, p. 1.

[73] Schulz, Frank J., Report to Chief of Detectives Austin J. Roche, Buffalo Police, July 15, 1926.

[74] Statements of Salvatore Insalaco and Michael Rizzo to Buffalo Police, July 16, 1926.

[75] "Tips on alleged slayers lead to moonshine still," *BDC*, Jan. 10, 1924; "Police find a still while seeking Pinnavaias," *Buffalo Enquirer*, Jan. 10, 1924, p. 12.

[76] Tona, Carmen, March 1981 interview with Pete Barbera, close acquaintance of Pietro Rizzo. Carlo Rizzo, another son of the murdered Pietro, became involved with the Buffalo crime family. He was found murdered in the trunk of a car April 10, 1980. The Flower Basket, located at 347 Niagara Street, was known as a "front" during Prohibition. Police officers regularly picked up bouquets of flowers and envelopes of cash as incentives to "look the other way" and ignore the bootlegging activities.

[77] "Police drive to break up vendetta," *BT*, July 18, 1926.

[78] Statement of Fred Ippolito to Buffalo Police, July 20, 1926.

[79] "Shot down as he begs for mercy," *BCE*, July 20, 1926.

[80] "Vassallo gives police lead on his murderers," *BCE*, July 21, 1926, p. 12.

[81] Buffalo Police arrest record for John A. Vassalo; Statement of Charles Pulvino to Buffalo Police, July 21, 1926.

[82] "Barber shot down in street is dying," *BEN*, July 20, 1926.

[83] "3d victim is shot down in street," *Buffalo Evening Times*, July 20, 1926.

[84] Madigan and Agaad, Report to Chief of Detectives Austin J. Roche, Buffalo Police, July 20, 1926. The information on the fistfight was provided in a statement from the victim's father, Matteo Vassallo.

[85] "Squads will patrol feud zone tonight," *BCE*, July 22, 1926, p. 11.

[86] Madigan, W.J. and squad, Report to Chief of Detectives Austin J. Roche, Buffalo Police, July 22, 1926. "Toto" is usually an affectionate form of the name "Salvatore." However, detectives believed Vassallo was trying to say either "Tony" or "Thomas."

[87] Vassallo homicide file, Buffalo Police, July 20, 1926; Report to Chief of Detectives

Austin J. Roche, Buffalo Police, July 20, 1926.

Chapter 12

[1] "90 are indicted in alleged rum plot," *BEN*, July 30, 1926, p. 1; Hunt, C.W., *Whisky and Ice: The Saga of Ben Kerr, Canada's Most Daring Rumrunner*, Toronto: Dundurn Press, 1996, p. 131-134. According to Hunt, an inspector with the Ontario police received information linking Joseph Sottile to the 1925 car bomb-murder of U.S. Customs Inspector Orville Preuster.

[2] United States v. Spallino et al., District Court, Western District of New York, 21 F.2d 567 (1927).; Hunt, C.W., p. 133. According to C.W. Hunt, Joseph Spallino and Joseph Sottile were related by marriage.

[3] Hunt, C.W., p. 134. Judge Emerson Coatsworth was previously mayor of the City of Toronto. He was appointed to the bench in March of 1914.

[4] Dubro and Rowland, p. 157-158; Nicaso, p. 103; "90 indicted as ring in big alcohol deal," *New York Times*, July 30, 1926.

[5] "Poison liquor floods border," *BEN*, July 28, 1926, p. 1. Alcohol Division leader Mark Crehan noted that the government formula for denaturing alcohol changed in spring, 1926, from the easily redistilled 39-D, contaminated with small amounts of pyrodene, gasoline and kerosene, to CD-5, which included deadly wood alcohol, or methanol. It was later learned that the product distributed through the regional bootlegging syndicate was almost entirely methanol.

[6] "Nine killed by poison booze here," *BCE*, July 25, 1926, p. 10.

[7] "Wood alcohol victim's babe also likely to die," *BCE*, July 26, 1926.

[8] "Poison liquor floods border."

[9] "31 arrests in alleged liquor plots," *Lockport NY Union-Sun and Journal*, July 30, 1926, p. 1.

[10] "Nine killed by poison...;" U.S. Census of 30. The 1930 census shows Sucharski, 34, his wife Carrie, 28, and their three children living on Hertel Avenue. In 1930, Sucharski was operating a lunch room.

[11] "Nine killed by poison..."

[12] "Nine killed by poison...;" U.S. Census of 1920. The 1920 census shows Banas living with his mother and siblings on Amherst Street and working as an electrician.

[13] "Federal officers to investigate alcohol deaths," *BCE*, July 25, 1926, p. 10.

[14] "Poisonous potions kill 9 persons across frontier," *BCE*, July 25, 1926, p. 10l; Hunt, C.W.

[15] "Poisonous potions kill 9 persons across frontier."

[16] "Poisonous portions kill 19..."

[17] "Wood alcohol victim's babe..."

[18] "Makes sworn statement as to where he purchased alcohol," *BCE*, July 26, 1926.

[19] "Voelker indicted on liquor charge four years ago," *BCE*, July 28, 1926, p. 5. Canandaigua, the county seat of Ontario County, New York, is southeast of Rochester. It sits about 90 miles east of Buffalo and 70 miles west of Syracuse.

[20] "Hunt vendor as poison booze death toll rises," *BDC*, July 26, 1926.

[21] "Seek to rend veil that covers bootleg traffic," *BCE*, July 27, 1926.

[22] "See arrest of king at early hour, wire says," *BCE*, July 27, 1926, p. 6.

[23] "Voelker will expose poison alcohol ring," *BCE*, July 28, 1926.

[24] "Voelker will expose…;" U.S. Census of 1900.

[25] "Voelker will expose…"

[26] "90 indicted in drive on liquor; source of poison bootleg found," *BEN*, July 29, 1926, p. 1; "90 are indicted in alleged rum plot," *BEN*, July 30, 1926, p. 1.

[27] "90 are indicted in alleged rum plot;" Dubro and Rowland, p. 159.

[28] Nicaso, p. 105.

[29] "Canadian officials bring bad liquor evidence here," *BCE*, Aug. 4, 1926, p. 1; "Man indicted here gives up in Canada," *BEN*, July 31, 1926, p. 1; "Five in poison rum case freed on $20,000 bail," *BEN*, Aug. 16, 1926, p. 3; "31 arrests in alleged liquor plots;" Nicaso, p. 103, 105.

[30] Nicaso, p. 107; Dubro and Rowland, p. 160-167.

[31] U.S. Census of 1930.

[32] Nicaso, p. 107.

[33] Dubro and Rowland, p. 167; Nicaso, p. 103; Hunt, C.W., p. 135, 137.

[34] "Must restore to the Third Ward Club the papers raiders took," *NG*, June 16, 1927, p. 22; United States v. Spallino et al.

Chapter 13

[1] Atlanta Federal Prison files for Giuseppe Morello, #2882, and Ignazio Lupo, #2883.

[2] Flynn, James P., "La Cosa Nostra, a.k.a. Cosa Nostra…," FBI file #NY 92-2300, July 1, 1963, p. 33. Flynn appears to have based much of his report on translations of Nick Gentile memoirs, notes and interviews.

[3] Gentile, p. 60-61.

[4] Gentile, p. 61. There are various English translations of the Italian word "Spirito." Given the circumstances, "Ghost" seems the most appropriate translation of the nickname. Since Valente and his associates generally spoke to each other in Sicilian, it seems unlikely that Valente was referred to by any English version of the nickname. If he was, it was probably by the close cognate "Spirit."

[5] Manifest of the *S.S. San Giovanni* arrived New York City on July 6, 1910; Umberto Valente World War I Draft Registration Card, June 5, 1917.

[6] Gentile, p. 69-70; "Shot in a feud in 'Little Italy,'" *NYT*, May 24, 1914, p. 22.

[7] Gentile, p. 70.

[8] Gentile, p. 68-69. According to Gentile, "D'Aquila had in every city a trusted secret agent…" Gentile indicated that Mafioso Mike LoBosco was a D'Aquila secret agent in Cleveland. (Later, Gentile states that D'Aquila installed two brothers named Sciortino as secret agents in the San Francisco Mafia.) While evidence is lacking, it seems likely that Pittsburgh's East End Mafia boss Giuseppe Siragusa was endorsed by D'Aquila. Setting a pattern that was followed later by Philadelphia boss Salvatore Sabella, Siragusa settled first in New York and then moved to Pennsylvania years later. Like Sabella, Siragusa's early claim to local Mafia authority seems to rest on his support from New York. Also like Sabella,

Siragusa opposed Masseria's Mafia network during the Castellammarese War.

[9] Joseph Lonardo Passport Application, March 22, 1919. According to the application, Lonardo was born on Oct. 20, 1884, and was naturalized an American citizen in Cleveland on Aug. 14, 1914. The application was witnessed by attorney Abraham E. Bernsteen. A decade later, the Harding Administration made Bernsteen a federal prosecutor. (A brief Bernsteen biography is included in Coates, William R., *A History of Cuyahoga County and the City of Cleveland*, Chicago: The American Historical Society, 1924.)

[10] Kelly, Ralph, "Murder in Cleveland: The Prohibition Toll, Chapter 6 – Passing of the Lonardos, Merchants," *CPD*, Jan. 1933; "Slayers of booze czar and kin are held, Barry says," *CP*, Oct. 14, 1927

[11] U.S. Census of 1920. According to the census, Frank reached the U.S. about 1901, Dominick in 1911, and John in 1912. Dominick and John lived in 1920 with Joseph Lonardo, his wife and their three children at 2534 East 38th Street, in Cleveland's "Big Italy" community.

[12] Kelly, "...Passing of the Lonardos, Merchants."; "Slayers of booze czar and kin are held, Barry says," *CP*, Oct. 14, 1927

[13] Kelly, "...Passing of the Lonardos, Merchants."

[14] "Slayers of booze czar and kin.."

[15] Gentile, p. 68.

[16] Morello, Celeste A., p. 41-47.

[17] SAC Philadelphia, "Angelo Bruno, AKA. AR. Daily Summary," FBI memo dated Jan. 21, 1965, file #92-444. Sabella's wife, Maria Galante, was Stefano Magaddino's cousin.

[18] Joseph Lonardo and his wife Concetta were godparents to Angelo Palmeri's daughter Rosaria, July 3, 1921, at St. Joseph's Church, Niagara Falls, New York. Vincenzo Mangano, arrested at the 1928 Cleveland convention, was godfather to Angelo Palmeri's daughter Rose, Sept. 29, 1925, at Holy Angels Church, Buffalo, New York.

[19] Paolino Palmeri and Elena Curti Certificate and Record of Marriage #19426, City of New York Department of Health, July 27, 1914.

[20] Frank Palmeri Baptism Record, St. Joseph's Church, Niagara Falls, NY, Dec. 27, 1924.

[21] Pistol permit applications, Erie County, New York. Angelo Palmeri's address, 295 Jersey Street, also was used for the pistol permit application of Brooklyn Mafioso Salvatore Maranzano, Aug. 10, 1925. The address of Filippo Mazzara, 203 Porter Avenue, a Mafia leader in Buffalo, was used when Salvatore Sabella sought a pistol permit there Oct. 14, 1925.

[22] Pollaccia and D'Aquila baptized children together at the Shrine Church of Our Lady of Solace, Coney Island, on Oct. 17, 1920. At that ceremony, D'Aquila served as godfather to Pollaccia's daughter Rosa. Descendants recall that Pollaccia soon thereafter became a supporter of Masseria and was a trusted Masseria adviser from the very beginning of his reign. Rosa Pollaccia baptism certificate and additional information provided by Louis P. Cafiero.

[23] Gentile, Chapter V. Gentile was in Sicily when D'Aquila condemned the dozen to

death. He recalled that he was met in Sicily by Morello, Lupo and Valente (and possibly others). However, documented travel dates do not match his recollection. Gentile returned to the U.S. through Boston in April 1921. Valente did not leave New York for Italy until July. Lupo's trip occurred in November. Morello's date of travel is not known.

[24] Manifest of the *S.S. Presidente Wilson* arrived New York City on Jan. 18, 1922. Valente and Pollaccia are not listed near each other in the manifest. Pollaccia had already been naturalized a U.S. citizen and was grouped on the manifest with other U.S. citizens. Valente was an American resident alien.

[25] Gentile, p. 78-79. It is conceivable that the arrangement also included Pollaccia.

[26] Warner, Richard N., "The Warner Files: On the trail of Giuseppe 'Joe the Boss' Masseria," *Informer: The History of American Crime and Law Enforcement*, February 2011, p. 56-58; Birth records of Menfi, Sicily, Certificate No. 29, Jan. 17, 1886.

[27] Manifest of the *S.S. California* arrived New York City Jan. 11, 1899; U.S. Census of 1910. Masseria's father, a 52-year-old tailor from Marsala, Sicily, entered the U.S. aboard the S.S. California. He headed to 243 Elizabeth Street to meet with Calogero Masseria. The relationship between the two men is uncertain. Census records indicate that Giuseppe Masseria arrived in the U.S. in 1902, followed a year later by mother Vita and brothers John and James. Brother Charlie Masseria crossed the Atlantic in 1904.

[28] U.S. Census of 1910. The census indicates that he was a tailor in a women's clothing factory. His father worked as a tailor in a men's clothing factory.

[29] "Connect prisoners with 12 burglaries," *NYT*, April 15, 1913, p. 7; "Girl, woman, 4 men shot in battle of two bootleg bands," *NYT*, May 9, 1922, p. 1.

[30] U.S Census of 1910.

[31] Giuseppe Masseria World War I Draft Registration. At the time of his 1917 registration, Masseria was said to be "stout" of build.

[32] U.S. Census of 1910; Social Security Death Index.

[33] "Thieves tear hole in pawnshop wall," *NYT*, April 14, 1913, p. 6. The authorities were convinced that the burglars would not have been able to access the pawnshop's vault. Build into the shop's foundation, vault was 30 feet by 18 feet. It had double masonry walls, each two-feet thick, and an inner metal foil liner linked to an alarm system.

[34] "A family of pawnbrokers," *NYT*, Aug. 2, 1878, p. 5; "Three golden spheres," *NYT*, June 16, 1878, p. 8.

[35] "Thieves tear hole in pawnshop wall," *NYT*, April 14, 1913, p. 6. The authorities were convinced that the burglars would not have been able to access the pawnshop's vault. Build into the shop's foundation, vault was 30 feet by 18 feet. It had double masonry walls, each two-feet thick, and an inner metal foil liner linked to an alarm system.

[36] State of New York against Pietro Lagatutta, Salvatore Rufino, Giuseppe Rufino and Giuseppe Masseria, New York Municipal Archives. Salvatore and Giuseppe Ruffino seem not to be related to the Joseph Ruffino who was convicted with Joseph DiCarlo in the 1924 witness intimidation case in Buffalo.

[37] State of New York against Pietro Lagatutta...; "Thieves tear hole in pawnshop wall."

According to the statement of Bartolomeo Fontana in the Good Killers case of 1921, an Angelo Lagattuta was wounded in an attack by the Good Killers gang in the Bronx. It is not known if Pietro and Angelo were related.

[38] State of New York against Pietro Lagatutta...

[39] State of New York against Pietro Lagatutta...

[40] "Connect prisoners with 12 burglaries," *NYT*, April 15, 1913, p. 7.

[41] "Girl, woman, 4 men shot in battle of two bootleg bands," *NYT*, May 9, 1922, p. 1. The news story looks back nearly a decade to report that Masseria was sentenced to four and a half years. Case documents do not specifically note his sentence. Documents state that codefendant Pietro Lagattuta was sentenced to state prison for not less than two years and six months nor more than five years. The Ruffino brothers appear to have been tried separately from Masseria and Lagattuta.

[42] Giuseppe Masseria World War I Draft Registration.

[43] Illegal activity in the New York City ice industry is documented as far back as 1900, when an ice wholesaling monopoly used Tammany Hall connections to obtain exclusive rights to Manhattan piers. ("Tammany calls a halt, *New York Tribune*, May 8, 1900, p. 11; "Special jury to probe ice trust," *New York Evening World*, May 18, 1900, p. 8.) As the monopoly formed, the price of ice in the city more than doubled. The American Ice Company was convicted of violating state anti-trust laws late in 1909. A fine of $5,000 was imposed. ("Ice trust guilty," *NYT*, Dec. 11, 1909, p. 1.) Several ice wholesalers subsequently formed. In 1911, these were found to be merely front operations for the continued monopoly of the American Ice Company. ("Says ice monopoly was never broken," *NYT*, July 19, 1911, p. 5.) In the 1930s, authorities discovered a layer of monopolistic racketeering between ice wholesalers and retailers. While the wholesale trust had been broken up and numerous small businesses dealt with the retail market for ice, a small number of middlemen appeared to be involved in every wholesale ice transaction. Suppliers sold only to them and retailers had no choice but to buy from them. New York City Deputy Commissioner of Markets Michael Fiaschetti, former leader of the NYPD Italian Squad, told the press the ice racket had existed since 1910. ("Middlemen forced out to end ice racket," *NYT*, April 21, 1934, p. 4.)

[44] Salvatore Mauro Passport Application, Jan. 19, 1908. The 239 Elizabeth Street address was the site of the F. Acritelli and Sons businesses and was also used by a number of other individuals and businesses. The Acritellis were bankers and steamship agents commonly employed by Italian immigrants to handle the transport of money and goods between the U.S. and Italy. Peter P. Acritelli, one of the principals in the business and also a city coroner and state deputy fire marshal, was the witness for Salvatore Mauro's 1908 passport application. Peter was accused just a few months earlier of aiding in voter registration frauds by allowing registrants to use the Acritelli business address as their own. Peter took control of the F. Acritelli & Sons business after the February 1908 death of his father. The business was pursued by creditors that spring. Its financial assets were gone by fall. Peter Acritelli died after a 1912 fall from an upper berth in a railroad Pullman car broke his collarbone and aggravated an old abscess near his ear. He died after undergoing an operation for mastoiditis, an infection of the back portion of the skull.

[45] "Murders ascribed to 'Bootleg Curb,'" *NYT*, Oct. 14, 1920, p. 6.

[46] "Bootleggers form rum 'curb market,'" *NYT*, Oct. 13, 1920, p. 1.

[47] "'Curb' whisky trail leads to 2 arrests," *NYT*, Oct. 16, 1920, p. 1.

[48] Thompson, Craig and Allen Raymond, *Gang Rule in New York*, New York: Dial Press, 1940, p. 10.

[49] Thomas Pennachio Prisoner File #11342, Atlanta Federal Prison, National Archives and Records Administration. Pennachio was sentenced by federal Judge Learned Hand on May 7, 1919, to serve one year and one day in prison. (Records show he previously served three months in Harts Island Prison for petit larceny in 1909 and served 18 months in Sing Sing Prison for burglary in 1915-16. His burglary prison term roughly coincided with Masseria's, though the two men appear not to have been in the same institution. In 1936, Pennachio and Luciano were indicted as leaders of a vast vice ring.) He remained free until July 28, 1920, while he appealed the decision. (This delay caused his sentence to begin about one month after Ignazio Lupo's release from Atlanta.) If Pennachio set up the Liquor Exchange, he must have done so at least two months before Prohibition agents were alerted to its existence in September 1920. Pennachio came up for parole in November 1920, but it was denied. With a "good time allowance," he was released from prison on May 17, 1921.

[50] Salvatore Mauro Passport Application; Salvatore Mauro Naturalization Petition, Kings County NY, Vol. 287, p. 161; U.S. Census of 1910.

[51] Salvatore Mauro Naturalization Petition.

[52] Salvatore Mauro Passport Application.

[53] U.S. Census of 1910.

[54] The Mauro and Masseria neighborhood of this period became the focus of an urban renewal project during the city administration of Mayor James Walker. Walker revealed in 1928 that he intended for the city to purchase 180 dilapidated properties along a seven-block stretch of the Lower East Side in order to widen Chrystie and Forsythe Streets and to build model low-cost housing. The project was momentarily derailed when property owners demanded exorbitant prices. It was resurrected in spring the following year, as property owners agreed to sales prices that were 25 percent over assessed value. The city took title to much of the land and began demolition work in summer of 1929, just before the stock market crash that led to the Great Depression. The seven blocks remained vacant through the Depression. Development plans were scrapped by Mayor Fiorello LaGuardia early in 1934. By then, the city had grown used to the open space and decided that a park would be its best use. Later that year, it was named Sara Delano Roosevelt Park in honor of President Franklin Roosevelt's mother.

[55] "Murders importer in East Side street," *NYT*, Dec. 30, 1920, p. 2.

[56] "Gunmen shoot six in East Side swarm," *NYT*, Aug. 9, 1922, p. 1; "Girl, woman, 4 men shot in battle of two bootleg bands," *NYT*, May 9, 1922, p. 1.

[57] United States Senate Special Committee to Investigate Organized Crime in Interstate Commerce (Kefauver Committee), Hearings, Part 2, 81st Congress, 2d Session, Washington: U.S. Government Printing Office, 1950, p. 132. Chicago Crime Commission Operating Director Virgil W. Peterson testified that Joe Masseria was the "head of the underworld activities of what is frequently called the Mafia" beginning in 1922.

58 "Gunmen kill cousin of 'Lupo-the-Wolf,'" *NYT*, May 9, 1922, p. 3.
59 Thompson and Raymond, p. 13.
60 "Girl, woman, 4 men shot in battle of two bootleg bands," *NYT*, May 9, 1922, p. 1.
61 "Girl, woman, 4 men shot…;" U.S. Census of 1920.
62 "Girl, woman, 4 men shot…"
63 "Gunmen shoot six in East Side swarm," *NYT*, Aug. 9, 1922, p. 1.
64 "Gunmen shoot six in East Side swarm."
65 "Gang kills gunman; 2 bystanders hit," *NYT*, Aug. 12, 1922, p. 20; "New Haven girl wounded in New York bootleggers' feud," *Bridgeport (CT) Telegram*, Aug. 12, 1922, p. 1. Eleven-year-old Agnes Egglinger was a resident of New Haven, Connecticut. She and her father Harry Egglinger were visiting with her maternal grandparents on 12th Street at the time of the attack. After the shooting, her father stopped a passing delivery truck to have her rushed to Bellevue Hospital.
66 "Gang kills gunman…"
67 "Faces 2 murder charges," *NYT*, Aug. 13, 1922, p. 5.
68 "Lucania aide held in taxicab racket," *NYT*, July 14, 1938, p. 1; Gentile, p. 97, 101. Gentile confirmed that his personal friend Biondo was a member of Masseria's organization.
69 "8 indicted in Brooklyn as counterfeiters," *NYT*, June 20, 1930, p. 48; "Genovese dies in prison at 71," *NYT*, Feb. 15, 1969, p. 29; Frasca, Dom, *King of Crime*, Crown Publishers, 1959, p. 80. The 1930 *Times* article noted that Genovese "has a long criminal record and is the leader of a gang on the west side of Manhattan." Genovese's 1969 obituary explained that Charlie Luciano and Vito Genovese both served as lieutenants to Masseria. Frasca stated incorrectly that Genovese was inducted into the Mafia on the East Side of Manhattan in 1915 during an induction ceremony was presided over by Ignazio Lupo. The author did not provide the source of his information. Lupo certainly could not have presided over a 1915 induction ceremony, as he was serving a counterfeiting sentence in Atlanta Federal Prison between 1910 and 1920.
70 "Marlow slayers said to be known," *NYT*, July 24, 1929, p. 19; "Police mystified in slaying of 'boss,'" *NYT*, April 17, 1931, p. 17. In the 1929 *Times* article written one year after the killing of Yale, New York Police Commissioner Grover A. Whalen noted that Masseria and Carfano used the same residential address. The 1931 article noted that Carfano and Masseria "had been partners in a racing stable of some twenty horses and also had been interested in a bookmaking enterprise."
71 Gentile, p. 96-97.
72 Gentile. p. 101.
73 Gentile, p. 90.
74 "Three slay man in street and flee," *NYT*, Oct. 11, 1928
75 "Three slay man in street and flee;" "Property valuation (tax assessments) of Southern Boulevard, Bronx, New York," city-data.com; Salvatore D'Aquila Naturalization Record, U.S. District Court of Brooklyn, July 13, 1926. The date of D'Aquila's move to the Bronx is in doubt. According to the news story, D'Aquila lived in Brooklyn until about 1926. His naturalization was processed on July 13, 1926. However, assessment records indicate that D'Aquila's two-story brick home

404 · *DiCarlo*

in the Bronx was completed in 1925. It is possible that the move was completed gradually. The Bronx home apparently still stands, though the character of the neighborhood has changed a bit with the more recent construction of multi-level apartment buildings. The D'Aquila home sat just outside the recognized boundary of the Belmont district, about half a mile from the Italian immigrant neighborhoods on Arthur Avenue.

[76] In this period, before the completion of the Triborough Bridge in the 1930s, travel between the Bronx and Brooklyn required passing through at least East Harlem and Upper Manhattan.

[77] Kobler, p. 162-163; "New rich rum chief slain by gunmen in car," *CT*, May 27, 1925, p. 2. Brothers Mike Genna and Tony Genna were murdered within weeks of Angelo Genna. Kobler cited evidence that Capone engineered the killing of Mike Genna. The plan failed, but Mike Genna was killed in a shootout with police moments later.

[78] Kobler, p. 209-210; Asbury, Herbert, *The Gangs of Chicago: An Informal History of the Chicago Underworld*, New York: New York: Thunder's Mouth Press, 1986, p. 361-362.

[79] The Unione Siciliana, which had recently been renamed the Italo-American National Union, was officially led by Judge Bernard P. Barasa. The press of the period considered Barasa a front man for Lombardo.

[80] "Hunt avengers in Loop murder of Mafia chief," *CT*, Sept. 9, 1928, p. 2.

[81] "Kill Lombardo, Mafia chief," *CT*, Sept. 8, 1928, p. 1; "Lombardo aide dies from his wounds," *NYT*, Sept. 10, 1928, p. 20; "Latest killing rival's bid to seat of power," *Buffalo Courier*, Sept. 9, 1928, p. 2; "Hunt avengers in Loop murder…"

[82] Though it made little difference to authorities, Joseph Lolordo denied he was a Lombardo bodyguard. Police had records showing that Lolordo's brother, Pasqualino, earlier had been a Lombardo bodyguard. It is possible that the identification of Joseph in that role was in error.

[83] "Hunt avengers in Loop murder…"

[84] Gentile, Chapter p. 88-89. Gentile did not identify Lonardo's Jewish employee. However, it seems likely that he was referring to Albert "Chuck" Polizzi (real name Leo Berkowitz). Polizzi, raised as a brother of Mayfield Road gangster Alfred "Big Al" Polizzi, was known to work with Cleveland Mafiosi, including "Big Al" and Lonardo lieutenant Lorenzo Lupo.

[85] Kelly, Ralph, "Murder in Cleveland: The Prohibition Toll, Chapter 4 – Murders Done - $25 a head," *CPD*, Jan. 1933.

[86] Lorenzo Lupo was born Feb. 15, 1886, to Giovanni and Elenora LoCastro Lupo in Vallelunga, Sicily. His mother and Joseph DiCarlo's mother were cousins. Lupo reached the U.S. on Jan. 3, 1902, aboard the *S.S. Santa Lucia*. He lived in Brooklyn in 1920. Wanted for murder in New York City in 1923, he fled to Buffalo. He was not related to Ignazio "the Wolf" Lupo.

[87] "Attacked by gunmen near home," *CPD*, Sept. 10, 1927, p. 1; "Sheriff denies Lupo shot in slot warfare," *CP*, Sept. 10, 1927, p. 1.

[88] "Attacked by gunmen near home."

[89] "Attacked by gunmen near home;" "Sheriff denies Lupo shot in slot warfare."

[90] Newton, Michael, *Mr. Mob: The Life and Crimes of Moe Dalitz*, Jefferson, NC: McFarland & Co., 2009, p. 40. According to Newton, Albert "Chuck" Polizzi's real name was Leo Berkowitz. When his Russian-Jewish parents died shortly after their arrival in Cleveland, he was informally adopted by the parents of Alfred "Big Al" Polizzi. Atlanta Federal Prison records show that "Chuck" Polizzi was imprisoned between April 21, 1921, and Jan. 25, 1925, for stealing government property.

[91] Kelly, Ralph, "Murder in Cleveland: The Prohibition toll, Chapter 7 – Nadel and Lupo: Both Died," *CPD*, Jan. 1933; "Hunt 6 gangsters as Lupo recovers," *CPD*, Sept. 11, 1927, p. 19; "Attacked by gunmen near home."

[92] "Lupo offers self-defense for slaying," *CP*, Oct. 4, 1927, p. 17.

[93] "Lupo is freed; grand jury to probe killing," *CPD*, Oct. 5, 1927, p. 1; "Lupo slaying fires Stanton to more action," *CP*, Oct. 5, 1927, p. 15.

[94] "Fails to indict in Lupo case," *CPD*, Oct. 12, 1927, p. 26.

[95] Kelly, Ralph, "Murder in Cleveland: The Prohibition toll, Chapter 5 – Death in Ambler Park: A bootleg joke," *CPD*, Jan. 1933.

[96] Kelly, Ralph, "Murder in Cleveland: The Prohibition toll, Chapter 6 – Passing of the Lonardos, merchants," *CPD*, Jan. 1933; Porrello, Rick, *The Rise and Fall of the Cleveland Mafia: Corn Sugar and Blood*, Fort Lee, NJ: Barricade Books, 1995, p. 68.

[97] Gentile, p. 90; "2 brothers murdered in bootleg war."

[98] Kelly, "...Passing of the Lonardos, merchants."

[99] "2 brothers murdered in bootleg war," *CPD*, Oct. 14, 1927; Kelly, "...Passing of the Lonardos, merchants." Angelo Caruso, at whose butcher shop John Lonardo died, was shot and mortally wounded Dec. 5 as he was closing the doors of his garage. He died early the next morning. Cleveland Police believed the men who killed the Lonardo brothers also killed Caruso, fearing that he could identify them.

[100] Report of the Detective Bureau, Police Department of the City of Cleveland, Oct. 13, 1927.

[101] "Hits new lead in murder of two Lonardos," *CPD*, Oct. 15, 1927.

[102] "Porello's bond set at $20,000," *CP*, Oct. 19, 1927.

[103] Reports of the Detective Bureau, Police Department of the City of Cleveland, Oct. 13-16, 1927. Eight boys were born into the Porrello family. An older Ottavio Porrello died in Licata, Sicily, on April 2, 1890, at the age of 11.

[104] Kelly, "...Passing of the Lonardos, merchants;" Kelly, "...Nadel and Lupo: Both Died;" Kelly, Ralph, "Murder in Cleveland: The Prohibition toll, Chapter 8 – The Ice Pick Murders," *CPD*, Jan. 1933.

[105] "Police seek gunman in yellow car," *CPD*, June 1, 1928, p. 1; "Seize gunman as suspect in Lupo murder," *CP*, June 1, 1928, p. 1.

[106] Kelly, "...Nadel and Lupo: Both Died."

[107] "Suspect booked as Lupo killer," *CP*, June 4, 1928, p. 1.

[108] "May free man in Lupo case," *CP*, June 6, 1928, p. 17; "Cut charge in Coletto case," *CP*, June 8, 1928, p. 23; "Drop murder charge," *CP*, June 22, 1928, p. 23.

[109] Salvatore and Vincenzo Callea appear to have first arrived in Buffalo as young men in the period 1912-1914. Salvatore settled on Seventh Street. Evidence suggests that Vincenzo moved periodically throughout the region (turning up in Cleveland

406 · DiCarlo

and in Ontario, Canada) and traveled back and forth to Sicily before making a permanent home in Buffalo in the early 1920s.

[110] Vincent Callea murder file, Buffalo Police; "Slaying here held result of dry raid," *BEN*, Aug. 27, 1933. Through documents found in Vincent Callea's possession and through testimony of witnesses, police were able to link the Calleas to the Porrellos of Cleveland. The *News* report of the Callea brothers murders noted that the brothers had been partners with an East Cleveland bootlegging gang. Vincent Callea's presence in Cleveland is documented by his arrest there on Jan. 18, 1921.

[111] "Brothers put on the spot near their saloon," *BEN*, Aug. 26, 1933; "U.S. joins search for slayers here," *BEN*, Aug. 28, 1933. In the Aug. 26 *News* story, Buffalo Deputy Police Commissioner William R. Connolly reveals his belief that the Callea brothers were murdered in 1933 because they had attempted to control distilleries in central and western New York and in Cleveland.

[112] City of Niagara Falls Directory, 1923. Paul Palmeri lived at 1538 Whitney Avenue. "Don Simone" Borruso resided at 1649 Whitney Avenue.

[113] City of Niagara Falls Directories, 1926-27, 1927-28. Falls Bottling Works was located at 1417 Walnut Avenue.

[114] City of Niagara Falls Directory, 1927-28.

[115] FBI report #BU 92-61. The document notes that naturalized citizen Magaddino was issued passport number 320287 at Washington, D.C., on Jan. 25, 1927. At that time, he announced his intention to travel from New York City to Europe on Feb. 17, 1927.

[116] Manifest of the *S.S. Presidente Wilson* arrived New York City on May 4, 1927. Calogero DiBenedetto, son of Antonino and Rosa Salvo DiBenedetto, was born March 2, 1906, in Brooklyn, New York. His father, Antonino DiBenedetto, brother of Giuseppe DiBenedetto, and Antonio Mazzara, brother of Filippo Mazzara, were murdered in a double-homicide in Brooklyn, New York, on Nov. 11, 1917.

[117] "Merchant in car is slain by gangsters," *BCE*, Dec. 23, 1927; "See murder as climax of big gang war," *BCE*, Dec. 24, 1927; "Rich dealer killed by gang," *BT*, Dec. 23, 1927, p. 22; "Local vendetta claims life of another victim," *BCE*, Feb. 28, 1929; "DiBenedetta shot down in store," *BT*, Feb. 28, 1929.

[118] Affidavits for License to Marry, State of New York, Aug. 23, 1910; Marriage Certificates, Aug. 29, 1910. Filippo Mazzara married Antonia Pampalone; Giuseppe DiBenedetto married Rosaria Pampalone. The witnesses to the marriage ceremonies were Leonardo Renda, Crocifissa Albanese, Vito Pampalona and Francesca Buccellato.

[119] U.S. Census of 1920. The census taken Jan. 3, 1920, listed Filippo Mazzara and Angelo Puma as boarders at 596 Niagara Street. Angelo Puma was born in Castellammare del Golfo, Nov. 9, 1884. He arrived at the port of New York aboard the *S.S. Napolitan* Prince on Sept. 27, 1903 (Petition for Naturalization). No direct family link could be found between Angelo Puma and the Francesco Puma of the Good Killers case.

[120] Buffalo City Directory, 1922. Giuseppe DiBenedetto was born March 7, 1890, in Castellammare del Golfo, son of Calogero and Antonina Mione DiBenedetto (Castellammare Birth Certificate #168). He arrived in New York City aboard the *S.S. Prince Albert* on Nov. 11, 1899 (Declaration of Intention).

[121] The LaRu Restaurant was owned by Salvatore LaMarca and Joseph Ruffino (Business Certificate #16437, filed Feb. 5, 1925, with the Erie County, NY, Clerk's Office).

[122] "Merchant in car is slain by gangsters;" "Rich dealer killed by gang;" "Extortion roundup snares two others," *BEN*, April 29, 1931, p. 3; *Annual Report Department of Police, Buffalo Police, 1927*, p. 62.

[123] "Rich dealer killed by gang."

[124] "Outside gunmen killed Mazzara, police theory," *BT*, Dec. 24, 1927; "See murder as climax of big gang war;" "Mazzara case stirs U.S. to halt killers," *BCE*, Dec. 26, 1927.

[125] "Police extend hunt for gang in murder case," *BEN*, Jan. 6, 1928, p. 1.

[126] Interview with Philip G. Mazzara, grandson of Filippo Mazzara, June 16, 2012.

[127] Monsignor Joseph V. Gambino was born to Giuseppe and Margherita Gambino in Poirino, Italy, on March 23, 1879. After an education in Turin, he was ordained in 1903. He came to the United States in 1907, arriving in New York harbor aboard the *S.S. Koenig Albert* on Jan. 30, and settled in western New York. He was naturalized an American citizen in 1912. Bishop Charles H. Colton of the Buffalo Diocese commissioned Rev. Gambino to begin Holy Cross Parish on Buffalo's West Side in 1914. Rev. Gambino led the parish for 54 years until his retirement in 1968. He died Jan. 20, 1975, in Southern Pines, NC. He was buried in Mount Olivet Cemetery in the Town of Tonawanda, NY. (Msgr. Joseph Gambino Certificate of Death #2891, North Carolina Department of Human Resources, Jan. 20, 1975; Social Security Death Index; U.S. Passport Application #34794, approved June 17, 1914; "Rev Joseph Gambino," Find A Grave (findagrave.com), accessed April 21, 2013.)

[128] "Final tribute paid to gunmen's victim," *BEN*, Dec. 27, 1927, p. 21; "Bury murder victim," *BCE*, Dec, 28, 1927.

[129] Probate court records, Estate of Philip Mazzara.

[130] "Police Italian Squad to seek to check slayings," *BCE*, Jan. 1, 1928.

[131] "Local vendetta claims life of another victim," *BCE*, Feb. 28, 1929; "DiBenedetta shot down in store," *BT*, Feb. 28, 1929.

[132] "Suspects are jailed in killing," *Erie Times*, Jan. 27, 1928; "Star witness 'forgets' as inquest opens," *Erie Times*, Jan. 31, 1928.

[133] "Randolph bank robbers receive stiff sentences," *Olean Evening Herald*, July 2, 1919. Corda was sentenced to between six and 10 years in Auburn State Prison after pleading guilty to robbery in the first degree. He and two accomplices robbed the Cherry Creek Bank. Anthony Palmisano and Patsy Corda were represented at trial by attorney Horace O. Lanza of Buffalo.

[134] "Phillip Mazzara's partner is killed," *BEN*, Jan. 27, 1928, p. 1.

[135] "Connect Erie slaying with inn murder," *BT*, Jan. 28, 1928, p. 1; "Corda to face murder charge in Erie crime," *BCE*, Jan. 28, 1928.

[136] "Star witness 'forgets' as inquest opens;" "Won't bring Corda back," *Erie Dispatch Herald*, Feb. 1, 1928.

[137] "Solution of murders centers in Buffalo, detective declares," *NG*, Jan. 28, 1928, p. 1.

[138] "Beau Brummel of East Side sent to serve year," *NG*, Feb. 23, 1921, p. 15; "Would

take case beyond bounds of Judge Piper's court," *NG*, Jan. 31, 1921; "Detectives tell judge of place whose secret rooms they say are guarded by electric door locks," *NG*, Feb. 10, 1921, p. 1.

[139] "Detectives tell judge of place whose secret rooms they say are guarded by electric door locks."

[140] "One man held; two sought in murder," *BEN*, Jan. 28, 1928, p. 1; "Suspect seen with victim," *Erie Times*, Jan. 28, 1928; "Detectives tell judge of place whose secret rooms they say are guarded by electric door locks."

[141] "Star witness 'forgets' as inquest opens," *Erie Times*, Jan. 31, 1928.

[142] Perry, Detective Sergeant Peter J., "Case of Salvatore Gagliono," report no. 2595, March 8, 1928, Buffalo Police Department.

[143] "Volley from auto kills pedestrian," *BCE*, March 7, 1928.

[144] Perry, "Case of Salvatore Gagliono."

[145] "Is vendetta victim here," *BCE*, May 8, 1928

[146] "No clues unearthed in recent murders," *BEN*, May 9, 1928.

[147] "Vendetta claims 2 lives in 24 hours," *BEN*, May 8, 1928.

[148] Statement of Carmela Falsone to Buffalo Police, May 7, 1928.

[149] Report of W.J. Madigan to Chief of Detectives Austin J. Roche, Buffalo Police, May 16, 1928.

[150] "Frank A. DeFusto dies in hospital," *BT*, May 10, 1928, p. 30; "DeFusta burial today," *BCE*, May 12, 1928, p. 24; "DeFusta funeral," *BT*, May 12, 1928, p. 2.

[151] Morello, p. 77.

[152] Morello, p. 56-64, p. 70-75. Immigration and draft registration records show a number of Philadelphia Zanghis were born in Umberto Valente's hometown of Barcellona Pozzo di Gotto in the Sicilian province of Messina and in the nearby community of Castroreale.

[153] Frank Yale Death Certificate #14764, Department of Health of the City of New York, July 1, 1928.

[154] "Capone subpoenaed in murder of Yale," *NYT*, July 8, 1928, p. 3. One ballistics expert determined that Thompson submachine guns later seized during an investigation of the St. Valentine's Day Massacre had also been involved in the Yale murder.

[155] The possibility that the Calabrian Yale objected to Masseria's inclusion of so many Neapolitan gangsters in his organization and grew closer to the conservative D'Aquila faction before his murder should be considered. Calabrian and Neapolitan gangsters were untraditional members of the Sicily-based Mafia. As the criminal groups were incorporated into the Mafia of the U.S. enmity between them became evident. Violent rivalries between Calabrians and Neapolitans included the Bazzano and Volpe factions in Pittsburgh and the Anastasia and Genovese organizations in New York.

[156] "Three slay man in street and flee."

[157] "Third gang killing reveals rum feud," *New York Daily News*, Oct. 11, 1928, p. 51.

[158] "Three slay man in street and flee."

[159] Salvatore D'Aquila Certificate of Death, Department of Health of the City of New

York; "Importer shot nine times," *NYT*, Oct. 12, 1928, p. 22.

[160] "Importer shot nine times," *NYT*, Oct. 12, 1928, p. 22.

[161] "Shot dead as he chats beside car with 3 men," *New York Herald*, Oct. 11, 1928, p. 18.

[162] Salvatore D'Aquila Certificate of Death, Oct. 10, 1928.

Chapter 14

[1] DiCarlo arrest record, Buffalo Police; FBI records; DiCarlo INS file, p. 41.

[2] Bureau of Prisons, *Prison Work as a Career*, Washington, D.C.: Press of Federal Prison Industries, Inc., 1947, p. 9.

[3] Lewisohn, Adolph, "Humane prison treatment," *NYT*, Letter to the Editor, Jan. 17, 1928, p. 28. Lewisohn quotes from Willebrandt's letter.

[4] According to Correctional Institution Inspection Committee, *Inspection and Evaluation of the Chillicothe Correctional Institution*, 2006, the completed facility was opened in 1936.

[5] Ruby, B.F., "DiCarlo – Public Enemy," *Town Tidings*, September 1933, p. 29. Ruby did not specify the source of the story.

[6] Erie County, New York, land records.

[7] Order of Judge John R. Hazel dated June 1, 1926. A June 26, 1926, notation on the document indicates that federal marshals could find no DiCarlo assets.

[8] FBI records; DiCarlo INS file, p. 41. The sources date his parole from Oct. 19, 1928.

[9] "Joseph J. DiCarlo... Personal History and Background," FBI records, 1952.

[10] DiCarlo, Joseph J., Oath of Convict, U.S. Court for the Western District of New York, Sept. 26, 1929.

[11] Certificate of Birth No. 11711, City of Buffalo, New York State Department of Health, Dec. 19, 1929.

Chapter 15

[1] "Police seize gang of 23 occupying luxurious suites," *CP*, Dec. 5, 1928, p. 1; "Mob looked hard, policeman says," *CPD*, Dec. 6, 1928, p. 2.

[2] "Nab 27 gunmen mobilized for Cleveland war," *Chicago Daily Tribune*, Dec. 6, 1928, p. 15.

[3] "2 brothers murdered in bootleg war," *CPD*, Oct. 14, 1927.

[4] Gentile, p. 90. The cause of the division between the once-close Lonardos and Porrellos remains a mystery. Gentile noted that Joe Lonardo passed a death sentence against Porrello-ally Todaro in 1926. Gentile talked Lonardo into removing that sentence. Gentile learned that Todaro engineered the later murders of Joe and John Lonardo.

[5] "Seize 27 gangsters in Cleveland raids," *NYT*, Dec. 6, 1928. Only the names of those arrested at the Statler Hotel were publicized.

[6] "Police link gunmen to rum fight," *CPD*, Dec. 6, 1928.

[7] "Police link gunmen to rum fight."

[8] Cook County, Illinois, Death Certificate #6004272; "Kill gang leader in home,"

Chicago Daily Tribune, Jan. 9, 1929, p. 1; "Police accuse Joe Aiello as Lolordo slayer," *Chicago Daily Tribune*, Jan. 10, 1929, p. 8..The Aiello family faction of the Chicago Mafia was believed responsible for Lolordo's murder. Lolordo's wife reportedly pointed to a photo of Joe Aiello when asked who killed her husband.

[9] Asbury, Herbert, *The Gangs of Chicago*, New York: Thunder's Mouth Press, 1986, p. 359-360; Kobler, John, *Capone: The Life and World of Al Capone*, New York: G.P. Putnam's Sons, 1971, p. 264-265.

[10] "Gang roundup questioned by city manager," *CP*, Dec. 7, 1928, p. 1.

[11] Cleveland Police Blotter, Dec. 6, 1928, copy provided by David Critchley; "Police link gunmen to rum fight."

[12] Manifest of the *S.S. Regina D'Italia* arrived New York City March 22, 1920. The ship's manifest shows Traina and D'Aquila traveling together from Palermo to New York. Both had previously lived in the United States.

[13] Davis, John H., *Mafia Dynasty: The Rise and Fall of the Gambino Crime Family*, New York: HarperTorch, 1994, p. 51-52.

[14] Kefauver Committee Hearings, Part 7, p. 746.

[15] Bonanno, Joseph, with Sergio Lalli, *A Man of Honor*, New York: Simon & Schuster, 1983, p. 85, 118, 124, 228; United States Treasury Department Bureau of Narcotics, *Mafia: The Government's Secret File on Organized Crime*, New York: Collins, 2007, p. 514, 596.

[16] "Cleveland friends aid 20 gunmen," *CPD*, Dec. 7, 1928.

[17] Kelly, Ralph, "Murder in Cleveland: The Prohibition Toll, Chapter 1," *CPD*, January 1933; Cavolo, Detective Charles, Memo to Deputy Inspector Chas. N. Sterling, Cleveland Police Department, Feb. 28, 1920.

[18] Giuseppe Vaglica Declaration of Intention, #4171, U.S. District Court, Tampa, Florida, April 19, 1928; Manifest of the S.S. San Giorgio arrived New York City Sept. 4, 1912.

[19] Hearings Before the U.S. Senate Select Committee on Improper Activities in the Labor or Management Field, June 30-July 3, 1958, 85th Congress, 2d Session; "Gangsters slay Tampa man with shotgun blast," *Tampa Tribune*, July 12, 1937, p. 1. The records of the Select Committee indicate that Vaglica was murdered on July 11, 1947. Tampa Mafia historian Scott M. Deitche found that date to be incorrect. As noted in the *Tampa Tribune* article, Vaglica was killed July 11, 1937.

[20] U.S. Census of 1920.

[21] Labadie, Stephen J., "La Cosa Nostra," Memo to SAC Tampa, Federal Bureau of Investigation, TP 92-218, Sept. 3, 1963. An earlier memo (April 10, 1959) by Elmer F. Emrich also mentions a fourth early Tampa crime boss, Thomas Zummo.

[22] Kefauver Committee Hearings, Part 7, p. 744, 749-750.

[23] Florida Death Index; L'Unione Italiana Cemetery records, Tampa, Florida. Italiano was born March 23, 1860, and died Aug. 11, 1930.

[24] "Police link gunmen to rum fight." Members of a SanFilippo family were linked with the Porrello-aligned Callea brothers of Buffalo, New York, during an investigation into the Aug. 25, 1933, double-murder of Vincenzo "Big Jim" and Salvatore Callea. Some of the Calleas lived in St. Louis for a time before settling in the Buffalo area.

[25] Salvatore DiCarlo was born April 2, 1904, in Vallelunga, Sicily, to Giuseppe and Vincenza DiCarlo. Giuseppe DiCarlo died of natural causes at his summer home in Bowmansville, New York, on July 9, 1922.

[26] Porrello, p. 89-90.

[27] "Gang roundup questioned by city manager."

[28] "Arrest blocks convention of 'cannon mob,'" *CP*, Dec. 6, 1928.

[29] "Told Capone was here after gangs," *CPD*, Dec. 12, 1928.

[30] "Cleveland friends aid 20 gunmen."

[31] "Arrest blocks convention…;" "Balk attempt of gunmen suspects to get freedom," *BCE*, Dec. 7, 1928, p. 2; "Gangsters move to gain freedom halted by police," *Chicago Times*, Dec. 7, 1928, p. 29.

[32] "Police seize gang of 23…"

[33] "Police link gunmen to rum fight."

[34] "Gang roundup questioned by city manager."

[35] "Why rush to bail gunmen? Hopkins asks," *CPD*, Dec. 9, 1928.

[36] "Why rush to bail gunmen?…"

[37] "Gunmen's bonds face test today," *CPD*, Dec. 10, 1928.

[38] "Gunman's bond is ruled out," *CP*, Dec. 15, 1928, p. 1.

[39] "Gangsters lose tussle for guns," *CPD*, Dec. 15, 1928, p. 4.

[40] "Frees 15 of gang if they quit city," *CPD*, Dec. 16, 1928, p. 1.

[41] "Frees 15 of gang…;" Gangsters lose tussle…"

[42] Porrello, p. 96.

[43] Allen, Edward J., *Merchants of Menace – The Mafia: A Study of Organized Crime*, Springfield IL: Charles C. Thomas, 1962, p. 35.

[44] "Nab 27 gunmen…;" "Seize 27 gangsters…;" "Arrest blocks convention…"

[45] "Nab 27 gunmen…"

[46] "Gang roundup questioned by city manager."

[47] "Arrest more than a score of alleged gunmen in a raid," *NG*, Dec. 5, 1928, p. 1.

[48] "Police link gunmen to rum fight;" "Nab 27 gunmen…"

[49] Gentile, p. 107, 109, 113. Gentile noted there were 300 representatives at a late 1930 Mafia general assembly meeting in New York and 500 attendees at a meeting held shortly after that in Boston. He did not specify the number of attendees at a Chicago convention held in honor of new boss of bosses Salvatore Maranzano in spring 1931 but stated that all the representatives from U.S. Mafia organizations attended.

[50] Gentile, p. 101; Warner, Richard N., "The Masserias of Cleveland," *Informer*, January 2010, p. 36-38. Gentile explained that a brother of Giuseppe Masseria was the leader of a Mafia faction in Cleveland. Warner noted that Masseria's father and several brothers and sisters relocated from New York to Cleveland.

Chapter 16

[1] Gentile, p. 96-97; Bonanno, p. 84. Gentile called Mineo and Ferrigno "*coadiutori*" or assistants of Masseria. He made it clear that the three men comprised a dictatorial

regime in the American Mafia. Bonanno called Mineo an "avowed ally" of Masseria. He clearly identified the Mineo organization with the earlier D'Aquila clan by noting Traina's membership in it.

[2] Gentile, p. 97, 101.

[3] Bonanno, p. 98, 100, 107. Bonanno stated that Morello was "the second most important man in Masseria's family," and "Masseria's brain trust, his chief adviser and chief strategist."

[4] Bonanno, p. 85.

[5] Bonanno, p. 93. Bonanno wrote, "The head of our Family was Cola Schiro, a compliant fellow with little backbone. Stefano Magaddino had used Schiro as a sort of puppet ruler in Brooklyn. During times of peace, Schiro was adequate. He appeased people, being extremely reluctant to ruffle anyone."

[6] Bonanno, p. 87-88.

[7] "Police accuse Joe Aiello as Lolordo slayer," *Chicago Daily Tribune*, Jan. 10, 1929, p. 8.

[8] Bonanno, p. 88.

[9] Birth and death records of Castellammare del Golfo, Sicily. Salvatore Maranzano, born July 31, 1886, was the third son of Domenico and Antonina Pisciotta Maranzano to be named Salvatore. The first was born in 1881 with his twin brother Antonio. That Salvatore died nine days after his birth. Antonio died two days later. A second Salvatore was born in 1884 and died the following year. Birth records describe Domenico Maranzano as "possidente" (landowner).

[10] Bonanno, p. 70.

[11] Records of the Erie County Clerk's Office.

[12] Bonanno, p. 70. Bonanno repeatedly used this "Turridru" spelling, though a more common spelling of the Sicilian nickname for Salvatore seems to be Turridu.

[13] Bonanno, p. 76.

[14] Bonanno, p. 70-71.

[15] Bonanno, p. 71.

[16] Report of Admissions and Rejections at the Port of Niagara Falls, Ont., for the month ending February 1926, Vol. 1, Pg. 146, Canadian Immigration Service. Saltfleet Township was incorporated into the town of Stoney Creek in 1974. Stoney Creek became part of the City of Hamilton in 2001.

[17] Manifest of the *S.S. Martha Washington* arrived New York City on May 19, 1922. Elisabetta sailed with sons Domenico, 13, Mariano, 5, and Angelo, 4; and daughter, Antonina, 11. Don Toto Minore probably had passed away by the time of the crossing. Elisabetta noted that her closest relative remaining in Italy was her uncle Giacomo Cascio of Via Onorato in Palermo.

[18] Canadian Immigration Service record, Niagara Falls, NY, May 22, 1927. It appears this location was outside of Saltfleet Township. If Maranzano ever actually worked a farm in Saltfleet, it must have been for a very short time.

[19] Critchley, David, *The Origin of Organized Crime in America: The New York City Mafia, 1891-1931*, New York: Routledge, 2009, p. 144; Census of 1920; Census of 1930; Manifest of *S.S. Lombardia* arrived New York City on Sept. 9, 1902; Castellammare del Golfo marriage certificate of Giuseppe Maranzano and Anna

Bevilacqua, July 28, 1901. At the time of the 1930 census, the home at 2706 Avenue J was occupied by Giuseppe Maranzano, his wife Anna, and their four children. Giuseppe, the president of an importing business and older brother of Salvatore, reported that he was renting the home for $150 a month. Giuseppe and Anna Bevilacqua Maranzano first arrived in New York on Sept. 9, 1902, aboard the *S.S. Lombardia.* Their first contact was Giuseppe's uncle Calogero Navarra of Eleventh Street in Manhattan. Giuseppe's appointment as president of the importing company appears to have coincided with Salvatore Maranzano's arrival in North America. Between 1911 and 1920, Giuseppe was known to be working as a New York City fireman. The marriage certificate of Giuseppe Maranzano and Anna Bevilacqua indicates that Giuseppe was 25 years old in 1901, establishing his position as Salvatore Maranzano's older brother.

[20] Bonanno, p. 74-75. This likely was the New Hamburg farm owned by Rocco Germano. New Hamburg sits just west of Wappingers Falls on the east bank of the Hudson River. It is possible that a fellow bootlegging racketeer from Castellammare del Golfo named Santo Vultaggio introduced Maranzano to the Wappingers Falls community. Vultaggio, a 1905 immigrant ostensibly employed as a baker, also had addresses in Brooklyn and Wappingers Falls.

[21] Bonanno, p. 85.

[22] SAC Buffalo, Memo to FBI Director, March 31, 1965, FBI file BU 92-61, enclosure p. 19. The enclosure is the translated text of electronic surveillance of Buffalo Mafia boss Stefano Magaddino. During a conversation with a number of associates, Magaddino reflects on Maranzano's ambition and his low opinion of the American branch of the Mafia.

[23] Gentile, p. 96-97.

[24] "Kill gang leader in home," *Chicago Daily Tribune*, Jan. 9, 1929, p. 1.

[25] Death certificate of Pasqualino Lolordo, registered no. 4272, filed Feb. 7, 1929, Cook County, Illinois. This death certificate is labeled, "Permanent." It was filed the day after the coroner's inquest. Another death certificate, registered no. 61, was labeled, "Temp." and was filed Jan. 11, 1929.

[26] "Kill gang leader in home."

[27] "Police accuse Joe Aiello as Lolordo slayer."

[28] Lyon, Chriss, "Capone's triggerman kills Michigan cop," *Informer*: The Journal of American Mafia History, Vol. 1, No. 1, September 2008, p. 21-23; Helmer, William J. and Arthur J. Bilek, *St. Valentine's Day Massacre*, Nashville: Cumberland House, 2004.

[29] Helmer and Bilek argue that Moran was the only target. Unable to locate Moran within the captured seven men, they say, the imported gunmen decided to kill all of their prisoners.

[30] Lyon; Hoover, John Edgar, "Memorandum for Mr. Joseph B. Keenan, acting attorney general," Aug. 27, 1936. Hoover wrote to Keenan about the confession of Byron Bolton, who described a number of events and individuals involved in the planning and execution of the massacre. According to Bolton, the Capone organization benefited at the time from the cooperation of a top Chicago police officer, John Stege, who was paid $5,000 a week for his help.

[31] Kobler, p. 246-254; Chepesiuk, Ron, *Gangsters of Miami*, Fort Lee, NJ: Barricade

Books, 2010, p. 47-48.

[32] Asbury, Herbert, *The Gangs of Chicago*, New York: Thunder's Mouth Press, 1986, p. 359-360; Kobler, p. 264-265.

[33] "Local vendetta claims life of another victim," *BCE*, Feb. 28, 1929; "Italians say police lax in death probe," *BT*, Feb. 28, 1929, p. 3.

[34] "Italians say police lax in death probe."

[35] "DiBenedetta shot down in store," *BT*, Feb. 28, 1929.

[36] "Local vendetta claims life of another victim."

[37] "Funeral rites for vendetta victim," *BT*, March 3, 1929.

[38] "Blast, razing hotel, traced to vendetta," *BCE*, April 29, 1929.

[39] "Mystery blasts level old hotel," *BN*, April 28, 1929; "3-story building at 981 Niagara is wrecked by blast," *BT*, April 28, 1929; "Blast, razing hotel, traced to vendetta."

[40] "Police hunt Lonardo, Jr. as slayer," *CPD*, June 12, 1929.

[41] Zicarelli, Detective George, Information report to Chief Inspector of Detectives Cornelius W. Cody, Oct. 16, 1927. The report indicated that Concetta Paragone had been previously married and had three children in a previous relationship before running away with Joseph Lonardo in 1906. She would have been only about 19 years old in 1906. According to the report, Concetta's first husband was also a resident of Cleveland.

[42] "Big Joe's girl calls Lonardo king of kings," *CP*, Oct. 28, 1927, p. 27; "Police hunt Lonardo, Jr. as slayer." A year before his death, Lonardo traveled to his native Licata, Sicily, and secretly returned through Havana, Cuba, and Key West, Florida, with a young woman named Concettina Bulone. The two shared a luxurious apartment in Cleveland. Bulone was deported after Lonardo's death.

[43] "Police hunt Lonardo, Jr. as slayer."

[44] Porrello, p. 98-99.

[45] Reports of the Detective Bureau of the Cleveland Police, June 13, 1929, and July 2, 1929.

[46] Porrello, p. 99; "Police hunt Lonardo, Jr., as slayer."

[47] Neilsen, Sgt. William T., Criminal Complaint, Cleveland Police, June 11, 1929; Porrello, p. 102-104. Porrello argued that Todaro's failure to financially assist the Lonardos played a large part in their decision to kill him. Angelo Lonardo did not mention financial concerns when he admitted his role in the killing in testimony before the U.S. Senate Permanent Subcommittee on Investigations in 1988. He said only, "In my case, my father was murdered by Salvatore Todaro in 1927. In revenge, my cousin, Dominic Sospirato, and I killed Todaro."

[48] "Lonardo's son indicted for feud killing," *CP*, June 12, 1929.

[49] "Mrs. Lonardo indicted with son in murder," *CPD*, June 13, 1929; "Lonardo's son indicted for feud killing."

[50] "Act to release Mrs. Lonardo," *CP*, June 18, 1929; "Wait surrender of Lonardo son," *CP*, June 19, 1929.

[51] "Slain 'baron' given gangster funeral," *CP*, June 15, 1929; Porrello, p. 108-109.

[52] "U.S. officials fear local killing will bring more deaths," *BT*, June 25, 1929, p. 1.

[53] "Former Batavia man murdered in Buffalo," *Batavia Daily News*, June 25, 1929.

[54] "Fear balks hunt for two killers," *BEN*, June 26, 1929.

[55] "Gunmen answer plea with shots," *BEN*, June 25, 1929; "Former Batavia man murdered in Buffalo;" "U.S. officials fear local killing will bring more deaths;" Ryan, Detective Sergeant James S., Investigation Report to Chief of Detectives John G. Reville, Buffalo Police Department, June 25, 1929.

[56] "Confident of arrest soon, sleuths say," *BCE*, June 26, 1929, p. 13.

[57] News reports of the period incorrectly identified Fred "Lupo" as Randaccio's stepson or son-in-law.

[58] "Two suspects in murder case rounded up by Buffalo police, one denied owning slayers' car," *Batavia Daily News*, June 26, 1929; "Discovery of death car is back of move," *BT*, June 26, 1929, p. 1; "Claim man held is murder car owner," *Buffalo Evening Times*, June 27, 1929.

[59] "Fear balks hunt for two killers."

[60] "Court releases two men held in murder case," *BCE*, June 29, 1929.

[61] Porrello, p. 111-113.

[62] Zicarelli, Detective Carl, Information report to Inspector Cody of the Cleveland Police Detective Bureau, Nov. 16, 1929.

[63] Porrello, p. 116-118; U.S. Census of 1930. At the time the census was taken on April 1, 1930, both Lonardo and Sospirato were inmates at the Cuyahoga County Jail.

[64] Porrello, p. 120-121.

[65] "Suspirato held in Porello quiz," *CPD*, Feb. 27, 1932; "Jail Lonardo in probe of feud killings," *CPD*, Feb. 28, 1932.

[66] "Pittsburgh gang leader murdered by racket rivals," *Clearfield PA Progress*, Aug. 7, 1929, p. 1; "Sleuths hunt gang killers of racketeer," *Pittsburgh Post-Gazette*, Aug. 8, 1929, p. 1.

[67] Hunt, Thomas and Michael A. Tona, "A test of resolve: The 1932 Mafia murder of Pittsburgh boss John Bazzano," *On the Spot Journal*, summer, 2008, p. 8.

[68] Giuseppe Siragusa Petition for Naturalization, May 23, 1923.

[69] Siragusa's alliance with the conservative Mafiosi in New York could have dated from the period 1910-1912, when he was a New York resident. It is possible that he was a D'Aquila disciple in the pattern of Philadelphia Mafia boss Salvatore Sabella.

[70] Ove, Torsten, "Mafia has long history here, growing from bootlegging days," *Pittsburgh Post-Gazette*, Nov. 6, 2000; Gentile, p. 113-114, 118.

[71] Terranova's Prohibition Era presence in the Buffalo area is documented. On Jan. 9, 1925, he was granted a pistol permit from Erie County, New York.

[72] World War I draft registration card, 1917.

[73] U.S. Census of 1930. Though Reina was killed in February 1930, he was listed at the Rochambeau Avenue address in the census taken on April 5, 1930.

[74] World War I draft registration cards, 1917. The cards of both brothers showed home addresses of 227 East 107th Street and business addresses of 313 East 103rd Street.

[75] New York assessment records indicate that the home was newly built in 1930.

[76] Their homes were located roughly within a city block of each other.

[77] Critchley, David, *The Origin of Organized Crime in America: The New York City Mafia, 1891-1931*, New York: Routledge, 2009, p. 149. Interestingly, the New York criminal case People v. Rizzo et al. of 1927 related to an attempt by Charles Rizzo, Anthony J. Dorio, Thomas Milo and John Thomasello to rob the $1,200 payroll of United Lathing Company on Jan. 14. The four men believed the payroll was being carried by Charles Rao, and they went in search of Rao. Rizzo was an employee of the firm and told his conspirators he could identify Rao. Police intercepted them before they located their target. In this case, the involvement of leading Mafiosi in the lathing enterprise was apparently insufficient to ward off robbers. However, it is possible that the company was targeted because of the involvement of underworld leaders. Years later, Milo and a son of his were linked with rackets controlled by the Genovese Crime Family.

[78] Maas, Peter, *The Valachi Papers*, New York: G.P. Putnam's Sons, 1968, p. 75.

[79] Maas, p. 82-83. Valachi might have saved his own life by refusing the contract on Livorsi. The Reina Mafia probably approached Valachi – known to be outside of the Mafia – in order to keep from being linked to the murder. If Valachi had done as asked, the Reina leadership could have killed Valachi to keep its involvement in the Livorsi slaying secret.

[80] Democratic Mayor James J. Walker defeated Republican challenger Fiorello H. LaGuardia by a more than two-to-one margin. LaGuardia ran an anti-Tammany campaign, and the Democratic machine mobilized to defeat him soundly. Charges that Walker's administration was corrupt and that Walker himself did not take his responsibilities seriously were largely ignored in the 1929 election. However, they later resurfaced, and Walker was forced to resign in 1932. A wave of reform brought LaGuardia into the mayor's office in 1933.

[81] "Vitale recognized ex-crooks at dinner; one suspect seized," *NYT*, Dec. 17, 1929, p. 1. Vitale said he vacationed at Hot Springs, West Virginia. There seems to be no community with that name. There is, however, a small unincorporated community named Hot Springs in the western portion of the state of Virginia. Ciro Terranova later also made reference to this community. It also is possible that Vitale was referring to White Sulphur Springs, West Virginia, a very popular resort community about 40 miles from Hot Springs, Virginia.

[82] "7 of Vitale guests had police records, Whalen declares," *NYT*, Dec. 13, 1929, p. 1.

[83] U.S. Census of 1930. Vitale lived with his wife and three children at 872 East 180th Street.

[84] "Vitale recognized ex-crooks..."

[85] "7 of Vitale guests had police records."

[86] "$5,000 loot taken at Vitale dinner," *NYT*, Dec. 9, 1929, p. 14.

[87] "Vitale told not to 'worry' in an underworld letter which said 'it's all fixed,'" *NYT*, Dec. 31, 1929, p. 1.

[88] "Judiciary: A judge's friends," *TIME*, Jan. 6, 1930; "Vitale recovered detective's pistol 2 hours after theft," *NYT*, Dec. 24, 1929, p. 1.

[89] "Vitale recovered detective's pistol...;" "Vitale must tell M'Adoo of dinner," *NYT*, Dec. 14, 1929, p. 3.

[90] "Seize three guests of Vitale dinner," *NYT*, Dec. 30, 1929, p. 1; "Terranova appears to talk to police; jailed in hold-up," *NYT*, Jan. 16, 1930, p. 1. Terranova claimed he

knew Vitale only casually, but he revealed that the two men met while both were vacationing far from the Bronx in Hot Springs, Virginia. Ciro Terranova also had ties to Buffalo. Records of the Erie County Clerk's Office listed Terranova's application for a pistol license on Jan. 9, 1925, with a 231 Niagara Street address.

[91] Terranova's wife, Teresa "Tessie" Catania, was the sister of Joseph and James Catania's father.

[92] " 'Dutch' Schultz seized, his companion shot as they show fight when accosted by police," *NYT*, June 18, 1931, p. 1; "Began as street hoodlum," *NYT*, Nov. 29, 1934, p. 2.

[93] "Vitale recognized ex-crooks at dinner..." Daniel Iamascia's older brother, Anthony Edward Iamascia, was educated at Fordham University and worked as an insurance agent.

[94] "Vitale must tell M'Adoo..."

[95] "Assails silence on Vitale dinner," *NYT*, Dec. 15, 1929, p. 18.

[96] "Vitale recognized ex-crooks at dinner..."

[97] "$5,000 loot taken at Vitale dinner;" "Vitale must tell M'Adoo..." A list of 60 attendees was reportedly created by police officers responding to the robbery. There was a delay in reporting the incident, and any number of guests could have departed before police arrived.

[98] "Vitale recognized ex-crooks at dinner..."

[99] Remarks attributed to both Terranova and Vitale indicated that the robbery was performed by "boys from downtown, around Kenmare Street." Some have misunderstood that as a reference to Masseria's Lower East Side organization. Police arrested one suspect, Joseph Bravate, 22, of 185 Chrystie Street, on Dec. 16. Bravate's home address was within two blocks of Kenmare Street. He told police he worked as a chauffeur. Though a number of the guests at the Vitale dinner identified Bravate as one of the robbers, he was not convicted. Later suspicion focused on gangster "Trigger Mike" Coppola. Decades later, Coppola served as a lieutenant in the Genovese Crime Family, which had once been Masseria's gang. Though this too seems to point an accusing finger in Masseria's direction, at the time of the Vitale dinner robbery, Coppola appears to have been associated with non-Mafia underworld organizations. Those gangs struggled against each other through the early 1930s. In 1929, Jack "Legs" Diamond, leader of one of the gangs - a Manhattan-based bootlegging ring - was fighting a losing war in the Bronx against Terranova's underworld ally Dutch Schultz.

[100] "Wealthy ice dealer slain in doorway," *NYT*, Feb. 27, 1930, p. 3; Maas, p. 86; Bonanno, p. 106. Reina's mistress, widow Mrs. James Ennis, told police she and Reina formerly shared an apartment on the Grand Concourse. The Sheridan Avenue apartment was rented about five months before Reina was killed.

[101] "Petrosino's successor terror of Italian criminals," *NYT*, Sept. 24, 1911, p. SM 8.

[102] Bonanno, p. 106, Maas, p. 86-87. Maas learned from Valachi that the Reina lieutenants were very cautious recruiting members for their splinter group. Valachi was only informed of their plot against Pinzolo after Valachi made clear his intense dislike of the new boss.

[103] Despite his nickname, Sharkey was born in Binghamton, New York. At the time of the match with Scott, promoters were working to arrange a championship fight

between Sharkey and Max Schmeling in New York City. The Sharkey-Schmeling fight was held in June at Yankee Stadium. Schmeling was awarded the heavyweight title after one ring judge ruled that he had been fouled by Sharkey.

[104] "Sport: Sharkey v. Scott," *TIME*, March 10, 1930. Scott insisted that Sharkey hit him low. Referee Lou Magnolia dismissed the claim and later called Scott "the yellowest bum I ever saw. For ten cents I'd take him into any cellar and give him a licking myself."

[105] "Arrest 19 at Miami in gambling clean-up," *NYT*, March 2, 1930, p. 33; "Gamblers held in Miami Beach raid," *Charleston WV Daily Mail*, March 1, 1930, p. 1; "Police find $73,000 cash in Miami gambling raid," *Syracuse NY Herald*, March 1, 1930, p. 1. Eighteen men were arrested at the hotel. They were Joe Masseria, John Masseria, Charles Luciano, Charles Harris, Philip Mayo, Michael George, James Lynch, Paddy Francis, Joseph Ross, Walter Hausen, William Gore, John Carnavale, Lon Shepard, James Murray, John Spiro, Harry Brown, Harry Eider and Harry Rosen. Frank Jacone was arrested when he arrived at the county jail to provide bond for the others. Harry Rosen was possibly Harry "Nig Rosen" Stromberg, a Philadelphia-based former ally of underworld financier Arnold Rothstein and a partner of Luciano's friend Meyer Lansky.

[106] Bonanno, p. 102.

[107] Kavieff, Paul R., *The Violent Years: Prohibition and the Detroit Mobs*, Fort Lee, NJ: Barricade Books, 2001, p. 57-58.

[108] Some researchers believe Milazzo was the sole boss of Detroit's East Side Mafia at this time.

[109] Morton, James, *Gangland International: An Informal History of the Mafia and other Mobs in the Twentieth Century*, Little, Brown and Company, 1999, p. 157; Kavieff, p. 58-59.

[110] "Riddled by lead slugs," *Detroit Free Press*, June 1, 1930, p. 1; Kavieff, p. 60; Gaspari Milazzo Death Certificate, reg. no. 7571, June 1, 1930, Michigan Department of Health.

[111] Bonanno, p. 102.

[112] Bonanno, p. 106-107.

[113] Bonanno, p. 100-101.

[114] Bonanno, p. 96.

[115] "Police guard at funeral," *NYT*, July 17, 1930, p. 2.

[116] "2 Brooklyn men die in shootings," *New York Evening Post*, July 15, 1930, p. 3. The *Post* reported that Bonventre closed up his bakery at 115 Roebling Street eight years earlier.

[117] Bonanno, p. 86-87.

[118] Vito Bonventre Death Certificate reg. no. 14800, July 15, 1930, Department of Health, City of New York.

[119] "Alcohol 'ruler' shot to death at Brooklyn home," *New York Herald*, July 16, 1930.

[120] "Alcohol 'ruler' shot to death at Brooklyn home;" "The King shot to death while opening garage," *New York Tribune*, July 16, 1930.

[121] "Alcohol 'ruler' shot to death at Brooklyn home."

[122] "Police guard at funeral."

[123] Bonanno, p. 103.
[124] Gentile, p. 97. Gentile recalled, "This situation profited Salvatore Maranzano who, then organizing a group of dissident hoodlums he called 'exiles,' began to inflame at first the minds of his [Castellammarese] countrymen, urging them to avenge Milazzo. He then turned to the Palermitani, urging them to revenge Toto D' Aquila, who also had fallen due to Masseria's material desires. This method of behavior yielded fruit, because many young men, yearning to avenge their friends, sympathized with the position of the new leader, and in this way the group soon became numerous."
[125] Bonanno, p. 104.
[126] Kelly, Ralph, "Murder in Cleveland: The Prohibition toll, Chapter 10 – (1930) The Porellos couldn't make any money," *CPD*, Jan. 1933; "Police have no corn sugar sales records," *CP*, May 11, 1931.
[127] "Porello brother is shot down in Woodland store," *CP*, July 26, 1930; Kelly, Ralph, "Murder in Cleveland: The Prohibition toll, Chapter 10…"
[128] "Only 3 left of seven Porrellos," *CPD*, Feb. 26, 1932.
[129] Kelly, Ralph, "Murder in Cleveland: The Prohibition toll, Chapter 9 – (1929-1930) Komissarow loved Lake Erie," *CPD*, Jan. 1933.
[130] Kelly, Ralph, "Murder in Cleveland: The Prohibition toll, Chapter 9…"
[131] Nicaso, p. 132-134.
[132] Nicaso, p. 135-136.
[133] Nicaso, p. 144.
[134] Nicaso, p. 135-136.
[135] Gentile, p. 97.
[136] Morello, p. 94, 96.
[137] Bonanno, p. 105; Maas, p. 88; Birth Certificate of Sebastiano Domingo. Domingo, born in Castellammare del Golfo on May 7, 1902, was known to Valachi as "Buster from Chicago." However, the gunman appears to have lived in Benton Harbor, Michigan, a town about 100 miles from Chicago. The Benton Harbor area often was visited by vacationing underworld figures from Chicago.
[138] Maas, p. 89.
[139] Bonanno, p. 96-97.
[140] Maas, p. 89; Bonanno, p. 96-97.
[141] Bonanno, p. 105.
[142] Maria Morello had married Gioacchino "Jack" Lima. The Limas had four grown children living with them at 352 East 116th Street. The youngest of those, 23-year-old Calogero, was Giuseppe Morello's godson.
[143] "Harlem racket gang murders two in raid," *NYT*, Aug. 16, 1930, p. 1.
[144] Maas, p. 88.
[145] Piraino was possibly related to a number of Brooklyn racketeers with the same surname. Bootlegger Stefano Piraino of Eighteenth Street in Brooklyn was killed in a liquor-related quarrel in December 1922 ("Dry navy laid up," *NYT*, Dec. 31, 1922, p. 1). Giuseppe "the Clutching Hand" Piraino of Seventy-seventh Street, a rackets leader in Brooklyn for at least a decade, was murdered March 27, 1930

("Racketeer slain in Brooklyn street," *NYT*, March 28, 1930, p. 1). Giuseppe Piraino's 21-year-old son Carmelo was killed about six months later. He was shot to death at dusk on October 6 in front of the Abyla Court Apartments, 1857 Eighty-fifth Street in Brooklyn. (Carmelo Piraino Death Certificate, reg. no. 19637, Oct. 6, 1930, Department of Health of the City of New York; "Son of 'the Clutching Hand' shot dead; fate of Piraino like that of his father," *NYT*, Oct. 6, 1930, p. 31.) The killing of Carmelo seems to have been unrelated to underworld feuds. It likely was a disciplinary action resulting from a domestic dispute five days earlier. Police were called after Piraino ended that quarrel by slashing his wife's face with a knife. In a March 12, 1932, interrogation at Sing Sing Prison's "death house," convicted killer Peter Sardini recalled that the subsequent order to kill Carmelo Piraino was given by Manfredi Mineo and executed by Salvatore "Sally the Sheik" Musacchio. Sardini's statement was discounted by the authorities as an effort to avoid capital punishment.

[146] "Harlem racket gang murders two in raid."

[147] Giuseppe Morello Death Certificate reg. no. 19631, Aug. 15, 1930, Department of Health of the City of New York.

[148] Maas, p. 88.

[149] "Man slain by five shots in Broadway office in mad-afternoon not discovered till 10 p.m.," *NYT*, Sept. 6, 1930, p.1; Bonaventura Pinzolo Death Certificate reg. no. 20943, Sept. 5, 1930, Department of Health of the City of New York.

[150] "Man slain by five shots in Broadway office...;" *NYT*, Sept. 6, 1930, p.1; Feinberg, Alexander, "Analysis of his testimony before board unfolds unsavory record," *NYT*, Nov. 22, 1952, p. 1; Maas, p. 87. Valachi recalled that Girolamo "Bobby Doyle" Santuccio was responsible for murdering Pinzolo.

[151] Maas, p. 88.

[152] LeGrand, Alexander P., "La Cosa Nostra," FBI file #92-262, May 28, 1964. The FBI noted that a number of Aiello's underworld associates migrated to Milwaukee, Wisconsin, in this period. Among them were his brother Sam, Joe Caminiti and Migele Mineo. In the few months leading up to Aiello's ambush, his ally Jack Zuta and his gunmen Peter "Ashcan" Inserio and Jack Costa were killed.

[153] Bonanno, p. 119-120.

[154] "Chicago warrants name 26 gangsters," *NYT*, Sept. 17, 1930, p. 26; Bonanno, p. 108. Bonanno appears to have incorrectly recalled that this arrest occurred on a Thursday. It occurred on a Tuesday. The newspaper account referred to Bonanno as "Joseph Bonventre" and to DiBenedetto as "Charles DeDenetto." According to the *Times*, police found two revolvers, two machine gun drums and ten small boxes of ammunition. Bonanno recalled that machine guns were discovered in the vehicle's back seat.

[155] "Bloodstained gun found in trunk," *BEN*, Sept. 17, 1930.

[156] A Bonanno driver's license was issued in the name "Giuseppe Bonventre" and included a Bonventre family address of 4009 Church Avenue, Brooklyn.

[157] Bonanno, p. 110-114.

[158] Calogero "Charley Buffalo" DiBenedetto's address in Buffalo, New York, was listed as 419 Prospect Avenue. According to the 1930 U.S. Census, other members of the household included his mother Rose, sister Sarah, brother Joseph, sister

Antonia Bonventre and her daughter Petrina.
[159] "Bloodstained gun found in trunk."
[160] Bonanno, p. 114.
[161] Bonanno, p. 119-120.
[162] "Slain Aiello's partner comes out of hiding," *CT*, Oct. 28, 1930, p. 4.
[163] "Joe Aiello slain in ambush," *CT*, Oct. 24, 1930, p. 1.
[164] "Slain Aiello's partner comes out of hiding."
[165] Bonanno, p. 107, 120.
[166] Maas, p. 88-92; Bonanno, p. 119-120.
[167] Manfredi Mineo Death Certificate, reg. no. 8617, Nov. 5, 1930, Department of Health of the City of New York.
[168] "Two men shot dead in Bronx gun-trap," *NYT*, Nov. 6, 1930, p. 27.
[169] Bonanno, p. 120.
[170] Bonanno, p. 120-121.
[171] Gentile, p. 104. According to Gentile, Masseria was warned by "*il capo della polizia*," or the chief of police. He was perhaps referring to New York Police Commissioner Edward P. Mulrooney, who took office in May 1930. Mulrooney was a uniquely streetwise commissioner, having risen through the ranks of the NYPD.
[172] Gentile, p. 102-103.
[173] Gentile, p. 104.
[174] Gentile, p. 103-104.
[175] Gentile, p. 105.
[176] Gentile, p. 106; Bonanno, p. 121.
[177] Gentile, p. 107-109.
[178] "Police slay thug who defied search," *NYT*, Jan. 20, 1931, p. 5; Giuseppe Parrino Death Certificate, reg. no. 2435, Jan. 19, 1931, Department of Health of the City of New York; Bonanno, p. 107. Bonanno made it appear that Parrino was murdered immediately after his appointment by Masseria.
[179] The candy store was located near an oddly shaped intersection of Belmont Avenue, Crescent Avenue and East 186th Street, two blocks east of Arthur Avenue in the Bronx.
[180] "Bail runner shot in street ambush," *NYT*, Feb. 4, 1931, p. 11; "Catania dies of wounds," *NYT*, Feb. 5, 1931, p. 26.
[181] Joseph Catania Death Certificate, reg. no. 1453, Feb. 4, 1931, Department of Health of the City of New York.
[182] Maas, p. 100-102.
[183] Maas, p. 102.
[184] "10,000 at funeral of 'Joe the Baker,'" *NYT*, Feb. 8, 1931, p. 30; Maas, p. 102. Maas estimated the price of Catania's coffin at $15,000. These coffin price tags were almost certainly exaggerations.
[185] "Mob leader 'put on spot,' belief of investigators," *Detroit Free Press*, Feb. 8, 1931, p. 1.

[186] "Craft link in LaMare case seen," *Detroit Free Press*, Feb. 9, 1931.

[187] "Loved LaMare, widow avows," *Detroit Free Press*, Feb. 8, 1931, p. 2.

[188] Gentile, p. 111.

Chapter 17

[1] Gentile, p. 111.

[2] Bonanno, p. 121-122; Maas, p. 103.

[3] Bonanno, p. 122.

[4] "Racket chief slain by gangster gunfire," *NYT*, April 16, 1931, p. 1. The Nuova Villa Tammaro restaurant was located between Hart Place and Neptune Avenue.

[5] "Gangster's death laid to 'friends,'" *Washington Post*, April 17, 1931, p. 4; "Police mystified in slaying of 'boss,'" *NYT*, April 17, 1931, p. 17.

[6] Bonanno, p. 122.

[7] Bonanno, p. 122; Gentile, p. 111-112; Maas, p. 104; Flynn, James P., "La Cosa Nostra," FBI file NY 92-2300, July 1, 1963, p. 14; "Questioned in murder," *NYT*, April 20, 1931, p. 4; Statement of confidential informant, Murder Inc. case files, Kings County NY District Attorney. Bonanno indicated that Luciano was present. Gentile explained that he was supposed to have lunch that day with Masseria, Genovese, Biondo, Mangano and LoVerde. Gentile insisted that he and LoVerde arrived at the restaurant moments after Masseria had been shot. Flynn reported that Masseria met Gentile, Biondo, Mangano and LoVerde for lunch. The *Times* article reported that police questioned Pollaccia in connection with Masseria's slaying. Authorities believe Pollaccia attended lunch with Masseria that day. (The article also stated that Pollaccia had been in the vicinity of the Alhambra apartments in the Bronx when Mineo and Ferrigno were shot to death.) The informant noted the presence of Carfano at the restaurant that afternoon. According to Maas, Valachi believed that Luciano, Genovese, Livorsi and Stracci were present.

[8] "Racket chief slain by gangster gunfire."

[9] Gentile, p. 112.

[10] "Racket chief slain by gangster gunfire."

[11] "Police mystified in slaying of 'boss.'"

[12] "Racket chief slain by gangster gunfire;" "Police mystified in slaying of 'boss;'" "Giuseppe Massaria, alias 'Joe-the-boss,' dec'd 4-14-31," Memo of the Kings County District Attorney's Office, DA-83, Nov. 27, 1940.

[13] "Racket chief slain by gangster gunfire."

[14] "Police mystified in slaying of 'boss.'"

[15] Gentile, p. 112; Flynn, "La Cosa Nostra," p. 14. The similarity in these accounts is no coincidence. Flynn based his report on Gentile's recollections.

[16] Gentile, p. 113; Flynn, "La Cosa Nostra," p. 15; Bonanno, p. 127.

[17] "Flowers fill 16 cars at gangster funeral," *NYT*, April 21, 1931, p. 34.

[18] McNeeley, Detective Patrick, Report to Inspector Cornelius Cody, Cleveland Police Department, May 10, 1931.

[19] McNeeley.

[20] "Police have no corn sugar sales records," *CP*, May 11, 1931.

[21] Cavolo, Detective Charles, Report to Inspector Cornelius Cody, Cleveland Police Department, May 10, 1931.

[22] "Lured to tenement, shot dead by gang," *NYT*, May 11, 1931, p. 4; Certificate of Death of John Giustra, No. 13268, May 10, 1931, Department of Health of the City of New York.

[23] "Giuseppe Massaria, alias 'Joe-the-boss,' dec'd 4-14-31." With the victory of the anti-Masseria forces, it seems unlikely that Johnny Giustra would have been killed for taking part in Masseria's assassination, as the informant suggested. It is more probable, given the circumstances and the emotional distress implied by the left-behind coat, that Giustra was murdered because he refused to participate in the anti-Masseria conspiracy.

[24] "Scarpato slain in reprisal for Joe the Boss," *New York Herald*, Sept. 12, 1932, p. 3. The *Herald* stated that Giustra and Liconti were partners in an undertaking establishment in Brooklyn. The newspaper appeared to be referring to the Guariano, Liconti and Giustra firm of Henry Street, which managed Giustra's funeral.

[25] The reputed underworld hostility toward Johnny Giustra and Carmelo Liconti is traditionally viewed as evidence that the two men had been the assassins of Masseria. However, following the assassination, Masseria opponents were in control of the American Mafia, and the hostility is easier to explain if Giustra and Liconti were Masseria loyalists.

[26] "Capone aide slain in midtown hotel," *NYT*, July 10, 1931, p. 40. According to "Police round up eight," *NYT*, Dec. 3, 1923, p. 19, Carmelo Liconti was arrested Dec. 2, 1923, in connection with the April 1923 murder of Biagio Giordano. The arrest occurred in a police raid on a restaurant dinner party on Columbia Street in Brooklyn. In addition to Liconti, police arrested Giovanni Mangravite (also charged in the Giordano killing) and Ignazio "the Wolf" Lupo (arrested for "acting in concert").

[27] Certificate of Death of John Giustra.

[28] "Trace gangster gun," *CP*, May 18, 1931.

[29] Information provided by Calvary Cemetery, Cleveland, Ohio.

[30] Maas, p. 104-107.

[31] Bonanno, p. 125-126.

[32] Bonanno, p. 127-128.

[33] Giovanni Montana was born in Montedoro, Sicily, on July 1, 1893, to Calogero Montana and Rosa Valenti (Birth Certificate #104).

[34] "John C. Montana," *BEN*, Sept. 11, 1931, p. 25.

[35] Bonanno, p. 128.

[36] Bonanno, p. 128.

[37] Flynn, "La Cosa Nostra," p. 15.

[38] Giuseppe Siragusa Naturalization Petition, U.S. District Court, Pittsburgh, May 23, 1923; Siragusa Declaration of Intention to Become a Citizen, Pittsburgh, Sept. 14, 1920.

[39] Ove, Torsten, "Mafia has long history here, growing from bootlegging days,"

Pittsburgh Post-Gazette, Nov. 6, 2000; "Siragusa, respected baker, yields to greed, dies in attempt to rule gangs," *PP*, Aug. 3, 1932.

[40] Marriage certificate of John Bazzano and Rosina Zappala, State of New York, Feb. 9, 1924; World War I Draft Registration, New Kensington, PA, June 5, 1917; Certificate of Arrival for Giovanni Bazsano [sic], U.S. Department of Labor Immigration Service; Bazzano Naturalization Petition, Feb. 22, 1915; "War to rule city rackets is revealed," *PP*, July 30, 1932.

[41] Gentile, p. 113-114.

[42] "4,000,000 payment offered by Capone," *NYT*, June 14, 1931, p. 1.

[43] "$4,000,000 payment offered by Capone."

[44] Wilson, Frank J., "In re: Alphonse Capone," report to chief of the Intelligence Unit of the Bureau of Internal Revenue, Treasury Department, Dec. 21, 1933.

[45] "Johnson bares Capone 'deal' in income case," *CT*, April 3, 1932, p. 1.

[46] The address of the Hotel Paramount was 235 West 46th Street.

[47] "Capone aide slain in midtown hotel," *NYT*, July 10, 1931, p. 40.

[48] Maas, p. 107.

[49] SAC Buffalo, Memo, March 31, 1965, enclosure p. 24.

[50] SAC Buffalo, Memo, March 31, 1965, enclosure p. 21.

[51] "5,000 dine in relays at religious feast," *NYT*, Aug. 2, 1931, p. 20; "Police search men at three-day dinner," *NYT*, Aug. 3, 1931, p. 4.

[52] Gentile, p. 115.

[53] Maas, p. 107.

[54] It is interesting that Maranzano chose to screen this fundraising dinner behind the Maritime Society of Sciacca. A Mafia network based in Sciacca threw its weight behind Maranzano's opponent Giuseppe Masseria in the Castellammarese War. The coastal city of Sciacca sits about a dozen miles southeast of Masseria's birthplace in Menfi. There is some suggestion that Maranzano called for retribution against all Sciaccatani following the close of the war.

[55] "5,000 dine in relays at religious feast."

[56] Gentile, p. 116.

[57] Bonanno, p. 129.

[58] Bonanno, p. 130; Maas, p. 108.

[59] Bonanno, p. 132.

[60] Bonanno, p. 133-134.

[61] The 34-story New York Central Building actually straddles Park Avenue. Built in 1929, it has more recently been known as the Helmsley Building.

[62] "Gang kills suspect in alien smuggling," *NYT*, Sept. 11, 1931, p. 1.

[63] Maas, p. 110.

[64] "Gang kills suspect in alien smuggling."

[65] Though not counted in this total, Giuseppe Morello's murder also fell within the timeframe. A former holder of the boss of bosses title, he did not hold the title at the time he was killed.

[66] "Gang kills suspect in alien smuggling;" "Suspect in alien smuggling ring killed by

gang," *CT*, Sept. 11, 1931, p. 8; "Clues to alien ring sought in notebook," *NYT*, Sept. 13, 1931, p. 4.

[67] "Seek official link in alien smuggling," *NYT*, Sept. 12, 1931, p. 14.

[68] "51 names listed in notebook of slain smuggler," *New York Herald*, Sept. 12, 1931, p. 3.

[69] Jackson later denied signing the pistol permit application and claimed the signature on it was a forgery.

[70] "Lee Jackson on pistol permit," *Poughkeepsie Evening Star*, Sept. 11, 1931, p. 34; "Tracing check in murder quiz," *Poughkeepsie Eagle News*, Sept. 12, 1931, p. 1.

[71] "Tracing check in murder quiz."

[72] "Seek official link in alien smuggling;" "Smuggler's murderers are traces to Buffalo," *BT*, Sept. 12, 1931, p. 1; "Detectives to visit Buffalo in killer hunt," *BCE*, Sept. 12, 1931, p. 18.

[73] Bonanno, p. 139.

[74] SAC Buffalo, Memo, March 31, 1965, enclosure p. 10. Magaddino recalled, "When Maranzano died, I was the one who managed things so that no one got killed."

[75] Bonanno, p. 137; Gentile, p. 118.

[76] Gentile, p. 118.

[77] "Siragusa, respected baker, yields to greed, dies in attempt to rule gangs," *PP*, Aug. 3, 1932.

[78] Maas, p. 119.

[79] Gentile, p. 118. According to Bonanno, Frank Scalise held the position of boss over the former D'Aquila-Mineo crime family during Maranzano's reign. After Maranzano's assassination, Scalise, who had been a strong Maranzano supporter, stepped down and was succeeded by Vincenzo Mangano.

[80] Bonanno, p. 141.

[81] Gentile, p. 119. Bonanno recalled the composition of the first Commission differently. He omitted Milano and included Magaddino. However, it seems likely that Magaddino was substituted for Milano shortly after the Commission was formed.

[82] Bonanno, p. 160.

[83] "Gang king is convicted of evading taxes," *BCE*, Oct. 18, 1931. Capone was sentenced Oct. 24 to serve 11 years in federal prison and to pay a $50,000 fine plus court costs. The Chicago boss was denied bail and held temporarily in Cook County Jail while he appealed. His appeals were exhausted on May 2, 1932. Two days later, he was transferred to Atlanta Federal Prison.

[84] Flynn, "La Cosa Nostra," p. 11.

[85] "Inn owner slain; body found in sack," *NYT*, Sept. 12, 1932, p. 11.

[86] "Translated transcription of the life of Nicolo Gentile," p. 115-116. This document, dating from the early 1940s, appears to be an FBI translation of the Gentile manuscript that through later edits became his book, *Vita di Capomafia*. No such document survives in FBI archives, however numerous Bureau documents refer to the translation. A May 15, 1963, memo from SAC New York to the FBI director, entitled, "La Causa Nostra," provided some explanation. According to the memo, Mario Brod, a former CIC operative in Sicily and later contract employee of the

CIA, developed Nicola Gentile as a source around 1942 – after Gentile had returned there to escape U.S. drug charges. At that time, Gentile may have been trying to negotiate for his return to the U.S. Gentile shared a copy of his manuscript with Brod, who discouraged the Mafioso from writing any more. A translation of the document shared with Brod, accompanied by a July 1, 1963, memo from Special Agent James P. Flynn of the FBI, was circulated among FBI field offices. The Pollaccia incident described in the manuscript was not mentioned in Gentile's *Vita di Capomafia*.

[87] "War to rule city rackets is revealed," *PP*, July 30, 1932; "Racket chiefs shot down by three gunmen," *Pittsburgh Post-Gazette*, July 30, 1932; "Three gang chiefs die in Pittsburgh," *NYT*, Sat., July 30, 1932, p. 28.

[88] Gentile, p. 121.

[89] Gentile, p. 122.

[90] "Spinelli linked to abandoned auto," *PP*, Aug. 12, 1932; "Underworld fears more killings," *PP*, Aug. 12, 1932.

[91] "Hotel record bares names of two men," *PP*, Aug. 15, 1932.

[92] Tito returned to Pittsburgh. Spinelli crossed into Canada and then sailed back to Italy. U.S. officials were unsuccessful in their attempts to have him extradited. Italian officials permitted him to be tried in that country in 1934 for the Volpe murders. He was convicted of premeditated homicide and sentenced to 30 years in prison. He died in prison in 1959 at the age of 65.

[93] Gentile, p. 122-123.

[94] Gentile, p. 123; "Man with face blacked found slain in sack," *Brooklyn Daily Eagle*, Aug. 8, 1932; "Body of man found in sack, victim knifed," *Brooklyn Daily Citizen*, Aug. 8, 1932, p. 1; "Arrest of 14 foils murder fete plan," *NYT*, Aug. 18, 1932, p. 20.

[95] Gentile, p. 123.

[96] "Man with face blacked found slain in sack;" "Body of man found in sack, victim knifed."

[97] "Arrests link Bazzano with slaying here," *PP*, Aug. 18, 1932; "Raid by police spoils party to pay off killers," *Zanesville (OH) Times Recorder*, Aug. 18, 1932, p. 1; "John Bazzano put on spot in New York," *PP*, Aug. 11, 1932; "Pittsburgh kin identifies sack murder victim," *New York Herald*, Aug. 12, 1932, p. 12; "Underworld fears more killings," *PP*, Aug. 12, 1932; "Home shaken, auto wrecked by explosion," *PP*, Aug. 13, 1932; Death certificate of John Bozzano [sic], Department of Health of the City of New York.

[98] "14 arrested in Volpe spite gang murder," *Syracuse Herald*, Wed., Aug. 17, 1932, p. 1; "Arrests link Bazzano with slaying here;" "Arrest of 14 foils murder fete plan."

[99] "7 seized as gangsters," *NYT*, Sat., Feb. 14, 1931, p. 3; "Suspects held without bail," *PP*, Aug. 17, 1932. Bonasera was seriously wounded in a January 1931 shootout. Police stated that he was shot at more often than the late Jack "Legs" Diamond. Oddo suffered a gunshot wound weeks later. Though they occurred during the period of the Castellammarese War, these shootings are generally not considered part of the war, as the Profaci organization maintained its neutrality.

[100] Birth record of Cassandro Salvatore Bonasera, Vallelunga, Sicily, certificate #123, June 18, 1897.

[101] Ellis Island passenger record, *S.S. Madonna*, Jan. 1, 1906; Deposition during Immigration and Naturalization Service deportation hearings, 1954; Marriage certificate for Cassandro S. Bonasera and Sarah Loretta DiCarlo, filed July 12, 1933, Erie County Clerk.

[102] Santo Angelo Volpe was born in Montedoro, Sicily Oct 20, 1879 (Birth Certificate #112). Volpe is widely credited with forming the first Mafia clan in Pennsylvania's coal-mining region in 1908. John Sciandra, formerly of Buffalo, succeeded Volpe as leader of the Scranton-Pittston crime family from about 1933-1940. Sciandra was born in Montedoro, Sicily April 10, 1899 (Birth Certificate #53). Joe Barbara led the crime family until his heart attack in 1956, when Rosario Bufalino became boss of the Scranton-Pittston crime family. Santo Volpe was not related to the Volpe brothers killed in Pittsburgh in 1932.

[103] "Witnesses to be called for DiCarlo today," *BCE*, May 4, 1932; "Samuel DiCarlo guilty," *BCE*, May 5, 1932; "Sack murder suspect brother of public enemy," *Syracuse Herald*, Wed., Aug. 17, 1932, p. 1.

[104] "14 arrested in Volpe spite gang murder."

[105] "14 men held for Bazzano killing freed," *Brooklyn Citizen*, Aug. 17, 1932; "Mystery hems 'murder ring' case collapse," *Brooklyn Daily Eagle*, Aug. 20, 1932..

[106] Statement of confidential informant, Murder Inc. case files, Kings County NY District Attorney. The informant noted that Scarpato began collecting protection payments from him after the 1930 murder of Joseph Piraino.

[107] "Inn owner slain; body found in sack;" "Scarpato slain in reprisal for Joe the Boss." The *Times* reported that Scarpato's tattoo was on his right arm. The *Herald* reported it was on his left. Scarpato's panic suggests that he considered himself a strong Masseria ally and felt that his fate was entwined with Masseria's.

[108] Manifest of the *S.S. Saturnia*, arrived New York City on June 1, 1932. The manifest notes that the Scarpato's obtained their passports on Aug. 8, 1931, within a week of the Maranzano banquet.

[109] "Inn owner slain; body found in sack."

[110] "Scarpato slain in reprisal for Joe the Boss." The address of the Seaside Inn was 1306 Surf Avenue. The Nathan's Famous delicatessen occupies 1308-1310 Surf Avenue.

[111] "Inn owner slain; body found in sack."

[112] "Scarpato slain in reprisal for Joe the Boss." This method of strangulation became known as the "Sicilian Knot" and as the "Italian Rope Trick."

[113] "Police question Pisano on slaying of Scarpato," *New York Herald*, Sept. 13, 1932, p. 1.

[114] Scarpato's wife continued to operate the Nuova Villa Tammaro restaurant for some time after her husband's murder. In September of 1936, she was convicted of possessing an unregistered 750-gallon still and a quantity of illicit alcohol. She was brought to trial with two codefendants, Gaetano Soporito and Paul Gelosi. Gelosi pleaded guilty. Soporito was acquitted.

Chapter 18

[1] "Ft. Erie man is kidnapped but refuses $6,000 ransom," *BEN*, Sept. 12, 1930, p. 1;

"Racketeer search reveals records," *BEN*, Sept. 13, 1930, p. 1; "Gangster drive fades as three men are freed," *BCE*, Sept. 13, 1930.

[2] "Gangster drive fades as three men are freed."

[3] "Trio held in kidnapping of Fort Erie man," *BCE*, Sept. 14, 1930, Section 7, p. 1.

[4] "Racketeer search reveals records."

[5] "Gangster drive fades as three men are freed."

[6] Roche was an appointee of Mayor Charles Roesch, who took office in 1930.

[7] "Roche says Buffalo free of gangsters," *BEN*, Sept. 15, 1930.

[8] "Police close office of rum racket union," *BEN*, June 23, 1931.

[9] "Police round up racketeers in guise of union," *BCE*, June 24, 1931, p. 1.

[10] "Racket probers hear extortion ring testimony," *BEN*, June 24, 1931; "Roche holds seven in drive on racketeering," *BCE*, June 25, 1931.

[11] "Man who threatens Joe DiCarlo sought," *BEN*, June 26, 1931, p. 25.

[12] "DiCarlo not held; grand jury reports," *BCE*, June 27, 1931.

[13] "Booze racket indictments to face attack," *BT*, June 28, 1931, p. 2; "Court to dismiss indictments soon," *BEN*, July 7, 1931, p. 36.

[14] Brown, Horace B., "Dynasty of murder," *True Crime*, April 1937, p. 36.

[15] Ritchie's real name was Alberto Verrusio Ricci. He claimed to be descended from Naples nobility.

[16] Brown, Horace B. p. 106; Knapp, Ellis E., "Al Ritchie murdered! Why?" *True Detective Mysteries*, July, 1931, p. 92; Ricci, Alberto Verrusio, "Black Hand exposed at last!" *True Detective Mysteries*, September 1930, p. 26. Brown and Knapp both indicated that Ritchie was born in the U.S. and was educated in Italy as a boy. Ritchie's own article does not mention a U.S. birth and indicates he traveled to the U.S. at the age of 18.

[17] "Buffalo Al not keen sleuth he pictured self," *BCE*, June 8, 1931, p. 1.

[18] "Buffalo Al not keen sleuth he pictured self."

[19] Silverman, William, "Joe Barber's gunmen put scars on Ritchie that gave him name," *BT*, June 10, 1931; Silverman, William, "Camorra spreads terror in Olean and Bradford," *BT*, June 9, 1931, section 2, p. 1; Brown, Horace B., p. 106. According to Silverman, the falling out between Ritchie and the Barbers stems from Ritchie's friendship with businessman Domenico Conte and brothers Fred and Tony Mussari. The Mussaris were set up for assassination by Barber in November of 1922. Conte was reportedly murdered in Salamanca, New York, in 1924 on Joseph Barber's orders. Brown links the feud to expansion of the Bradford-based Barbers into Olean.

[20] "John Barber, Olean man, expires from attackers' bullets," *Olean Evening Times*, May 15, 1925, p. 1.

[21] "Buffalo Al not keen sleuth he pictured self."

[22] "Al Ritchie shot down by gunmen who make escape," *Olean Evening Times*, Sept. 27, 1929, p. 3.

[23] "Ritchie's cunning fools authorities, politicians," *BCE*, June 11, 1931, p. 1; "Ritchie twice narrowly escapes arrest as fixer," *BCE*, June 11, 1931, p. 1.

[24] Knapp, Ellis E., p. 46, 91.

[25] Ricci, Alberto Verrusio, p. 27.

[26] "Joe Barber, alleged Bradford gang leader, taken for last ride," *Olean Evening Times*, May 4, 1931, p. 8; "Allison told of death of Joe Barber by call from Olean is belief," *Olean Evening Times*, May 5, 1931, p. 3.

[27] Knapp, Ellis E., p. 95.

[28] Knapp, Ellis E., p. 44.

[29] Knapp, Ellis E., p. 46; "Al Ritchie victim of slayer's gun fire," *Olean Evening Times*, June 6, 1931, p. 3; "Bradford County official slain, suspect hunted," *New Castle (PA) News*, June 6, 1931, p. 2.

[30] Knapp, Ellis E., p. 96; "Pall bearers for Ritchie get threats," *Olean Evening Times*, June 8, 1931, p. 3.

[31] "Man who threatens Joe DiCarlo sought." Angelo Palmeri gained his U.S. citizenship through naturalization on Jan. 7, 1925.

[32] "Arrest four in alleged attempt to extort money from Falls man," *NG*, Sept. 8, 1931. The 1920 U.S. Census shows brothers Anthony, Frank, Harry and Bernard Falcony, residing together at 205 Main Street, Niagara Falls, and partnering in a restaurant business. (The family name at that time was written "Falcone.") The 1930 U.S. Census shows Anthony Falcone, his wife Mary and their children living at 345 Main Street. The family seems to have immigrated to the U.S. from Caturano, near Naples on the Italian mainland.

[33] "3 held in assault freed," *BEN*, Sept. 28, 1931, p. 28. The 1930 U.S. Census indicated that Amico was the owner of a market in Rochester, NY.

[34] "Free Mangano and gang, held as kidnappers," *CT*, Nov. 12, 1931, p. 7; "Sensational rumors set afloat by Falls undertaker's arrest," *NG*, Nov. 11, 1931, p. 1.

[35] "Free Mangano and gang, held as kidnappers."

[36] "Kidnap victim freed as police hold Mangano," *CT*, Nov. 11, 1931, p. 6.

[37] "Paul Palmeri one of gang suspected of abducting Berg," *NG*, Nov. 10, 1931.

[38] "Seven held in murders," *NYT*, Dec. 28, 1925, p. Amusements 17; Schoenberg, Robert J., *Mr. Capone*, New York: HarperCollins, 1993, p. 143. Agoglia and Capone were among the men arrested following the December 1925 murders of "Peg Leg" Lonergan, Neil "Needles" Ferry and Aaron Heins in the Adonis Social Club, 152 Twentieth Street in Brooklyn. Agoglia's brother Angelo was reportedly one of the owners of the Adonis Club.

[39] "Free Mangano and gang, held as kidnappers;" Bonanno, p. 107. Caruso remained a group leader within the Bonanno Crime Family through the 1960s.

[40] "Sensational rumors set afloat by Falls undertaker's arrest."

[41] "Kidnap victim freed as police hold Mangano."

[42] "Sensational rumors set afloat by Falls undertaker's arrest."

[43] "Free Mangano and gang, held as kidnappers."

[44] "Pair shoot man through the heart, flee," *BCE*, Nov. 22, 1931.

[45] World War I Draft Registration Card for Faulkner E. Vanderburg, June 5, 1917; U.S. Census of 1930.

[46] "Pair shoot man through the heart, flee."

[47] Kefauver Committee Hearings, Part 2, p. 128, Part 5, p. 692-693, 759; Demaris,

Ovid, *Captive City: Chicago in Chains*, New York: Lyle Stuart, 1969, p. 98-99; Kobler, p. 114; Poundstone, William, "Fortune's formula," *NYT*, Sept. 25, 2005; "Mont Tennes, headed Chicago racing ring," *NYT*, Aug. 7, 1941, p. Obits 17; "Gambling in Chicago traced to overlord," *NYT*, June 8, 1928, p. 9; "Ask Capone to aid gambler's release," *NYT*, Aug. 25, 1931, p. 13; "Buys racing form stock," *NYT*, Aug. 16, 1933, p. Amusements 20; "Moe L. Annenberg, publisher, is dead," *NYT*, July 21, 1942, p. Obits 19. There was evidence of opposition to the General News Bureau's growing monopoly in summer of 1931, when Bureau co-owner Lynch was kidnapped and held for $250,000 ransom. By 1934, the Annenberg-Lynch partnership had crumbled. Annenberg moved on to start a rival wire service, called Nationwide. Using strong-arm tactics, Nationwide succeeded in taking many of General News Bureau's clients. Later in the year, Annenberg bought out Lynch's share of General News Bureau.

[48] "Clue in death gets nowhere," *BT*, Nov. 24, 1931, p. 3.

[49] "Pair shoot man through the heart, flee."

[50] "Shoes thought clue in slaying," *BEN*, Nov. 23, 1931, p. 21; "Clue in death gets nowhere."

[51] "Ex-convict quizzed in murder," *BEN*, Dec. 2, 1931.

[52] "DiCarlo nabbed on vote charge," *BT*, Dec. 2, 1931; "Police are seeking to deport DiCarlo," *BEN*, Dec. 3, 1931, p. 1.

[53] "Argue dismissal tomorrow of charge against DiCarlo," *BCE*, March 6, 1932; "DiCarlo nabbed on vote charge."

[54] "Records of aliens and others checked," *BEN*, Dec. 4, 1931, p. 1.

[55] "Judge explains DiCarlo bond," *BT*, Dec. 4, 1931; "DiCarlo auto case held honest error," *BEN*, Dec. 23, 1931, p. 17. New York State Commissioner of Motor Vehicles Charles A. Harnett investigated DiCarlo's driver's license and found that it was issued as the result of a processing error by Buffalo District DMV Director Henry Seilheimer.

[56] "DiCarlo's case adjourned at police request," *BCE*, Dec. 4, 1931, p. 24.

[57] "Judge Rowe says he is not amendable to police head," *BEN*, Dec. 4, 1931; "Records of aliens and others checked;" "Judge explains DiCarlo bond."

[58] "Illegal registry charged," *BEN*, Dec. 10, 1931, p. 1.

[59] "Public enemy quizzed," *BCE*, Jan. 11, 1932, p. 1; "DiCarlo grilled by director of U.S. alien drive," *BCE*, Jan. 12, 1932; "DiCarlo is grilled again in alien drive," *BEN*, Jan. 12, 1932.

[60] According to *BCE* reporter Clarence Bull, the 1933 Public Enemy List included: 1. Joseph DiCarlo, 2. Sam "Toto" DiCarlo, 3. John Fina, 4. Sam "Scar Face" Coppola, 5. Joe "The Goose" Gatti, 6. Anthony "Baby Face" Palmisano, 7. Frank DeGoris, 8. Anthony "Lucky" Perna, 9. Joseph Ruffino, 10. Joseph Aleo, 11. Sam Pieri, 12. Sam "Doc" Alessi, 13. John Cammilleri, 14. Anthony Tutino.

[61] Record of Examination, Jan. 11, 1932, Joseph DiCarlo INS file, p. 133. Giuseppe DiCarlo was naturalized a U.S. citizen on July 7, 1920 (Certificate No. 1397587).

[62] "Unable to find data on DiCarlo naturalization," *BCE*, Jan. 13, 1932.

[63] "DiCarlo's citizenship claim accepted," *BEN*, March 5, 1932.

[64] "Argue dismissal of charge against DiCarlo," *BCE*, March 6, 1932; "Signed

registration blank, DiCarlo says," *BEN*, March 7, 1932, p. 17; "DiCarlo goes free," *BEN*, March 8, 1932, p. 34.

[65] "Joe DiCarlo's brother held on U.S. charge," *BCE*, April 16, 1932, p. 22.

[66] The address of Joe Todaro's tobacco shop's was 11103 Woodland Avenue. It stood near Cleveland's "bloody corner" – Woodland and East 110th Street. The shop was two doors from the Porrello-owned barbershop where Joe and John Lonardo were killed in 1927, across the street from the spot where Salvatore "Black Sam" Todaro was murdered in 1929 and diagonally across the intersection from the grocery where James Porrello was murdered in 1930. Joe Todaro denied he was any relation to the late Salvatore Todaro.

[67] Kelly, Ralph, "Murder in Cleveland: The Prohibition toll, Chapter 11," *CPD*, January 1933; "Cleveland gunmen slay two more Porrello brothers," *BCE*, Feb. 26, 1932, p. 1; "2 others near death; feud suspect wanders to hospital, wounded," *CPD*, Feb. 26, 1932; "Only 3 left of seven Porrellos," *CPD*, Feb. 26, 1932. Angelo, Ottavio and John Porrello were the three surviving Porrello brothers.

[68] USA v. Samuel DiCarlo, U.S. District Court of Western District of New York, Indictment No. 8947, April 6, 1932.

[69] "Joe DiCarlo's brother held on U.S. charge."

[70] Indictment No. 8947.

[71] "Joe DiCarlo's brother held on U.S. charge."

[72] "Witnesses to be called for DiCarlo today," *BCE*, May 4, 1932; "Sam DiCarlo guilty," *BCE*, May 5, 1932; USA v. Samuel DiCarlo, U.S. District Court of Western District of New York.

[73] Petition for appeal, U.S. Circuit Court of Appeals for the Second Circuit.

[74] "DiCarlo is held in July fourth bombing probe," *BEN*, July 11, 1932, p. 1; "Sheriff orders DiCarlo freed after quizzing," *BCE*, July 12, 1932, p. 9; "James Dyke dead," *BEN*, July 5, 1932. James Dyke was just 27 years old when he died suddenly July 3, 1932, in Saratoga Springs, NY. His brother Thomas J.B. Dyke was in Chicago, attending the Democratic National Convention, when he received the news and rushed to Saratoga Springs. Burial was arranged in New York City.

[75] "Slot machine war resumed with new raid," *BCE*, Sept. 10, 1932, p. 20.

[76] The decision was rendered on January 18, 1932.

[77] "100 slot machines in storage seized," *BEN*, Sept. 9, 1932, p. 21.

[78] "Roche plans to seize all slot devices in city," *BCE*, Sept. 11, 1932; "100 slot machines in storage seized."

[79] "Two injured in explosion at Erie, PA," *BCE*, Aug. 7, 1932.

[80] Benedetto Palmeri Certificate of Death, New York State Department of Health, Dec. 21, 1932.

[81] "Buffalo Bill, police figure, dies in his car," *BEN*, Dec. 21, 1932, p. 1; "Record funeral is expected as hundreds mourn Palmeri," *BEN*, Dec. 22, 1932.

[82] "Record funeral is expected as hundreds mourn Palmeri."

[83] Benedetto Palmeri Certificate of Death; "Palmeri funeral services Saturday," *BT*, Dec. 22, 1932, p. 15; "Buffalo Bill services to be held tomorrow," *BCE*, Dec. 23, 1932; Burial records of Pine Hill Cemetery; "Record funeral is expected as hundreds mourn Palmeri."

[84] Pine Hill Cemetery records list the Panepinto & Palmeri Funeral Home in Niagara Falls, co-owned by Paul Palmeri and Alfred Panepinto, as the undertaker of record. The Mascari Funeral Parlor, 860 Niagara Street, Buffalo, in which Samuel Mascari and Marcantonio Palamara were partners, assisted with the funeral arrangements.

[85] Statement of Sam Varisco, Buffalo Police Department, January 13, 1933; "Committeeman is accused of murder," *Buffalo Evening Times*, Jan. 14, 1933.

[86] In his statement to police, Varisco claimed only one of his shots struck Angelo Porrello.

[87] Statement of Sam Varisco; "Committeeman is accused of murder."

[88] "Hearing Friday for Varisco in Porrello death," *BCE*, Jan. 15, 1933.

[89] "Two figures in fatal shooting are arraigned," *BCE*, Jan. 17, 1933.

[90] "Sister of slain Porello tries to commit suicide," *CPD*, Jan. 16, 1933.

[91] "Defense moves to end Varisco murder charge," *BCE*, Jan. 31, 1933; "Grand jury to get case of Varisco," *BEN*, Feb. 1, 1933; "Judge Keeler holds Varisco for grand jury," *BCE*, Feb. 2, 1933.

[92] "Pleads guilty after trial is half over," *BCE*, May 23, 1933; "5-10 years is term in landlord slaying," *BEN*, June 2, 1933.

[93] Vincent Anconitano was born Aug. 10, 1901 in Castellammare del Golfo, Sicily (Declaration of Intention, July 21, 1914). Anconitano, known as a member of the DiCarlo Gang, resided at 419 Prospect Avenue in 1933, the same address as "Charley Buffalo" DiBenedetto.

[94] "DiCarlo denies, police insist night club shots for him," *BEN*, Jan. 25, 1933, p. 17; "Special squad airs 'ambush' of DiCarlo," *BT*, Jan. 25, 1933, p. 1.

[95] "DiCarlo denies, police insist night club shots for him."

[96] "Special squad airs 'ambush' of DiCarlo."

[97] "Two seized here as links in big counterfeit ring," *BT*, Feb. 23, 1933; "Trio under arrest in quiz of crimes," *BEN*, Feb. 23, 1933, p. 1.

[98] "Two quizzed in regard to bogus money," *BCE*, Feb. 25, 1933, p. 1.

[99] "Man is held as alleged passer of bogus money," *BCE*, July 21, 1932.

[100] "Randaccio will hear sentence on April 10th," *BCE*, April 6, 1933, p. 17; "Gets seven-year term on bad money charges," *BCE*, April 11, 1933, p. 15. The date of Randaccio's sentencing coincided with the beginning of the end of national Prohibition. On April 10, Michigan became the first state to ratify the 21st Amendment.

[101] "Public enemy convicted of passing spurious bill," *BCE*, April 20, 1933, p. 1.

[102] "Ruffino sentenced," *BCE*, April 27, 1933, p. 9.

[103] "Palmisano blamed for bad bill flow," *BEN*, Aug. 16, 1933.

[104] "Palmisano is held in bail of $50,000," *BEN*, Aug. 16, 1933.

[105] "'Baby Face' Palmisano murdered," *BT*, Feb. 20, 1934.

[106] Cullen-Harrison allowed for the manufacture and sale of beer with 3.2 percent alcohol by weight (approximately 4 percent alcohol by volume). Under the Volstead Act, only near-beer with 0.5 percent alcohol or less was permitted.

[107] "DiCarlo beer plans under police probe," *BEN*, June 20, 1933, p. 19; "Roche sees DiCarlo," *BCE*, June 21, 1933.

[108] Bonasera criminal record, Police Department of the City of New York.
[109] "Weddings and Engagements: Bonasera-DiCarlo," *BT*, June 28, 1933, p. 4; "Wedding attracts crowd to church," *BEN*, June 28, 1933; "DiCarlo nuptials," *BCE*, June 29, 1933.
[110] "Seek Buffalo aid in Albany disappearance," *BCE*, July 12, 1933; "DiCarlo goes to aid hunt for O'Connell," *BEN*, July 12, 1933, p. 6.
[111] "DiCarlo goes to aid hunt for O'Connell." Thomas J. B. Dyke had moved to Albany, where he became an active participant in the Democratic machine run by brothers Dan and Ed O'Connell. Dyke's old underworld ties had come to light earlier in 1933, when he was proposed for the position of State Senate Sergeant-at-arms. Dyke died on June 21, 1945, in Albany at the age of 49. He was survived by his wife, Rose Ercolino Bellantoni, and four daughters. ("Thomas Bellantoni, East Side figure, 49," *NYT*, June 22, 1945, p. 12.)
[112] Eight men from Albany, New York City, and Hoboken, New Jersey, were successfully prosecuted in 1937 for the John O'Connell kidnapping. Two original defendants in the case pleaded guilty just as the trial began. They confessed to guarding O'Connell while he was held in a Hoboken gang hangout, and they identified the other defendants as their accomplices. O'Connell took the stand to identify two other defendants as the men who seized him. The men who pleaded guilty were sentenced to prison terms of 36 and 49 months. The other defendants were sentenced to longer terms. Manning Strewl, the gang member who directly negotiated with the O'Connell family, was sentenced to 58 years in prison and a $10,000 fine.
[113] "DiCarlo move to get share in slot machines revealed," *Buffalo Evening Times*, Aug. 22, 1933.
[114] The address of the saloon was 367 Connecticut Street. The business had been open since May, 1933.
[115] "Girl, 14, caught in bullet hail, is badly hurt," *BCE*, Aug. 26, 1933, p. 1; "Brothers put on spot near their saloon," *BEN*, Aug. 26, 1933, p. 1; Report of Callea murder investigation by Detectives Connors, Crotty and Donahue, Buffalo Police Department.
[116] "Brothers put on spot near their saloon."
[117] "Girl, 14, caught in bullet hail, is badly hurt;" "Brothers put on spot near their saloon."
[118] "Confident of making five arrests soon," *BCE*, Aug. 27, 1933, section 7, p. 1; Report of Callea murder investigation. The automobile was registered to James Gagna of 175 Sycamore Street.
[119] Supplementary Investigation Report, Buffalo Police Department, Oct. 16, 1933. Joseph Carlisi, born March 28, 1886, was the father of Roy, Anna and Sam "Wings" Carlisi. Roy Carlisi later became a top capodecina in the Buffalo crime family. Sam Carlisi, born Dec. 15, 1921, later became boss of the Chicago crime family and was suspected of involvement in the murders of the Spilotro brothers.
[120] "Slaying here held result of dry raid," *BEN*, Aug. 27, 1933; "U.S. joins search for slayers here," *BEN*, Aug. 28, 1933.
[121] "Funeral of Calleas guarded by police," *BEN*, Aug. 29, 1933.
[122] "Uncover still in police raid in Jamestown," *BCE*, Aug. 30, 1933, p. 1.

[123] "Suspects not identified by bullet victim," *BCE*, Aug. 31, 1933, p. 11.

[124] "Two more slayings thought possible," *BEN*, Aug. 30, 1933.

[125] Supplementary Investigation Report, Telephone Record Log, Buffalo Police Department, Aug. 31, 1933.

[126] Calogero Romano Passport Application No. 424140, issued May 23, 1924; Passenger manifest of S.S. Gallia, arrived New York City on April 21, 1905; Calogero Romano Pistol Permit Renewal Application No. 950, Erie County NY Clerk's Office, dated Dec. 9, 1930, filed March 4, 1931. Calogero Romano, born in Pietraperzia, Sicily, on July 29, 1886, settled in Chicago after his immigration to the U.S. on April 21, 1905. He was known to be close to Roy Carlisi's father, Joseph Carlisi, also a Chicago resident. Romano relocated to Buffalo, where he was held in high esteem by Magaddino. Magaddino was repeatedly noted offering deferential cheek-kiss greetings to Romano at regional meetings held in Buffalo. The gesture was conspicuous, as other meeting attendees greeted Magaddino in that manner. Roy Carlisi married Romano's daughter.

[127] Statement of Carmela Callea, Buffalo Police Department, Sept. 1, 1933; Statement of Giovanna Callea, Buffalo Police Department, Sept. 1, 1933. Vincenzo's wife Giovanna Casano Callea remained behind in Sicily when Vincenzo traveled to the U.S. Vincenzo made regular visits before bringing her and their children to Buffalo in February 1924.

[128] "Buffalo man, gun unfired, found slain," *BEN*, Sept. 5, 1933; "Man murdered, scent alcohol feud as cause," *BCE*, Sept. 6, 1933.

[129] "Motive for murder sought by police," *BEN*, Sept. 6, 1933; "Jealousy was crime cause, deputy, "*BCE*, Sept. 7, 1933, p. 18.

[130] "Police holding three men in Callea murder," *BCE*, Sept. 13, 1933.

[131] "Three suspects in twin murder freed by court," *BEN*, Sept. 13, 1933.

[132] "Fire in Jamestown stirs Callea hunt," *BEN*, Oct. 12, 1933; "Callea quizzed about slaying of two cousins," *BCE*, Oct. 14, 1933; "Police say cousin not double slayer," *BEN*, Oct. 14, 1933; Interrogation of Joseph Callea, Buffalo Police Department, Oct. 14, 1933; Distillery seizure, U.S. Attorney Richard H. Templeton, Western Judicial District, June 9, 1933. Joseph Callea and three others were arrested and charged with the manufacture and possession of alcohol after Prohibition agents raided an Amherst distillery on June 2, 1933. The distillery was located within a two-story frame house on the old L.R. Steel Farm, one-half mile from the intersection of Campbell Boulevard and North Forest Road in the hamlet of Getzville. In the raid, agents seized a 3,000-gallon steel still, a 1,000-gallon copper still, 38,000 gallons of molasses mash, two 1,000-gallon wooden vats full of molasses and 800 gallons of first-run alcohol.

[133] Supplementary investigation report from Buffalo Police detectives to Chief of Detectives Emanuel Shuh, Oct. 28, 1933. The Callea brothers were likely suspects in the February 1929 murder of Joseph DiBenedetto, uncle of "Charley Buffalo" DiBenedetto. The Calleas operated a soft-drink saloon at 124 Dante Place. That was located within a block of Vincent Paladino's grocery at 116 Dante Place, where DiBenedetto was murdered. DiBenedetto and the Calleas competed for bootleg liquor profits.

[134] "First arrests near in war on alcohol," *BEN*, Sept. 7, 1933.

135 "Roche directs drive against liquor makers," *BCE*, Sept. 8, 1933, p. 9.
136 "Roche directs drive against liquor makers."
137 "Plant largest ever seized by Buffalo force," *BCE*, Sept. 9, 1933, p. 1.
138 "Anti-gambling squad used in latest forays," *BCE*, Sept. 10, 1933.
139 Giovanni (John) Tronolone was born in Buffalo on Dec. 12, 1910. He was the son of Vincenzo Tronolone and Maria Gnozzo, natives of San Fele, a region of Basilicata in Italy.
140 "Gangs, driven out elsewhere, settling here," *BCE*, Oct. 5, 1933, p. 11.
141 Adeline Pieri's sister Elsie was Joseph DiCarlo's wife. Her brother was Sam Pieri.
142 "Cops attend dance, though not invited," *BEN*, Oct. 5, 1933.
143 The last Democrat elected before the consecutive Republican administrations was Louis P. Fuhrmann. He was first elected mayor in 1910 and was re-elected in 1914.
144 Charter rules prohibiting a mayor from succeeding himself were enacted late in the second term of Roesch's predecessor, Mayor Frank X. Schwab.
145 "Buffalo today elected," *NYT*, Nov. 8, 1933, p. 15. In addition to the mayoralty, Democrats took control of the city council and won three city court judgeships.
146 "Schwab quits Buffalo race," *NYT*, Oct. 12, 1933, p. 14; "NRA support seen in Buffalo result," *NYT*, Nov. 12, 1933, p. E6.
147 "Gets third term as head of police in Buffalo," *NYT*, March 18, 1934, p. E6.
148 "DiCarlo benched as #1 enemy," *BEN*, March 12, 1934.
149 "2 of 5 identified in bandit showup," *BEN*, Jan. 18, 1934; "Identified as raider, stands trial today," *BCE*, Jan. 19, 1934, p. 13.
150 "City combed after 3 men menace girl," *BEN*, Jan. 20, 1934.
151 "2 aides hunted in Palmisano racket killing," *BEN*, Feb. 20, 1934; "'Baby Face Palmisano murdered."
152 "2 aides hunted in Palmisano racket killing," *BEN*, Feb. 20, 1934.
153 Antonio Palmisano birth record, Montemaggiore, Sicily, Oct. 15, 1898.
154 Passenger manifest of the *S.S. Re D'Italia* arrived New York on May 15, 1913. Anthony Palmisano's married sister Rosalia, 20, also made the trip along with her two-year-old daughter Domenica. They were also heading to Buffalo, where Rosalia's husband Carmelo Patti lived.
155 Passenger manifest of the *S.S. Sant'Anna* arrived New York on March 10, 1912. The manifest showed Domenico Palmisano, 48, traveling with a 17-year-old son also named Domenico. The document indicated that the older Domenico had lived in the U.S. between 1906 and 1911.
156 "Nab suspect in Palmisano investigation," *BT*, Feb. 21, 1934.
157 "2 aides hunted in Palmisano racket killing."
158 "DiCarlo seized in slot flareup," *BEN*, Aug. 17, 1934.
159 "2 aides hunted in Palmisano racket killing."
160 "4 human hairs clue in slaying," *BT*, Feb. 23, 1934.
161 "'Baby Face Palmisano murdered."
162 "Police tracing Mafia's hand in gang death," *BEN*, Feb. 21, 1934.
163 "2 muscle men destroy three digger devices," *BEN*, April 6, 1934; "Police open war

on muscle men," *BEN*, April 7, 1934.

[164] "Machine wreckers continue slot war," *BEN*, April 8, 1934.

[165] "Two seized as slot war muscle men racketeers," *BEN*, April 12, 1934.

[166] "Auto is bombed in digger strife," *BEN*, Aug. 16, 1934.

[167] "Thinks Falls pair killed undertaker," *BCE*, April 30, 1934; "Callea case link hinted in murder," *BEN*, May 2, 1934.

[168] "Terror killing will be probed by grand jury," *BEN*, April 30, 1934.

[169] Statement of Antonino Sacco to Buffalo Police, April 29, 1934.

[170] "Terror killing will be probed by grand jury;" Carroll, Assistant Chief of Detectives James L., Supplementary Report to Chief of Detectives John J. Whalen, April 29, 1934.

[171] "Terror killing will be probed by grand jury."

[172] "Think Falls pair killed undertaker;" "Police say killers imported for gang slaying in Buffalo," *NG*, April 30, 1934, p. 1; "Callea case link hinted in murder," *BEN*, May 2, 1934.

[173] Benedetto Palmeri Certificate of Death, Dec. 21, 1932.

[174] Carroll, James L., Supplementary Report; Statement of Antonino Sacco; Statement of Vito DeNitto to Buffalo Police, April 29, 1934; Statement of Michael Pellettiri to Buffalo Police, April 29, 1934.

[175] "Callea case link hinted in murder;" "Man questioned in murder case," *BT*, May 2, 1934.

[176] "Man questioned in murder case;" "Judge frees three in Palamara death," *BEN*, May 3, 1934.

[177] "Two Falls men held for assault after cop is beaten and stabbed," *NG*, May 21, 1934, p. 1; "Falls assault case is in hands of jury," *Lockport Union Sun and Journal*, July 11, 1934; "Pair convicted of assaulting officer," *Lockport Union Sun and Journal*, July 12, 1934.

[178] "Two Falls men held for assault after cop is beaten and stabbed."

[179] "Policeman charges men with assault," *Lockport Union Sun and Journal*, July 10, 1934; "Falls assault case is in hands of jury."

[180] "Pair convicted of assaulting officer."

[181] "Seven sentenced to Attica Prison in county court," *Lockport Union Sun and Journal*, July 13, 1934.

[182] "Buffalo faces new slot war," *BEN*, July 31, 1934.

[183] "Trio's arrest believed end of slot war," *BEN*, Aug. 10, 1934.

[184] "Auto is bombed in digger strife;" "Police reveal auto bombing second effort," *BCE*, Aug. 17, 1934.

[185] "DiCarlo seized in slot flareup."

[186] "Eight held for questioning in auto bombing," *BCE*, Aug. 18, 1934.

[187] "Question 5 in enquiry into 'digger' blowup," *BCE*, Aug. 19, 1934.

[188] "5 are released in bomb inquiry," *BEN*, Aug. 20, 1934.

[189] "Two more arrested in digger bombing," *BEN*, Aug. 21, 1934; "DiCarlo, two others freed in bomb quiz," *BEN*, Aug. 23, 1934.

190 "Women hunted in death ride of Joe Mule," *BT*, Oct. 22, 1934; "Man tortured to death, body left in ditch," *BCE*, Oct. 22, 1934.

191 Birth records of Racalmuto, Sicily, certificate no. 595, Dec. 15, 1904. Mule was born to Calogero and Calogera Mule Mongiovi. His parents were married Oct. 31, 1896. Calogero Mongiovi was a sulfur miner.

192 Manifest of the *S.S. Berlin* arrived New York City on Feb. 23, 1912.

193 Manifest of the *S.S. Patria* arrived New York City on Jan. 21, 1921.

194 Interview with Pete Barbera, 1981.

195 "Gang gunman is put on the spot to silence him," *BEN*, Oct. 22, 1934.

196 Interview with Pete Barbera, 1981.

197 "Woman hunted in death ride of Joe Mule;" "Woman linked by police in Mule slaying," *BCE*, Oct. 23, 1934; "Cappola to sift slaying of Mule," *BEN*, Oct. 23, 1934.

198 "Man tortured to death, body left in ditch."

199 "Man tortured to death, body left in ditch."

200 "Riddled body of Palamara found in auto," *BCE*, Aug. 19, 1935; Officer Frank Felicetta and Officer John Mahoney, Supplementary Investigation Report to Chief of Detectives, Buffalo Police Department; Calhan, Captain John, Correspondence sent to Commissioner James W. Higgins, Buffalo Police Department.

201 "Riddled body of Palamara found in auto."

202 "Police quiz man in murder here," *BEN*, Aug. 19, 1935; "Mystery auto, bearing Ohio plates, is clue," *BT*, Aug. 19, 1935.

203 "Riddled body of Palamara found in auto."

204 "Mystery auto, bearing Ohio plates, is clue."

205 "Mystery auto, bearing Ohio plates, is clue;" "Racket studied as murder clue," *BT*, Aug. 20, 1935; "New facts bared in gang slaying," *BEN*, Aug. 20, 1935; Palamara business records, Buffalo Police Department.

206 "Mystery auto, bearing Ohio plates, is clue."

207 "Riddled body of Palamara found in auto."

Chapter 19

1 "Public enemy act signed by Lehman," *NYT*, May 16, 1935, p. 19; "Drastic crime law opposed by board," *NYT*, Feb. 28, 1935, p. 7; "Anti-crime bill gains at Albany," *NYT*, April 2, 1935, p. 4; "Brownell crime bill passed by Assembly," *NYT*, April 9, 1935, p. 12; Pace, Eric, "Herbert Brownell, 92, Eisenhower attorney general dies," *NYT*, May 2, 1996. The bill was named for its author, state Assemblyman Herbert Brownell Jr., Republican of New York City. New York Police Commissioner Lewis J. Valentine was a strong supporter of the anti-consorting measure. Brownell served in the Assembly from 1933 to 1937. He later served as chairman of the Republican National Committee and as U.S. attorney general in the Eisenhower Administration.

2 "The crime of consorting," *NYT*, July 13, 1935, p. 12. The *Times* story recalled the objection of Dean Burdick of Cornell Law School: "A statute which prohibited objectionable persons from merely associating, without regard to the reason for

their association, would be in effect a statute which made their guilt depend solely upon the fact of their being objectionable."

[3] "Police open drive on public enemies," *NYT*, May 21, 1935, p. 1. The arrested men were Rocco Bellarmino, 24; Saul Berman, 28; Barney Gambino, 22; Joseph Laurette, 20; Irving Moskowitz, 23; Jerry Pietrafesa, 21; Ralph Rabiner, 22; William Rabinowitz, 21; Irving Schenker, 22; and Oscar Shapiro, 23.

[4] "Trial date set for 10 nabbed under new law," *BCE*, May 26, 1935.

[5] "Police arrest Joe DiCarlo under new Brownell law," *BCE*, June 3, 1935; "DiCarlo in court on Brownell charge," *BT*, June 3, 1935, p. 1.

[6] "Pleads not guilty," *BCE*, June 4, 1935, p. 4.

[7] "Brownell law will be tested in court today," *BCE*, June 11, 1935, p. 22.

[8] "Brownell law ruled valid; 4 men convicted," *BCE*, June 12, 1935, p. 1.

[9] "Four convicted under new law press appeal," *BCE*, June 19, 1935, p. 22.

[10] "Admission laid to Tronolone," *BEN*, March 13, 1937; "Term of month given to Tronolone," *BEN*, March 15, 1937, p. 17.

[11] "County judge upholds Brownell convictions," *BCE*, July 30, 1935, p. 9.

[12] "Brownell law appeal record is put on file," *BCE*, Aug. 13, 1935, p. 11.

[13] "New law jails 7 as public enemies," *NYT*, June 2, 1935, p. 1. The convicted men were Rocco Bellarmino, Saul Berman, Barney Gambino, Irving Moskowitz, Jerry Pietrafesa, Irving Schenker and Oscar Schapiro.

[14] "Public enemy law tested by 11 victims," *NYT*, Nov. 26, 1931, p. 1.

[15] "Public enemy law voided on Spitale," *NYT*, Jan. 8, 1936, p. 5.

[16] Frahm, Chief of Detectives Fred W., Letter to Buffalo Police Department Chief of Detectives John J. Whalen, Sept. 23, 1935.

[17] Salvatore Pieri Certificate of Birth, City of Buffalo, No. 405, filed Feb. 2, 1911.

[18] "3 alleged rum runners caught at Hudson Street," *BEN*, Sept. 3, 1931, p. 39.

[19] "Two Sentenced As Suspicious Persons", *CPD*, Jan. 25, 1936.

[20] "2 Buffalonians jailed," *BEN*, Jan. 25, 1936, p.3.

[21] "Selection of gang murder trial jury may take a week," *Toledo Blade*, Jan. 28, 1936.

[22] Thomas Licavoli was a cousin of Pete Licavoli, a leader in the Detroit Mafia at the time.

[23] "Licavoli gangsters hunted for Toledo girl's murder," *Toledo Blade*, Dec. 1, 1932; "Government strikes powerful blow at gangster control in Toledo," *Toledo Blade*, Dec. 8, 1932; "Sensational testimony due in Licavoli trial," *Toledo Blade*, Oct. 8, 1934.

[24] Illman, Harry R., *Unholy Toledo: The True Story of Detroit's Purple-Licavoli Gangs' Take-over of an Ohio City*, San Francisco: Polemic Press Publications, 1985, p. 113, 120.

[25] "Licavoli, 13 others indicted in slayings," *Toledo Blade*, March 8, 1934.

[26] Illman, p. 122-123.

[27] Illman, p. 124; "Licavoli gangsters hunted for Toledo girl's murder."

[28] "Mayor hints at shakeup in gang war," *Toledo Blade*, Dec. 2, 1932; "Licavoli, 14 others indicted on federal liquor charges; three hunted in girl's slaying," *Toledo*

Blade, Dec. 5, 1932.

[29] Point Place was later incorporated into the City of Toledo.

[30] "Licavoli, 13 others indicted in slayings," *Toledo Blade*, March 8, 1934; Illman, p. 127.

[31] Illman, p. 135-137.

[32] Illman, p. 167-168.

[33] Illman, p. 160-161; "4 murders considered in trial of Licavoli," *Toledo Blade*, Nov. 9, 1934; "Licavoli sentenced to life in prison," *Toledo Blade*, Nov. 9, 1934. Licavoli's appeals of the verdict continued for decades. On Jan. 28, 1968, Ohio Governor James A. Rhodes commuted the conviction to second-degree murder, making Licavoli eligible for parole. Licavoli won parole four years later. He died Sept. 17, 1973.

[34] Leo Moceri was named underboss of the Cleveland Mafia in 1976. He disappeared later that year, as Cleveland underworld factions entered into a power struggle.

[35] "Hotel maid links Carsello and Rai to Licavoli gang," *Toledo Blade*, Feb. 6, 1936; "Stein charges third degree in murder quiz," *Toledo Blade*, Feb. 14, 1936.

[36] "Rai-Carsello mistrial motion is overruled," *Toledo Blade*, Feb. 19, 1936; Illman, p. 167.

[37] "State asks chair verdict for 2 Licavoli gangsters," *Toledo Blade*, Feb. 20, 1936.

[38] "Reams charges gang treason," *Toledo Blade*, Feb. 21, 1936.

[39] "Rai, Carsello get life terms," *Toledo Blade*, Feb. 23, 1936.

[40] "Mother is dead, three daughters injured in blast," *NG*, May 19, 1936; "Police say 2 bombs used in Falls blast," *BEN*, May 20, 1936.

[41] "Mystery veils motive for Falls bombing outrage as police study theories in hunt for some clue," *NG*, May 20, 1936.

[42] "Mother is dead, three daughters injured in blast."

[43] "Mystery veils motive for Falls bombing outrage…"

[44] Nicolo Longo birth record, no. 891, Castellammare del Golfo, Sicily, Dec. 13, 1897.

[45] Passenger manifest of the *S.S. Friedrich der Grosse*, arrived New York City April 23, 1910.

[46] Passenger manifest of the *S.S. France*, arrived New York City Jan. 16, 1921.

[47] Nicolo Longo Naturalization Certificate No. 1991793, June 9, 1924.

[48] Passenger manifest of the *S.S. Conte Verde* arrived New York City Oct. 25, 1924.

[49] Arcangela Longo Naturalization Certificate No. 3995930, Sept. 16, 1935.

[50] "Mystery veils motive for Falls bombing outrage…" Decades later, Buffalo reporters Lee Coppola and Tony Cardinale learned from an underworld source that Longo had served as a top lieutenant in the Magaddino Crime Family. They revealed in "Family man Magaddino shunned violence," *BEN*, Feb. 25, 1974, that Magaddino became enraged at Nicolo Longo for exposing Arcangela and their daughters to harm and banished Longo from the Buffalo territory. Longo moved to New York City. His three daughters were subsequently raised in Magaddino's home.

[51] "Search for bombers of Falls home is extended out of city," *NG*, May 21, 1936.

[52] "Huge throngs attend last rights for Falls bombing victim today," *NG*, May 23, 1936.

[53] Coppola, Lee, and Tony Cardinale, "Family man Magaddino shunned violence,"

BEN, Feb. 25, 1974.

[54] Anna LoTempio Panepinto was married to Anthony Panepinto in Batavia on Sept. 3, 1912.

[55] The cousin's name, omitted from the text to prevent confusion, was also Frank LoTempio. His bride was Caroline Rizzo.

[56] Rose LoTempio Panepinto was married to Anthony Panepinto's brother Alfred, partner in the Panepinto and Palmeri Funeral Home of Niagara Falls. They were married in Batavia on June 27, 1928. Alfred did not attend the LoTempio wedding due to an injured knee. Rose was driven to the ceremony by James Cardone, a friend from Niagara Falls.

[57] Sam Pieri was married to Carrie LoTempio, sister of the groom and cousin of Frank LoTempio of Batavia. Pieri's marriage took place in Tonawanda, New York, on Jan. 23, 1934. John "Peanuts" Tronolone served as a witness.

[58] "Police head assails murder witnesses who keep silent," *BCE*, June 28, 1936.

[59] Statement of Mrs. Josephine LoTempio to Buffalo Police, Sept. 9, 1936.

[60] "Batavia murder victim's funeral planned for tomorrow morning, service at St. Anthony's Church," *Batavia Daily News*, June 29, 1936, p. 1; Birth records of Valledolmo, Sicily. The Panepinto family also had its roots in Valledolmo.

[61] "Investigators obtain number of death auto," *BCE*, June 28, 1936.

[62] "DiCarlo halted at Peace Span, held by police," *BEN*, June 30, 1936.

[63] Detective Sergeant Frank N. Felicetta later served as Buffalo Police Commissioner in 1958-1961 and 1966-1973.

[64] "Crowd watches thugs riddle body," *BT*, June 27, 1936.

[65] Nine year old Mary Petruzzi was standing on the sidewalk in front of her home at 547 Seventh Street and witnessed the shooting of Frank LoTempio.

[66] "Police head assails murder witnesses who keep silent."

[67] "Tempio rites held today, clue lacking," *Batavia Daily News*, June 30, 1936.

[68] "Murder probers free DiCarlo without a hearing on writ," *BEN*, July 1, 1936.

[69] "Tempio rites held today, clue lacking."

[70] Ford, Leslie N., "Police reveal reputed bookie payoff scheme," *BCE*, July 31, 1936.

[71] "Prosecutor tries new tack in 'racket' quiz," *BCE*, Aug. 1, 1936; Ford, Leslie N.

[72] "Prosecutor tries new tack in 'racket' quiz;" "Hearing delayed while police probe rackets," *BEN*, July 31, 1936, p. 1.

[73] "Immunity offer made," *BEN*, Aug. 1, 1936, p. 3.

[74] "Tronolone is nabbed," *BCE*, Aug. 4, 1936; "Tronolone arrested," *BEN*, Aug. 3, 1936, p. 1; "Tronolone wins 6-week stay and is remanded to jail," *BEN*, Aug. 4, 1936, p. 17.

[75] Wake services for Maria Concetta Grimaldi, mother of Batavia racketeer Louis Grimaldi, were held at 242 Seventh Street.

[76] "Gunmen in Buffalo murdered a Batavian," *Batavia Daily News*, Aug. 26, 1936.

[77] "Gunmen in Buffalo murdered a Batavian."

[78] "Gun used to slay Izzo found, police believe," *BEN*, Aug. 27, 1936, p. 25.

[79] "Bullet tests show no link in 2 slayings," *BEN*, Aug. 26, 1936.

80 "Gunmen in Buffalo murdered a Batavian."
81 "DiCarlo witness held as perjurer," *BEN*, Sept. 19, 1935, p. 3.
82 "DiCarlo surrenders on assault charges," *BEN*, Sept. 23, 1936, p. 1.
83 "DiCarlo gives self up, denies assault count," *BEN*, Sept. 24, 1936.
84 "It was hid in auto; one man loses leg," *Medina Journal Register*, Oct. 30, 1936.
85 "It was hid in auto; one man loses leg;" "Gangland killers strike again blasting Batavians from a car," *Batavia Daily News*, Oct. 30, 1936; "Blast wrecks automobile of LoTempio kin," *BCE*, Oct. 30, 1936; "Every clue followed in bombing case," *Medina Journal Register*, Nov. 5, 1936.
86 "Every clue followed in bombing case;" "Gangland killers strike again blasting Batavians from a car."
87 Strickland, J.C. Jr., "Joseph J. DiCarlo," FBI memo, MM 92-104, Dec. 27, 1957. According to the memo, DiCarlo first registered with the Miami Beach Police Department as a convicted felon on Feb. 6, 1937.
88 "Attorney ill, DiCarlo's trial again delayed," *BEN*, Feb. 24, 1937.
89 "Accuser tells of hiding head during attack," *BEN*, March 1, 1937; "Jurist rejects motion to end DiCarlo trial," *BCE*, March 2, 1937.
90 "Jurist rejects motion to end DiCarlo trial."
91 "Mystery calls over telephone are reported," *BEN*, March 2, 1937; "Warning of death received by juror," *Buffalo Evening Times*, March 2, 1937.
92 "Accused loses plea for second mistrial," *BEN*, March 3, 1937.
93 "Accused loses plea for second mistrial."
94 "DiCarlo is acquitted of assault charge: Co-defendant in case also freed by jury," *BCE*, March 4, 1937.
95 Yocum, H.V. and E.H. Adkins, City of Miami Beach Police Department letter to Chief of Buffalo Police, March 5, 1937.
96 "Tronolone files not guilty plea," *BEN*, March 6, 1937, p. 3.
97 "Jury trial demanded by Tronolone, Miller," *BEN*, March 9, 1937, p. 1.
98 "Admission laid to Tronolone."
99 "Term of month given Tronolone."
100 Alfred Panepinto was married to Rose LoTempio Panepinto, Frank and Russell LoTempio's sister.
101 The Panepinto and Palmeri Funeral Home was later taken over by the Magaddinos and became the Magaddino Funeral Home.
102 "Outside gangsters move their war to Batavia slaying Niagara Falls man in midnight card game," *Batavia Daily News*, Aug. 14, 1937; "Five questioned here about Batavia murder," *BCE*, Aug. 15, 1937; "Former Falls man shot while playing cards in poolroom," *NG*, Aug. 14, 1937.
103 "Outside gangsters move their war to Batavia…"
104 "Five questioned here about Batavia murder;" "Former Falls man shot while playing cards in poolroom."
105 "Outside gangsters move their war to Batavia…" Salvatore Lagattuta also served as a pallbearer at Arcangela Longo's funeral. He was married to Filippo Mazzara's sister Vincenza in Buffalo, NY, June 20, 1922.

[106] "Murder trail leads toward Niagara Falls," *BCE*, Aug. 16, 1937.

[107] "State police investigators join the hunt for gang slayers," *Batavia Daily News*, Aug. 16, 1937.

[108] "Hunt for Batavia gang killers extends today to Niagara area," *Batavia Daily News*, Aug. 17, 1937.

Bibliography

Following is a list of major sources consulted during research for *DiCarlo: Buffalo's First Family of Crime*. More specific citations and additional sources will be found in the endnotes.

Interviews:
Rose Lombardo, Ben LaMonte, Philip G. Mazzara, Joe Giambra, Ronald Fino and Pete Barbera.

Federal Bureau of Investigation Files:
Joseph J. DiCarlo, Stefano Magaddino, Frederico Randaccio, Salvatore Pieri, Salvatore DiCarlo, Rosario Carlisi, Daniel G. Sansanese, John Cammilleri, Sam Frangiamore, Joseph Fino, Antonino Magaddino, Peter A. Magaddino, Albert Billiteri, William Sciolino, Daniel Domino, Carl J. Rizzo, John R. Catanzaro, Charles Anthony Cassaro, James V. LaDuca, Joseph A. Pieri, Laborers Union Local 210, Frank Sinatra.

Newspapers and Magazines:
Albany Times-Union, Batavia Daily News, Brooklyn Daily Eagle, Brooklyn Standard Union, Buffalo Commercial Advertiser, Buffalo Courier Express, Buffalo Daily Courier, Buffalo Enquirer, Buffalo Evening News, Buffalo Morning Express, Buffalo News, Buffalo Times, Cleveland Press, Cleveland Plain Dealer, Chicago Tribune, Detroit Free Press, Hamilton Herald, Il Corriere Italiano, Lockport Union Sun and Journal, Miami Daily News, New York Daily News, New York Evening World, New York Herald, New York Post, New York Sun, New York Times, Niagara Gazette, North Tonawanda Evening News, Olean Evening Times,

Pittsburgh Post-Gazette, Pittsburgh Press, Rochester Democrat and Chronicle, Rochester Times-Union, Syracuse Herald Journal, Toledo Blade, Toronto Daily Star, Troy Times Record, Utica Daily Press, Youngstown Vindicator, LIFE magazine, *TIME* magazine and other periodicals. (See endnotes for specific article citations.)

Police, Court, Prison Records:
Buffalo Police Department reports, correspondence, witness statements and arrest records.
Cleveland Police Department reports.
State of New York v. Pietro Lagatutta, Salvatore Rufino, Giuseppe Rufino and Giuseppe Masseria, 1913.
State of New York v. Joseph DiCarlo, 1938.
State of New Jersey v. Bartolomeo Fontana, Francesco Puma, Giuseppe Lombardi, 1921-1922.
State of New Jersey extradition records, 1844-1968.
U.S. v. Giuseppe Calicchio et al., 1910.
U.S. v. DiCarlo, Capodicaso, Ruffino and Gialelli, 1924.
U.S. v. Spallino et al., 1927.
U.S. v. Samuel DiCarlo, 1932.
U.S. v. Charles Caci, Stephen A. Cino, Pasquale A. Natarelli, Frederico G. Randaccio and Louis Sorgi, 1967.
U.S. v. Thomas J. Carella, Daniel J. Domino, Joseph C. Erhart and Salvatore Pieri, 1967.
U.S. v. Mason Tenders District Council of Greater New York, 1994.
U.S. v. Laborers' International Union of North America, AFL-CIO, draft complaint, 1995.
U.S., appellee, v. Russell A. Bufalino, et al, 1960.
U.S., appellee, v. Vito Agueci, et al, 1962.
U.S., appellee, v. Charles Caci, Stephen A. Cino, Pasquale A. Natarelli, Frederico Randaccio and Louis Sorgi, 1968.
Stern v. United States, 1953.
Giordano v. United States, 1953.
Jin Fuey Moy v. United States, 1920.
Bankruptcy docket, Buffalo, NY, 1910.
Bankruptcy docket, Buffalo, NY, 1912.
Last Will and Testament of Vincenza DiCarlo.
Probate court records for the estate of Philip Mazzara.
Prisoner information for Joseph DiCarlo.

New York State inmate registers for Sing Sing Prison.
New Jersey State inmate registers for Trenton.
Atlanta Federal Prison files for Giuseppe Morello, Ignazio Lupo and Thomas Pennachio.

Other Government Sources:

Naturalization documents for Giuseppe DiCarlo, Gaspare Magaddino and others.

Immigration and Naturalization Service files for Joseph DiCarlo, Umberto Randaccio, Cassandro Bonasera.

Immigration and Naturalization Service investigation of Panaro's Lounge raid, 1967.

Passenger manifests of arrivals in New York City and Niagara Falls, NY.

Hearings of the House Subcommittee on Crime, 1996.

Hearings before the Permanent Subcommittee on Investigations, "25 Years After Valachi," 1988.

New Jersey State Commission of Investigation, "Report and Recommendations on Organized Crime Infiltration of Dental Care Plan Organizations," 1981.

New York State Commission of Investigation, "An Investigation of Certain Organized Crime Activities and Problems of Law Enforcement in Rochester, New York," 1966.

McClellan Committee, U.S. Senate, Hearings, 1957-58.

Reuter, Arthur L., "Report on the activities and associations of persons identified as present at the residence of Joseph Barbara, Sr., at Apalachin, New York, on November 14, 1957, and the reasons for their presence," State of New York Commissioner of Investigation, April 23, 1958.

Kefauver Committee, U.S. Senate, Hearings and Committee Reports, 1950-51.

Immigration Commission report to U.S. Senate, 1911.

U.S. Secret Service daily reports of William J. Flynn, 1909.

U.S. Secret Service daily reports of John A. Adams, 1911.

U.S. Census records.

Military draft registrations.

Pistol permit applications.

Passport applications.

Public school records.

Other Records:
Birth, marriage and death records in the United States and Italy; land and business records; and local business and residential directory information.

Published Books:
Abadinsky, Howard, *Organized Crime, Ninth Edition*, Belmont, CA: Wadsworth, 2010.

Alexander, Shana, *The Pizza Connection: Lawyers, Money, Drugs, Mafia*, New York: Weidenfeld & Nicolson, 1988.

Allen, Edward J., *Merchants of Menace – The Mafia: A Study of Organized Crime*, Springfield IL: Charles C. Thomas, 1962.

Allen, Oliver E., *The Tiger: The Rise and Fall of Tammany Hall*, Reading, MA: Addison-Wesley Publishing Company, 1993.

Asbury, Herbert, *The Gangs of Chicago: An Informal History of the Chicago Underworld*, New York: New York: Thunder's Mouth Press, 1986.

Asbury, Herbert, *The Gangs of New York: An Informal History of the Underworld*, Garden City, NY: Garden City Publishing Co., 1928.

Bonanno, Bill, *Bound by Honor*, New York: St. Martin's Press, 1999.

Bonanno, Joseph, with Sergio Lalli, *A Man of Honor*, New York: Simon & Schuster, 1983.

Butler, Joseph Green, *The History of Youngstown and the Mahoning Valley, Ohio, Volume 1*, Chicago: American Historical Society, 1921

Chepesiuk, Ron, *Gangsters of Miami*, Fort Lee, NJ: Barricade Books, 2010.

Cipolla, Giuseppe, *Le Famiglie Di Vallelunga*, Commune di Vallelunga Pratameno, 1995.

Critchley, David, *The Origin of Organized Crime in America*, New York: Routledge, 2009.

Damone, Vic, with David Chanoff, *Singing Was the Easy Part*, New York: St. Martin's Press, 2009.

Davis, John H., *Mafia Dynasty: The Rise and Fall of the Gambino Crime Family*, New York: HarperTorch, 1994.

Deitche, Scott M., *The Silent Don: The Criminal Underworld of Santo Trafficante Jr.*, Fort Lee, NJ: Barricade Books, 2007.

Demaris, Ovid, *Captive City: Chicago in Chains*, New York: Lyle

Stuart, 1969.
Demaris, Ovid, *The Last Mafioso*, New York: Times Books, 1981.
Downey, Patrick, *Gangster City: The History of the New York Underworld, 1900-1935*, Fort Lee, NJ: Barricade Books, 2004.
Dubro, James, *Mob Rule: Inside the Canadian Mafia*, Toronto: Macmillan of Canada, 1985
Dubro, James and Robin F. Rowland, *King of the Mob: Rocco Perri and the Women Who Ran His Rackets*, Markham, Ontario: Viking, Penguin Books Canada, 1987.
Earley, Pete and Gerald Shur, *WITSEC: Inside the Federal Witness Protection Program*, New York: Bantam Books, 2002.
Edwards, Peter, *Northern Connection: Inside Canada's Deadliest Mafia Family*, Montreal: Optimum Publishing, 2006.
Edwards, Peter and Antonio Nicaso, *Deadly Silence*, Toronto: Macmillan Canada, 1993.
Fentress, James, *Rebels and Mafiosi: Death in a Sicilian Landscape*, Ithaca NY: Cornell University Press, 2000.
Fenwick, Charles G., *Political Systems in Transition: War-Time and After*, New York: The Century Co., 1920.
Fiaschetti, Michael, as told to Prosper Buranelli, *The Man They Couldn't Escape: The Adventures of Detective Fiaschetti of the Italian Squad*, London: Selwyn, 1928.
Frasca, Dom, *King of Crime*, Crown Publishers, 1959.
Flynn, William J., *The Barrel Mystery*, New York: The James A. McCann Company, 1919.
Gentile, Nick, *Vita di Capomafia*, Rome: Editori Riuniti, 1963.
Gentry, Curt, *J. Edgar Hoover: The Man and the Secrets*, New York: W.W. Norton & Company, 1991.
Griffin, Joe with Don DeNevi, *Mob Nemesis: How the FBI Crippled Organized Crime*, Amherst, NY: Prometheus Books, 2002.
Gryta, Matt, with George Karalus, *The Real Teflon Don: How an Elite Team of New York State Troopers Helped Take Down America's Most Powerful Mafia Family*, Buffalo: Cazenovia Books, 2012.
Guthman, Edwin O. and Jeffrey Shulman, editors, *Robert Kennedy: In His Own Words*, New York: Bantam Press, 1988.
Hamill, Pete, *Why Sinatra Matters*, Boston: Little, Brown and Company, 1998.
Helmer, William J. and Arthur J. Bilek, *St. Valentine's Day*

Massacre, Nashville: Cumberland House, 2004.

Hess, Henner, translated by Ewald Osers, *Mafia and Mafiosi: Origin, Power and Myth*, New York: University Press, 1998.

Hill, Henry Wayland, editor in chief, *Municipality of Buffalo, New York: A History, 1720-1923*, New York: Lewis Historical Publishing Company, 1923.

Humphreys, Adrian, *The Enforcer*, Toronto: HarperCollins Canada, 1993.

Hunt, C.W., *Whisky and Ice: The Saga of Ben Kerr, Canada's Most Daring Rumrunner*, Toronto: Dundurn Press, 1996.

Illman, Harry R., *Unholy Toledo: The True Story of Detroit's Purple-Licavoli Gangs' Take-over of an Ohio City*, San Francisco: Polemic Press Publications, 1985.

Jacobs, James B., with Christopher Panarella and Jay Worthington, *Busting the Mob: United States v. Cosa Nostra*, New York: New York University Press, 1994.

Kavieff, Paul R., *The Violent Years: Prohibition and the Detroit Mobs*, Fort Lee, NJ: Barricade Books, 2001.

Katz, Leonard, *Uncle Frank: The Biography of Frank Costello*, New York: Drake Publishers, 1973.

Keefe, Rose, *Guns and Roses: The Untold Story of Dean O'Banion*, Nashville: Cumberland House, 2003.

Keefe, Rose, *The Starker: Big Jack Zelig, the Becker-Rosenthal Case, and the Advent of the Jewish Gangster*, Nashville: Cumberland House, 2008.

Kefauver, Estes, *Crime in America*, Garden City, NY: Doubleday and Company, 1951.

Kennedy, Robert F., *The Enemy Within*, New York: Harper and Brothers, 1960.

King, Russell, *Sicily*, Harrisburg: Stackpole Books, 1973.

Kobler, John, *Capone: The Life and World of Al Capone*, New York: G.P. Putnam's Sons, 1971

Lacey, Robert, *Little Man: Meyer Lansky and the Gangster Life*, Boston: Little, Brown and Company, 1991.

Lait, Jack, and Lee Mortimer, *Chicago Confidential*, New York: Dell Publishing, 1950.

Lamothe, Lee and Antonio Nicaso, *Blood Lines: The Rise and Fall of the Mafia's Royal Family*, Toronto: HarperCollins Canada, 2001.

Lay, Shawn, *Hooded Knights on the Niagara: The Ku Klux Klan in Buffalo, New York*, New York: New York University Press, 1995.

Lewis, Jerry, *Dean & Me: A Love Story*, New York: Broadway Books, 2005.

Lewis, Norman, *The Honored Society*, New York: G.P. Putnam's Sons, 1964.

Maas, Peter, *The Valachi Papers*, New York: G.P. Putnam's Sons, 1968.

McClellan, John J., *Crime Without Punishment*, New York: Duell, Sloan and Pearce, 1962.

McPhaul, Jack, *Johnny Torrio: First of the Gang Lords*, New Rochelle, NY: Arlington House, 1970.

Meyer, Joseph J., *The Wet City: Buffalo, New York, During the Prohibition Era, 1920-1933*, Allegheny College, 1996.

Morello, Celeste A., *Before Bruno: The History of the Philadelphia Mafia, Book 1, 1880-1931*, published by the author, 1999.

Morton, James, *Gangland International: An Informal History of the Mafia and other Mobs in the Twentieth Century*, Little, Brown and Company, 1999.

Navasky, Victor S., *Kennedy Justice*, New York: Atheneum, 1971.

Nelli, Humbert S., *The Business of Crime: Italians and Syndicate Crime in the United States*, Chicago: University of Chicago Press, (Phoenix edition) 1981.

Newark, Tim, *Lucky Luciano: The Real and the Fake Gangster*, New York: Thomas Dunne Books, 2010.

Newton, Michael, *Mr. Mob: The Life and Crimes of Moe Dalitz*, Jefferson, NC: McFarland & Co., 2009.

Nicaso, Antonio, *Rocco Perri: The Story of Canada's Most Notorious Bootlegger*, Mississauga, Ontario: John Wiley & Sons Canada, 2004, p. 60

Pietruszka, David, *Rothstein: The Life, Times, and Murder of the Criminal Genius Who Fixed the 1919 World Series*, New York: Carroll & Graf, 2004.

Pistone, Joseph D., with Richard Woodley, *Donnie Brasco: My Undercover Life in the Mafia*, New York: New American Library, 1987.

Porrello, Rick, *The Rise and Fall of the Cleveland Mafia: Corn Sugar and Blood*, Fort Lee, NJ: Barricade Books, 1995.

Raab, Selwyn, *Five Families: The Rise, Decline and Resurgence* of America's Most Powerful Mafia Empires, New York: Thomas Dunne Books, 2006.

Reid, Ed, *Mafia*, New York: Random House, 1952.

Reid, Ed, *The Grim Reapers: The Anatomy of Organized Crime in America*, Chicago: Henry Regnery Company, 1969.

Reid, Ed, *The Shame of New York*, New York: Random House, 1953.

Roemer, William F. Jr., *Roemer: Man Against the Mob*, New York: Donald I. Fine, 1989.

Rowe, Thomas C., *Federal Narcotics Laws and the War on Drugs: Money Down a Rat Hole*, Binghamton NY: Haworth Press, 2006.

Schiavo, Giovanni, *The Truth About the Mafia*, New York: Vigo Press, 1962.

Schneider, Stephen, *Iced: The Story of Organized Crime in Canada*, Mississauga, Ontario: John Wiley & Sons Canada, 2009.

Schoenberg, Robert J., *Mr. Capone*, New York: HarperCollins, 1993.

Scott, Peter Dale, *Deep Politics and the Death of JFK*, Berkeley, CA: University of California Press, 1993.

Servadio, Gaia, *Mafioso: A History of the Mafia from its Origins to the Present Day*, London: Secker & Warburg, 1976.

Shelton, Brenda K., *Reformers In Search of Yesterday / Buffalo in the 1890s*, Albany: State University of New York Press, 1976.

Smith, Dennis Mack, *A History of Sicily: Medieval Sicily, 800-1713*, New York: Viking Press, 1968.

Sterling, Claire, *Octopus: The Long Reach of the International Sicilian Mafia*, New York: W.W. Norton & Company, 1990.

Thompson, Craig and Allen Raymond, *Gang Rule in New York*, New York: Dial Press, 1940.

Turkus, Burton B. and Sid Feder, *Murder, Inc.: The Story of the Syndicate*, New York: Da Capo Press, 1992.

Ungar, Sanford J., *FBI*, Boston: Little, Brown, 1976.

United States Treasury Department Bureau of Narcotics, *Mafia: The Government's Secret File on Organized Crime*, New York: Collins, 2007.

Valentine, Douglas, *The Strength of the Wolf: The Secret History of America's War on Drugs*, London: Verso, 2009.

Vogel, Michael N., Ed Patton and Paul Redding, *America's*

Crossroads: Buffalo's Canal Street / Dante Place: The Making of a City, New York: Western New York Heritage Institute, 1993.

Wolf, George, with Joseph DiMona, *Frank Costello: Prime Minister of the Underworld*, New York: William Morrow and Company, 1974.

Index

A.D.L. Holding Corporation, 260, 276
Ace in the Hole, 98
Ackerman, Dr. Joseph, 80
Acquisto, Angelo, 339
Adams, John A., 20
Adrano, Frank, 282
Agoglia, Sylvester, 292
Agro, Thomas, 98, 106, 108, 110, 111
Aiello family, 194
Aiello, Joseph, 34, 168, 194, 230, 233, 236, 237, 255, 257, 258; and Antonio Lombardo, 194; and Gaspare Milazzo, 233; flees to Buffalo, 257; murder of, 258
Akron, OH, 204
Albano, Michael, 323
Albany, NY, 296, 299, 308
Albion, NY, 351
alcohol distilleries, 171, 178, 179, 184, 198, 236, 300, 310, 311, 313, 314
alcohol distillery explosion, 300
alcohol redistilling, 152, 171, 174, 180
Alden, NY, 61
Aleo, Joseph, 286, 287, 288
Alessi, Frank, 268, 297
Alessi, Louis, 148
Alessi, Sam "Doc", 315
Alfano, Vincenzo, 86
Allison, Detective Jack, 289, 290
Alo, Frank, 224
Amara, Caterina, 168
Amatuna, Samuzzo "Samoots", 163, 165, 166
American Temperance Society, 40
Amherst, NY, 310, 311
Amico, Patsy, 292
Anastasia, Albert, 280, 281
Anawanda Club, 276
Anconitano, Vincent "Jimmy the Tough", 305
Andrews, William, 128

Angersola, John, 197, 253
Annenberg, Moses, 294
Anselmi, Albert, 163, 164, 165, 166, 238
Antinori, Ignazio, 225
Anti-Saloon League, 41, 42
Antonelli, Albert, 268
Archie, Joseph, 59
Arlington Hall, 67
armed robbery, 52, 158, 245, 246, 316, 343
arson, 85, 239
Artichoke King. *See* Terranova, Ciro
assault, 246, 303, 322, 324, 343, 344, 345
Atlanta Federal Prison, 97, 102, 111, 129, 144, 182, 188, 219
Attell, Abe, 71
attempted murder, 285
Attica State Prison, 322
Auburn State Prison, 180
Augello, Joe, 315
Austaro, Charles, 149, 150, 151
Auto Inn. *See* Auto Rest roadhouse
Auto Rest roadhouse, 69, 70, 93, 94, 95, 103, 104, 111, 113, 116, 117, 123, 124, 127, 136, 220; Ku Klux Klan raid, 136; liquor raids, 93, 94, 103
automobile theft, 251, 265, 282, 298
Baer, Charles, 284
Bagheria Club, 303
Bagheria, Sicily, 34, 168
Baglio, Joe, 149
Bain, U.S. Commissioner Donald, 95
Baldelli, Ecola "the Eagle", 163
Balli, Charles, 52
Baltimore, 97
Banas, Joseph "Patsy", 176
bank robbery, 201
bankruptcy fraud, 13, 22, 23, 24, 77, 200
Barber, Joe, 289, 290
Barber, John, 289
Barbera, John, 94, 287, 288
Barbera, Pietro, 52

Barcellona Pozzo di Gotto, Sicily, 183
Barone, Anthony, 349
Barone, Dr. Anthony, 46, 73
Barone, Frank, 323
Barone, Frank E., 101, 104
Barone, John, 125
Barone, Rosario, 115
Barrel Murder. *See* Madonia, Benedetto
Barrel Mystery, The, 48
Barry, Safety Director Edwin D., 226, 227, 241
Bartkowiak, Joseph, 63
Bartlett, Prohibition Enforcement Chief Allan, 154
Bascone, Vito, 163
Basile, Joseph, 28
Batavia, NY, 33, 149, 241, 340, 341, 342, 344, 345, 346, 350, 351
Battaglia, Anthony, 314, 315, 329
Battaglia, Orazio, 21
Battaglia, Peter, 337
Baucina, Sicily, 188
Bauder, June, 310
Bazzano, John, 270, 277, 279, 280, 281, 282, 299, 308; "Sack Murder", 281; and Nicola Gentile, 271; and Volpe brothers, 279, 280; military service, 270
Bazzano, Santo, 279
Beck, Frederick C., 69
Beckerman, "Little Abie", 68
Bell, Louise, 334, 335
Bella, Tony, 224
Bellantoni, Angelina, 66, 68
Bellantoni, Gaetano. *See* Dyke, Thomas J.B. "Tommy"
Bellantoni, Rocco, 66
Belleville, NJ, 225
Belliotti, Rev. Domenico, 144
Bellissimo, Dominico, 18
Bello, Tony, 229
Belmar, NJ, 80
Benk, Sergeant Joseph, 252
Bennett, Charles, 80
Benovitz, Emil and Sylvia, 267
Bentz, Dr. Charles A., 179
Berg, Alexander, 292, 293
Bernardo, Rev. Alfonso, 339
Bertoni, Ernest and Angela, 228
Beyer, Albert, 299
bichloride of mercury, 135
Billerio, Rev. Austin, 151
Bingeman, Detective Sergeant George, 115
Biondo, Joseph, 192, 264, 280, 281
Bishop, Health Officer John L., 58
Bison Trio, 70
Black Hand extortion, 12, 13, 18, 19, 27, 28, 29, 45, 47, 77, 135, 187, 247, 290
Black Sox scandal of 1919, 70
Blackmon, M.F., 131, 154

Blaine, Senator John, 301
Blatt, Norman "Big Agate", 334
Bocchimuzzo. Maurizzio, 63
bombing, 18, 27, 60, 153, 165, 166, 239, 247, 299, 304, 323, 336, 346
Bonadonna, Anthony, 158
Bonadonna, Rocco, 135
Bonanno family, 26
Bonanno, Caterina Bonventre, 75
Bonanno, Joseph, 75, 235, 251, 257, 268, 274, 275, 276, 278; birth of, 75; family background, 75
Bonanno, Salvatore (Joseph Bonanno's father), 75
Bonarrigo, Ben, 345
Bonasera family, 9
Bonasera, Cassandro "Tony the Chief", 281, 329; and Salvatore Lucania, 281; and the DiCarlo family, 281; arrest record, 308; marries Rosaria DiCarlo, 308
Bonasera, Charles, 34, 299
Bond Chemical Company, 125
Bonfiglio, Albert, 203
Bonventre family, 26, 75, 81
Bonventre, Antonia DiBenedetto, 299
Bonventre, Carmela Magaddino, 75
Bonventre, Frank, 201
Bonventre, Martino, 75
Bonventre, Peter, 60
Bonventre, Vito, 76, 82, 88, 251, 258; funeral of, 252; murder of, 251
bookmaking, 221, 293, 294, 304, 330, 336, 340, 343, 346, 347, 349, 350
bootlegging, 2, 40, 43, 51, 54, 59, 60, 62, 63, 69, 71, 106, 108, 125, 145, 146, 150, 151, 163, 171, 174, 183, 204, 221, 235, 241, 252, 254, 266, 286, 310, 313, 318, 324, 333, 334
Borruso, Samuel, 204
Borruso, Simone, 40, 198
Borsellino, Anthony, 253
Boston, 32, 33, 40, 72, 97, 162, 261
Bowmansville, NY, 72, 104, 116, 123, 124
Bradford, PA, 289, 290
Brancato, Frank, 297
Brancato, Sam, 315
Brantford, Ontario, 64
Brehm, Allen K., 141
Brezing, Rev. Herman, 155
bribery, 130, 154
Broadway Central Hotel, 81
Bromley, Patrolman Elmer, 317
Bronx, NY, 70, 86, 193, 194, 232, 244, 245, 246, 247, 249, 256, 259, 260, 262, 275; Alhambra Apartments, 259; Belmont Avenue, 262; Fordham Hospital, 262; Our Lady of Mount Carmel Church, 262; Pelham Parkway, 259; Roman Gardens, 247; Roman Gardens

454 · *DiCarlo*

restaurant, 245; Washington Avenue, 268
Brooklyn, 48, 77, 224, 232, 251, 260, 281, 292; Bath Beach, 193; Bensonhurst, 193; Bushwick, 163; Coney Island, 264, 273, 274, 283; Del Pezzo Restaurant, 261; Kings County Hospital, 267; Mount Carmel Roman Catholic Church, 252; Prospect Park South, 284; Red Hook, 280; Seaside Inn, 283; Tin Can Mountain, 281; waterfront rackets, 224; Williamsburg, 76, 78, 79, 82
Brown, Helen, 163, 167
Brownell Law (consorting), 328, 329, 330, 331, 333; nullified, 330
Brownstein, Jack, 196
Bryan, William Jennings, 41, 42
Bryant, William, 349
Bua, Michael, 282
Buccellato family, 26, 75, 81, 86
Buccellato, Felice, 75
Buccellato, Giovanni, 76
Buccellato, Vito, 88
Bufalino, Rosario "Russell", 294
Buffalo, 1, 15, 276, 281, 351; Amherst Street, 177; Black Rock, 176, 178, 179; Broadway Auditorium, 127; Broadway Brewing Company, 158; Buffalo Trust Company, 141; Canal District, 2, 16, 17, 21, 27, 199; Central YMCA, 105; Chippewa Street, 105; City Court, 134, 295; Columbus Hospital, 46, 106, 169, 172, 310; Connecticut Street, 178, 309, 312; Delaware Avenue, 103, 105; dock workers, 16; economy, 15; Efner Street, 171; Elmwood Hotel, 179; Emergency Hospital, 113, 135, 238; Erie Canal, 17; ethnic conflict, 16, 24; Federal Building, 105; Front Avenue, 21, 43, 47, 170; General Electric building, 239; General Hospital, 61; Georgia Street, 52; host site of Mafia meetings, 91; Italian immigration, 15; Jersey Street, 234, 301; Marine Bank, 141; Maryland Street, 199; Michigan Avenue, 285; Moose Hall, 315; narcotics trafficking, 97; New York Central Station, 127, 128; Oak Street, 112; Pan-American Exposition, 1; Pearl Street, 349; police corruption, 99, 100, 102; politics, 17, 73, 315; population growth, 15; Prospect Avenue, 33, 72, 92, 104, 115, 258; River Road, 63; Seventh Street, 23, 27, 172; Sisters of Charity Hospital, 204; South Side, 16; St. Anthony's Hall, 169; St. Mary's Maternity Hospital, 221; Thompson Street, 179; Trenton Avenue, 169, 345; Vermont Street, 314; West Eagle Street, 21, 23; West Side, 16, 302, 310; West Tupper Street, 106
Buffalo Al. *See* Ritchie, Alberto
Buffalo Athletic Club, 348
Buffalo Bill. *See* Palmeri, Benedetto Angelo
Buffalo Commercial Advertiser, 116
Buffalo Courier, 159
Buffalo Courier Express, ix
Buffalo Crime Family, 71, 199; "the Arm", 3; assistance to Gervase family, 161; collapse of, 3; early factions, 92
Buffalo Enquirer, 94
Buffalo Evening News, 322, 332
Buffalo Evening Times, 123, 309
Buffalo Italian Importing Company, 22, 23
Buffalo Morning Express, 94
Buffalo Pitts Company, 19
Buffalo Police Department: Italian Squad, 201
Buffalo Times, 161
Buffalo, Charley. *See* DiBenedetto, Calogero "Charley Buffalo"
Buffalo, Rochester and Pittsburgh Railroad, 145
Burd, Judge George P., 328
Burfeind, Police Chief John, 100, 102
Burg, George, 125
Burgio, John, 157
Burgio, Louis, 291, 328
burglary, 45, 71, 185, 187, 225, 244, 246, 333
Burns, William J., 131
Buster from Chicago. *See* Domingo, Bastiano "Buster"
Busti, Paolo, 17
Cacera, Michael, 306
Caietta, Julius, 80
Caiozzo, Camillo, 80, 82, 83, 90
Calabrian organized crime, 36, 51, 63, 64, 164, 193, 254, 289; cooperation with Mafia, 63; led by Rocco Perri, 65
California Dry Fruit Importers, 256
Callea, Carmela, 312
Callea, Joseph, 312, 313
Callea, Salvatore "Sam", 198, 240, 303, 309
Callea, Vincenzo "Big Jim", 198, 240, 303, 309
Callinan, Detective Sergeant George H., 56, 150, 153, 337
Callinan, Patrolman Simon, 100
Caltanissetta, Sicily, 8
Caltavuturo, Sicily, 59, 149
Camerano, Sylvester. *See* Cameron, Lester
Cameron, Lester, 70, 105, 106, 108, 109, 110, 111, 120, 121, 143
Cammarata, Emanuele, 224
Cammilleri, John, 315; murder of, xii, xiv
Camorra. *See* Neapolitan organized crime
Canandaigua, NY, 177

Cannatta, Luigi, 22
capodecina, 193
Capodicaso, Gaetano, 113, 114, 117, 118, 119, 124, 125, 126, 127, 129, 130, 135, 139, 141, 142
Capone, Alphonse, 164, 167, 193, 194, 205, 226, 227, 233, 237, 238, 257, 258, 259, 264, 265, 266, 268, 269, 271, 272, 276, 277, 278, 292; and Giuseppe Masseria, 193, 194, 233, 259; and Nicola Gentile, 271; tax evasion, 271, 279
Capone, Ralph, 271
Caputo, James "Julie", 315
Capuzzi, Nick "the Thief", 259
Caradonna, Vito, 88
Carallo, Frank, 51
Carfano, Anthony, 193, 205, 264, 284; and Gerardo Scarpato, 284
Carillo, Peter, 151
Carlisi, Joseph, 311
Carlisi, Roy, 310, 311, 312
Caroddo, Carlo, 78
Carr, Deputy Police Chief Frank J., 173
Carr, Lieutenant Robert, 292
Carroll, Assistant Chief James, 318, 321
Carsello, Ralph, 334, 335, 336
Carubba, Serafino, 24
Caruso Restaurant, 320
Caruso, Angelo, 196, 292
Cascio Ferro, Vito, 12
Cascio, Dr. Daniel, 205
casino gambling, 340
Castellammare del Golfo Society, 338
Castellammare del Golfo, Sicily, 26, 31, 40, 64, 75, 77, 79, 81, 184, 200, 234, 337
Castellammarese Mafia network in the U.S., 32, 40, 77, 79, 81, 84, 87, 198, 233, 234, 236, 244, 249, 251, 255
Castellammarese War, 234–65; postwar meetings, 268
Catalano, Philip, 201
Catania, James, 246
Catania, Joseph "Joe the Baker", 246, 261; funeral of, 262; murder of, 262
Catania, Sicily, 34, 163, 262
Cavallero, 165
Cavaretta, Rosario, 98, 101
Cavolo, Detective Charles, 45, 253
Cecala, Antonio, 21
Cefoli, Bruno, 19
Celona, James, 35, 36, 37, 38, 39, 63
Celona, Joseph, 168
Cerda, Sicily, 225
Cerrito, Nicholas, 291
Certo, Peter, 198, 312
Cesare, Michael, 350
Cheektowaga, NY, 299, 311, 312, 326, 343, 344
Chiaravalloti, Frank, 292

Chicago, 16, 20, 34, 70, 72, 77, 78, 79, 86, 91, 162, 163, 164, 165, 167, 168, 173, 193, 194, 196, 204, 223, 224, 225, 230, 233, 236, 237, 238, 248, 250, 255, 258, 259, 264, 265, 268, 269, 271, 276, 277, 278, 279, 282, 292, 293, 298, 301, 307, 311, 315, 339; Amato's restaurant, 166, 168; Bridewell Hospital, 194; Hotel Congress, 268, 269, 271; Jefferson Park Hospital, 166; Kolmar Avenue, 258; North Clark Street, 237; North Side, 164, 194; politics, 78; S.M.C. Carting, 237; South Side, 163; West Garfield Park, 258
Chicanno, Francesco, 22
Chiesa Maria Santissima di Loreto (Church of Mary Most Holy of Loreto), 7
Chillicothe, OH, 219
Chirico, Toto, 232
Christiano, Vito V., 73
Church of the Annunciation, 311
Cicatello, Anna, 170
Cicatello, Anthony, 169
Cicatello, Joseph, 169
Cicero, IL, 238
Cieravo, Salvatore "Rose", 80, 83, 89, 90
Circolo Musicale Bellini, 72
Clark, "Jew Minnie", 69, 72, 93, 103, 123, 137, 143
Cleveland, 3, 34, 44, 45, 55, 72, 96, 107, 109, 128, 138, 139, 141, 144, 173, 183, 193, 194, 195, 196, 198, 200, 204, 222, 223, 224, 225, 226, 227, 229, 230, 231, 237, 240, 241, 242, 243, 249, 252, 253, 254, 258, 266, 267, 278, 279, 282, 296, 297, 302, 304, 308, 310, 312, 329, 333; Kinsman Road, 266; Mayfield Road, 195, 228, 253, 296; Our Lady of Peace Church, 241; St. John's Hospital, 297; St. Luke's Hospital, 253, 297, 304; Venetian Cafe, 253; White Rock Inn, 195; Woodland Avenue, 45, 196, 223, 228, 240, 253, 297
Closs, Edward, 61
Clum, Alfred, 228
Coatsworth, Judge Emerson, 175
Coca-Cola, 95
cocaine, 95, 96, 97, 98, 101, 103
Coll, Vincent "Mad Dog", 276
Colletti, Charles, 196, 197, 253
Collins, Rev. James, 339
Cologna, Joseph, 161
Colosimo, "Big Jim", 164
Colton, Bishop Charles H., 72
Connolly, Detective Sergeant William, 113, 115, 116, 124, 135, 140, 310, 314
Connors, Lieutenant Vincent J., 345
Consolo, Biagio, 228
Constantino, Samuel, 321

construction workers strike of 1910, 24
Conte di Torino Lodge, Order Sons of Italy, 72
Cook, Harold V., 101
Cooley Motor Company, 342
Coonan, Detective Sergeant Joseph, 190
Coppola, Frankie, 315
Coppola, Iggy, 315
Coppola, Samuel, 287, 288, 315, 322
Coppola, Steve, 315
Corda, Pasquale "Patsy", 201, 202, 300, 312
Corleone, Sicily, 12, 244
corn sugar, 183, 223, 227, 230, 326
Corrado, Pete, 334
Corrigan, Magistrate Joseph E., 85
Cortelli, Margaret, 308
Cosenza, Joe, 266, 268
Costanzo, Salvatore, 21
Cotroni, Raphael, 127
counterfeiting, 11, 12, 20, 48, 77, 78, 182, 305, 306, 307, 315, 318
Crage, Joseph, 127
Creahan, Captain John J., 102
Crehan, Mark, 174
Cridino, Augustine, 118, 125
Crissey, Mae, 93
Crocevera, Isidoro, 8, 11, 20, 48, 106
Cronin, Commissioner Jeremiah R., 154, 180
Cronin, Patsy. *See* Curione, Pasquale
Cullen, William, 200
Cullen-Harrison Amendment, 307
Curione, Pasquale, 153, 154, 180, 312
Cusick, Joseph, 175
Custodi, Frank "Cakes", 323, 343
customs violations, 180
Cuyahoga County OH Jail, 243
D'Andrea, Anthony, 77, 91, 163, 224; family background, 77; priesthood, 77
D'Andrea, Francesca Miceli, 77
D'Andrea, Giuseppe, 77
D'Andrea, Lena Wagner, 77
D'Angelo, Bert, 176, 180
D'Aquila, Marianna, 205, 206
D'Aquila, Salvatore "Toto", 77, 79, 164, 182, 183, 184, 185, 190, 193, 194, 198, 204, 205, 206, 224, 230, 232, 234, 236, 252, 259, 261, 266, 278; and Umberto Valente, 185; death sentence against Morello faction, 182; murder of, 205; police record, 206
Damanti, Joe, 297
Danser, Medical Examiner Earl G., 46, 160, 179
Dante Place (Canal Street), 17, 24, 26, 27, 30, 72, 142, 157, 158, 159, 160, 169, 170, 238, 239, 302, 303, 326
Davenport, Detective Charles C., 89
Davis, attorney J. Mercer, 90

Davis, John, 128, 130
Davis, Ralph S., 345
Dayton OH Workhouse, 197
DeCalo, Joseph, 24
DeCaro, John, 170
DeFusto, Frank A., 204
DeGoris, Frank, 318
Delahunt, Raymond, 114, 117, 128, 130, 131
Dempsey, Jack, 71
Dempsey, Justice John P., 229
DeNitto, Vito, 320
DePalma, Biagio, 195
DePasquale, Thomas, 118, 125
Depew, Assistant U.S. Attorney Ganson Goodyear, 107, 109, 110, 117, 118, 132, 147
DePrima, Giuseppe, 11, 12
DeSalvo, Anthony, 316
DeStefano, Daniel, 262
Detroit, 33, 34, 72, 76, 79, 81, 85, 86, 87, 102, 107, 109, 163, 168, 196, 200, 233, 248, 249, 250, 255, 262, 308, 314, 331, 332, 334, 336, 339; Grandville Avenue, 262; Vernor Highway, 248
Devlin, U.S. Attorney Frederick T., 298
DiBenedetto, Calogero "Charley Buffalo", 198, 255, 257, 258, 299, 313
DiBenedetto, Giuseppe, 161, 198, 199, 338; arrival in Buffalo, 199; murder of, 238
DiCarlo Gang, 220, 285, 291, 300, 316, 336, 341, 343
DiCarlo, Francesco, 5, 9; death of, 31
DiCarlo, Francesco (JD grandfather), 7
DiCarlo, Giuseppe, 2, 7, 15; "Don Pietro", 27; and Angelo Palmeri, 25, 26; and Giuseppe Morello, 12, 20; and Isidoro Crocevera, 48; and Minnie Clark, 69; and Tommy Dyke, 66, 69; bootlegger, 43; boxing fan, 70; business failure, 22, 24; commission merchant, 31; death of, 2, 71; funeral, 72; grocery business, 9, 21; health failing, 32, 66; Mafia boss, 20, 34, 71, 87, 91; marriage of, 8; narcotics, 119; naturalization, 29; restaurateur, 50; saloon operator, 27, 31, 50
DiCarlo, Joseph J., 49, 111, 129, 144, 149, 285, 292, 294, 308, 314, 315, 323, 333, 341, 342, 345, 347, 350; ancestors of, 7; and Angelo Palmeri, 27, 30; and Anthony Palmisano, 317; and John Fina, 315; and Joseph Lonardo, 139; and Joseph Ruffino, 125; and Lester Cameron, 120; and Lorenzo Lupo, 195; and Minnie Clark, 94; and Peter Gallelli, 127; and Philip Mangano, 115; and Salvatore Callea, 312; and Salvatore Todaro, 139; and Stefano Magaddino,

92; and Whitey Kroll, 343; arrival in Buffalo, 19; author Tona's encounters with, xi–xiv; Auto Rest roadhouse, 69; birth of, 9; bootlegging, 93, 103; brewery sales representative, 307; childhood, 28; childhood homes in Buffalo, 21, 23; consorting with criminals, 329; death of, 3; draft registration, 29; education, 10, 29; FBI file, xiv; federal fine, 220, 221; florist, 296, 344; gambling devices, 300, 309; illegal voter registration, 294, 295; immigration, 5, 10; in Brooklyn, 10; in Detroit, 331; in federal custody, 219, 220; in Florida, 347, 349; in Manhattan, 10; life as parallel for Buffalo Crime Family, xv, 1–4; marriage to Salvatora "Elsie" Rose Pieri, 143; motor vehicle violations, 51; narcotics, 97, 99, 104, 109, 112, 119, 133, 136; naturalization, 296; parole, 220; passed over as father's successor, 73; pauper's oath, 221; portrayed as extortion victim, 288; Public Enemy No. 1, xi, 295, 316; quotes from, xiii, 103, 132, 221, 288, 294, 296, 305, 307, 308, 344, 347, 348; targeted by rivals, 304; trial for assault of Whitey Kroll, 347; witness intimidation, 112, 114, 119, 121, 129, 131
DiCarlo, Marino, 7
DiCarlo, Rosaria "Sarah", 5, 9, 30, 104, 118, 125, 127, 132, 220; marries Cassandro Bonasera, 308
DiCarlo, Salvatore "Sam", 5, 9, 50, 116, 220, 225, 228, 229, 281, 285, 286, 295, 298, 309, 329; transporting stolen vehicle, 282
DiCarlo, Vincenza Grasso, 5, 8; death of, 32; funeral of, 33
DiCarlo, Vincinetta Sarah, 221
DiCaro, John, 275
Dickey, Assistant U.S. Attorney Samuel, 117
Dickey's Roadhouse, 69
Dickson, Chief Constable S.J., 149
DiGregorio, Bartolo, 78, 82
DiGregorio, Gaspare, 275
DiGregorio, Rosaria Caroddo, 78
DiMarto, Liborio, 19
DiNieri, Vincenzo "James", 59, 60, 61, 62, 149, 150, 151; murder of, 150
DiRosa, Calogero, 157, 158
DiSalvo, Cerio, 312
DiStefano, James, 312
DiTulio, James, 52
DiVita's restaurant, 64
Doane, U.S. Commissioner Charles, 95, 96
Dolce, Sam "Shoes", 323

Dold Farms, 150
Domingo, Bastiano "Buster", 255, 256, 259, 262
Dominico, Albert "Kid Ginger", 99, 101, 102
Don Nitto. *See* Palmeri, Benedetto Angelo
Don Turridru. See Maranzano, Salvatore
Donahey, Governor A. Victor, 229, 254
Donovan, Colonel William J. "Wild Bill", 96, 97, 100, 103, 104, 105, 106, 111, 114, 115, 117, 118, 119, 120, 121, 123, 124, 125, 126, 128, 130, 131, 135, 136, 138, 139, 141, 142, 143
Dovern, Mildred, 160
Doyle, Assistant District Attorney David F., 350
Draper, Coroner W.L., 57
drivers licenses, 295
Duquette, District Attorney Burt A., 150
Dwyer, Detective James, 284
Dyer Act, 282, 298, 309
Dyke, Edward "Eddie", 68
Dyke, John B. "Johnny", 96
Dyke, Thomas J.B. "Tommy", 66, 67, 73, 97, 132, 204, 299, 308; move to Buffalo, 68; restaurateur, 69
East Cleveland, OH, 311
Eastman, Monk, 67
Egan's Rats, 238
Elardo, Anthony, 323
Elk Street Market, 21, 173, 202
Elks Lodge, 200, 202
Ellis Island, 10, 76, 82, 96, 225
Elmira NY Reformatory, 97, 106
Emky Shoe Company, 309
Endicott, NY, 76
Enea, Pasquale, 9, 12
English, Joseph "Wop", 335
Erie Beach, 160
Erie County Jail, 96, 98, 106, 111, 118, 130, 320, 333, 344
Erie, PA, 201, 300, 339
extortion, 12, 13, 14, 19, 45, 47, 66, 71, 77, 163, 166, 185, 187, 221, 225, 286, 287, 288, 291, 319, 336, 343, 344
Fairbanks, Chief Garner R., 290
Falcone, Salvatore, 339
Falcony, Anthony, 291
Falcony, Frank, 291
Falls Bottling Works, 198
Falls Tonic Company, 180
Falsone, Carmela, 204
Falsone, Santo, 169, 203
FBI, ix, xiv, 73, 131
Fein, Benjamin "Dopey Benny", 66, 67
Feiner, Phoebe, 110
Felicetta, Detective Sergeant Frank N., 341, 344
Ferrara, Tony "the Pelican", 194

Ferrigga, Joseph, 158
Ferrigno, Steve, 232, 259, 260, 278
Fiaschetti, Captain Michael, 81, 82, 84, 87
Fina, Adeline Pieri, 315
Fina, Frank, 34
Fina, John, 287, 288, 315, 329
Fina, John A., 96
Finazzo, Francesco, 86
Fino, Joe, xii
Fino, Ronald, xii
Fitzgibbons, Detective Sergeant William, 303
Fitzmartin, attorney John, 243
Flegenheimer, Arthur, 246
Fleischman, attorney Samuel M., 110, 118, 130, 328, 329, 330, 349
Flynn, Immigration Inspector William H., 227
Flynn, Secret Service Agent William, 11, 48
Folwell, Magistrate George H., 282
Fontana, Bartolomeo, 80, 81, 82, 83, 84, 86, 87, 88, 89
Ford Hotel, 103
Fort Erie, Ontario, 285
Forti, Jim, 64
Fox, Harriet, 109
Fox, Kitty, 96
Frahm, Chief of Detectives Fred W., 331
Frascella, Patrolman Soldano, 30
Fraterizo, Joseph, 47
Fraterrigo, Salvatore, 321, 351
Fredonia, NY, 144
Freiberg, Sheriff Charles F., 299
Fremming, LeRoy, 125
Friberg, Assistant County Prosecutor Harry, 336
Fritsch, U.S. Marshal Joseph, 132
Frontier Hotel, 239
Fuhrmann, Mayor Louis P., 25
Gagliano, Antonio, 168
Gagliano, Tommaso, 244, 256, 259, 275, 278; and Giuseppe Morello, 244; and Joseph Valachi, 245; immigration, 244
Gagliardo, Toto, 64
Galante, Mariano, 82, 88
Gallagher, Detective George, 284
Gallelli, Helen, 104, 114, 129
Gallelli, Peter, 103, 104, 105, 112, 113, 114, 117, 118, 119, 122, 124, 126, 127, 129, 130, 131, 132, 135, 136
Gallo, Ciro, 281
Gambino, Carlo, 260
Gambino, Carmelo, 157
Gambino, John, 157, 159, 160
Gambino, Rev. Joseph, 33, 72, 200, 308
gambling, 2, 3, 17, 27, 36, 70, 71, 105, 111, 163, 187, 195, 196, 221, 248, 293, 299, 314, 316, 319, 334, 336, 340, 341, 343, 346, 350
gambling devices, 299, 319, 322
Gandolfo, Filippo and Giuseppina, 39
Gant, John, 80
garrote, 284, 325
Garson, Murray, 295
Garwood, Samuel, 161
Gary, IN, 224
Gatti, Joseph, 314, 315, 323, 331
Gatti, Nick, 315
Gattozzi, Luigi, 228
Gaudiosa, Daniel. See Rogers, Daniel J.
Gayety Theater, 329
General News Bureau, 293
Genna family, 34, 162, 164, 194
Genna, "Bloody Angelo", 163, 165
Genna, "Little Mike", 163, 164, 165
Genna, Antonio "Tony the Gentleman", 163, 165
Genna, Pete, 163
Genna, Sam, 163, 165
Genna, Vincenzo "Jim", 163
Genova Inn, 145, 146, 148
Genovese, Frank, 158, 159
Genovese, Vito, 193, 264, 276, 278, 280, 281
Gentile, Nicola, 184, 185, 195, 264, 265, 270, 277, 279, 280
Gentile, Sam, 98, 101
Gerace, Philip, 319
Geraci, John, 116, 117, 123
Geraci, Joseph, 239
Gerard, Charles, 126
Germano, Rocco, 276
Gervase, Fortunato, 161, 162
Gervase, Joseph, 160
Gervase, Vincent, 161
Giallombardo, Giuseppe, 11
Giambra, Detective Joseph G., xi, xii
Giambrone, Joseph, 169
Giannola family, 86
Gilman, Mary, 175
Gilmore, May, 110, 112, 116, 120, 121, 122, 123, 128, 134, 143; and Joseph Patitucci, 122; perjury, 134
Giunta, Giuseppe "Hop Toad", 223, 224, 228, 238
Giustra, Johnny "Silk Stockings", 267
Glaefke, Patrolman Elmer, 254
Gloeckner, Lieutenant Kurt, 222
Glor, Detective Sergeant Charles, 178
Gnazzo, Emilio C., 55
Gnazzo, Lillian, 55, 58
Gold, Beatrice, 163, 167
Gold, Benjamin, 163
Gold, Donald, 167
Gold, Esther, 163
Goldstein, Harry, 180
Good Killers case, 79–91, 199, 252; Buffalo

"chief", 84, 87; press sensationalism, 86, 88
Good, Clarence E., 159
Goodrich, Jimmy, 71
Gorski, Stanley, 62, 150
Granatelli, Joseph "Longo", 86
Grand Central Terminal, 84, 87, 88
grand larceny, 333
Grande, Detective John B., 168
Grant, Edward, 158
Grasso, Luigi, 5
Greco, John and Antoinette, 228
Greenfield, Henry N., 103
Greenwald, "Little Maxey", 67
Greenwald, Assistant District Attorney Clarence W., 337
Griffin, Irene, 160
Grill, Charles, 103
Gryniewicz, Charlotte, 306, 307
Guagliano, Salvatore, 202
Guarino, Frank, 19
Guarino, Salvatore, 149
Guarnieri, Giuseppe, 21
Guastaferro, Detective Sergeant Ralph, 200, 201
Gueli, Dominic "Mangino", 296, 297
Guelph, Ontario, 36, 44, 63, 64
Gugino, attorney Frank, 295, 296, 298
Gugino, Carmelo, 21
Guzik, Jake "Greasy Thumb", 272
Guzik, Sam, 272
Haas, Valentine, 103
Hamilton, Ontario, 35, 36, 40, 44, 63, 64, 149, 180, 202, 235; General Hospital, 175
Hamlin, Chauncey J., 22
Hammacher, Schlemmer & Company, 187
Hamtramck, MI, 248
Harcourt, Judge Bertram E., 322
Harding, U.S. Commissioner Harry E., 221
Harris, Judge Samuel J., 347, 348, 349
Harrison Narcotics Act, 95, 104
Harry Lenny and Tommy Dyke Association, 66, 67
Hartman, Evelyn, 50
Hawthorne Inn, 238
Hayes, James A., 103
Hazel, Judge John R., 107, 109, 110, 111, 114, 181, 220
Hemstock, Gladys, 50
Henner, Edward, 178
Hennessy, Thomas M., 155
heroin, 95, 98
Higgins, Police Chief James W., 87, 316, 318, 323, 329, 341
Hinkley, Justice Alonzo G., 242
Hoak, Undersheriff George W., 59, 60
Hofheins, Assistant District Attorney Walter W., 54, 55, 295

Hollywood Inn, 308
Holy Angels Church, 302
Holy Cross Church, 33, 72, 200, 308, 340, 341
homicide, xii, xiv, 11, 12, 35, 36, 37, 38, 44, 45, 46, 49, 53, 54, 55, 56, 57, 58, 59, 62, 63, 64, 66, 67, 76, 79, 80, 81, 82, 83, 84, 85, 86, 88, 89, 90, 107, 114, 115, 147, 148, 149, 150, 151, 153, 154, 155, 157, 158, 159, 160, 162, 163, 164, 165, 166, 168, 169, 170, 171, 172, 176, 179, 183, 189, 190, 192, 194, 195, 196, 197, 198, 199, 201, 202, 203, 204, 205, 224, 225, 227, 229, 230, 237, 238, 239, 240, 241, 243, 245, 246, 247, 249, 251, 253, 254, 256, 257, 259, 261, 262, 265, 267, 268, 272, 275, 276, 277, 278, 281, 282, 284, 289, 290, 291, 293, 294, 295, 296, 299, 300, 302, 303, 308, 309, 311, 312, 313, 317, 320, 321, 324, 325, 332, 333, 334, 335, 336, 341, 342, 345, 350, 351
Hoover, J. Edgar, 131
Hoover, President Herbert, 301
Hopkins, William R., 226, 228
horse races, 105, 349
Hotel Statler (Buffalo), 308
Hotel Statler (Cleveland), 222, 223, 226, 227, 229, 230
Hudson, William M., 310
Iacuzzo, Joseph, 323
Iamascia, Anthony, 246
Iamascia, Daniel J., 246
ice racket, 187, 244
illegal possession of a revolver, 304
informants, 62, 81, 99, 102, 108, 177, 195, 281, 282, 289
Ingrassia family, 20
Insalaco, Salvatore "Sam", 170
Internal Revenue Service, 97, 271
International Groceries Corporation, 200
Intravia, James, 224
Ippolito, Fred, 172
Iraci, Anthony, 294
Iroquois Hotel, 149
Iselin, NJ, 225
Italian Gardens restaurant, 68
Italiano, Ignazio, 225, 228, 229
Italo-American Importing Company, 258
Izzo, Sam "Salvie", 344, 345, 346
Jackson, Town Supervisor Lee, 276
Jackson, Willie, 70, 71
Jamestown Cafe, 319, 323
Jamestown, NY, 148, 310, 311, 313
Jamison, Dr. Charles E., 80
jewelry, 246
Jewish organized crime, 67
Joe the Boss. *See* Masseria, Giuseppe "Joe the Boss"
Johnson, Detective Arthur C., 246

Johnson, Detective James, 127
Johnstown, PA, 270
Joliet Prison, 78
Jopp Drug Company, 180
Jordan, Detective William "Stormy Bill", 100, 103
jury tampering, 107, 348
Kaba, Immigration Inspector John, 296
Kalisch, Judge Samuel, 89
Kamarek, Felix, 146
Kansas, Rocky, 70, 71, 73, 99, 127
Kaplan, Rubin, 68
Karnes, Belle, 96
Kaufman, Abe, 110
Keating, U.S. Commissioner George P., 95
Keeler, Judge Patrick J., 304
Keenan, Detective James, 58
Kelley, "Lucky Lou", 145, 148
Kelly, Patrolman Thomas, 57
Kelly, Paul. *See* Vaccarelli, Paolo "Paul Kelly"
Kennedy, Jack, 334
Kenney, Narcotics Agent Stanley, 110
Kenney, Stanley, 101
Kenny, Detective Sergeant Ed, 238
Kerr, John Benjamin "Ben", 180
kidnapping, 187, 285, 286, 292, 293, 308, 329
Kingston Penitentiary, 38
Kirk, Detective William D., 192
Klein, U.S. Commissioner John H., 95, 98, 104, 105, 114, 115, 116, 117
Klippel, Peter, 69
Knibloe, attorney John, 105, 342, 346, 347, 350
Knight, Judge John, 298, 306
Knowles, District Attorney Raymond A., 337
Knox, Judge John Clark, 101
Kroll, Roman C. "Whitey", 343, 345, 347, 348
Ku Klux Klan, 136, 137, 138, 155
Kuhn, Leo, 62
La Salle, NY, 153, 180
LaBarbara, Joseph, 291
LaBarbara, Michael, 291
Laborers Local 210, ix, xii
Lacatto, Andrea, 86
LaChiusa, Albert, 323
LaChiusa, William "Billy", 305, 319, 323
Lachman, Arthur, 22
Lackawanna, NY, 304, 305, 319
Ladonna, Paul, 80
LaFata, Salvatore, 168
Lagattuta, Angelo, 86
Lagattuta, Pietro, 186
Lagattuta, Salvatore, 339, 351
Lakrewski, Alexander, 63
Lama, Gus, 127

LaMarca, Salvatore, 125
LaMare, Anna, 262
LaMare, Cesare "Chester", 248, 249; flees to New York, 262; murder of, 262
Lansone, Fannie, 240
Lanza, attorney Horace O., 19, 138
Lanzetti gang, 204
LaPaglia, Joseph, 159
Larkin, Judge George A., 344
LaRu restaurant, 199
LaSalle, Ernest, 334
Lascola, Dr. August, 132, 301
LaSina Restaurant, 202
Laughlin, Leo, 93
Lavigne, George "Kid", 71
Lawrence, Belle, 101
Lawrence, Jack, 70
Lazzi, Stanley, 203
Leach, Coroner G.E., 37
Lehman, Governor Herbert H., 328
Leibowitz, attorney Samuel Simon, 282
Leigh, Detective Frank, 169
Lenny, Harry, 66, 67
Leonard, Benny, 71
Leone, Christina, 54
Leone, Constantino, 54
Levinson, attorney Adrian, 293
Lewiston, NY, 51, 63, 153; Mount St. Mary's Hospital, 337
Licata, Carmelo, 254
Licata, Sicily, 96, 183, 195, 198, 226
Licato, Richard, 203
Licavoli Gang, 334, 335
Licavoli, Jimmy, 334
Licavoli, Thomas "Yonnie", 334, 335
Liconti, Carmelo, 267, 272, 283
Lima, Mary, 255, 256
Lipsitz, attorney Harry, 114, 118, 130
Liquor Exchange, 188
Livaccori, Philip, 113, 118, 125, 201, 202, 300
Livorsi, Frank, 245, 264
loan sharking, 71
LoBosco, Joseph, 86
LoBosco, Michael, 52, 184, 266, 268
LoBosco, Pietro, 86
Lockport, NY, 59
LoDestro, Louis, 118, 125
LoGrasso, Dr. Horace, 21
Lojacono, Dr. Salvatore, 46, 72, 73
Lolordo, Joseph, 194, 224
Lolordo, Lena, 236, 237
Lolordo, Pasquale "Patsy", 223, 228, 236; murder of, 237
Lombardi, Giuseppe, 82, 83, 88, 90
Lombardino, Andrea, 225
Lombardino, Salvatore, 225, 227, 229
Lombardo, Antonio, 167, 194, 224, 230
Lombardo, Peter, 282

Lombardo, Philip, 311
Lombardo, Samuel, 344, 346
LoMonte, Fortunato "Charles", 183
Lonardo family, 96; grocery business, 183
Lonardo, Angelo, 241, 243
Lonardo, Concetta Paragone, 55, 240, 243
Lonardo, Dominick, 183
Lonardo, Frank, 183, 243
Lonardo, John, 183, 196, 200, 223
Lonardo, Joseph, 55, 138, 183, 184, 193, 194, 195, 196, 198, 200, 223, 240; and the Callea brothers, 312
Long, Medical Examiner Charles E., 46, 135, 170, 175, 179, 325
Longo, Antonina, 337, 339
Longo, Arcangela Magaddino, 336, 337, 338, 339; funeral of, 338
Longo, Francesco, 338
Longo, Josephine, 337, 339
Longo, Matteo, 337
Longo, Nicholas, 336, 337, 338, 339; and Giuseppe DiBenedetto, 338; immigration, 337; marriage to Arcangela Magaddino, 338
Longo, Rosa Ruggieri, 337
Longo, Rose, 337, 338, 339
LoPiccolo, Stefano, 265
LoPresti, attorney Salvatore, 226
Loreto, Sicily, 7
Los Angeles, 163, 168
LoTempio, Antonino, 340
LoTempio, Frank, 340, 344, 345, 346, 350; background, 340; funeral of, 342; murder of, 341
LoTempio, Josephine Mancuso, 340
LoTempio, Pietra Castellana, 340
LoTempio, Russell, 340, 346
Louisville, KY, 262
LoVerde, Salvatore, 264, 265
LoVullo, Sam, 52, 167, 168, 171, 204, 351
Lubitsky, Abe "Punk", 334
Lucania, Salvatore "Charlie Luciano", 192, 248, 264, 278; and Salvatore Maranzano, 264, 265, 276; and Stefano Magaddino, 276; betrayal of Giuseppe Masseria, 264, 265
Lucchese, Thomas, 244, 257, 275, 276
Luciano, Charlie. *See* Lucania, Salvatore "Charlie Luciano"
Lumetto, Joseph, 351
Lumia, Frank, 112, 116, 134
Lupo, Ignazio "the Wolf", 12, 13, 20, 21, 182, 184; 1909 extortion charge, 13; business failure, 23; counterfeiting conviction, 20
Lupo, Lorenzo, 121, 195, 196, 197
Lynch, John L., 294
Maccio, Tony "Mike", 290
Mack, Detective Sergeant Richard C., 310

Madigan, Detective William, 173
Madison Square Garden, 67, 70, 71
Madonia, Benedetto, 11, 12, 20
Mafia convention in Chicago, 1931, 269, 270, 271
Mafia convention in Cleveland, 1928, 222–31, 230; arraignment, 227; arrests, 222; attendees escaped notice, 226; bail, 227, 228; criticism of police, 226; five go to trial, 229; guilty pleas, 229; interrogation of suspects, 227; known attendees, 223; two suspects released, 227
Mafia of Sicily, 8, 26, 75
Mafia of United States, 29, 36, 77, 78, 223, 230; "boss of bosses", 12, 77, 79, 164, 182, 184, 185, 189, 193, 194, 198, 205, 206, 223, 224, 230, 231, 232, 233, 234, 236, 248, 250, 251, 255, 256, 259, 261, 264, 269, 270, 272, 273, 274, 275, 277, 278; Castellammarese War, 234–65; Commission, 270, 278, 279; crime family reorganization, 268; factions, 236, 255; post-Castellammarese War meetings, 268
Magaddino family, 26, 81
Magaddino, Angela, 79
Magaddino, Anna Buccellato, 76
Magaddino, Carmela Carodddo, 78
Magaddino, Gaspare, 76, 78
Magaddino, Giovanni, 75
Magaddino, Giuseppa Ciaravino, 75
Magaddino, Josephine, 79
Magaddino, Pete (Stefano's cousin), 269
Magaddino, Peter (Stefano's son), 78
Magaddino, Pietra Carodddo, 78
Magaddino, Pietro (Stefano's brother), 76, 78, 82
Magaddino, Stefano, 2, 82, 84, 85, 88, 233, 250, 254, 258, 269; and Giuseppe DiBenedetto, 198; and Giuseppe Masseria, 234, 250; and Michele Merlo, 78; and Salvatore D'Aquila, 184; and Salvatore Lucania, 276; and Salvatore Maranzano, 273, 275, 276; and Sam DiCarlo, 226; and the Callea brothers, 198, 312; arrival in western New York, 64, 91; death of, 3; family background, 75; home damaged by bomb, 337; immigration, 76; induction into Mafia in Chicago, 77; installed as Buffalo Crime Family boss, 92; marriage of, 78; member of Commission, 283; rebellion against, 3; salesman, 76
Magistrale, Tony, 126
Magliocco, Giuseppe, 224, 228, 229
Maher, attorney Michael H., 101
Mahoney, Detective Sergeant John, 345
Mahoney, Detective Sergeant John F., 344

Maier, Ann, 306, 307, 317
malicious mischief, 332
Mancusa, Samuel, 57, 58
Mancuso, Charles, 310
Manestri, John, 158, 159
Mang, Chief Elmer, 318
Mangano, "Dago Lawrence", 292
Mangano, John J., 97, 99, 106, 121; government witness, 108
Mangano, Philip, 115, 131, 224
Mangano, Vincenzo, 224, 227, 232, 264, 278, 281
Mangus, Joseph, 312
Manor, Phil. *See* Livaccori, Philip
manslaughter, 180
Manzella, Carmelo, 21, 22, 24
Manzella, Giovanni, 21
Manzella, Lucia LoGrasso, 21
Manzella, Pietro, 21
Manzella, Salvatore, 9, 13, 21
Maranzano, Elisabetta Minore, 234, 235
Maranzano, Giuseppe, 236
Maranzano, Salvatore, 234, 235, 236, 250, 251, 252, 255, 256, 257, 258, 259, 260, 261, 262, 263, 264, 265, 268, 269, 270, 271, 272, 273, 274, 275, 276, 277, 278, 283, 292; alienates supporters, 274; and Giuseppe Masseria, 236; banquet, 272; bootlegging, 236; Brooklyn residence, 235; immigration, 234; import-export business, 236; in Canada, 235; in Wappingers Falls, NY, 236, 268; memo book, 276; murder of, 275; smuggling aliens into U.S., 276
Marchino, Ercole, 265
Marchione, Paul, 247
Marinaccio, Detective Sergeant Anthony, 201
Marinelli, Albert, 68
Maritime Society of Sciacca, 273
Marnon, Deputy Police Chief John S., 102, 178
Martin, Jack, 54
Martino, Mike, 45
Mary Help of Christians Church, 27, 39, 266
Mascari Funeral Parlor, 302
Mascari, Joseph, 127, 201, 320
Mascari, Louis, 72
Mascari, Samuel, 320
Mascato, Filippo, 36
Masseria, Giuseppe "Joe the Boss", 164, 168, 185, 186, 187, 188, 189, 190, 191, 192, 193, 194, 196, 198, 204, 205, 206, 223, 230, 231, 232, 233, 234, 236, 240, 247, 248, 249, 250, 251, 252, 255, 256, 257, 259, 260, 261, 262, 263, 264, 265, 266, 267, 272, 273, 276, 278, 283, 284; and Alphonse Capone, 193, 194, 233, 259; and Joseph Aiello, 233; and Steve Ferrigno, 259; birth of, 185; dodges assassin's bullets, 191; funeral of, 265; immigration, 185; murder of, 265; orders men to disarm, 261
Masseria, Joseph (Giuseppe's son), 185
Masseria, Marie, 185
Masseria, Sam, 267
Masseria, Vita Marceca, 185
Maul, Judge Peter, 319
Mauro, Salvatore, 86, 187, 188, 189
Maybee, William, 176
Mayfield Road Gang, 253
Mazzara, Filippo, 31, 87, 92, 113, 144, 161, 162, 170, 171, 172, 173, 198, 199, 200, 201, 202, 238, 240, 324; and Giuseppe DiBenedetto, 199; arrival in Buffalo, 199; estate, 201; funeral of, 200; murder of, 199
Mazzara, Lena, 144
McAdoo, Chief Magistrate William, 247
McCall, Donald B., 178
McCarthy, Assistant Detective Chief Frank J., 332
McCormack, attorney Martin, 226
McHugh, Secret Service Bureau Chief Edward J., 154
McIntyre, attorney Ernest, 110, 118, 120
McLaughlin, Judge Clifford, 303
McNamara, Patrolman Edward, 30
McNaughton, attorney Daniel N., 23
McPherson, Detective Lieutenant Bert, 85, 86, 87
McTigue, Patrolman Robert, 319
Medina, NY, 346, 351; Medina Memorial Hospital, 346; Van's Grill, 346
Meli, Angelo, 248
Mello Bottling Works, 312
Menfi, Sicily, 185
Menneci, Michael, 287
Mercer, Rev. A.B., 155
Mercurio, August, 106, 108
Merlo, Michele "Mike", 78, 163, 166, 224, 271
Messina, Gaspare, 261
Messina, Sicily, 183
Metz, Joseph & Sons, 24
Meyer, Deputy Sheriff Ralph H., 195
Meyer, Teddy, 127
Miami, 205, 248
Miami Beach, FL, 248, 347, 349
Milano, Frank, 253, 278, 279, 282
Milazzo, Gaspare, 34, 79, 84, 233, 234, 248, 250, 252; murder of, 249
Miller, William, 349
Milne, Justice of the Peace Benjamin P., 344
Milwaukee, 72
Mineo, Manfredi "Alfred", 232, 259, 260,

276, 277, 278
Minnolera, Frank, 323
Minore, "Don Toto", 234
Mirabella, Giovanni, 225
Mirabella, John, 334
Mistretta family, 308
Mistretta, Loretta, 9, 39
Mistretta, Rosaria, 9, 27; death of, 31
Mitchell, Ritchie, 127
Moceri, Joe, 336
Moceri, Leo, 334, 335
Monaco, John, 294
Monastero, Stefano, 243, 270
Mongelluzzo, Amato, 168
Mongiovi, Calogero, 324
Mongiovi, Giuseppe. *See* Mule, Joseph
Monmouth County NJ Jail, 80, 89
Monreale, Sicily, 225
Monroe County Jail, 118, 148
Montana, John, 269, 338; influence in Buffalo, 269; politics, 269
Montana, Joseph, 24
Montana, Peter, 171
Montante brothers, 118
Monteleone, Domenico, 7
Montemaggiore Belsito, Sicily, 143, 317
Montesano, attorney Michael, 60, 118, 130
Moore, County Attorney Guy B., 103, 114, 137, 179
Moran, George "Bugs", 237, 238, 257
Morello, Giuseppe, 12, 13, 20, 77, 182, 184, 189, 232, 244, 250, 255, 256; counterfeiting conviction, 20; murder of, 256
Morello, Thomas, 52
morphine, 96, 97, 98, 101, 103, 108, 109, 110, 119
Morris, Edward "Fat Bull", 68
Morris, Judge George, 117, 118, 119, 123, 129, 142, 143
Moundsville WV Prison, 161
Mount Calvary Cemetery, 321
Mount Carmel Church, 161
Mucha, James, 178
Mule, Joseph, 118, 125, 318, 321, 323, 324, 325; immigration, 324
Mule, Martino, 77
Mule, Vito, 77
Murphy, Joseph, 98
Muscarella family, 9
Naples, Italy, 5, 6, 105
narcotics, 95, 96, 108, 119, 141, 188
Natarelli, Pasquale, 316
Nathan's Famous, 283
Neapolitan organized crime, 193, 201, 204, 289
Neeb, Norman J., 348
Neptune City, NJ, 80, 83
New Jersey State Prison, 91

New Kensington, PA, 270
New Orleans, 16, 20, 72
New York City, 9, 10, 12, 13, 16, 18, 19, 20, 21, 23, 25, 26, 27, 31, 32, 34, 40, 53, 54, 55, 58, 66, 71, 76, 80, 83, 85, 91, 96, 97, 104, 110, 112, 117, 120, 127, 162, 168, 171, 178, 182, 183, 186, 187, 198, 199, 223, 234, 235, 244, 245, 246, 250, 251, 252, 255, 257, 268, 277, 292, 299, 306, 307, 309, 318, 324, 328, 329, 330, 337, 338; Bellevue Hospital, 90, 190; Bowery, 185, 186, 187, 188; Brokaw Brothers Building, 257; Broome Street, 68, 188; Canal Street, 188; Chrystie Street, 86, 88, 188, 189; Delancey Street, 86; East Harlem, 10, 19, 183, 189, 244, 255; East Village, 183; Elizabeth Street, 9, 11, 12, 13, 17, 21, 26, 66, 185, 186, 187, 273; ethnic conflict, 67; Hotel Paramount, 272; Mafia bosses, 232; Monroe Street, 267; Mulberry Street, 66, 188; New York Central Building, 275; Park Avenue, 275; Prince Street, 12, 188; St. Mark's Hospital, 192; Stanton Street, 26; Times Square, 256
New York Police Department Italian Squad, 81, 84, 87
New York Times, 90
Newark, NJ, 106, 225
Newburger, Deputy Police Commissioner Harry, 68
Newton, attorney Thomas L., 347
Niagara County Court, 322
Niagara County Jail, 59, 202, 322
Niagara District Association, 315
Niagara Falls, NY, 2, 15, 21, 28, 31, 39, 40, 51, 55, 58, 60, 63, 64, 91, 146, 149, 152, 174, 235, 266, 291, 292, 312, 318, 339, 350, 351; Council of Churches, 155; Third Ward Political Club, 174, 180, 181; Whitney Avenue, 92, 198, 336
Niagara Gazette, 58
Niagara Mint Company, 300
Niagara Storage Warehouse, 300
Nichols, Patrolman Ben, 57
Nickerson, Patrolman Thomas, 321
Nitti, Frank, 271
Nobile, Sam, 195
Noonan, Judge Thomas Hazard, 148
Norris, Chief Medical Examiner Charles G., 257
Norvew, Edward, 126
Notarbartolo family, 6
Nowakowski, Stanley, 61, 62
Nuova Villa Tammaro restaurant, 264, 265, 267, 273, 283
Nyler, Celia, 145, 146
O'Banion, Dean, 164, 278

O'Connell family, 308
O'Connell, John J. Jr., 308
O'Grady, Detective Thomas, 20
O'Leary, Detective Sergeant Bartholomew, 115
O'Neill, Rev. George, 339
Oakville, Ontario, 176
Oddo family, 20
Oddo, John "Johnny Bath Beach", 281, 308
Ohio State Penitentiary, 243, 254
Ohio State Police, 220
Old Timer's Tavern, 322
Olean, NY, 289, 290
Oliveri, Sam, 224, 228
Olson, Patrolman Harold F., 165
Ontario Temperance Act, 39
opium, 97, 188
Orlando, Matteo, 27
Ormand, James, 284
Osowski, Patrolman Frank, 222, 226
Oyler, Ralph Hunter, 97, 99, 101, 102, 109
Paladino, Ida, 238
Paladino, James, 238
Paladino, Vincent, 238
Palamara, Anthony, 320, 325, 327
Palamara, Marcantonio "Mike", 320, 324, 325; and Anthony Palmisano, 321; funeral of, 321; murder of, 320
Palamara, Rose, 326
Palamara, Rose Mascari, 320
Palazzola, Paul, 224
Palermo, Giuseppe, 225, 229
Palermo, Sicily, 6, 7, 8, 49, 75, 87, 234, 243, 270
Palm Island, FL, 238
Palmeri family, 26, 266
Palmeri, Angelo. *See* Palmeri, Benedetto Angelo
Palmeri, Anna, 39
Palmeri, Anna Caleca, 26
Palmeri, Benedetto Angelo, 2, 25, 26, 30, 31, 32, 39, 40, 55, 56, 58, 73, 87, 91, 92, 113, 117, 127, 128, 142, 161, 184, 234, 274, 291, 296, 299, 318, 320, 321; and Philip Mangano, 115; and Salvatore D'Aquila, 184; and Salvatore Maranzano, 274; death of, 301; funeral of, 302; immigration, 26; marriage, 27; perjury, 291; saloon operator, 27; severely beaten, 291
Palmeri, Francesco, 26
Palmeri, Frank, 184
Palmeri, Helen, 55
Palmeri, Laura, 298
Palmeri, Paul, 26, 55, 151, 184, 198, 276, 281, 292, 299, 321, 339, 350
Palmeri, Rosaria, 55
Palmisano, Anthony "Baby Face", 306, 307, 315, 317, 318, 321, 324, 325; family background, 317; immigration, 317; murder of, 317
Palmisano, Benedetta, 317
Palmisano, Domenico, 317
Palmisano, Maria, 317
Palmisano, Salvatore, 317
Pampalona, Antonina, 199
Pampalona, Rosaria, 199
Panepinto and Palmeri Funeral Home, 302, 350
Panepinto, Alfred, 350; funeral of, 351; murder of, 350
Panepinto, Anna, 340
Panepinto, Anthony, 345
Panepinto, Rose, 340, 341
Panic of 1907, 19
Panzarella, Dr. Charles, 73
Papaleo, Nicola, 58
Papalia, Tony, 254
Paparone, Dominic, 35, 36, 37, 38
Pariso, Joseph, 310, 311
Parrino, Giuseppe, 249, 261
Parrino, Sam, 249
Patitucci, Joseph "Busy Joe", 96, 98, 99, 101, 103, 104, 112, 113, 116, 126, 134; and Salvatore Todaro, 139; attacked, 113, 119; confession, 135, 142; government witness, 102, 119; immigration, 96; military service, 96; suicide, 134
Patitucci, May. *See* Gilmore, May
Patitucci, Natalia, 140
Patricola, Vincent, 54
Payne News Agency, 293
Peace Bridge, 342
Pecoraro, Rose, 166
Pelletier, Joseph, 202
Pellettiri, Michael, 320
Pennachio, "Tommy the Bull", 188
Penney, Assistant U.S. Attorney Thomas Jr., 116
Pennsylvania Hotel, 178, 280
Pennsylvania Sugar Company, 326
perjury, 291, 345
Perna, Angelo, 201
Perna, Anthony, 294, 305, 312, 318, 322, 323, 328, 330, 333
Perri, Bessie, 254
Perri, Rocco, 36, 37, 39, 40, 44, 63, 64, 149, 152, 174, 176, 180, 181, 235, 254; "King of Bootleggers", 39
Perry, Detective Sergeant Peter, 201
Peschio, John, 323
Peters, Anthony, 349
petit larceny, 323
Petrash, Judge Louis, 333
Petrella, Thomas, 70
Petrelli, Dominic "the Gap", 244, 245
Petrosino, Lieutenant Joseph, 87

Pezzino, Calogero, 21
Philadelphia, 76, 79, 97, 184, 196, 204, 255, 293
Picogna, Carolina, 118, 125
Picogna, Joseph, 118, 125
Pieri, Giovanni, 143, 332; death of, 143
Pieri, Giuseppe, 143
Pieri, Horace, 315
Pieri, Ignazia "Anna" Ciresi, 143, 332
Pieri, John, 220, 335, 336
Pieri, John Rai, 333
Pieri, Joseph, 220, 314, 315, 316, 323, 328, 330, 333
Pieri, Rosolino, 143
Pieri, Salvatora "Elsie" Rose, 143, 220, 335
Pieri, Sam, xii, xiv, 220, 315, 316, 317, 323, 328, 330, 332, 333, 340, 341; and Frank LoTempio, 340; childhood, 332; criminal record, 332
Pieri, Stefano, 143
Pieri, Steven, 315
Pine Hill Cemetery, 31, 32, 33, 34, 72, 302
Pinnavaia, Michele, 148
Pinnavaia, Ralph, 147
Pinnavaia, Salvatore "Sam", 146, 147, 148
Pinzolo, Bonaventura "Joseph", 247, 256
Piper, Judge Charles, 57, 58, 59, 60
Piraino, Joseph, 256
Pisa, Italy, 75
Pisano, Little Augie. See Carfano, Anthony
pistol permit applications, 142, 148, 184, 234, 276, 291
Pittsburgh, 33, 86, 163, 168, 225, 243, 270, 271, 277, 278, 279, 280, 281, 282, 299, 308; East End, 243; Empire Yeast Company, 270; North Side, 243, 277; Rome Coffee Shop, 279; Squirrel Hill, 270; Virogo Yeast Company, 270; Wylie Avenue, 279
Pittston, PA, 171
Pizzuto, Flo, 53
Pizzuto, Frank, 53, 54
poison, 175, 176, 179, 180, 304
police brutality, 85, 258
Polino, Samuel, 349
Polizzi, Albert "Chuck", 195, 197, 253
Polizzi, Angelo, 281, 315
Pollaccia, Saverio "Sam", 164, 168, 184, 264, 278; murder of, 279
Pollaro, Gaspare, 256
Ponzo, Joseph, 86
Pooley, Justice Charles A., 59
Porrello family, 96, 183, 196, 198, 231, 266, 296, 311, 312
Porrello, Angelo, 196, 197, 302, 303; move to Buffalo, 302
Porrello, Frances, 304
Porrello, James, 197; murder of, 253
Porrello, John, 197, 303, 304, 310, 311; and the Callea brothers, 312
Porrello, Joseph, 197, 223, 226, 228, 241, 252, 268; murder of, 253
Porrello, Josephine, 304
Porrello, Mary, 228
Porrello, Ottavio, 197, 304
Porrello, Raimondo, 197, 228, 296, 297
Porrello, Rosario, 197, 296, 297
Potts, Detective Captain Emmett, 223
Poughkeepsie, NY, 276
Power City Distributing Company, 338
Prestogiacomo, Pasquale "Patsy Presto", 258, 259
Preuster, Lucas, 154, 155
Preuster, Orville A., 152, 153, 154, 155, 156
Privitera, Vincent, 125
Profaci Crime Family, 281, 308
Profaci, Giuseppe, 224, 228, 229, 232, 278; and Giuseppe Magliocco, 224; and Ignazio Italiano, 225; Mama Mia Importing Company, 225
Prohibition in Canada, 39
Prohibition in the United States, 40, 42, 43; Department of Treasury, 43; repeal, 301, 305, 307, 314, 316
prostitution, 82, 121, 202, 221
protection racket. See extortion
Provenzo, Samuel, 147
Pulvino, Angelo, 172
Puma, Angelo, 199, 200, 239, 240
Puma, Francesco, 82, 83, 85, 88, 89, 90
Quattrone, Joseph, 326
Quattrone, Joseph A., 168
Racalmuto, Sicily, 324
Ragone, Charles, 106
Randaccio, Frederico: "Lupo", 242
Randaccio, Umberto, 34, 242, 306
Rangatore, Frank, 32, 39, 55
Rangatore, Salvatore Jr., 339
Rangatore, Sam, 56
Rawls, Audrey, 334
Raymond Street Jail, 85
Realbuto, Louis, 205
Reams, County Prosecutor Frazier, 335
receiving stolen property, 323
Red Bank NJ Borough Jail, 80
Regan, Police Superintendent Michael, 18, 25
Regan, Prohibition Chief Leo, 179
Reilly, Detective Sergeant Terrence M., 56
Reina, Antonino, 244
Reina, Gaetano, 232, 244; ice racket, 244; immigration, 244; murder of, 247
Reppetto, Detective Silvio A., 84
Reuben Social Club, 304
Reville, Detective Chief John G., 242
Ricca, Paolo, 279
Riccio, Edward, 298

Rine, Deputy U.S. Marshal Frank, 102
Ritchie, Alberto, 127, 288, 289, 290, 291; assistant county detective, 289; informant, 289; journalist, 290
Ritchie, Anna Ciscone, 290
Ritz, 69, 132
Rizzo, Carl, xii; murder of, xiv
Rizzo, Joseph, 171, 172
Rizzo, Lucia, 299
Rizzo, Michael, 170
Rizzo, Peter, 47, 52, 54, 170, 171, 292
Rizzo, Pietro (Peter's cousin), 171
Rizzo, Pietro (Peter's cousin), 170
robbery, 324
Roberto. Joseph, 158
Roche, Police Commissioner Austin J., 100, 102, 172, 173, 176, 178, 179, 286, 287, 294, 295, 296, 299, 300, 301, 305, 306, 307, 312, 313, 314, 316, 323, 329; public enemies list, 295, 316
Rochester, NY, 32, 118, 132, 148, 149, 158, 171, 292, 333, 351
Rocky Kansas Jazz Band, 70
Roesch, Mayor Charles E., 315, 316
Rogers, Daniel J., 70, 73, 104, 118, 125
Roma Café, 202
Romano, Calogero, 312
Romano, Dr. Giuseppe, 283
Romano, Sam, 328
Romeo, Joe, 180
Roosevelt Cafe, 319
Roosevelt, President Franklin D., 301
Rosenberg, attorney Emanuel, 330
Rosenow, Patrolman Louis H., 102
Rothstein, Arnold, 70, 71, 230, 245
Rowe, Judge George H., 295
Rue, Detective Jacob B., 85
Ruffino, Anna, 125
Ruffino, Giuseppe, 186
Ruffino, Joseph, 113, 114, 124, 125, 129, 139, 144, 199, 305, 306, 312, 315
Ruffino, Salvatore, 186
Ruhl, Judge James, 243
Russell, Howard Hyde, 41
Russo, John, 98, 106, 108
Russo, Michael, 44, 225, 282; criminal background, 225
Russo, Salvatore P., 44, 48
S.S. Fitch, 285
S.S. Indiana, 5, 6
S.S. Lombardia, 9, 26
S.S. Martha Washington, 235
S.S. Perugia, 78
S.S. Presidente Wilson, 198
S.S. Re D'Italia, 317
S.S. San Giorgio, 76
S.S. Saturnia, 283
S.S. Saxonia, 40
Sabella, Maria Galante, 79

Sabella, Salvatore, 79, 84, 184, 204, 255
Sacco, Antonino "Nino", 320, 324
Sacco, Antonio, 30
Sacco, Giuseppe, 224
Sacco, Nino and Antonio, 50
Sacco, Stephen, 320
Salamanca, NY, 145, 289, 290
Saltfleet Township, Ontario, 235
Samuels, Frances, 275
San Francisco, 22, 72
San Pietro Apostolo, Italy, 40
Sanborn, NY, 151
SanFilippo, Calogero, 225
Santa Caterina Villarmosa, Sicily, 8
Santasiero, Joseph, 287, 288
Santasiero's Restaurant, xi, xii, xiii
Santuccio, Girolamo "Bobby Doyle", 245, 259, 277
Sanzone, Joseph, 115
Sarandrea, Loreto "Jumbo", 290
Sarcona, Luca, 86
Sargent. U.S. Attorney General John G., 178
Savini, Patrolman Donald, 100
Savino, James, 247
Savino, John, 247
Sayer, Frank E., 148
Sbarbaro, Assistant State's Attorney John, 165
Scalia, Augustus, 33, 339
Scalise, Frank, 260, 277
Scalisi, John, 163, 164, 165, 166, 238
Scalzo, attorney Angelo F., 57, 58, 59, 60, 322
Scanlon, Detective Michael, 169
Scarpato, Elvira, 283
Scarpato, Gerardo, 264, 265, 273, 283, 284
Schaefer, Philip C., 315
Scherer, Mina, 124
Schiro, Nicola, 232, 249
Schmelzer, G.F., 153
Schreiber, attorney Cornell, 336
Schultes, Glen, 295
Schultz, Dutch. *See* Flegenheimer, Arthur
Schwab, Mayor Francis Xavier, 100, 102, 137, 138, 148, 315, 316
Sciacca, Sicily, 236
Sciandra, Andrew, 201
Sciaroni, Domenic, 36, 38, 44, 63, 64
Sciaroni, Joseph, 64
Sciaroni, Salvatore, 64
Sciascia, Angelo, 321
Scibilia, Gaspare. *See* Milazzo, Gaspare
Scilla, Italy, 66
Scillia, Edward, 328
Scimeca, Michael, 187
Scinta, Serafino, 33
Scola, Carmen, 328
Scott, Edward J., 345, 347, 348

Scott, Phil, 248
Scott's Roller Rink, 345
Scranton, PA, 288
Selvaggi, Assistant District Attorney Nicholas, 85
Selzer, Judge Charles, 229
Seville, Spain, 290
Sexton, Charles F., 89
Shadow and Confetti Ball, 315
Shaker Heights, OH, 196
Shapiro, Herman, 187
Sharkey, Jack "Boston Gob", 248
Shaw, Ellsworth H., 152
Sheehan, John, 98
Shelper, Raymond, 60
Shisler, William, 285, 286
Shlenker, attorney Edward F., 109
Shoemaker, Chief of Detectives William, 293
Shuler, Carl F., 229
Sicilia Bella tavern, 324
Simon, Deputy Police Commissioner Carleton, 84
Simon, G.J., 224
Simpson, J.B., 186
Simpson, John E., 185
Simpson, William, 186
Sing Sing Prison, 11, 246
Siragusa, Giuseppe, 168, 243, 270, 277; immigration, 270; murder of, 277
Sirianni, Joseph, 40, 51, 61, 64, 154, 155
Sirianni, Samuel, 51, 61, 62
Sirocco, Jack, 66, 67
Slade, Fred, 326
slot machines, 195, 309, 319, 324
Smaldino, Detective Sergeant John, 157, 201
Smith, Albert, 60
Smith, Governor Al, 89
Smith, Leonard, 113
Smolarek, Leo, 62
smuggling, 180
Snyder, Patrolman John H., 251
Societa Castellammare del Golfo, 200
Societa Sant'Angelo di Licata, 311
Society of the Madonna, 151
Solomon, John, 300
Sorrell, Isaac, 80
Sospirato, Dominic, 240, 241, 243
Sottile, Joseph Henry, 40, 57, 58, 59, 151, 152, 154, 155, 174, 175, 180, 181
South Haven, MI, 163
Spallino, Calogero, 282
Spallino, Joseph, 174, 180
Spang, Charles, 158
Spera, Giuseppa, 7
Speranza, Dominic, 35, 36, 37, 38
Spero, Joe, 125, 127, 131
Spica, Mary, 98

Spica, Samuel, 98, 104
Spinelli, Giuseppe "Big Mike", 280
Spinelli, Louis, 292
Spingola, Henry, 166
Sposato, Caesar, 307, 318
St. Anthony of Padua Roman Catholic Church, 21, 143, 199
St. Anthony's Church (Batavia), 342
St. Anthony's Roman Catholic Church (Fredonia), 144
St. Catharines, Ontario, 36, 37, 204
St. Joseph's Cemetery (Niagara Falls, NY), 339, 351
St. Joseph's Church (Niagara Falls, NY), 151
St. Joseph's Church (Niagara Falls, NY), 339
St. Louis, MO, 223, 225, 238, 292, 293
St. Valentine's Day Massacre, 238
Stanton, County Prosecutor Edward, 196
Stapleton, Michael H., 146
Star Spangled Banner, 136
Staten Island, NY, 232
steerage travel, 5, 6
Stella Restaurant, 98, 99, 101
Stevenson, Walter, 186
Stewart, Prohibition Agent George H., 145, 146, 147
Stickney, U.S. Commissioner Charles D., 95
Still, John A., 290
Stone, Jack, 298
Stracci, Joseph "Joe Stretch", 264
Strauss, Frederick, 67
Strong, Justice Selah B., 190
Sucharski, Carrie, 176
Sucharski, Joseph, 176
suicide, 135, 252, 304
Sullivan Law, 85
Summers, Judge Robert J., 329, 349
Sunset Inn, 50
Surf Democratic Club, 283
suspicious persons, 222, 227, 333
Sweeney, Patrolman William, 165
Syracuse, Joseph, 241, 242
Syracuse, NY, 148, 279, 307, 318
Syracuse, Russell, 334
Tagliagambe, Silvio, 184, 190
Tagliarano, Matthew, 50
Talluto, Angelo, 328
Tammany Hall, 17, 66, 187, 245, 276
Tammaro, Anna, 265
Tampa, FL, 223, 225
Tardino, Angelo, 311
Taylor, attorney Alexander, 73
Taylor, George, 162
Templeton. U.S. Attorney Richard H., 154, 179
Tennes, Mont, 293

Tepecano Democratic Club, 245, 247
Terranova, Ciro, 244, 245, 246, 262
Terranova, Vincent, 189
Testa, Biaggio, 118
Testa, Elizabeth, 118
Thierfeldt, Captain Edward, 113, 115, 295
Thomas J.B. Dyke Association, 68, 73
Thomas, Judge E.H., 11
Thompson submachine gun, 237
Thompson, Elmer, 160, 162
Thorn, County Judge F. Bret, 296, 304, 330, 350
Thrasher, attorney Louis, 143
Tilocco, Sam, 226, 229, 253
Tito, Joe, 280
Tivoli Restaurant, 324
Todaro, Salvatore "Black Sam", 96, 138, 139, 140, 183, 193, 195, 196, 223, 231, 240; funeral of, 241; murder of, 241
Todaro, tobacconist Joe, 297
Toledo, Joseph, 60
Toledo, OH, 331, 334, 335, 336
Tombs Prison, 85, 89
Tonawanda, NY, 50, 308, 316, 317, 318, 324, 325
Toronto, Ontario, 36, 64, 180
Torrio, Johnny, 164
torture, 285
Tozzo, Rocco. *See* Kansas, Rocky
Tracey, Detective Sergeant Edward, 190
Trafficante, Santo Sr., 225
Traina, Giuseppe, 79, 184, 224, 227, 232, 260, 281
Transit Inn, 69
Trapani, Sicily, 229, 236
Travale, Alphonse, 328
Travis, Tony, 57
Trench, George A., 348
Trenton, NJ, 282
Tricca, Frank "Chick Tricker", 66, 67
Troia, Vincenzo, 265, 269, 274
Tronolone, John "Peanuts", 314, 315, 323, 328, 330, 333, 343, 344, 345, 346, 347, 348, 349, 350; and Whitey Kroll, 343
Tropea, Orazio, 34, 162, 163, 164, 165, 166, 167, 168, 194, 278; addressbook, 167
True Detective Mysteries, 290
Tuanos, Philip, 201
Tyler, Sheriff Frank, 137
U.S. Customs Department, 152, 155
U.S. Industrial Reformatory, 219
U.S. Secret Service, 20, 48, 305, 306
Ulizzi, Frank, 34, 44, 45, 48; Buffalo "safe house", 45
Union Carbide Corporation, 59
Unione Siciliana, 34, 77, 78, 167, 194
United Lathing Company, 244
Utica, NY, 28, 33, 34, 58, 168, 194, 339

Vacante, Salvatore, 28
Vacanti, Florence, 344, 346
Vacanti, Josephine, 104
Vaccarelli, Nick, 67
Vaccarelli, Paolo "Paul Kelly", 66, 67
Vaccaro family, 34
Vaccaro, Anthony, 45, 47, 49
Vaccaro, Vincent, 46, 49, 106
Vaglica, Giuseppe, 225, 229
vagrancy, 176, 286, 314, 321, 323
Valachi, Joseph, 244, 245, 256, 259, 262, 273
Valarosa, Charles, 30
Valente, Rev. Donato Gregory, 72
Valente, Umberto, 182, 184, 185, 190, 191, 192, 230, 278
Valentine, Commissioner Lewis J., 328
Valenzano, Michael. *See* Russo, Michael
Valle, Domenic, 345
Valledolmo, Sicily, 7, 15, 19, 21, 59, 77, 143, 340
Vallelunga, Sicily, 5, 6, 7, 8, 9, 15, 19, 34, 125, 281, 308
Vamos, Justice of the Peace Stephen, 196
Van Dyke Taxi Company, 269
vandalism, 319, 323
Vanderburg, Faulkner E., 293, 294, 295
Vario, Nicola, 19
Varisco, Antonio, 304
Varisco, Samuel, 303, 304
Vassallo, Frank, 54
Vassallo, John Anthony, 172, 173
vending machines, 300
Venice Restaurant, 50, 66, 68, 139
Verona, Joe. *See* Sciaroni, Domenic
vice, 196, 334
Villardo, Vincent, 28
Vinciguerra, Giuseppe, 229
Viola, Paul, 201
Viola, Sam, 201
Visconti, Rosalino, 47
Vitale, John, 34
Vitale, Magistrate Albert H., 245, 246, 247
Voelker, Carl, 179
Voelker, James C., 177, 178, 179, 180
Volpe, Arthur, 279
Volpe, James, 279
Volpe, John, 279
Volpe, Santo, 281
Volstead Act, 42
von Hagen, Pauline, 272
Waldow, Sheriff William, 61
Walsh, Assistant District Attorney John T., 348
Wappingers Falls, NY, 236, 268, 276
Wartime Prohibition Act, 42
Washington, D.C., 97
Weinshank, Albert, 238
Weinstein, Herman, 132

Westphal, Assistant Corporation Counsel Frank C., 102
Wexler, Irving "Waxey Gordon", 68
Whalen, Police Commissioner Grover A., 247
Wheatfield, NY, 150
Whiteacre, Elmer J., 152
Wilkerson, Judge James H., 272
Wilkes, Edward N., 141
Willebrandt, U.S. Assistant Attorney General Mabel Walker, 219
Williamsville, NY, 69, 94
Wilson, Patrolman Charles B., 165
Wilson, President Woodrow, 42
Windsor, Ontario, 286
wine bricks, 257
Winfield, John, 319, 323
Winspear, William and Robert, 53
wire service, 293, 294
Wisch, Assistant District Attorney George E., 329, 330, 344
Wise, Justice of the Peace Edward W., 85
Wisniewski, Detective Thaddeus, 345
Wolcott, "Jersey" Joe, 71
Women's Christian Temperance Union, 40
wood alcohol, 175, 178
World Series of 1919, 70

World War I, 29, 39, 41, 96, 270, 293, 311, 340
Wortzman, Max, 180
Wyandotte, MI, 248
Wynne, attorney Edward A., 85
Yale, Frank, 164, 193, 204, 230, 278
Yates, Samuel. *See* Izzo, Sam "Salvie"
Yates, William, 346
Yellow Cab Company, 269
Yonkers, NY, 11, 260
Yorkell, Ernest J., 196
Youngstown, NY, 51, 52
Youngstown, OH, 3, 72, 268
Zabito, Joseph, 160
Zanghi gang, 204
Zappala, Andrew, 281
Zelig, "Big Jack", 66
Ziegele Brewing Company, 31
Zimmerman, Chief of Detectives Charles F., 48, 49, 107, 149
Zimmerman, Mayor George J., 315
Zion Lutheran Church (Niagara Falls), 155
Zito, Antonio, 45
Zuckenberg, Samuel, 192
Zuzze, Jennie, 118
Zuzze, Salvatore, 118, 125

Made in the USA
Middletown, DE
18 August 2022